INTRODUCTION TO

Linguistic Structures

INTRODUCTION TO

Linguistic Structures

FROM SOUND TO SENTENCE IN ENGLISH

Archibald A. Hill

UNIVERSITY OF TEXAS

HARCOURT, BRACE AND COMPANY
NEW YORK

For M. B. H.

FOREWORD

This book is intended for students on the college or graduate level, whether their interests are primarily in the English language or in linguistics. It presupposes no prior knowledge of language analysis, so that it may well be made the text for a first course in linguistics or for the course in the English language now offered by many English faculties. On the other hand, there is no reason that it should not be used in classes which follow the type of introductory course offered in a number of institutions under the rubric "General Linguistics." It is designed for those who wish to know something of the structure of the native tongue; it is neither a textbook of composition nor a manual for the teaching of composition. Equally, it is not a text for learners of English as a second language nor a handbook for teachers of English to foreigners. While it is none of these things, it presents the fundamentals necessary to all of them. It is therefore a book which may be of use to many types of students—those who wish to pursue linguistics as a profession, those who wish to know enough of the science to be able to use it in studying and teaching English and other languages, and those who wish merely to add breadth to a liberal education by examining the most important of human symbolic activities.

The description of English which forms the body of the book is not intended as a complete reference grammar. The results of linguistic investigation since 1933 have been so considerable that it is necessary to make the first task that of redrawing the broad outlines of language study on newer lines, before attempting exhaustive description of all details. Linguistics has also produced so much new knowledge of the use and structure of English that it is doubtful if a work intended to be as definitive as Poutsma's *Grammar of Late Modern English* is any longer to be undertaken by a single scholar. Though not exhaustive at any stage, the book moves through the hierarchy of English structure, from the smallest elements, sounds, up to the largest elements, sentences. There is a balanced amount of attention to each level, so that the result is unified. In this, the book differs from previous attempts to apply newer techniques to English, the most notable of which treats primarily sounds and another of which treats syntax only. In attempting a balanced description of English, the author has been not unmindful of an accusation almost as old as language science—that linguists die before completing a description of the vowel *a*.

Readers of such monumental works on English as the grammars of Jespersen and Luick will miss the copious apparatus of footnotes and bibliography which have become traditional in historical treatments of language. In a structural description, rigorous analysis occupies much the place of experimentation in laboratory sciences. Step-by-step exposition of analytical procedure becomes all-important. The results of analysis are deprived of their full importance if presented without the steps by which they were reached, since a healthily growing science is one in which students should participate and to which they should contribute. It is not a body of facts to be memorized.

The absence of reference to many great scholars, European and American, who are not interested in structural techniques is not a sectarian insistence that a single group are the sole possessors of the truth. At this stage of language science, no point of view, no set of techniques, and no conclusions can be categorically designated right to the exclusion of all others. Each must be pursued until its possibilities are exhausted, and must then be judged in the agora of scholarship by the totality of its results. It is in this spirit that controversial matters have been handled. They have been frankly faced, and it is the author's belief that in science, decisions must always be made. Yet all decisions are tentative and capable of being upset by new evidence or by better interpretation of the evidence already at hand. In all those matters where interpretations are both variant and important, the endeavor has been to present both the evidence and the alternatives.

A book such as this could not have been written without a heavy debt to other scholars. The primary debt has been to the Linguistic Society of America and the scholars who have taken part in its meetings and contributed to its journal, *Language*. To one group of scholars, who have been both friends and linguistic mentors, I owe even more, as the pages of this book make evident. These men are George Trager, Henry Lee Smith, Jr., Bernard Bloch, and Martin Joos. To W. Freeman Twaddell, Robert P. Stockwell, and Werner Winter I am indebted for reading the manuscript. It is scarcely enough to pay them the usual thanks for fruitful suggestions. These three careful scholars have contributed in large measure to whatever virtues the book may have, not at all to its faults. To many students I also owe a debt, often for objections raised with determination and defended with skill. Together with all linguists of my generation I owe a pervasive debt to Bloomfield and Sapir, without whose work this book and all of American linguistics would be impossible.

A. A. H.

Austin, Texas
February 1957

CONTENTS

INTRODUCTION TO

Linguistic Structures

1.... WHAT IS LANGUAGE?

1. Some basic assumptions

The subject of linguistics presents an initial difficulty because the word which designates it is unfamiliar. The word can easily be defined as the scientific analysis of language, but it is doubtful if such a definition is meaningful to anyone who lacks familiarity with this kind of analytic activity. It is far better to begin by defining language, since language is closer to the reader's experience. Yet even the definition of language presents unsuspected difficulties and needs preliminary discussion before it is attempted directly.

If a group of educated speakers are asked to define the language they are using, the reply will probably be "All the words and sentences used to express our thoughts." The definition is satisfactory in everyday situations, since long practice has made plain what is meant, and consequently most hearers know how to respond accurately. But for all that, the definition is not sufficiently accurate to be the basis for analysis. Terms like "words and sentences," which seem transparent to a speaker of a Western language, would be more misleading than enlightening if applied to some languages. Moreover, there are phenomena similar to language which this definition does not identify. Most important, the definition identifies language activity by thought. Language activity can be observed, and is therefore subject to verification. Thought can be observed only by subjective introspection, and so is not subject to verification. Language activity is therefore more knowable, thought less knowable. Obviously a definition must define the less knowable by the more knowable if it is to cast light. In what follows, such a definition will be attempted. There must first be a warning, the need for which will be clearer as we advance. A definition is not a description. A definition gives only those characteristics which have diagnostic value for recognition. A description attempts to give all characteristics, preferably in the order of their importance. A definition necessarily leaves out much and may make use of relatively trivial characteristics, but it is not to be condemned for that reason.

Most professional students of language proceed from a few assumptions, one of which is that the fundamental forms of language activity are the sequences of sounds made by human lips, tongues, and vocal cords—the phenomena usually distinguished by the narrower name of "speech." Though this first assumption may seem like a truism, it is important, since many who accept it verbally still act as if they did not believe it. Some few even deny it. There are only two reasons for questioning the assumption. Writing has great permanence and great prestige. Further, the basis of our education is training in the manipulation of written symbols of ever-increasing complexity. Highly literate people, and those who would like to be literate, are therefore apt to think of writing as the real center of language and of speech as peripheral and derived—often badly—from the written forms.

There are a number of facts which should settle this question of priority. First, speech reaches back to the origins of human society; writing has a history of only about seven thousand years.[1] Also, no contemporary community of men is without language, even though it is probably still true that most of the world's several thousand language communities remain in the preliterate stage, without benefit of alphabet or even picture symbol. Individual members of literate communities, furthermore, learn their language some years before they learn to read or write it; and adults, even adults who are professional writers, carry on a good deal more speech activity in daily living than activity involving writing. The final fact is that all writing systems are essentially representations of the forms of speech, rather than representations of ideas or objects in the nonlinguistic world. There are exceptions to this statement, like the Arabic numbers which work independently of the words for numbers in the Western languages. The exceptions, however, are in a minority disproportionate to the majority of symbols which always indicate the forms of language. The point can be driven home by a pair of simple examples. The symbol for *one* in Japanese writing is a single stroke, that for

---

[1] The great antiquity of language, as compared with writing, is a reasonable assumption, but it is often presented without evidence. To arrive at the conclusion that language is older than writing, linguists and anthropologists start from the observed fact that in modern communities, all organized cooperative activity rests firmly and necessarily on language as the means of controlling and directing interaction. This being so in all observed communities, it is assumed by archaeological anthropologists that when remains of past communities show material evidence of social organization, these remains are those of communities which possessed language. Communities which show such evidences of social organization also show artifacts or other evidences which are much older than the remains of any communities which show evidences of even primitive systems of writing. It is possible that early human communities possessed some other form of highly organized communication, such as the gesture language which has been occasionally proposed since the days of Locke (cf. Max Müller, *Lectures on the Science of Language*, London, 1862, p. 31). But though possible, such a nonvocal symbol system is unlikely. Language is now a universal activity; it is an extra and unnecessary hypothesis to suppose something else.

two two strokes, and so on. It might be thought that such a symbol has no relation to the Japanese word for *one* (*ichi*) but represents instead the non-linguistic idea of "oneness." Actually the occurrence of the single stroke is correlated with the occurrence of the word. It occurs not only in the number but also in such forms as *ichiji, primary*. The Japanese symbol, therefore, has a quite different range from the letter sequence *one* of English, which is not used in the dissimilar word *primary*. The one-stroke symbol corresponds with the occurrence of the Japanese word *ichi*, proving that the one-stroke symbol is a representation of the word (though an understandably pictorial one), and not a direct representation of the idea of oneness.

Written symbols can be understood, furthermore, insofar as they fit into a linguistic structure, even when they refer to nothing in the nonlinguistic world. Thus, if an English text should have the sentence "He *sprashes* it," the second word could immediately be recognized as a verb in the third person singular and as a sequence of sounds quite in accord with English structural habits, though it represents nothing in the outside world at all. For the purposes of this book, therefore, the linguist's assumption that language is a set of sounds will be adopted. It is no contradiction of this assumption that the sounds can be secondarily translated into visual marks, grooves on a wax disk, electrical impulses, or finger movements.

Linguists assume that the description and analysis of language must begin with description of the sounds and their patterning and that description of meaning must be put off until the first task is done. Such an attitude is often misunderstood to be a denial of meaning, but this is not true. The linguist's desire to put off analysis of meaning is no more than an application of the principle of working from the more knowable to the less knowable, and though linguistics has not as yet had very striking results in semantic analysis, it can be hoped that the next few decades will see results of real value in semantics.

2. The defining characteristics of language

Working with the assumptions given above, linguists can offer a set of five defining characteristics which serve to set off language from other forms of symbolic behavior and to establish language as a purely human activity. Often animal communication will have one or more of these five characteristics, but never all of them.

First, language, as has been said, is a set of sounds. This is perhaps the least important characteristic, since the communication of mammals and birds is also a set of sounds. On the other hand, the system of communication which is in some ways most strikingly like language, that of bees, is a set of body movements, not sounds. It would be easy, further, to imagine a language based on something else than sound, but no human language is so constructed. Even the manual language of the deaf is derived from the pre-existent spoken language of the community.

Second, the connection between the sounds, or sequences of sounds, and objects of the outside world is arbitrary and unpredictable. That is to say, a visitor from Mars would be unable to predict that in London a given animal is connected with the sound sequence written *dog*, in Paris with the sequence *chien*, in Madrid with *perro*. The arbitrary quality of language symbols is not infrequently denied, for a number of reasons. Sometimes the denial is based on nothing more than the notion that the forms of one's native language are so inevitably right that they must be instinctive for all proper men. Sometimes the denial is more subtle. It is often maintained that all language, even though now largely arbitrary, must once have been a systematic imitation of objects by means of sound. It is true that there are some imitative words in all languages, but they are at best a limited part of the vocabulary. It is easy to imitate the noise of a barking dog, for instance, but difficult if not impossible to imitate a noiseless object, such as a rainbow. Though imitative words show similarity in many languages, absolute identity is rare. A dog goes "bow-wow" in English, but in related languages he often goes "wow-wow" or "bow-bow." The imitative words do not, after all, entirely escape from the general arbitrariness of language. The imitative origin of language appears, therefore, at worst unlikely and at best unprovable. The same injunction holds for theories of language origin which speculate that it is an imitation of facial or other gestures.

If it is assumed that language is arbitrary, what is meant by the statement? Just that the sounds of speech and their connection with entities of experience are passed on to all members of any community by older members of that community. Therefore, a human being cut off from contact with a speech community can never learn to talk as that community does, and cut off from all speech communities never learns to talk at all. In essence, to say that language is arbitrary is merely to say that it is social. This is perhaps the most important statement that can be made about language.

In contrast, much of animal communication is instinctive rather than social. That is to say, all cats mew and purr, and would do so even if they were cut off from all communication with other cats. On the other hand, some animal communication seems to share the social nature of human speech and is therefore learned activity. A striking example is the barking of dogs, which is characteristic only of the domesticated animal, not of dogs in the wild state. Similarly, the honey dances of bees may not be altogether without an arbitrary element. It is also likely that when more is known of the cries and chatterings of the great apes in the wild state, a considerable social element in their communication may be found. Nor should it be thought that all human communication is social. A part of our communication consists of instinctive reactions which accompany language, like the trembling of fear or the suffusion of blood which accompanies anger. Yet even in the nonlinguistic accompaniments of speech, the tones of voice and the gestures, it is now clear that there is more of arbitrary and socially learned behavior than had at one time been supposed.

Third, language is systematic. I cannot hope to make this statement completely clear at this point, since the whole of this book is devoted to an exposition of the system of language. However, some observations may now be made about the system of language. As in any system, language entities are arranged in recurrent designs, so that if a part of the design is seen, predictions can be made about the whole of it, as a triangle can be drawn if one side and two angles are given. Suppose there is an incomplete sentence like "John —s Mary an —." A good deal about what must fill the two blanks is obvious. The first must be a verb, the second a noun. Furthermore, not all verbs will go in the first blank, since it requires a verb whose third person singular is spelled with –s and which can take two objects (that is, not such a verb as *look* or *see*). Nor will all nouns fit in the second place, since an initial vowel is required, and the noun must be one which takes an article. There is no difficulty in deciding that the sentence could be either "John gives Mary an apple" or "John hands Mary an aspirin," but not "John *gaves* Mary an *book*."[2]

Another observation that can be made about language systems is that every occurrence of language is a substitution frame. Any sentence is a series of entities, for each of which a whole group of other entities can be substituted without changing the frame. Thus the sentence "John gives Mary an apple" is such a substitution frame. For *John* there can be replacements like *he, Jack, William, the man, her husband*, or many others. For the verb, entities like *buys, takes, offers*, as well as the alternatives *hands* or *gives*, may be used. This characteristic of extensive substitutability for all parts of any language utterance is of some importance in that it enables us to say that parrots, no matter how startlingly human their utterances may be, are not carrying on language activity. A parakeet may produce the sentence "Birds can't talk!" with human pitch, voice tones, and nearly

---

[2] In this book, an asterisk placed before a form means that it is believed to be impossible. In historical treatments of language, on the other hand, an asterisk before a form indicates that it has been reconstructed by comparison but is not actually recorded. These two uses of the asterisk should not be confused.

perfect sounds. But the bird never says "Dogs can't talk!" or "Birds can't write!" His utterance is a unit, not a multiple substitution frame.

Still another characteristic of language systems is that the entities of language are grouped into classes, always simpler, more predictable, and more sharply separated than the infinite variety of objects in the world. For instance, a whole series of objects is grouped under the single word *chair*, and *chair* is put into the large class of nouns. In dealing with objects in the outside world it may be difficult to decide whether something is a chair, a stool, or merely a rock. In language, we think of nouns and verbs as quite separate and are apt to say that the one class represents things, the other events. But in the outside world, as the physicists tell us, it is often hard to decide whether an object is best described as thing or as event.

To return once more to the defining characteristics of language, the fourth characteristic is that it is a set of symbols. That is to say, language has meaning. In this form the statement is a platitude and does not distinguish language from other activities which are also symbolic. The nature of language symbols turns out to be rather different from the symbols of other types of communication. The simplest nonlinguistic symbol can be defined as a substitute stimulus. Pavlov's famous dogs, fed at the sound of a bell, eventually began to drool at the sound of the bell even when no food was present. The dogs were responding to a substitute stimulus. Nonlinguistic symbols can also be substitute responses, and these can also be taught to animals. A dog who learns to "speak" at the sight of food has learned such a substitute response. In human speech, however, one of the most striking facts is that we can talk about things which are not present, and we can talk about things which ordinarily produce a strong physical reaction without experiencing that reaction. For instance, I can talk about apples even though there are none in the room, and I can talk about them without always making my mouth water, even when I am hungry. This type of language, which occurs without an immediately present stimulus or response, is called "displaced speech," and it is obviously of great importance. It is what enables man to know something of the past and of the world beyond the limited range of his vision and hearing at a given moment.

The crucial fact in producing this almost miraculous and purely human effect seems to be that a given language entity can be both substitute stimulus and substitute response, and can also be a stimulus for further language responses or a response to other language stimuli. I can talk about apples when they are absent because "something reminds me of them." That is, I can make language responses to what is before me, and these language responses can stimulate the further response *apple* without any direct physical stimulus to my vision, touch, or smell. *Apple* can call forth still further language entities, like *pear* or *banana*, in an endless chain; these entities are also both stimuli and responses. When human speakers do this, they are setting up what philosophers call a "universe of discourse." The ability to make connected discourse within the symbol system is what enables men to talk at length, and profitably, about things they have never seen. By means of language men make elaborate models of distant experience and eventually test their accuracy by acting upon them. All that is known of animal communication leads to the supposition that precisely what is absent from it is the kind of symbolic activity here described, symbolic activity connected not merely with experience but with all parts of the symbol system itself. We believe, in short, that animals are incapable of displaced speech.

The paragraphs above are rather general, so that a concrete example may be helpful. Let us suppose that two speakers of English are together in a room. One of them is cold. A direct response for him would be to close the window.

Instead of this he can use the substitute response, which is also substitute stimulus: "John, please close the window for me." John can either close the window or reply with a further substitute: "Just a minute. Wait until I finish this page." Such a reply may produce acceptance or may lead to a discussion of John's procrastinating character, of the fact that his parents did not discipline him properly in youth and that modern young people are generally rebellious and unmannerly. To all of this John may reply that modern times are marked by progress and the disappearance of old taboos. In the meantime the window may have been quietly closed, or completely forgotten in the warmth of discussion. What is important is that each speaker has begun reacting, not to the immediate situation, but to the other speaker's language and to his own. And in so doing, each has been building a model of general social conditions, of wide scope and ultimately of some value, even in a random and unchecked conversation of the sort described.

We are now ready to turn to the last defining characteristic of language, the fact that it is complete. By this is meant that whenever a human language has been accurately observed, it has been found to be so elaborated that its speakers can make a linguistic response to any experience they may undergo. This complex elaboration is such a regular characteristic of all languages, even those of the simplest societies, that linguists have long ago accepted it as a universal characteristic. Nevertheless, in early books about language, and in the descriptions by linguistically untrained travelers today, there are statements that tribe X has a language with only two or three hundred words in it, forcing the tribe to eke out its vocabulary by gesture.[3] Linguists maintain that all such statements are the product of lack of knowledge, and are false. Skepticism about such statements is borne out by the fact that in all instances where it was possible to check on tribe X, its language proved to be complete as usual, whereupon the statement was transferred to tribe Y, whose language was as yet unknown. The statement that human language is complete once again serves to distinguish it from animal activity. In the communication of bees, for instance, the subjects of systematic discourse are severely limited. Bees cannot, apparently, make an utterance equivalent to "The beekeeper is coming."

The statement that human language is always complete should not be interpreted to mean that every language has a word for everything. Obviously the ancient Greeks had no words for automobiles or atom bombs, and probably the modern Yahgan of Tierra del Fuego lack them as well. The completeness of language lies rather in the fact that a speaker of ancient Greek would have been perfectly capable of describing an automobile had he seen one, and further that had automobiles become important in ancient Greece, the speakers of Greek would have been perfectly capable of coining a word for them. It is a characteristic of vocabulary that, except in languages which have gone out of use, it is always expansible, in spite of the fact that resistance to new forms may frequently appear. Since language enables the user to make appropriate responses to all things and since vocabulary is thus characteristically "open," differences in vocabulary between two languages are not an accurate measure of the difference in efficiency or excellence of the two tongues. The fact that Eskimo does not have as highly developed a vocabulary of philosophy as does German merely indicates that the Eskimos are less interested in philosophy; on the other hand, Eskimo has a highly developed vocabulary for various kinds of snow, indicating that snow is important in Eskimo society. The completeness of

---

[3] A typical recent statement of this sort was reported by Leonard Bloomfield in "Secondary and Tertiary Responses to Language," *Language*, XX, 1944, p. 49 *n*.

"A physician, of good general background and education, who had been hunting in the north woods, told me that the Chippewa language contains only a few hundred words. Upon question, he said that he got this information from his guide, a Chippewa Indian. When I tried to state the diagnostic setting, the physician, our host, briefly and with signs of displeasure repeated his statement and then turned his back to me. A third person, observing this discourtesy, explained that I had some experience of the language in question. This information had no effect."

For a good general account of the completeness of primitive languages and the use of gesture as a substitute among mutually unintelligible language groups, consult Ralph L. Beals and Harry Hoijer, *An Introduction to Anthropology*, Macmillan, New York, 1956, pp. 508–11.

human language and the openness of vocabulary make a groundless chimera of the occasionally expressed fear that a language might so degenerate as to become useless.

We can now attempt a definition of language, though the definition will be cumbersome. Language is the primary and most highly elaborated form of human symbolic activity. Its symbols are made up of sounds produced by the vocal apparatus, and they are arranged in classes and patterns which make up a complex and symmetrical structure. The entities of language are symbols, that is, they have meaning, but the connection between symbol and thing is arbitrary and socially controlled. The symbols of language are simultaneously substitute stimuli and substitute responses and can call forth further stimuli and responses, so that discourse becomes independent of an immediate physical stimulus. The entities and structure of language are always so elaborated as to give the speaker the possibility of making a linguistic response to any experience. Most of the above can be paraphrased by saying that every language is a model of a culture and its adjustment to the world.

3. Language and the study of its nature

Since language is something that we habitually take for granted, it may not be clear, even after this discussion, why language and, even more, the study of language are important. Primarily they are important because language is a solely human activity, which separates man from other living beings. But though this may be readily granted, it is not always realized how fundamentally language is a defining characteristic of man. Even among students of man it is probably more common to define him as "the tool-making animal" than as "the talking animal." But it is quite possible that tool making is less crucially human than talking is. For one thing, it is natural that an archaeologist's attention should turn toward tools, which can be dug up, rather than toward language, which cannot. For another, it is not always easy to recognize how fundamental language is, even in our own society. There are individuals who lead nearly normal lives in spite of being deprived of speech, so that it may be argued that speech —admittedly the fundamental form of language—is a dispensable form of activity. Yet such speechless individuals always develop some form of substitute language, and all such substitutes presuppose the individual's membership in a society fully provided with speech. There are many things, such as wearing neckties, making movies, or cooking, which only human beings do. But many of these are not universal among men, and all of them are secondary. As for tool making, this activity is universally human, but it is in some sense shared with the higher primates. When, however, it is argued that tool making involves more than the use of a convenient stick or stone and is the purposeful molding of an object for future use, it would seem that the tool maker is an individual capable of displaced speech and of shaping his activity in accord with a symbolic model. In other words, as soon as man is defined as a maker of tools whose use lies in the future, we presuppose the existence of language. Therefore linguists, and many anthropologists, believe that language is the phenomenon most basic in human society. Historical anthropologists assume that when humanoid remains are found in a situation indicating an organized community, they are necessarily remains of a group possessed of language. If, then, it is language more than anything else we can observe which makes us men, it is ultimately the study of language which is most likely to throw light on the essential humanness of human beings. I wish at this point, however, to make a specific disclaimer. There are characteristics inaccessible to science which also distinguish man; the science of language is not concerned with these and should under no circumstances be understood as denying them. On the other hand, the existence of spiritual qualities ought equally to be understood as not being a bar to the study of those things which can be investigated by science.

If scientific study of language can throw light on human qualities and activities, there is no direction in which there is greater likelihood of illumination than in the investigation of thought, whether that investigation be understood as a part of psychology or a part of logic. It was said earlier that linguists do not deny the existence or importance of mind. The American linguist insists that language entities cannot be profitably investigated in terms of the mental concepts or thoughts back of them, but this insistence ought always to be understood as carrying with it the corollary that mental concepts can be profitably investigated in terms of the language entities which are so largely instrumental in their formation. It has also been said that language is basic to society. It is therefore probable that increased knowledge of language will mean increased knowledge of society. The promise is already recognized and has already borne fruit, since anthropologists have made brilliant use of linguistic insights. Less broad than thought and society, another area in which linguistic knowledge is beginning to prove useful is in the study of literature, if for no other reason than that literature is an art constructed in language. Similarly, the practical activity of language instruction, whether that of a foreign or the native tongue, can profit by knowledge of the nature of the material which is to be imparted.

I have up to now spoken of the importance of language study from the broad aspect of human knowledge; for the individual student the impact of language study is different. The native language provides its speakers an ever-present and deeply habituated instrument by which they measure and control experience. All adults have had a long indoctrination in the attitude that language is both a transparent glass through which we see the world and a tool by which we mold it. Therefore the first stages of study of language for the sake of knowledge rather than with a practical aim are apt to be disquieting, or even to seem useless. A somewhat parallel case can be drawn from optics. We think of our eyes as instruments which transmit the "real" appearance of objects directly to our minds. It is often disturbing to realize that our eyes necessarily influence the appearance of objects and that a surface which appears flat to us can scarcely appear so to the nearly spherical eye of a fly. Yet to say that language study is apt to be difficult or disquieting is not the same thing as to say that it is of no value to the individual. An important aim of education is the adjustment of the individual to the world in which he has to live, and linguistic knowledge is a help toward that end. The individual's understanding of reality is increased if he can learn to distinguish the ways in which the structure of his language may influence his perception of reality. Study of language is one of the best ways in which a narrow belief in the rightness of one's own ways of doing things, and the wrongness of every other way, can be broken down. It is instructive to find that some languages, even among the European group, are not felt to be inadequate because they do not distinguish between fingers and toes by separate vocabulary items. The knowledge that there are languages which have no tenses at all and others which attach tenses to their nouns is a good introduction to the myriad ways in which men channel the basic human needs, experiences, and activities which indeed remain much the same throughout the world. A student trained in language is aware, on the practical level, of language pitfalls. A very little training may prepare him for failure of communication when an Englishman and an American talk about *corn*. More sophistication is needed for dealing with the situation reported by Bloomfield in which an Englishman misunderstood his American pronunciation of *Comedy Theatre* as a request for a nonexistent *Carmody Theatre*.[4] In all such instances, the student trained in language will deal with the inevitable failure of understanding in realistic terms, without wasting time in denouncing one group or the other for not knowing its own language. And similarly, he is prepared to deal with the difficulties of a foreign language on a more realistic level than by supposing that there is a one-to-one correspondence between its forms and those of English.

By now, I hope that some meaning has been given to the definition of linguistics as the scientific study of language. Linguistics has for its goal

---

[4] *Language*, Holt, New York, 1933, p. 81.

the understanding of language, and it is secure in the belief that such understanding will increase human knowledge. It strives to present a picture of language as complete as possible, as consistent as possible, and as simple as possible, again secure in the belief that if these conditions are fulfilled it will be as truly and revealingly a science as is chemistry or astronomy. This book is an attempt to take the reader through some of the first steps in this young science. The means chosen have been an explanation of the techniques and entities of linguistics in an extended sketch of English, followed by shorter sketches of different language structures. It is not assumed that a sketch of Eskimo will make the reader more capable of finding his way about in Greenland; rather it is hoped that he may gradually come to accept a scientific attitude in a kind of activity where most people, even those thoroughly educated, have not tried to be scientific, and where some, indeed, have resisted the suggestion that they should be. The first stages of investigation and statement may seem to be disturbing and even to introduce confusion where none existed before, but as the design of language and its analysis unfold, clarity emerges, and with it the security of understanding.

2.... STRESS, JUNCTURE, PITCH

1. The data and the method of analysis and presentation

In this chapter and all of those which follow, the English which is described is the personal dialect of a single speaker or, to use the technical term, a single idiolect. The person whose idiolect is thus presented is, again to use a technical term, the informant. It is not true that a description thus based on a single idiolect is inapplicable to the speech of others or to other dialects. The idiolect used is made up of characteristics shared with millions of speakers. Rather, the choice of a single idiolect is dictated by the necessity of basing statements on a body of data which are verifiable. If they had not been, or had been based on the idiolect of a fictitious average speaker, the results would have been confusing because those based on observation would have been indistinguishable from those which were not and comparable and noncomparable data might have been treated together. The statements based on the informant's idiolect have been compared with other observed idiolects, or groups of idiolects, as often as knowledge and the limits of space mad ; it possible to do so, but no reader should be alarmed because his usage differs from that presented here. Statements that so-and-so does not or cannot occur mean that the informant rejects them as foreign to his habits.

Because there is available to me no exhaustive body of information on language items and structure other than in my own language habits, I have had to use myself as the informant.[1] This is the usual practice of

---

[1] Since I have acted as my own informant, it is probably of some importance to describe for the reader what my idiolect is and something of the social and other influences which have formed it. I am a mature speaker, educated, and by profession academic. I belong to the urban middle class, and my contacts with other speech than American English have not been significant in molding my speech habits. I have been exposed to formative influences from the following regions, named approximately in chronological order: New York City, northern Kentucky, California, New Haven, Maine, Michigan, Piedmont Virginia. My dialect is a variety of the type called Midland, and my speech is usually commented on less frequently when I am in Michigan or California than when I am in the Southwest or anywhere along the Atlantic seaboard. I have picked up a good many items and some structural

linguists describing their native speech for the benefit of other native speakers of the same tongue. The practice has disadvantages, since it is notoriously easy to deceive oneself about language and to mistake rationalizations for actual use. For that reason I have tried to test my conclusions against other idiolects and the opinions of qualified linguists, particularly as to their interpretations of the forms they have heard me use.

The method of work has been to try to group my utterances into those which are the same and those which are different. As is the practice with most current analysis, attention has been focused on the differences—the contrasts. Classifications and formulations have been tested by variation and new combinations, with the purpose of arriving as nearly as possible at the limits of combination. As a result, a statement that "it is a rule that so-and-so must happen" is a statement that, so far as I have been able to test, it always does happen. Such statements are purely descriptive and have predictive value only in that what has often been observed to happen is likely to continue to happen in the future.

The order of presentation is from the smallest items, sounds, to the largest items, sentences. This is not the only presentation which might have been used. In analysis, however, this procedure has the advantage of presenting, at each stage, small lists of items, which can then be used to describe larger lists in terms of combinations of items from the smaller list. There are relatively few sounds, which are combined to make a great many words. The several thousands of words in any idiolectal vocabulary are, in turn, combined to form still larger numbers of sentences. Once analysis of the sort here attempted is complete, on the other hand, a reverse approach is useful, one in which the largest units are broken down into successively smaller units. The second approach probably more nearly approximates the way a child learns his native language; the first is on the whole more nearly the way an adult learns a second tongue.

2. Stress

Within the sphere of sound, we shall begin with loudness, which is familiar to most readers under the name of accent but which in linguistics is called stress. This feature is described first because many, if not all,

characteristics from each of the speech types to which I have been exposed. To name a few characteristics of my pronunciation, I pronounce *r* in all situations, distinguish between *wail* and *whale*, pronounce *can't* and *aunt* to rhyme with *slant*, make no distinction between *horse* and *hoarse*. These are characteristics which mark my speech as a type of Midland. Perhaps from New England influence is my pronunciation of *whole* in phrases like *on the whole*, and from the South I may have my tendency to diphthongize the vowel of *leg*.

stress distinctions are readily recognizable to most speakers. Stresses can therefore be used as a good first example of the way in which linguistic entities contrast with one another. Stress can be handled without the necessity of mastering a systematic respelling of English, so that the student can delay the study of a special alphabet until he has acquired some useful understanding of linguistic processes.

All languages are characterized by differences in loudness in the chain of utterance, but not all languages employ these differences so as to set up contrasts among them. For instance, suppose that in any utterance a language always stresses the second syllable, the fourth, the sixth, and so on. It follows that all utterances are stressed alike and that no two utterances could contrast in stress. In terms of meaning, and so in terms of the structure which signals the meaning, it is the contrasts alone which are relevant and significant. An actual language which has an arrangement of stresses like that I have described, in that there are no contrasts, is the nearly extinct Indian language Tonkawa. In this tongue a heavier stress falls on the second syllable of any two-syllable utterance and on the next to last syllable (penult) of any utterance of more than two syllables.[2] Here, as in the hypothetical language described above, stress can never constitute a contrast between utterances.

In English, the situation is quite different. The extremes of contrast in stress can be readily established by comparing two utterances such as *differ* and *defer*. In many dialects, the two forms are exactly alike except that in the first it is the initial syllable which is loudest and in the second it is the final syllable. The position of the heaviest stress, called primary stress, can be indicated by a mark, thus:

díffer   defér

The syllables left unmarked have weak stress. When it is convenient, these also can be marked:

díffĕr   dĕfér

Minimal pairs such as *differ* : *defer* are somewhat rare. Pairs such as *Sátan* : *satánic*, where the vowels differ as well as the stress, are more common. But when stress differentiates phrases or sentences, as it regularly does, the variations are often minimal, unaccompanied by differences in vowels and consonants. Thus, in most American speech, the greeting "How are you?" varies between "How áre you?" (the form used by the first speaker) and "How are yóu?" (the form used by the speaker who replies). Indeed,

---

[2] Harry Hoijer, "Tonkawa," in *Linguistic Structures of Native America*, ed. by Cornelius Osgood, Viking Fund Publications in Anthropology, No. 6, New York, 1946.

successive utterances of any sentence, such as "Rose is a girl," can vary in this way. As ordinarily pronounced, *is* lacks stress, but if it is emphasized it can get the heaviest stress in the sentence.

If we take two words, such as *dústy* and *wíndows*, and pronounce them alone as citation forms, we see that both have the same primary-weak stress sequence. But if we put them together in a construction and then make a complete utterance of the construction, the pattern varies. The first syllable of *dusty*, though still stronger than the second, is now weaker than the first syllable of *windows*. The first syllable of *dusty* has an intermediate grade of stress, called secondary. We would write the construction:

dûsty wíndows

Contrast between primary and secondary stress can be seen on *brief* in *bríefcase* (portfolio) and *brîef cáse* (case at law which is brief). The first of these forms does not, however, have a weak second syllable. Rather, in many but not all idiolects, it has still another grade of stress, called tertiary.[3] It must then be written:

bríefcàse

American speakers have no difficulty in recognizing three grades of stress, but a fourfold distinction causes trouble for many. There are two kinds of difficulties involved. It has at least once been reliably reported to me that a certain idiolect had only three contrasting forms. In any idiolect under analysis, the possibility of lack of distinction has always to be taken into account. Yet, since a four-stress system is the general rule and since, as we shall see, a four-stress system is in accord with the arrangement of contrasts elsewhere in the pattern of sounds, the four-stress system is to be regarded as the normal one, and any three-stress system is a departure from the normal. In three-stress systems, it is the two middle grades, secondary and tertiary, which are thrown together. In recording such an idiolect, the transcriber should use the symbols for secondary or tertiary in accord with what he hears and arrive at the conclusion that the two are noncontrastive later, when their distribution has been studied.

Much more common is the kind of difficulty caused by variation in key words. Thus in my idiolect, for instance, there is a whole series of compounds which have tertiary on the second syllable. In a good many idiolects some or all of them have secondary on the second syllable instead. The student should therefore go through the list carefully, deciding whether the items are alike or different:

---

[3] The names of these four grades—primary, secondary, tertiary, and weak—are those which have become traditional in American linguistics. Students sometimes find more descriptive names helpful. A satisfactory set of descriptive names is strong-loud, loud, weak-loud, and weak.

White House: Whíte Hòuse or *Whíte Hôuse*
greenhouse: gréenhòuse or *gréenhôuse*
blackboard: bláckbòard or *bláckbôard*
blackbird: bláckbìrd or *bláckbîrd*

It is common for these, and all like them, to have tertiary on all the second syllables. It is perhaps equally common for them to differ, some having secondary, some tertiary. It is apparently rare—at least in most regions—for them all to have secondary. A student who finds that he treats these words as not all alike has therefore provided himself with a good list of key words for his own idiolect. Those which have a slightly louder second syllable have secondary stress, those with a weaker second syllable have tertiary stress.

For a student who pronounces the whole list alike, the chances are that he is using tertiary stress, though if he comes from the Southwest, he may be using secondary. The problem is to distinguish. For my own idiolect a contrast can be set up between these two forms:

gréenhòuse   Gréen hôuse (house belonging to Mr. Green)

If such a contrast exists, the forms can easily be sorted into secondary and tertiary. If there is no contrast, contrast can be hunted for in another situation. A word like *necessary* as a citation form has *nécessàry*. Placed in a construction, it then usually becomes

a nêcessàry stép

illustrating all four stress contrasts. Yet, even here difficulty can arise, and a good many students find trouble in hearing these distinctions because instead of making a single construction of article, adjective, and noun, they give two citation forms:

a nécessàry   stép

If there is trouble in hearing a distinction between tertiary and secondary, it is also likely that there will be trouble in hearing a distinction between tertiary and weak. No quite minimal pair can be found, but the following citation forms are near-minimal, and work for many idiolects:

Phárĭsèe contrasted with *fállăcў*

It is the contrast in the final syllables which is here being illustrated.

In this discussion a somewhat radical position has been implied throughout. Until a few years ago, it was an assumption almost universal among linguists that a speaker, even without special training, would infallibly and automatically hear the contrasts in his own speech and that the only things he would not hear would be sounds which are not contrastive.

Consequently, it would at that time have been necessary to say that any speaker who had trouble in hearing four grades of stress would be one who had only three contrasts. We have taken the position that there are speakers who have four contrasts but who still have difficulty in hearing all the distinctions they make. Such difficulties occur not only in the system of stresses, but with other sounds as well. In every instance where a speaker has difficulty in hearing a distinction which he actually makes, the reason can be found in the kind and frequency of variation. If most words have a form in secondary and another in tertiary and if a speaker has become habituated to hearing words with both varieties, he will be accustomed to disregard the difference. But it is a principle in analysis that sounds are contrastive, even if there is only one pair in the whole system where the contrast is firmly established. It is the analyst's task to find this one pair, and he cannot be satisfied that there is no contrast until he has examined all possible pairs. It is necessary to advise the reader that, if he still has trouble with four stresses after having worked through the possible distinctions which have been given, he should consult a competent analyst and let the analyst sort out contrasts for him.

A discussion of some sets of variations in sentences may be helpful. I give first two sentences differentiated by spelling and then take up the ways in which these may be differentiated by stress or by stress and other features:

> *Drive it into the garage.*
> *Drive it in to the garage.*

There is a difference in meaning between the two sentences. The first is one which is a directive to drive the car, now in the yard, into the garage. The second is a directive to drive the car, now on the road, into town to the garage, probably for repair.

In my own idiolect, the clearest possible pronunciation of the first sentence is to give a pause before *into* and secondary stress on *into*:

> *Dríve it ìnto the garáge.*

Slightly less clear is a form with tertiary stress:

> *Dríve it ìnto the garáge.*

In my idiolect if the pause is not given, the sentence may become:

> *Drîve ĭt ĭntŏ thĕ găráge.*

The situation here, with five weak syllables in succession, is rare in English and does not mean that all these weaks are absolutely alike in loudness. When there are several syllables alike in contrastive stress grades and which are placed in succession, there is a simple rhythmic rule which assigns a slightly stronger value to alternate syllables beginning with the second. Thus, in this sentence, *into* has this slightly stronger weak on its first syllable.

In my idiolect the clearest form of the second sentence is:

Drîve it ín   to the garáge.

If the pause is not given, the sentence may become:

Drîve ĭt ín tŏ thĕ găráge.

In my idiolect, there can be reduction of the secondary stress to tertiary:

Drîve ĭt ìn tŏ thĕ găráge.

In my idiolect, then, the minimal form of distinction for these two sentences can be the difference between a slightly stronger weak and a tertiary:

FIRST SENTENCE *Drîve ĭt ĭntŏ thĕ găráge.*
SECOND SENTENCE *Drîve ĭt ìn tŏ thĕ găráge.*

This distinction has been carefully tested in my own idiolect and is one that is normal for me. If it is made similarly for the reader, it then illustrates a sentence difference between tertiary and weak. However, in testing this against other idiolects, I have found that my distinction seems to be somewhat uncommon. For other idiolects, a commoner minimal distinction is between tertiary for the first sentence and secondary for the other:

FIRST SENTENCE *Drîve ĭt ìntŏ thĕ găráge.*
SECOND SENTENCE *Drîve ĭt ín tŏ thĕ găráge.*

It should be instructive for the reader to experiment to find which type of distinction he uses. So far as I know, the two sentences are usually distinct, though the distinction is not necessarily made in the same way.

A second pair of sentences is interesting not only in the distinctions but in the fact that this pair is not differentiated in spelling. I shall give the two sentences in their maximally differentiated forms first:

Whât ăre yŏu wôrkĭng fór? (What are you trying to obtain?)
Whât ăre yŏu wórkĭng fòr? (Why are you working?)

In my idiolect, and in most others, the first sentence, with difference of emphasis, may also be:

Whât ăre yŏu wórkĭng fôr?

The pair of sentences gives, therefore, a good differentiation between secondary and tertiary. In my own idiolect, however, the difference does not have to be between secondary and tertiary, since with a pronunciation which

is apparently uncommon for others, I can reduce *for* in the second sentence
to weak:

Whât ăre yŏu wórkĭng fŏr? (Why are you working?)

Once again, the reader should compare his own usage.
In sentences, none of the stress patterns are absolutely fixed. The
content of the sentences in the context produces changes. Indeed, any
syllable in a given utterance can on occasion receive primary stress. The
sentence "John went home" is usually "Jôhn wênt hóme." But if it answers
the question "Who went home?" it will probably be "Jóhn wênt hôme," and
if it answers the question "Is John on his way home?" or "Is John at home
now?" it will probably be "Jôhn wént hôme." Similarly, the construction
dusty windows was given with secondary stress on *dusty*, and primary stress
on *windows*. Under conditions of emphasis, the stress relations change:

Nó, nôt múddy wîndows, dústy wîndows.

But even though stresses vary widely, they remain within limits and do
not change merely at random. For instance, *a vèry grêen hóuse, a véry grêen
hôuse,* and *a vèry gréen hôuse* are all possible, with varying emphasis. But
*a vèry gréenhòuse is not, since *gréenhòuse,* as its stress shows, is a compound,
before which *a very* does not occur.

Up to this point we have been discussing individual stresses and how
they vary. Stresses also form patterns which are meaningful. The patterns
/ˆ ´/ and /´ `/[4] commonly distinguish a construction consisting of an adjective
and noun from a compound noun:

> *bîg héad* and *bíghèad* (conceit)
> *hôt ród* and *hótròd* (a "souped-up" car)
> *Chrîstian Bróthers* (a religious order) and *Chrístian Bròthers*
>   or *Chrístian Brôthers* (a firm of brothers named Chris-
>   tian)

The same contrast also distinguishes verb constructions from compound
nouns which contain verbal elements:

> *hôok úp* and *hóokùp*
> *pîck póckets* and *píckpòckets*
> *kíss me quíck* and *kíss-me-quìck* (an old fashioned type of
>   bonnet)

---

[4] Sequences of symbols for contrastive sounds are enclosed in slant lines. Symbols
for sounds which are not contrastive or for sounds whose contrastive quality has not
yet been established are enclosed in brackets. Thus *yes* may be recorded /yés/ or
[yés·] indicating a noncontrastive variety of *s*-sound.

The pattern /ˊ ˋ/ characterizes some verbal compounds, so that there are also contrasts like:

Týpe rîght! and týpewrìte

In some instances it is possible to carry the variation in stress patterns through a series of three, all correlated with differences in meaning:

> the grêen hóuse and the whîte hóuse (houses which are green
>   or white)
> the gréenhòuse and the White Hòuse (a conservatory and
>   the residence of the President)
> the Gréen hôuse and the White hôuse (houses belonging to
>   Mr. Green and Mr. White)
> a blâckbìrd's nést (nest of a blackbird)
> a blâck bírd's-nèst (bird's-nest which is black)
> a blâck bírd's nést (nest of a black-colored bird)

English punning habits often make use of a sentence with the stress pattern so distorted as to suggest a ridiculous utterance. A simple example is the catch sometimes posed for children:

Dìd you êver sêe a hôrse flý?

The sentence is a distortion of the more expected:

Dìd you êver sêe a hórseflỳ?

3. Junctures

An utterance does not necessarily become understandable even when all its vowels, consonants, and stress patterns have been recognized. It is still necessary to recognize where the boundaries fall. A typical pair of sentences is "He will act, roughly in the same manner" and "He will act roughly, in the same manner." In presenting the pair in writing, *roughly* is assigned to what follows or what precedes by the position of the comma. In speech, the two are equally distinct and in no danger of confusion. The position of the boundary is signaled by elements in the sound system, which are imperfectly represented in writing by punctuation marks. These boundary signals are called junctures, and it is these which we are about to describe.

Junctures distinguish utterances not only by where they fall but by the differences between the several types of juncture. We can conveniently begin with the two which most frequently mark the ends of sentences and which are therefore called terminal. The following sentences are examples of the types:

John went home.   John went home?

That is, if the first sentence is pronounced as a simple statement and the second as a question, the ordinary description is to say that the second is distinguished by a "rising inflection," a rise in pitch. The statement is essentially right, though it needs more precision. A sentence otherwise indistinguishable from a statement becomes a question if it has a sharp rise in pitch at the end. The sharp rise is related to a second kind of pitch, which we will describe in the next section of this chapter. This second kind of pitch consists of the levels of pitch which characterize the whole of the preceding material. But though terminal upturn is related to the pitch levels which precede, the upturn is a distinct phenomenon. The levels may be spread over several syllables; the upturn occurs on the last syllable only. Moreover, the upturn may be started from a high or low level; it is the upward direction rather than the starting point which matters. It is true, however, that the type of upturn we have illustrated in the second of our two sentences starts from a relatively high level—this is the pattern which we recognize as indicating a question. Before we return to other instances of the upturn, we will take up the other sentence, the one punctuated with a period.

In this sentence, which would presumably be described as having a "falling inflection" if we continued the type of language used to describe the question sentence, it is easy to hear that the general direction of pitch moves downward on the last word. A part of this movement belongs to the level, since a statement usually has a relatively low level on the last syllable or syllables. Another part of the pattern, however, is a downturn on the last syllable only, which is analogous to the upturn we have already described. It should be stated, however, that the downturn is somewhat less noticeable than the upturn, because it does not move as far.

These two entities, which we can preliminarily identify as upturn and downturn, are two of the four English junctures. The first is called double bar and is written /||/; the second is called double cross and is written /#/. Double bar corresponds to a comma when it occurs on a relatively low level; when it occurs on a relatively high level, to a question mark. Double cross is primarily the sound spelled with a period, but the correspondence is not exact.

We can illustrate with a counting sequence:

one, two, three, four

One way of saying this sequence is with the upturn which characterizes /||/ after the first three numbers and the downturn of /#/ at the end. It is to be noted that *óne* || in this sequence is not the same as *one*(?). The two are differentiated by the difference in the preceding level. Also important is the fact that the sequence *óne* || *twó* || *thrée* || leaves the hearer with the expectation that counting will continue, whereas when *fóur* # is reached, it is interpreted as a signal that counting is complete.

The third type of juncture is one which has neither upturn nor downturn. One way of arriving at recognition of it is to try the counting sequence over again. If the reader has practiced it in the fashion described, he will have recognized the occurrence of /||/ by its upturn. The sequence should now be tried with pitch held level on the first three numbers. The task is not very difficult, since though it may be strange to produce such a pronunciation by direction, a little experimenting with natural forms of the sequence will enable the reader to recognize what is being described. This juncture is called single bar and is written /|/.

The two forms of the counting sequence are then:

óne || twó || thrée || fóur # and óne | twó | thrée | fóur #

Further practice in recognizing /|/ can be gotten by taking a pair of sentences which might be ambiguous in rapid speech and then pronouncing them in careful fashion so as to distinguish them. Such a pair are:

The sûn's râys méet # and The sôns râise méat #

If pronounced in the fashion indicated, the two sentences are quite indistinguishable, though of course, the surrounding context will usually lead the hearer to interpret without hesitation. In more careful speech, or if the context does not clarify, the first sentence is:

The sûn's ráys | méet #

And the second is:

The sóns | râise méat #

The more careful pronunciation also introduces some variations in the stress pattern. The sentences are instructive not only because they are good keys for identifying /|/ but also because they demonstrate that /|/ can be heard without the speaker's giving a true pause, that is, without cessation of sound.

The single bar is not as frequent at the ends of sentences as are the other two, but /|/ can and does occur in sentence final. When it does so, it usually creates the impression of an utterance left incomplete, as if there were hesitation or something else that the speaker might say. The following short quotation from a current novel seems to indicate a terminal /|/, since the "upward inflection" is explainable simply as absence of a downturn:

". . . Johnny had to get his car—"
Her voice ended on an upward inflection, letting the explanation hang suspended on the air.

So far as there is a punctuation mark which corresponds to a terminal /|/, it is the dash which is used in this bit of quoted dialogue.

We have preliminarily defined the three terminals as upturn, downturn, and level. The definition is inadequate, since it will distinguish the three from one another but will not tell us that /|/ is occurring. That is, /|/ can be recognized in these terms only if we already know that there is a juncture of some sort present. This fact means that there must be some sound, or quality of sound, which identifies the whole class, the members of which are then distinguished from one another by the differences which we have already described. The general identifying characteristic is to be found in timing. All of the junctures prolong the immediately preceding sound or sounds, but in varying degrees. These can be described—tentatively only, since the necessary instrumental measurements are not fully available—as prolongation equal to about the length of one average sound for /|/, one and a half average sounds for /||/, and two sounds for /#/. It should also be mentioned that the identification of /#/ as two-unit prolongation with downturn is disputable. One of the features which accompanies /#/ is a gradual cessation of sound, so that the voice may be said to "trail off." It is still not clear whether it is actually the downturn or the trail-off which is the distinguishing feature of /#/. The definitions that have been given here must be taken as a working formulation only, subject to correction when the physical measurements have been made and published.[5]

The definition of terminals as prolongation phenomena must also be made precise in relation to pause. A non-linguist's description of the entities we have been identifying is often to speak of them as pauses of varying length. We have already implied that they are not true pauses, in that sound does not cease. True pause plays no part in linguistic signaling, though as we shall eventually see, it plays a part in a larger area of the communication situation, that which covers the relationship between sentences. It is the prolongations characteristic of the junctures which are responsible for the identification of them with pauses in our ordinary statements about language.

The three junctures we have described are terminals, in that all can occur at the ends of sentences and of phrases. No sentence or phrase can end without one of these occurring. The remaining type of juncture occurs within the borders of a phrase and cannot occur at the end of either sentence

---

[5] The formulation of junctures as time phenomena is due primarily to the investigations of Martin Joos, who has worked extensively with a relatively new instrument, the sound spectrograph. Joos is uniquely qualified for such investigations, since he is both acoustically and linguistically trained. It is to be hoped that he will publish his results not only on junctures but on the meaning of the loose term "length of an average sound."

or phrase. It is called internal, or plus, juncture and is written $/+/$. When sounds are given without juncture, they are said to be in smooth transition, though in this book, in certain situations, it will prove convenient to speak of smooth transition as absence of juncture, or zero.

A minimal pair involving variant position of $/+/$ are *that stuff* and *that's tough*. English speakers sometimes maintain that there is no difference between the pair, but it is easy to show that they do indeed contrast. If the pair are repeated several times and a group of listeners is asked to identify which construction is occurring, there is always agreement. Other minimal pairs are *an aim : a name* and *we'll own : we loan*. Another pair which is minimal if the two constructions are stressed alike is *Í scréam : íce créam*.

In all such distinctions several things happen. Probably most speakers of English would be tempted to say that the distinction lies in syllable division, the various sounds belonging now to one syllable, now to the other. The statement turns out to be ultimately true, but it is certainly inadequate. For one thing, it is only much later in analysis that the syllable can be defined, and for another, there must be some sound which signals for us what the syllable division is. If a pair like *that stuff : that's tough* are again repeated several times, the distinction begins to be audible in terms of prolongation. In the first utterance, the *t*-sound which occurs before *s* is prolonged, in the second it is the *s*-sound. Plus juncture is then like the others in being a phenomenon of timing. The prolongation differs, however, in being a half-unit only, "unit" being used in the sense given above as a period of time about equal to the length of one average sound. Plus is like $/|/$ in lacking any feature of pitch modification.

One of the interesting results of defining $/+/$ as a half-unit prolongation is that the definition fits with a loss of distinction which seems to take place in many, though possibly not all, idiolects. In English, two identical consonant sounds (not letters!) can be brought together by the loss of an intervening sound. A pair showing such loss would be:

touris(t)s are   las(t) Saturday

We should expect a distinction, since the second $/s/$ belongs to the first syllable in the first utterance, and to the second in the other. Moreover, it can be proved that a juncture is occurring, since the *s*-sounds occupy two and a half units. Yet for most speakers there is no distinction. That is, a hypothetical $/-s + s-/$ is no different from a hypothetical $/-ss + -/$. When prolongation of identical sounds occurs, the juncture cannot be placed as falling between them or after them. This loss of distinction is exactly what we should expect if the juncture is a tempo feature alone.[6]

---

[6] It is possible that some idiolects preserve a distinction under these circumstances. If they do, $/+/$ would have to be defined as containing some other differentiating

If we can define /+/ as a time phenomenon, we should still point out that it has important effects on the sounds around it. That is, the kind of *t*-sound which follows the /+/ in *that's + tough* is the sort which regularly begins an English syllable. That which follows the *s* in *that + stuff* is a non-initial variety. The difference is audible. Yet it can be defined as non-contrastive. By this statement we mean that if the presence or absence of /+/ is a contrast, then we can describe the kinds of *t*-sounds as dependent on the contrastive plus. Such noncontrastive differences are called redundant sounds by the specialists in communication theory; the linguist's name for such sounds is "allophones." At this point we shall make no statement about how the linguist decides which sounds are contrastive and which redundant, except the general one that the aim of linguistic analysis of speech sounds is to account for all differences with as few contrasting sounds as possible, reducing as many differences as possible to redundant status.[7]

4. Pitch

The contrasting pitches of utterance, whether terminal or not, are produced by varying rapidity in vibration of the vocal cords. As the rapidity increases, the pitch rises. Pitch in speech, unlike pitch in singing, is relative rather than absolute. A linguistically high pitch for a bass voice may differ considerably from the same pitch for a soprano, but as long as the levels are parallel in the two voices, the patterns which result are recognizable.

Terminal pitches, as we have seen, consist in an upturn and a downturn, though the upturn is greater than the downturn. The terminal pitches do not move as far as the difference between two adjacent levels, and the terminals can fall on varying levels. They can, for instance, produce a fall from the lowest level or a rise from the highest level.

----

characteristic, perhaps the increase of energy which marks the beginning of a syllable, or the decrease which marks its end, or the dip between the two. This point also will have to await acoustic analysis.

[7] A serious difficulty has arisen over just this decision as to whether differences in sounds surrounding /+/ are or are not redundant. A /+/ is often so short as to be below the duration (five centiseconds) which the human ear can hear. Under these circumstances, what we actually do hear is the effect on the surrounding sounds. The result is naturally to make many linguists believe that the surrounding sounds are contrastive. The answer has been best formulated by Robert P. Stockwell, using material from Joos. The Stockwell formulation will appear in the forthcoming report of the Texas Conference on Problems of Linguistic Analysis. According to Stockwell, the juncture can be proved to be occurring by acoustic measurement; what we hear are the redundant sounds which are the only audible indication that the juncture is there.

The pitch levels are written with figures /1/ to /4/, with /1/ for the lowest, /4/ for the highest pitch.

2   3   1
Jôhn + wênt + to + schóol + to + dày #

The transcription indicates that the sentence starts on the second level of pitch, goes on without change to the syllable *school*, which occurs with pitch /3/, and thereafter falls gradually, ending with pitch /1/ on the final syllable. This contour is then followed by a further, but very slight fall, which is the terminal pitch. This pattern, /2 3 1/ followed by /#/, is typical of simple declaration and also of the citation forms of single words.

There is a partial correlation between pitch and stress, since the highest pitch normally falls on the syllable with primary stress. Though the correlation is common, it is not absolute, so that it remains necessary to treat pitch and stress independently. There are, for instance, occurrences of primary stress with pitch /1/, as in

1 1   1 1   1 1
yés | yés | yés #

when the utterance implies the attitude "Don't be foolish, of course it is."

Pitch patterns in English are best analyzed as belonging to the sentence as a whole, rather than to the word. The pitch patterns—together with their terminals—distinguish one sentence from another, as the sentence above is distinguished from a more normal sequence, such as:

3 2   3 2   3 1
yés | yés | yés #

The pitch patterns might, it is true, be assigned to phrases, but there are instances in which a single contour is spread over a sentence of more than one phrase, as in:

2   3   2   2   2
I + thínk + so | sâid + Jóhn |

Here the contour seems to be simply /2 3 2/, though extended over the final phrase. This is not to say that a sentence cannot have more than one contour, since we can certainly think of plenty of sentences like:

2   3 2   2   3 1
Jôhn + wênt + físhing | Mâry + wênt + to + tówn #

The intention of these statements is to associate the pitch pattern with the sentence, an association expressible by the statement that a sentence must have one or more patterns (or contours); a sentence of a single contour may have one or more phrases; a sentence of more than one contour is a sentence which is a construction of more than one phrase. These statements are necessarily made as first approximations, however. We have not been able to define such concepts as "phrase" and "sentence." We can, however, define a pitch contour at this point. It is a pattern of pitch levels rising to and falling from a single peak and ending in a terminal juncture.

The pitch contour, defined as a sequence of pitches with only one peak, may extend beyond the boundary of a single phrase as it does in the sentence "'I think so,' said John." Stress patterns also show contours, in that the sequence of stresses between terminal junctures always shows a single peak, the primary stress. Stress contours differ from pitch contours in that two phrases are never united into a single stress contour. For this reason, stress patterns can be defined as belonging to the phrase, whereas pitch patterns may appear at the phrase level but may also characterize sentences composed of more than one phrase. In placing pitch patterns on the sentence level, we are following a usual type of analysis, but in placing stress as a part of the phrase we run counter to the usual statement that stress characterizes words. We should clarify the statement that a pair of words such as *differ* and *defer* have stress patterns of $/'\ ^{\vee}/$ and $/^{\vee}\ '/$ by explaining that these are the patterns these two words have when pronounced as citation forms, that is, when treated as phrases made up of single words. No word can be pronounced except as a phrase or a part of a phrase, so that any pronunciation of a word receives either the stress pattern of a complete phrase or the partial stress pattern characteristic of it as part of a phrase.

We shall not in this chapter attempt to describe the pitch patterns of English, other than to say for illustrative purposes that a typical question pattern is $/2\ 3\ |||/$ as in:

$$
\begin{matrix}
2 & & & 3 \\
\text{Jôhn} & + & \text{wênt} & + & \text{hóme} \ ||
\end{matrix}
$$

The patterns are relatively few and will be described in Section 6 of Chapter 7. Our task in this chapter is only to establish contrasts for all four pitch levels.

The easiest contrast to establish independently of the contrastive terminal junctures is that between $/3/$ and $/4/$. We have seen $/3/$ occurring in such a sentence as:

$$
\begin{matrix}
2 & & & 3\ 1 \\
\text{Jôhn} & + & \text{wênt} & + & \text{físhing} \ \#
\end{matrix}
$$

If this sentence occurs as an answer to something like "Didn't John go hunting?" it will become:

$$
\begin{matrix}
2 & & & 4\ 1 \\
\text{Jôhn} & + & \text{wênt} & + & \text{fìshing} \ \#
\end{matrix}
$$

Nothing is changed except the pitch which falls on the primary stress. Some practice in hearing the distinction may be necessary, since in habitual talk about language we would call this modification merely one of "emphasis," which does not distinguish it from stress.

If /3/ and /4/ are now established as levels which the reader is able to hear, we then go on to contrasts for the other two pitches, still independent of the terminals, and of the stress variation. We can return to the type of sentence we spoke of earlier, in which a single contour is spread over two phrases:

$$\begin{array}{cccc} 2 & 32 & 2 & 2 \end{array}$$
Lêt's gó | Jôhn + ánswered |

If we now turn this sentence around, we get a construction of two phrases with two contours:

$$\begin{array}{ccccc} 2 & 3 & 2 & 2 & 31 \end{array}$$
Jôhn + ánswered | Lêt's gó #

The sequence *John answered* is occurring under identical conditions of stress and following terminal, but with /2/ on the primarily stressed syllable in one instance and /3/ on it in the other.

The same sort of device can be used for establishing contrastive value for /1/:

$$\begin{array}{cccc} 2 & 31 & 1 & 1 \end{array}$$
Ì + dó | Jôhn + ánswered #

Here the second phrase continues the last level of the preceding /2 3 1/ contour. If the reader is able to identify /2 3 1/ he should then have no difficulty in recognizing that the second phrase continues the same level. Again we turn the sentence around:

$$\begin{array}{ccccc} 2 & 3 & 1 & 2 & 31 \end{array}$$
Jôhn + ánswered # Ì + dó #

The /1/ occurs with primary stress and identical terminal in both instances of the phrase. We have not attempted to show all the types of contrast which occur. For absolute completeness we would have to show contrast between /4/ and all the others in turn, /3/ and all the others in turn, and so on. Those here given are enough to indicate that such a permutation of contrasts should be easily constructible. A final warning is that we have used several merely typical and common pitch patterns in differing sentences. It is hoped that by now the reader is sufficiently aware of possibilities of variation so that he realizes that none of these common pitch patterns are meant to be the only ones under which the several sentences could occur.

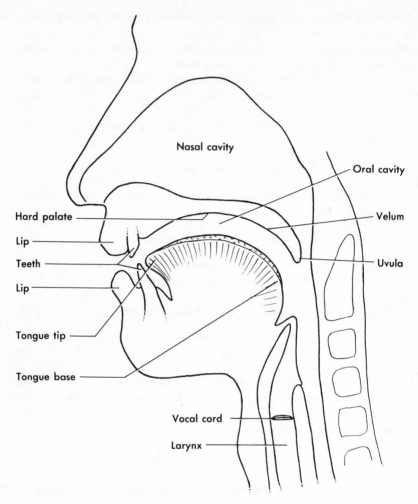

THE SPEECH ORGANS

The ridge immediately behind the upper front teeth is the alveolar ridge (from the alveoli, the sacs in which the teeth are set).

The portion of the upper throat above the larynx and below the oral cavity is the pharynx. It extends above the velum to the beginning of the nasal passage. This upper portion is called the nasopharynx.

The larynx is a cartilaginous box whose inner surfaces are clothed with flesh and muscle. The forward surface of the larynx is the "Adam's apple." It contains two retractile, muscular lips, capable of producing a continuous sound by vibration. They are the vocal cords, only one of which can be seen in this sectional view. The opening between them is the glottis.

Below the larynx is the trachea, or windpipe.

3.... CONSONANTS

1. Introduction

The names "consonant" and "vowel" are familiar to everyone by long usage and will be used throughout this book. Definition of these two classes of sounds rests not on their phonetic quality but on their differing distribution. There have been, however, a good many efforts to define consonants as a universal class of sounds marked by some phonetic feature always found among them and always absent from the class of vowels. Such efforts are less than completely successful for the reason that what is distributionally a consonant in one language may be distributionally a vowel in another. There are also languages—Chinook is apparently one—in which classification of sounds into consonants and vowels is irrelevant. For these reasons, the definition of consonants must be made language by language rather than universally. In this chapter there is no attempt to define the class of sounds described as consonants. They are instead merely listed, and definition of the class must wait until Chapter 6, "Phonotactics," in which we take up the distributional characteristics of English sounds.

Before consonants are considered a set of symbols to designate them unambiguously must be introduced, as has already been done for stresses, junctures, and pitch. The list of key words which follows gives the symbols at the left, and as far as possible each consonant is then illustrated in initial, final, and medial position. This list is further chosen so as to give words which are as nearly as possible alike in pronunciation, at least in their consonants, in all dialects:

1. /p/ *pat, cap, Cappy*
2. /b/ *bat, cab, cabby*
3. /t/ *tap, cat, catty*[1]
4. /d/ *dab, cad, caddie*
5. /k/ *cat, tack, tacky*
6. /g/ *gat, tag, baggy*
7. /c/ *chap, patch, patchy*
8. /j/ *Jack, cadge, badges*
9. /f/ *fat, laugh, taffy*
10. /v/ *vat, love, covey*
11. /θ/ *thigh, teeth, ether*
12. /ð/ *thy, teethe, either*

[1] In some dialects, the distinction between *catty* and *caddie* is lost, both being pronounced with a /d/.

13. /s/ *sap, pass, classy*   19. /ŋ/ ——, *slang, slangy*
14. /z/ *zoo, ooze, choosey*   20. /l/ *lass, Sal, Sally*
15. /š/ *shack, cash, mashie*   21. /r/ *rot, tar,[3] sorry*
16. /ž/ ——, *rouge,[2] measure*   22. /y/ *yacht*
17. /m/ *mat, cam, clammy*   23. /w/ *watt*
18. /n/ *gnat, can, canny*   24. /h/ *hot*

Numbers 16 and 19 have blanks in the first column, since these consonants do not occur in initial position (except that 16 occurs in some foreign words). Numbers 22, 23, and 24 are not taken up in final and medial positions because in postvocalic occurrences they are better taken up with the vowels.

The twenty-four sounds here given are distinguished from one another by a relatively small number of articulatory differences, called distinctive features. The arrangement of these features is such that each sound shares some distinctive features with others although each sound is set off from every other sound by a difference in at least one distinctive feature. As a result, the sounds can be arranged in a series of intersecting classifications, making a striking, though imperfect, pattern. The distinctive features, furthermore, sometimes fall into pairs, sometimes form a larger series.

2. Voice versus voicelessness

When the vocal cords are vibrating, they impart musical quality—regular vibration—to the column of air that passes between them, and so to the resultant sound. This vibration of the vocal cords is called voice, and its absence—when the vocal cords are drawn back so that air passes freely between them—is called voicelessness. Voice can be isolated and heard by contrasting a voiced with a voiceless sound. Such a pair are the voiced /z/ and the voiceless /s/. The vibration of the /z/ can be felt by putting a finger on the Adam's apple.

The voice-voicelessness distinction appears as one which sets up some English consonants in opposed pairs, the members of each pair differing only in voice. The consonants paired by voice are as follows:

VOICELESS /p t c k f θ s š
VOICED   b d j g v ð z ž/ .

---

[2] *Rouge* is often pronounced with /j/ rather than /ž/, which is rare in final position.
[3] In eastern New England and much of the coastal South, /r/ is usually absent in postvocalic position.

In addition, there are a number of consonants which are normally voiced but are not opposed to corresponding voiceless sounds to make pairs. Such sounds are the nasals, /m/, /n/, and /ŋ/; the linguals /l/ and /r/; and two sounds of the class called semivowels, /y/ and /w/. In these unpaired consonants, voice ceases to be a distinctive feature, and there are a number of varieties of these unpaired sounds which are more or less unvoiced. These occur in the neighborhood of voiceless sounds, as with the /w/ of *sweet* and the /r/ of *tree*.

3. Closure versus constriction

The oral cavity can be completely closed by placing the tongue against the roof of the mouth or by pressing the lips together, though to secure such closure, the velum must be raised to prevent air from passing through the nose. A sound characterized by closure is called a stop. The contrasting type of sound is made by merely narrowing the oral cavity by means of tongue or lips, again with raised velum. When the oral cavity is thus narrowed, friction is set up at the point of greatest narrowness, and the resulting sound is called a spirant.

The stops of English, voiceless and voiced, are:

> VOICELESS   /p t c k
> VOICED   b d j g/

The spirants of English, similarly voiceless and voiced, are:

> VOICELESS   /f θ s š
> VOICED   v ð z ž/

It will be observed that there are four pairs of both stops and spirants,[4]

---

[4] This listing of stops and spirants makes two controversial statements. The sounds here written /c/ and /j/ are often analyzed as sequences, namely /tš/ and /dž/. Second, the sound /h/ is often classed among the spirants, or even as an isolated sound not placed in the intersecting system of distinctive features, but in any event not placed among the semivowels, where it will be described in this chapter. Unfortunately, it is not possible to make any statement on these matters which is not controversial. Even to compromise, as one recent book on linguistics has done, by setting up a special symbol for the third semivowel, which does not place it at all with relation to other sounds, is to be controversial. Such compromises only ensure that all parties to the dispute will be dissatisfied. Both these disputes involve matters which must somehow, and sometime, be answered positively on an all-or-none basis, and I have therefore assumed that it is the linguist's duty to come to a definite position as best he can about both of them. Later in this chapter there is some discussion of the reasons for these two decisions and a presentation of the structural alternatives involved. It is, of course, the reader's privilege to disagree, since it is his task also to come to the best conclusion of which he is capable.

but stops and spirants do not themselves pair off as perfectly as do voiced and voiceless sounds, since there are also differences in articulation. The most perfect pairs are /p/ : /f/ and /b/ : /v/, though even here there is a slight difference, since the stops are made with both lips, and the spirants with lower lip and teeth.

4. Position of articulation in four-way distinctions

Up to this point, we have dealt with distinctive features which are in binary arrangement. Position of articulation, however, gives a multiple differentiation. By position of articulation is meant the point in the oral-nasal cavity at which there is either closure or constriction. Considerable discussion will be necessary to present this type of differentiation clearly. The position which is furthest forward is that achieved by closing both lips. This position is known as bilabial, and English /p/ and /b/ are thus made. Next back is the position in which the lower lip is placed against the lower edge of the upper front teeth. This position is called labiodental, and this is the position of the spirants /f/ and /v/.

The third position can be called interdental, though the description is not accurate for all varieties of pronunciation. The blade of the tongue narrows the opening of the oral cavity by approaching the lower edge of the upper front teeth, or may actually protrude between the upper and lower teeth. There are two interdental sounds, the spirants /θ/ and /ð/.

There is a larger series of sounds which can be called dental. Two are stops, two are spirants. In all, the tongue either closes the mouth in the general region of the base of the upper front teeth, or the tongue narrows the opening so as to produce friction at that point. There is considerable variation, however, in the exact point of articulation. It may be on the back surface of the upper teeth, at their base, or on the ridge behind them, which is called the alveolar ridge. All these variations are covered by the term "dental." The following are the dentals:

/t d s z/

Next is a position on the back surface of the alveolar ridge, which can be called postdental. There are four postdental sounds, /c j š ž/. The first two of these are paired stops, and their analysis presents a number of problems. The release of these stops, characterized by a high degree of friction, will be discussed under nondistinctive features. The two spirants present only a very minor problem, one of variation. The sounds can be made either with the tip of the tongue up (apical articulation), so that constriction is produced over the tip, or with the tip down (dorsal articulation), so that the constriction is produced by the surface of the tongue.

The position farthest back is known as velar. That is, the back surface of the tongue produces closure or constriction against the soft palate, or velum. The stops /g/ and /k/ are velar.

In surveying stops and spirants, we have now enumerated a total of six articulatory positions, namely, bilabial, labiodental, interdental, dental, postdental, and velar. They give a diagrammatic arrangement as follows:

BILABIAL	LABIODENTAL	INTERDENTAL	DENTAL	POSTDENTAL	VELAR
/p			t	c	k
b			d	j	g
	f	θ	s	š	
	v	ð	z	ž	/

The diagram is symmetrical, but only partly so. The stops and spirants are each arranged in four positional pairs, from front to back, but the positional groups in stops cover a wider range than do those for spirants, which run only from labiodental to postdental instead of all the way from bilabial to velar.

The positional arrangement can be much more symmetrically stated if we disregard exact location and reduce our six positions to four, numbered from front to back for both stops and spirants:

POSITION 1	POSITION 2	POSITION 3	POSITION 4
/p	t	c	k
b	d	j	g
f	θ	s	š
v	ð	z	ž/

The two diagrams introduce a problem. Which diagram is the better? The first diagram states the phonetic facts more accurately and groups together sounds which are alike in both articulation and acoustic quality, as in the series of sounds labeled postdental. Yet the first diagram, by its phonetic accuracy, sacrifices an underlying structural symmetry which can be expressed by an analogy: as bilabial, dental, postdental, and velar are to the stops, so labiodental, interdental, dental, and postdental are to the spirants. The second diagram brings out this structural relation, but sacrifices phonetic accuracy, as when it groups the postdental spirants not with the postdental stops but with the velar stops. The two diagrams taken together express one of the constantly recurring qualities of language, the occurrence of both regularity and irregularity. The analyst has a choice as to whether he will emphasize the symmetry or the irregularity; perhaps better, he has a choice as to whether he will say that the pattern is one of phonetic congruity with partial structural symmetry or one of structural symmetry with only partial phonetic congruity. At present it would seem necessary to use both types of statement, the one supplementing the other. The first type of diagram is much the more common in books on phonetics, and it is clearly needed since exact phonetic knowledge of sounds is necessary to understand both their arrangement into groups of contrastive sounds and the shifting development of these groups. Yet, though linguists are hesitant to commit themselves fully, it also seems that some phenomena, particularly in histori- cal development, are intimately related to, if not caused by, structural symmetry.

5. Some controversial classifications

As was intimated earlier (footnote 4, p. 33), the listing of the initial sounds of *chump* and *jump* among the stops is not by any means universally accepted among American linguists. The alternative is to classify these sounds as sequences of stop and spirant, /tš/ and /dž/. The controversy has at times seemed to be settled, but has each time broken out afresh. At an early period of phonetic study, the International Phonetic Association devised an alphabet for the writing of sounds, familiar to many students under the name "IPA." The background of this alphabet was largely the sounds of French, and since in French a sound like that of *chump* is indeed a sequence, the IPA wrote the English sounds as sequences. For long this analysis was accepted uncritically, and many older books on phonetics present it without discussion. In the early 'thirties, Bloomfield presented a contrast which can be illustrated by the pair *white shoes*: *why choose*. One of these is a sequence, the other something different and therefore apparently a single sound. This contrast seemed to settle the matter in favor of classifying the sounds in question as units in English. In 1940, the Bloch and Trager analysis of English sounds set up /+/ as a unit, and it became evident that the Bloom- field distinction could be easily handled by assuming that *white shoes* con- tained the sequence /-t + š-/, while *why choose* could be analyzed as con- taining /- + tš-/. Since that time there has been no agreement.

The basic reason that I have chosen to present the sounds as units is that I believe there are contrasts in my idiolect which make such an inter- pretation necessary. These can be illustrated as follows:

/–t + š–/   *whîte shóes, whàt shĕbáng? wheát shèaf, whàt shĕ díd*
/–tš–/   *cóurtshìp, Whéatshèaf* (name of an inn), *whàt shĕ díd*
/– + c–/   *whỳ chóose, ă chúmp, séa chèst, blûe chéese, kăchóo*
/–c + –/   *cátch 'ĭm, Dûtch élm, pítch-òut, Dútchỷ*
/–c–/   *cátch 'ĭm, kéchŭp, dúchy, kítchĕn, kăchóo*

It is not contended that these distinctions exist in all idiolects, nor, as the examples show, does every word or construction have to be pronounced with only one of the sequences. It is rather contended that all the sequences occur in one idiolect under conditions of stress sufficiently varied to make it necessary to provide for the five differing sequences which can be set up only by recognizing /c/ as a unity.

It should also be pointed out that the issue is not always clear in discussions of the problem. It is sometimes assumed that all dialects and idiolects are alike, so that the problem is one of analysis alone. At other times it is assumed that idiolects differ, some having a sequence, others a unity. Unfortunately it has not been conclusively proved that there are idiolects which have only a sequence, so that at the present it can only be stated that such idiolects are possibilities.

As for distributional evidence on whether we are dealing with sequences or with unities, it is inconclusive. There is good distributional evidence for both conclusions. The intersecting patterns of distinctive features, which have been presented here, probably have little evidential value. It is rather that the relations of stops and spirants in parallel sets of fours is a product of the decision to place /c/ and /j/ among the stops than that it is a necessity to place them there because the symmetrical arrangement forces it. Section 9 of this chapter will present the kind of symmetrical arrangement which is the result of removing /c/ and /j/ from the list of stops.

The second controversy is over /h/, which we have called a semivowel. The controversy is even more violent, though in fact the necessary conclusions are at least a little clearer. The initial /h/ of *home, heat, huge,* and *what* was certainly, at one time in the past, a spirant in all its occurrences. In its present distribution, as we shall see in Chapter 6, it still shows itself in some sequences which are typical for spirants, and in some of the occurrences listed above, it shows the feature of friction which, as we saw in Section 3, is characteristic of spirants. If we consider the initial /h/ a spirant, however, it is one which is quite unlike other spirants in English, in that it is not paired with a voiced counterpart. Further, the friction which characterizes some initial /h/-sounds is not generally found in all occurrences and can be described as a noncontrasting variety of sound which occurs only under statable conditions which prevent contrastive quality. Sometimes /h/ is stated to be a spirant, not because of the friction heard in *huge*, but because there is another kind of friction, taking place at the glottis or in the pharynx. But glottal or pharyngeal friction is something which appears nowhere else in the system of nearly symmetrical distinctive features which characterize English sounds. To rely on this kind of friction to identify /h/ as a spirant is therefore to isolate it still further from the rest of the system.

The distributional features which make /h/ look like a spirant can be disregarded, since as we shall see, they are capable of a different explanation. In other words, whatever /h/ may be, classification as a spirant is to be avoided if some other classification for it can be discovered which leaves it less isolated.

A phonetic description of /h/ which is as good as any is as normally a voiceless vowel which has varieties corresponding to many different vowels —even to some things which are not vowels, as in the interjection often written *hmm*, where it is a voiceless nasal. As for the statement that there are varieties corresponding to most vowels, note the way the /h/ is pronounced in *aha, teehee, yoohoo*, and *behest*. The statement that /h/ is a voiceless vowel will hold except for forms like *hmm*, where its nonvocalic quality can be assumed to be accounted for by the nature of the sound which follows. But even if we accept this phonetic statement, to classify /h/ as a vowel is obviously rather worse than to classify it as a spirant, since no vowels show voiceless quality in English. The statement has value, however, in two ways. First, the sound has some phonetic resemblance to vowels, and second, it is clear that the sound is without any closely fixed point of articulation as a distinctive feature.

The semivowels /y/ and /w/ similarly vary in position; compare /y/ in *Bayonne, he yipped, a yacht*; and also compare /w/ in *to woo, he weds, a war*. A distinctive feature for semivowels as a class can then be set up as "lack of fixed position." Since, as will be shown later, there is structural gain if a third semivowel can be found and used in analysis in ways parallel to the use of /y/ and /w/, /h/ can be pressed into service as the third semivowel. It is important to note that this is a classification the reasons for which lie in the symmetrical structure of distinctive features and which can be defended because it removes a needless asymmetry. What we have is an /h/ which under other classifications is a "leftover," at the same time that there is a "hole" in the class of semivowels. Under such circumstances the analyst is under obligation to re-examine his system to find if the leftover cannot be made to fill the hole.

The explanation adopted here was first announced by George Trager in a talk before the Yale Linguistic Club. It later appeared in joint publications by Trager and Bloch and by Trager and Smith, and has been perhaps most widely circulated in the series of books for English as a second language put out under the auspices of the American Council of Learned Societies.[5] As intimated, it has often been attacked, and it is almost certain that no one would have suggested this solution had the starting point been only observation of the phonetic characteristics of the sounds in question. It is the solution adopted here because I know of no other which will not leave the general sound system violently skewed. To any student or analyst who does not accept the working principle that skewness is to be avoided in shaping a description, the inclusion of /h/ among the semivowels will seem a needless and grotesque break with tradition.

The status of /c j/ and /h/ is different. With /c j/ the pattern statement offers no convincing solution, and the solution must be sought in the number and kinds of contrasts. With /h/, the pattern is the sole important reason for the final classification of the sound. Since the status of the two problems is thus different, Section 9 of this chapter offers an alternate pattern statement for /c j/ but none for /h/, since a different classification of /h/ would largely destroy the pattern.

6. Fixed position versus nonfixed position

This opposition has already been described. Nonfixed position characterizes the three sounds called semivowels, all of which have an unusually large number of noncontrastive varieties in accord with what sounds surround them. The semivowels /y/ and /w/ can be described as sounds moving away from, or gliding from, a generally high front or high back position to any position which is less high front or less high back, respectively. The /h/-sound, notably different from these two in many ways, also has a large number of noncontrastive varieties, dependent on the surrounding sounds. All three then have nonfixed positions and are thus negatively distinguished from all other sounds. It can be mentioned in passing that /h/, though often not a glide in the same sense as /y/ and /w/, has varieties in which it can be said to glide, as when an /h/ is placed between vowels of

---

[5] The first publication arguing for treatment of /h/ as the third semivowel was George L. Trager and Bernard Bloch, "The Syllabic Phonemes of English," *Language*, XVII, 1941, p. 239–41. The more extended publication by Trager and Henry Lee Smith, Jr., was *An Outline of English Structure*, Studies in Linguistics: Occasional Papers 3, 1951. See particularly p. 20–30. Typical of the volumes in the Spoken English Series done under the auspices of the American Council of Learned Societies is *El Inglés Hablado* by F. B. Agard and Assistants, Holt, New York, 1953. This volume provides extensive dialogues in complete phonemic notation.

differing character. Nonfixed position might seem to make it impossible to distinguish the semivowels in terms of position of articulation. This is not the case, however, since even though their positions are not narrowly fixed, they can still be described as generally front, or generally back, with relation to each other.

7. Position of articulation in three-way distinctions

We have described at length the appearance of position of articulation in stops and spirants, where there are (in our analysis) four differing positions from front to back. There are two sets of sounds in which position of articulation appears as a three-way distinction, rather than as a four-way system. These are the semivowels and the nasals. The three nasals are:

$$/\text{m n ŋ}/$$

For the first, /m/, the actual position is bilabial; for the second, /n/, it is dental; for the third, /ŋ/, it is palato-velar. These have, in short, the same positions as the stops /b/, /d/, and /g/.

The three semivowels (in our analysis) can be described as containing one sound, /y/, which is generally front, or more exactly a glide starting from a generally front position. A second sound is /w/, which can similarly be described as starting from a back position. The third sound, /h/, in these terms, is best described negatively—it is non-front and non-back. In this negative sense, but perhaps in this negative sense only, it can be assigned to the remaining position, that which is non-front and non-back, i.e., center.

Unlike as semivowels and nasals are in many ways, they share some characteristics. They are unpaired as to voice, none of them having counterparts different in voice only. Also, they share the three-way, rather than the four-way, distinction in position. Here, as with stops and spirants, the positions are different in detail for the two sets and can be equated only at the expense of disregarding phonetic and acoustic accuracy. But as with stops and spirants, structural analogy justifies the equation, provided only that the statement is not made so as to suppress the facts of difference. Nasals and semivowels are therefore assigned to a three-distinction system, looking like this:

FRONT	CENTER	BACK
/m	n	ŋ
y	h	w/

The distinctive features which separate the two sets are double, however.

The nasals have the positive feature of nasality, but lack the nonfixed position of the semivowels. The semivowels, in turn, have the positive feature of nonfixed position, but lack nasality.

8. Lateral versus nonlateral consonants

There are two remaining consonants, made in a rather similar position, /l/ and /r/. The usual name for them is liquids, though since it is primarily the tongue which produces them, a better name might be linguals. The two are paired by their lingual quality, and are not set off from any other consonants by point of articulation; the four- and three-point articulatory opposition of stops and spirants, on the one hand, and of nasals and semivowels, on the other, is here still further reduced to one position only. Or put otherwise, in this set articulatory position has ceased to be a distinctive feature, just as in nasals and semivowels, voice and voicelessness ceased to be distinctive features. The pair, then, have a simple binary opposition, which can be easily described. The first of them, /l/, has lateral quality. That is to say, the tip of the tongue is placed against the roof of the mouth —the exact position does not matter—but the sides of the tongue are narrowed so that air passes freely around them. The second of the pair, /r/, is without this quality and has instead a bunching of the tongue in the midmouth at the same time that the surface of the tongue is widened and flattened. At least, this is probably a common way of making the sound, though older books describe a variety which is used in a number of dialects where the tip of the tongue is turned upward and backward toward the roof of the mouth. The opposition between /l/ and /r/ can then be called simply lateral and nonlateral, and both sounds can be called linguals.

9. Structural statements

It will now be seen that the consonants are arranged in three structural sets. The first is that of stops and spirants, where there are four quadrilateral sets, the first one of which is:

	STOPS	SPIRANTS
VOICELESS	/p	f
VOICED	b	v/

This gives a figure for all of this system which would look like this:

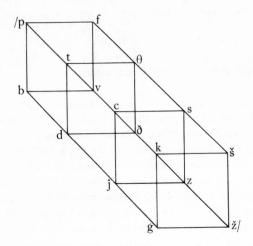

In this figure, every line represents opposed distinctive features. That is, /p t c k/ are all opposed to /f θ s š/ by the opposition between stops and spirants, and both of these are opposed to /b d j g/ and /v ð z ž/ by the voiced-voiceless distinction. The four connected squares represent the four articulatory positions.

In nasals and semivowels, however, the system is on one plane, since the voiced-voiceless distinction is dropped:

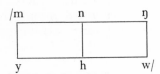

There is one series /m n ŋ/, differentiated by position, and a second series, /y h w/, differentiated in the same way. Each series is differentiated from the other by the distinction between nasality with fixed position and non-nasality with nonfixed position.

Finally, the linguals are distinguished by a simple opposition:

LATERAL   /l/
————————————————
NONLATERAL   /r/

The descriptions and patterns we have thus far stated can be summarized in a single table:

		VOICELESS	/p	t	c	k
STOPS		VOICED	b	d	j	g
		VOICELESS	f	θ	s	š
SPIRANTS		VOICED	v	ð	z	ž
	NASALS			m	n	ŋ
	SEMIVOWELS		y	h	w	
	LATERAL			l		
	NONLATERAL			r	/	

It was said earlier that an alternative structural statement, that which would result from removal of /c j/ from the list of stops, would be given. It is herewith appended, though in briefer form than that which we have been developing at length:

/f θ s š
v ð z ž
p t k
b d g
m n ŋ
y h w
l
r   /

In this arrangement, only one set has a fourfold-distinction system, the spirants. They are thus isolated from the rest of the system, and the skewness of the front to back positions for spirants and for stops is no longer strange, since difference in distinctions does away with any need for equating four-way and three-way sets. Another advantage to this system is that it draws together the stops and nasals, in accord with the phonetic fact that the two sets share the feature of oral closure. The rest of the pattern remains the same.

As a pattern, there are many things to be said for this arrangement, not least of which is that this is an arrangement which is closer to the historical one which must once have existed. The reason this pattern has not been adopted has been made clear: it is believed that the distinctions found in at least one idiolect prevent it. Should this belief prove to be mistaken, the alternate pattern would be forced upon us. It should be evident that such a change would be relatively minor in its effects, not at all a major revolution.

10. Contrastive and redundant features

In describing consonants, we have several times met with a feature of sound which is contrastive in one part of the system but which ceases to be so in some other part. When a feature ceases to be distinctive, sounds can have it or be without it, and it will no longer make any difference to the signal system, becoming redundant. Thus, in all of the system except stops and spirants, voice is no longer a distinctive feature. Most of the eight remaining sounds are normally voiced, but all have voiceless varieties. The /h/, however, is normally voiceless in prevocalic position, though voiced postvocalically. A second feature which becomes nondistinctive in a part of the system is position of articulation, since the linguals have only one position, with nothing opposed. As we should expect, the linguals can therefore vary widely from front to back.

In the system of classification which places /c j/ among the stops, the friction which characterizes their release and which ordinarily is a distinctive feature of the spirants has been classified as nondistinctive. A current name for stops with spirant release is "affricates," and the friction release is spoken of as affrication. In the system we have adopted, therefore, affrication has not been mentioned, since /c/ is distinguished from /t/ by its position, and the affrication is redundant.

Often a set of sounds has some feature which is quite constant but which is redundant as long as some other feature has been decided upon as distinctive. An example of such a relatively constant feature is found among the voiceless stops. All have varieties which have the quality known as aspiration, a puff of air accompanying the release, which can be felt with the hand held before the lips if a series of words like *pool, tool, Charles, cool* are pronounced in isolation. The aspiration varies somewhat in intensity for the different stops, but occurs for all of them in postjunctural position. As long as voicelessness is held to be the distinctive feature, aspiration is redundant. It is interesting, therefore, that there has been at least one attempt to describe aspiration as the distinctive feature and voicelessness as redundant. The attempt has not been very actively pressed and is not adopted in this book, since it would result in a rather more complex classification of the stops. In a classification based on aspiration and the lack of it, the stop of *stew* would have to be described as a variety of the sound found in *do*, not as a variety of the sound found in *two*. Difficulty would arise with the variety of sound found in *water*, which is unaspirate, as is the sound found in *ladder*. For dialects which keep the two sounds distinct, an aspirate-nonaspirate classification would at least be no better than one based on voice. We shall return to this variety of /t/ shortly.

Among other redundant features of stops is their length. Generally, voiceless stops are shorter than voiced stops, though one of the peculiarities of /c j/, which falls in with classifying them as sequences, is that their length approximates that of two sounds. The relative shortness of /t/ as opposed to /d/ is a normally redundant feature which has a unique relation to the variety of voiced /t/ we have just been describing. Redundant features of some other sounds are that /y/ is normally made with a slitlike opening made by spreading the lips, while /w/ has a tubelike opening made by rounding the lips. Similarly, /s/ and /z/ have slitlike openings between the tongue and roof of the mouth, while /š/ and /ž/ have tubelike openings between tongue and roof of the mouth.

Nondistinctive features can also be correlated with some varieties of a class of sounds rather than with all; strictly speaking, aspiration thus distinguishes only some varieties of stops. Another such feature, which accompanies stops in some positions, is absence of release. This lack of release is normal for a stop followed by another stop, as in *doctor, Atkins, captain,* and *abdomen.* Stops before a terminal juncture may or may not have a release. In my own idiolect there are certain styles of talking in which the release is characteristic—the styles characteristic of lecturing, of talking into a recording machine, of repeating for someone who has not understood. In normal conversation, the release is absent.

All sounds have varieties which vary in position, particularly noticeable if such variation produces no overlapping with the positional range of some opposed sound. Variation is quite wide with a sound like /l/; the series found in *filth, Olga, million, feel,* and *cool* makes an excellent opportunity for observing variation in fronting and backing. A similar variation can be found in the /t/—if that is the sound used—of *width,* as contrasted with the /t/ of *act.*

Akin to fronting and backing, but differently accomplished, is the variation known as brightening and darkening. The variation can be heard in the *m*-sounds of *seem* and *zoom.* There is no variation of position, since both varieties are firmly bilabial. Some of the quality of the preceding vowel is carried over into the following /m/, since the tongue position of the vowels (and the rounded or slit position of the lips) persists after closing the lips. It is possible to make a series of /m/'s or /l/'s with the qualities of each of the vowels of English in turn. Somewhat the same thing can be done with the spirants /s z š ž/, though not with as perfect a series. Even with sounds involving the tongue, as with those just mentioned and with /n/, it is possible to produce this kind of variation by varying the position of the part of the tongue behind the tip, or varying the lip position, or both. A consonant is called bright if it approaches the quality of the vowels in *peal* and *pail,* dark if it approaches the quality of those in *pool* or *pall.* In English, variation in brightness is of some importance for /l/, at least.

Generally, initial or postjunctural /l/'s are brighter than those after vowels, but in large areas of the South, /l/'s are bright (or at least brighter than those of other dialects) in all positions. A bright variety of /l/ in *college* is a striking Southernism.

Glottal action presents a somewhat special type of nondistinctive feature. The glottis—the opening between the vocal cords—can be tightly closed so as to prevent escape of air. This is what happens when we hold our breath. In speech, closing the glottis occurs as a momentary interruption, the glottal stop, written [ʔ]. It can be heard in the form *ah-ah* [áʔa] which means "Stop it!" This interjection, however, is not a part of the regular linguistic structure and is a sort of verbal gesture. In normal English speech, the glottal stop occurs in some idiolects before any primarily stressed vowel after pause. It is a way of beginning the vowel (what is called a vowel onset) which does not contrast with other ways of beginning the vowel, and so is nondistinctive. In other situations, and in some dialects of the Eastern metropolitan area, a glottal stop occurs in words where a /p/, /t/, or /k/ precedes an unstressed syllable ending in a nasal of the same point of articulation as the stop, or when the unstressed syllable ends in /l/ after any of these stops. Examples are *cap'm* (for *captain*), *kitten*, and *bottle*. In all these words, what is most audible is the glottal stop, but the glottal stop occurs with simultaneous oral closure. As a result we have glottalized varieties of /p/, /t/, and /k/, rather than new contrastive sounds.

This description of nondistinctive features is meant to be illustrative rather than exhaustive and could well take up many more pages. We will close the subject, however, by returning to the /t/ which in my idiolect occurs in *water*. In my speech this contrasts with /d/—*latter* and *ladder* are not homonyms—but only in one quality, time. That is, the voiced variety of sound which I still classify as a /t/ has the shortness of a voiceless stop, contrasting with the greater length of /d/. In this one variety of /t/, a feature of time otherwise nondistinctive has been made distinctive. Should time become a general distinctive feature, it would obviously have a very considerable effect on the patterning of English sounds. At present it constitutes a sort of footnote, an exception of detail to the general statement that the length of stops is a nondistinctive feature. This process whereby a nondistinctive feature becomes distinctive when the normally distinctive feature has been lost has been called "rephonologizing" by the linguists of the Prague school. It is one of the most important ways in which change in the patterning of sounds can develop.

4.... PHONEME AND ALLOPHONE

1. The classification of sounds

Throughout the preceding chapters we have used a rather cumbersome terminology, speaking of sounds, varieties of sounds, groups of sounds, and contrastive sounds. By this time the reader should have some experience with how sounds function in language and with some of the kinds of articulations which distinguish them. It is therefore possible to replace this cumbersome terminology with the unfamiliar but far more exact terms used by linguists. Among linguists, a group of sounds is called a phoneme and the members of the group are called allophones. When we described the several kinds of *t*-sounds in the preceding chapter, we were describing the allophones which make up the phoneme /t/. The reader has probably tacitly assumed that sounds are grouped into classes (which we now call phonemes) by physical similarity, about as we group certain objects into the classes *ball* and *cube*, for example. Even in the physical world it is something more of a problem to describe just how we draw the line between such things as balls and cubes than it might at first sight appear, and in language, grouping sounds into phonemes such as /t/ or /d/ is a problem which occupied a whole generation of linguists.

The results of their concern with the methods of classification have established the principle that sounds are grouped into phonemes primarily in terms of their distribution, not in terms of their physical similarities and differences. Thus, no articulatory noise can be classified until its distribution is known. Suppose the reader hears a man whose language is unknown to him—a native of Fiji, perhaps—saying something which contains an initial articulatory noise identical, or nearly identical, with the articulatory noise used in such an English word as *tap*. The Fijian sound cannot be classified as a variety of the English /t/; in fact, it cannot be classified at all, since its distribution is unknown. It is, as far as the hearer knows, only a sound, not either a phoneme or an allophone. Until enough of the distribution is known so that distributional classes can be formulated, all that can be done with sounds such as our Fijian consonant is to describe their phonetic or physical characteristics, a necessary preliminary process before classification begins.[1]

In general, the classification of sounds gives relatively few contrasting classes (the phonemes), each of which contains very many varieties of sound which do not contrast with each other (the allophones). Classifications of the sounds of any language are judged as to their rightness by three criteria, used not only in classification of sounds but in all parts of language analysis, and probably basic to most kinds of scientific analysis. The classification must be complete; no classification of English sounds into phonemes would be satisfactory if it failed to take account of the initial contrast between:

$$\overset{3\ 1}{bat \text{ /bǽt \#/}} \text{ and } \overset{3\ 1}{pat \text{ /pǽt \#/}}$$

The classification must be consistent; if /b/ and /p/ are recognized as a contrast in *bat* and *pat*, then the contrast must also be recognized in asbestos, which is /æz + béstis/ or /æs + péstis/, to name only two varieties of pronunciation. Even if here the contrast between /b/ and /p/ makes no difference to the word, we must recognize it if we are to be consistent. The classification must be simple; it must classify all the varieties of sounds with as few statements and, other things being equal, into as few phonemes as possible. In this sense, simplicity is not the same thing as being easy to understand. It may take a good deal of explanation to show that the [t]-sounds in *top, stop, pot, button,* and *atom* are all allophones of /t/, particularly if the person to whom the explanation is made does not have the often misleading signposts of spelling to guide him. Yet a classification which makes all these sounds allophones of one phoneme is simpler than one which presents them all as possible contrasts. By simplicity is meant, in other words, the logical concept of parsimony of hypotheses.

The principles given above are by no means as clear-cut as they appear in this first approximation. None of the three criteria is easy to apply in practice, particularly when the analyst is faced with sacrificing something which falls under one criterion for something which falls under another. We shall go on to be more precise, hoping that some of the difficulties will gradually emerge, together with solutions for them so far as solutions are possible. When sounds occur in the same environment, they are said to

---

[1] We can now revise the explanation given in Chap. 2, footnote 4, of the use of slant lines and brackets. Slant lines enclose a notation which indicates the phonemes, instances of which occur in utterance, as in:

$$\overset{3\ 1}{\text{/yés \#/}}$$

Brackets enclose the phonetic entities, without reference to their classification into phonemes, as in our Fijian sound [t].

contrast, and their distribution with respect to each other is contrastive. Sounds which contrast are always members of different phonemes. An example of contrastive distribution is that of /m/ and /n/, both of which occur in the environment

$$-ap \ \overset{3\ 1}{/-\text{ǽp }\#/}$$

giving the citation forms:

$$\overset{3\ 1}{map\ /\text{mǽp }\#/}\ \text{and}\ \overset{3\ 1}{nap\ /\text{nǽp }\#/}$$

This example is conclusive evidence that /m/ and /n/ form a contrast, since the environment is manifestly the same and both occur in it. Unfortunately, difficulties arise over just what is meant by identical environments. A part of the difficulty is revealed if the definition of identical environments is put in the form "in environments consisting of the same phonemes in identical order." There is danger of circularity, in that the surrounding sounds must first have been classified into phonemes before the sound under analysis can be classified. The problem is then how to begin. In practice the analyst must proceed by a series of intelligent guesses, which he then checks, stage by stage, as the analysis continues. Thus if a Fijian linguist were analyzing English and he found the forms we have written

$$\overset{3\ 1}{/\text{mǽp }\#/}\ \text{and}\ \overset{3\ 1}{/\text{nǽp }\#/}$$

he would probably say that he heard two sounds [m] and [n] occurring after silence, with following vowels, consonants, pitch, and stress which sounded similar. He would set up two possible phonemes, /m/ and /n/, as a first guess, testing for other contrasts and checking his guess by whether the contrast existed in other positions as well, for instance *Pam* and *pan*. As he built up other guesses, he would return to see whether his /m/ : /n/ guess was in accord with them, resulting in a consistent and simple total analysis. If it did, it would be accepted in his final statement, a hypothesis consisting of a total inventory of phonemes and their pattern. Thus the inventory of contrasts is built up in much the same way that a cryptogram is solved. Starting assumptions are made and abandoned if they do not prove fruitful; as long as they lead to other assumptions consistent with the first, they are continued as working hypotheses, until finally all contrasts have been accounted for.

An even more serious difficulty arises in defining identical environments. Sometimes a whole class of words is pronounced with one or the other of two differing sounds, with no resultant difference in meaning. An instance of this kind of variation was cited in Section 10 of Chapter 3, where it was said that any word ending in a final voiceless stop could be pronounced with either a fully released or an unreleased stop in pre-terminal position. Thus, if we bring this statement to bear on one of the words we have been discussing,

3 1
/mǽp #/

we see that both the released and unreleased variety of [p] occur in the phonemic environment

3 1
/mǽ– #/

and would therefore seem to be in contrast. Yet no difference in meaning results in any of the words pronounced with final [p] when there is variation in the release. Two sounds which occur in identical phonemic environments without producing difference in meaning are said to be "free variants." The concept is troublesome, since either there must be a reliance on meaning or the definition of contrastive distribution is contradicted. A possible way out of the logical difficulty was also suggested in the earlier discussion. In my own idiolect a finally released [p] is characteristic of certain formal styles of speaking. We can then say that free variation is variation without function, in that the variation does not distinguish forms, in the way that /m/ and /n/ distinguish *map* and *nap*. Free variation, in turn, is believed to be correlated with a difference in style, though it must be admitted that this belief is a hypothesis based on inconclusive and incomplete evidence but adopted for the sake of consistency. We can then return to our definition of identical environments and revise it in accord with the hypothesis just adopted. Identical environments consist of the same phonemes in the same order and in the same style. It should be pointed out that analysts do not work from the stylistic differences first. Instead they check to see that there is no pair of forms distinguished by an observed variation, and if there is none, they then label the variation as without function, or free. Under our hypothesis functionless variation is taken to be prima-facie evidence of difference in style.

The two types of situation in which differing sounds may occur are phonemically identical and phonemically different situations. Differing sounds which occur only in differing phonemic environments are always in noncontrastive distribution. Further, if a sound or sound feature always occurs in conjunction with a single phoneme, or group of phonemes, that sound is redundant. That is, the distinctions will always be carried by the phoneme or phonemes in the environment. Such a redundant feature in English is vowel nasalization, which always occurs when there is a contiguous nasal phoneme /m/, /n/, or /ŋ/. The distinction betweeñ the nasalized vowel of

and the oral vowel of

$$\overset{3\quad 1}{/\text{mǽp}\ \#/}$$

$$\overset{3\quad 1}{/\text{kǽp}\ \#/}$$

is typical—it is redundant because the distinction is carried by the consonants /m/ and /k/.

When nasalization has thus been shown to be redundant, the way is left open for classifying the oral and nasalized varieties of /æ/ in the same phoneme. When they have been so classed, the oral and nasalized varieties of /æ/ are said to be in the special subtype of noncontrastive distribution which is called complementary. That is, the total distribution of /æ/ consists of the distribution of the oral varieties, complemented by the distribution of the nasalized varieties. Complementary distribution thus characterizes the distribution of the allophones of a phoneme. If for any reason the sounds in question are not assigned to the same phoneme, their distribution is merely noncontrastive.

The first step in classification of sounds is a study of their distribution. If the distribution is contrastive, they are assumed to belong to differing phonemes. If the distribution is noncontrastive, they may or may not be members of the same phoneme, and it is necessary to use a further criterion to reach a final decision. This criterion is physical similarity, or more exactly, whether or not physically observable distinctive features are shared. An example of the use of such a criterion can be drawn from the sounds [h] and [ŋ]. The [h] here meant is the initial of *home*, a variety that occurs only before vowels. The [ŋ] of *sing*, on the other hand, occurs only after vowels, so that there is no environment in which the two sounds can contrast. Yet analysts have not assigned them to the same phoneme, and as Daniel Jones pointed out, the reason is lack of physical similarity. Put more exactly, what has happened is that when the phonemes of English had been examined for their distinctive features, it was found that no reasonably complete, consistent, and simple arrangement of distinctive features would assign a distinctive feature, or combination of features, to [h] and [ŋ] in common.

At one time it was assumed that possession of a single distinctive feature, or combination of features, different from those found in all other phonemes was a necessary condition before two sounds could be classified as allophones of one phoneme. Further, a corollary of this assumption was that no two identical sounds could belong to different phonemes. Indeed, many, if not most, analysts would assume that these two statements still hold as basic postulates, as announced in Bernard Bloch's extremely important study,

"A Set of Postulates for Phonemic Analysis."[2] Yet it now seems inescapable that distributional criteria take precedence over physical similarity and dissimilarity. Some overlapping of identical sounds, as when a segment of consonantal sound is distributed between the consonant and a following juncture, must be reckoned with. Recent work by researchers at the Haskins Laboratories and by Stockwell, and the continued work of Jakobson, all have tended to establish the existence of some overlapping and therefore the priority of distribution over physical features. Yet the physical criterion is not abandoned. It is now reduced to the status of an operating procedure, instead of a postulate. That is, the statement of phonemic patterning should, in rigorous method, involve a minimum of overlapping rather than a maximum. Some examples of how analysts now operate with the criterion of physical similarity will make these statements clearer.

Let us suppose that /n/ and /ŋ/ have been established as two phonemes. It is then observed that in the sequence consisting of nasal and immediately following /k/, no distinction is possible between /n/ and /ŋ/, in that only one variety of nasal occurs. No matter how spelled, sequences like *ink*, *sink*, *think* do not contain sounds some of which are /n/, some /ŋ/. In spite of the fact that no opposition is possible, American analysts have no hesitation in assigning the sound which occurs before /k/ to /ŋ/ rather than to /n/ or to some independent phoneme. The sound is noticeably more like the /ŋ/ of *sing* than any other sound, and to set up independent phonemes in such situations would be to complicate the analysis greatly. Another example can be drawn from the words *sphere* and *svelte*. Many speakers, including the author, pronounce this initial sequence alike, and no contrast between /sf–/ and /sv–/ is possible. Since the sound which follows /s–/ is voiceless and since voicelessness has been set up as a distinctive feature, the sound is assigned to /–f–/, even though the sound is not necessarily identical with the /f–/ of *fall*. An example of another sort is found in the [^t_v] of *water* already discussed. This sound has been assigned as an allophone of /t/ on distributional grounds, since it contrasts in my idiolect with /d/ and with all other phonemes. Yet it lacks the distinctive features which are found in all other allophones of /t/, preserving only the otherwise redundant feature of time. Here, then, physical similarity has been disregarded in favor of distribution, because to do otherwise would produce an uneconomical type of analysis.

The analyst, it ought to be clear from this discussion, is often faced with the possibility of more than one classification, as he is with [^t_v]. In my

---

[2] *Language*, XXIV, 1948, pp. 3–46. The statement that identical sounds cannot be members of more than one phoneme was not one of Bloch's numbered postulates, but was contained in the definition of the phoneme, part of which read: "[a system of] mutually exclusive, and conjointly exhaustive [set of classes]." The postulate underlies numbered postulate 6 and is basic to most of the discussion which follows.

speech two kinds of things happen in pairs like *writer* and *rider*. In *writer* not only is the stop distinctly shorter than it is in *rider* but the preceding vocalic elements are distinctly shorter as well. The shorter vocalic sequence occurs before all voiceless stops and [$\overset{t}{\underset{v}{}}$], while this sound never occurs after a long vocalic sequence. We thus have a choice. We could regard the vowel length as contrastive and the difference between [$\overset{t}{\underset{v}{}}$] and [d] as redundant, or we could regard the consonantal difference as contrastive and the vowel length as redundant. If we take the first choice, we either double the number of vowel phonemes or introduce a new contrast of length. We also make transcription more difficult in pairs like *bat : bad*, where length variation also occurs but correlated with the difference in following consonant phonemes. If we assign the flapped [$\overset{t}{\underset{v}{}}$] to /t/, we do not increase the number of phonemes. There is consequently a considerable gain in simplicity, over against which we can count only a slight loss in consistency, namely, that the voiced-voiceless distinction generally found in stops does not distinguish all allophones of /t/ from /d/. The situation is typical; there is no uniquely right answer in scientific analysis. Yet in phonemic analysis as in any other, insofar as different answers are not merely verbally or mechanically different, there is always one answer which is better than the others, because it is more in accord with the criteria of completeness, consistency, and simplicity.

The illustration just given is typical in that it represents a choice involving a loss in one direction outweighed by a gain in another. Of the three criteria, completeness is the most important. In phonemics and elsewhere in language, all contrasts must be accounted for, and any system which fails to do so is to be rejected. Consistency in phonemics often works out in terms of symmetrical arrangements like those in our diagrams of consonants. Yet we have seen that these diagrams may take varying shapes, since symmetry in the diagram may conceal a lack of symmetry elsewhere. Similarly, simplicity, which is measured by the number of statements necessary to give a description or explanation, can be gained in one department of description at the expense of complexity somewhere else. The result of this uncertainty is not unreliability for the products of analysis; it is rather that any analysis is a scientific hypothesis assumed to be valid only so long as no better hypothesis is devised.

It will be worthwhile to give an example of a serious and farreaching problem in English, which has already been mentioned and on which analysts are not yet fully in accord, though to do so will necessarily carry us ahead into the analysis of vowels. Older phonemic analyses present the vowels of both *bit* and *beat* as single segments. The analysis offered here presents *beat* as a complex nucleus consisting of the two segments /iy/. Phoneticians have long been in agreement that the vowel of *beat* is physically complex, but those analysts who write *bit* as /bɪt/ and *beat* as /bit/ choose to regard the "off-glide" as redundant. The phonemic analysis here adopted is most radical, not in the analysis of *beat* as /biyt/ and *boat* as /bowt/, both of which were proposed long ago by the English phonetician Sweet, but in the analysis of *idea* as /aydíh/, that is, in setting up the centering off-glide as a third semivowel, to be identified as an allophone of the initial of *home*.

Its advantages are principally in the direction of consistency. There results from it an arrangement of semivowels which fits neatly into the general consonantal structure, and as will be seen later, the vowels also become strikingly symmetrical. Under the other type of analysis, considerable inconsistency results. Words like *bite* and *bout* are stated to contain diphthongs, [ɑɪ] and [aʊ], which are regarded as two segments, while the sequences (much like these two) of *beat*, *boat*, and *boot* are stated to be simple vowels. The number of vowels is increased, usually to thirteen, in an arrangement which is notably less symmetrical and which often does not take account of all possible contrasts.

Yet some loss is involved in an analysis setting up three semivowels. The loss is primarily in phonetic congruity and, on a different level, in the symmetry of sequences of phonemes. The semivowel /h/ is normally voiceless in prevocalic position, the other two are normally voiced everywhere. In some phonemic sequences, initial /h/ has a distribution characteristic of spirants, /y/ and /w/ do not. It is primarily these facts of difference between /h/, on the one hand, and /y/ and /w/, on the other, which have been responsible for the rejection by some phonemicists of the analysis which places /h/ among the semivowels. Yet it seems that the gain in consistency and simplicity is sufficiently great to warrant the kind of choice made in this book.

We have given something of the criteria and methods used by analysts in grouping sounds into phonemes, and some illustration of the problems which are encountered. It is then time to give a more formal definition of the terms "phoneme" and "allophone." A phoneme is a group of sounds all the members of which are in complementary distribution with one another, or in free variation. The group must contrast with all other groups, or more exactly, all members of the group must contrast in some position with the members of all other groups. The members of a phoneme are its allophones. The allophones of a phoneme normally share a distinctive feature or combination of features not found in the allophones of other phonemes, and overlapping of allophones (identical sounds as members of more than one phoneme) is minimized in rigorous analysis.

The statement just made, that the allophones of a phoneme must somewhere contrast with the allophones of all other phonemes, can be expanded for some classes of phonemes. The class of phonemes called consonants are sounds which may be present or absent in a given utterance. The allophones of a consonant phoneme must therefore not only contrast with the allophones of all other consonant and vowel phonemes but must also contrast with the absence of consonant and vowel phonemes, as the initial of *cup* contrasts with the absence of any comparable initial in *up*. For other classes of phonemes, such as those of pitch, no such contrast with zero is possible. No utterance can be made without a phoneme of pitch, so that there is necessarily no absence with which to contrast whatever pitch phoneme occurs.

From the point of view of all the possible utterances in English, a phoneme is a large class of sounds. In an individual utterance, the situation is different. In a form like

$$\overset{3\ 1}{/\text{mǽp}\ \#/}$$

if we disregard for the time being the phonemes of stress, pitch, and juncture, we have an abstracted sequence which we can write /mæp/. There can be a contrast at the beginning with *nap* /næp/, in the middle with *mop* /map/, at the end with *mat* /mæt/. Other contrasts are possible only if something is added, as in *maps* /mæps/. We therefore say that there are only three segments in *map*, and allophones of only three phonemes occur in it, except for the phonemes of stress, pitch, and juncture, which we have left out of account. It is usual, indeed, to say that there are only three phonemes in *map*, but it is more accurate to use the cumbersome statement just given. Obviously, the class does not occur in a given item; only the representative of the class occurs. From this point of view, an allophone can be called the smallest linguistic unit which can be arrived at from the analysis of meaningful forms, and the number of allophones can be identified with the number of contrast points characterizing any utterance. Allophones of phonemes are not the smallest linguistic units, however. They are only the smallest units arrived at by the kind of analysis we have just described. When these units have been arrived at, they may themselves be compared and analyzed. The units arrived at by analysis of phonemes—the type of analysis called componential—are the distinctive features. These distinctive features are smaller than the allophones of phonemes, since any distinctive feature is a part of the allophone which occurs. It is characteristic, however, that the distinctive features recur in successive allophones, as the distinctive feature of voice occurs in the two first phonemes of /mæp/ and oral closure occurs in the first and third. Allophones, indeed all the allophones of any phoneme, can then be described as bundles of distinctive features, a different bundle occurring with each segment of the utterance.

We have been presenting the problems encountered by well-trained analysts. The reader may be a beginner. Fortunately, therefore, it is possible to present the phonemes of English largely as the results of classification by analysts, with a minimum of attention to problematical classification and subtleties of method. Some appreciation of the difficulties is necessary, since otherwise even simply stated phonemic groupings will be misunderstood. We can, however, leave the subject of problems and method by outlining some of the misconceptions and inconsistencies which are apt to plague, not the serious analyst, but the beginning student.

The most disastrous type of misconception is to allow phonemic classification to be influenced by spelling, with which it has little to do and which it often contradicts. Thus, the spelling *th* conceals an English phonemic contrast which is revealed by the pair:

$$\begin{array}{cc} 3 \quad 1 & 3 \quad 1 \end{array}$$
ether /íyθər #/ and *either* /íyðər #/

In other instances, spelling makes a difference where none exists phonemically. Such a pair is *Thomas* and *Tom*, where the initial phoneme is /t/ for both. The warning is worth giving since it is often hard for literate persons not to be influenced by spelling, even if they know that it is not the same as sound.

A second major pitfall is disregard of rare contrasts. It has been said that only /ŋ/ of the nasal phonemes occurs before /k/. Yet /ŋ/ contrasts with /n/ in the pair *sing : sin*. Further, while only /ŋ/ occurs immediately before /g/, just as it occurs before /k/, an /ŋ/ without following consonant contrasts with the sequences /ŋk/ and /ŋg/, in *singer : sinker : finger*. In short, no matter how limited the contrasts between /ŋ/ and /n/ may be, they are still contrasts and must be the deciding factors in classification. The beginning analyst is apt to disregard the rare contrasts, particularly if there is identity of words. For instance, *income* patently contains the words *in* and *come*. Yet, in this situation the resultant form may be:

$$3 \quad 1$$
/íŋkəm #/

The beginner, and even some who should no longer be beginners, will sometimes assume, therefore, that here /ŋ/ is "serving as an allophone of /n/." Such a statement maximizes rather than minimizes the amount of phonemic overlapping, and would produce a phonemic classification so conflicting as to be both arbitrary and confusing.

Related to this kind of confusion, since it often has its source in the same kind of reliance on meaning, is the assumption that whatever does not distinguish words is not phonemic. Thus *either* can have the vowel of *beat* or of *bite* without effect on the meaning of this particular word. Yet the pair we have just given show that /iy/ and /ay/ are contrastive. There are statements in some beginning books that the use of /iy/ and /ay/ in *either* is "not a phonemic" difference. All such statements should be revised to read "is not meaningful on the word level."

Difficulty can also arise from inaccurate segmentation. In many regions of the coastal South, *house* is [háws] but *houses* is [hǽwzɨz], the two diphthongs being in complementary distribution. The statement is sometimes made that therefore the two diphthongs are allophones of the same phoneme. But since /a/ and /æ/ are themselves separate phonemes and, since the diphthongs contain a separate second element, /aw/ and /æw/ cannot be allophones of one phoneme. To make them so would necessitate setting up an elaborate set of new phonemes, one for every diphthong in the language.

2. Phonemes of the individual and the community

We have talked about contrast, or the lack of it, and have said nothing at all about dialect variation. Yet dialect differences can seriously affect phonemic contrasts. If a speaker has forms like

$$\text{/mǽp #/ and /nǽp #/}$$

it is clear that there is a contrast in his speech, at least. But suppose that speaker A—to set up for the minute an impossible hypothetical situation— has only

$$\text{/mǽp #/}$$

and speaker B has only

$$\text{/nǽp #/}$$

would /m/ and /n/ then contrast, since both forms do not occur in the speech of either individual? If we move ahead again to vowel phonemes and their problems, the hypothetical situation I have just set up can be illustrated with a real and important difference. There is a variety of vowel, [ɨ], which occurs in contrast with all others in the speech of many Americans. It may be used in the phrase *just a minute*, where *just* is stressed, and if so, *just* will contrast with the *just* of *a just decision* and will also contrast with *jest* and *gist*. If the reader has such a set of contrasts, there is no doubt that there is a phoneme /ɨ/ (barred *i*) in his speech. But there are other varieties of American speech to which the reader may belong. There are speakers who also have the sound [ɨ] but use it only under weak stress and only before dentals, as in *hunted* [hɔ́ntɨd]. For such speakers also, this is the only variety of [i]-like sound which occurs in this position, so that [i] and [ɨ] no longer contrast.

If they do not, are we still justified in setting up [ɨ] as a separate phoneme on the basis of contrasts in the speech of others? We can do so, but this requires recognition of two kinds of phonemic structure, in one of which the two sounds would contrast, while in the other they would not.

It was once assumed that contrast had to occur in the speech of a single individual, speaking in a single style, and at a single time. That is, it was assumed that the only meaningful phonemic structure was individual. There is no doubt that such individual structures are indeed meaningful. Since individual speech defined as above has been called an idiolect, phonemes in individual speech can be called "idiophonemes." But important as idiophonemic structure is, if we limit our discussion to it, we have no framework for description and analysis of a whole language like English or French, or of any large speech community in which there are widespread individual differences. Since it is necessary to study languages as wholes, it is important to provide an over-all pattern for that purpose.

Until the last few years, discussions of the phonemics of languages relied on description of an "average speaker," who was at best an abstraction and at worst a fiction. Descriptions based on the average speaker, therefore, were often confusing when compared with the usage of a real individual. Recently, however, phonemicists working with structural characteristics and pattern congruities have postulated symmetrical patterns for phonemic contrasts which are characteristic of whole speech communities, though idiolects within the community might not make use of all contrasts which the diagram provides.

The [ɨ] we have just been describing is a pertinent example of this kind of procedure. An entity of some sort different from those of *bust*, *gist*, and *jest* was first suggested, but for his own idiolect only, by Benjamin Lee Whorf. Smith and Trager, in working through the vocalic structure of English, noted the absence of a distinctive entity in the otherwise symmetrical set of vowels they postulated.[3] Proceeding to experiment with Whorf's suggestion, they found that it indicated a distinction actually needed to describe a large number of idiolects, though it was a vowel phoneme whose existence had not previously been suspected. Working through dialect differences in this way, with full attention to pattern congruity, Trager and Smith would now define the largest kind of speech community, equivalent to a language, as a group of speakers the sum of whose speech is characterized by a single, symmetrical diagram of possible phonemic contrasts. Such a

---

[3] Whorf's identification of a high central phoneme in his own speech is to be found in "Phonemic Analysis of the English of Eastern Massachusetts," *Studies in Linguistics*, II, 1943, pp. 21–40. It was reviewed by Trager in the pages immediately following. Trager and Smith discuss the various dialectal uses of the high central phoneme fairly fully in *An Outline of English Structure*, Studies in Linguistics: Occasional Papers 3, 1951.

symmetrical diagram is called an over-all pattern, or dialectal pattern. It includes all dialects of the language, and each dialect uses some, but not necessarily all, of the contrasts found in the pattern. The contrasts within the pattern are diaphonemes, and the structure is a diaphonemic pattern.

To return to the usage of a speaker who has both [ɨ] and [i] but who lacks a contrast between them, it is now possible to describe both his individual usage and his relation to the over-all pattern. In his own idiolect, the noncontrasting occurrences of [ɨ] are allophones belonging with /i/. This arrangement, to use our slightly redundant kind of terminology, constitutes an idiophoneme. From the point of view of the language as a whole, where it has been established that there are contrasts between /ɨ/ and /i/, the two sounds are members of differing groups, that is, two differing diaphonemes. The proper description of any idiolect is, then, a statement of the relation of its idiophonemes to the diaphonemes; the analyst must say which idiophonemes correspond to diaphonemes and what the differences are. The over-all pattern constitutes the best basis yet devised for a systematic and structural approach to dialectology.

In describing the consonants, the relation of idiophonemes to diaphonemes was not mentioned. Though there are differences in consonants among American speakers, the consonants, on the whole, offer fewer and less noticeable divergences from one dialect to another than do the vowels. It was therefore possible to describe consonants without stating whether they were idiophonemes or diaphonemes, since by judicious choice of examples it was usually possible to present them as the same from both points of view. With vowels the differences are more numerous and more varied in kind. Therefore in the description which follows, it is to be assumed that the term "phoneme" is always used as the equivalent of "diaphoneme," unless the contrary is explicitly stated.

The over-all pattern is a hypothesis of structure which is a contribution of Trager and Smith.[4] It has met with resistance and is, like all hypotheses, one which is being tested by use in further investigation. When new evidence disproves it, suggesting a different over-all pattern, or an over-all pattern differently arrived at and defined, the hypothesis will be revised or rejected as the new evidence demands. In the meantime, two statements can be made about the nature of the hypothesis regarding the existence of an over-all pattern. Language is a predominantly regular structure, on all its levels. If it were not, it would be so chaotic that we could not master it. It is this regularity which is the ultimate justification for belief in the possibility of an over-all pattern in sounds. Language is also characterized by irregularities on all its levels. If it were not, language would be so rigid that its patterns could not be applied to new situations, and there would be no pos-

---

[4] See *An Outline of English Structure*, p. 9 and *passim*.

sibility of the change which we know characterizes all languages at all periods of their history. If all language structures are both regular and irregular, with the regularities outnumbering the irregularities, there is no reason to suppose that an over-all pattern is any more rigidly regular than any other of the patterns that students have been able to arrive at by analysis of the buzz of talk. In short, irregularities can characterize the over-all pattern as well as the idiophonemic patterns, but in the over-all pattern, as elsewhere in language, the regularities must outnumber the irregularities.

Irregularities are of several sorts. The pattern can show skewing, or an idiolect or idiolects can show skewing in relation to the pattern; either case shows asymmetry which must be described. An example of this skewing was found in an idiolect which was analyzed at the recent Texas conference on phonemic problems. This speech would have called for ten, rather than the usual nine, vowel phonemes provided for in the Trager-Smith pattern, had the various sounds been described in terms of non-overlapping phonemes. But considered as contrasts in differing situations, there were always only nine contrasts in any one situation. This speech therefore represented an idiolect in which the over-all pattern applied only at the expense of recognizing skewing, in that ten physically different sound types were arranged under nine contrasts, with asymmetry between contrasts in one situation and another.

A second type of irregularity is the existence of holes. We have seen that idiolects have holes, in that any given idiolect may make no use of some of the possible pattern contrasts. These idiolectal holes may become holes in the over-all pattern if eventually all idiolects come to show the same lack. No good example can be pointed to from English structure, but at least an analogous situation can be found in Latin. The over-all pattern of that language called for an [h] which was the third in a series of three spirants, corresponding to the general arrangement of Latin consonant phonemes in sets of threes. Such a phoneme at one time existed, but so far as we know the idiolects of Imperial Latin, they had all come to lack the inherited /h/—the Latin over-all pattern showed a hole.

Third, an idiolect, or indeed the over-all pattern, may show an item over and above the possible contrasts provided for by the symmetrical structure. Such an item is a leftover. Here there is an instance from English. James Sledd suggested in an important review of the Trager and Smith *Outline* that in his own idiolect—that of Atlanta—a tenth vowel was necessary to account for all contrasts.[5] He has been able to show ten contrasting vowel sounds in a single type of situation. There was therefore no possibility

---

[5] Review of Trager and Smith, *An Outline of English Structure*, and Fries, *The Structure of English*, in *Language*, XXXI, 1955, pp. 312–45.

of accounting for this idiolect as having merely skewness in its relation to the over-all pattern. The idiolect, previously mentioned, which showed nine vowels but in a skewed arrangement comes from the same southeastern region. Yet it should be emphasized that the two situations were different; one idiolect showed only skewing, the other showed a genuine and unmistakable leftover.

A fourth kind of irregularity is much less important, though common enough. As a result of dialect mixture, a given idiolect may be a mixture of sound-types which present what were originally differing idiophonemes as free variants. Such idiolects give more contrasting sound-types than are provided for in an over-all pattern of nine phonemic contrasts. In my own idiolect, for instance, I have no contrast between /o/ and /ɔ/ before /r/, but I have been exposed to dialects other than my own, and as a result, now have a higher and a lower allophone of /ɔ/, both of which I use as free variants before /r/. Should these free variants acquire function, of necessity either skewing or the production of a leftover would be the result.

Thus, it may be said of the hypothesis of an over-all pattern, in our present knowledge of it, that the pattern is one of contrasts, not of sound entities. Use of the over-all pattern by no means absolves the student of dialectology from observing and analyzing distribution and formulating statements of contrast and complementation. The analysis of an idiolect or a group of idiolects cannot be done merely by equating an item heard in the idiolect with an item from the over-all pattern simply because the two are physically similar. From the other point of view, since all language structures are characterized by both regularity and irregularity, the presence of irregularities such as those which have been described is not evidence warranting rejection of the hypothesis that over-all symmetry of contrasts exists. He who uses over-all pattern analysis and he who does not use it must recognize that no over-all pattern can ever be completely rigid, if over-all patterns are at all like other language structures.

This chapter can be concluded with a final statement on the phonemic analysis used in this book. It is hoped that controversial positions have been presented with full acknowledgment of the existence of controversy, but with equally full awareness that decisions must be made in scientific matters, even when controversial. The phonemic analysis presented here is that of the Trager and Smith over-all pattern, and it has been chosen for the reason that it is the most complete, consistent, and simple analysis of English phonemes in existence. It is an analysis capable of being revised when revisions are shown to be needed, but it is not an analysis capable of being refuted except by another analysis more complete, more consistent, and more simple.

5.... VOWELS AND VOWEL NUCLEI

This chapter is short, since the features which distinguish vowels from one another in English are two only: position in a plane from front to back and position in a plane from high to low. We here describe only the minimum necessary to establish contrasts, without presenting a description of the many noncontrastive varieties of vowels which often characterize individual dialects. Yet, though this chapter is short, it is crucial, and the student should not merely read it but should practice the distinctions described until he is certain what his individual usage is.

The vowels of English are arranged, as has been said, in a diagram of three columns and three rows, as below, where they are written with their respective phonemic symbols:

/i ɨ u
e ə o
æ a ɔ/

For several of these, key words can be given with little trouble. The key words will so far as possible be in the shape of a consonant, a stressed vowel, and a consonant, since this is the situation in which the simple vowels occur without any following semivowel and in which they are most clearly isolable:

/i/ *bit, pit*
/e/ *bet, pet*
/ə/ *but, putt*
/u/ *put*

For the others, varying degrees of difficulty, because of dialectal variation, arise. For the vowels on the bottom line, there is considerable agreement in most of America on /æ/ and /a/. Nearly all the United States employs the two in the following key words:

/æ/ *bat, pat*
/a/ *pot*

The second key word, *pot*, is /pɔt/ or the like in British English and eastern New England. Probably the best key word is therefore *father* /fáðər/ which has /a/ nearly everywhere, though the /a/ is often followed by /h/, /fáhðɚr/. With or without /h/, *father* can be used as a test comparison for *pot*. If both have the same vowel it is /a/; if they are different *pot* has /ɔ/.

Again, most of America has a clear distinction between the low central and the low back vowels, but there are some regions, such as the Rocky Mountain area, where the distinction is apparently absent, and a good many other areas where distribution of the two phonemes is irregular, so that key words are hard to give. The key words for most of America, then, are:

/ɔ/ *bought, want*

In much speech, however, the /ɔ/ does not occur in these words as a simple vowel but is accompanied by the semivowel /h/. Since, however, the vowel itself is clear enough in general American speech, we can for the minute disregard differences such as /bɔt/ and /bɔht/, /wɔnt/ and /wɔhnt/.

In the Rocky Mountain area, /ɔ/ is often lacking, so that words like *pa* and *paw*, *knotty* and *naughty* sound alike, and all use /a/, though the collective idiophonemic allophone of /a/ may be somewhat farther back than that used for *pa* and *knotty* in most of America.

In southern New England, words like *cod* and *cawed* often have /ɔ/ and /ɔh/: thus, /kɔd/ and /kɔhd/; or they may even vary with /a/ and /ah/, creating confusion in the use of key words. As suggested earlier, however, in this area *father* has /a/: /fáðəh/, /fáðɚr/, or /fáhðɚr/.

The midback vowel offers difficulty only because it rarely occurs without a following semivowel. In almost all of America, *boat* is /bówt/, and most *o*-sounds have the same diphthong. In a good deal of the Atlantic coast, however, *going to* is /gónə/, with a simple vowel (a commoner form is, however, /gónə/). In coastal New England also, a simple vowel is used in *whole* /hól/, *road* /ród/, *home* /hóm/.

The high central barred *i*, /ɨ/, causes perhaps the greatest amount of trouble, as the previous discussion of it suggests. As there indicated, the adverb *just*, when stressed, is probably the best key word for it. There are others, however. In the coastal South, *sister* is often /sístər/, contrasting with *lister* /lístər/. In the metropolitan area of the Atlantic coast, *willies*, as in "I've got the willies," is /wíliyz/, contrasting with *Willy's* /wíliyz/. And in much of the non-coastal South, *whip* is /hwíp/, a pronunciation rather commoner than its variant /hwɔ́p/, the form seemingly implied by such a dialect writing as *whup*.

For the student who is attempting to learn the sounds indicated by the symbols, the dialectal differences which affect key words make it necessary that he do a good deal of comparing of his own speech with that of others. The ideal situation is to be able to listen to examples of variant pronunciation given and recorded by a trained instructor. Failing this opportunity, the student must try the key words over in his own speech, and then compare them with the pronunciations of his friends. Needless to say, if such a form as *can't* had been given as a key for /æ/ and the student uses a "broad *a*," /kánt/ or /káhnt/, his understanding of the difference between /æ/ and /a/ would be confused.

Not only do dialect differences make trouble for a student who is trying to identify key words in his own idiolect, but the student must also be warned against unconscious distortion in pitch, stress, and juncture. If, for instance, one tries to compare two citation forms such as *hot* and *hat*, it is an English habit to give the first one as

3 2
/hát ‖/

and the second as

3   1
/hæt #/

with quite different pitch and juncture patterns and consequently with less than perfectly comparable results. This particular difficulty can be met by consciously giving all citation forms with the pattern /3 1 #/ or possibly even /4 1 #/. Distortion in stress is even more troublesome, particularly in trying to isolate the vowels of unstressed syllables. Thus, the unwary student, called on to observe the second syllable of *kitchen*, is all too likely to give the distorted form /kìc+én/, which completely disguises the vowel that would occur in actual speech. The best way of guarding against such stress distortion is to put contrasting forms into sentences, seeing that the sentences are naturally pronounced. For instance, "I have a new kitchen" can be contrasted with "I have a new apron."

Once the nine simple vowels are identified, the student should then learn to understand the distinctive features back of the diagrammatic arrangement with which this section started. The distinctive features are only two, vertical and horizontal position of articulation. The position of the narrowest opening between the tongue and the roof of the mouth is what is here meant by the position of articulation, and its variant positions should be observed by watching with a mirror and feeling the tongue with a finger. The vowels in the left-hand column, /i e æ/, are spoken of as front, those in the right-hand, /u o ɔ/, as back, the remaining three, /ɨ ə a/, as central. The three rows are called high, mid, and low, respectively, so that any vowel is described by a combination of the two terms, as high front, or midcentral, and so on.

Observation of these positions can be begun by comparing *pit* and *put*, then taking the /i/ and /u/ out of their contexts and pronouncing them alone, watching and feeling the point of articulation until the difference in position is learned, and identified with the resultant sound-quality. After /i/ and /u/ are mastered, the /ɨ/ should be added, so that the three high positions can be compared, by moving from front to back and the reverse. A final stage of practice and observation is learning to pronounce a series of vowels like /i e æ/ continuously, moving through all the intermediate stages from highest to lowest without a break. This exercise is excellent for learning to manipulate vowel sounds consciously and for learning the sound qualities which result from lowering, raising, fronting, or backing the point of articulation.

While the simple vowels are adequately described in terms of two distinctive features only, there are nondistinctive features which are of phonetic importance. The back vowels, for instance, are round, that is to say, the lips are more or less pursed. The front vowels are unround, with the lips in a slitlike opening. Other nondistinctive features characterize the arrangement of allophones. Thus, all vowels are more or less nasalized before and after nasal consonants. All vowels have allophones varying in length. In general, vowels are longest in stressed syllables before voiced consonants, shorter before voiceless consonants and in polysyllabic forms not broken by juncture, shortest of all when weakly stressed. Vowels also vary in height when they occur before semivowels, the situation which will be next described.

The semivowels /y h w/ have already been discussed. The name "semivowel" is given because the sounds in question structure with vowels when they occur in postvocalic position, the combination of vowel and semivowel making up what is known as a complex nucleus. In any sequence ending in a consonant before which a simple vowel occurs, a complex nucleus can be substituted for it, as in *lot* /lát/ and *light* /láyt/, or *bit* /bít/ and *beat* /bíyt/. When the semivowels occur before vowels, however, they structure with the consonants and enter into consonant clusters in the same way and in the same position as simple /l/ and /r/, as in such series as *screw* /skrúw/ : *skew* /skyúw/ and *train* /tréyn/ : *twain* /twéyn/. It is sharing of structural habits with both consonants and vowels which is indicated by the name.

The prevocalic and postvocalic positions can be illustrated by *yes* /yés/ and *say* /séy/, which make a mirror image (a phonemic palindrome) of each other. In description of the semivowels as consonants, it was said that the distinctive quality of /y/ is a downward glide from the upper front corner. In postvocalic position, the distinctive feature is a glide in the reverse direction, that is, upward toward the high front corner. Similarly, postvocalic /w/ is a glide upward toward the high back corner, and postvocalic /h/ is a glide toward center. The structural and phonetic parallel between /h/ and the other two semivowels is not perfect, however, since prevocalic /h/ is normally voiceless and postvocalic /h/ normally voiced. The other two semivowels are normally voiced in both positions. In prevocalic position also, /y/ and /w/ enter freely into consonant clusters; /h/ does not.

The English over-all pattern provides the possibility of combination of any vowel with any following semivowel, making 27 complex nuclei or diphthongs, which, with the 9 simple vowels, make a total of 36 vowels and nuclei. No single dialect employs them all, but all 36 are found somewhere among the English dialects. Not all of the combinations will be described, and I shall begin with those which are most widespread.

COMBINATIONS WITH A FOLLOWING /y/ IN CONTRAST
WITH THE VOWEL ALONE

/a/ *lot* /lát/; /ay/ *light* /láyt/ (In some areas, notably Oklahoma and Texas, however, *light* becomes /láht/. In Virginia *ride* similarly becomes /ráhd/, but *light* and *write* retain /ay/.)

/i/ *bit* /bít/; /iy/ *beat* /bíyt/

/e/ *bet* /bét/; /ey/ *bait* /béyt/

/o/ *Boyd* /bóyd/ (This nucleus frequently varies with /ɔy/, *Boyd* /bɔ́yd/.)

COMBINATIONS WITH A FOLLOWING /w/ IN CONTRAST
WITH THE VOWEL ALONE

/a/ *pot* /pát/; *pout* /páwt/

/u/ *look* /lúk/; *Luke* /lúwk/

Nuclei with /h/ are more confusing, since in many words variation between vowel and vowel with /h/ is nonsignificant, even though phonemic. One form, however, in which an /h/ nucleus practically always occurs, except in trisyllabic pronunciations, is *idea* /aydíh/, or possibly /aydíh/. In the dialects of New England and the coastal South, the areas in which postvocalic /r/ is absent, the /h/ is regularly substituted for /r/, so that *barn* becomes /báhn/, *fear* becomes /fíh/, *cord* becomes /kóhd/, *mourn* becomes /móhn/, and so on.

Occurrence of /h/ after /æ/ or /e/ before a nasal is common over most of the country, so that *land* is either /léhnd/ or less commonly /léhnd/. Also, after /a/ the allophone of /h/ which frequently occurs is simply a lengthening of the vowel, giving pairs like *bomb* /bám/ : *balm* /báhm/; *Polly* /páliy/ : *Pali* /páhliy/ (a dialect of Middle Indic); *sorry* /sáriy/ : *sari* /sáhriy/. In all of these, the distinction may be phonetically a short opposed to a long /a/.

Among the rarer and more dialectal nuclei are such forms as *cash* with /æy/, /kǽyš/, heard in western Virginia and Tennessee and elsewhere; /uy/ which occurs generally in *buoy* and *chop suey* and *phooey* when these forms are pronounced as one syllable, thus /búy/ (varying with a learned or sometimes nautical /bóy/), /câp + súy/, /fúy/. The dissyllabic forms are /búwiy/, /câp + súwiy/, /fúwiy/. The nucleus /əy/ has acquired a good deal of undeserved notoriety. It occurs in the variety of New York City speech supposedly associated with Brooklyn, in *bird* /bə́yd/, *burl* /bə́yl/, *shirt* /šə́yt/. A word like *burl* may or may not be distinguished from *boil*, but New Yorkers do not symmetrically transpose *burl* to /bóyl/ and *boil* to /bə́rl/. It is also curious that /əy/ in *bird* can occur as far away from New York as New Orleans, where it has none of the low prestige it has in Manhattan.

In Tidewater Virginia, *houses* has the nucleus /æw/, and as mentioned previously, this nucleus is there in complementary distribution with the /aw/ of *house*. In much British speech, the nucleus /əw/ is used in place of /ow/, as in *note* /nə́wt/. Even more striking is another British form, *note* /néwt/.

The list of dialectal forms is not complete, but is sufficient for our purposes. Once he has learned to hear the nuclei given above, and their component parts, the student should check his own speech to find out what forms he uses—particularly to decide on his use of nuclei with /h/.

The presentation of English phonemes here given is not meant to be a complete account of either English phonetics or English dialects. The purpose has been to identify the significant elements in English structure. Similarly, there is no attempt to drill the reader in transcription of English utterances, since that is something best done in a classroom. Nevertheless, the materials here presented are sufficient so that a careful reader, willing to work out details for himself, can use them to transcribe not only his own speech but most of the types that he may hear.

6.... PHONOTACTICS

1. Distributional classes of phonemes

The area of phonemics which covers the structural characteristics of sequences is called phonotactics.[1] It is essentially a description of the distribution of phonemes, once they have been identified. Since phonemics proper makes use of distributional criteria in identification, phonotactics is an extension of phonemics.

Phonotactical description of a language defines the phoneme classes which occur in it. Traditionally, phonemes have been divided into such classes as consonants and vowels on the basis of their phonetic characteristics. Yet a phonetic division of phoneme classes is never fully successful, since there are sounds which sometimes act like consonants, sometimes like vowels. And, further, sounds more or less on the borderline will be treated as vowels by one language, as consonants by another. In the preceding description of English phonemes, it was convenient to use the traditional terms without definition. We can now proceed to define vowels and consonants, together with other phoneme classes, on a more rigid distributional basis.

The smallest utterance which occurs in English has a phoneme or phonemes of pitch, a phoneme of stress, a terminal juncture, and at least two other phonemes. A typical minimal utterance is then:

$$3\ 1$$
$$/\text{ów} \#/$$

The pitch and stress phonemes represent our first class and have the following distributional characteristics: they are necessary, in that no utterance occurs without them; they occur at the same time with each other and at the same time as the type of phoneme here represented by /ow/. The members of the class cluster; that is, there are successive pitch or stress phonemes.

---

[1] The term "phonotactics," now widely used, as well as other terms in "–tactics" to indicate sequences of items, such as "morphotactics" and "logotactics," I owe to an unpublished lecture by Robert P. Stockwell delivered before the Linguistic Institute held at the Georgetown University Institute of Languages and Linguistics in 1954.

This characteristic of simultaneous occurrence with other phonemes is what is responsible for the name of the class, "suprasegmental phonemes," in that they "spread over" several segments.

The second class is that of junctures. They also are necessary, in that every utterance has at least one of the class. They are not strictly suprasegmental, however, and occur in sequential order with vowels and consonants. As we shall see in Chapter 7, they have morphemic distribution which groups them with the suprasegmental phonemes. They do not cluster, since there are never two junctures in succession. The class is divided into two subclasses: one consists of /#/, /‖/, and /|/, all of which occur before silence and are therefore called terminal junctures; and a second consists of /+/ alone, which never occurs in this position and is therefore sometimes called an internal juncture.

The third phoneme class is that of vowels, which can be distributionally defined as necessary, since no utterance occurs without at least one member of the class and since in the minimal two-segment utterance, the vowel is always the first of the two, as in /ow/. The fourth class, consonants, is the first class which is not necessary, since in minimal utterances of the /ow/ type, the second position can as well be filled by a semivowel as by a consonant. Consonants often occupy the second position in minimal utterances, as in /it/. In nonminimal utterances, they also occur before the vowel, as in /bit/. Consonants alone among the segmental phonemes occur in clusters, English permitting as many as three consonants before or after vowels, as in *spray* /spréy/ and *corpse* /kɔ́rps/.

The last class contains the three semivowels, which are like consonants in being unnecessary, since there can be utterances like /it/ without them. They form a special class because, as explained above, they structure with both consonants and vowels, depending on whether they are prevocalic or postvocalic.

2. Phoneme clusters

We can now proceed to describe phoneme sequences, which can be done in terms of clustering habits. A cluster is a sequence of two or more phonemes of the same class without the intervention of a phoneme of another class. The phoneme types which cluster are the suprasegmental phonemes and the consonants. The clustering of the suprasegmental phonemes is of a different kind from that of consonants, since suprasegmental phonemes cannot occur without simultaneous segmental elements.

There are limitations on the clustering of stresses. First, the number of stress phonemes (in our system of analysis) always corresponds to the number of vowels in the utterance; and, second, a primary stress cannot cluster with itself unless there is an intervening terminal juncture. Otherwise, the stresses can cluster with themselves and with any other stress. The limitations on clustering of pitches will be described in Section 6 of Chapter 7.

3. Prevocalic consonant clusters

Vowels, as said earlier, do not cluster. That is, no two vowels can occur without an intervening semivowel, consonant, or juncture. Thus the clustering habits of phonemes are almost altogether the clustering habits of consonants alone. In describing these, we will begin with the clusters which are postjunctural and prevocalic—the groups that would ordinarily be described as initial. In this position, the largest number of consonants which can occur is three, and the clusters are as follows:

/spl–/		/skl–/
/spr–/	/str–/	/skr–/
/spyu–/	/styu–/	/skyu–/
		/skw–/

Examples are: /spl–/ *splash;* /spr–/ *spray;* /spyu–/ *spew;* /str–/ *straw;* /styu–/ *stupid;* /skl–/ *sclerotic;* /skr–/ *scream;* /skyu–/ *skewer;* /skw–/ *squirt.* There are a number of peculiarities about the occurrence of these clusters. Those containing /y/ have all been written with a following /u/. This is because /u/ is the only vowel before which they occur. That is, we have forms like *spew* and *skew*, but no form like */spyah/ or */skyah/, unless in a carefully learned pronunciation for a foreign word or name, like *Schiaparelli.* A second peculiarity is in the /styu–/ group. In much American speech, there is no word in which /styu–/ occurs which does not also have a variant /stu–/. Thus, besides the pronunciation /styúwpid/ (often regarded as elegant), there exists a commoner variant /stúwpid/. Similarly beside /styúw/ there is /stúw/, *stew.* Curiously, however, there are words in /stu–/ which never have a variant /styu–/, so that the variation does not work equally in both directions. That is, *stool* is never /styúwl/ in any kind of speech which is at all natural. There is also considerable variation in the number and kind of words which employ these clusters. The most frequent are /spl–/, /spr–/, /str–/, /skr–/, and /skw–/. The clusters with /y/ are all low in frequency as might be expected, in accord with the strictly limited environment in which they occur. The group /skl–/ is very rare and is practically limited to learned and foreign words like *sclerosis* and its derivatives. This last group, then, hardly seems thoroughly established in the general language, and the same statement can be made of /styu–/, which, as we have seen, often exists only as a variant of /stu–/. There must, therefore, be many speakers for whom the clusters are only seven:

/spl–/
/spr–/   /str–/   /skr–/
/spyu–/   /skyu–/
                    /skw–/

This underlying arrangement is strikingly symmetrical, though, as often with symmetrical arrangements in language, we do not know why it occurs. Yet some things can be said about it. Thus the absence of */stl–/ is in accord with a general limitation on initial clusters, in that no dental stop clusters with /l/ initially. That is, we do not have either */tl–/ or */dl–/. The behavior of /styu–/ is also reflected in two-consonant clusters, where /tyu–/ and /dyu–/ also alternate with /tu–/ and /du–/. Finally, the limitation that /y/-clusters only occur before following /u/ is rather faintly reflected in the behavior of /skw–/, which occurs before /i/ in *squeeze*, but not before /u/—there being no such form as */skwúwz/. The limitation is not perfectly worked out, but suggests an underlying pattern of distribution in which the high front semivowel did not occur in a cluster before a high front vowel, and a high back semivowel similarly did not occur in a cluster before a high back vowel.

The most notable feature of these clusters, however, is their great similarity. That is, only /s/ goes in the first position, only /p t k/ in the second position, only /l r/ and /y w/ in the third.[2] The positions, moreover, are never reversed; that is, in spite of spelling, there is no such 2-1 cluster as */ps–/. This fact of arrangement is one of the reasons why it seems best to analyze the initial of *chump* as a single segment, rather than as a cluster of /t/ and /š/.

These positional groups can be used to describe the two-consonant clusters as well. For these, we can set up two classes: a "derived" class, those which are contained in the three-consonant clusters just described but with one position vacant, like /sp–/ which is a 1–2 cluster with position 3 empty; and a "nonderived" class, with clusters like /fl–/ which contains a consonant not found in any clusters of three. The derived 1–2 clusters which are possible are /sp–/, /st–/, and /sk–/. All occur, as in *spoon, stone, school,* and all are frequent, there being approximately 500, 1,000, and 400

---

[2] In accord with the structure of these initial groups, positional classes are assigned to consonants. Positional group 1 contains /s/ and all other spirants; positional group 2 contains stops and nasals; positional group 3 contains linguals and semivowels.

dictionary entries for the respective groups.[3] This is much greater lexical frequency than for any of the three-consonant clusters, the most frequent of which is /str–/ with 200, and the least frequent of which is /spyu–/ with only 4.

The possible 2–3 clusters are /pl–/, /pr–/, /pyu–/, /tr–/, /kl–/, /kr–/, /kyu–/, and /kw–/. Again all occur, as *play, pray, pew, true, clue, crew, cue,* and *queen.* The lexical frequencies are high, running from /pr–/ with approximately 1,000 entries to /pyu–/ with 70. With 1–3 clusters, the situation is different. Of the four possible clusters, only /sl–/ and /sw–/ are found. The possible groups */sr–/ and */syu–/ are both absent. Examples of /sl–/ and /sw–/ are *sleep* and *sweep,* and both groups are frequent, having frequencies of approximately 200. The missing clusters have some peculiarities, however. The missing /sr–/ is in a sort of complementary distribution with /šr–/ as in *shrink,* in that the initial /š/ does not cluster freely with other consonants than /r/ and that /šr–/ therefore fills the place of the missing /sr–/. This complementarity results in the appearance of allophones of /š/ in /šr–/ which are often rather /s/-like, and there can easily be dialects in which /šr–/ has become /sr–/, supplying the place of the expected /s/-cluster. The other missing cluster, /syu–/, has a shadowy existence as an elegant variant in words like *suitor* /syúwtər/.

In general, limitation on the occurrence of consonants increases with the number of consonants in a cluster. Thus, if there is no clustering at all, there is the maximum of freedom, in that all the consonants except /ŋ/ and /ž/ occur before vowels. If two consonants occur, very considerable limitation begins, since the first consonant is then a spirant or a stop, and the second is stop, nasal, lingual, or semivowel. If three consonants occur, there is a maximum of limitation as we have seen, in that the first is always /s/, the second a voiceless stop, and the third lingual or nasal. If we work downward, then, from three-consonant clusters, to those of two, and to single consonants, we should always expect the two-consonant groups to contain all those possible in groups of three and others as well. This is what happens most of the time. If we leave position 1 vacant, we have not only clusters like /pr–/, /tr–/, and /kr–/, which occur as parts of three-consonant clusters, but sequences like /br–/, /dr–/, and /gr–/, which do not. The 1–3 clusters, in which /sr–/ and /syu–/ are missing, constitute the only exception to the general rule that any two-consonant cluster should contain all the combinations which occur as parts of clusters of three. This non-

---

[3] All frequency figures in this chapter refer to the number of dictionary entries containing the cluster in question, not to the number of times items containing the cluster occur in continuous text. The dictionary used was *The American College Dictionary,* ed. by C. L. Barnhart, Random House, New York, 1948.

occurence of /sr-/ and /syu-/ is made up for by the occurrence of non-derived clusters like /fl-/, as we shall see.

When we pass to a general description of nonderived clusters, it is convenient to begin with the special group of 2–3 forms represented by /pw-/ and /tw-/. The phonemes of which these two-consonant clusters are made up, however, all occur in various of the three-consonant groups. Of the two, /tw-/ is certainly more fully established, since it occurs in thoroughly native forms like *twist* and *twin*, while /pw-/ is not only infrequent, but limited to foreign forms like *pueblo* /pwéblow/, besides which there is a variant /pyuwéblow/. If the /skl-/ of *sclerosis* is not regarded as an established part of the language, then /kl-/, which is a very frequent cluster, must also be put in the same group of nonderived clusters with /pw-/ and /tw-/.

Two consonant clusters of the 1–2 type increase the number of phonemes which can occur in the first position by adding /š/ and of those which can occur in the second by adding /m/ and /n/. The new groups are then /sn-/ as in *snow* and /sm-/ as in *small*. Both these groups are frequent and well established. The groups with initial /š/ are /šp-/, /št-/, /šk-/, /šm-/, and /šn-/. All are of very low frequency, the highest having 5 dictionary entries, and the lowest, 1. All occur in place or proper names like *Schmidt* and *Schneider* and almost all have variants with simple /s/. The whole group, then, represents an expansion of the English clustering pattern under foreign influence. Yet foreign in origin as these clusters are, they are sufficiently similar to established groups so that there is no great resistance to them. Thus, for instance, the vogue of the comic-strip coinage *shmoo* makes it quite clear that /šm-/ is reasonably well established, even if still in a somewhat special category.

The nonderived 2–3 clusters are sufficiently numerous so that they are best handled with a tabular list. The first group of them, shown with examples, is that in which position 2 has a voiced stop:

/bl-/	*blame*			/gl-/	*gleam*
/br-/	*bread*	/dr-/	*drain*	/gr-/	*grain*
/byu-/	*beauty*	/dyu-/	*dew*	/gyu-/	*gewgaw*
/bw-/	*bwana*	/dw-/	*dwell*	/gw-/	*guava*

In these, the clusters in /l/ and /r/ all have frequencies in the hundreds, but those in /–yu-/ and /–w-/ are again very low. The cluster /dyu-/ again has a nonclustering variant /du-/, as in *duty* /dyúwtiy/ or /dúwtiy/. It should be said in passing that with the cluster written /gyu-/, there are rare and sporadic occurrences of /gy-/ where some other vowel than /u/ follows. Such a sporadic and dialectical form is *girl* /gyə́hrl/ found in Tidewater Virginia. The same remark applies to other two-consonant clusters with

/–y–/ as second member, for instance *car* /kyáhr/ and the more widespread form *piano* /pyáhnow/. The three /–w–/ clusters in this group seem to have only one thoroughly established representative, /dw–/. The least established is /bw–/, represented only by foreign forms like the Bantu form given above or Spanish words like *bueno*. It is evidence of some resistance to the cluster that the Virginia place name *Buena Vista* is usually /byùwnə + vístə/ with spelling pronunciation. There is no such resistance to /gw–/, which is employed in the common name *Gwen*.

The second group of nonderived 2–3 clusters are those which have a nasal before the representative of group 3. Most of the group are rare, and all are of recent origin. Nonetheless some are quite well established, and the whole group is of importance to the clustering pattern, since it is these clusters which establish that the nasals belong in position 2. Clusters described earlier, like /sm–/, might have been called 1–3, and as we shall see later in postvocalic clusters, it is necessary there to assign the nasals to position 3. Moreover, as spellings like *know* and *gnaw* still testify, English once had /kn–/ and /gn–/ which would force assignment of the nasals to position 3 in initial clusters as well. There is thus an interesting hint of language history in the present position of nasals in the clustering pattern. It is possible, though unproved, that the loss of /kn–/ and /gn–/ is connected with the development of new clusters like /myu–/ in which the nasals occur before a form belonging to position 3. The clusters in question are:

/myu–/ /nyu–/
/mw–/ /nw–/

Of the group, only /myu/ is frequent, being found in such words as *music* and *mute* and without a following /–u/ in *mirror*, often /myírər/. As is usual with dentals before /–yu–/, /nyu–/ has a variant without /–y–/, as in *news* /nyúwz/ or /núwz/. The clusters with /–w–/ are limited to French words and names, like *moire* /mwáhr/ and *noire* /nwáhr/.

The nonderived 1–3 clusters again add new spirants to position 1. The first group, shown with examples, is that of voiceless spirants other than /s/:

/fl–/	*flame*		/šl–/	*Schlitz*
/fr–/	*free*	/θr–/ *three*	/šr–/	*shriek*
/fyu–/	*few*	/θyu–/ *thews*		
		/θw–/ *thwack*	/šw–/	*schwa*

The first two columns offer no peculiarities; all are thoroughly established, and most of them are frequent. The groups in /–yu–/ are rare as usual, and /θw–/ is also rare, but thoroughly native. The expected limitation on dental clusters in /l/ reappears, since there is no */θl–/.

As mentioned, /š/ does not cluster freely in initial position with any consonant except /r/. Therefore as one might expect, /šr-/ is the only cluster in the third column which is frequent, having approximately 40 entries. The other two clusters in the column are again of foreign origin, though now common in German names. The 1–3 clusters with /s/ and /š/ could, if we disregard recent additions, be put together in a single column:

/sl-/
/šr-/
/sw-/

As well as this group of 1–3 clusters with voiceless spirants, there are nonderived clusters with voiced spirants. The group is not well filled out, there being only two spirants, /v/ and /z/, which appear at all. The reason for the absence of /ð/ and /ž/ is historic: both are phonemes of recent development, and the allophones or phonemic sequences from which they arose did not occur before other consonants:

/vl-/   *Vladivostok*
/vr-/   *Vries* (a name)
/vyu-/   *view*   /zw-/   *zouave*

None of these clusters is frequent, and only /vyu-/ appears in forms which occur often in speech, yet all of them are sufficiently similar to established clusters so that there is no resistance to them.

There is, however, a pair of nonderived clusters which are at least historically of the 1–3 type and which are of great importance. They are /hw-/, as in *wheel*, with a lexical frequency of approximately 300, and /hyu-/, as in *human*, with a frequency of 40. One of the general characteristics of English clustering is that two successive consonants cannot be members of the same positional group, at least in initial clusters. Since the third-position consonants include the semivowels, these clusters of two semivowels break the rule. There is a historical explanation. The modern phoneme /h/ is from two sources, a Proto-Germanic spirant and a glide in postvocalic position much like that of Modern English. After the loss of friction in the spirant ancestor, the two fell together in a single phoneme. The clusters with initial /h/ represent the spirant ancestor, so that these were originally normal representatives of the 1–3 type. They now constitute an exception, and it is likely that their exceptional quality is connected with the loss of these clusters in much American speech of the Atlantic seaboard and South, where *wheel* becomes /wíyl/ and *human*, more rarely, becomes /yúwmən/.

The clustering peculiarities of /h/ were earlier alluded to in Section 5 of Chapter 3, where it was said that these clustering characteristics are capable of an explanation other than the assumption that /h/ is still a spirant. Part of this explanation, the diverse origins of the /h/-phoneme, has just been given, but the historical facts are certainly not conclusive in themselves. They bear the possible interpretation that initial [h] is a spirant and that the postvocalic entity still belongs to a differing phoneme. More important is the fact that in the situation in which a vowel nucleus occurs before a consonant, there are idiolects which have contrasts of the type *road* /rówd/ and *rowed* /róhwd/ or *lies* /láyz/ and *Lisa* /láhyzə/. Though these are not the forms he cited, James Sledd's review of *An Outline of English Structure*[4] discussed a number of contrasts which could be easily explained in this way, as are a number of forms once differently analyzed by Bernard Bloch. Such distinctions are not present in my own idiolect, but are by no means rare. The interesting feature of such sequences is that when they occur, the postvocalic entity now assigned to /h/, but admittedly of different origin from the prevocalic [h], is showing the same kind of clustering habits as the initial /h/. That is, clusters of two semivowels can occur in either prevocalic or postvocalic position if the first member of the cluster is /h/. The peculiarities of initial /h/ in these idiolects are no longer that it shares distributional features with spirants but that it shares distributional features with the postvocalic entity.

In our description of initial clusters there has been no attempt to describe all rare and aberrant groups, like the /ts-/ which is the dictionary pronunciation of *tsetse fly*. Such groups can safely be ignored since they do not follow normal patterns, and when the words containing them penetrate everyday speech, they promptly acquire variants more in accord with English habits. There is one exception to the normal pattern which has become firmly established. This is the /sf-/ of *sphere*, *sphinx*, and *svelte*, for the last of which the dictionaries recommend /sv-/. The cluster is a genuine 1–1 group, the only one found in the language, and its adoption indicates the prestige of the languages from which the forms were taken, since otherwise it is likely that the words would have become /spíhr/ and /spíŋks/, as they not infrequently do in the speech of children.

The rules for initial clusters, generally stated, are the following: position 1 includes spirants, position 2 sounds with oral closure (stops and nasals), position 3 linguals and semivowels. All clusters follow the order 1–2–3, though not all positions have to be filled. With the exception of the clusters /hw-/, /hyu-/, and /sf-/, no initial cluster has more than one representative

---

[4] Review of Trager and Smith, *An Outline of English Structure*, and Fries, *The Structure of English*, in *Language*, XXXI, 1955, pp. 312–45.

of any one position. Finally, the less strict limitation on clusters of the 2–3 and 1–3 type is explained by a rule which carries over to final and medial clusters as well. Stops and spirants are arranged in voiced and voiceless pairs, while nasals, linguals, and semivowels are not. It is a rule, then, that paired consonants cannot cluster if they differ in voice quality. Thus, in 1–2 clusters we can have only /sp–/ or a possible /zb–/ (notice the bookish "Zblood!"); never */sb–/ or */zp–/. It is this rule which makes the "correct" pronunciation of *svelte* with /sv–/ seem un-English. Many speakers who use it seem to preserve the rule, however, by breaking up the cluster with an intervening juncture.

As stated, the rule indicates that as long as the initial consonant of a three-consonant cluster must be /s/, then only the voiceless stops can occur in position 2. If position 1 is vacant, we can have either voiced or voiceless stops in position 2, since the consonants in position 3 are not paired by voice. That is, we can have clusters like both /bl–/ and /pl–/. Similarly, in 1–3 clusters we can have both /sw–/ and the much rarer /zw–/.

4. Prejunctural consonant clusters

From initial clusters we will pass to final groups, that is, postvocalic, prejunctural clusters. Some of these clusters preserve the same order of positions as in initial clusters, but with the limitation that phonemes of position 3 do not occur, so that only 1–2 clusters are possible.[5] The list of 1–2 clusters, with examples, is as follows:

	/–ft/ *aft*	
	/–vd/ *bereaved*	
	/–θt/ *toothed*	
	/–ðd/ *wreathed*	
/–sk/ *risk*	/–st/ *list*	/–sp/ *lisp*
	/–zd/ *raised*	
	/–št/ *cashed*	
	/–žd/ *rouged*	

The limitations which appear here have some relation to the limitation on

---

[5] The type of phonemic analysis and transcription used in this book interprets all instances of syllabic linguals and nasals as instances of vowel and following consonant. Thus a phonetic [bə́tn̩] is always analyzed as phonemic /bə́tən/ or /bə́tin/. If the phonemic transcription used recognizes syllabic quality as an independent phoneme, the rule that linguals and nasals do not cluster in final position is still valid, but is then expressed in the form that syllabicity rather than an intervening vowel breaks up such clusters.

1–2 initial clusters. It will be remembered that in initial clusters the established groups were /sp–/, /st–/, and /sk–/, as here, and the groups like /št–/ were recent importations. The phonemes /c/ and /j/ did not figure in initial clusters, just as they do not here. The rest of the limitation here present—namely, that all the spirants occur in position 1, but only with /t/ or /d/ in position 2—bears no relation to the structure of initial clusters, except to suggest as there, that /s/ is a special phoneme in its clustering habits.

In final position, however, these 1–2 clusters can be expanded by the addition of a third consonant, which can be /s/ or /z/, and after /p/ or /k/ can also be /t/. This is the first of three such special positional groups. We shall write it –3[†], with the statement that it occurs only in clusters of a forward type:[6]

/–fts/ *rafts*
/–vdz/ *the bereaved's*

/–sps/ *lisps*   /–sts/ *lists*   /–sks/ *risks*
/–spt/ *lisped*   /–skt/ *risked*

It is noteworthy that position –3[†] is not filled after all the 1–2 clusters, and it seems likely that some of them would be resisted. Such a group as /–zdz/ would at least pile up a number of dentals with minor distinctions in articulatory position, which seems unlikely for English, as the development of the parallel /–sts/ suggests. Furthermore, all 1–2–3[†] clusters are subject to various developments that suggest that they are not thoroughly established. For instance, the colloquial form almost universally used for *asked* is /æst/, with loss of /k/. Similarly, *lists* is often reduced to /lís + s/, or simply to /lís/. For *lists* there are also older dialect forms such as /lísiz/ or /lístiz/. Even in the other clusters which have not been thus reduced, breaking up the cluster with a juncture is common, as in /lís + ps/ or /lísp + s/.

In the 1–2–3[†] groups just given, reduction to a two-consonant cluster when one position is unfilled gives rather surprisingly few new clusters. If –3[†] is left vacant, the resultant cluster is a normal 1–2 formation of the type already described. If position 1 is left vacant, the resultant cluster is of a normal reversed type, which will be described below. If position 2 is left vacant, the result may be simply /–st/, again a normal 1–2 cluster. Since clusters of identical consonants do not occur in English, the groups /–sps/, /–sts/, and /–sks/ cannot be reduced by leaving position 2 vacant.

---

[6] The special groups which are always preceded by a consonant or cluster will be written with a dash before them: –3[†]. Groups always followed by a consonant or cluster have a dash after them: 3[†]–. The dagger indicates "special group."

The result of these several limitations is that the only two-consonant clusters derivable from this group are the 1–3[†] pair, /–fs/ and /–vz/. They are found in forms like *scuffs* and *leaves*.

The forward groups are by no means the only, or the simplest, clusters that occur finally. We have, for instance, a form like *corpse*, with /–rps/, which is a reversed cluster, consisting of 3–2–1. There are six of these which are nearly exact palindromes of the forward clusters found in initial position. They are therefore quite predictable. They are the /–rps/ already mentioned; /–rts/ as in *hearts;* /–rks/ as in *parks;* /–lps/ as in *Alps;* /–lts/[7] as in *halts;* and /–lks/ as in *hulks.* Again all are frequent and thoroughly established.

The semivowels, of course, also occur before final consonants and consonant clusters, but it will be remembered that in this position the semivowels are classified as members of the vowel nucleus. There are therefore no 3–2–1, 3–2, or 3–1 final clusters in which position 3 is filled by a semivowel.

There are, however, reversed clusters which are not exactly similar to the forward clusters. It was said on page 74 that in reversed clusters it is necessary to assign nasals to position 3, the position they once held in forward clusters as well. In final position, nasals occur before stops (e.g., *limp*) and before spirants (e.g., *swims*), so that there is no possibility of assigning them elsewhere than to position 3. In reversed clusters, however, a nasal clusters only with a stop of the same order, that is, labials with labials, dentals with dentals, and velars with velars. There are apparent exceptions to this rule as in *ringed* ("ringed with steel") but the exceptions are only apparent, since such forms are interrupted by a juncture, e.g., /ríŋ + d/. The result of this rule of articulatory congruence is that the 3–2–1 clusters in which nasals occur are only three: /–mps/, as in *glimpse*; /–nts/, as in *tents* (this is the maximal form of the cluster, which may be reduced to /ns/ only); and /–ŋks/, as in *lynx* or *inks.* Again, all three are fully established and quite frequent.

The nine 3–2–1 clusters already described could theoretically be increased by nine more, consisting of the same position 3 consonants, voiced stops in position 2, and /z/ in position 1. Not all of the nine occur, the list being as follows:

/–rbz/ *herbs*
/–rdz/ *words*
/–rgz/ *bergs*

---

[7] The limitation which prevents initial */stl–/ and */tl–/ does not apply to 3–2–1 groups.

/-lbz/ (rare, but may occur in *bulbs*, commoner
forms of which are /bɔ́hbz/, or
/bɔ́lb + z/)
/-ldz/ *yields*
/-ndz/ *mends* (the maximal form of the cluster, which
may be reduced to /-nz/)

We have already met a situation in which it was necessary to set up a
special position, –3† in final 1-2-3† clusters, in order to deal with forms like
lisps. In reversed clusters, we must also set up a special position, –1†, which
occurs when the preceding group is 1 or any member of 2 other than /t/ or
/d/. The sole membership in –1† is /t/ and /d/. Examples of 3-1-1† are:

/-lst/   *pulsed*
/-rst/   *first*
/-mst/ *glimpsed* (In this cluster the smooth transition form is as given. If all four consonants are present, the cluster is often
broken by a juncture, /glímp + st/.)
/-nst/ *fenced*
/-ŋst/ *jinxed* (As with /-mst/, if four consonants are
present, often there is a juncture,
/jíŋk + st/.)
/-nzd/ *cleansed*

With other than /s/ or /z/ in position 1, we have:

/-lft/   *selfed* (past tense of *self* as verb, meaning
"inbred")
/-rft/   *scarfed*
/-mft/ *humphed*
/-lvd/ *shelved*
/-rvd/ *carved*

The forms with /-θ-/ are, with the exception of /-rθt/, all rare, and
essentially nonce formations:

/-lθt/   *healthed* (provided with health)
/-rθt/   *earthed*
/-mθt/ (possible in *warmthed*, but see below, p. 82)
/-nθt/ *plinthed*
/-ŋθt/ *strengthed*
/-rðd/ *birthed* (the voiced variant)

If the position 1 consonant is /š/, only two clusters are found, though these are commoner than most of those we have been dealing with. The two forms are /-lšt/ in *welshed* and /-nšt/ in *bunched*. Both clusters, however, alternate with forms in /-c-/, /wélct/ and /bɔ́nct/.

The 2-1-1[†] cluster type is composed of stops in position 2 and spirants in position 1:

> /-pft/ (rare, but known to the writer in *Zipfed*, past
> tense of verb *Zipf*, "to analyze language
> in the manner of G.K. Zipf")
> /-pθt/ *depthed* (a nonce form)
> /-pst/ *lapsed*
> /-tθt/ *widthed* (a rare form, but possible in *gener-*
> *ously widthed)*
> /-dzd/ *adzed* (a rare form)
> /-tst/ *blitzed*

The remaining type of cluster in which –1[†] occurs is 3-2-1[†]. Clusters of this type have lingual or nasal in position 3, and any stop except /t/ or /d/ in position 2. There are the usual general limitations; for instance, those against paired consonants of differing voice quality and the limitation which prevents a nasal from clustering with a stop of differing order of articulation. As a result of this last limitation, there are only three nasal clusters, since each nasal can cluster with only one following stop:

> /-lpt/ *scalped*
> /-rpt/ *usurped*
> /-mpt/ *exempt* (may be reduced by loss of /p/, which
> is then replaced by /+/; or /+/ may
> appear after the /p/ without loss)
> /-lct/ *belched* (varies with /-lšt/, /bélšt/)
> /-rct/ *arched*
> /-nct/ *bunched* (varies with /-nšt/, /bɔ́nšt/)
> /-lkt/ *hulked*
> /-rkt/ *worked*
> /-ŋkt/ *linked*

We would expect a similar set of nine voiced clusters, but only six appear:

> /-lbd/ *bulbed*
> /-rbd/ *orbed*
> /-ljd/ *bulged* (varies with /-lžd/, /bɔ́lžd/)
> /-rjd/ *diverged*

/–njd/ *arranged* (varies with /–nžd/, /əréynžd/
/–rgd/ *berged* (or similar rare forms)

Before we leave the groups with –1†, we can return for a minute to the clusters of *glimpsed, jinxed,* and a possible third in *chintzed.* If four consonants are present, without juncture, the clusters are of the 3-2-1-1† type, representing an extension of the usual rule that clusters are limited to three. Such four-consonant clusters cannot be said to be very thoroughly established, but they have something more than a theoretical possibility. They are structurally interesting in that they establish that –1† is rather an extension of the three basic positional groups than a substitution for one of them.

There is still another special group beside the –3† and –1† which we have now taken up. This group can be called 3†–, consisting of /r/ alone, and occurring only in reversed clusters. The special group is necessary in order to handle all instances of /r/ before the other members of positional group 3 in reversed clusters, that is, before /l/ or a nasal.

EXAMPLES OF 3†-3-2

/–rlt/   (rare, but occurs in the facetious pronuncia-
              tion /spɔ́rlt/ for *spoilt*)
/–rld/ *world*
/–rnt/ *burnt*
/–rnd/ *spurned*

Examples of 3†-3-2 with other stops than /t/ or /d/ in position 2 are not well established, though there is no reason why such a sequence as /–rmp/ or /–rŋk/ could not occur.

EXAMPLES OF 3†-3-1

/–rlz/ *Charles*
/–rnz/ *burns*
/–rmz/ *charms*
/–rmθ/ *warmth*
/–rns/ (rare, but possible in the facetious pronunciation
              /pɔ́rns/ for *prince* and *points*)

As often, not many of the expected clusters appear. Forms like *warmth* are interesting, therefore, in establishing the possibility of extending the pattern to other than /z/ and /s/. These forms in 3†– are still more interesting in another way, in that, as with –1†, they give the possibility of four-consonant clusters. The commonest four-consonant cluster is /–rldz/ in *worlds,* but the two last forms in the list above have four-consonant variants,

/wɔ́rmpθ/ and /pɔ́rnts/. It is noteworthy, then, that the theoretical limit on final clusters is five, 3†-3-2-1-1†, a type which is not found but which would probably strike most speakers as at least pronounceable, in some such form as /–rmpθt/, */wɔ́rmpθt/. Even the four-consonant clusters, however, are less than fully established, since they are commonly subject to loss of position 2 or to breaking up by a juncture.

As with initial clusters, there are a few isolated exceptions, with a special history. The exceptions here are in the three words *fifth, sixth,* and *twelfth.* The irregularity consists, as with *sphere,* in the clustering of two spirants, a type our description does not provide for. A special formula could of course have been set up to take care of these three forms, but the clusters are closely related morphologically and semantically, so that it seems more economical to lump all three, /–fθ/, /–ksθ/, and /–lfθ/ as a single type of exception. Moreover, the history of all three shows development toward forms which would fit the general pattern. Thus *twelfth* has a common 2-1 variant, /twélθ/, and *fifth* and *sixth* had earlier forms with 1-2 /fíft/, and 2-1-1† /síkst/. Historically, the forms are special in that, though they are thoroughly native, they have arisen not from normal phonological habits but from the analogical regularizing of the /–θ/ which appears in *fourth* and *seventh.*

We can now summarize briefly the types of final clusters which we have presented. The first type is forward clusters, which have the varieties 1-2 as in *lisp* and *raft,* and 1-2-3† in *lisps* and *rafts.* The second type is the simple reversed cluster, 3-2-1 as in *corpse* or *words.* The third type contains –1†, a type which reaches its maximum in the possible but not invariant 3-2-1-1† of *glimpsed.* The type has subdivisions in 3-2-1† in *worked;* 3-1-1† in *pulsed;* and 2-1-1† in *next.* The fourth type contains 3†–, which again reaches a maximum in the somewhat variable 3†-3-2-1 of *worlds.* The subdivisions are 3†-3-2 in *burnt* and 3†-3-1 in *burns.* The theoretical limit is reached in such a nonexistent 3†-3-2-1-1† as *warmthed* /wɔ́rmpθt/.

A final observation about the special positional groups –3†, –1†, and 3†– is that their peculiarities are due to rather different causes. The groups –3† and –1† are mainly, though not solely, due to the presence of a few endings, commonly added to all sorts of stems. The second factor in these clustering groups is that dentals such as /s/ and /t/ are clearly, even in initial clusters, in a rather special position. In the group 3†–, however, no morphological factor is at work. The presence of sequences like /–rl/, where there is no such sequence as */–lr/, is evidence that /r/ is structurally different from /l/, the phoneme which is otherwise nearest like it. The fact that /r/ can occur before heavy consonant clusters suggests strongly that /r/ is much more like the semivowels than is the other lingual and that, in some dialects at least, it might be possible to avoid setting up a position 3†– by making postvocalic /r/ a member of the preceding vowel nucleus rather than of a following consonant cluster.

The remaining final clusters are two-consonant groups. The forward two-consonant groups, those in 1-2, have already been treated, so that reversed two-consonant clusters are all that remain to be described. All but one of these groups will be very briefly given, with no attempt to list all the examples, since they can be very readily constructed:

3†-3	3-1
/-rl/ *twirl*	/-rs/ *coarse*
/-rn/ *burn*	/-ls/ *pulse*
/-rm/*charm*	/-lθ/ *health*
	/-rf/ *scarf*

3-2	2-1
/-rt/ *hurt*	/-ks/ *tax*
/-lt/ *halt*	/-dz/ *adze*
/-rk/ *work*	/-tθ/ *width*
	/-pf/ *Zipf*

The last group is 2-1† in forms like *act*. Such a cluster might have been counted as a forward cluster of the 2-3† type, since forward clusters gave us such forms as *risked*. It has seemed better to place *act* among the reversed clusters, however, since it will be remembered that a /t/ belonging to –3† could appear only after /k/ or /p/. There is no such limitation on the reversed clusters, and groups not only like *act* but like *robbed* are therefore better accommodated here. There are six such clusters:

/-bd/ *robbed*	/-ct/ *itched*
/-pt/ *apt*	/-gd/ *dragged*
/-jd/ *judged*	/-kt/ *act*

5. Intervocalic consonant clusters

We have now surveyed the final clusters and can pass on to medial clusters. As usual, we will define medial clusters as intervocalic clusters not immediately preceded or followed by a juncture and not interrupted by one. Some general description of this type of sequence is necessary before we take up the groups in detail. First, if we have such a sequence as /-st-/ in *dusty*, it is genuinely medial as long as there is no juncture before or after the group. If what is uttered is /dɔ́ + stiy/, the cluster is treated as initial. Contrariwise, an utterance such as /dɔ́st + iy/ treats the cluster as a final group. If /dɔ́s + tiy/ is the form spoken, then the cluster is broken up into final and initial elements.

Syllable division also complicates the treatment of medial clusters, since there can be no intervocalic cluster without syllable division before, after, or within it. Syllable division, however, is not a phoneme, so that a sequence of intervocalic consonants is still a genuine cluster, even though the consonants of which it is composed may belong to different syllables. Juncture produces syllable division in medial clusters, and some types of syllable division do not occur without it. Others, however, occur with or without a juncture. Thus a sequence /dáktər/ will always be divided between the /k/ and /t/ when there is no juncture. It will be divided in the same way with a juncture in that position—/dák + tər/. The sequence, of course, represents the word *doctor*, which is commonly pronounced either with or without the juncture. If the sequence should represent the phrase *docked 'er*, however, syllable division after the /t/ could be accomplished only by a juncture, /dákt + ər/. In the discussion of medial clusters which follows, account will be taken of both syllable division and juncture, and it will be seen that junctures are particularly likely to occur at points of normal syllable division, though they may occur at other points also.

The first group of medial clusters are those composed of two consonants. To understand this very large group of clusters, it is necessary to point out that a frequent situation is a sequence in which a consonant ends a preceding element and another consonant begins that which follows, with a juncture marking the division. That is, if we write /C/ to mean any consonant, and /V/ to mean any vowel, or vowel nucleus, we can symbolize this situation as /–VC + CV–/. If the juncture is lost in any such situation, the two consonants then become a true medial cluster, regardless of any morphological boundaries or of syllable division. The limitation on clusters of the type /–VCCV–/ are essentially limitations on the loss of juncture between consonants. These limitations are considerable, but are simple to state. First, juncture is not lost between identical consonants, that is, a sequence like /–p + p–/ in *stop payment* does not become a true cluster. A juncture is not lost between paired consonants if they differ in voice quality, so that /–p + b–/, as in *stop Bill*, also does not become a cluster. Juncture is preserved between a nasal and a stop of differing order, as in *Tom Carter*, /–m + k–/ and *Jack Myers*, /–k + m–/. Finally, juncture is in many idiolects preserved between differing nasals, as in *damnation*, /–m + n–/ and *inmost* /–n + m–/.

The juncture losses give consonant clusters of two types, those which conform to the patterns of initial and final clusters, like /–sp–/, and those which do not, like /–tk–/. In a cluster of the first type, a juncture lost between the consonants can be replaced by a juncture before or after them, making the cluster conform to either initial or final clusters. That is, a phrase like *this policy* occasionally varies between /ðis + pálisiy/, /ði + spálisiy/, and /ðisp + álisiy/. With a cluster of the second type, as in *hot cakes*, a juncture lost between the consonants is not replaced by one before the /t/ or after the /k/. At present it cannot be said that loss of juncture between consonants which make up a noninitial, nonfinal cluster is less frequent than in groups which are possible as initials or finals. It can be said, however, that whenever there is a cluster of the /–VCCV–/ type without juncture, syllable division falls between the consonants. Syllable division before or after the cluster is possible only if a juncture can be so placed.

As just said, the limitations on loss of juncture between consonants are considerable. Even under these general limitations, however, the number of possible two-consonant medial clusters is very large, no less than 264. Most of them actually occur, though a number of expected combinations are prevented by the fact that /ŋ/ and /ž/ do not occur in prevocalic position in clusters. Since the number of clusters is so large, we will content ourselves with giving illustrations of one set only, that in which one member is /p/. Some of these examples are drawn from phrases, some from forms ordinarily printed as one word. In both types of illustration, however, only the forms without a juncture constitute genuine medial clusters:

/–pt–/   *helicopter* /hélikàptər/
/–pc–/   *stepchild* /stépcàyld/, more usually /stép + càyld/
/–pk–/   *Kipke* /kípkiy/ (the proper name)
/–tp–/   *output* /áwtpùt/, more usually /áwt + pùt/
/–cp–/   *catchpole* /kǽcpòwl/, more usually /kǽc + pòwl/
/–kp–/   *jackpot* /jǽkpàt/, more usually /jǽk + pàt/
/–pf–/   *up for* (election) /ə́pfɚr/, usually /ə́p + fɚr/
/–pθ–/   *depthen* /dépθin/ (a rare form)
/–ps–/   *capsule* /kǽpsùwl/, often /kǽp + sùwl/
/–pš–/   *Upshur* /ə́pšər/ (the proper name)
/–fp–/   *half-pay* (officer) /hǽfpèy/, usually /hǽf + pèy/
/–θp–/   *southpaw* /sáwθpòh/, usually /sáwθ + pòh/
/–sp–/   *wispy* /wíspiy/
/–šp–/   *Ashby* /ǽšpiy/ (the proper name, in the smooth transition form; usually /ǽš + biy/)
/–pm–/   *shipment* /šípmint/, often /šíp + mint/
/–mp–/   *limping* /límpiŋ/
/–pr–/   *April* /éypril/
/–pl–/   *deeply* /díypliy/, often /díyp + liy/
/–rp–/   *sharper* /šárpər/
/–lp–/   *helper* /hélpər/

A cluster of this type, say /–kp–/, which arises only by the loss of juncture and is noninitial and nonfinal, can at least possibly be expanded so as to make the first consonant the last member of a final cluster, as in *inkpot*, and the second the first of an initial cluster, as in *ink-press*. When this happens, however, juncture between /k/ and /p/ is always preserved, so that we are no longer dealing with a medial cluster.

We can, then, make some further general statements about medial clusters. First, any initial cluster can become a medial cluster if juncture before it is lost. Thus, the /spl–/ of *splash* is a medial cluster in *display*. Similarly, any final cluster can become medial by the loss of a following juncture. Thus, the /–rps/ of *harps* becomes (or may become) medial in *harpsichord*. For this reason, it is unnecessary to describe further those medial clusters which correspond to initial or final types.

There is, however, a large group of apparent medial clusters which must be described in order to exclude them properly from true clustering groups. A frequent medial situation is, as just said, a final cluster before a following initial cluster. Such a situation is represented by forms like *work-plan*, in which there is first a final cluster of a 3-2 type and then an initial cluster of a 2-3 type, so that two consonants of the same positional group are brought together. Such groups normally have a juncture, giving a formula –3-2 + 2-3–, making the occurrence of the juncture predictable and breaking up the apparent medial cluster into a final and an initial pair. The rule can be generally stated as follows: whenever a reversed cluster is followed by an initial cluster, a juncture is required between any two consonants of the same positional group. There are several types of sequences which illustrate this rule. We have already given an example of –3-2 + 2-3–; an example of –2-1 + 1-3– is *tax-flow*. The types can, in short, be reduced to those with successive consonants of group 2 and those with successive consonants of group 1.

A second general type of situation can be represented by such a form as *ink-spreader*. The sequence of consonants is such as to give an overlap, since the /s/ could be the last of a final cluster or the first of an initial cluster. The series might be represented thus:

$$3 \ \ 2 \ \ 1$$
$$/\eta \ \text{k} \ \text{s} \ \text{p} \ \text{r}/$$
$$1 \ \ 2 \ \ 3$$

With clusters of this type, it is possible to predict the occurrence of a juncture only in part. That is, a juncture must occur in such sequences, but its location may be either before or after the overlapping consonant. In the form given, it is before; in such a phrase as *inks producer*, it is after. In such another phrase as *Hank's praying* (i.e., "Hank is praying"), it may be both before and after.

In simple reversed clusters and simple forward clusters, it is always /s/ which is the overlapping consonant in a group of five. But since there is a group –1†, which contains /t/ and /d/, these also can overlap, sometimes producing an overlap of two consonants:

$$\begin{array}{ccc} 2 & 1 & 1\dagger \\ /\text{k} & \text{s} & \text{t} \quad \text{r}/ \\ 1 & 2 & 3 \end{array}$$

This is the sequence of *extra*. There will be a juncture in the sequence somewhere, breaking it into final and initial elements. But the location of the juncture now has pretty wide possibilities. It may be before the /s/, breaking the group into a simple final consonant and a normal initial cluster; after the /s/, setting up two two-consonant clusters; after the /t/, setting up a final cluster of three, as in *next*, and a single initial consonant. Judging from my own idiolect, it would seem that a division /–k + str–/ and /–ks + tr–/ in this particular item are about equally frequent and that a division /–kst + r–/ is rare. A simpler group is the /–kst–/ of *Baxter*. Here there is a possibility of juncture after the /t/, treating the whole sequence as a final cluster. But in my speech, such a division is rare. The usual one is /–k + st–/, and even /–ks + t–/ is uncommon. With this group it should also be noted that the whole sequence can be given without juncture, /bǽkstər/, since /–kst/ is a possible final group, yet even this treatment seems to be less common than /–k + st–/.

It is possible to summarize the behavior of overlapping or possibly overlapping sequences by saying that initial clusters tend to take precedence over final ones. The precedence is not an absolute rule, but seems to govern the most frequent treatment of groups which overlap. Thus, a sequence such as /–tst + r–/ remains possible in such a rare phrase as *chintzed room* ("a heavily chintzed room"), but if there is any disturbance of the juncture situation, it will tend to fall so as to produce the initial cluster /str–/. Within the boundaries of fixed constructions, therefore, juncture divisions in accord with initial clusters are commoner than those in accord with final clusters. A form like *hamstrung* is in no particular danger of displacement of juncture so as to produce /–mst + r–/, but a form like *vestry* can easily give either /vé + striy/ or /vés + triy/, both in accord with initial clusters, while the etymological /vést + riy/, with a final cluster, is rare.

A final note on medial clusters is that the special limitations on initial clusters, such as the absence of /stl–/, /tl–/, /dl–/, and /sr–/ do not apply. All of these groups occur as medials when a juncture is lost, though all frequently have junctures which break the clusters. Examples are forms like *lastly*, *butler*, *saddler*, and *disregard*.

7 .... MORPHEMICS

1. Morph, allomorph, and morpheme

As we continue the process of working from smaller to larger units of structure, the morpheme is the unit we encounter immediately after the phoneme. No phoneme can occur in speech without being a part of one of these units, and no morpheme can occur without being a member of some still larger construction. The morpheme is larger than the phoneme in that every morpheme must contain one phoneme and may contain several.

As a first definition of the morpheme, we can say that a morpheme is a recurrent sequence of phonemes, or a class of recurrent sequences of phonemes, which contrasts with other sequences or classes of sequences. The contrasting sequences, however, contrast only with sequences of phonemes of the same type. That is, morphemes made up of segmental phonemes contrast with all other morphemes made up of segmental phonemes; morphemes made up of suprasegmental phonemes of stress contrast with all other morphemes made up of stress phonemes; morphemes made up of pitches contrast with all other morphemes made up of pitches. Thus a form like *yes* contrasts with *no, ouch, up, policy,* and so on. It cannot be said to contrast with the stress morpheme which accompanies it, nor with the also accompanying pitch morpheme. On the other hand if *yes* has the pitch and terminal sequence which marks a question, this pitch morpheme contrasts with the morpheme which would mark a statement. There are, therefore, three kinds of morphemes, according to the type of phonemic material they contain. The kinds are segmental morphemes, stress morphemes, and pitch morphemes. As we shall see later, the stress morphemes also contain $/+/$; the terminal junctures are assigned to the pitch morphemes.

The members of a morpheme are its allomorphs, so that there is an exact terminological parallel between allomorph and morpheme, on the one hand, and allophone and phoneme, on the other. Further, a sequence which has been isolated by being cut away from the surrounding sequences but which has not yet been classified as to membership in a morpheme is called a morph. This term is then parallel to "sound," an entity within phonemics which has similarly been isolated, but not classified as to membership in a phoneme.

We shall begin our discussion with segmental morphemes. In doing so we shall treat them as abstractions, in that the transcription will remove the phonemes of stress and pitch without which segmental material cannot be pronounced. Transcription intended for morphemic analysis will be enclosed in braces—{ }—though unless otherwise stated, the symbols employed will still be phonemic. A cut, or possible cut, between morphemes will be written thus: –. Thus a morphic notation for *dogs* is {dɔhg–z}.[1]

A general difference between segmental morphemes and phonemes is that phonemes do not have meaning; they are distinguishers only, the elements which keep larger constructions apart. Many segmental morphemes have meaning, in the sense that they carry a reference to something in the nonlinguistic world, as does the morpheme {dɔhg}. Yet, even with segmental morphemes this referential meaning is not always as clear as it is in the example given. Can, for instance, a general definition be written to cover instances of *dog*, in *putting on the dog* and *dogfish?* With suprasegmental morphemes, referential meaning is absent, and they act as distinguishers of larger constructions much as phonemes do. A question sentence, for instance, is often kept apart from a statement solely by its pitch and juncture pattern, yet {2 2 3 ‖} does not refer to anything in the nonlinguistic world, as {dɔhg} does. It is thus not possible to say that morphemes are necessarily referentially meaningful elements; it is only possible to say that they are elements which may have referential meaning.

As with other elements in language, identification and classification must rest firmly on formal and distributional characteristics rather than on meaning. One reason for this statement as it applies to morphemes has just been given. Morphemes do not always have meaning, and even when they do, the meaning is not always clear. The basic reason, however, is that reliance on meaning as a primary tool of analysis produces circularity. Meaning is the end product of language differences, and we cannot therefore both define the differences by the product and define the product by the differences. Analysts nevertheless make use of meaning in spite of the danger. As we go on, we shall attempt to discuss how far it is possible to do so and yet avoid the ever-present danger of circularity.

----

[1] The most widely used symbol for morphemic notation is one identical with the root sign of mathematics. It has not been adopted in this text, since in most transcriptions offered, the material transcribed is not analyzed into its ultimate morphemic components. Our transcription is therefore morphic rather than strictly morphemic, and the use of root signs is reserved for transcriptions in which morphemes and allomorphs are fully identified.

2. Segmental morphs — first cuts

Structural linguistics has worked out a number of precise processes by which morphs, once identified, can be classed into morphemes and by which still further cuts can be made, once some of the morphs have been identified. But as with phonemics, the real problem is how to begin. If the process of morphemic analysis is to be orderly, it must be based on observable and previously defined phonemic entities. Clearly the best phonemic guides are the junctures. In Chapter 2 we saw variant constructions like *an aim : a name* distinguished from each other by the position of /+/. A common-sense decision here would be that the /+/ corresponds to the boundaries of variant morphs. A similar common-sense decision would be that terminal junctures normally occur at boundaries. We shall, therefore, examine the possibility that our first cuts into morphs should be rigorously in accord with the occurrence of junctures.

Such a possibility is a somewhat uncomfortable nettle to grasp, since acting on it produces some surprising results. Yet if it is granted that junctures normally occur at boundaries, cuts made in accord with them would have a probabilistic justification in that they would more often be right than wrong. To test the possibility on other than gross probabilities, it is necessary to examine the consequences of junctural cutting and of cutting done without reference to junctures.

A first difficulty in junctural cutting is that junctures are sometimes predictable in terms of phonotactic sequences, without reference to meaningful constructions. The proper name *Anchises*, dictionaries tell us, should be pronounced /æn + káysiyz/. In this pronunciation the /+/ is predictable because of the preceding and following phonemes, /n/ and /k/, giving a nasal of differing order from the following stop. The name is certainly a unit, in both its distributional behavior and its meaning, so that nothing beyond the phonological level suggests cutting it into two morphs.

The soundest argument against cutting the name into two morphs is that such cutting would needlessly increase the number of morphs and give morphs which are unique. It would seem possible to counter this argument by stating that rejection of wasteful cutting properly belongs to a later step, that of making further cuts when the possibility of junctural cuts has been exhausted. If objection to cutting *Anchises* at the juncture is based on the fact that it does not produce a pair of morphs which mean anything, the answer is clearly that morphemes do not necessarily have meaning. If objection to cutting is based on the fact that *Anchises* is a nonseparable syntactic unit, the answer is that *greenhouse* is also a syntactic unit, yet is accepted by all analysts as a two-morph construction. If objection to junctural cutting of such forms is based on the fact that it would often contradict etymology, the answer is that history and analysis are separate fields of study.

Another type of objection to junctural cutting is that /+/ does not always appear in the same place in two differing dialects. In my own idiolect there is no reason, formal or otherwise, for cutting *winter* into morphs. Yet a common New York City pronunciation is /wín + tər/, with two morphs, where my idiolect has one. The two pronunciations of *winter* are not only variations of the same syntactic and semantic entity, they are examples of nonsignificant dialect variation. Again, nothing beyond phonology suggests the possibility of a cut. To this it can be answered that variation in morphemic structure between dialects is not surprising. In my idiolect *lean-to* is /líyn + tùw/, which I should unhesitatingly cut into the morphs {liyn} and {tuw}. Yet in much of rural America the form is /líntər/, phonologically as much a single morph as *winter*. The etymological relation between the two pairs of variants is different, it is true, but this is a fact which need not concern us.

Probably the most serious objection to junctural cutting is that junctures can vary in a single entity within a single idiolect. The phrase *at all* offers a good, and a rather extreme, example in my own idiolect. I have three variants of this phrase /ətóhl/, /ət + óhl/, and /ə + tóhl/. They are nonsignificant varieties and are apparently correlated with differences in style. Thus, the last form is characteristic of an extremely emphatic way of talking. All forms can be treated therefore as "allos" of the phrase, with varying morphemic structure. The complexity which such variation produces, when we are stating morphemes and their allomorphs, is removed when we state the variations of the larger entity, so that nothing is permanently lost by junctural cutting even in this example.

The disadvantages of junctural cutting can then be summarized in the statement that junctural cutting gives morphs which are not required by analysis of larger entities. This statement can be met by the statement that nothing on the higher levels prevents such cutting. We can now examine the results of nonjunctural cutting. One method of nonjunctural cutting was recently proposed by Zellig Harris.[2] The method is admirably rigorous, and therefore cannot be objected to on the same grounds as other attempts at cutting without use of junctures. Harris proposed to make use of informants to find the points in any given sentence where the largest number of other items could be substituted. His first cuts were then made at these substitution points. But though rigorous, the method is laborious. Furthermore, it does not seem to be necessary. The substitution points are also the points at which junctures are most likely to occur. It therefore appears

---

[2] Published as "From Phoneme to Morpheme," *Language*, XXXI, 1955, pp. 190–213. It is interesting that Harris notes a correlation with junctural cutting in the following statement: "Indeed, when junctural phenomena are specified, the segmentation accords all the better with morphological analysis." p. 196.

that there is correlation between Harris' method and junctural cutting; they are variant processes which achieve the same results.

In truly nonjunctural cutting, the analyst works with the once accepted definition of a morpheme as a unit of recurrent phonemic-semantic similarity. If this is our criterion, one of the results can be shown in a series of forms like *snoot, snooty, snout, sneer, snake, snow,* and several others. There is phonemic similarity in the initial /sn–/, and there is semantic similarity in that most of the words are more or less unpleasant. As a result, there have been occasional suggestions that we should recognize initial /sn–/ as a morpheme (or at least a meaningful entity) with the meaning "unpleasant." Yet not all words in the list are unpleasant, at least not for everyone. In the midst of a hot summer, I find it difficult to react to *snow* with distaste, and one word, *snood,* has romantic associations for me. We are clearly in a realm of subjective reaction, where one student can set up a morpheme meaning "unpleasant," another can set up two, one meaning "unpleasant," and the other "pleasant." Neither analysis can be either denied or verified. Such cutting, extreme as it is, is still a fair example of the arbitrariness and confusion which result from abandoning a formally based procedure. It is interesting also that formal procedures would make such cuts seem unlikely. In no one of the whole list of words is /sn–/ set off from what follows by /+/—suggestive, though not conclusive, evidence that /sn–/ is not a morpheme.

A less important result of nonjunctural cutting can be described in terms of the resultant attitude for the analyst. If he assumes that boundaries are to be identified on syntactic and semantic grounds, then /+/ is an entity whose appearance is controlled by the occurrence of the otherwise defined boundaries. Under these circumstances, /+/ is an irregular phoneme which appears and disappears in a meaningless fashion—one colleague has referred to /+/ as "floating juncture" and has proposed (with hesitation, it is true) that no entity which thus "floats" should be set up as a phoneme. If we proceed in the other direction, assuming that /+/ signals a boundary which would otherwise be unrecognizable, the occurrence of /+/ becomes understandable.

The alternatives here presented have been carefully weighed, and as a result a hypothesis has been adopted. It is adopted with full knowledge that it is controversial, but also in the belief that the consequences of rejecting it would be more serious than those of adopting it. As with any hypothesis, it must be tested by its results in further investigation, and in this instance, the test is essentially all the material which follows this chapter. It is believed that the hypothesis is valid for English, and for some other languages, though not necessarily all. The hypothesis is that the occurrence of any juncture always marks the boundary of an entity larger than a phoneme.

The entity thus bounded may be word, phrase, or sentence, but must always be at least a morph.

Two concluding statements can be made about cutting based on junctures. The first is that morph boundaries certainly occur where there is no /+/ to mark them. An example is *dogs* {dɔhg–z}. That is, the correlation between /+/ and morph boundary works in one direction only; the absence of /+/ does not establish the absence of a boundary. The second statement is that the entities which emerge after cutting in accord with junctures are morphs only. They cannot be classified into allomorphs and morphemes until they have been further studied, primarily for their distributional characteristics. For the reasons indicated in these two statements, the cuts indicated by junctures are a first step only, and require a second step in which careful distributional study and further cuts are both made.

3. Segmental morphemes — second cuts and classification

Let us suppose that we have identified a morph, {yes}, which occurs between silence and a terminal juncture in a sentence like "Yes, Mr. Jones." We now find another sentence such as "Yesterday we went to the movies." This sentence begins with a phonemic sequence, /yes/, which is identical with the sequence we have already set up as a morph in the first sentence. It is possible that it may be a second instance of the same morph, here occurring with no /+/ after it, or it may be an unrelated phonemic sequence. Admittedly, the easiest procedure is to dismiss the question with the statement that the two sequences mean different things and so cannot be instances of the same morpheme. Probably most analysis is considerably influenced by meaning, and the use of meaning can be defended as a short cut. But, as in phonemic analysis, it is a dangerous short cut. Therefore, even if an analyst has used meaning as an initial guide, he should back up his decisions by distributional statements. Meaning should be no more than a hint of what to look for, never a primary criterion of classification.

We can now label our two instances of phonemic sequences—one of which we know to be a morph—as /yes/1 and /yes/2 and use them as illustrations of the procedure of comparison. Both sequences, as the two sentences show, can be preceded by silence. But with following environments, the situation is different. We have seen that /yes/1 is followed by a terminal, /yes/2 is not. Further, /yes/1 can be followed by other segmental material, since "Yes I will, Mr. Jones" is a normal utterance. We cannot place new segmental material after /yes/2. Such a sentence as "*Yes-* I will, *terday* we went to the movies" is unnatural.

In this kind of testing, we are operating much as an anthropologist

operates with an unknown language, which he tests by means of the responses of a native informant. Having been given an utterance, the anthropologist proceeds to vary it systematically, to find out how many of the
variations make possible utterances. The artificially varied *"Yes- I will,
terday we went to the movies" is a typical example of the sort of experiment
which would be tried with an informant. The informant could be relied
on to state that the sentence is impossible. The procedure outlined is far
preferable to that of asking the informant—in this case oneself, as a native
speaker of English—whether the two sequences mean the same thing. The
method of variation to test for the possible has the advantage of minimizing
the reliance on meaning.

Further test sentences for /yes/2 tell us still more about its distribution.
We can vary the construction *yesterday* by giving a form *yesteryear*, either
one of which could occur in a sentence—"Where are the snows of yester-?"
Further, *year* in my idiolect can be established as a morph in this situation,
since the phonemic sequence can be /yéstər + yìr/ when pronounced as
an utterance set off by terminals. Thus, we have presumptive evidence
that {yestər} is a morph, evidence borne out by the fact that we cannot
split *yesterday* so as to place *-terday* after silence or a terminal. We proceed
to examine as fully as we are able and find no instances of other constructions which conflict with the view that {yestər} is a constant sequence,
in other words a morph. Our original question is now fully answered. As
we knew at the beginning, /yes/1 is a morph, {yes}. The second sequence
is not an instance of this morph, and not even a morph at all; it is merely
a part of the morph {yestər}. We can restate these results in the form of a
principle of classification. Identical sequences must be assigned to different
morphemes when it is shown that their environments are different.

We are not at the end of our difficulties. We have found a morph,
{yestər}, which occurs with the following morphs *day* and *year*. The two
are identical sequences, and we may therefore label them arbitrarily {yestər}1
and {yestər}2. We could now say that {yestər}1 occurs only with following
day, and {yestər}2 only with following *year*. The situation has something
of the paradoxical, but such an argument is possible and would have the
result of assigning these two instances of identical sequences to different
morphemes. Once again the short cut is to say that the two sequences
mean the same thing and so must be instances of the same morpheme.
There is a possibility, however, of making a different kind of statement,
and if the reader agrees that premature reliance on meaning is to be avoided,
the necessarily cumbersome, though more rigorous, statement is worth
making.

The two constructions *yesterday* and *yesteryear* have distributional
similarity in that in almost any sentence where one occurs the other can be

substituted without producing an unsatisfactory sentence. The two environments in which the sequence {yestər} occurs are *day* and *year*, which we have already identified as morphs. We can then say further that {yestər}1 and {yestər}2 occur in environments where the immediately following morphs are different, but that the constructions resulting are distributionally similar. We can express this in analogical form: {yestər}1 is to *day* as {yestər}2 is to *year*. Whenever it is possible to make such an analogical statement, identical sequences are occurring with differing immediate environments but in constructions which occur in the same larger environments. When two or more instances of identical sequences occur in this way, they will be said to have structurally similar larger environments and to be instances of the same morpheme.

If, however, we are dealing with differing sequences of phonemes instead of identical sequences, the distributional criterion is applied differently. If we compare the two utterances "Yes, Mr. Jones" and "No, Mr. Jones," we know that {yes} and {now} are morphs, since they are occurring between silence and a terminal. The environments for the two morphs are identical, and, to use terminology now familiar, the morphs are in contrastive distribution. The two morphs are then members of different morphemes.

Yet, with differing sequences, distributional similarities have also to be taken into account, just as with identical sequences. We can set up a series of utterances:

> *I saw a dog.*
> *I saw two dogs.*
> *I saw a cat.*
> *I saw two cats.*
> *I saw a horse.*
> *I saw two horses.*

There is no difficulty in picking out three morphs, examples of differing morphemes, since all occur after $/+/$ and before a terminal in the environment "I saw a ——." The three differing morphemes are {dɔhg}, {kæt}, and {hɔhrs}. Further, these morphemes recur in the environment "I saw two ——," where each is followed by a differing phoneme or sequence. We can use our already established morphemes to give us further cuts; they are {dɔhg–z}, {kæt–s}, and {hɔhrs–iz}. We have, then, established a new series of morphs, all three of which are phonemically different. The problem now is that of deciding whether these morphs do or do not belong to the same morpheme. The three constructions containing these differing morphs all occur in the same environment, as we have just seen; the constructions, therefore, have distributional similarity. We can form our analogical statement: as {z} is to {dɔhg}, so {s} is to {kæt}, and so {iz} is to {hɔhrs}. The three morphs are then in complementary distribution and are members of the same morpheme.

It so happens that this set of forms, introduced as an example of classification of differing morphs, also illustrates something else. The series shows second cuts based on junctural cuts, but at one remove. That is, morphs established on formal grounds, as were *dog*, *cat*, and *horse*, can be used as the basis of second-step cuts when they recur with additional segmental material, even though that additional material is not set off by /+/. This statement is a first principle of second-step cutting.

The method of classification of the morphs thus isolated from the series of sentences quoted can also be formulated as a principle which constitutes a definition of complementary distribution of morphs. When morphs, whether differing or identical, are found in an immediate environment which contains representatives of different morphemes, the distribution of the morphs in question is complementary if the constructions, consisting of the morphs in question and the different morphemes in their immediate environment, have distributional similarity.

We have given a first principle of second-step cutting, to the effect that formally established morphs could be used as a basis for second-step cuts when the formally established morphs recur. This principle can be slightly expanded, so as to establish a basis for a large number of other cuts. A morph may be established formally in one sentence by being set off by /+/. It may recur in another sentence without being thus set off, even though it is in the same immediate environment. The cut can then be made on the basis of the previously observed form with /+/. In my idiolect this sort of variation often takes place in constructions which have primary stress followed by tertiary stress, with or without an intervening weak. An example is *table top*. Phonemically this is probably most often /téybil + tàp/, a form which satisfactorily establishes the morph {tap}. A not uncommon variant is /téybiltàp/, without /+/. A cut before {tap} is justified in the second pronunciation since the form with /+/ has already been observed. All such examples of variation consisting of forms with and without /+/ will be spoken of as instances of loss of juncture. The statement that /téybiltàp/ has lost a /+/ is, however, only a convenient way of describing the situation. I do not have figures of frequency or knowledge of history sufficient to prove that there was a normal and pre-existent form with /+/, which later disappeared. As with other descriptive statements, a statement that /+/ has been lost is not to be understood as indicating historic fact.

Morphs which are somewhere established by being set off by junctures can be used to justify cuts in other constructions where the morph reappears, so long as there is a distributional parallel between the construction in which the morph was first established and those in which the morph reappears. An illustration can be drawn from a proper name like *Tomkins*. In my speech this is often /tám + kìnz/, establishing a morph {kinz}. Since there is a close distributional parallel between *Tomkins* and other names, like *Watkins, Atkins, Hopkins,* I am justified in cutting these into morphs, even though they may not all have a /+/. An illustration drawn from the normal vocabulary, and so less special than proper names, can be found in *warmth*. In my speech this form is often /warm + θ/, establishing the last phoneme as a morph. The first morph is one which often occurs without the following {θ}, and it is one which is then describable as an adjective, whereas we describe the construction with {θ} as a noun. A parallel construction is the form *coolth*—often described as a nonce form, though certainly a commonly recurrent one. In this form there is no /+/ in my speech, but the construction contains an underlying sequence, {kuwl}, easily establishable as an independent morph and an adjective. The total construction is also a noun, so that there is distributional parallel between *warmth* and *coolth*, shown both in the distribution of the constructions and in the parts of which each is made up. *Coolth* then contains the morphs {kuwl} and {θ}, and the cut is justified. Suppose, however, that the form under examination had been *path* rather than *coolth*. There is a general similarity in distribution between *warmth* and *path*, but not a close one. Both are nouns, but only *path* takes a plural and only *path* occurs with any frequency after an indefinite article. Further, if we attempt a cut in *path*, we get the sequence /pæ–/, which does not occur as an independent morph. There is thus no parallel between the construction *warmth* and *path*, and no cut is justified in the second form.

We have been working with two criteria in arriving at the second-step cuts we have described above. No form should be cut unless one or another of its suspected morphs is somewhere established by a juncture. Further, no form should be cut unless structural and distributional parallelism exists between the form under examination and some other form already cut on formal grounds. Both criteria are necessary, and it will be instructive to give an example of cutting which is wasteful because it disregards one of them. This example of cutting is presented, however, with the warning that it is to be rejected, and is therefore not to be confused with cutting which is justified. There is a pair of English forms which have a close distributional parallel, *stalactite* and *stalagmite*. If we deliberately disregard junctural divisions we could record the two as containing the following sequences of segmental phonemes: /stælæktayt/, /stælægmayt/. We could then go further, cutting out a hypothetical morph, *{stalæ}, to which we might assign the meaning "water borne deposit," and a second hypothetical morph, *{ayt}, to which we might assign the meaning "mineral substance."

We have now two residues, /–kt–/ and /–gm–/, which we would also have to describe as hypothetical morphs, with the meanings "down" and "up," respectively.

The analysis is deliberately chosen as an example of the grotesque. These cuts can, of course, be objected to on the grounds that they are wasteful, since they produce two unique morphs, and a third morph which is found only in this pair. It is indeed a general principle of second-step cutting that it should be done with a minimum rather than a maximum of resultant unique morphs. Yet there is an even more important reason why this particular analysis should be rejected. It deliberately disregards the juncture pattern, and so produces a series of cuts with no phonological basis. In my speech both forms have a /+/: /stæláek + tàyt/ and /stæláeg + màyt/. The morph structure is therefore very different from that which was set up on the basis of parallelism alone. An example of cutting erroneous because it disregards the second criterion, structural parallelism, has already been shown by the discussion of *path*.

It will probably be helpful if at this point we give an example of justified cutting, which makes proper use of the phonological basis and of structural parallelism, and also chooses between possible alternatives with proper regard to economy. Suppose we have the sentence:

She is very boisterous.

We can easily isolate the last word as a form set off by junctures: {boystrǝs}. As the transcription just given shows, however, there may be no juncture to use as a guide in further cutting. We have, then, several choices, for all of which some phonological basis can be found. We could find in this form a repetition of the established morph {boy} with a following *{strǝs}. We might find here a unique morph, {boystr–}, and following {ǝs}, and we might even find {boy} with a following unique *{str} and {ǝs}. The closest structural parallels for *boisterous* are the series *monstrous, lustrous, wondrous,* and *thundrous*, all of which contain a series of morphs for which phonological justification is readily available, *monster, luster, wonder, thunder*. In combination these are regularly modified by loss of /ǝ/ before /r/. All then give phonological justification for setting up a following morph {ǝs} which occurs throughout the series. We can use the parallel to establish the fact that *boisterous* also contains {ǝs} rather than *{strǝs}, checking by *lustrous* and *monstrous*, the only other forms which give even a possibility of *{strǝs}. A cut such as to give *{strǝs} would result in setting up two unique morphs for which there is no phonological basis, namely *lus–* and *mon–*. The cut is therefore unjustified. The same reasoning applies to a cut setting up a separate *{str}. Our conclusion must be that *boisterous* does not contain {boy}, but only {boystr–}, and the number of unique morphs is reduced to this one form.

Throughout this discussion we have also been making use of a criterion of classification and cutting which has not been explicitly mentioned, for the reason that it cannot be properly applied until other criteria which take precedence over it have been fully exploited. This criterion is phonemic similarity. If we are analyzing a form like *dogs*, it is true that we can find phonological basis for the form *dog*, but we can find no phonological basis for such a form in the construction *dogs*, which never occurs (in my idiolect at least) with /+/ before the final consonant. In short, the final step was the assumption that *dogs* contains the morph {dɔhg} because it is phonemically identical with instances of {dɔhg} which are elsewhere established phonologically.

In classification of morphs, phonemic similarity must also be used. Suppose that on phonological and structural grounds we have split *health* into the morphs {hel} and {θ}. There is no morphologically independent morpheme identical with {hel} to which this morph can be assigned. There are, however, two forms which are similar, namely, *whole* {howl} and *hale* {heyl}. Each would be structurally satisfactory, and {hel} might be an allomorph of either. Yet {hel} shares one more phoneme with {heyl} than it does with {howl}, and for that reason should be assigned to {heyl}.

The fact that phonemic similarity is a criterion of classification outranked by others results in the fact that morphs which have no similarity, and so share no phoneme in common, can be assigned to the same morpheme. When this happens the two or more allomorphs so assigned are said to be in suppletive relation. A clear example of suppletive allomorphs is to be found in the forms of the verb *to be*. The two forms *am* and *is* are both to be analyzed into base and suffix, giving an allomorph {æ} for the base in the first form and {i} in the second. The structural and paradigmatic parallels justify classing these two forms together, in spite of their lack of any phonemic similarity. It should be said, however, that rigorous analysis should strive to keep suppletive allomorphs at a minimum, just as rigorous phonemic analysis strives to keep overlapping allophones at a minimum.

Phonemic similarity is a necessary criterion; meaning is not. This statement disposes of classification difficulties in some instances where there is identity of phonemes but semantic divergence. In a form like *foxglove* there are two morphs, and these are identical with morphs which occur elsewhere, independent of each other. In *foxglove* neither morph can be shown to have an environment which differentiates it from the independent forms *fox* and *glove*. The two forms must then be assigned the status of allomorphs of the identical and independent morphemes, in spite of the fact that the flower has nothing to do with foxes or gloves. The semantic peculiarities are a property of the construction as a whole and do not affect our identification of the component allomorphs.

4. Segmental morphemes — nonsequential occurrence

The segmental morphs we have so far been describing all occur in simple sequential order, with consequently clear boundaries marking the point at which one leaves off and the next begins. Sequential order is a necessary characteristic of morphs whose boundaries are marked by $/+/$, but on occasion morphs established by second-step cutting occur in such a fashion that border lines are less sharp. A relatively simple example is to be found in a form like *division*. No plus occurs, so that cutting must be done on other grounds. We can find in the form a contained construction, *divide*, in which the last phoneme is $/d/$. If we go on to constructions like *commune* : *communion*, we can discover a following morph, {yən}, of which the form in *division* is an allomorph. When the {yən} is added to a preceding morph ending in $/d/$, without a following $/+/$, the expected sequence $/-dy-/$ is replaced by $/-\check{z}-/$. The problem then is to find the boundary between morphs. A cut before or after the $/-\check{z}-/$ would require a statement for the allomorphic development of both morphemes and would be equally arbitrary made in either position. A more economical statement is to say that when $/d/$ is thus followed by $/y/$ over a morphemic boundary not marked by $/+/$, the result is $/-\check{z}-/$, which then belongs to both morphemes, giving a cut which can be represented thus:

$$/divi\check{z}ən/$$

In more extreme overlapping, a morph can occur completely within the boundaries of another morpheme, with replacement of some of the material of the enclosing form. There is reason, as we shall see in Section 3, Chapter 9, for analyzing *took* as containing a morph consisting of {-u-}, which occurs in nonsequential order with {teyk}, replacing its vowel nucleus. In other languages such nonsequential morphemes often occur without replacement of any of the material of the morpheme to which they are added, and they are then called infixes. An example is from Chamorro, where the borrowed Spanish word *planta* is used to mean "plant; shrub." With infixed {um}, $/plumanta/$, it means "collection of plants; plantation."

Still another class of nonsequential morphemes are the dovetailed, discontinuous morphemes characteristic of Semitic languages. The lexical morphemes in Semitic tongues are often an unpronounceable abstraction consisting of three consonants, which are always united with vocalic morphemes, grammatical in character and occurring between the consonants. An example can be drawn from Arabic. A typical lexical morpheme is {k t b}, which can be represented as {C_1 C_2 C_3}. This then occurs with vocalic morphemes, which can be generalized as {V}. It will be noted also that, in the list of examples, there are more normally sequential morphemes which occur as well:

/katab/ {$C_1VC_2VC_3$} (he wrote)
/ktaab/ {$C_1C_2VVC_3$} (book)
/kutub/ {$C_1VC_2VC_3$} (books)
/maktab/ {$maC_1C_2VC_3$} (office)
/maktabe/ {$maC_1C_2VC_3V$} (library)
/maktuub/ {$maC_1C_2VVC_3$} (letter)
/kaatib/ {$C_1VVC_2VC_3$} (clerk)
/kattab/ {$C_1VC_2C_2VC_3$} (he dictated)

A final type of nonsequential occurrence is that in which two morphs, whose existence can be postulated on structural grounds, are replaced by an unanalyzable whole. The classic example is the French *à le*, which is replaced by the unanalyzable *au*. Charles F. Hockett, who first called attention to this type of form, coined for them the name "portmanteau morphs."[3] The name might well be extended to all forms in which there is blurring of sequential boundaries, with consequent difficulty of analysis. A form like *took* is then a portmanteau, though its components can eventually be analyzed.

5. Stress morphemes

It is usual to say that English segmental morphemes do not have stress as an integral part of their structure. The statement can be agreed to, since it is easy to find given segmental morphemes occurring now under one stress phoneme, now under another. However, the statement is often followed by another: that English words have stress patterns which are an integral part of their structure. If stress phonemes and patterns are denied to morphemes, they should also be denied to words. For instance, a word such as *house* also has no inherent stress phoneme which must always accompany it. Under variant conditions *house* can appear under /´/, *the hóuse;* under /ˆ/, *the White hôuse;* or under /`/, *the White Hòuse.* The construction

---

[3] "Problems of Morphemic Analysis," *Language*, XXIII, 1947, p. 333.

where stress patterns unmistakably appear is the phrase, which can be defined as a morpheme or sequence of morphemes bounded by a terminal juncture. Thus, when it is said that an English word such as *twenty* has the stress pattern /′ ˇ/, what is meant is that it has this stress pattern when it is treated as a phrase. If it is merely a part of a phrase, it may have instead a pattern of /ˆ ˇ/. It should be remembered that no English word can be pronounced except as either a phrase or a part of a phrase.

Let us begin with a construction such as *the White House*, treated as a minimal utterance consisting of one terminal-juncture group or phrase. Phonemically it will be:

$$\overset{2}{/ðə} + \overset{3}{hwáyt} + \overset{1}{hàws} \#/$$

It has a pitch and terminal pattern /2 3 1 #/ which we can at the minute disregard, since this pattern is a property of the sentence. What remains is a pattern /ˇ + ′ + `/. Such a sequence is called a phrase superfix and is made up of phonemes of stress together with pluses. We should expect such a superfix pattern to show combinations of phonemes into units analogous to segmental morphemes, which are then the components of the larger construction, the superfix.

A first statement concerns the fact that we have assigned /+/ to superfixes consisting otherwise of stress phonemes. A principal reason is that /+/, which occurs between segmental phonemes, can scarcely be a component of segmental morphs and morphemes. In a form like *White House* it would be awkward indeed to assign the boundary-marking /+/ to either the preceding or the following morph. Yet /+/ is a phoneme, and if it is like other phonemes, it must be a component of morphemes. We have already assigned stress sequences to phrases, and /+/ is the only juncture which can occur within a phrase. The conclusion is clear that /+/ is a component of phrase morphemes whose other type of component is stress phonemes. The phrase pattern we isolated was /ˇ + ′ + `/. If this is to be split into morphs, does /+/ go with what precedes or what follows? In our system of symbolization it must go with what follows, since /+/ cannot appear at the end of such a sequence, a position which is necessarily occupied by a terminal. In our superfix, however, there is no /+/ before the initial /ˇ/. A phrase must begin either after silence or after a terminal juncture—it never begins after /+/. Thus, we can say that in initial position in the phrase, /+/ is replaced by the initial onset after silence or by a terminal.

Thus, if we take a phrase such as *a house*, the superfix is /ˇ + ′/, and we have seen that /+/ goes with what follows, while what precedes is an initial allomorph. In other words, a stress morpheme can be defined as a combination of /+/ with one or more following stress phonemes. Disregarding for the minute the possibility of morphemes containing more than one stress phoneme, we have stress morphemes of the following types:

$\{+\ '\}$ a *house*
$\{+\ ^\}$ a *green* house
$\{+\ `\}$ a green*house*
$\{+\ ˇ\}$ stop '*er* (contrasts juncturally with *stopper*)

Each of these morphemes has a phrase-initial allomorph which differs by absence of $/+/$.

Stress phonemes can be located, in that they always (in our system of analysis) fall on the vowels. The element in these morphemes whose location is unpredictable is $/+/$. It follows therefore that if the location of $/+/$ is indicated, the location of the morpheme as a whole is then fully predictable. This fact enables us to write a phrase in morphemic notation in which the morphemes are linearly written, though the phonemes are not in sequential order. The system of writing has many advantages for morphemic analysis, and phrases written in this way would look like the following:

a house /ə + háws/ $\{ˇ\}$ {ə} $\{+\ '\}$ {haws}
greenhouse /gríyn + hàws/ $\{'\}$ {griyn} $\{+\ `\}$ {haws}

The morpheme $\{+\ ˇ\}$ has an allomorph with zero stress. It is to be found in forms like warmth /wɔrm + θ/, where the juncture falls before a consonant so that there is no vowel on which stress can fall. The allomorph is predictable, therefore, in terms of surrounding significant elements. It is assigned to $\{+\ ˇ\}$ for the obvious reason that zero stress is more like weak stress than any other. There is the rarer allomorph of $\{+\ ˇ\}$, which consists of zero stress and zero juncture, that is to say, a zero allomorph. It can be found in such a form as:

(It')s cool /s + kúwl/ {ø} {s} $\{+\ '\}$ {kuwl}

In some idiolects, indeed, a further form might be:

(It')s cooled. /s + kúwl + d/ {ø} {s} $\{+\ '\}$ {kuwl} $\{+\}$ {d}

This latter form is one of the reasons for a decision which has been implied in the previous statements. No stress morpheme contains more than one $/+/$. If a morpheme is to be written thus linearly, it must contain only one element the location of which is unpredictable. To set up a morpheme with two occurrences of $/+/$ would be to give two unpredictable elements.

It remains only to examine those morphemes which contain more than one stress phoneme. In my idiolect any combination of /´/ with /ˆ/ has an intervening /+/ and is therefore a combination of two morphemes. Combinations of /´/ and /`/ may or may not have an intervening /+/, but a construction like /kán + tènt/ is spoken of as having lost juncture when it appears without /+/. A pronunciation such as /kántènt/ can therefore be analyzed as {´} {kan} {`} {tent}, where {`} is assigned the status of allomorph of {+ `}—an allomorph believed to be the product of rapid speech. The same conditions apply to combinations of /ˆ/ and /`/—they are more usual with intervening /+/ than without.

In short, it turns out to be only /˘/ which combines with other stress phonemes into a single morpheme. A weak stress can combine with any preceding stronger stress, giving three more stress morphemes:

$$\{+ ´ ˘\} \quad \text{about } \textit{twenty} \quad \{+ ´ ˘\} \text{ \{twentiy\}}$$
$$\{+ ˆ ˘\} \quad \textit{twenty} \text{ men} \quad \{ˆ ˘\} \text{ \{twentiy\}}$$
$$\{+ ` ˘\} \quad \textit{very} \text{ new house} \quad \{+ `˘\} \text{ \{veriy\}}$$

Similarly, a weak stress can combine with a following stress, so that there are morphemes like {+ ˘ ´}, as in "What's all this *about?*" It is not necessary to list and exemplify these morphemes, since they can be readily constructed by the reader. An example of {+ ˘ ´ ˘} can be found in *eleven*, for instance. Furthermore, it seems likely that the limit on numbers of weak stress phonemes in a single morpheme is two, so that {+ ´ ˘ ˘} *twentieth* is a normal but extreme example.

6. Pitch morphemes and superfixes

The analysis and description of pitch morphemes present problems more complex than those of stress morphemes, but a number of preliminary statements can be made about them with little likelihood of serious disagreement. In the previous section, analysis led to the conclusion that stress morphemes contain a /+/ in combination with one or more following stress phonemes. Several stress morphemes combine into a larger construction, the stress superfix, characteristic of the phonological phrase. The unifying characteristic of the stress superfix is its possession of a single primary stress.

Building on these conclusions, we can define a pitch morpheme as a construction containing a terminal juncture and several pitch phonemes. As with stress morphemes, it is advisable to assign no more than one juncture to a morpheme. Just as we have bounded the stress morphemes by an initial /+/, we will bound the pitch morphemes by a final terminal.

A phonological phrase therefore has the following characteristics: It has a morpheme or morphemes usually consisting of /+/ followed by one or more stress phonemes, and these make up a stress (or phrase) superfix. It also has a single pitch morpheme. Pitch morphemes combine into larger constructions, pitch superfixes. Since each phrase has a single pitch morpheme, pitch superfixes necessarily characterize constructions consisting of more than one phrase. It is because pitch morphemes thus combine into superfixes in constructions larger than phrases that pitch constructions can be said to belong to the sentence. Similarly, it is because stress morphemes combine into stress superfixes within the phrase that stress can be said to belong to the phrase.

Pitch morphemes belong to a level higher in the language hierarchy in quite a different sense as well. As we have seen, the stress morpheme is located when the /+/, its one unpredictable element, is placed. The position of the pitch morpheme is—or ought to be if the analysis is consistent and successful—located when its terminal juncture is placed. When stress morphemes have been placed in terms of the position of /+/, the stress phoneme or phonemes are then automatically correlated with the underlying material, the consonant, vowel, and semivowel phonemes. In successful analysis of pitch, a pitch morpheme should contain pitch phonemes predictable in location because correlated similarly with the underlying material. Further, with pitch morphemes, the underlying material should be not the segmental morphs and phonemes but the stress morphs and phonemes. The analysis here presented is an attempt to set up just such a three-layer system: pitch morphemes correlated in position with stress morphemes, stress morphemes correlated with segmental morphemes. The junctures of the two top layers are the unpredictable elements in each.

Before we go on to develop the analysis of pitch morphemes in detail, we can make a preliminary demonstration of the fact that the position of junctures is unpredictable and that, when these are placed, there is correlation of pitch with stress, and stress with segmental material. We shall use an utterance which contains no difficulties of analysis. The utterance is "He got 'em." If this utterance is part of a larger sequence, the terminal which concludes it must first be placed. The segmental material of "He got 'em" is identical with the segmental material of the larger utterance "He got a mighty fine wife." That is to say, /#/ might or might not fall after the /m/ of "He got 'em."

Having placed the /#/ and stated further that this is the only terminal in the utterance, we know that we are dealing with a minimal sentence consisting of a single phonological phrase with only one pitch morpheme. Let us state that the pitch morpheme contains the pitch sequence /2 3 1/ and that the stress sequence is /ˋ ́ ˘/. It is agreed by all analysts that under these circumstances the initial pitch /2/ must coincide with /ˋ/, /3/ with /ˊ/, and /1/ with /ˇ/. The pitches in this sentence correlate neatly with the stresses.

We have stated the stress sequence as /ˋ ˊ ˇ/. This is not a statement of stress morphemes, since we as yet know only the stress phonemes and do not know the number and position of the plus junctures. In the utterance we started with, there is a /+/ after *he* and another after *got*. The position of these is likewise unpredictable; the first one might be before or after /g/, the second one before or after /t/.

We can now write a complete transcription of the superfix structure of our utterance, independently of the segmental material underlying it. Such a transcription is:

$$\{ˋ\} \{+ ˊ\} \{+ ˇ\} \{2\ 3\ 1\ \#\}$$

In turn, we can also write a partial phonemic transcription including only the segmental material and the junctures:

$$/hiy + gat + \ni m \#/$$

From this partial phonemic analysis, the rest follows: knowing the stress sequence and the pitch sequence, we can then fit the three layers together with perfect confidence.

With this sentence, then, a transcription which gives all the phonologically bounded morphs is as follows:

$$\{ˋ\} \{hiy\} \{+ ˊ\} \{gat\} \{+ ˇ\} \{\ni m\} \{2\ 3\ 1\ \#\}$$

The notation we have just given is, strictly speaking, morphic rather than fully morphemic. The segmental material it contains is analyzed only into those morphs which contain prima-facie evidence of their boundaries —in actual fact, all three of the words the sentence contains can be broken down further into smaller morphs by paradigmatic analysis. The suprasegmental material, however, is fully morphemic in the form here given. The ultimate segmental morphemes do not here concern us; what is of interest is that the transcription just given has been shown to be exactly equivalent to phonemic notation and can readily be reconverted into it without uncertainty at any point:

$$\overset{2}{}\ \ \overset{3}{}\ \ \overset{1}{}$$
$$/hìy + gát + \ni m \#/$$

The sentence we have been analyzing represents one in which there are correlations between pitch and stress accepted by all analysts. Before correlation of the same degree of neatness can be established for all phrases and sentences, a number of decisions have to be made about the nature of pitch morphemes. The first of these decisions concerns the number of pitch phonemes in a pitch morpheme. For this decision we can turn to monosyllabic utterances. If we use such a form as *sure*, one of the ways in which it can be pronounced is with three differing pitches, as follows:

$$\begin{array}{c} 2\ 3\ 1 \\ /\text{šúhr } \#/ \end{array}$$

There are other pronunciations, such as the following with two pitches:

$$\begin{array}{c} 3\ 1 \\ /\text{šúhr } \#/ \end{array}$$

And there are also pronunciations with only one pitch:

$$\begin{array}{c} 2 \\ /\text{šúhr } |||/ \end{array}$$

It is clear, therefore, that the maximum number of differing pitches is three.

Considered purely phonemically, these three utterances can be described as containing patterns of one, two, and three phonemes. Yet pitches can be described differently from the morphophonemic point of view. Monosyllabic utterances can be said to have three pitch points at which contrasts are possible, so that a fully morphemic notation would indicate the pitches which fall at each one of these points, whether that particular pitch happened to contrast with the others or not. Thus, recording the initial, middle, and final pitches, we find that our three utterances of *sure* contain the morphemes {2 3 1 #}, {3 3 1 #}, and {2 2 2 ||}. That is, in the second, the initial and middle pitches are the same, and in the third, all three are alike. Similarly if *sure* is pronounced as a question, it becomes:

$$\begin{array}{c} 2\ 3 \\ /\text{šúhr } |||/ \end{array}$$

And again two of the pitches are identical. The form introduces a minor problem, since such a rise might be recorded as either {2 2 3 ||} or {2 3 3 ||}; either writing would indicate a rising pattern. Phonetically {2 2 3 ||} is the preferable writing, however, since the rise in pitch on such an utterance is observably nearer the end than the middle of the syllable.

If we adopt the conclusion that the number of pitch phonemes morphemically considered is three in monosyllables, it follows that this number is also the minimum in polysyllabic utterances. In polysyllabic utterances the initial pitch becomes that of the first vowel, the middle pitch that of the syllable with primary stress, and the final pitch that of the last vowel. If, however, the utterance contains only two syllables, two of these pitch points coincide, falling on the syllable with primary stress. Thus we have the following two instances of {2 3 1 #}:

$$\begin{array}{ccc} 2 \ 3 \ 1 & & 2 \quad 3 \ 1 \end{array}$$
/šúhrliy #/ and /əv + kóhrs #/

In the first, the initial and middle pitch points occur on the first syllable, and in the second, the middle and final pitch points occur on the last syllable. The placement is fully automatic, and once the rule is given, the morphemes are unambiguous as to where the pitches fall.

In all three-phoneme pitch patterns, the middle pitch is always the syllable with primary stress. Furthermore, two pitch points always coincide on the syllable with primary stress whenever this syllable is either initial or final. Thus, there are two pitches on each of the primarily stressed syllables in the following utterances, though each has more than two syllables:

$$\begin{array}{ccc} 23 \quad 1 & \quad 2 & \quad 3 \ 1 \end{array}$$
/sɔ́rtinliy #/   /ðə + nûw + bîl + pǽst #/

Both of these utterances then also contain {2 3 1 #} with all pitches automatically placed. It should not be thought, however, that {2 3 1 #} is the only morpheme which can fall on an utterance like *certainly;* somewhat more characteristic of my idiolect is {3 3 1 #} with initial and middle pitches alike. The same remark applies also to monosyllables like *sure.* Some analysts have said that {2 3 1 #} has an allomorph consisting of {3 1 #} when the morpheme falls on a monosyllable. The statement can hardly be true, since {2 3 1 #} and a phonetic /3 1 #/ contrast on monosyllables. The phonetic /3 1 #/, as we have said, is an instance of the morpheme {3 3 1 #} and is very common on monosyllables, whereas {2 3 1 #} is much rarer.

While the middle pitch of a three-phoneme pattern necessarily falls on the syllable with primary stress, it should not be thought that the middle pitch is necessarily the highest pitch. It is the highest pitch only if the contour is rising-falling. If the pattern is falling, the highest pitch is initial. If the pattern is rising, the highest pitch is the final pitch. Two three-phoneme patterns which illustrate these patterns are:

$$\begin{array}{cc} 3 \quad\quad 2 \ 2 & \quad 2 \ 3 \end{array}$$
/àym + kɔ́miŋ |||/   and   /ríhliy ||/

The first of these has the morpheme {3 2 2 ‖} and the second {2 2 3 |}. In the second utterance, initial and middle pitch fall on the first syllable since it has primary stress.

So far as we have gone, we have spoken only of morphemes which have three pitch points. There are, however, more than three pitch points in some utterances. There are in all a total of five, since some utterances have a pre-middle pitch distinct from initial pitch, and others have a post-middle pitch distinct from final pitch. No single utterance has contrasting pitches at both the pre-middle and the post-middle, however. Further, the nature and arrangement of contrasts are such as to make it possible to analyze all pitch morphemes as having no more than four phonemes.

A fairly well known variety of pitch pattern is the following, commoner in British than American English:

$$2 \qquad 3 \qquad\qquad 3 \quad 1$$
/hìyz + gôwiŋ + təðə + múwviyz #/

Here the highest pitch is not a peak but, so to speak, a plateau which begins on a syllable with secondary stress which occurs before the primary, and extends through the primary. Pre-middle pitch, of which this utterance is an example, falls always on a secondary stress which occurs before the primary. In this utterance, the morpheme will be written {2 3 3 1 #} with four phonemes.

A morpheme with pre-middle pitch does not have to have this plateau pattern, however. The pattern can be that of a peak, with the highest point falling on the pre-middle, as in:

$$2 \qquad 3 \qquad 2 \qquad 2$$
/sòw + dôwnt + ráš + mìy ‖/

The morpheme is to be written {2 3 2 2 ‖}, again with four phonemes.

A type of utterance with post-middle pitch is one which has received its widest attention in a paper by James Sledd which he read before the Modern Language Association in 1955 and which remains unpublished at this date. The utterance is:

$$2 \quad\;\; 3\,1$$
/wə́ndərfil #/

The peculiarity in this utterance is that the peak falls not on the syllable with primary stress but on the syllable immediately after it. The post-middle pitch occurs only on the first syllable after primary, and only when there is more than one such syllable. Morphemically, the utterance has four pitch phonemes, to be written {2 2 3 1 #}, and the utterance is therefore one which contains a different morpheme from the pronunciations:

$$
\begin{array}{cccc}
2\,3 & 1 & 3 & 1 \\
/\text{wə́ndərfïl} \#/ & \text{and} & /\text{wə́ndərfïl} \#/
\end{array}
$$

These latter contain, respectively, the morphemes {2 3 1 #} and {3 3 1 #}, both differing from the first pronunciation in that they contain only three phonemes. It should also be said of an utterance like *wonderful* with peak on the second syllable that the morpheme is not affected by the addition of a tertiary or weak syllable, or series of syllables, before the primary. If this is done, as in

$$
\begin{array}{ccc}
2 & 2 & 3\ \ 1 \\
/\text{ìt} + \text{s} + \text{wə́ndərfïl} \#/
\end{array}
$$

the only change is that initial pitch then occurs before the primary syllable.

What happens to an utterance of this type if an initial secondary is added is not fully known. No instances of rise on a pre-middle pitch point with carry-over of the plateau to post-middle have been observed; and instances in which it was thought that there was a pre-middle rise, with fall on the middle and again rise on the post-middle, have so far proved illusory. That is, on closer examination all such contours turned out to be instances of two phrases broken by a /||/. For these reasons it seems a good assumption that pre-middle and post-middle are never of importance in the same utterance.

We have, then, the following types of four-phoneme pattern:

{2 3 3 1 #} *He's going to the movies.*
{2 3 2 2 ||} *So don't rush me.*
{2 2 3 1 #} *Wonderful.*

The problem is whether or not a morpheme having four phonemes can be identified as one having pre-middle or post-middle pitch. The problem is answered by the pattern type. Pre-middle and post-middle pitches are of importance only as locations of the peak pitch or (in the case of pre-middle pitch) the start of a plateau. It therefore follows that if the first two digits in a morpheme of four phonemes contain a rise to the highest pitch, the morpheme is one in which pre-middle pitch is significant, and conversely, if the first two digits do not show this rise, the morpheme is one in which post-middle pitch is significant.[4]

---

[4] Robert P. Stockwell first called my attention to the problems in the number and placement of pitch phonemes morphemically written. We have carried on an extensive discussion and correspondence about the problem; the solutions presented in this chapter are the result of collaboration.

We can, then, summarize by saying that pitch morphemes can be analyzed tentatively into three- and four-phoneme patterns, with the type of pattern relied on to determine which of the five possible pitch points are significant in four-phoneme patterns.[5] So far as is known, two pitch points fall automatically on any initial or final syllable with primary stress, and on such syllables only. The placing of pitch phonemes is therefore believed to be fully automatic, and it is further believed that the framework here presented will be sufficient for taking care of all pitch patterns not yet observed, with only minor modifications.

At the start of this section, it was observed that pitch morphemes make up unified larger constructions with boundaries wider than the single phrase. It should be frankly admitted that we do not as yet have sufficient data to identify and describe such unified larger constructions fully, but we can point to some of them. These unified larger constructions involve the notion of contour. In general a single phrase is a contour, in that it has only one point before which pitch can rise and after which pitch can fall. That is to say, a typical contour is /2 3 1/, where the middle pitch is preceded and followed by lower pitches. In these terms, the initial and final pitches are not capable of giving a contour, since they cannot be both preceded and followed by lower pitches. The statement is of importance, since there are sequences like the following:

3   2 3 1

/ìts + wə́ndərfil #/

That is, there are two high points, but only one contour, since only the post-middle is both preceded and followed by lower pitches. A sequence such as */ 2 3 2 3 2/, however, would be one of two genuine contours, a type which does not occur in English. Except for sentences like that just quoted, most English phrases contain only one high point, not merely only one contour. The high point may be either a peak or a plateau. As has been pointed out, phrases can occur on a monotone, with no peak at all and consequently no contour. Such monotone phrases often occur under conditions in which they

---

[5] The statement that the occurrence of pre-middle and post-middle pitch points can be identified by the contour is, it is now evident, valid only for instances of rise on the pre-middle pitch point. In a paper presented at the Second Texas Conference on Problems of Linguistic Analysis in English, Stockwell was able to introduce examples in which there was a fall on the pre-middle pitch point from a relatively higher initial pitch point. All such sentences would require that all five pitch points be written and would then contain something more than a single contour. It therefore is probable that English pitch patterns will be found to contain three-, four-, and five-digit sequences, or that they will eventually be shown to contain either three or five. Until Stockwell's results are published and evaluated the statement in the text can be allowed to stand.

are no more than continuations of the final pitch phoneme of the preceding phrase. The following is an example of conversation constructed to show several such concluding monotone phrases:

> Hè's gône to Páris {2 4 4 |} sâid Jóhn {4 4 4 ||}
> To Bèrlín {2 3 1 |} Ì replíed {1 1 1 #}
> Yòu súre {2 2 3 |} Jôhn ásked {3 3 3 ||}
> Ì guéss sò {2 3 2 |} Ì hédged {2 2 2 #}

Under these circumstances, each of the concluding phrases of these sentences continues the pattern of the preceding, so that the sentence as a whole is unified by having a single contour. It is not to be thought, however, that the instances of {3 3 3 ||}, {2 2 2 ||}, and so on are mere allomorphs. Monotone morphemes occur independently, and in ways not related to continuation of the preceding. They are therefore independent morphemes, but here occurring in ways which unify the larger construction, the pitch superfix.

The second way in which pitch superfixes show unity is that they sometimes appear in what may be called a complex sentence contour. That is, each phrase is itself a single contour or monotone, and the individual phrases may involve falls from their individual high points. Yet the succession of phrases shows a progression of high points which itself makes up a unified rise and fall. The following is an example:

> 2   2   2   3   2   4   1
> Pôrt ôf Nèw Yórk Aŭthóritў | tícket bòok | sóles òffice #

The construction is here presented as an isolated phrase; it was actually given to informants as the subject of a sentence concluding with "... is a block up the street."[6] What is significant here is that in each of the phrases which make up the construction there is a progression from /2/ to /3/ to /4/, so that the whole makes up a complex contour, broken only by the descent from /3/ to /2/ in the second phrase. Little is known about such complex contours, and a number of questions are in need of solution. For instance, it is not known how many phrases can be thus unified—probably three is close to the maximum, since progression from /2/ to /4/ is as wide a range of phonemic variation as is common, which gives sufficient peaks to accommodate only three phrases. Further, we do not know whether such complex

---

[6] The construction here quoted was originally supplied by Uriel Weinreich, *The Field of Yiddish*, Linguistic Circle of New York, 1954. It is discussed by Stockwell in his review of Weinreich in *Language*, XXXII, 1956, p. 380. Stockwell would now analyze the second and third phrases, here written with only two pitches each, as containing three, {3 3 2 |} and {4 4 1 #} respectively.

contours can occur over the boundaries of phrases marked by other terminals than /||/, though a good guess is that such constructions would be unlikely. Finally, this superfix shows a single dip in the progression of higher to higher pitches. We do not know if superfixes can show more than one dip, though here also a guess is that they do not.

The quoted construction is of further interest in that it occurs not on a sentence but on a sentence element. It might, however, have fallen on a sentence, since the construction would have been essentially the same with an initial "That's . . ." and /#/ after *office*. Our initial statement that pitch superfixes occur on constructions larger than phrases can now be made more precise. Pitch superfixes with unifying characteristics may occur on complete sentences, but may also occur on major elements within the sentence. In any case a pitch superfix always involves more than one phrase, and any sentence of more than one phrase shows a pitch superfix, though such a pitch superfix may not show characteristics of unity that we can as yet point to.

8.... MORPHOTACTICS

1. Morpheme, word, phrase, and sentence

In the previous discussion of segmental morphemes, it was seen that any sequence which can stand under a stress morpheme is one which contains at least one morph, though on further examination it might prove to contain more than one. Thus the occurrence of morphs is something which can in large part be observed and verified in terms of phonemes produced and heard. Beyond the morph and morpheme units, the only larger units which can be observed and verified are phrases and sentences. These can be defined as morphs or sequences of morphs which can stand under a pitch morpheme. It is not, however, possible to tell by observing the pitch morpheme alone whether what is heard is phrase or sentence. The occurrence of a pitch morpheme tells the hearer only that a terminal juncture group is occurring; it does not by any means always tell him whether this terminal juncture group is linked to others, and is therefore a phrase only, or whether it is independent, and is therefore a sentence. Thus, for instance, the pitch morphemes {2 3 2 |} and {2 3 2 ||} are commonly characteristic of phrases only, but may occur as sentence superfixes. Conversely, the morpheme {2 3 1 #} is generally characteristic of sentences, but may occur linked and thus be a phrase superfix.

There is, therefore, a series of entities between the morph, which occurs marked off by /+/, and an entity which must be a sentence because it is preceded and followed by silence. These entities are the various classes of words and phrases. They must be examined in detail, and, if possible, a phonological basis must be laid for definition and distinction, though it is obvious from what has just been said that definition cannot be accomplished by phonological criteria alone.

One entity which can be set up is the phonologically minimal word. Any sequence which has a single stress morpheme and can stand under a pitch morpheme is a phonologically minimal word; it is a morpheme which is phonologically minimal and at the same time a minimal terminal-juncture group. It is possible to narrow this definition even further. The stress morpheme which characterizes a segmental morpheme as one which is a minimal word, phrase, and sentence is {′}, that is, the allomorph of {+ ′}, which stands after silence. Characteristically, though not by any means necessarily, the pitch morpheme under which such a segmental morph occurs is {3 3 1 #}. Stress morphemes which contain lower grades of stress than /′/ do not occur in isolation, and the stress morphemes which contain a combination of /˘/ and /′/ are not the minimal form of the stress morpheme. Furthermore, such nonminimal forms of the stress morpheme always invite the possibility that second-step analysis may show that there are two stress morphemes and therefore two segmental morphemes. We can rephrase our definition of the phonologically minimal word, then, as a sequence of segmental phonemes which can stand under {′} and at the same time under any pitch morpheme possible when there is only one stress phoneme present.

Our task is therefore to enumerate the sequences of segmental phonemes which can appear under these conditions. The smallest such sequence, as we saw in Chapter 6, is one of two phonemes, the first of which is a vowel and the second of which is a consonant or semivowel. The two types can be represented by the following:

$$\overset{4\,4\,1}{Up\,!} \;\; /\acute{\text{э}}\text{p}\,\#/ \quad \{'\} \; \{\text{эp}\} \; \{4\,4\,1\,\#\} \qquad \overset{4\,4\,1}{Ow\,!} \;\; /\acute{\text{a}}\text{w}\,\#/ \quad \{'\} \; \{\text{aw}\} \; \{4\,4\,1\,\#\}$$

Each of these two types can be expanded either before the vowel or finally by the addition of a consonant or consonants, so long as the resultant clusters conform to the structure of clusters as described in Chapter 6. Thus an artificially constructed minimal word which contains as many phonemes as possible is the following nonexistent form:

$$\overset{3\,3\,1}{*/\text{skl\'awrmpst}\,\#/} \quad \{'\} \; \{\text{sklawrmpst}\} \; \{3\,3\,1\,\#\}$$

Such a form reaches the maximum sequence which is pronounceable without breaking English phonotactic sequences and is the maximum which would be possible under the formulas given by Whorf for English monosyllabic words.[1]

There are forms, however, which have all these characteristics except for the fact that there may be a /+/ contained somewhere within the sequence. Indeed, the nonsense word we have just created might well have the variant form */skláwrm + st #/, and an example from the real vocabulary is:

$$\overset{3\,3\,1}{warmth} \;\; /\text{w\'orm} + \theta\,\#/$$

---

[1] *Language, Thought, and Reality. Selected Writings of Benjamin Lee Whorf*, ed. by John B. Carroll, John Wiley, New York, 1956, pp. 222–25. Whorf's paper, "Linguistics as an Exact Science," originally appeared in *Technology Review*, XLIII, 1940.

Such forms are words, but they are no longer phonologically minimal words, in that these forms now contain allomorphs of two stress morphemes, {+ ′} and {+ ˚}. Forms like *warmth*, when occurring under a single pitch morpheme, can be defined as words because, though they contain more than one morph, only one of these morphs corresponds to the structure of a sequence which can stand isolated under a single pitch morpheme. We can add to our definition of word forms, therefore, by describing a phonologically nonminimal word as one containing more than one phonologically established morph only one of which corresponds to the structure of a phonologically minimal word.

This concept can be brought to bear on a problem in which levels of analysis and terminology can often become confused. Suppose we hear an utterance such as:

3 3 1

(It')s cool. /s + kúwl #/   {ø} {s} {+ ′} {kuwl} {3 3 1 #}

By the definition we have just given, this is a phonologically nonminimal word, since the morph {s} is not one which corresponds to anything which can stand under a pitch morpheme. The whole construction, however, is a variant of what is ordinarily written as "It is cool" and is thought of as containing three "words." The construction as a whole is an "allo" variant of a phrase, containing a zero variant of *it* and a variant of *is* which consists of a single phoneme. Variants of words are called allologs, and a variant of a phrase might well be called an allophrase. To recapitulate,

3 3 1
/s + kúwl #/

contains a zero allolog of the minimal word *it*, shown to be present only by the fact that the following form has the phoneme characteristic of the allologs of *is* which appear after morphs ending in voiceless stops. Next comes the allolog of *is* which consists of a single phoneme and so is an allolog incapable of standing isolated, though of course another allolog of this word— the form {iz}—is a minimal word sequence. The final sequential morph is {kuwl}, the sole form in the construction which has the structure of a phonologically minimal word. Morphs such as {s} and the {θ} of *warmth* are then morphs which have a phonemic structure such as to mark them as "bound," or incapable of standing under a pitch morpheme. The morph {θ} has no allomorph which is not thus bound, but the morph {s} is an allolog, which means that it is a variant of a morpheme which on occasion does stand isolated under a pitch morpheme.

Thus, under phonological scrutiny alone, we know of the construction

3 3 1
/s + kúwl #/

only that it is a phonologically nonminimal word. When we advance to morphological scrutiny and thereby identify the various morphemes to which each morph belongs, we find that the morphemic, though not the morphic, structure of the two constructions

$$\overset{3\ 3\ 1}{/s + k\acute{u}wl \#/} \quad \text{and} \quad \overset{3\ 3\ 1}{/w\acute{o}rm + \theta \#/}$$

is quite different. The first is a phonologically nonminimal word which is an allophrase of a construction containing three morphemes capable of standing as minimal words; the second is a phonologically nonminimal word and no more. The analysis of an utterance like

$$\overset{3\ 3\ 1}{/s + k\acute{u}wl \#/}$$

has been given at this length because this is an important instance of a situation in which description must be precise about the analytical levels under discussion. The construction is one thing phonologically speaking; quite a different thing when we are analyzing it morphologically.

A phonologically minimal word may be morphologically nonminimal. A typical example is a construction like

$$\overset{3\ 3\ 1}{dogs \ /d\acute{o}hgz \#/}$$

We have seen that under second-step cutting, a morph, {z}, is isolable here, though in many idiolects it always occurs without being marked by $/+/$, that is, it is a morph and morpheme which occurs without an accompanying stress morpheme. A final morphemic transcription for *dogs* is $\{'\} \{dɔhg\} \{z\} \{3\ 3\ 1\ \#\}$. Phonologically minimal words which are morphologically nonminimal, containing a second morph which is without a stress morpheme, may also be allophrases. Thus, *cant* may appear as

$$\overset{3\ 3\ 1}{/k\acute{æ}nt \#/}$$

and *can't* as the identical utterance

$$\overset{3\ 3\ 1}{/k\acute{æ}nt \#/}$$

The first, under morphological analysis, shows a simple structure—$\{'\}$ $\{kænt\} \{3\ 3\ 1\ \#\}$; the second shows the more complex structure—$\{'\} \{kæ\}$ $\{nt\} \{3\ 3\ 1\ \#\}$. In the latter form, a single stress morpheme is distributed over two bound allologs, and the whole is an allophrase with the phonological structure of a minimal word. Phonologically minimal allophrases and word allophrases even when nonminimal can then be treated on two levels: phonologically based morphology and a level much higher in the ascending structure, that of syntax.

The statements given in the preceding pages define for us the phonological basis for a classification of segmental morphs and a description of the kinds of larger constructions into which they enter. These larger constructions will be described in terms of the kinds of morphemes found in them and the sequences in which these morphemes occur.

2. Types of segmental morphemes

The starting point for classification of morphemes is a sequence of phonemes which appears as a phonologically minimal word. If such a sequence is shown to contain only one morph when it has been subjected to second-step analysis, it is also a morphologically minimal word. All forms which are phonologically and morphologically minimal words can be called bases. Examples of bases are *up, out, down, eye, dog, catch, run, green, slow,* and most of the monosyllabic vocabulary.

Furthermore, any form which appears with a single stress morpheme, even though that stress morpheme is composed of more than one stress phoneme, is a base if second-step analysis shows that it does not contain more than one morph. Examples of this type of base are *window,* with the stress morpheme $\{'\ \check{\ }\}$, and *erase,* with the stress morpheme $\{\check{\ }\ '\}$. A form which is not a base but a larger construction, even though it has the same stress morpheme, is *twenty* /twéntiy/. The form never has /+/ in my idiolect (though I have heard a form /twén + tǐy/ rather often from radio announcers) and therefore has only one stress morpheme. Secondary analysis shows that the form contains a morpheme {tiy} which recurs in forms like *seventy, ninety,* and others. A morphemic transcription of *twenty* is therefore: $\{'\ \check{\ }\}$ {twen} {tiy} {3 3 1 #}.

A morpheme which has thus been established as a base may occur with other segmental material before it, as in *kind* and *unkind.* Whether the preceding material has a stress morpheme of its own or whether the new construction merely has a differing single morpheme makes little difference to our classification. In this particular instance, the usual structure of the larger form is /ən + káynd/, with $\{\check{\ }\}$ on the initial vowel. It happens, also, that this initial sequence has a phonemic structure which would be possible under a pitch morpheme. Yet the morph {ən} can be safely said not to occur normally in any such hypothetical form as *$\{'\}$ {ən} {3 3 1 #}. We can, therefore, set up a second class of segmental morphemes, which we will call prebases. Prebases are morphologically bound morphemes since they do not occur isolated under a pitch morpheme; it is characteristic of them, however, that they are not usually phonologically bound. Like {ən}, they usually have the phonemic structure characteristic of minimal words. Thus, with most prebases, it is a morphotactic characteristic which identifies them, in that they belong to morphemes which have the morphotactic property of not occurring with a morpheme of pitch. In other instances, however, phonological characteristics are of help in the identification. Thus a form like *potato* has been described as having a phonemic structure as follows: /pə + téytə/, or in more formal style, /pə + téytow/. Morphemically, the first pronunciation is {ˇ} {pə} {+ ´ ˇ} {teytə} {2 3 1 #}. The morpheme {teytə} rarely occurs without the preceding morph {pə} and never in combination with any other sequence which is a recognizable prebase. Thus the two segmental morphs are normally an indivisible construction. Under these circumstances, the natural decision is to label {teytə} as the base, since it is the stressed form and can occasionally occur without preceding {pə}; the morph {pə} is therefore assigned the status of prebase, even though the morph is unique and so not one to which a meaning can be assigned. An even more striking case is the pronunciation /s + vélt/ for *svelte*, mentioned in Chapter 6, Section 3. The morph {s} must be a prebase (and one of the rare instances of a prebase which does not contain a vowel) since it has the type of phonemic structure which marks it phonologically as bound. The morphemic structure is therefore {ø} {s} {+ ´} {velt} {3 3 1 #}. As with *potato*, the construction is an indivisible semantic unit in which it is not possible to assign separate meaning to either morph, since both are allomorphs of unique morphemes.

If we turn from what may precede a base to what may follow it, we find that there are certainly morphs which are parallel to those we have called prebases. It turns out, in fact, that there is more than one kind of segmental morph which can follow a base, so that it becomes necessary to set up distinctions. One kind of entity occurs in partially symmetrical sets in which each member of the set occurs with a given base and, indeed, with large numbers of individual bases. These are the "grammatical endings" of familiar terminology. They can be defined morphotactically as morphemes which stand frequently before terminal junctures. They contrast with prebases which stand frequently in initial position and are always followed by a segmental morph of some sort with no intervening terminal juncture. The type of morpheme we are talking about here must always be preceded by a segmental morph with no intervening terminal juncture. These characteristics, however, do not serve to distinguish a "grammatical ending" from any other type of morpheme which is noninitial.

In English, grammatical elements have two striking characteristics. In any morphologically nonminimal word there is generally only one such element present, though in one set there are two. Their position is fixed, in that if there is one of these elements present, it occupies the last position, and if two, the last two positions. The characteristics here mentioned can be rephrased to take care of both the instances of two grammatical elements and of the commoner instances in which there is only one. One grammatical ending (exemplified by the plural of such nouns as *child*, which is a segmental morph, {in}), may occur either before the terminal juncture when a construction containing it is placed under a pitch morpheme or before the ending of the "possessive" of nouns, which then stands before the terminal of the pitch morpheme. Except for this one type of ending, which can be followed by a second ending, it is a rule that there is only one ending in each construction. The endings are therefore said to close the construction, since a terminal juncture must always fall after the ending, never before it.

For the class of morphemes ordinarily called endings, we shall adopt the name "suffix." The class will be described in detail in the next chapter, and the lists there given will fully define the class and all members of it. The other class of morphemes which can follow a base, we shall call postbases. Here we shall do no more than attempt to distinguish between the two classes. Postbases, like suffixes, are noninitial. Since more than one postbase can be added to a single base, as in *boy-ish-ness*, a postbase must be described as a morpheme which can follow a base or another postbase. Postbases can be followed by other postbases, by suffixes, or by a terminal juncture. As with a suffix, the terminal must always fall after a postbase, never before it.

Postbases do not fall into the limited classes characteristic of suffixes; a typical noun paradigm contains only two suffixes combined to give a maximum of four forms. In contrast, there are a large number of postbases, and their morphotactic limitations and affinities are largely unpredictable, necessitating elaborate listing. For instance, the postbase {θ} is added to adjectival forms like *warm, strong, true*. It is not added to *green* or *blue*, forms which take the different postbase *–ness*. Postbases can occur piled up in multiple sequences, so that it is possible to build constructions containing them with considerable freedom. Such a freely constructed form, which I have never heard in conversation, is the following:

$$\overset{2}{} \qquad \overset{3}{} \quad \overset{1}{}$$
**beautificationistically* /byùwtifi + kêyšən + ístik + əliy #/

In a morphic transcription, this form is:

{ˋ ˇ} {byuw} {ti} {fi} {+ ˆ ˇ} {keyŠ} {Šən} {+ ´ ˇ} {ist} {ik} {+ ˇ ˇ} {ə} {liy} {2 3 1 #}

In the transcription above, the symbol {Š} is adopted for the purpose of showing that the single phoneme overlaps, in that it belongs to both the preceding and the following morphemes, as with the /ž/ of *division* mentioned in Chapter 7, Section 4. The same form can be retranscribed with normalization of the morphemes, leaving out of account the suprasegmental morphemes which have been fully given:

{byuwt} {tiy} {fay} {ik} {eyt} {yən} {ist} {ik} {əl} {liy}[2]

At the moment, there is no need to discuss and justify the segmentation and normalization given here. Our hypothetical form is of interest in several ways. Because it follows normal sequences, it is sufficiently natural so that it seems to mean something, even if we are not sure exactly what. It is also pronounceable, and would probably be pronounced by a reader, in just about the form that I have given here, without the benefit of a transcription. On the other hand, though natural, it is a form which must approach the theoretical limit on the number of postbases. While I have made no exhaustive search, in forms known to me from actual conversation the greatest number of postbases seems to be six, and the hypothetical form given above is the longest that I have been able to construct. An example of an actual form with six postbases is *conservationistically*, all of the morphemes of which are also employed in our hypothetical form. The hypothetical form also illustrates another feature of postbases. Sequences of them may contain recurrences of the same morpheme, as our sequence shows by the two occurrences of {ik}.

Another one of the properties which distinguish postbases from suffixes is syntactic. Suffixes often occur in correlated arrangements, so that if a given suffix occurs in an initial pronoun or noun, a special suffix also occurs in a following verb. Thus a sentence like "The cows —— grazing" cannot be filled by all forms of the verb *to be*. The normally expected forms are *are* or *were*; *is* or *was* do not occur here, at least in standard speech. Conversely, if *cow* had been without suffix, the expected forms would be *is* or *was*. This kind of correlation is familiar under the name "concord," though in describing the limited and rather special kind of concord characteristic of English we shall use the term "selection" instead.[3] Whenever selection exists, the correlated suffixes make it impossible to substitute a form without a suffix for one with it; to do so produces an abnormal sentence. With postbases, on the other hand, correlation and selection are absent, so

---

[2] There is an apparent contradiction in this segmentation into morphs, in that the /š/ of *−ation* was assigned to both morphemes, whereas the single /t/ in *beauty* and the single /l/ in /−əliy/ are presented as belonging to the following morphs only. Assimilations of identical consonants over morphemic boundaries are handled differently from assimilations of unlike consonants. See below, p. 171.

[3] See below, Chap. 15, Section 2.

that a sentence containing a form consisting of base and postbase will often be satisfactory grammatically—even though not the same semantically—if the base alone is given, without the postbase. Thus, "John shot a *tigress*" can be varied by dropping the postbase, giving "John shot a *tiger*." In other instances, it is not possible to substitute the same base without postbases, but it is nearly always possible to substitute a different base. Thus, in a sentence like "John shows great *manliness*," it is not possible to substitute the base *man*. It is possible, however, to substitute a large number of other bases, such as *fear, wit, courage, joy*. In this kind of substitutability, the criterion used is always whether the varied form is a normal utterance. No attention is paid to whether the variant sentences mean the same thing. The fact that suffixes are often required when selection exists, whereas postbases are not, has occasionally been used as a means of distinguishing the two classes of morphemes. Selection, however, is a very limited feature in English syntax, so that suffixes are by no means always required as they are in the sentences we used as illustrations.

We have so far been able to identify four classes of segmental morphemes. They are bases, prebases, postbases, and suffixes. To these four there can be added a fifth, prefixes. A prefix is distinguished from a prebase in exactly the same way that a suffix is distinguished from a postbase. Prefixes, however, are extremely limited and special in English and are not usually recognized as occurring at all. Yet if pronoun forms are carefully analyzed, as will be done in Section 2 of Chapter 9, it is possible to identify the initial consonants of forms like *he, she, we*, and *me* as grammatical elements occurring before an invariant base which consists of a vowel alone. Prefixes can then be said to have a shadowy existence as products of analysis; they are not immediately recognizable forms like the suffixes of *dogs* or *loved*. A sixth class might also be possible, since the variation between *goose* and its plural, *geese*, might be analyzed as an infix consisting of the vowel nucleus alone. This analysis is rejected (see Chapter 9, Section 1), so that it is not necessary to recognize this sixth type.

A possible seventh type may also be mentioned briefly at this point. Some suffixes occasionally appear as something which might be called a postphrase.[4] Thus {z} is a suffix in a construction like *John's house*. The same morpheme appears also in forms like *the King of England's crown*, where it is traditional to describe the construction as a group genitive. The appearance of {z} at the end of such a long construction is the only one of these forms which is commonly described in grammars, but in conversation other endings can be treated in much the same way. Note such a sentence as:

---

[4] For a parallel, see the postphrases of Eskimo, described in Appendix A.

Mary *dear John–ed* him all over the place.

It is unnecessary to set up a special class of postphrases for English, since the morphemes which occur in this position are the same as those which appear as suffixes. We need only make the statement that suffixes can appear, under rather limited and special conditions, as phrase terminals.

We are now ready, then, to give a definition of a simple, but morphologically nonminimal, word. A word is a construction capable of standing isolated under a pitch morpheme and consisting of segmental morphemes of up to four types. The types are prebase, base, postbase, and suffix. There may be multiple prebases and postbases, but there is only one base, and there are never more than two suffixes.

In Section 4 of this chapter we shall return to the morphotactics of the classes of morphemes we have here described in general terms. It is our task, at this point, to describe the remaining types of construction which fall between the morpheme and the phrase. The two types thus far described consist of base alone (the minimal word), and base together with prebases, postbases, and suffixes. Units larger than these can all be described as phrases, though to do so means that the term "phrase" is used with variant definitions. One definition of the term "phrase" has already been given: that it is a morpheme or series of morphemes marked by a pitch phoneme. This definition identifies the entity which can be called a phonological phrase. Another use for the term "phrase" is to identify it with the potential phrase. As we have seen, every base, and every nonminimal word form, is a potential phrase in that it can be spoken in a fashion which places it under a pitch morpheme. The minimal potential phrase is therefore identical with the word, and so is a term for which we have no need.

In order to make clear what is meant by a potential phrase, we can consider the sentence:

$$\overset{2}{\text{Hè's}} + a + vèry + óld + \overset{31}{mán} \,\#$$

This is a sentence composed of only one pitch morpheme and is thus a minimal sentence. Within it, however, the italicized construction *a very old man* can itself be treated as a terminal juncture group and is therefore a potential phrase. Within this group there are others which could be so pronounced. *Very old* is a potential phrase, as are *old man* and *very old man*. Other partial sequences are not potential phrases, since their appearance set off by terminals is unlikely. Such partial sequences, which are parts of a potential phrase, rather than themselves potential phrases, are *a very* and the larger sequence *a very old*.[5] The only other potential phrases here

---

[5] The sequences *a very* and *a very old* appear as phonological phrases only if there is repetition, as in *a very, very old man*.

are the four minimal potential phrases, the units we have called words.

A nonminimal potential phrase is then a sequence which contains more than one base and which is of such a nature that it is normally capable of being set off by terminals. This entity is what is usually meant by the term "phrase" and may be more strictly identified as the morphological and syntactic phrase. It is a relatively loose concept, but is useful. It is used throughout this book, but when there is danger of misunderstanding, the phonological phrase is called a terminal juncture group, or the morphological phrase is explicitly specified. A useful characteristic of the morphological phrase is that it is usually a form for which a single base, or base construct, can be substituted. Thus for the morphological phrase *a very old man*, the single form *John* is substitutable.

If we continue with the entities which can fall within the phonological phrase, we find two types of morphological phrases. The type which is least interesting to us at the minute can be called the free phrase, consisting of words in normal sequence and called free because sequences of this sort can be constructed almost without limit, whether the speaker has ever heard the sequence before or not. Such a free phrase is our *a very old man*, above. On the model of this, I can construct *a very young man*, *a very old woman*, and even *a very superstitious button*, a sequence I believe I have never heard. It is characteristic of the various groups of free phrases that each group has stress-morpheme constructions which identify it. The morphological free phrase *a very old man* has the stress construction {ˇ} {+ ˋ ˇ} {+ ˆ} {+ ´}, the construction which is characteristic of the sequence article-adverb-adjective-noun. If we make allowance for the varying number of weak syllables, we find that the same construction appears in all the examples we have given, and the stress construction marks all free phrases of the same type. Free phrases will be described in detail in the chapters which deal with syntax. Here they can be dismissed.[6]

---

[6] In certain rather specialized phrases, phonologically of the free-phrase type, there are traces of a type of morpheme which occurs with much greater frequency and importance in other languages. The English examples are found in forms like *roly-poly* /rôwliy + pówliy/, *Georgy-Porgy* /jɔ́rjiy + pɔ́rgiy/, and the now much more productive type:

332   331
cheese-shmeese /cíyz | šmíyz #/
332   331
money-shmoney /mə́niy | šmə́niy #/

The striking feature of these sequences is that they consist of partial repetition of a preceding morpheme, together with a fixed recurrent element, /p/ in the first type, /šm/ in the second. As morphemes, therefore, these vary in phonemic content from one occurrence to the next, though the pattern is readily describable. These mor-

The phrases which are not free are relatively fixed entities and function as units. They have several characteristics, of which the most important is that their stress constructions depart from those characteristic of the corresponding free phrases. Thus, for instance, the stress construction characteristic of adjective and following noun when these are a free phrase is {+ ^} {+ ʹ}. This is the construction found in *the green house* {ˇ} {ðə} {+ ^} {griyn} {+ ʹ} {haws} {2 3 1 #}. When this sequence of segmental morphemes is no longer a free phrase, the stress construction becomes {+ ʹ} {+ ˋ}, giving the construction *the greenhouse* {ˇ} {ðə} {+ ʹ} {griyn} {+ ˋ} {haws} {2 3 1 #}. The free-phrase construction does not always become {+ ʹ} {+ ˋ}, however. It may also become {+ ˋ} {+ ʹ}. Thus, notice the contrast in stress in the following pair of sentences:

The colonists settled a *new England*.   {+ ^} {+ ʹ ˇ}
The colonists settled *New England*.   {+ ˋ} {+ ʹ ˇ}

The contrast in stress construction is the necessary defining characteristic of the fixed phrase; if the contrast is not there, the form remains a free phrase, no matter how special its meaning. In my speech the sequence *old fox* has {+ ^} {+ ʹ} and is thus a free phrase, though it is fully specialized in meaning in any such sentence as "John is an old fox." The fixed phrase can also show variation in the phonemic structure of one or more of its components, resulting in allologs correlated with the fixed phrase construction. An example is the construction *Russophobe* {ʹ ˇ} {rəsow} {+ ˋ} {fowb} {3 3 1 #}. It is to be noted that this form has the stress construction of a fixed phrase, and not the free-phrase construction of such a sequence as *Rússiăn phóbĭă*. In addition, however, both the forms of which the construction is made up are allomorphs which appear only in constructions of this particular kind.

Not infrequently, also, the fixed phrase and the free phrase differ in syntactic distribution. An instance of such difference has already been shown. The fixed phrase *New England* is one before which an indefinite article is not used, as long as *New England* appears before the terminal. An indefinite article can be used only in a sequence like *a New England town*.

phemes can be called calques. A symbol for them can be written with a sequence of dots, indicating repetition. Thus:

{^ ˇ} {rowliy} {+ ʹ ˇ} {p ...} {2 3 1 #}
{ʹ } {ciyz} {3 3 2 | } {ʹ } {šm ...} {3 3 1 #}

The most commonly encountered type of calque is that which is called reduplication. It consists in repetition of the consonantal framework, typically of a following morpheme, with a usually invariant vowel. In Latin forms such as *cecidi, tetigi*, reduplication is one of the types of grammatical affix. In languages of the Malayo-Polynesian group, reduplication is a major structural device, occurring in words and phrases of all types.

The free phrase *a new England* is one before which the indefinite article regularly appears.

More important, at least at this stage of discussion, is the fact that fixed phrases are expandable by means of prebases and postbases. A good example is *un-get-at-able*. The core of this construction is *get at*, here shown to be a fixed phrase since it has the stress construction $\{+\;`\}\{+\;´\}$, which differs from the stress construction the same sequence would have as a free phrase. The free phrase occurs in:

He's a hard man to *get at*. $\{+\;^\}\{+\;´\}$

To this core there has been added the postbase *-able* and the prebase *un-*. The layers of accretion are as follows:

1. *Get at* becomes a fixed phrase by the addition of the stress construction $\{+\;`\}\{+\;´\}$.
2. To the fixed phrase (which does not occur alone) is added the postbase *–able* defining the new construction as adjectival.
3. To this construction is added the prebase *un–*, a form freely added to adjectival material.

The order of these accretions can be checked by one of the principles of the kind of cutting called immediate constituent analysis. Immediate constituent analysis is the process of segmenting a complex construction by successive single cuts. In these terms, the process of accretion, described above, can be reversed to state that the first cut is made between *un–* and *get-at-able* and that these two forms are then the immediate constituents of the construction. The immediate constituents of *get-at-able*, in turn, are *get-at* and *–able*. When all cuts have been made, the total of morphemes found in the original construction are its ultimate constituents. The principle, which we referred to above, is that immediate constituent analysis should be made with cuts which give a maximum number of actually occurring words or phrases at each step. Thus our first cut is better than a first cut into **un-get* and **at-able*, or into **un-get-at* and *–able*, since either of these cuts would produce nonexistent constituents. The discussion of the process of immediate constituent analysis is introduced here for the reason that it shows that one of the constituents is the stress construction which marks the sequence *get-at* as a fixed phrase. In short, it is not the presence of prebase and postbase which marks *un-get-at-able* as a unit; rather the prebase and postbase are possible accretions to something which has already been defined as a fixed phrase by the stress construction.

Fixed phrases can also be expanded by means of suffixes. Characteristically, these fall at the end of the fixed phrase, and so are often preceded by morphs which would not take the suffix which occurs were the preceding morph occurring in a free phrase. A typical example is *two teaspoonfuls*. This is defined as a fixed phrase by its stress construction, in my idiolect {+ ´ ˇ} {+ ˇ}. The stress construction of the free phrase can be seen in:

Fill the two *teaspoons full*. {+ ^ ˇ} {+ ´}

It should be said that *teaspoon* itself is a fixed phrase, and one of the immediate constituents of *teaspoonful*. As with *un-get-at-able* it is not the presence of the suffix which characterizes the construction as a fixed phrase but its stress pattern, since suffixes can appear at the ends of free phrases, as with the group genitive. Thus, the presence of a suffix cannot define the type of phrase for us.

Fixed phrases, particularly those with suffixes, are sometimes divided into two types, called endocentric and exocentric.[7] A fixed phrase like *táble-tòp* is called endocentric because the phrase as a whole belongs to the same form-class (noun) as its "head," in this instance presumably *top*. An exocentric phrase is one represented by such a form as *forgét-me-nòt*, where the phrase as a whole does not belong to the same class as any word in it. The difficulty in this type of distinction is that it involves a series of decisions as to what constitutes the "head" of the construction. Such decisions invite reliance on meaning, as when it is said that *road* is the "head" of *railroad* since a railroad is a kind of road, not a kind of rail. It is this difficulty which Harold Whitehall has recently attempted to deal with by calling forms like *table-top* "headed" groups, and forms like *forget-me-not* "non-headed" groups.[8] Whitehall's distinction is useful but, as far as phrases are concerned, unnecessary. All decisions as to what is the head, or whether a head is present or not, can be avoided by merely classifying fixed phrases into those types in which the suffix would be added to the preceding morph in a free phrase and those types in which it would not. Thus *table-top* is an example of the first type, *teaspoonfuls* of the second.

It was stated earlier that fixed phrases are normally inflected by addition of the suffix at the end of the fixed phrase. This is not an absolute rule. Not infrequently an element in a fixed phrase other than the final one will receive the suffix. An example is *courts-martial*. It is important to remember that it is the stress construction of this form which defines it as a fixed phrase, not its unusual order characteristics, or its semantic content. The stress construction is {+ ´} {+ ` ˇ}. It does not have the free-phrase construction of a sequence like *(the) body beautiful*, which has the same unusual order but which has {+ ^ ˇ} {+ ´ ˇ}. Somewhat commoner as examples

---

[7] Cf. Bloomfield, *Language*, pp. 194–96.

[8] Harold Whitehall, *Structural Essentials of English*, Harcourt, Brace, New York, 1956, pp. 9–17.

of inflected first members in fixed phrases are constructions like *ménfòlk* and *wómĕnfòlk*.

The entities which can be contained within a single phonological phrase are then: minimal words or bases, nonminimal words, fixed phrases, and potential free phrases. Suffixes are characteristically added to bases, to nonminimal words, and to fixed phrases. There are, however, some instances of suffixes which are added to free phrases. If a postbase or prebase is added to a minimal word, it becomes nonminimal, but further prebases and postbases can be added to constructions which are already nonminimal. Prebases and postbases can also be added to fixed phrases, but cannot be added to free phrases. When a postbase is added to the last form in a free phrase, it is a constituent of that form alone, not of the whole phrase.

Now that we have labored over the distinctions between various kinds of words and various kinds of phrases, it may seem a paradox to end the discussion with the statement that the distinctions are not always important, since there is a good deal of variation in the treatment of morphemes, tending to blur the lines of division. A sensible analysis of *communism* would say that it is a nonminimal word and that the last morpheme, *–ism*, is a postbase. The statement is not invariably true of all occurrences of the morpheme, since there are sentences like "He was exposed to all the *isms* of the radicals." The decision that *ism* is a postbase must then be made on a probabilistic basis, on the ground that its occurrences in situations like *communism*, *Methodism*, *Gallicism*, and the like, far outnumber occurrences like that in the sentence just quoted. This probabilistic method is the one used here, but it should be firmly stated that such a probabilistic formulation always involves an obligation to list the exceptions.

3. The phonemic structure of segmental morphemes

Now that we have isolated the classes of segmental morphemes, it is possible to describe the sequences of phonemes which occur in the various classes. The area covered by such a description would ideally include not only the phonemic shape of various morphemic norms but the phonemic variations between allomorphs. The latter type of information will be scanted in our description, for the compelling reason that detailed and systematic information on this kind of variation is not available. A description of the phonemic structure of morphemes, and of variations in that structure, is a description of phonemes as constituents of morphemes and constitutes the subject called morphophonemics.

Bases, the natural class with which to begin our description, must be syllabic, that is, must contain a vowel or vowel nucleus. Without recapitulating in detail the description given in Section 1, we can devise a symbolic representation for the several morphophonemic types, and go on to add some characteristics of structure which we have not yet mentioned. In this symbolization, V stands for any vowel or vowel nucleus, and C stands for any consonant or permitted consonant cluster:

V: *owe*   CV: *toe, stow*   VC: *oat, oast*   CVC: *tote, stoat, toast*

The maximum consonant cluster of five, described in Chapter 6, never occurs in a base morpheme. A cluster of five consonants always occurs over a morphemic boundary which is revealed by second-step analysis. The longest cluster I have ever heard in a base morpheme is /–rmpf/, and this occurs in a highly special form. A colleague has it in an idiolectal construction /mɔ́rmpf/, which he uses as a word with the meaning "to make a noncommittal noise." Such a form can hardly be used to establish four-consonant clusters as normal for base morphemes. In generally used forms, the limit on clusters within the base is three, in both prevocalic and postvocalic position. Examples are *splash* and *calx*. There is a further limitation, since there are no bases which contain maximal clusters in both positions at the same time.

Bases may also contain more than one vowel. The limit seems to be three syllables, since sequences of four and five syllables—in my idiolect, at least—are always broken into two morphs by /+/, though it must be admitted that the /+/ is lost in some individual utterances of the sequences. Examples of two- and three-syllable forms which are without /+/ in my speech are *window* and *eleven*. The situation in longer sequences can be represented by what happens to forms like *tarantula* and *sarsaparilla*. The first of these is normally /tə + rǽncilə/, though a second form I also use is /tə + rǽnc + lə/. The sequence is therefore to be analyzed as a word consisting of prebase, base, and postbase. The normal pronunciation, for me, of *sarsaparilla* is /sàrsə + pərílə/. Such a pronunciation indicates the presence of two morphs, both unique. The second of them can be identified as the base, since it is stressed. The occurrence of /+/ is explained by the stress sequence of tertiary and primary, with intervening weaks. It will be remembered that in Chapter 7, Section 5, we described such sequences as normally having a /+/, though the juncture could be lost. In this sequence, the location of /+/ is not predictable and may well vary from speaker to speaker.

In a pronunciation like /tə + rǽncilə/, the appearance of /+/ cannot be explained in the same way. A hypothesis, at present unproved, is that two is the maximum number of weaks which can combine with a stronger stress in a single morpheme. If the hypothesis should be verified by further study, it would establish an important fact for formally based morphemic analysis

Two further structural characteristics of base morphemes can be added

When bases are polysyllabic, there is some limitation ·on clustering of the medial consonants, since there are no bases with maximal clustering in all positions. The second structural characteristic belongs rather to their morphotactics than to their phonemics. Normally the base receives the heaviest stress within the sequence of morphs which make up the word. This stress characteristic is not an absolute rule, however, since there are instances of stressed prebases. Stress on the base is common enough, nevertheless, so that position of the stress can be used to identify the base in forms where there is nothing which contradicts such an identification.

We have seen one instance of a prebase which contains no vowel, *svelte* when pronounced /s + vélt/. A closely parallel form is the medical term *sthenic*, which can be /s + θénik/. Both are words which contain unique morphs, so that there is no possibility of assigning meaning to the recurrent morpheme {s}. In both instances, the /+/ and the resultant morphemic division is correlated with the rare consonant sequence, so that the morpheme {s} could be spoken of as phonotactically generated.

While there are, then, somewhat limited and special cases of prebases which contain no vowels, the widely recurrent and easily recognizable prebases, which make up the normal structure, all contain a vowel or vowel nucleus. There are a fair number of prebases which have two syllables, as in *intramural* or *interurban*. There are no prebases with three syllables, since forms like *deuterocanonical*, with a first element /dùtərow/ followed by /+/, all seem to be instances of fixed phrases. That is, the same first element appears as a base in *Deuteronomy*. Even with the two-syllable forms, it is often difficult to decide whether a first element is a prebase or a first base in a fixed phrase. A form like *anticommunist* shows /æ̀ntiy-/ as a prebase, if we ignore the occurrence of sentences like "John's always an *anti.*" The decision as to whether *anti* is base or prebase can be made on the basis of frequency— the use in the sentence quoted is rarer than occurrences of *anti* as a prebase.

If prebases can be described as having a maximum of two vowels, where bases may have three, prebases are then simpler in structure than bases. They show greater simplicity also in their consonant structure. Three-consonant clusters do not occur; the typical cluster type in prebases is the /pr-/ of *pre-* and *pro-*.

Postbases, in distinction to the classes already described, need not be syllabic. In *warmth, depth, length* the postbase is the single consonant {θ}. In *linguistics*, the final postbase is {s}; the form is not identical with the suffix of plurality in nouns, since we say "Linguistics *is* a science." Monosyllabic postbases may have the following forms:

V: *mud* becomes *muddy*   VC: *type* becomes *typist*
CV: *normal* becomes *normalcy*   CVC: *establish* becomes *establishment*

Dissyllabic postbases are fairly common, as with the *–itis* of *appendicitis*, the *–able* of *actionable*, and the *–ary* of *voluptuary*. There are no trisyllabic postbases.

Prefixes will not be described at this point, since the only entities which can be assigned to this class in English, the initial elements of pronouns, require detailed analysis before discussion. The remaining forms are, then, the suffixes. Like postbases, suffixes may be nonsyllabic. Examples are the {z} of *dogs* and the {d} of *loved*. Suffixes may also be syllabic, as in *horses, loaded,* but there are no polysyllabic suffixes. The syllabic suffixes are limited to the patterns V and VC.

Examples of vocalic suffixes are found in the allomorphs of the plural morpheme in nouns; they occur in nouns of foreign origin, with modification of the base morpheme, and often also with a stress morpheme different from that which occurs in the singular:

> *femur : femora*   {ˊ ˇ} {fiymər}: {ˊ ˇ ˇ} {femər} {ə}
> *alumnus : alumni*   {ˇ ˊ ˇ} {əlumnəs}: {ˇ ˊ ˇ} {əlumn} {ay}
> *bolshevik : bolsheviki*   {ˊ ˇ} {bowlšə} {+ ˋ} {viyk}: {ˋ ˇ} {bowlšə}
>   {+ ˋ ˇ} {viykiy}
> *stigma : stigmata*   {ˊ ˇ} {stigmə}: {ˇ ˊ ˇ} {stigmat} {ə}

In all these examples, the suffixes have been analyzed as consisting of vowel or vowel nucleus alone. The variations in the preceding base are meaningless and allomorphic, and the variations in stress morphemes are redundant though not allomorphic.

Dissyllabic suffixes were once common in English, but are now unknown. The learned nouns given above might seem in some instances to contain dissyllabic suffixes, but in every instance it turns out that it is more economical to analyze such forms as containing a monosyllabic suffix only. *Stigmata* is a good example. If we should cut so as to give a plural suffix **–ata*, we should still have to recognize a base allomorph **{stigm–}*, which occurs before the plural suffix so analyzed. If we cut so as to give a suffix **–ta* of the pattern CV, we have then to recognize the base allomorph **{stigma}*, and the plural suffix we set up is without parallel. If, then, we cut as was done above, we have the base allomorph {stigmat} (a base allomorph is necessary with any cut) and a suffix {ə}, which is paralleled by forms like *femur : femora* or *genus : genera*.

In the description of suffixes, the last type which needs to be mentioned is one which is, in a sense, a product of the type of analysis used. In a pair of verb forms like *drive : drove*, we have elected to describe the variation between the present and past tenses as a vowel morph, {ow}, which can be called a suffix only by the arbitrary process of describing all grammatical inflection in nouns and verbs as suffixational. A terminological alternative is to call this element an infix, which is satisfactory enough. With either term, however, the facts of occurrence must be described. Grammatical morphs of this type occur in nonsequential order, replacing the vowel or vowel nucleus which falls under stress. They thus produce, in sum total of base and grammatical morpheme, a subtype of portmanteau construction, one in which normal sequential order is departed from and in which it is impossible for the boundaries of the two segmental morphemes to be marked off by stress morphemes.

These grammatical variations constitute an exception to the general character of grammatical morphemes which are added after the base. There is some advantage in applying the term "suffix" to all grammatical morphs, though such a terminological procedure requires that these exceptions be taken account of and be reconciled to the general type. In linear analysis these forms can be presented sequentially even though they do not occur so, if a statement of their order peculiarities is given. A morphophonemic writing such as {OW} can be adopted for the vocalic portion of *drove*, with the statement that such a writing always indicates a suffix which occurs in nonsequential order.[9] A transcription of *drove* would appear thus:

drove   {′} {drayv} {OW} which equals /drówv/

In suprasegmental morphotactics, suffixes rarely have a stress morpheme of their own, at least in my idiolect. That is, the morpheme {′} occurs without modification or variation in both *dog* and *dogs*. An example of a suffix with its own stress morpheme (but zero stress) is *ringed* {′} {riŋ} {+} {d}.

As intimated at the start of this section, the subject of morphophonemics takes up phonemes as members of morphemes and thus includes the phonemes and their order in all morphemes. Usually, however, morphophonemics is more narrowly defined as covering the differences in phonemic structure between allomorphs of the same morpheme. There have been studies of this type of morphophonemics for a number of languages, but unfortunately no thorough study for English. The reason for the lack is primarily that the preliminary and extensive task of preparing a complete inventory of English morphemes has not been done. A large part of what is available on morphophonemics is, at present, isolated treatment of irregular and unsystematic changes in base morphemes when suffixes are added. Dictionaries and grammars give information on such variations as that between a singular *fungus* and the plural *fungi* {′ ˇ} {fənj} {ay}. In some instances the changes are sufficiently systematic so that they can be described in general statements. One such morphophonemic statement is

---

[9] See below, pp. 140–41.

that when /d/ is followed by /y/ over a morphemic boundary not marked by /+/, the sequence is replaced by the single phoneme /ž/, which we have stated to belong to both the preceding and following morphemes. Under similar circumstances /ty/ is replaced by /š/. Examples of the two changes are *divide : division* and *inflate : inflation*. If, on the other hand, the sequence is /d + y/ or /t + y/, the replacements are /j/ and /c/ as in:

$$\overset{33\ 3}{Did\ you?}\ /díjə\ |||/ \quad \text{and} \quad Can't\ you?\ \overset{3\ 3\quad 3}{/kǽncə\ |||/}$$

In other instances, a change will be found in some morphemes, but not in others of similar phonemic structure. Thus, *knife, life, wife, calf, thief, leaf, loaf,* all substitute /v/ for the final /f/ of the base when the plural suffix is added. Other forms ending in /f/, such as *cough, laugh, muff,* do not vary before the suffix. Variations of this sort can be handled by use of the concept of the morphophoneme. It will be remembered that the morphophoneme has been defined as a phoneme considered as a member of a morpheme. Thus, a pair of forms like *calf* and *laugh* contain instances of the same phoneme /f/, but the /f/ in *calf* is a member of that morpheme, the second a member of *laugh*. The alternation {kæf} : {kæv-} is a property of the morpheme {kæf} and is not in any way related to the phonemic situation in which /f/ is found. We can express this fact by saying the morphophonemic alternations undergone by the /f/ in /kǽf/ show it to be different from the /f/ in /lǽf/, which remains constant. We can then further set up a class of /f/'s which have the morphophonemic alternation found in /kǽf/, and devise a special symbol for them. One which has frequently been chosen is /F/, a symbol the meaning of which is: "a phoneme /f/ which is replaced by the phoneme /v/ in this morpheme when the plural suffix is added." Such symbols are morphophonemic symbols, and transcription which employs them is morphophonemic transcription. It is of some interest that systems of conventional orthography are not infrequently more or less morphophonemic. An example is the pair *Dach* and *Tag* from German. In many dialects of German, the final consonants of these two morphemes are alike before juncture; the spelling indicates that one of these forms, *Dach*, retains its voicelessness before a suffix beginning with a vowel, whereas the other, as in *Tages*, has a voiced phoneme under similar circumstances.

4. Morphotactics of segmental morphemes

The subject of morphotactics falls into two divisions. The suprasegmental morphotactics of segmental morphemes is a description of the stress morphemes which occur with individual morphemes and with classes of morphemes. Segmental morphotactics describes the sequences of segmental morphemes which occur before and after individual morphemes and classes of morphemes. Some statements which properly belong to each area have been anticipated in the preceding sections, for reasons of convenience.

In suprasegmental morphotactics, it can be said that the citation forms of bases, when without prebases, postbases, and suffixes,[10] always occur with a morpheme which contains primary stress, the possibilities being {′} {′ ˘} {′ ˘ ˘} {˘ ′} {˘ ′ ˘}. Examples of each of these types are:

{′} *horse*   {′ ˘} *window*   {′ ˘ ˘} *idiot*   {˘ ′} *about*   {˘ ′ ˘} *eleven*

It may be said that the several stress patterns are separate morphemes because, though the number of stress phonemes is predictable, their position is not.

In the citation forms of morphologically nonminimal words, it is normal for the base to have one of the morphemes given above and for the affixed material to be unstressed. This is by no means a universal rule, however. A good many nouns have primary stress on the first syllable, whether this is base or not. Thus we have forms like *réject, rétread, réwrite*. In a good many instances of successive postbases, the stress may fall on one of them, as in *linguístic*. Even though allocation of the heaviest stress to the base is thus by no means universal, it is still a tendency common enough so that stress can be used as a means of distinguishing the base from the affixed elements when there is no conflicting morphological or other evidence. Thus, in our earlier discussion of *potato* {˘} {pə} {+ ′ ˘} {teytow}, the unstressed first syllable could be safely called a prebase.

In fixed phrases, the characteristic—but again by no means universal—stress pattern is tertiary stress on one base, primary stress on the other. There are instances of tertiary stress on one of the affixes, as in *rè-tíre* (tire over again) and *nécessàry*; there are also instances of fixed phrases where one of the bases receives weak stress, as in *nèverthĕléss*, but it is noteworthy that these are all instances of phrases containing more than two bases. The combination of tertiary with a stronger stress can, as with the position of the heaviest stress, often be used as a means of identifying the construction type. Thus a form like *dèuterocanónical* has two indications that it is a fixed phrase rather than a word. The first element, *deutero–*, has three syllables, rather than two as expected in prebases, and also receives the characteristic tertiary stress.

In my idiolect, primary stress and secondary stress make a construction which is characteristic of a free phrase. In many idiolects this does not

---

[10] A general term for any segmental morpheme which is not a base is "affix."

seem to hold, since a very common variation is that between *bláckbìrd* and *blàckbírd*. It is to be doubted, however, that the sequence secondary-primary occurs, even in these idiolects, as anything other than a free-phrase pattern.

In the morphotactics of postbases, a minor detail is that they are often correlated with the occurrence of a stress morpheme on a preceding element. An example is the postbase {ik}. The form *linguist* {′ ˇ} {lingw} {ist} has stress on the first syllable. If {ik} is added, the form becomes {ˇ ′ ˇ} {lingw} {ist} {ik}. Yet not all instances of {ik} have this stress correlation, as is shown by the pair *Arab : Arabic*. Another postbase which has the same kind of stress correlation is that which has the morphemic norm {yən}. Note *cómmune* (noun): *commúnion*; *dúplicàte* (verb): *duplicátion*.

In free phrases, the actually occurring stress morphemes are correlated with the form classes of words and fixed phrases. Thus, for instance, a noun in final position has a morpheme containing primary stress, as in "John drank *mílk*." In a similar position, a pronoun would have weak stress, as in "John drank *ĭt*." The occurrence of stress morphemes can therefore be used to define the form classes, and will be so used in describing syntax. From the point of view taken in this chapter, however, it is enough to point out that there is no correlation between the fact that a morpheme is a word and the stress it receives when it is in a free phrase.

Several important statements covering segmental morphotactics have already been made. Thus, it has been said that there may be, at least theoretically, as many as nine postbases with a single word. Prebases can occur in sequences of three, as in *pre-re-exportation*. A further characteristic of prebases and postbases is that they can be repeated in the same construction, as in *un-re-untied*, or the two instances of {ik} in *beautificationistic*. Prebases can also occur in variant order, as in *unretied* and *re-untied*. The order in these forms certainly affects the meaning, but only insofar as is covered by the statement that the immediate constituent consists of the base and the form nearest to it.

Beyond these relatively simple statements, there is little which can be said with authority on morphotactics. The subject is one urgently in need of investigation, but until the investigation has been performed, all statements are necessarily tentative and sketchy. There are undoubtedly limitations on the order of postbases: though we have *–ishness* in *boyishness*, there are no examples of **-nessish*; while we have *–icize* in *publicize*, there are no examples of these postbases in reversed order. Whether these limitations on order can be systematically stated is not at present known. Postbases also occur in favorite sequences, such as *–fication* in *purification*, *qualification*, or *–istically*, in *statistically*, *linguistically*. It is a striking fact that not all the layers of accretion, as found in these sequences, represent constructions used as independent words. Thus with the base *publ–*, there is the construction *publication*. This contains *public*, but there is no independent **publicate*. With *duplication* there is an underlying *duplicate*, but no **duplic*. This distribution indicates that the sequences have been added to bases not individually, but as wholes. Such favorite sequences often form immediate constituents which should be cut off from the underlying forms in conglomerates, rather than by the simpler process of always cutting off the last one.

Edward Sapir, in a work which never reached full publication, observed that a given base often occurs with a set of alternating postbases which make up a partially symmetrical family. The instances cited were the postbases {ər} and {id}, both of which tend to occur with any single base, though there are instances in which only one of the two is found:

pale					
pallor	*splendor*	*squalor*	*rigor*		
pallid	*splendid*	*squalid*	*rigid*	*frigid*	*chrysalid*
					chrysalis
					chrysaloid

As can be seen from the examples, the symmetry is far from perfect.

An observation can also be made about the differing sequences characteristic of prebases and postbases. Both types can repeat the same morpheme, as we have seen. Prebases can repeat the same morpheme in immediate contact, as in *un-un-tied*, *re-re-tied*; postbase series do not show repetition unless other material intervenes between the repeated forms. The repetition in postbase sequences occurs because the same morpheme happens to be a member of two successive favorite sequences.

There is little to add to the morphotactics of suffixes beyond what has already been given, and what will be more carefully presented in the chapters on inflection. At this point we need only to qualify our earlier statement that no segmental morphemes are added after the suffix. There are a few exceptions to this general statement. Occasionally, there is a double plural. For instance, *scissors*, even though it has no singular, certainly contains a plural suffix, since we say "The scissors are ——." There are, however, occasional occurrences of the word—at least in very informal speech—where the final element is treated as part of the base, giving some such sentence as "No, not the scissors, the *scissorses*." In *shambles*, what was once a suffix is now firmly a part of the base: "The room *was a shambles*." A form which seems also to be established is *bobby-soxer*, where the spelling *sox*, instead of *socks*, is evidence, though slight, that the suffix is now part of the base. All such forms, many of which are objected to as incorrect, are evidence of variant morphemic structure and are only etymologically instances of addition after a suffix.

9.... INFLECTION

1. Nouns

In English, words and fixed phrases are divided into two groups: those which can take suffixes and prefixes, that is to say, those which are inflectable; and those which can take only prebases and postbases and which are therefore uninflectable. Suffixes and prefixes are added to bases in intersecting and largely symmetrical sets called paradigms. A typical paradigm is that for nouns, where a given form is classified according to the two variations, or categories, of case and number. Since the paradigmatic sets are sharply different for large groups of words, words fall into classes defined by their paradigms. These large groups are called form classes, though the traditional name for them is parts of speech.

English possesses three classes of inflected words: nouns, pronouns, and verbs. Without defining the first of these classes, we can begin our analysis with the forms of the noun *ox*, chosen because, though it is a rather rare form, it is one which offers the clearest approach to noun inflection. The forms are:

1. *ox* /áks/
2. *ox's* /áksɨz/
3. *oxen* /áksɨn/
4. *oxen's* /áksɨnz/

The four forms are made by means of two suffixes, one of which we can call the case suffix and the other of which is the number suffix. Each suffix contrasts only with its absence, and the order is fixed—when both suffixes occur, as in form 4, it is the number suffix which occurs first.

The great majority of nouns, however, do not have forms like those for *ox*, with the two suffixes clearly distinguished from each other. Much more typical is a noun like *boy*:

1. *boy* /bóy/
2. *boy's* /bóyz/
3. *boys* /bóyz/
4. *boys'* /bóyz/

Here forms 2, 3, and 4 are exactly alike, though spelling has introduced artificial differences among them. It is clear that in this paradigm the case and number suffix are homonymous, both occurring as {-z}. But the real difficulty of this set is in form 4. Here there is only one suffix, instead of two as in. *oxen's*. If only one suffix, which one is it, case or number?

If we go to still another noun, *wife*, we get evidence we can use to answer the question we have just raised. The forms of *wife* are:

1. *wife* /wáyf/
2. *wife's* /wáyfs/
3. *wives* /wáyvz/
4. *wives'* /wáyvz/

The forms are irregular in that there is a second allomorph of the base, {wayv}, which appears in 3 and 4. This allomorph does not appear in form 2, where we know the ending is the case suffix. It appears in form 3, where we know also that the ending is the number suffix. Since the second allomorph appears in form 4, this is evidence that the overtly present ending in form 4 is the number suffix, not that for case. We can account for the irregularities in *wife*, then, by saying that the second base allomorph appears only before the number suffix, and that in form 4, the case suffix has a zero allomorph.

Further evidence for explanation of the variations in noun paradigms can be drawn from the forms of *sheep*:

1. *sheep* /šíyp/
2. *sheep's* /šíyps/
3. *sheep* /šíyp/
4. *sheep's* /šíyps/

Form 3 is a plural, since the form occurs in such plural phrases as *two sheep*. But the number suffix is zero, the kind of zero which can be given allomorphic status as a member of the number-suffix morpheme. Form 4 here must be assumed to be the case suffix, since the number suffix is a zero.

The several variations we have so far met can be put together in a single series of statements. Whenever the case and number suffix are not homonymous (as in *oxen's*), both suffixes are present in form 4, with the number suffix first. Whenever the number suffix is a zero allomorph, form 4 consists of the number suffix in zero, followed by the case suffix. Whenever the case and number suffix are homonymous (as in *wife*, *boy*), the number suffix appears, followed by the case suffix in a zero allomorph. In short, it is possible to reconcile all differences on the basis of an assumption that the number suffix is always given first and that, of two homonymous suffixes, the second is always reduced to zero.

A special type of noun is that represented by *man*. For this noun, as for *ox*, there are four differentiated forms:

1. *man* /mǽn/
2. *man's* /mǽnz/
3. *men* /mén/
4. *men's* /ménz/

The difficulty, of course, is that the two plural forms are shown not by an ending added after the base but by an internal vowel change. We have seen that forms like *wife* have a second base allomorph which appears before the number suffix, so that a possible analysis of the forms like *man* would be to say that they have a zero allomorph of the number suffix, before which the base appears in an allomorphic— and so meaningless— variation. Such an analysis, however, is to be rejected for distributional reasons. First, the paradigm of *man* is exactly parallel to that of *ox*, making it almost mandatory to assign plural meaning to the vowel change, and second, the form *men* does not have the distribution of a base allomorph. For the allomorph {wayv–}, there is a second appearance in the verb *wiving*, and for *thief* the allomorph {θiyv–} occurs in *thievish, thievery*. That is, the second base allomorph of such nouns often occurs in other secondary formations. For nouns like *man, mouse, woman*, and so on, the secondary formations employ the base without modification, as in *manly, mousey, womanish*. Even when there is modification of the base as in *mouser, teething*, the form of the base which appears is different from that which appears in the plural of the noun. For these distributional reasons, then, forms like *men* and *women* will not be described as allomorphs of the base before a zero allomorph of the plural.

A second possibility of analysis is also to be rejected. The vowel change of these forms is sometimes described as a "replacive," but in English, all morphemes except those which are occurring in zero allomorphic shape consist of one or more observable phonemes, and it is cumbersome at best to equate a process such as replacement with an overt phoneme sequence. To describe *foot : feet* as containing a replacement of /u/ by /iy/ is also somewhat uneconomical, since we are then forced to say that *goose : geese* contains a different replacement, that of /uw/ by /iy/.

The analysis here adopted is therefore of a third type, one which has already been briefly suggested. The vowel of *men* will be stated to be a suffix, but one which has the property of occurring in nonsequential order, since it always replaces the stressed vowel (or vowel nucleus) of the base. Such nonsequential suffixes are extreme examples of the kind of overlap which is only partial in such a form as *division*, where we have seen that the /–ž–/ belongs to both the base and the postbase. This type of analysis will be employed again in describing the forms of verbs, where it is ᴗven more useful than it is in nouns. In nouns, the assumption that the vowel of *men* is a form of the number suffix has another minor structural advantage. It was stated above that the number suffix always occurs in first position, the case suffix in second. The vocalic suffixes preserve this order, since they occur actually within the borders of the base itself. A further generality is that in nouns, whenever there is a second base allomorph, it occurs only with the number suffix, as with *child : children : children's*. Again, the vocalic suffixes preserve this characteristic. Strictly analyzed, *men* contains a second allomorph of the base, which consists of the consonantal framework alone. This allomorph appears only with the suffix {–e–}, in *men : men's*, which is then parallel to *children : children's*.[1]

If we now turn to the variant shapes of the case and number suffixes, we find that some of them are capable of orderly statement. For the case suffix and the form of the number suffix which is homonymous with it, three regularly distributed allomorphs appear, as in *dog's* {–z}, *cat's* {–s}, and *horse's* {–iz}. The first variety occurs after all voiced phonemes except /z ž j/; the second after all voiceless phonemes except /s š c/; and the third after /z ž j/ and /s š c/, that is, after the sibilants and the two affricated stops. There are also suffixes of the same shape in pronouns *(yours, its)* and verbs *(he plays, he drinks, he rises)* which have the same distribution in terms of preceding segmental phonemes. There is no further variation in the case suffix, except the occurrence of a zero allomorph. We have seen that this occurs regularly after the homonymous number suffix;[2] it also occurs, particularly with proper names, after bases which end in a sibilant or affricate, as in *Mr. Jones' house*.

The number suffix is far more complex. There are, first, occasional rather traditional occurrences of {–s} where the normal distribution would give {–z}, as in *dice, pence*. There are irregular sequential suffixes, such as the {–in} of *oxen, children, brethren*; the {–ə} of *phenomena, curricula*; the {–iy} varying with {–ay} in both *alumni* and *alumnae*; and the four non-sequential suffixes {–iy–}, in *goose, foot, tooth*, {–ay–}, in *mouse, louse*, {–e–}, in *man*, and {–i–}, in *woman*. Nearly all these suffixes occur with a second

---

[1] It would be quite possible to analyze this {–e–} as an infix. We have not done so on account of the overwhelmingly suffixational character of English inflection, so that it is structurally simpler to define all inflectional morphemes in nouns and verbs as suffixes, though with provision for exceptions. In a scheme of analysis like that presented here, "infix" is a term reserved for affixes added within the boundaries of a segmental morpheme, without replacement of any material. No instances of infixes thus defined are found in English.

[2] I have been anticipated in this statement by Leonard Bloomfield. See his statement in *Language*, p. 223, that a form such as *actresses'* contains a zero form of the case suffix.

base allomorph, as in *children*. They also frequently have a different stress morpheme, as with *stigma* which has the base allomorph {stigmə} in the singular, with the stress morpheme {ˊ ˇ}, and a second base allomorph {stigmat-} with the stress morpheme {ˇ ˊ} before the number suffix {-ə}. We have also seen, in *sheep*, that there is a zero allomorph of the number suffix. Irregularities of the base are sometimes associated with this allomorph also. Indeed, we have become so accustomed to preserving the foreign plural—if there is one—of a borrowed noun, that we sometimes use forms quite out of accord with normal structure. Such a noun is *jinni*, "Islamic supernatural being," for which dictionaries give a singular /jíniy/ and a plural *jinn* /jín/. For anyone who follows this rather puristic recommendation, *jinn* must be analyzed as a second base allomorph with loss of /-iy/ before a number suffix in zero. When it is remembered that /-iy/ is normally an allomorph of the plural suffix, the pair *jinni : jinn* seems strange indeed.

I have made no effort to collect all the variants of the suffixes, and of bases before them, since such a list would assume the proportions of a small dictionary.[3] Some statements can be made, however, about the morphemic status of the dozen or more varieties. There is no doubt that the case suffix is a morpheme contrasting with its absence and with the number suffix. That is, all four noun forms contrast with one another, as in "This is a picture of the child," "This is a picture of the child's," "This is a picture of the children," and "This is a picture of the children's." For the case suffix, it is probable that the zero forms which appear in *the actress' studio* or the rarer *mathematics' great advance* are explainable as controlled variants, that is allomorphs of a single case-suffix morpheme. The first form is controlled by the following consonant, the second by the fact that *mathematics* ends in a postbase (not the number suffix, since we say *mathematics is a science*) which does not take any further suffixation. In forms like *Mr. Jones'* or *Mr. Jones's*, the variation is controlled by differing styles.

The variants of the number suffix could certainly be grouped into relatively few morphemes. Most of the time a given base, like *child*, selects a given form of the suffix, so that the {-in} of *children* is here in complementary distribution with the {-z} of *boys*. But not all variation can be so explained. Thus, variants such as "All men are brothers" and "All men are brethren" can occur even in the same kind of style. The plural suffix must then be described as a family of morphs, all having the same paradigmatic distribution, but containing more than one morpheme.

The morphemic status of the noun suffixes having been described,

---

[3] A readily available list of variants is to be found in *Webster's New International Dictionary*, 2nd ed., pp. 1895–97. Unfortunately the list is based, at least in part, on spelling.

meanings for them can be rather quickly given. The number suffix occurs with all such forms as *two boys*, *three boys* whose meaning is indicated by the traditional name "plural." The case suffix is often called possessive, but the name does not fit all occurrences of the form. *John's enemy* is not the same kind of possession that is found in *John's hat*. The name "genitive" has the advantage of being merely arbitrary, since we do not stop to etymologize it. Yet it would be possible to find a more indicative name. All instances of the case suffix occur either when the noun with suffix is followed by another noun which is the head of the phrase or when such a second noun can be readily added, as when we expand "This is John's" to "This is John's house." This relationship, noun with case suffix preceding second noun, is one of those that constitute modification in English. As will be shown later, such modifying nouns belong to the fifth order group of modifiers, a general name for which is "determinatives."[4]

Early in our description of noun inflection, we made the statement that the several varieties of it could be reduced to a consistent type of structure. We can now proceed to demonstrate that statement by a series of diagrams, first for the general type, and then in more detail for the various inflectional classes. The general type is as follows:

	POSITION 1	POSITION 2
1. base	——	——
2. base	——	determinative suffix
3. base	plural suffix	——
4. base	plural suffix	determinative suffix

The general type found here, where each suffix is in a fixed position and each suffix contrasts only with its absence, is different from that found in verbs. There only one suffix can occur at a time, and each suffix therefore contrasts with all others and with the absence of all suffixes. The noun paradigm is reminiscent of paradigm formation in language structures which have been called agglutinating. In Tonkawa, for instance, there are nine positions following the base, in each of which only one suffix can occur, the suffix contrasting therefore only with its absence. The English noun paradigm is no more than a rudimentary development of positional inflection, and the nature of the inflectional structure has been obscured by the frequency of forms like *boys'*, where the second suffix is a zero allomorph. Yet, so long as we still have forms like *oxen's*, the noun paradigm will remain of the positional type.

---

[4] Other members of the fifth order group are articles. The name "determinative" has recently been used by Donald J. Lloyd and Harry R. Warfel, *American English in Its Cultural Setting*, Knopf, New York, 1956, p. 111. They prefer the slightly variant form "determiner."

In describing the classes in detail, we shall introduce morphemic symbols which have been somewhat generalized. The base will be written BASE or BASE-2 when there is allomorphic variation. The number and case suffix will both be written {-z} when they are homonymous, but the number suffix will be written {X} when it is distinct. The symbol {ø} indicates a zero allomorph of either suffix and is not to be confused with absence of a suffix, which is shown by a dash: ——.

CLASS I, NUMBER SUFFIX {X}

		POSITION 1	POSITION 2	EXAMPLES
1.	BASE	——	——	*ox, man*
2.	BASE	——	{-z}	*ox's, man's*
3.	BASE	{X}	——	*oxen, men* {m–n}
	or BASE-2			plus {-e-}
4.	BASE	{X}	{-z}	*oxen's, men's*
	or BASE-2			{m–n} plus
				{-e-} plus {-z}

CLASS II, NUMBER SUFFIX {-z}

		POSITION 1	POSITION 2	EXAMPLES
1.	BASE	——	——	*boy, wife*
2.	BASE	——	{-z}	*boy's, wife's*
3.	BASE	{-z}	——	*boys, wives* {wayv}
	or BASE-2			plus {-z}
4.	BASE	{-z}	{ø}	*boys', wives'*
	or BASE-2			{wayv} plus
				{-z} plus {ø}

CLASS III, NUMBER SUFFIX {ø}

		POSITION 1	POSITION 2	EXAMPLES
1.	BASE	——	——	*sheep, jinni*
2.	BASE	——	{-z}	*sheep's, jinni's*
3.	BASE	{ø}	——	*sheep, jinn*
	or BASE-2			(the latter is
				BASE-2)
4.	BASE	{ø}	{-z}	*sheep's, jinn's*
	or BASE-2			{šiyp} plus {ø}
				plus {-z}; and
				{jin} plus {ø}
				plus {-z}

The statement here given is a structural, not a historical, analysis. Thus, for instance, it has been said that form 4 of such nouns as *boys'* contains a zero allomorph of the determinative suffix in second position. The statement does not mean that this zero allomorph developed historically from a form which once had two suffixes, one of which was dropped. In point of fact, the historical development was quite different. The forms with a nonhomonymous number suffix added the modifying suffix for form 4, thus creating, so to speak, the zero in form 4 of *boys'*. Structural statements are never to be read as historical, and new structural relations can come about in more than one way.

2. Pronouns

The paradigmatic class most like nouns are the pronouns. The class is small, and indeed most members of it fall within the one subgroup which is fully inflected, the personal pronouns. We can consequently begin with that group. The forms are:

	I	II	III	IV	V	VI	VII
1.	*I*	*we*	*you*	*he*	*she*	*it*	*they*
2.	*me*	*us*	*you*	*him*	*her*	*it*	*them*
3.	*my*	*our*	*your*	*his*	*her*	*its*	*their*
4.	*mine*	*ours*	*yours*	*his*	*hers*	——	*theirs*

At first sight, the forms seem to be almost without system, yet some analysis is possible. We shall present first a relatively practical analysis, which stays fairly close to the forms as they actually appear.

A first assumption is that there are four distinctions in each set, though only sets I, II, and VII present all four forms. The others will be assumed to have reduced these distinctions by homonymity, though in differing ways. Set VI, however, lacks one form, that which would be found in such a sentence as the very rare "This book is *its*." Form 1 in all seven sets can be assumed to be unmarked, though it may be pointed out that all these first forms have a partial similarity, in that all except *it* end in a semivowel, /w/ after /u/, /y/ elsewhere. A semivowel is not to be expected after the consonant /t/. We shall make no use of these similarities in this first type of analysis. Sets I, II, and V present a second form in the second line of examples, and this form may be suppletive as in set II, that is to say, may show no segmental phoneme in common with form 1. The other sets, III, IV, VI, and VII, employ the same bases throughout, but make distinctions by means of suffixes.

If we then reduce our list of forms to those characterized by suffixes only, we have:

	III	IV	VI	VII
2.	you	him	it	them
3.	your	his	its	their
4.	yours	his	——	theirs

These endings can be quickly normalized, giving these morphemic norms: for form 2, {–m} (it cannot be the zero which appears in III and VI, since to normalize as zero would be to destroy one of the four distinctions); for form 3, {–r}; and for form 4, {–rz}. The presence of any one of these suffixes is incompatible with a final semivowel in the preceding base, and there is therefore a full set of automatic base allomorphs. If we look at the suffixes, however, we can see that two differing processes occur. One we can call syncretion, which we can illustrate by the forms *you* and *it*, both of which have, not the expected {–m}, but the suffixless construction of form 1. The second we can call allomorphic development, which we can illustrate by the form 3 of VI, *its*. In this form the morphemic norm is replaced by a form which is not itself a morphemic norm and which is therefore an allomorph of that norm.[5]

At this point, one further analytic possibility emerges. It is possible to analyze the fourth form, whose morphemic norm has been stated to be {–rz}, into two suffixes, {–r–z}. Even in a practical analysis there is some advantage in doing so, since as we shall see later, there is good syntactic evidence for considering this suffix a separate form and one not to be identified with the determinative ending of nouns.

We now turn our attention to the forms which employ a variant base in form 2. The employment of a second base is not incompatible with the employment of a suffix as well, since set V has forms 2 and 3 as *her*, with a second base and the suffix which is the morphemic norm for form 3. It follows that *us* and *me* are instances of zero allomorphs of the suffixes after the second bases. *Our* and *ours* are then seen to be allomorphs of the second base before the suffixes of forms 3 and 4. *My* presents a problem. It is not in suppletive relation with *me*, since it shows two phonemes, /m–/ and /–y/, in common with it. Yet the form makes the same distinction which is elsewhere made by the addition of the suffix /–r/. The /–a–/ which distinguishes *my* from *me* could be identified as an allomorph of {–r} only at the expense of a complicated statement of allomorphs and their order of occurrence. It will therefore be assumed, in this practical type of analysis, that *my* represents the type of combination of two morphs where it is not possible to

---

[5] For a fuller discussion of these two processes and examples of their use in paradigmatic analysis of a more complex sort, see Appendix B, "Latin."

analyze the result into its components. Such combinations, as said before, have been called by Hockett "portmanteau morphs."[6] Our statement for this form would then read "{miy} plus {-r} equals {may}"; that is, a statement of the combination by merely listing the resultant form. *Mine* can then be analyzed by cutting it into the portmanteau {may} plus an allomorph of final {-z}.

This process of analysis gives us a picture of the personal pronoun inflection which looks like this:

SET I

1. *I*   {ay} BASE-1, without suffix
2. *me*   {miy} BASE-2, with zero allomorph of {-m}
3. *my*   {may} portmanteau, consisting of BASE-2 plus {-r}
4. *mine* {may-n} portmanteau as above, plus allomorph of {-z}

SET II

1. *we*   {wiy} BASE-1, without suffix
2. *us*   {əs} BASE-2, with zero allomorph of {-m}
3. *our*   {aw-r} allomorph of BASE-2, with morphemic norm of suffix
4. *ours* {aw-r-z} allomorph of BASE-2, with morphemic norms of suffixes

SET III

1. *you*   {yuw} BASE-1, without suffix
2. *you*   {yuw} BASE-1, with loss of suffix and loss of distinction
3. *your* {yu-r} allomorph of BASE-1, with morphemic norm of suffix
4. *yours* {yu-r-z} allomorph of BASE-1, with morphemic norms of suffixes

SET IV

1. *he*   {hiy} BASE-1, without suffix
2. *him*   {hi-m} allomorph of BASE-1, with morphemic norm of suffix
3. *his*   {hi-z} allomorph of BASE-1, with syncretistic suffix identical with the {-z} of form 4
4. *his*   {hi-z} allomorph of BASE-1, with zero allomorph of {-r-} and morphemic norm of second suffix

SET V

1. *she*   {šiy} BASE-1, without suffix
2. *her*   {hə-r} BASE-2, with syncretistic suffix identical with that of form 3
3. *her*   {hə-r} BASE-2, with morphemic norm of suffix
4. *hers* {hə-r-z} BASE-2, with morphemic norms of suffixes

---

[6] Charles F. Hockett, "Problems of Morphemic Analysis," *Language*, XXIII, 1947, pp. 321–43. The article should be consulted entire, particularly for the analysis of pronouns, which differs from that presented here.

SET VI

1. *it*   {it} BASE-1, without suffix
2. *it*   {it} BASE-1, with loss of suffix and loss of distinction
3. *its*   {it–s} BASE-1, with syncretistic suffix, an allomorph of the second
    suffix of form 4
4. —

SET VII

1. *they*   {ðey} BASE-1, without suffix
2. *them*   {ðe–m} allomorph of BASE-1, with norm of suffix
3. *their*   {ðe–r} allomorph of BASE-1, with norm of suffix
4. *theirs*   {ðe–r–z} allomorph of BASE-1, with norms of suffixes

The analysis here given is pressed as far as would be useful if we were considering these personal pronouns alone, and even this analysis is carried further than the needs of a teacher of English as a second language, who would find it far easier simply to tell his students to learn the forms. Something, however, has been accomplished from the point of view of the analyst, since the system has been shown to be one containing four distinctions, and the suffixes have been arrived at by consistent cutting and statement. The analysis has given us, also, several terms for concepts which will prove useful later. The crucial point, at which this analysis left off, was the point at which the relation between morphs was one of suppletion, though one instance of a portmanteau not involving suppletion is included in the analysis.

It is possible to analyze the suppletive forms only at the expense of greater complication in description of pronoun forms, and therefore any analysis which considers these forms as an isolated class stops at this point. It can be given as a general principle of analysis that under these conditions, where suppletion is met, analysis should stop. If on the other hand, there is another class of forms which can be clarified by carrying analysis further, then we are forced to carry analysis as far as we can. In general, incomplete analysis is practical in that it produces less abstraction and complication, and thus throws more immediate light on the set of forms under scrutiny. These facts should not, however, be taken as invalidating more complete analysis when something can be gained by it, just as the possibility of complete analysis should not be taken as invalidating practical analysis for its own purposes.

In English there is a class of forms, characterized by initial variation, which have proved difficult to define. They are represented by forms like:

here	*there*	*where*
hence	*thence*	*whence*
	then	*when*

They are a series characterized by partially systematic recurrence of initials in /h–/, /ð–/, and /hw–/. They have syntactic similarities to pronouns and have stress characteristics which they also share with pronouns. But for all that, they have most often been called adverbs. It would therefore be desirable to find out if they possess formal characteristics sufficiently clear to justify grouping them with pronouns. The existence of this doubtful class of forms constitutes justification for pushing the analysis of personal pronouns further, in the hope that analysis will reveal structural characteristics which throw light on the *here, there, where* group.

Our analysis of pronoun suffixes was relatively complete, but aside from the setting up of some allomorphs, the pronominal bases have been left largely unanalyzed. We are left with a series of bases for form 1 as follows:

{ay}   {wiy}   {yuw}   {hiy}   {šiy}   {it}   {ðey}

There is certainly a frequently recurring element, a final /–y/. We have seen, also, that the occurrence of final /–w/ in /yuw/ can be associated with the preceding /–u–/, giving the possibility of reducing all forms except *it* to combinations of a preceding form and a following /–y/. Without deciding the status of this /–y/ but provisionally cutting it off as a separate morph, we find our form 1 forms are now:

{a–}   {wi–}   {yu–}   {hi–}   {ši–}   {it}   {ðe–}

The element which obviously carries most of the differentiation is the initial consonant, the following vowel being commonest in the recurrent form /–i–/. The form *it*, furthermore, contains the recurrent vowel and a consonant, though, in its order, the form is abnormal by comparison with the others. If we regularize this order and normalize the vowels of *you* and *they*, all forms would then be hypothetically alike in construction, except the first, which lacks a consonant. Yet the second base of this first set contains a consonant, /m–/, which can be pressed into service. As a result we get a set of forms for all pronouns in form 1 consisting of initial consonant, invariant vowel, and final /–y/. In this abstract form of the system, it is clear that the initial consonant carries the person, number, and gender distinctions, the vowel is a base meaning merely "personal pronoun," and the {–y} is a suffix for form 1. The initial consonants are then true paradigmatic affixes and the only instance of inflection by prefixes in English.

We can conclude this complete, nonpractical, and abstract analysis by giving one example of the statements necessary to convert the abstract forms into those actually found. In this example all forms not actually found are marked with an asterisk:

1. *we:*   {w–i–y}
2. *us:*   *{w–i–m}; {–m} after {w–i–} becomes {–s}; *{w–i–} before re-
            sulting {–s} becomes {ə–}, a portmanteau
3. *our:*   *{w–i–r}; before {–r} and {–r–z}, initial consonant and vowel are
            transposed, giving *{i–w–}; initial *{i–} becomes {a–} before
            {–w–}
4. *ours:* *{w–i–r–z} (See rules given for 3.)

One immediate though nonpractical result is that we have now a tool for working out the morphs contained in a form like *us.* It contains {ə–}, which is a portmanteau of {w–i–}, and {–s}, which is an allomorph of {–m}. The same kind of procedure can be applied to all forms in the several sets, giving consistent steps of analysis for all forms whether suppletive or not.

Much more important, we have the criterion for *here, there, where* which we were in search of. All these forms can now be defined as being classifi- able with pronouns, since they are formed by initial consonantal variation. Most of them, however, are pronominals rather than pronouns, since they lack the suffix characteristics of true pronouns. Yet, among them is at least one true pronoun, *who,* which has suffixes in *whose* and *whom.* As with *how,* its initial morph can be defined as an allomorph of {hw–}, reduced to {h–} before any following element containing /–w/. The series {h–}, {ð–}, {hw–}, while a series of morphemes, is not an example of a series of prefixes, since the forms do not belong to a paradigmatic set. These morphemes are rather a set of prebases closely parallel to the elements which appear as true prefixes in the inflection of personal pronouns.

Some observations about history can be made at this point. The analysis of the personal pronouns may seem to be so abstract as to be one which could be made for any similar set from any period of the language. This is not the case. In some idiolects and in some styles, an older pronoun *thee* is still preserved. The existence of this pronoun in any idiolect makes it im- possible to analyze as we have done, since *they* cannot then be normalized without loss of distinction between *thee* and *they.* The loss of *thee* has there- fore had structural effects well beyond the mere loss of an item.

Second, there are still idiolects in which instead of *it* we have *hit,* a form which not only makes the analysis we have given again impossible but has a quite different relationship to the pronominals. In such an idiolect, there is striking parallelism between the series *here, there, where* and the series *hit, that, what.* That is to say, there is crossing between the pronominal and pronoun series in their initial elements. There are syntactic traces of this kind of arrangement in the forms *he* and *who* of Modern Standard Eng- lish, all of which suggest earlier structural arrangements which grouped pronominals and pronouns together, but in different ways from that of current English. These states would well repay study.

The pronominals will be fully described in Chapter 20, Section 1. Here we can stop with merely the fact that we have achieved a means of formal definition. No form class has been more confusingly defined, since the reliance is almost always on semantic characteristics. Thus, no less a scholar than George O. Curme was led to define *others* as a pronoun since it is a substitute.[7] Yet, since it shows all the formal characteristics of a noun, it must belong to that form class rather than to pronouns.

We have not yet examined the morphemic status of the various morphs which appear in pronouns, nor have we written meanings for them. The initial consonants, the only true examples of prefixation in English, are certainly morphemes, since contrasts like *we went : she went* can be found for all of them. Similarly, the base morph {–i–} is a morpheme, since it is the invariant element left after all variations are taken account of. The suffix morphs, however, cannot all be shown to be in contrast with one another. Thus, there seems to be no utterance in normal style which contrasts forms like *I* and *my*, *he* and *his*. Always one form or the other is required by the larger syntactic framework. The suffix morphs, then, form part of a paradigmatic family in which each has status as a structural element in the total set, though not all represent independent morphemes. It is primarily in the belief that the results of paradigmatic analysis result in paradigmatic elements, rather than in morphemes, that the study of pronouns here presented differs from that of Hockett, mentioned above.

Meanings for the suffixes can in some cases be written without much departure from the traditional. Form 1 in all sets is subjectival, the form which selects concording verb forms and which often—though not always—stands before the verb. Form 2 is that which belongs in the complement. The traditional name is objective, and in most instances this will be satisfactory, though we shall return to such terms as object and complement later in taking up the larger utterance units. Form 3 is the determinative case of pronouns, which corresponds exactly to the determinative case of nouns. Form 4, however, is a little more complicated. The forms like *hers, ours, theirs* never occur with a following noun in the same phrase. Further, a form 4 can always be replaced by a form 3 and a noun. A sentence like "This is one of hers" can always be replaced by "This is one of her books." Form 4 is then a phrase substitute. Since it contains the suffix {–r–}, that of the determinative case, it is necessarily the suffix {–z} which is acting more narrowly

---

[7] *Principles and Practice of English Grammar*, Barnes and Noble, New York, 1946, p. 50.

as the specific substitute for the noun member of the replaced phrase. It is therefore necessary to set up this pronominal suffix as {-z}3, the third suffix in this phonemic shape, different from the two which we have already found in nouns.

The prefixes contain rather varying semantic components, so that each will have to be considered separately. The set I prefix, *{m-}, contains two components: speaker and exclusiveness. The latter term means that no other persons are included with the speaker. The contrasting set II prefix, *{w-}, contains speaker and inclusiveness, that is, others are included with the speaker. Set III, {y-}, contains person addressed, with no distinction as to inclusiveness or exclusiveness. Sets IV, V, and VI all contain three components: the person neither the speaker nor person addressed, gender, and exclusiveness. The remaining set, VII, contains two components: (1) neither the person addressed nor the speaker and (2) inclusiveness, in that others are included with the "third person" individual. For all these sets, the traditional names are convenient enough. They are, in order, first person singular, first person plural, second person, third person singular (with three genders), and third person plural.

3. Verbs

Pronouns are a small class, but the class of verbs is not only the most complex of English inflected groups, it is also large and divided into several large subgroups. Three of the five forms for the verb *drink* represent a good starting point for discussion:

1. I, you, we, they *drink*

                3. I, you, we, they, he, she, it *drank*

2. He, she, it *drinks*

The suffix which appears in form 2 is again a sibilant with the same three shapes which we have met before: {-z}, {-s}, and {-iz}. This is the fourth such suffix we have met, and when it is necessary for clarity, it will be numbered {-z}4. It is distributed like the other similar suffixes, in accord with the preceding phonemes, that is, {-z} after all voiced phonemes except sibilants and affricates, {-s} after all voiceless phonemes except sibilants and affricates, {-iz} after sibilants and affricates. Form 3, it is apparent, covers the range of forms 1 and 2 together; that is, there is no differentiation for the *he, she,* and *it* pronouns. For that reason, in the tabulations given later, form 3 will be aligned so as to be on a line halfway between the line on which form 1 falls and that on which form 2 falls. Form 3 contains a vowel change, which will again be treated as a vocalic suffix occurring in nonsequential order.

Forms 1 and 2 are traditionally called present, though they are not very closely associated with present time. Often, as in "He drinks," the action is habitual—past, present, and presumably future as well. Often enough it is future, as in "The train leaves in fifteen minutes." There are also narrative uses in which this form occurs with lexical items indicating past time, as "Yesterday, when I get up, I notice this fellow hanging around." These uses with past-time indication have been traditionally called by the rather inaccurate name "historical present." Essentially all uses of this form are merely unmarked, just as the singular of nouns is an unmarked number. We shall call forms 1 and 2 the non-past, and describe the so-called historical present as a use of the unmarked non-past believed to be a stylistic variant.

Form 2 is traditionally called the third person singular, a name which designates the form well enough, but in a rather wasteful fashion, since it designates the form by the intersection of two categories and therefore implies that there are six forms for the non-past verb, even though five of them are exactly alike. A single component can be found for this $\{-z\}4$ suffix, however. The sentences where it is required can be illustrated by:

John stands on the corner.
Mary stands on the corner.
The house stands on the corner.

In each of these sentences, the noun can be replaced by one of the gender pronouns, *he, she,* or *it.* If the sentence is "John and Mary stand on the corner," it is true that we can use the two gender pronouns *he* and *she,* but we can also use the genderless *they.* The suffix $\{-z\}4$ is required, then, whenever the actor is *he, she, it,* or any form capable of being replaced by one of these alone. The suffix correlates with a gender-bearing subject and can therefore be called the gender form.

If we take up verbs such as *drink* or *drive,* we find that they have two more forms. Form 4 is *drinking, driving,* and form 5 is *drunk, driven.* These forms are usually spoken of as present and past participles, respectively. If the name "present" is replaced by "non-past," the designations are acceptable, though it is not usual to show any reason for the names. The justification for assuming a non-past and past component in these forms is that it is possible to draw up an analogical statement: "the snow *drives*" is to "the snow *drove*" as "the *driving* snow" is to "the *driven* snow." The two forms are rather unlike in distribution otherwise, however. Both function as modifiers, as in *a driving lesson* and *a badly driven car,* but form 4 also occurs in sentences like *he likes driving,* where form 5 cannot occur. That is, form 4 has syntactic affinities with both adjectives and nouns, form 5 only with adjectives. Again, if the phrases *the driving snow* and *the driven snow* are expanded so as to express the agent of the action, the phrases are developed differently. One becomes *the wind is driving the snow*, and the other *the snow is driven by the wind*. The differing form for these two expansions is often expressed by calling form 4 active and form 5 passive. The name "participle" applied to both indicates the syntactic affinities of both forms with adjectives.

With this introduction, we can now set up our first class of normal verbs. The symbolization of the suffixes is morphemic, even when phonemes are employed in them. Thus, $\{-z\}$ indicates any one of the normal shapes of the gender suffix; $\{-V-^1\}$, the nonsequential vowel suffix added to the base in form 3; and $\{-V-^2\}$ the vowel change in form 5 when this vowel is different from $\{-V-^1\}$:

CLASS I

NON-PAST	PAST
1. BASE ——	
	3. BASE $\{-V-^1\}$
2. BASE $\{-z\}$	
4. BASE $\{-iŋ\}$	5. BASE $\{-V-^2\}$

For all of this class $\{-V-^1\}$ is /-æ-/, and $\{-V-^2\}$ is /-ə-/. Thus the five forms for *drink* are:

1. *drink* 2. *drinks* 3. *drank* 4. *drinking* 5. *drunk*

Membership in this class consists of *begin, drink, ring, shrink, sing, spring, stink, swim*. In this list and those which follow, no attempt is made to be exhaustive, and no systematic account will be taken of variations such as that of *stink*, which often has a form 3 *stunk*. The occasional variations which appear are illustrative only, and the list is meant as an extended sketch rather than a complete reference list.

Class II verbs are similar to those of class I in that these two are the only classes which regularly differentiate all five forms. Class II, however, often has a sequential suffix for form 5. The allomorphs of this suffix are $\{-in\}$ and $\{-n\}$, the latter occurring after bases ending in a vowel, semivowel, or /-r/. The nonsequential form 5 suffix consists of both vowel change and the sequential element just described. This form of the suffix can be written $\{-V-\cdots-in\}$. Examples of the two types of form 5 are *know : known* and *break : broken*. More narrowly classified, $\{-V-\cdots-in\}$ may be either $\{-V-^1\cdots-in\}$ or $\{-V-^2\cdots-in\}$, so that there are three forms of the suffix: $\{-in\}$ in *known*; $\{-V-^1\cdots-in\}$ in *break, broke, broken*; and $\{-V-^2\cdots-in\}$ in *drive, drove, driven*. The first subclass is that with $\{-in\}$:

CLASS II, 1

NON-PAST		PAST	
1. BASE	——		
		3. BASE	$\{-V-^1\}$
2. BASE	$\{-z\}$		
4. BASE	$\{-iŋ\}$	5. BASE	$\{-in\}$

With $\{-V-^1\}$ as /–uw/, there are six verbs: *blow, grow, know, throw, draw,* and *slay*. They can be illustrated by *know*:

1. *know* 2. *knows* 3. *knew* 4. *knowing* 5. *known*

Take and *shake* have $\{-V-^1\}$ as /–u–/; and *bid* ("command") and *forbid* have $\{-V-^1\}$ as /–æ–/. Two unique verbs are *fall* and *see*, where $\{-V-^1\}$ is /–e–/ and /–ɔh/ respectively.

CLASS II, 2

NON-PAST		PAST	
1. BASE	——		
		3. BASE	$\{-V-^1\}$
2. BASE	$\{-z\}$		
4. BASE	$\{-iŋ\}$	5. BASE	$\{-V-^1\cdots-in\}$

The largest group of verbs in this subclass are those which have $\{-V-^1\}$ as /–ow–/, which in turn varies with /–ɔh–/ or /–oh–/ by a regular morphophonemic alternation when it occurs before /–r/. Here belong *break, choose, freeze, speak, steal,* and *weave*; the /–r/ forms are *bear, tear, shear, swear*. Three verbs have $\{-V-^1\}$ as /–i–/: *bite, chide, hide*. The verbs *get, beget, forget* have $\{-V-^1\}$ as /–a–/, and *lie* ("recline") has /–ey/.

CLASS II, 3

NON-PAST		PAST	
1. BASE	——		
		3. BASE	$\{-V-^1\}$
2. BASE	$\{-z\}$		
4. BASE	$\{-iŋ\}$	5. BASE	$\{-V-^2\cdots-in\}$

In this subclass there is a close-knit group for which $\{-V-^1\}$ is /–ow–/ and $\{-V-^2\}$ is /–i–/: *drive, ride, rise, thrive, shrive, smite, strive, write*. A possible further member of the group is *stride*, which is usually defective, lacking form 5. There is, finally, one verb, *fly*, where $\{-V-^1\}$ is /–uw/ and the suffix of form 5 is $\{-own\}$.

The classes which follow, except for the last, which is mixed, all reduce the number of differentiated forms to four or less, having form 3 and form 5 identical. The first of these classes has the same vowel change in forms 3 and 5:

CLASS III

NON-PAST		PAST	
1. BASE	——		
		3. BASE	$\{-V-^1\}$
2. BASE	$\{-z\}$		
4. BASE	$\{-i\eta\}$	5. BASE	$\{-V-^1\}$

In this class the shape of $\{-V-^1\}$ varies widely, there being nine vowels and nuclei which occur for it. The largest group has $/-\vartheta-/$: *cling, sling, spin, swing, win, wring, hang, dig, stick, strike.* The group with nasal consonants among these verbs recalls the nasal consonants of class I, and verbs with nasals not infrequently are given alternate treatment, existing as members of both I and III. A second group all have bases ending in $/-d/$ or $/-t/$ and take $/-e-/$ for $\{-V-^1\}$. These are *bleed, breed, feed, lead, read, speed, hold,* and *meet.* For bases which end in $/-nd/$, there is the group *bind, find, grind,* and *wind,* all with $\{-V-^1\}$ as $/-aw-/$. Two verbs have $/-i-/$, *light* and *slide*; and two have $/-a-/$, *shoot* and *tread.* There are three single verbs, with $/-æ-/$, $/-\text{ɔh}-/$, and $/-ow-/$ respectively. They are *sit, fight,* and *shine.* One verb, *stand,* is unique not only in having $\{-V-^1\}$ as $/-u-/$ but also in having a base allomorph which loses its nasal consonant when $\{-V-^1\}$ occurs.

The fourth class is that to which the great majority of English verbs belong. It is distinguished not only by having a homonymous form 3 and form 5, but by the fact that both of these forms have a suffix containing a dental stop. The suffix has three forms, $\{-d\}$, $\{-t\}$, and $\{-id\}$, and their regular distribution is that $\{-d\}$ occurs after all voiced phonemes except $/-d/$, $\{-t\}$ occurs after all voiceless phonemes except $/-t/$, and $\{-id\}$ occurs after $/d/$ and $/t/$. The suffix also has an irregular form, which consists in the appearance of $\{-t\}$ after a voiced phoneme where $\{-d\}$ would be expected. The regular forms of the suffix will be written morphemically as $\{-d\}$, the commonest form. The irregularly occurring suffix will be written $\{-t\}$. The first subgroup in this class is of those with no irregularities:

CLASS IV, 1

NON-PAST		PAST	
1. BASE	——		
		3. BASE	$\{-d\}$
2. BASE	$\{-z\}$		
4. BASE	$\{-i\eta\}$	5. BASE	$\{-d\}$

The class is very large and is therefore the one whose membership need not be listed. Unless a verb is stated to belong to another class or subclass, it can be assumed to belong here. It is unnecessary to do more than illustrate the three regular forms of the suffix. Examples of {-d} are *play, pin, fear*; examples of {-t} are *miss, scratch, bake*; and of {-id} are *load, note*.

The second subclass has a regular suffix but allomorphic variation of the base. In the writing of these forms, C indicates any consonant or consonant cluster:

CLASS IV, 2

NON-PAST		PAST	
1. BASE	——		
		3. BASE-ALLOMORPH-2	{-d}
2. BASE	{-z}		
4. BASE	{-iŋ}	5. BASE-ALLOMORPH-2	{-d}

Creep, keep, leap, sleep, sweep, and *weep* all have their second base allomorph in {Cep-}. *Leave, cleave, reave,* and *bereave,* have {Cef-}; and *sell, tell* have {Cowl-}. The rest are single verbs. *Make* has {mey-}; *clothe* has {klæ-}; *hear* has {hər-}; *lose* has {lɔs-} (or {lɔhs-}); and *flee* has {fle-}. The final verb in the subclass is *say,* which has a second allomorph, {se-}, and is unique in that this allomorph appears in form 2 as well as in 3 and 5.

The next subclass is very small, only one verb belonging to it without alternate forms made according to class IV, 1. The irregularity in this subclass consists solely in having the dental suffix in the irregular allomorph {-t} where {-d} would be expected.

CLASS IV, 3

NON-PAST		PAST	
1. BASE	——		
		3. BASE	{-t}
2. BASE	{-z}		
4. BASE	{-iŋ}	5. BASE	{-t}

The only verb which is always a member of this subclass is *dwell,* forms 3 and 5 of which are /dwélt/; but *burn, smell, spill, spoil,* and, in substandard speech, *kill* are sometimes treated in this way. Usually, however, there is some difference in distribution between the forms with {-t} and {-d}. Thus, for instance, we usually say "spilt milk," but "I spilled the milk."

The remaining subclass has both the irregular {–t} suffix and allomorphic variation of the base:

CLASS IV, 4

NON-PAST		PAST	
1. BASE	——		
		3. BASE-ALLOMORPH-2	{–t}
2. BASE	{–z}		
4. BASE	{–iŋ}	5. BASE-ALLOMORPH-2	{–t}

Bring, beseech, buy, catch, seek, think, teach have the second base allomorph in {Cɔh–}. *Bend, lend, rend, send, spend, build,* and *gird* have a second allomorph which loses the final /–d/. *Deal, dream, feel, kneel, lean,* and *mean* have the second allomorph in {CeC–}, though *dream* and *lean* also have forms in accord with IV, 1.

The fifth class are those verbs which have a zero allomorph of the suffix in forms 3 and 5. In consequence, these verbs differentiate only three forms. All of them have bases which end in /–d/ or /–t/. Those forms which are marked with a double dagger (‡) also have inflection according to IV, 1.

CLASS V

NON-PAST		PAST	
1. BASE	——		
		3. BASE	{–ø}
2. BASE	{–z}		
4. BASE	{–iŋ}	5. BASE	{–ø}

The members of this class are *bet, bid* ("make an offer"), *outbid, overbid, burst, cast, cost, cut, hit, hurt, knit‡, let, put, quit‡, rid, set, shed, shred‡, spread, shut, slit‡, split‡, sweat‡, thrust, wed‡, wet‡, whet‡.*

Three verbs can be placed in this class as irregular members, having a zero in only one of the two forms. *Come* has {–V–¹} as /–ey–/ in form 3 and zero in form 5. *Run* has {–V–¹} as /–æ–/ in form 3 and zero in form 5. *Beat* has zero in form 3 but {–in} in form 5.

In the five classes which have been described, there has been a regular correlation in suffix types. That is, a verb which has a dental suffix in form 5 also has it in form 3. Similarly, a verb which has {–in} or any of its variants in form 5 has {–V–¹} in form 3. There are a few verbs which break this correlation in suffixes of forms 3 and 5, though for all of them there are alternate forms which are regular. These verbs constitute a sixth, mixed, class:

CLASS VI, 1

NON-PAST		PAST	
1. BASE	——		
		3. BASE	{-d}
2. BASE	{-z}		
4. BASE	{-iŋ}	5. BASE	{-d} or {-in}

The members of this subclass are *hew, prove, show, sew,* and *sow.* For most of them there is some difference in the distribution of the alternates for form 5, as in "hewn stone," but "He has hewed to the line."

CLASS VI, 2

NON-PAST		PAST	
1. BASE	——		
		3. BASE	{-d} or {-V-¹}
2. BASE	{-z}		
4. BASE	{-iŋ}	5. BASE	{-d}

In this subclass *wake, awake, dive* have {-V-¹} as /-ow-/; and *crow* has {-V-¹} as /-uw/. The variation between *dived* and *dove* is dialectal, and the form with vowel change is often frowned on.

These six classes cover the inflectional characteristics of normal verbs, except for the highly irregular *go,* which requires separate description. *Go* has a first base allomorph, {gow}, which appears in forms 1, 2, and 4, all of which are normal. It has a second base allomorph, {wen-}, which appears in form 3 alone with the irregular suffix {-t}. There is, last, a third base allomorph which appears only in form 5, {gɔh-} or {ga-}, giving *gone* /gɔ́hn/. A paradigm of this sort, in which base allomorphs share no segmental phonemes in common, is of the type that has been called suppletive. There is thus a strong suggestion that these several forms do not belong together in the same paradigm, though it is traditional to group them thus. The justification for grouping the forms in a single paradigm is that distributionally *go : went* covers the same range as *come : came,* as in "John goes to school every day," "John went to school yesterday"; and "John comes to school every day," "John came to school yesterday." That is, the two base allomorphs complement each other, so as to make up a single distributional unity. Historically, the situation is different, since *went* was once the form 3 of the verb *wend. Wend,* however, has now acquired a new form 3, *wended.*

The verbs not yet described fall into a single group, though one with several subclasses. These are the verbs which can form a negative by means of {-nt} or {-int}. As stated in Chapter 8, Section 1, these negative forms are phonologically minimal words, which are allophrases, varying with forms like /kǽn + nát/, the full phrase form. On the phonological level, then, the negative forms will be treated as words, and the negative element as a suffix. The forms with a negative suffix vary considerably in use of the syllabic or nonsyllabic allomorph. Thus, *aren't* can appear as either one or two syllables. The two forms {–nt} and {–int} would seem to be linguistically free variants, though presumably the variation is stylistically explainable. Most of the distribution of these allomorphs is predictable, however, since the nonsyllabic form occurs regularly after vowels and semivowels. The syllabic form occurs regularly after consonants. Variation is possible after /–r/ and after the /–y/ of *may*.

These allophrases were spoken of as phonologically minimal words, and the negative element as a suffix. It might have been possible to describe the negative element as a postbase, which we have not done. It is preferable to assign it the status of a suffix, since we have found several instances of double suffixation, while instances of a postbase added after a suffix are all rare and special.

Class VII then are the negatively inflected verbs. They can be further classified on the basis of their inflection when the negative suffix is absent. The first group are those which have a full inflection, that is to say, have a non-negative set of forms which accord with some one of the classes of normal verbs already described. It will be unnecessary to draw up schemes for these verbs, since they will be described in detail and with reference to the inflectional class.

CLASS VII, 1

a. Two verbs in this group are inflected like regular verbs of class IV, 1 in their non-negative forms. They are *dare* and *need*, the forms for which are:

1. *dare, need*	4. *daring, needing*
2. *dares, needs*	5. *dared, needed*
3. *dared, needed*	

These verbs have negatives for forms 1 and 2, with loss of {–z} before the negative suffix, so that forms 1 and 2 are alike: *daren't* /dérint/, *needn't* /níydint/.

b. *Have* is a verb of Class IV, 2, that is to say, it has a regular suffix, but an irregular base allomorph. The second allomorph of the base is {hæ–}, giving the following forms:

1. *have* /hǽv/ 2. *has* /hǽz/ 3. *had* /hǽd/ 4. *having* /hǽviŋ/ 5. *had* /hǽd/

It is to be noted that the second allomorph appears before {–z} as well as in the forms with dental suffix. In this, *have* is like *say*, above, and *do*, below. The negatives are regular:

    1. *haven't* /hǽvint/   2. *hasn't* /hǽzint/   3. *hadn't* /hǽdint/

c. *Do* is a verb of class VI, that is, it has form 3 with {-d}, form 5 with {-n}. In addition, its base allomorphs are complex, BASE-1 is {duw}, BASE-2 is {də-}, BASE-3 is {di-}, and BASE-4 is {dow-}. The forms are then as follows:

    1. *do* (with BASE-1) /dúw/   4. *doing* (with BASE-1) /dúwiŋ/
    2. *does* (with BASE-2) /dɔ́z/   5. *done* (with BASE-2) /dɔ́n/
    3. *did* (with BASE-3) /díd/

The negatives are regular except for form 1, which employs BASE-4. They are:

    1. *don't* /dównt/   2. *doesn't* /dɔ́zint/   3. *didn't* /dídint/

Besides these, form 2 occurs in some speech with a zero allomorph of the gender suffix, *he don't*. The form has been violently objected to, in spite of the analogy of *he daren't* and *he needn't*.

CLASS VII, 2

These are defective verbs, lacking forms 4 and 5, and with a zero allomorph of the suffix in form 2. On the basis of their inflection in form 3, they could be described as defective verbs of class IV. The members of the class are *can, may, shall,* and *will*. *Can* has three base allomorphs: BASE-1 is *can* {kæn} (varying with {kæhn} and {kehn} dialectally); BASE-2 is {ku-}; and BASE-3 is {kæ-} (varying dialectally with {ka-}, {keh-}, and {kah-}). The forms are:

    1. *can* (with BASE-1)
    2. *can* (with BASE-1 and zero allomorph of the suffix)
    3. *could* (with BASE-2, /kúd/)

In the case of this form, which is here called form 3 of *can*, and that of the corresponding forms of *shall, will, may,* there are syntactic reasons for doubting that they are past tenses. A clear instance of occurrence without a component of past time is the childhood rhyme "wish I *may*, wish I *might*, have the wish I wish tonight." Formally, however, all these forms contain a final phoneme easily identifiable with {d} or one of its allomorphs. Further, there are still a good many situations in which the forms in question show parallelism with normal past forms. Thus in my speech a normal form is "Yesterday John ate all he *could*," and *can* would be impossible. The non-past is similarly the normal form in "Every day John eats all he *can*." In this particular pair of sentence frames, only *should* occurs unexpectedly, appearing as *should* in both. All these uses of this group of form 3 verbs seem to represent an extension of the uses of normal verbs with {d} or its equivalent in situations like "If he *came* tomorrow . . ." In normal verbs such uses show a component of unreality, associated with *if*. In view of the formal similarity of these verb forms with those containing a form 3 suffix and in view of the close semantic parallelism between all members of this small group, it is simplest to call them all form 3 verbs, each with a corresponding non-past form, as given. In these forms, however, the suffix varies in meaning from that which it has with normal verbs, in that here the component of unreality has become generalized.

The negatives of *can* are: 1 and 2, *can't* (with BASE-3 and a zero allomorph of the gender suffix in form 2) /kǽnt/, {kæ} {nt}; the dialectal variants are /kánt/, /káhnt/, etc.

May has only two base allomorphs, {mey} and {may–} which appears in form 3. The forms are:

1. *may* {mey}
2. *may* /méy/ {mey} plus {–ø} (the allomorph of the
     gender suffix)
3. *might* /máyt/ {may} plus {t}

The negatives are: 1 and 2, *mayn't* /méynt/ or /méyint/, both somewhat rare, and often with the syllabic form of the negative suffix, contrary to expectation. Form 2 contains the {–ø–} allomorph of the gender suffix, but form 1 only the allomorph of the base and an allomorph of the negative suffix. Form 3 is *mightn't* /máytint/, {may} plus {t} plus {int}.

Shall has three base allomorphs: BASE-1 {šæl}, BASE-2 {šu–}, BASE-3 {šæ–}. The forms are:

1. *shall* {šæl} (with variants in accord with the stress
     morpheme
2. /šǽl/ {šæl} plus {–ø} for the gender suffix
3. *should* (with BASE-2) /šúd/, {šu} plus {d}

The negatives are: 1 and 2 *shan't* /šǽnt/ with dialectal variation. The form contains BASE-2, and the negative suffix; form 2 also contains {–ø–} for the gender suffix, giving {šæ–} plus {–ø–} plus {–nt}.

Similarly, *will* has base allomorphs with parallel distribution: BASE-1 {wil}, BASE-2 {wu–}, and BASE-3 {wow–}. The forms are:

1. *will* {wil}   2. *will* {wil} plus {–ø}   3. *would* {wu–} plus {–d}

The negatives are: 1 and 2 *won't* /wównt/, where form 2 as usual analyzes into {wow} plus {-ø-} plus {-nt}. Form 3 is *wouldn't* /wúdint/, {wu-} plus {-d-} plus {-nt}.

CLASS VII, 3

Here belong two words, *ought* and *must*, which have a zero allomorph of the gender suffix and which lack forms 3, 4, and 5. They are therefore so little differentiated that they are identified as verbs only by their syntactic characteristics and by the negative suffix. The forms for *ought* are:

1. *ought* {ɔht}   2. *ought* {ɔht} plus {-ø}

Negative 1 and 2 is *oughtn't* /ɔ́htint/.
   Must has:

1. *must* {məst}   2. *must* {məst} plus {-ø}

Negative 1 and 2 is (with a second base allomorph {məs-}) *mustn't* /mə́sint/.

CLASS VII, 4

This class consists solely of the verb *to be*, which as in most languages of the Indo-European family, is the most irregular in the language. Its forms are notably out of line with those of other verbs, making more distinctions than are found anywhere else, and with a large number of irregular and suppletive base allomorphs. The non-negative inflection is as follows (no account is taken of stress and dialect variants):

NON-PAST	PAST
1*a*. *be* /bíy/	
1. *are* /áhr/	3. *were* /wɔ́hr/
1*b*. *am* /ǽm/	
	3*a*. *was* /wáhz/
2. *is* /íz/	
4. *being* /bíyiŋ/	5. *been* /bín/

These forms require considerable analysis to be made intelligible. Forms 1*a*, 1, and 1*b* taken together cover the range of form 1 in a normal verb; in this verb, 1*a* and 1*b* have been split off by distinctions not found elsewhere. Form 1*a* is required after *to*, as in "He wants *to be* good," and when it stands first in subjectless sentences of the type "*Be* good!" Form 1*a* also occurs in sentences like "If he *be* elected . . ." and "I suggest (that) it *be* done." These uses are those which are traditionally called infinitives, imperatives, and subjunctives. The last term is less satisfactory than the other two, and the use of it here is not to be understood as meaning that there is a subjunctive mood in English. There are, rather, occurrences of forms from the normal verb paradigm in special syntactic situations which can be summed up as subjunctive uses. Form 1*b* is for action by the speaker alone, as in "I am talking." Form 1 is what is left of the usual range of form 1, that is, it is used with the pronouns *you*, *we*, and *they*. In the past forms, 3 corresponds to the usual range of a form 3, except that 3*a* has again been split off. *Was* occurs with the pronouns *I*, *he*, *she*, and *it*, and thus corresponds to the combined range of forms 1*b* and 2 in the non-past forms.

One set of forms occurs with the base found in 1*a*, 4, and 5. The occurrence of /bíy/ is usually syntactically controlled, as was indicated above, but some contrasts can be found for it with forms like *is* and *was*. After *if* we can use *be*, *is*, *were*, or *was*, as in "If this be treason . . ." or "If this is treason . . ." We can thus set up {biy} as a base morpheme, occurring in 1*a* without suffix, in 4, and in 5, where it assumes the allomorph {bi–}.

In the other non-past forms, *are* can be equated with the usual suffixless form 1; it is, therefore, the morphemic norm of a second base morpheme. Form 1*b* will, in turn, be analyzed as containing the suffix {–m}, which carries the meaning "action by speaker alone," and a second allomorph of the base morpheme of *are*, namely {æ–}. Form 2 as usual contains the suffix {–z}, but a third allomorph of the same base morpheme, {i–}.

In the past forms, *was* contains the usual non-past gender suffix {–z}, though in an unusual range, since it is used for the pronoun *I* as well as for the gender pronouns. It covers, that is, the combined range of the forms 1*b* and 2 in the non-past forms. Since, however, no other verb differentiates two forms in the past, there is a difficulty in analyzing the forms *were* and *was*. It seems best to meet it by describing *were* as the unmarked base of a third independent morpheme, which carries the meaning of "past being" and is more nearly parallel to the unmarked form of a verb like *love* than to such a marked past form as *loved*. This third base morpheme, then, has its second allomorph {wa–} or {wə–} before the usual {–z} ending.

In its negative forms, the verb *to be* is the same in standard and non-standard speech for forms 3 and 3*a*, which are *weren't* /wə́hrint/, /wə́rint/, or /wə́rnt/; and *wasn't* /wáhzint/, /wázint/, or /wə́zint/. In the non-past forms, standard and nonstandard forms are sharply divided. The standard forms are:

> 1. *aren't* /áhrint/, /árint/, or /árnt/   1*b*. ——   2. *isn't* /ízint/

The most interesting feature of this set is the absence, at least in the United States, of a negative for 1*b*. For this form, there exists only the phrase variant *am not*. British English carries 1 over to 1*b*, giving *aren't*, which is then to be analyzed as the base allomorph 1, followed by a zero of the 1*b* suffix (like the loss of the form 2 suffix in *he needn't*) before the negative.

British speakers can therefore use such negative questions as "I'm a teacher, aren't I?" without embarrassment. In American speech, such a question often has to be rephrased, since the approved form "Am I not?" seems bookish, and the nonstandard form is stringently avoided.

Nonstandard speech uses *ain't* /éynt/ for all three forms of the non-past. The form is to be analyzed as a fourth allomorph of the non-past base, occurring only before the negative suffix, like the negative allomorph of *will*, which appears in *won't*. With this fourth allomorph, the suffixes of 1*b* and 2 both have zero allomorphs.

Social attitudes toward *ain't* are both very real and very curious. There is no form in the language whose inappropriate use more firmly marks the user as careless or uneducated. Yet the form is structurally parallel to other forms which are not objected to, and it certainly has a venerable history. It seems in no danger of disappearing, and even educated speakers use it in ways usually inadequately described as "jocular" or "informal." On the other hand, it equally shows no likelihood of becoming accepted usage. Since its peculiar status cannot be explained structurally or historically, it is a form which offers a tempting opportunity for study of social attitudes toward language.

10.... FORM CLASSES MARKED BY DERIVATIONAL MORPHEMES

Up to this point we have been able to isolate the classes of nouns, pronouns, and verbs. Paradigmatic characteristics will not, however, identify all members of these classes since some of them are defective, lacking all or some of the expected set of suffixes. In complex words which are thus defective, the normal next step is to look at any postbases the form may contain, since other constructions containing the same postbase may be fully inflectable. If this should be the case, the postbase defines the class of the defective construction. Thus the analyst may find himself with such a form as *greenness*, which cannot be immediately classified as a noun, since it is not usually inflected for number or case. But the same postbase occurs in *kindness*, where it is regularly inflected for number, giving *kindnesses*. As a result, the analyst has no hesitation in calling *greenness* a noun. One of the advantages of a complete and indexed morphemic lexicon of English would be that it would bring together all constructions containing the same postbase, so that this kind of analysis would be greatly simplified.

Prebases are of relatively little classificatory value, and we will therefore spend little time on them. The value that they have is usually limiting rather than firmly diagnostic. Thus such a prebase as *un–* can be added to verbs, and to adjectives, a class we have not yet set up, but not directly to nouns. There are, however, a good many nouns like *unfriendliness*, which would seem at first sight to disprove the statement just made. Yet the statement is valid, and the order of adding pre- and postbases demonstrates it. That is, we do not add *un–* to the noun *friend* to get such a form as "my **unfriends*"—at least in normal style, though such forms occur in poetry. The order of addition is therefore:

> *friend* (noun) plus *–ly* gives *friendly* (adjective)
> *friendly* (adjective) plus *un–* gives *unfriendly* (adjective)
> *unfriendly* (adjective) plus *–ness* gives *unfriendliness* (noun)

Such another prebase as *re–* is of slightly more value, since it is normally added to verbs only, occurring with adjectives and nouns only when there is an underlying verb, as in *repainted* and *repaintable*.[1] Still other common prebases, such as *pre-* itself, can be freely added to bases of most of the form classes. Thus, about all that can be gained from a knowledge of the prebases is that, even in isolation, an occasional construction like *reties* or *unties* is a verb, not an inflected noun.

If there were a morphemic lexicon, the formation of English words could be much more fully described than is possible at present, and individual postbases and prebases could be extensively used in assigning words to their proper form classes. In the absence of such a lexicon, this chapter will be confined to considering only two sets of postbases: those which mark a core group of adjectives and those which mark a core group of adverbs. The chapter is therefore shorter than the importance of derivational processes would warrant were more known of the subject.

It was said immediately above that postbases serve to isolate core groups within the large classes of adjectives and adverbs. The groups thus isolated are called cores, since they do not by any means make up all the membership in each class. Rather they identify a first group in each class, which serves as a means of isolating the phonological and syntactic characteristics occurring with the core group. These further characteristics can then be used to identify the remaining members of the class.

We can start with a series like *the slow cars, the slower cars, the slowest cars*. Phonologically each series is a single phrase, that is, is not interrupted by any juncture other than $/+/$. We know that the last word in each is a noun, as proved by the suffixes it may appear with. We can then use the series to set up a tentative definition of one group of adjectives: any word which can be modified by the addition of {-ər} and {-ist} is an adjective. The definition is not complete, however, since the resultant word has to have the syntactic and morphological characteristics of *slow, slower, slowest* and, negatively, must lack the characteristics of any other form class. Thus, for instance, *type, typer, typist* might be thought of as a series which contains adjectives. The series does not have the distribution of *slow, slower, slowest*. We can say *a slower car than mine* or *the slowest car in the group*. We cannot

---

[1] An apparent exception to this statement is the occurrence of nouns like *rejects* /riy + jèks/ and *retreads* /riy + trèdz/, in contrast to the verbs *reject* /riy + jékt/ and *retread* /riy + tréd/ or /riy + tréd/. With these also there is an underlying verb, which has been made over into a noun by change in the superfix, in much the same way that the superfix distinguishes *hóok + úp*, verb, and *hóok + ùp*, noun. Nouns with this prebase and the noun superfix are very much less frequent than verbs with the verb superfix, and comparative frequency is presumptive evidence that the nouns are derived from the verbs, rather than the reverse. The process is similar, therefore, to the derivation of *revision* from an underlying verb, *revise*, by the addition of the morpheme {yən}.

fit *typer* or *typist* into this series, or even into a series involving other nouns, such as *boy* or *talk*. Negatively, a form such as *typist* has the inflectional characteristics of a noun, as in *the typist's coat*. For these reasons, then, the series *typer*, *typist* does not contain the same morphemes as *slower*, *slowest*; and *type*, *typer*, *typist* are not adjectives. To be complete, our preliminary definition should read: any word having the distributional characteristics of *slow* and capable of being modified by the addition of *–er* and *–est* is an adjective, and the resultant constructions containing the postbases *–er* and *–est* are also adjectives.

There is an old discussion, dating back at least as far as Sweet in 1891, as to whether the *–er: –est* (the morphemes of comparison, to give the usual name) are postbases or suffixes. Sweet spoke of them as inflectional, but was in doubt:" [They] may be regarded as being almost as much a process of derivation as of inflection"[2]—that is, as much postbases as suffixes. Since then, many competent analysts have spoken of comparison as belonging with the suffixes. The discussion is not of the greatest importance, but there are a number of reasons for putting comparison together with the postbases. First of all, suffixes are regularly characteristic of the great majority of the members of any form class they characterize, as the case and number suffixes are characteristic of nouns. The endings of comparison do not thus characterize adjectives, since a great many adjectives, like *beautiful*, do not take these endings, using *more* and *most* instead. Further, suffixes are frequently tied to something else in the sentence, and are therefore required. A form with a suffix, like *horses*, normally occurs with the following verb form in "The horses are grazing," and we do not say "The **horse are* grazing." Comparative forms are rarely thus correlated. In "Mary is prettier, but Jane is brighter," we can produce a perfectly sensible sentence without the comparative forms: "Mary is pretty, but Jane is bright." Finally, we have a good many forms, like *my betters*, *my elders*, where there is an added noun suffix. Such forms are more easily handled if we treat the *–er* as postbase followed by suffix than if we assume that there are two suffixes.

More important than this difficulty in terminology is the fact that our definition—any word with the distribution of *slow* and capable of being modified by the addition of *–er* and *–est* is an adjective, and the resultant constructions are also adjectives—runs counter to most, if not all, traditional definitions. It is usual, for instance, to define *slower* as an adverb in such sentences as "The car runs slower," which our definition denies. The traditional definition is based on meaning, whereas ours has as usual attempted to rely on form and distribution. Even in this situation, then, we shall call

---

[2] Henry Sweet, *A New English Grammar*, Oxford, 1891, Part I, Par. 65.

slower an adjective and shall describe the peculiarities of distribution of adjectives after verbs when we describe the elements of sentences.

As was said earlier, words like *beautiful*, which have the distributional characteristics of words like *slow*, do not take the postbases of comparison, but make phrasal comparisons, *more beautiful* and *most beautiful*, instead. The distributional characteristics of *beautiful* prove it to be an adjective, but *more* and *most* can occur with other words like *rapidly*, words which there is good reason to define as adverbs. The use of *more* and *most* does not narrowly define the form class of the word with which it occurs and will therefore have to be supplemented by distributional characteristics. At this point, even though some anticipation of later statements is involved, it is convenient to assume that there is a group of adjectives which use *more* and *most*, as well as a group which uses *–er* and *–est*, and then proceed to make what statements are possible about the occurrence of the two types of comparison. At least one advantage of such a procedure is that there is a good deal of variation, so that the two types of comparison are best handled together. For instance, it is usual in Modern English to say *slower*, but Andrew Marvel's "vaster than ages, and *more slow*," produces no sense of strangeness. For variation in the other direction, in the kind of informal speech in which we indulge in nonce formations, we can certainly say things like "Mary, you're *beautifuller* than ever!"

Normally, monosyllabic adjectives take *–er* and *–est*, for example, *young, kind, green, vast, false, full*, and many more. For all of these, *more* and *most* can occasionally occur, particularly when more than one adjective is in postverbal position, as in "I never knew anyone *more proud and brave*," or "She is *more kind and more beautiful* than her sister."

For *like, real, right, true*, and *wrong* there is variation, with phrasal comparison generally the more common. Adjectives of two or more syllables usually take *more* and *most*, but there are a good many exceptions which can be only partially systematized. The first group are adjectives like *muddy*, which has *muddier, muddiest* more commonly than *more muddy, most muddy*. These forms contain an adjectival postbase, {–iy}, which can be added to nouns as in the example given, to bases which occur as verbs, as with *lazy* ("He lazed around all day"), or to bases which occur only as bound forms and so cannot be assigned to any form class. Such a word is *pretty*. A second postbase which acts similarly in comparison is an adjectival *–ly* which will be called {–liy}1. This postbase differs from a second *–ly* in that {–liy}1 can be added directly to noun bases to form an adjective, as in *manly, friendly, earthly*. It can also be added to bound bases, as in *ugly*. The same postbase occurs in a limited number of adjectives formed by the addition of {–liy}1 to adjective bases or their allomorphs, as in *cleanly, goodly, kindly, lowly*, and *sickly.* All of these forms are proved to be adjectives by the occurrence of comparison by postbases, and so in turn identify the postbases as instances of {–liy}1.

One adjective in *–some, handsome,* commonly takes *–er* and *–est.* Other adjectives with the same postbase, *gruesome, lissome, toilsome, toothsome, troublesome,* and *winsome* usually have *more* and *most.* Another group where there is hesitation are adjectives in /–ər/, /–il/, and /–in/, where these terminations need not be morphemes. A number of adjectives of this type compare with postbases and often reduce the number of syllables in the compared form by loss of the vowel. Such forms are *clever, sober, noble, able, common,* and *rotten.* The type is unpredictable, however. *Hostile,* for instance, has only *more hostile.* To complete this representative list, there is a group of miscellaneous polysyllabic forms which often have *–er* and *–est.* They are *narrow, pleasant, profound, quiet, serene,* and *severe.*

The comparative postbases are unstressed and may be preceded by /+/, though they are usually without it, as in *wetter,* which has the intervocalic allophone of /t/. In phrasal comparison, *more* and *most* normally have tertiary stress, though this may be raised to primary under contrastive conditions. *More* and *most* in comparison are not themselves adjectives, though there are adjectival forms, as in *môre bútter, môst bútter.* The distinction is one of stress.

The second form class for which a core group can be isolated by observation of postbases is that of adverbs. The postbase in question, *–ly,* is homonymous with {–liy}1, and we shall accordingly call it {–liy}2. This postbase differs from {–liy}1 in that it cannot be added to noun bases. Thus, such forms as *manly, friendly* contain {–liy}1. There are some distributions in which {–liy}1 and {–liy}2 overlap with each other, however. Both can be added to simple monosyllabic adjective bases, though the number of such forms with {–liy}1 is strictly limited and can easily be taken care of by listing. The postbase {–liy}2 is added only to adjectives and always results in an adverb. The adjectival postbase is distinguished from {–liy}2 by the fact that it cannot be added to a complex adjective *(passionate* gives only adverbial *passionately)* or to a polysyllabic adjective, even though not complex. Thus *common* gives only adverbial *commonly.* Again, a form made with {–liy}1 can be distinguished from one with {–liy}2 by the fact that forms with {–liy}1 take comparison with postbases. Thus, in isolation the forms *sickly* and *quickly* look much alike, and both are formed from simple adjective bases. The first is an example of {–liy}1 since it gives *sicklier* and *sickliest,* while the second is an example of {–liy}2, since it has only *more quickly, most quickly.*

The distributional characteristics of adverbs are described in the treatment of phrases in Chapter 14, Sections 1 and 2, but it is useful at this point to state that adverbs and adjectives have a large and, in the history of English analysis, a troublesome area of overlap. Both adjectives and adverbs can occur in postverbal position in sentences like "The car runs slow" and "The car runs slowly." In the analysis here proposed, *slow* is described as an adjective since it is compared with *–er*, while *slowly* is called an adverb with {–liy}2 since its comparison is *more slowly*.

The phonemic shape of {–liy}2 differs in some of its occurrences from that of {–liy}1. The shape of {–liy}1 is relatively constant and is only rarely preceded by /+/. For {–liy}2, a preceding plus is also rare, but there is one situation in which it may occur. In forms like *real*, if there is no /+/, the resultant adverb is /ríhliy/, that is one /l/ has been lost. There exists however, a contrasting form with plus, /ríhl + liy/, as in "The picture is drawn very *really*." The form with loss of /l/ produces a difficulty in analysis. One solution might be to adopt the procedure given above in Section 4 of Chapter 7, where the /–ž–/ of *division* was said to be a member of both the preceding and the following morphemes. Another procedure, which has not appeared in print to my knowledge, is to say that assignment to either the preceding or following morpheme is arbitrary and that the only way of avoiding arbitrariness is to cut off the single /l/ from both morphemes, setting it up as a predictable empty morph. A third possibility is to assign the single /l/ to one morpheme or the other. It is this third possibility which has here been adopted, even though this choice seems to contradict the one made with *division*. It is a very general rule of English morphophonemics that any sequence which consists of /C$_1$ + C$_1$/ (where C$_1$ indicates two occurrences of the same consonant) always becomes /C$_1$/ with loss of /+/. There is no such general rule governing assimilation of unlike consonants when /+/ is lost. Therefore it is practical to treat the analysis of *division* and *really* differently, assigning to one morpheme only the single consonant resulting from assimilatory loss of one of a pair of identical consonants. The decision as to which morpheme the single consonant should be assigned to is governed by the normal direction of assimilation in English. It is more usual for the first of two consonants to become like the second than for the second to become like the first, as long as there is no intervening /+/. Thus, for instance, *width* gives /–tθ/ rather than /–dð/, and when /+/ is lost in *income*, the result is /–ŋk/ rather than /–nd–/. For these reasons the morphemic boundary in the junctureless forms of *really* is placed before the simple /l/, giving a complete morphemic structure as follows:

$$\{\acute{\ }\ \} \ \{rih\} \ \{liy\}^3$$

---

[3] *Division* has been treated as an example of morphemic overlap, yet it would be possible to analyze so as to avoid such a conclusion. The single /–ž–/, which is the result of assimilation of /–dy–/, could be assigned to either the following or the

preceding morpheme, depending on which of two alternate hypotheses were adopted.

The first of these hypotheses would assume that the immediate result of assimilation of /–dy–/ was */–žž–/. The further result would then be loss of the first of the two identical consonants. Such a development would assign the single /–ž–/ to the following morpheme.

Under the second hypothesis, the first step of assimilation would be assumed to be from /–dy–/ to */–žy–/. The second step would then be loss of the /–y–/ after /–ž–/, an assumption which receives some support from the rarity of /y/ /ž/ elsewhere in English phonotactics. Neither hypothesis can be established by historical evidence, but of the two, the second is slightly preferable, since the final step in it is supported by some evidence from structure.

As the earlier treatment of *division* indicates, I have rejected both of these hypotheses and have assumed the existence of overlap instead. The decision is based partly on the criterion of simplicity, since it avoids the necessity of either of the two-step hypotheses just outlined, but more importantly the decision is based on the belief that English morphemes have an important structural feature—the possibility of occurring in phonemically nonsequential order. The phonemically nonsequential order is not the same thing, of course, as morphemically nonsequential order.

11.... THE STRUCTURE OF FREE PHRASES

1. General phonological characteristics

In Section 1 of Chapter 8 several kinds of phrases were described. The type which will be described here are phonological phrases, that is, terminal juncture groups. They are nonminimal in that all contain more than one base or base construction. They are free in that all have the phrase superfixes characteristic of normal collocations of words, rather than the phrase superfixes characteristic of fixed phrases. Thus, to repeat an example used earlier, *blâck + bírd* is a free phrase with the superfix {ˆ} {+´} characteristic of adjective and following noun, while *bláck + bìrd* is a fixed phrase marked by the superfix of primary-tertiary characteristic of compound nouns. A free phrase may of course contain a fixed phrase as one of its constituents, as in *an + ôld + bláck + bìrd*, where *blackbird* again has primary-tertiary. In *an + ôld + blâck + bírd*, on the other hand, the superfix identifies the construction as a free phrase none of whose constituents is a fixed phrase. In short, a fixed phrase has the distributional characteristics of a word, and, as a constituent of a free phrase, it is not to be distinguished from a word. It should also be noted that other constituents than the noun at the end of the adjectival phrase can be fixed phrases rather than words. Thus *greenhouse* is a fixed phrase in final position in *an ôld gréenhòuse*, but in *an ôld gréenhòuse plánt* it no longer occupies the position of the head of the phrase and is rather a modifier. There are occasionally some surprises in free phrases which contain a fixed phrase as one of its constituents, and there are also dialect differences. In general a superfix consisting of /ˆ + ´ + ˋ/ is characteristic of an adjective modifying a following compound noun, as in *ôld bláckbìrd*. Yet, in one phrase, *wîld bírdsèed*, the expected semantic relationships do not appear. That is, we should expect the phrase to mean *birdseed gathered wild*, with *wild* modifying the fixed phrase which follows. Yet this particular product is sold under conditions which make it clear that it means rather "seed for wild birds." As usual we shall follow the formal characteristics in dissecting phrases of the type now under discussion, and we shall handle exceptional constructions of the type of *wild birdseed* by listing them when necessary. It is worth pointing out that the peculiar semantic characteristics of such phrases are a quality of the construction considered as a unit, with a distribution of its own. Thus, if the sentence were "I spent the morning gathering *wild birdseed*," the normal semantic relations would be restored. The semantic peculiarities are parallel to those of *old fox* in "John is an *old fox*," where the phrase is specialized, and "John shot an *old fox*," where no specialization exists. As for *wíld bírdsèed*, there are probably historical facts which would explain it were they known. It is quite possible that underlying its present form is something like **wîld-bìrd bírdsèed*, in which the type of development known as haplology (the loss of one of two repeated identical sequences) has taken place. It is also possible that the underlying construction was something like **wîld-bìrd séed*, which has been analogically leveled under the superfix of *bírdsèed*. In the absence of evidence, the historical development can only be guessed at.

Sometimes, also, there are dialect differences in which one pronunciation is more or less ambiguous or surprising, while the other is clear. Thus in my own idiolect, *Îrish + lâmb + stéw* is structurally ambiguous, since it has the superfix of a free phrase and might therefore be interpreted either as "stew made from Irish lambs" or "lamb stew made in the Irish manner." In point of fact, the latter interpretation happens to be the correct one, parallel to that of another pronunciation *Îrish + lámb + stèw*, the interpretation of which is clear.

In this particular phrase, the ambiguity is not very important and could scarcely lead to genuine misunderstanding, since "stew made from Irish lambs" is a rather improbable interpretation in a country which does not import lambs from Ireland. On occasion, however, the ambiguity can be real. Thus a construction such as *Wêstvìew Róad* makes clear that the name of the street is *Westview*. At least once in giving this street name, I was misheard, and the name was interpreted as *View*, an interpretation which would have been possible only if I had said *Wêst Víew Róad*.

We shall take up ambiguities of various types as we come to them, but at the moment a general explanation can be given for a number of them. In most nominal phrases, the immediate constituents are arrived at by cutting off the first word, as in *Irish lamb stew*, where the cut is after *Irish*. Since semantic specialization is always possible, the constituent *lâmb + stéw*, even though it has the superfix of a free phrase, is itself somewhat ambiguous. There is, in short, no formal signal which tells us, in such a pronunciation, whether this immediate constituent is a semantic unit or not. The pronunciation *lámb + stèw* is of course clear, since the superfix identifies it as a fixed phrase, and therefore a unit. A theoretically possible pronunciation which would be equally clear would be **Îrish + làmb + stéw*, which would define the immediate constituents as *Irish lamb* and *stew*. The ambiguity can then be stated as follows: a phrase with successive secondaries before the primary normally consists of successive modifiers before the head of the phrase. Whenever there has been specialization of meaning in the constituent which consists of the secondary and immediately following primary, ambiguity results. The chief means by which such ambiguities are resolved is by modification of the superfix in the direction of a superfix characteristic of a fixed phrase.

In the descriptions of free-phrase types which follow, the method will be to set up model phrases which are as close as possible to the maximum of the type. Stress and order characteristics will both be described, and these stress and order characteristics will be used to set up further form classes of words, as well as subclasses within the groups, such as adjectives which have already been identified by their postbases.

2. Noun phrases

Noun phrases are phrases in which the last word is a noun or fixed noun phrase. The noun is shown to be the head of the phrase by its primary stress and, syntactically, by the fact that the whole group can be replaced by a simple noun. The characteristic stress pattern of such phrases is a series of secondaries preceding the primary stress on the noun. There may be intervening weaks, and there can also be tertiaries under statable conditions.

We can start our examination of phrases of this type with the following model: *all the ten fine old stone houses*. The phrase can be broken up into smaller phrases, of course, but normally it is not, there being no intervening junctures other than pluses. The total pattern is /ɔ̂hl + ðə̀ + tên + fâyn + ôwl + stôwn + háwzĭz/. The first observation is that there are rules of order which govern the occurrence of the words of which the phrase is made up. Some of these rules are absolute—that is, *the* and *ten* cannot be reversed without producing an unsatisfactory utterance. With *fine* and *old*, however, reversal is unusual, but possible. Yet, when reversal occurs, the phonological conditions are markedly and necessarily altered. If the sequence *old fine houses* is used, then a terminal juncture, normally /||/, must be used after *old*, and may very well appear after *fine* as well. That is, *fine* and *old* must come in normal order as long as they are in the same phrase. If they are reversed, the phrase is then broken up into smaller phrases. If we now add such a word as *gray* to the group *fine old stone houses*, we find that its position is limited, but not completely fixed. *Gray* must normally follow *fine*, and precede *stone*, but it can either precede or follow *old*. Yet, whether it precedes or follows *old*, *old* and *gray* must be separated by a terminal juncture, again characteristically a /||/. A final item in the relationship of two such forms as *old* and *gray* is that if *old* is removed from the model phrase *all the ten fine old stone houses* and *gray* is substituted, the phrase is not affected. *Gray* fits into the position occupied by *old* and requires no terminal juncture or breaking up of the phrase.

The data just given are sufficient to establish order classes for the words in the model phrase. Two words belong to the same order class if one can substitute for the other without affecting the framework of the phrase. Two words belong to different order classes either if they occur in a fixed sequence, as do *the* and *ten*, or if their sequence can be broken only by placing a terminal juncture between them. Finally, two words belong to the same order class if they can occur in the order AB or BA, but require a terminal, A | B or B | A, between them, as do *old* and *gray*.

We can then return to our model phrase, numbering the various words in it, according to their closeness to N, the noun which is the head of the phrase:

VI	V	IV	III	II	I	N
all	*the*	*ten*	*fine*	*old*	*stone*	*houses*

/ɔ́hl + ðə + tên + fâyn + ôwl + stôwn + háwziz/

It is not certain that there are not more order groups than those here given, but there are at least this many. It is characteristic that all six may be present, though it is perhaps a little unusual. More often one or more of the order groups are absent without other effect on the phrase.

It is not possible at present to give an exhaustive and authoritative list of the membership in the various order groups, but even a sketchy listing is useful. In group VI go *all*, *both*, and *half*.[1] In group V go the definite and indefinite articles; *this*, *that* and their plurals; form 3 of all personal pronouns *(my*, *their*, etc.); and the case-inflected forms of all nouns, whether singular or plural *(child's*, *children's*, etc.). In group IV go the numerals, both the forms like *third* and those like *three*, but not those constructions which while made up of numeral morphemes yet do not belong to the ordinary

---

[1] The *half* which is a modifier of group VI is to be distinguished from the homonymous noun *half*. The noun form has a normal plural, *halves*, the modifier does not. In such a construction as *half the boys*, the form found is the group VI modifier, as its position and the fact that it cannot be pluralized demonstrate. In *the half of it*, *half* is the noun form and can be pluralized to *the halves of it*.

A form not found in my idiolect is *the both of them*, which similarly treats *both* as a noun, though one which is without a plural. Such variation is natural enough, since all three words, *all*, *both*, and *half*, have as one of their syntactic characteristics that they can be followed by *of* constructions, as in *all of them*, *both of them*, *half of them*, making the dividing line between these forms and nouns a rather slight one.

decimal number system. An example is *ten-fifteen* as in *the good old ten-fifteen train*, where *ten-fifteen* belongs to the time system, not the counting system. *Dozen* and *half-dozen*, on the other hand, belong to group IV.

Although it is taking the groups out of order, it is convenient to jump to group I. Here belong all uninflected noun forms, when shown to be in modifying relationship by being reduced to secondary stress and being placed before another noun on which the primary stress falls. Examples are *silk hat, coal stove*, or slightly more complex, *jacknife dive*. Here also go minimal phrases which consist of numerals followed by an uninflected noun of measure or price. In these, the numerals are reduced to tertiary stress. Note "the gôod ôld five-cênt cigár," rather than "the *five- good old -cent cigar," which we should have expected were *five-cent* not itself a fixed phrase. These uninflected nouns as modifiers of a second noun are to be sharply differentiated from the first form in fixed nominal phrases, with the superfix primary-tertiary. Examples of fixed phrases are *cánnon-bàll*, *Návy màn*, *White Hoùse*, and of course many more.

Other members of group I are modifiers derived by means of a postbase from nouns that would normally fall in group I. Examples of such modifiers are *stoney, wooden, silken*, and *golden*. As a result of this relationship, national adjectives fall in group I. Thus in "these fine old *chîna dólls*," *china* is a nominal modifier of group I. (Notice that, in contrast, *Chîna tràde* is a fixed noun phrase). From *china dolls*, the postbase *–ese* gives us "these fine old *Chinese dolls*," where *Chinese* is evidently of the same order group as *china*.

Group II is the most troublesome to define, and the group has characteristics which are still uncertain. There is a subgroup within it, to which *old, new*, and *little* belong, which has a peculiarity of stress in that its members can make up a minimal noun phrase with the superfix tertiary-primary, as in *old maid* /òwl + méyd/ ("spinster"); *New Deal* /nùw + díyl/; and *little man* /lìtil + mǽn/ ("boy"). All of these forms, however, can be paralleled by fixed phrases with the more usual primary-tertiary, as in *old country* /ówl + kòntriy/; *newcomer* /núw + kòmər/; and *little-neck* /lítil + nèk/ ("a kind of clam").

We can therefore set up a class IIa, consisting of these forms and any others which have the same stress characteristics, that is, a possible use of the fixed-phrase superfix tertiary-primary. The color adjectives, such as *red, white, green*, are typical of II. When we have both a IIa form and a II form, the IIa usually precedes, as in *old gray mare*, which is /ôwl + grêy + méhr/, without a terminal juncture after *old*. This usual order and the absence of intervening terminal juncture suggest that *old* and *gray* should be assigned to different order groups. However, reversed order is possible, also without intervening /||/, as in *gray old man* /grêy + ôwl + mǽn/. With other adjectives of group II, similar reversals are also possible. Thus *big thick steak* /bîg + θîk + stéyk/ is usual, but *thick big steak*, though commoner with /|/ after *thick*, can certainly occur as /θîk + bîg + stéyk/. In the present state of knowledge, then, it would seem that order characteristics within group II are peculiar in that there are preferred orders but that these are reversible without intervening terminal juncture.

The membership of group II could be accurately described only by a complete listing, and the list in turn could be made up only by a survey of a large corpus of speech, which would take into account the order in which the modifiers occur, and what stresses and what junctures accompany them. In the absence of such a list, the group can be very roughly described semantically by saying that its membership consists of the color adjectives; the age group, *old, new, young*; and the shape-size group, *big, huge, little, small, tall, high, thick, thin, slim, fat,* and *stout*.

The membership in group IIa has already been described as consisting of *old, new,* and *little*. I cannot, in my own speech, find other examples of adjectives which can take the tertiary-primary superfix to make a fixed phrase with a following noun, except for one nearly isolated example. This is the adjective *black*, in the three phrases *Black Beauty, Black Sambo,* and *black mammy*. All can occur with the phrase pattern of secondary-primary, as in *his old black mammy* /hìz + ôwl + blǽk + mǽmiy/. But all can occur with tertiaries, as in /hìz + ôwl + blæ̀k + mǽmiy/. The first two phrases are proper names drawn from books, the third is more nearly a current speech form. Needless to say, behavior in these phrases has nothing to do with the meaning of *black* as a color term or a racial term. Ordinarily, *black* in either meaning takes the stress superfix primary-tertiary as in *blackbird* /blǽk + bə̀rd/ and *black man* /blǽk + mæ̀n/.

If *black* is then admitted to the group IIa, the subgroup cannot be correlated with preferred order. That is, we have the order IIa-II in *new white house*; IIa-IIa in *old black horse*; and II-IIa in *big black horse*. The property which puts a form in IIa is a stress peculiarity alone.

The stress characteristics of IIa give rise to an ambiguity. If we have the phrase pattern secondary-tertiary-primary without an intervening single bar to guide us, the stress pattern does not tell us whether we are dealing with a fixed adjective phrase, as in *ostrich-fan dance* /âstric + fæ̀n + dǽns/ (in contrast with the ludicrous *ostrich fan-dance* /âstric + fæ̀n + dǽns/), or with an adjective followed by a fixed noun phrase, as in *beautiful New Haven* /byûwtifil + nùw + héyvin/. The ambiguity is real when we are dealing with the two phrases which would be written as *near New Jersey* and *near-new jersey*. Both can be /nîhr + nùw + jɔ́rziy/. Though real, the ambiguity in this particular phrase is not very troublesome, since it can be solved if *New Jersey* is pronounced with weak stress on *New*, if there is a single bar at the proper boundary, or if there is something like an indefinite article preceding, which fits with one phrase but not the other.[2]

It has been said that the characteristics of group IIa do not correlate with the preferred order within group II. It is still impossible to describe this preferred order exactly, but the observation of older grammarians that the color adjectives follow others of group II seems to be sound. Besides the fact that order within group II is merely preferred, instead of relatively fixed, one other characteristic of the group can be mentioned before we leave it. This is that all its members are compared with postbases. In this, the group forms a partial contrast with group III, which can be compared either with postbases or with *more, most.* The test is not complete, however, since *wise* is also a member of group III in spite of having *wiser, wisest.*

Besides the partial morphological test for membership in group III which has just been described, an adjective can be phonologically assigned to group III if it regularly precedes a known group II adjective such as *old* and if the order cannot be reversed without stress or juncture modification. Were the members of group II fully listed, however, we would then describe group III by saying that it contains all the modifiers whose position is not otherwise defined. It is worth pointing out that group III has by far the largest membership and that it is normally the group into which fall new or learned adjectives, such as *dolichocephalic* or *phonemic.*

The normal stress pattern for all modifying groups is secondary stress, except for group V, where our model phrase showed a form with weak stress. Group V does not always have weak stress, though the possibility of weak stress in this group distinguishes it from all others. There are only two members of the group which are regularly weak, the definite and the indefinite articles. *This, that,* and their plurals, together with all the pronoun forms which fall in the group, normally take tertiary stress. The case forms of nouns have secondary stress. In this group we therefore have three stress types, depending on the type of morpheme which occurs:

/ɔ̀hl + ðə̀ + búks/   /ɔ̀hl + mày + búks/   /ɔ̀hl + jǽks + búks/

As usual, the weak and tertiary stresses, like secondary stresses, can be raised under conditions of contrast, but not without affecting the stresses of the rest of the phrase.

Group V modifiers, having the possibility of tertiary and even weak stress, constitute a second instance in which the stress pattern alone is not enough to determine boundaries, just as was true with a tertiary stress on an

---

[2] The fullest discussion of adjectival order groups is that of Carlyle Westbrook Barritt in his unpublished dissertation, *The Order Classes of English Modifiers,* University of Virginia, 1952. Barritt is the discoverer of the stress peculiarities of group IIa, and to him I owe much in the discussion here given.

adjective of 11a. That is, *all my books* has the same secondary-tertiary-primary pattern which we found to be ambiguous in *near New Jersey* and *near-new jersey*. But the group v modifiers with weak or tertiary stress have syntactic characteristics which serve to clarify their status even when there is no /||/ to make the boundaries of the constituents clear. The definite and indefinite articles are never final, that is to say, they do not occur immediately before /|||/ or /#/, and only rarely before /||/. It is clear, therefore, that the weakly stressed forms are always to be referred to the same minimal potential phrase with the material which follows. Similarly for the forms with tertiary stress, all but *his, this, that* are nonfinals, since as described in Chapter 9, pronouns have distinct forms like *my* and *mine* for nonfinal and final positions. Furthermore, even with *his, this,* and *that,* they do not receive tertiary stress when final. As a result of these characteristics, it can be set up as an invariable rule that any weak or tertiary modifier of group v will always be interpreted as belonging with what follows rather than with what precedes.

With modifiers of other groups, the situation is not so clear. As has been stated, reduction of a word from secondary to tertiary, when that word is preceded by another which preserves its secondary stress, often indicates that the second word is now making up a fixed modifying phrase with the preceding word. We have met examples of this sort of reduction already, but it would be well to give some others, with their effect on meaning:

> *light gray stone walls* /lâyt + grêy + stôwn + wóhlz/ (walls which are light in weight, gray, and made of stone)
> *light-gray stone walls* /lâyt + grèy + stôwn + wóhlz/ (walls which are light-gray in color and made of stone)
> *light graystone walls* /lâyt + grêy + stòwn + wóhlz/ (light walls made of the kind of stone called graystone)

A more invariant rule is that in phrases which follow our model, a tertiary stress following the primary stress makes up a fixed noun phrase together with the preceding primary. This rule applies quite without distinction as to the nature of the form on which the new primary stress is made to fall. We thus get distinctive sets like the following:

> *big green house* /bîg + grîyn + háws/
> *big greenhouse* /bîg + gríyn + hàws/
>
> *new Cannon sheets* /nûw + kǽnən + šíyts/
> *new cannon-balls* /nûw + kǽnən + bòhlz/

In the two examples given, the forms *green* and *cannon* are adjective and noun, respectively, as independent forms. As the first members of fixed phrases, however, their membership in separate form classes becomes irrelevant. It is the fixed constructions of which they are parts which have membership in form classes. The first two elements in these constructions can no more be said to belong to one form class or another than can the bound form *heal–* in the noun construction *health.*[3]

The rule that primary-tertiary in nominal phrases is always the stress superfix of a fixed noun phrase explains a number of constructions which would otherwise seem to have abnormal order of modifiers. The common phrase *poor little rich girl*, if the three first forms were treated alike in stress, would require a terminal juncture after *little* which belongs to group II, since *rich* which follows it belongs to group III and there is thus a reversal of order. As actually pronounced, the phrase is / pûr + lîtil + ríc + gɔ̀rl/. *Rich girl* is a fixed noun phrase, here treated like any noun. A somewhat similar nonce phrase which I once heard was *the mahogany new mirror*. The phrase breaks normal order rules, since *mahogany* should follow *new*. The speaker gave *new mirror* the pattern primary-tertiary, /núw + mìrər/, thus making of it a fixed phrase before which the modifier *mahogany* was possible.

The rule that primary-tertiary makes a fixed noun phrase does not apply to the pattern primary-secondary. Such patterns are somewhat rare and often consist of the raising of a secondarily stressed modifier and the lowering of the primarily stressed noun under conditions of contrastive stress. Native speakers find such patterns confusing when pronounced in isolation, a reaction which is understandable, since in isolation the contrastive situation is absent. An example of such a pattern is:

the big white house /ðə + bîg + hwáyt + hâws/

Such a pattern could mean either the house which is white, not black, or the house which belongs to Mr. White, not Mr. Black.

There are thus only two stress patterns of three parts which give unambiguous directions to the hearer for recognizing the boundaries of the phrase constituents. The pattern secondary-secondary-primary is that of two modifiers and a following noun. Such a phrase is always to be cut by taking off the first modifier, leaving the second modifier and the noun, which are then split in a second operation. To return to the example *Irish lamb stew*, with the pronunciation secondary-secondary-primary, the cutting

---

[3] For those interested in the history of English grammatical analysis, *cannon-ball* is an important form. Otto Jespersen, in *A Modern English Grammar on Historical Principles*, Heidelberg, 1914, Vol. II, Par. 310, reports a discussion among the leading English linguists of his day in which the authorities divided evenly as to whether *cannon* in this construction was noun or adjective. The discussion still goes on in school grammar, and there has been no more agreement than there was in the discussion of 1881. Such discussion is an interesting example of the futility of analysis based on meaning.

there given followed this principle, giving *lamb stew* as one constituent. The phrase was spoken of as seeming ambiguous to some speakers only because they expected *Írish lámb stèw*; the cutting into constituents would be the same for both stress patterns.

The second unambiguous pattern is secondary-primary-tertiary, that of modifier and following fixed noun phrase. As just said, the splitting of such a phrase into its constituents falls at the same points as in the pattern secondary-secondary-primary, but this identity of boundaries is not to say that the two patterns are not often sharply different in meaning, as a pair like *bêautiful líttle róck : bêautiful Líttle Ròck* can testify. As a sort of variant of this pattern, it might be added that the pattern secondary-primary-weak would be equally unambiguous.

Fixed noun phrases with a superfix consisting of either $/'~/$ or $/' + ~/$ are, however, unknown. These two patterns are characteristic of non-minimal words, such as $\{'~\}$ *hussy* or $\{'\}$ $\{+~\}$ *Tomkins*. That is, the morphemes which receive weak stress are not bases. It is irrelevant, of course, that *hussy* contains a second element which is etymologically an old base, *wife*. At present, at any rate, it is no longer a base.

All other stress superfixes of three or more morphemes produce ambiguity which must be resolved by identifying the words or morphemes on which they fall. We have taken up one of these ambiguities, that of *near-new jersey* and *near New Jersey*. An ambiguity which has not been taken up is that which is caused by the fact that extended noun phrases may contain fixed adjectival phrases, formed by the reduction of a normally secondarily stressed element to tertiary. Such a tertiarily stressed element may go either with what precedes or with what follows, producing un-certainty about the boundaries of constituents. Whether a fixed adjectival phrase is formed with tertiary-secondary or with secondary-tertiary seems to be a matter of dialect. Thus a phrase such as *red-ink stained papers* may show that *red-ink* is a fixed adjectival phrase by the pattern /rêd + iŋk + stêynd + péypərz/ or /rèd + îŋk + stêynd + páypərz/. Either pattern, however, is distinct from /rêd + îŋk + stèynd + péypərz/, where *ink-stained* is the fixed adjective phrase. Thus, a tertiary among a series of secondaries produces ambiguity as to the boundaries of fixed adjectival phrases; it also, however, produces a still further ambiguity, since such a tertiary can also be an adverb and will then go with what follows.

We can now add a further characteristic to the description of adverbs which we have already given. In a series of modifiers, an adverb is a form receiving tertiary stress, though this alone will not identify it. A further negative identification is that an adverb cannot appear immediately before the noun in phrases of this type. This negative characteristic is what makes it necessary to define *very*—whatever it may be elsewhere—as an adjective in "The very thing!" /ðə + vêriy + θíŋ/. Thus, it is always necessary to identify the form class of the material on which the stress pattern falls before the stress pattern can be used to identify the phrase type. Suppose that we have the phrase *more beautiful women*, which is ambiguous as written. If the phrase has the pattern secondary-secondary-primary, /môhr + byûwtifəl + wímin/, the result is always unambiguous; *more* is an adjective. If the pattern is tertiary-secondary-primary, it is at least clear that *more* is not an independent adjective. The phrase now has the pattern of *thèse bêautiful wómen*, but a speaker of English knows (even though he may not be able to put his knowledge into words) that *more* is not a member of group v with tertiary stress. The tertiary-secondary-primary pattern can also occur in such a phrase as *blàck-bîrd's nést*, though in some dialects the pattern used there would be secondary-tertiary-primary. A speaker of English thus realizes that *more* is a form that has the order characteristics of an adverb. As a result, in practice /mòhr + byûwtifəl + wímin/ is never ambiguous. The hearer interprets as "women who are more beautiful," the meaning which is appropriate to the adverb.

We can now return to our model phrase and describe the ambiguities which result from tertiaries in all positions. If the phrase pattern is secondary-tertiary-primary, the cut may be before or after the tertiary. If the cut is after it, the phrase contains a fixed adjectival phrase before a noun. If the cut is before the tertiary, the phrase consists of an adjective before a fixed noun phrase. One possibility is ruled out; the tertiary cannot here represent an adverb.

If the pattern is tertiary-secondary-primary, there are three possibilities. The tertiary may be a group v modifier. It may be an adverb followed by a modifier of any group, since all groups can be preceded by some at least of the adverbs. There are limitations, it is true, but these are a part of the individual lexical characteristics of the items themselves. Thus, though "*suddenly stone* houses" is not very likely, "*nearly stone* houses" is possible enough. The third possibility, of course, is that the tertiary may be the first member of a fixed adjectival phrase.

If the basic pattern is secondary-secondary-primary, the addition of a tertiary between the secondaries makes for even more uncertainty. We may have a phrase of the type *âll mỳ gôod bóoks*, with a group vi modifier, a group v modifier, and a modifier from any one of the following groups. The phrase may be of the type *âll mòre expênsive bóoks*, where we have modifier, adverb, modifier. We can have *nêar-nèw wôol jérsey*, where we have a fixed modifying phrase, a modifier, and then the noun. In *ôld Nèw Jêrsey hóuses*, we have modifier, fixed modifying phrase, and noun.

There are some limitations on adverbs, or, if the order groups are identifiable, on the formation of fixed modifying phrases, which remove some of the ambiguities. Thus, if both groups VI and V are present, an adverb cannot come between them. Conversely, a tertiary before a group VI must be an adverb, since there are no fixed phrases in group VI.

The description just given emphasizes the amount of ambiguity with each of the various phrase patterns. In actual speech the real ambiguity is surprisingly slight, and the phrase patterns serve to distinguish constructions quite clearly. Thus, for instance, I once inadvertently addressed a class as "fôrty ôdd péople." I was quite properly greeted by laughter—the proper phrase was "fôrty-òdd péople." That is, *odd* with secondary stress is always an adjective, and with tertiary is always the second component of a minimal phrase of group IV. My mistake produced an interesting example of a clear reaction by a group of linguistically untrained but native speakers to a distinction between secondary and tertiary stress. A different series in which there is no real ambiguity is:

/flǽt + hwâyt + rák/ (a rock which is flat and white)
/flǽt + hwáyt + ràk/ (flat Whiterock water)
/flǽt + hwàyt + rák/ (a rock painted with flat-white)

Here the first two patterns are unambiguous, the first that of two modifiers followed by a noun, the second that of a modifier followed by a fixed noun phrase. In effect, the third is also unambiguous, since *white* is not an adjective which takes the superfix tertiary-primary when it forms a fixed noun phrase—as the second example shows.

A more complicated example can be found in the sequence *pretty long-stemmed American beauties*. A part of the stress pattern on this phrase is fixed, since *stemmed* always receives tertiary stress. *Stemmed* could then conceivably be an adverb or a reduced adjective going with what follows or what precedes. The first possibility is ruled out by the fact that the form contains a postbase {-d}, one of the forms used to construct adjectives, as in *a bearded man*. Further, such adjectives do not form fixed phrases with what follows under a superfix of tertiary-secondary; that is, we do not say "*stèmmed Amêrican* béauties." Still further, adjectives in {-d} regularly form fixed phrases with what precedes, as in *ă blâck bèarded ănd vèry hâiry mán*. For these reasons, the hearer readily interprets *long-stemmed* as a fixed phrase. As for *pretty* in this example, it is unambiguously adjectival if it has secondary stress. If it has tertiary stress, it is an adverb, or conceivably the first member of a fixed modifying phrase. What then identifies *pretty* as an adverb? The problem arises with a good many forms which occur with both secondary and tertiary stress, and the problem is settled, if at all, by characteristics of order. *Pretty* with tertiary stress can occur freely before modifiers of groups I, II, and III, as in *prètty Amêrican áccent*, *prètty ôld hóuse*, and *prètty cômfortable hóuse*. Furthermore, *pretty* is not a form which makes a noun phrase with tertiary-primary, like the *new* of *New Jersey*. It is again interesting that native speakers react to *prètty lóng-stèmmed Amêrican béauties* without hesitation over the interpretation. Long familarity with *pretty* and its order characteristics makes the stress pattern clear.

A different kind of situation exists with phrases like *tâll òld máid* and *yêar-òld máid*. Again the native speaker unhesitatingly cuts out the constituents *old maid* and *year-old*, though the stress does not make the division clear. The cuts here are apparently made on the basis of greatest probability, checked by the points at which division by /||/ is possible. That is, there is no common modifying phrase *tâll-òld*, but there is a fixed noun phrase *òld máid*. Similarly, *yêar-òld* is a common fixed phrase of group I, though *year* alone does not occur freely before all classes of nouns. That is, *yêar máid* would be uncommon at least, even though *yêar subscríption* is quite possible. As to the checking by /||/, what is meant is that *tall|old maid* is a possible variant for the first phrase, *year-old|maid* for the second.

The behavior of *year-old* gives us, finally, a further series in which complex stress variations, all without real ambiguity, are possible:

twò-hûndred-yèar-òld hóuses	(houses two hundred years old)
twô hûndred-yèar-òld hóuses	(two houses, a hundred years old)
twô-hùndred yêar-òld hóuses	(two hundred houses, a year old)

Here the fact that what precedes *year-old* is a set of number morphemes is enough to make the stress patterns clear.

It is not maintained that these examples clear up all ambiguities. They are rather meant to be an exemplification of the way we thread our way through the complicated patterns of speech. Sometimes, indeed, there is ambiguity in the stress pattern which makes no difference in the meaning but may make considerable difference to the analysis. Such an ambiguity is that of the phrase *a grèat bíg bóy*. Since the stress pattern is not that of two adjectives, it is not clear whether *great big* is composed of adverb and adjective or whether *great* is the first component of an adjectival phrase. The only criterion that seems usable here is that *great* with tertiary stress seems limited to occasions when the following form is *big*. It therefore seems preferable to call *great big* a fixed adjectival phrase.

We are now ready to gather together what can be learned from this extended discussion of noun phrases and bring it to bear on the description of the form classes which occur within them. Words in all six of the modifying groups can now be called adjectivals, a name which indicates that the whole set shares some of the characteristics of the adjectives, the smaller group which is contained within the maximal set. The characteristic stress for all groups is secondary, except for group V which contains forms which have tertiary and weak stress. Group I contains adjectivals, that is, nouns occurring as modifiers, as in *stone house,* and true adjectives, as in *American house.* Groups II and III are all true adjectives. Group II forms are all compared by means of postbases, whereas the adjectives of group I are compared by *more* and *most,* and the forms of group III vary, some having postbases, like *rich, richer,* and others, like *expensive,* having only *more* and *most.* Group IV are adjectivals, and all members of it, except for a few forms like *odd,* which appears in fixed group IV phrases *(fôrty-òdd),* are numerals. Not all numerals occur here, since when followed by adjectivals of group V like *dollar, pound,* and even the phrase *year-old,* numerals reduced to tertiary stress can make up a fixed modifying phrase with the following adjectival, which then belongs to group I.

Group V again contains adjectivals, that is, articles and demonstratives, the third form of pronouns, and the determinative form of nouns. The stress characteristics have already been described. They have, however, another characteristic which has not yet been mentioned. They fall into two subgroups, a group Va with weak or tertiary stress, which comprises all group V forms except the determinative cases of nouns. Group Vb has secondary stress, and there are sequences of Va followed by Vb, as in *the boy's mother,* but there cannot be two Va forms in the same phrase. That is, forms like the Italian *il mio padre* do not occur. The Va-Vb sequence gives rise to a curiously complex construction, since it is possible to take a long phrase of some such type as *all the ten pretty young American children,* where all six groups of modifiers are represented, and then place the noun at the head of it in the determinative case, making a Vb adjectival. When this is done, it is possible to build up a further maximal phrase repeating modifiers of groups IV, III, II, and I, ending with a noun which is then the head of the whole group. Here, then, is an example of a noun phrase which reaches the theoretical limit of complexity:

VI	Va	IV	III	II	I	N (Vb)	IV	III	II	I	N

all the ten pretty young American children's twenty little old china dolls

Such a sequence as this is not likely to occur in ordinary conversation, and even less likely to occur without being broken up by the occurrence of /||/ after the Vb noun. Yet, even though unlikely, it is constructed in strict accord with our habits of phrase structure and is therefore at least theoretically possible as well as understandable. It is interesting that the groups VI and V which occur in the first half of the maximal phrase cannot be repeated in the second half. That is, we do not say:

VI	Va	Vb	VI	V	I	N

all the children's *both their china dolls*

The construction here described is the so-called group genitive, the longest natural example of which, known to me, is a sentence recorded by the field workers of the *New England Atlas:* "She goes with *the boy who lives across the street's* brother." This particular example happens to fall at the end of a phrase of a different type, it is true, but the function of the phrase ending {-s} is the same as in the phrases we have been examining.

The most striking fact about this use of the determinative case ending is that it is still a bound morpheme, and so not an independent word; but though bound, it is not a component of the word to which it is added. It is, for instance, not possible to drop out *boy who lives across the* ("She goes with the . . . street's brother") and get a sensible sentence, while if we drop out *who lives across the street* we get the perfectly possible "She goes with the boy . . . –'s brother." That is, the case ending is a component only of the whole preceding phrase. It thus constitutes two exceptions to the usual rules of structure. First, it is an instance in which a free phrase is end-inflected, and second, it is one of the chief exceptions to the rule that morphemes are components of words or fixed phrases. It can therefore be called a phrasally bound inflectional morpheme, or postphrase.

We have called the modifiers of group v adjectivals, since they do not have the characteristics of true adjectives and since the noun and pronoun forms which appear here are special phrasal forms of words belonging normally to other form classes. It is worth mentioning that other analyses sometimes differ. Thus Curme has called *this* and *that* the only adjectives in English which are inflected for number.[4] To do so is to make an unnecessary distinction—*this* and *that*, whether we call them adjectives or adjectivals, belong to group v and share their characteristics with other members of the group. Number inflection appears in the pronouns of v*a* and in the nouns of v*b*. If it is argued that the number inflection of these forms is not governed by the number of the following noun (*the children's book*), as *these books* is governed, it can still be pointed out that the indefinite article (a group v modifier) is correlated with the number of the following noun, since the form of the indefinite article with a following plural is zero (*a book : books*).

We have had to deal at length with group v, so that it is pleasant that we can deal with group vi quickly. As already said, its membership is limited (*all, both, half*). All members are adjectivals rather than adjectives, since none of them are compared. They share with v*a* the characteristic that no more than one member of the group can occur in a single construction. They differ from most of the members of v*a* (all but *this* and *that*) in that group vi

---

[4] George O. Curme, *A Grammar of the English Language*, Vol. III, *Syntax*, Heath, New York, 1931, p. 508.

modifiers stand before /|||/ and /#/, while v*a* forms do not. The group are not all alike in distribution, however. *All* and *both* have a unique characteristic in that they alone stand as modifiers in pronoun constructions and with the pronoun preceding: *they all, they both.* All three forms have a further distributional feature, which they share with *some* (see below) and *more, most,* in that they occur in constructions which follow the model of *(the) top of (the) table, (the) top of it.* That is, these modifiers act as nominals in constructions with following preposition and noun or pronoun. Examples are *all of them, both of them, half of them, some of them, more of them, most of them.* While this characteristic differentiates group vi rather sharply from group v, it is shared with other modifying groups, since we have forms like *the blue of the sky.*

Before we leave the six groups of modifiers and pass on to adverbs, it should be said once more that it is quite possible that there are more groups than six. There are at least four modifiers with special characteristics which call for further investigation. *Same* and *very* (with secondary stress) normally fall between v and iv as in *"the same ten houses"* and *"the very ten* houses (we were talking about)." *Same* and *very* differ, however, in that *same* can occur finally, before any modifier of groups iv, iii, ii, or i or before a noun, whereas *very* must be followed by a group iv modifier or a noun. Adjectival *more* and adjectival *pretty* fall between iv and iii, as in *"tên môre bêautiful* wómen" and *"tên prêtty expênsive* hóuses." All of these unique forms are adjectivals, rather than adjectives, since none are compared.

Still another modifier with special characteristics is *some.* The most striking characteristic of this form is its variation in stress. It may occur with secondary stress before a following noun, as in "That was *sôme dínner!"* (i.e., "a remarkable dinner"). It may occur, again before a noun, with tertiary stress, as in *"Sòme bóys* | did it." If the form following *some* is adjectival *more,* that is, *more* with secondary stress, *some* may even have weak stress, as in "I want *sŏme môre bútter."* These several sets of stress forms are not, therefore, all the same thing. *Some* with secondary stress is an adjectival, though not a true adjective since it cannot be compared. It cannot be assigned to any one of the order groups, though its order characteristics can be described easily enough. That is, it is a unique form which precedes group iv, as in:

IV   III   II   I

sôme tên fíne ôld stône hóuses

It may, of course, precede a modifier of any lower group, if modifiers of the groups higher than the one preceded by *some* are absent. Another of its unique characteristics, at least in my idiolect, is that *some* with secondary stress cannot be preceded by a modifier of group v or vi, at least in the same phrase, though forms like "They were *bóth* | *sóme dínners*" are perfectly possible.

The form of *some* with tertiary stress belongs to group v—it cannot be an adverb, since it occurs immediately before the noun. Its position is partially verified by a construction like:

III   II   I

sòme fíne ôld stône hóuses

That is, it occurs before group III. It cannot, however, occur before group IV, since it is only the secondarily stressed *some* which occurs there. *Some* with tertiary stress can hardly be assigned to group IV, since it is not a numeral and does not form part of a fixed numeral phrase. Its stress characteristics therefore safely assign it to group v, and therefore the fact that it can be neither preceded nor followed by a modifier of group v*a* is what we should expect. It can, however, be followed by a modifier of group v*b*, as in *sòme mân's clothing*, but since we can have other v*a* modifiers followed by a v*b* modifier, as in *the man's clothing*, this also is normal. As a modifier of group v*a*, its chief peculiarity is that it cannot, like others of the group, be preceded by a member of group VI.

The form of *some* with weak stress is again unique and occurs only before adjectival *more*. It can then be stated to be a reduced form of the tertiarily stressed *some*, which makes the first component of a fixed phrase with the following *more*.

Our final statement about phrases of this type concerns adverbs. Again, it can be quickly made. Adverbs are forms which characteristically receive tertiary stress when they occur within nominal phrases, whereas the adjectives characteristically receive secondary. Adverbs also have relatively great freedom of order, since they can occur before a modifier of any one of the six groups, though not before the noun and not between VI and v. Adverbs always "modify" the following modifier, that is, they form a constituent with it. Adverbs can be confused with reduced adjectival forms, which also receive tertiary stress and which make constituent phrases with modifiers which precede or follow. If /|/ occurs after a tertiary form, the form is a reduced adjective making a fixed phrase with the modifier which precedes. If the /|/ occurs before the tertiary form, the order characteristics must be relied on to identify the form. Thus, tertiary *more* is an adverb because it can go before modifiers of groups III and I and, negatively, because it cannot occur before the noun. *Great* in *grèat bíg* was treated as a reduced adjective in a fixed phrase because it occurs only before the one modifier, *big*.

In this chapter, we have found it convenient merely to number the order groups of modifiers, which is clear enough, when as here, the model phrase is before us. In later chapters, however, we shall have occasion to refer to order groups again, where it will be inconvenient to repeat the model phrase. In such situations, descriptive names are more useful. So far as such names can be given, they are as follows: Group I, (*"stone* houses") are nominal modifiers. Group IV (*"ten* houses") are numerals. Group V (*"the* houses"), (*"Jack's* houses") can be called determinatives, and the case form of nouns is then the determinative case. Group VI (*"all* the houses") can be described as predeterminatives, making use of their position, the only group which can occur before the determinatives. Groups II and III, the true adjectives, cannot be conveniently named. They will, however, be referred to as adjectives of groups II and III, which should be sufficiently clear.

12.... VERB PHRASES, I

Two-Verb Constructions

1. Formal characteristics

Verb phrases form the heart of most English sentences and are of greater complexity than other sentence elements. They can contain multiple verb forms, like "I *want to try to get going* by ten"; they can contain multiple nonverbal elements, like *so thoroughly* in "I don't want to be *so thoroughly* examined"; and they may be discontinuous, interrupted by nominal material, as in "I want to try to have *these papers* gotten out by noon." Yet, in spite of this great complexity, it is possible to find in them a few relatively simple patterns, which are then combined to build up complicated series of the types illustrated. If the point of attack is on phrases containing no more than two verb forms, disregarding for the time being both those phrases with three or more verbs and those containing nonverbal material other than *to*, we find three basic types which may be exemplified as follows:[1]

TYPE A₁

I *can* (F1)
He *can* (F2) } *go* (F1—infinitive)
I *could* (F3)

TYPE A₂

I *want* (F1)
He *wants* (F2) } *to go* (F1—infinitive)
I *wanted* (F3)

TYPE B

I *keep* (F1)
He *keeps* (F2) } *trying* (F4—present participle)
I *kept* (F3)

TYPE C

I *have* (F1)
He *has* (F2) } *taken* (F5—past participle)
I *had* (F3)

---

[1] For the sake of convenience, verb form 1, form 2, etc. will be designated as F1, F2, etc. in this treatment of verb phrases.

As the table indicates, the types are based not on the forms of the first verb but on those of the second. It is also immediately noticeable that the only form found in both the first and second position is F1, the uninflected base. But even in constructions like *will go*, which have F1–F1, the first F1 is distinguishable from the F1 in second position. The first F1 is simply the common form of the non-past and varies with F2 when there is a gender-bearing subject. The second F1 does not thus vary, is often preceded by *to*, and in one verb has a separate form, *be*, which differs from its common non-past, *are*. For these reasons it is traditional to call the uninflected verb in second position an infinitive. In the discussions which follow, the traditional term will be adopted. Similarly, since forms 1, 2, and 3 can all appear in first position, we shall symbolize this range of possible variation as F1 (2,3). As is indicated in the table, there are two forms of the first type of phrase, which may be symbolized as F1(2,3)Inf. and F1(2,3)*to*-Inf. Only a few verbs can fit into the first position in the subtype without *to*, and since this subtype is therefore much more limited, it will be described first.

The most important verbs which do not take *to* are *can* ("can go"); *do* ("do go"); *may* ("may go"); *will* ("will go"); *shall* ("shall go"); and *must* ("must go"). All of these verbs take the negative suffix *–nt*, but not all negative verbs pattern in this fashion, since we have *oughtn't to go, isn't to go*. Some negative verbs vary. The older treatment of *dare* was without *to*, as in "I *dare do* all that may become a man"; and the construction lingers in some set phrases like "I dare say." Otherwise, forms like "He finally *dared to speak*" are now characteristic. *Need* usually has *to* in the positive ("He *needs to go*"),[2] but is without it in the negative ("He *needn't go*.")

A few non-negative verbs make constructions of this type, though the constructions are few in number and strictly limited. The most notable is *let*, which has *let go, let drive, let fly*, and occasionally *let pass* and *let be*. It is curious that the only other type of construction in which *let* appears is that with an intervening noun or pronoun, as in *let him talk*. That is, there are no constructions with *to* and other verbs in second position. *Make* appears in one construction of this type, *make do*. A final somewhat special case is *hear tell*, as in "I *hear tell* (or *say*) that he's leaving."[3] All of these non-negative verbs enter into the type of construction mentioned above with *let*, in which

---

[2] *Needs must*, a bookish construction, does not contain a verb as its first member, since we have forms like *we needs must*, which show that the morpheme which is added to *need* is not the suffix of F2. The morpheme found in *needs* is a now nearly isolated adverbial postbase.

[3] It has been suggested by Bernard Bloch that *better* in the colloquial *I better go* fits the pattern of verbs like *must*. Traditionally, of course, *better* is called an adverb. The traditional analysis then requires a zero allolog of *had* in the preceding position. Bloch's suggestion is found in an important study, "English Verb Inflection," *Language*, XXIII, 1947, pp. 399–418.

there is an intervening noun or pronoun, *make it do, hear it ring*. A number
of other verbs act similarly: *help him work, saw it fall*. In these constructions,
the intervening form belongs to another main division of the sentence, and
the total construction cannot be profitably discussed until we take up the
sequences of main sentence elements.

Syntactically, all examples of the subtype F1(2,3)Inf. are the same.
In stress superfixes which accompany the constructions there is sharp
variation. There are four superfixes: weak-primary, characteristic of most
of the negative verbs; tertiary-primary (varying with secondary-primary),
for some of the negative verbs like *must* and the non-negative *let*; secondary-
primary (without variation), for non-negatives like *make* in *make do*; and
primary-secondary in *he does go*. These superfixes have variants characterized by variation in the number of weak syllables, the most notable of
which is reduction of the weak-primary of *will go* to primary alone when the
first verb loses its syllabic quality in *I'll go*. Further, the phonemes of
primary stress described as occurring here are all subject to reduction to
secondary stress, but since these reductions are unpredictable except in
terms of units ultimately larger than the sentence, occurrence of weak-
secondary instead of weak-primary is stylistic variation.

The verbs which take the superfix weak-primary are *can, shall, will*, and
usually *must*. All have allologs which differ from their citation forms in the
segmental material contained, as, for instance, does weakly stressed *shall*
/šil/[4] from /šǽl/. The weak forms, however, are also influenced by the
juncture conditions, which vary even more widely than do the stress morphemes. If a verb phrase of the F1(2,3)Inf. type is preceded by a noun or
pronoun, the nominal material may be followed by /|||/ (rare), /||/, /+/, or no
juncture at all. Between the first and second verb of a phrase of this type,
there will be /+/ or no juncture. The presence or absence of the first and
second junctures makes for many phrase variants, not all of which are yet
fully known.

For *will*, the first juncture is regularly absent after pronouns, and the
forms of the verb then become {l} after semivowels and {il} after consonants,
as in *I'll go* /àyl + gów #/ and *It'll go* /ìtil + gów #/. The same forms of the

---

[4] In this chapter there is a necessary departure from the usual form of transcription.
Generally, a word like *shall* is given as /šǽl/, the citation form which necessarily has
primary stress. In this chapter verb forms are being discussed as members of phrases,
often with stress other than that which they would receive as citation forms. For this
reason a phrase such as *shall go* /šil + gów/, with superfix of weak-primary, is treated
as an entity from which /šil/ with weak stress is abstractable. The reader is warned
that transcriptions like /kǽnt/, an abstraction from the stress pattern of *can't go*, is
not the citation form, nor do we mean to imply that in other constructions *can't* must
necessarily have tertiary stress. In a situation like "No, I can't," *can't* receives primary
stress.

verbs appear after nouns, though here the first juncture is usually preserved. We thus have minimal distinctions involving /+/ and its absence in pairs like "The cat'll eat it" /ðə + kǽt + il + íyt + ìt #/ and "The cattle eat it" /ðə + kǽtil + íyt + ìt #/. Among verbs in the group now being described, only *will* has allologs consisting of the final consonant, or vowel and final consonant alone. The type is found elsewhere among negative verbs and will be fully discussed in connection with *be*.

Besides the weak forms of *will* just described, there is a third form, {wil}. The occurrence of this form can be predicted if for any reason the stress is raised to tertiary or if the first juncture is a single or double bar, as in /jǽk | wil + ɡów #/ *JACK will go*. Yet {wil} is not predictable in terms of either juncture or stress, since we can also have it after /+/ and with weak stress, where we should expect one of the forms without the initial consonant. A sentence like *Jack will go* is often /jǽk + wil + ɡów #/. The occurrence of such forms may turn out to be stylistically controlled, but even though {wil} and {l}∼{il} are paradigmatic equivalents and are both in complementary distribution with stressed {wíl}, they cannot be assigned to the same morpheme.

The F3 form of *will* has a similar set of weak forms, {d}∼{id}, on the one hand, and {wid}, on the other. Their distribution is the same as the F1 forms. That is, juncture is usually lost after a pronoun, as in *I'd go* /àyd + ɡów #/, while after a noun we may or may not keep the juncture, as in *Bob'd go* /bâbid + ɡów #/ or /bâb + id + ɡów #/. In forms with a plus, we may also get {wid}, as /bâb + wid + ɡów #/. In neither the F1 nor the F3 forms of this verb in phrases is the second juncture very commonly lost, nor does it produce any further assimilatory changes if it is. For *can* the weak forms may be somewhat more neatly sorted out. If both the first and second juncture are present, the weak form is {kin}, as in *Pete can go* /pîyt + kin + ɡów #/. If the second juncture is lost, the vowel remains, but the nasal is subject to assimilation by a following velar, as in /pîyt + kiŋɡów #/. If, on the other hand, the first juncture is lost, the form becomes /kin̩/, where the allophone of /i/ is syllabicity of the nasal consonant. The second juncture is then usually preserved, as in *I can try* /àykin̩ + tráy #/, but may be lost before a velar, as in *I can go* /àykiŋɡów #/. In this last form, however, the nasal remains syllabic. The F3 form is {kid}, and is subject to assimilation of the last consonant if the second juncture is lost, as in *I could see* /ày + kitsíy #/ or *I could try* /ày + kitráy #/. The preceding juncture maý or may not be present with the weak forms of *could*, and its absence produces no assimilatory effect.

The F1 and F2 forms of *shall* under weak stress are {šil}, and loss of the first juncture has no effect on the form. The second juncture is usually preserved. For F3, the weak form is {šid} if both junctures are present, as in *I should go* /ày + šid + gów #/. If the following juncture is lost, we again get assimilation of the final consonant, as in *I should see* /ày + šitsíy #/. If the preceding juncture is absent, the form becomes {št} whether or not the following juncture is present. We thus get *I should go* /àyšt + gów #/ and *I should eat* /àyštíyt #/. The latter form is interesting, since though the syllable division is before /t/, there is no aspiration. The aspirate /t/ occurs only after juncture.

The last verb which takes the superfix weak-primary is *must*, though this verb may also take tertiary-primary. With either superfix the weak form is {mìs} or {məs} before the sequence juncture-consonant, or consonant alone, as in *we must go* /wìy + mìs + gów #/, *we must come* /wìy + mìs + kə́m #/ or /wìy + miskə́m #/. Before the sequence juncture-vowel, or vowel alone, the form may retain its final /t/, *we must eat* /wìy + mìst + íyt #/ or /wìy + mistíyt #/. Absence of the first juncture produces no further effect on the form of the verb, /wìymistíyt #/.

The second stress superfix is tertiary-primary. It has already been mentioned that it may occur with *must*. When *must* receives tertiary stress, the junctures are present, but there are no differing forms of the base. A negative verb which regularly receives the superfix tertiary-primary is *may* and its F3 form, *might*. The forms are then *I may go* /ày + mèy + gów #/ and *I might go* /ày + màyt + gów #/. The latter form, however, rather frequently receives contrastive stress, with primary-secondary, /ày + máyt + gôw #/.

The non-negative verb which takes tertiary-primary is *let*, usually in the phrase *let go*. The usual form of the verb is /lèt/ if /+/ follows, as in /lèt + gów #/ or /lèt + dráyv #/. *Let go*, however, often lacks /+/, becoming /lègów #/. Often the juncture is then restored, giving /lèg + gów #/, presumably the form indicated by the common dialect spelling *leggo*. The first juncture is not usually absent.

The tertiary-primary superfix, more generally speaking, is characteristic of the negative forms of negative verbs, all of which take it, though with individual variations in the juncture pattern. For *can* the F1 negative form is /kænt/ (with dialectal variations, of course), and this form may be preserved if the second juncture is present, *I can't go* /ày + kænt + gów #/, *I can't eat* /ày + kænt + íyt #/. It may also be preserved, even without the second juncture, if the following phoneme is a vowel, /ày + kæntíyt #/. A second weak form consists simply of /kæ̀–/, or whatever vowel nucleus may be used, plus nasality. The nasal quality is then to be interpreted as an allophone of /n/, /m/, or /ŋ/, depending upon the articulatory position of the following phoneme, as in *I can't tell* /ày + kæntél #/, *I can't pass* /ày + kæmpǽs #/, *I can't go* /ày + kæŋgów #/. The forms with nasal vowel or vowel nucleus are not used before vowels even when the second juncture is present. Somewhat surprisingly, these forms with nasalized vowel are also used before the sequence juncture-consonant, as in /ày + kæ̀n + téll #/, /ày + kæ̀m + pǽs #/, /ày + kæ̀ŋ + gów #/. Such occurrences are surprising because the presence of a plus, with its resultant lengthening of the preceding phoneme, normally acts to protect that phoneme from loss. The development here is understandable, however, if we assume that the juncture has been restored after reduction of the nasal consonant.[5]

The F3 negative form for *can* is usually /kùdin/ with syllabic nasal and following juncture. Before juncture and vowel, or before vowel alone, it may be /kùdint/, as in *I couldn't eat* /ày + kùdint + íyt #/ or /ày + kùdintíyt #/. The negative verbs, *shan't : shouldn't* and *won't : wouldn't* have forms strictly parallel to *can't : couldn't*. That is, the F1 forms are /šæ̀nt/ and /šæ̀n/, /šæ̀m/, /šæ̀ŋ/ with nasalization of the vowel, and /wòwnt/ besides /wòwn/, /wòwm/, /wòwŋ/, again with nasalized vowel. The F3 forms are /šùdin/ and /wùdin/ with syllabic nasal and usually with following juncture. The distribution of these forms, and the problems they raise are exactly similar to those for *can't : couldn't*.

The negative forms of *may* are peculiar only in that the non-past form, /mèyint/, is very rarely used in the United States, though it is more frequent in England. The negative of the F3 form, *mightn't*, is commoner and has the expected form /màytin/, with loss and preservation of the final consonant under conditions similar to those for forms like *couldn't*. *Don't : didn't* also take tertiary-primary, though as has been said, the positive forms of this verb ordinarily take a quite different stress superfix. The variants of *don't* and *didn't* are similar in shape and distribution to *can't : couldn't*; that is, there are forms which are to be phonemicized as /dòwn/, /dòwm/, /dòwŋ/ according to the position of the following consonant, though all actually occur as mere nasalization of the vowel nucleus. All occur both with and without a following /+/. The F3 form is /dìdin/, with variations exactly parallel to those for /kùdin/. There is one feature which is of interest in the negative forms of *do*. *Do*, alone among the negative verbs which occur regularly before a following infinitive without *to*, has a differentiated F2

---

[5] There are difficulties in the interpretation of these forms. A possibly serious one is in phonemic interpretation. If we contrast the juncture form of *until* /ən + tíl/ with *can't tell* /kæ̀N + tél/ (where N is written to indicate nasalization of the vowel without full /n/ articulation), the nasal quality and the fully articulated /n/ would seem to be in contrast. I have chosen to disregard the possibility that nasality and nasal consonants contrast, largely for reasons of structural simplicity which make me believe that the difficulty can be resolved when more evidence has been gathered.

There is further difficulty in a historical interpretation of forms which have nasality followed by /+/. In Early Middle English, the sequence unstressed vowel-nasal-juncture regularly lost the nasal consonant. The mechanism of this change has not been investigated in the light of juncture.

form, *does*, and a negative for it, *doesn't*. The negative form, as has been said earlier, is often undifferentiated, that is, *he don't*, a construction which has been one of the shibboleths of normative grammar. As might be expected, the weak form of *doesn't* is /dəzɪnt/ or /dəzɪn/, with loss or preservation of the final consonant as in *couldn't*.

The verb constructions of this type without *to* before the second member which we have so far described have had the superfixes {`+´} or {˘+´} often with loss of /+/. Other superfixes occur, however. The superfix {ˆ + ´}, normally characteristic of other types of verb phrases, occurs with two relatively isolated phrases without *to*, *hear tell* and *make do*, in both of which juncture loss is unusual. The superfix {´ + ˆ} also occurs with the verb *do* when it is the first member of this phrase type, as in *he does go* /hìy + dɔ́z + gôw #/. Though this superfix is now normal with *do* phrases in the positive, other superfixes occurred with it in earlier English, as in "The Northwind *dòth blów*." The superfix {´ + ˆ} with other than *do* phrases is characteristic of contrastive sentences as in "He *will* go" /hìy + wíl + gôw #/, and therefore *do* phrases can also be said to contain an element of contrast. That is, "He does go" is not the normal answer to a question like "Is he going?" but is rather the normal positive response to a negative form like "He doesn't go."

Our second subtype is F1(2,3)*to*-Inf. This is one of the commonest verb phrases, and most verbs can occupy first position in it. Yet some limitation there is, since we do not say, as some foreigners do, "He **accepts to take* the position." The limitations on verbs which enter this construction could be profitably studied only by listing all the verbs in the language, and the task has not been done. It would be worth doing as a part of the information which should eventually be available to dictionary makers and as a means of settling a minor but troublesome point of difficulty for learners of the language. In the meantime, however, it is worth pointing out that the phrase type is sufficiently common so that new and nonce formations which conform to it are readily acceptable, as in such a form as "His sentences fairly *explode to signify*."

The normal stress pattern for the type is secondary-primary, or more exactly, secondary-weak-primary, since *to* intervenes between the first and second verb and receives weak stress. The juncture pattern of an example of the phrase like *he wants to go* admits of considerable variation with consequent variation in stress. We can have /hìy + wɔ́nts + tə + gów #/, with a total of three junctures, all /+/; or we may have /hìy + wɔ́nts | tə + gów #/ with the juncture following the first verb raised to /||/. The /+/ following *to* may be lost, but it is not normally raised to /||/. The fact that the juncture after the first verb may often be a terminal indicates that the phrase should be divided into immediate constituents before rather than after the *to*. Yet, in larger syntactic contexts, phrases of this type pattern in a way which is a little surprising in the light of the immediate constituent boundaries. That is, in repetitions of the phrase type, where there is a differing first verb but identical second verb, as in "He not only *wants to go*, he *plans to*," it is not the whole of the second constituent which is represented by zero, but only the verb form. It is worth noting, however, that in such repeated forms with zero second verb, the juncture before *to* may still be a single bar, /hìy + nàt + ôwnliy + wónts + tə + gôw ‖ hìy + plǽnz | túw #/. That is, the possible terminal juncture here also demonstrates that a major boundary occurs before the *to*.

The conditions just described for *want*, in both stress and juncture patterns, apply to nearly all verbs which can occupy first position in phrases of this type. This is true even for such negative verbs as *ought* and for *need* (in the positive only) when they occur in this type of phrase. Two verbs, *have* and *used*, are peculiar in their juncture pattern, in that both have lost the juncture before *to* and consequently have undergone assimilation of the final consonant. The forms of *have* which occur in this phrase are /hǽf/, *I have to go* /ày + hǽftə + gów #/; and /hǽs/, *he has to go* /hìy + hǽstə + gów #/. The form of the past is sometimes /hǽ/, *he had to go* /hìy + hǽtə + gów #/, but is often /hǽt/ with a restored juncture, *he had to go* /hìy + hǽt + tə + gów #/. The form spelled *used* is phonemically /yûws/, *I used to go* /ày + yûwstə + gów #/, so that a near-minimal distinction is set up between pairs like "This is the pen I use to write with" /ðìs + izðə + pén + ày + yûwz + tə + ráyt + wìð #/ and "This is the pen I used to write with" /ðìs + izðə + pén | ày + yûwstə + ráyt + wìð #/. The first sentence means "This is the pen I employ in writing," while the second means "This is the pen I formerly wrote with." The form /yûws/ is historically a past tense of *use* but can no longer be referred to the same base, since both forms can occur in identical environments. That is, though /yûws/ normally occurs without following juncture, the juncture may be restored, giving /yûws + tə + ráyt #/, which is then in contrast with *use to write* /yûwz + tə + ráyt #/.

Somewhat similarly, even though it is less commonly realized, the *have* which occurs in the phrase *have to go* is best not analyzed as an allolog of *have*, "to possess." The phrase *he has to* may be /hìy + hǽs + tùw #/ with contrastive stress and juncture. The phrase *he has two* may occur in the shape /hìy + hǽz + tûw #/, thus constituting a minimal contrast between the two morphemes. These somewhat rare types of contrast are supported by nonminimal contrasts like "These are the ones I *have to go*" /. . . hǽv + tə + gów #/ and *have to go* /hǽf + tə + gów #/. Strictly speaking, our previous description of *have* as a negative verb does not apply to the *have* which occurs in this phrase, nor to the *have* which means "possess." Both verbs, at least in American English, construct negatives with *don't*, "I don't have to go" and "I don't have it," though British English also has the construction "I haven't it," which seems unnatural in America. There are, thus, three entities which are often lumped together as forms of a single verb: *have*-1 ("possess"), which is a non-negative verb and which does not enter into the F1(2,3)*to*-Inf. construction; *have*-2 ("be under obligation [to . . .]"), a non-negative verb characteristic of the F1(2,3)*to*-Inf. construction, but with a different phonemic shape from *have*-1; and *have*-3, the only negative verb of the group whose syntactical characteristics will be described below.

In colloquial American English there is still another verb which is subject to loss of following juncture and which has developed from an old past form in a way similar to that which gives us *used to*. This is the *got* of phrases like "When you gotta go, you gotta go." The form is then an uninflected verb like *used* and gives contrasts like /ày + gâtə + gów #/ ("I must go") and /ày + gât + tə + gów #/ ("I was given the opportunity of going"). Needless to say, the formal equivalent of *I gotta go* is *I've got to go*, containing a minimal allolog of *have*-3 and a following past participle.

Relatively complicated as these phrases with *used to*, *have to*, and *got to* are, they are far surpassed by the complexity of the verb *be* in phrases of the type *I'm to go*.[6] The forms of these phrases are best approached in terms of the weakest forms of the verb *be*, not merely in these phrases but in fully articulated sentences where some form of *be* is the only verb. These can be illustrated by the following sentences:

F1 *We're men.* /wìr + mén #/ or /wìy + ər + mén #/
F1*b* *I'm a man.* /àymə + mǽn #/ or /ày + əmə + mǽn #/
F2 (A) *John's a man.* /jân + zə + mǽn #/ or /jânizə + mǽn #/
 (B) *Jack's a man.* /jæ̀k + sə + mǽn #/ or /jæ̀kizə + mǽn #/
 (C) *Rose's a girl.* /rôwz + izə + gə́rl #/ or /rôwzizə + gə́rl #/
F3 *They were men.* /ðèy + wər + mén #/ or /ðèywər + mén #/
F3*a* *I was a teacher.* /ày + wəzə + tíycər #/ or /ày + wizə + tíycər #/ or /àywizə + tíycər #/

These forms are interesting if for no other reason than that they give a contrast between two such utterances as *Jack's driving*, that is, "Jack is driving," and *Jack's driving*, which is the simple possessive. The first is /jæ̀k + s + dráyviŋ #/ or perhaps /jæ̀k | s + dráyviŋ #/, while the second is /jæ̀ks + dráyviŋ #/. Yet, as can be seen from the examples, it is not adequate merely to say that a juncture is always preserved before these weak forms. For F1, the full form *are* is reduced to /r/ alone, which occurs

---

[6] See pp. 200–01.

without juncture after semivowels or vowels. After a semivowel the form is /ər/ if the juncture is present. On the other hand, in forms like *sheep are animals*, the juncture and allolog distribution is different, since after a consonant the reduced form is /ər/ with or without a preceding juncture. For F1*b*, the distribution is somewhat simpler, since it occurs only after the pronoun *I*, that is, after a semivowel. Here /æm/ is reduced to /m/ alone if there is no juncture, but to /əm/ if the juncture is present. It is in the forms of 2, here divided into three allologs, A, B, and C, that the greatest complexity arises. When *is* occurs after consonants, as above, there is preservation of the base morpheme only after the sibilant spirants and /c/, and /j/, as in the example *Rose's a girl*. After other consonants and vowels and semivowels, the base is represented by a zero allomorph, and the final consonant is assimilated across the juncture to a preceding voiceless phoneme, giving the /s/ of the example *Jack's a man*.

The treatment of *is* after consonants and with preservation of juncture throws light on the history of noun forms with case and number suffixes, since as we have seen, the case and number suffixes are assimilated to the consonant of the preceding base in a fashion exactly similar to the forms of *is*, though there is now no juncture before the suffixes. It can be stated as a law of English sound-change that the normal direction of assimilation is for the first consonant to be assimilated to the second when there is no intervening juncture, as in *has to* /hǽstə/; *in case* /iŋkéys/; *width* /wítθ/. When, however, there is an intervening juncture, as with the weak forms of *is*, the first consonant is lengthened, and the result is then assimilation of the second consonant to the first. It can therefore be assumed that the case and number suffixes, both of which once contained a vowel, must have developed through a stage in which the vowel was replaced by a juncture, producing the assimilatory developments which differentiated the three allomorphs of the suffixes. After the assimilations had occurred, the junctures were then lost, giving the present forms.

The weak and nonsyllabic forms of *am, is, are*, all occur in phrases of the F1(2,3)*to*-Inf. type, giving forms like *I'm to go* /àym + tə + gów #/; *we're to go* /wìr + tə + gów #/; *John's to go* /jân + z + tə + gów #/ or /jânz + tə + gów #/ or, with juncture loss and consequent normal assimilation, /jânstə + gów #/. The assimilated form of *is* occurs in *Jack's to go* /jǽk + s + tə + gów #/, and the form with preserved vowel occurs in *Rose's to go* /rôwz + iz + tə + gów #/ or /rôwziz + tə + gów/.

Beside these nonsyllabic forms, however, there is a second set of forms of *am, is, are*, with full vowels and tertiary stress, giving *I am to go* /ày + æ̀m + tə + gów #/; *we are to go* /wìy + àr + tə + gów #/; *Jack is to go* /jǽk + ìz + tə + gów #/. Historically it would seem likely that the forms of *be* in this construction normally took the stress superfix tertiary-primary, as in these examples, since these are the normal forms and the superfix weak-primary is not usually found. The nonsyllabic forms of *be* have been, then, analogically extended to this construction from sentences like *Jack's a man*; they did not originate in this construction.

The F3 forms normally have tertiary stress: *I was to go* /ày + wɜ̀z + tə + gów #/; *we were to go* /wìy + wɜ̀r + tə + gów #/. The stress superfix weak-primary is found, however, giving /ày + wìz + tə + gów #/. The negative forms all occur with tertiary-primary: *he isn't to go* /hìy + ìzin + tə + gów #/; *he wasn't to go* /hìy + wɜ̀zin + tə + gów #/. They may, of course, have primary stress under conditions of contrast.

Our second main type of verb phrase is that which can be symbolized as F1(2,3)F4, as in *he keeps trying*. The phrase type is common, but a curious limitation on its construction is that none of the negative verbs except *be* and *need* enter into it. That is, we say, "He is going" and "It needs washing," but not "He *can going*" or "He *will going*." It is noteworthy with *need*, however, that its negative forms do not enter into the construction, the negative of "It needs washing" being "It doesn't need washing," not "It *needn't washing*."

It is usual for non-negative verbs to occur in this construction with the superfix secondary-primary, as in such common examples as *stop talking* /stâp + tɔ́kiŋ #/; *try writing* /trây + ráytiŋ #/; *start moving* /stârt + múwviŋ #/. The same superfix can occur with two other constructions which are therefore homonymous with the verb phrase in *–ing*. One of these is verb and following object in *–ing*, as in *buy toweling* /bây + táwəliŋ #/; and the other is verb and following *–ing* form as a modifier, as in *eat standing* /îyt + stǽndiŋ #/. Though such forms are often enough homonymous with the verb phrase, they are distinguished from it by the ways in which each is expandable. That is, *buy toweling* can be expanded to *buy some toweling* or *buy towelings*, where it is then clear that *toweling* is a noun. Forms like *keep talking* cannot be thus expanded. Similarly *eat standing* can be expanded to *eat while standing*, which is again impossible for *keep talking*. Further, a construction like *buy toweling* is not merely a phrase, since it consists of two main sentence elements, verb and object. It is therefore capable of being said with /‖/ instead of /+/ between its two parts. The same observation applies to *eat standing*, which consists of verb and modifier. It is, of course, possible to use /‖/ between the two parts of *keep talking*, but this is much less likely and will occur only when something in the stylistic situation calls for an unusual type of utterance. Such considerations enable the analyst to separate the several constructions which may be homonymous, but it is not at all likely that interpretation of ambiguous constructions is done by this sort of testing in everyday language use. The ordinary user of language is apt merely to say that *standing* is not something that can be eaten, so that to interpret *eat standing* as if it were parallel to *eat bread* is impossible. The appeal to meaning is here a convenient short cut, though as usual it is an inexact method of analysis. More exactly, one can say that the most probable type of noun which occurs after a verb like *eat* is a simple base, without such postbases as *-ing*. Only with an occasional form such as *seasoning* is the relation verb-object possible if the verb is *eat*. Thus, to interpret *eat standing* as verb and modifier is more probable than to interpret it as verb and object. Similarly, there are no frequently occurring verb phrases in *-ing* where *eat* is the first verb; that is, there is nothing like **eat talking* parallel to *stop talking*. The interpretation of *eat standing* follows lines of probability.

It was said above that verbal phrases in *-ing* are rather common, but it is still true that the number of normal verbs which enter into them as first component is not large. A partial list of them is *begin* ("begin talking"), *get* ("get going"), *keep* ("keep trying"), *need* ("it needs washing"), *quit* ("quit pushing"), *remember* ("I remember meeting him"), *seem* (Curme quotes a rather rare form—"He seems waiting"), *start* ("start talking"), *stop* ("stop talking"), *want* ("it wants doing"). It is probable that an accurate check on all verbs in the language would not increase the list very greatly. In all these forms the superfix is secondary-primary, and the juncture sequence is /||/ or /+/ before and after the phrase, with /+/ between the two verbs. The statement that phrases of this type are common means, then, that examples of it occur with great frequency, rather than that the list of verbs which enter into the construction is large.

By far the most frequent example of the phrase type is that in which the verb *to be* occupies the first position. When this happens, the set of weak and nonsyllabic forms described for *be* on page 199 are most commonly employed, giving sentences like *I'm talking* /àym + tókiŋ #/, *Jack's talking* /jæ̀k + s + tókiŋ #/. But besides these nonsyllabic forms, there is a set of relatively full forms which occur with weak stress, /jæ̀k + iz + tókiŋ #/, as well, of course, as forms which occur with one of the stronger grades of stress, *I am talking* /ày + æ̀m + tókiŋ #/. The past tense and negative forms are the same as those described for constructions of the type *isn't to go*. The fact that the several forms of the verb *be* occur in identical environments proves that these forms are not allomorphs of the same morpheme. They are, however, members of the same paradigmatic family, just as, in the inflection of nouns, the suffixes which occur in *brethren* and *brothers* are different morphemes but members of the same paradigmatic family.

The third and last type of verb phrase is F1(2,3)past-participle, as in *he has gone*. Phrases of this type also occur frequently, but the number of verbs which enter into the first position in the construction is even smaller than for the verb phrase in *-ing*. Among negative verbs only *have* ("He hasn't gone") and *be* ("He isn't gone") appear here. Among non-negative verbs, the only clear member of this construction is *get* ("He got gone by ten o'clock.")

A difficulty arises, however, with verbs like *seem* and *become*. There are constructions, *seemed taken* and *became taken*, which look much like *had taken*. The difficulty arises from the fact that many adjectives make use of postbases which are homonymous with the suffixes of past participles (*wooden, wooded*). If we then say that *seemed taken, became taken* contain adjectives as their second members, we would seem to be appealing to meaning, or being merely arbitrary. The decision is based, however, on satisfactorily formal, though syntactic, grounds. The construction *seemed taken* can be expanded by the addition of *very*, which is characteristic of adjectives ("He *seemed very taken* with her"). Further, there are some past participles, like *died*, for which there is no corresponding homonymous adjective. *Seem* and *become* do not occur before such participles—that is, we do not say "He **seemed died."* These characteristics give us a fairly clear picture. All instances of ambiguity in constructions with *seem* and *become* can be resolved as adjectives, and none need be analyzed as past participles.

The same ambiguity exists with *be* and following forms which may be either adjectives or past participles, but unfortunately the ambiguity here is not so readily solvable. Though we do not say **was been* or **was died* any more than we say **seems been* or **became died*, there is at least one unambiguous past participle before which *be* can occur. This is *had*, as in the favorite example of triteness, "A good time *was had* by all." In my idiolect *seemed* cannot appear here without additional material—"A good time seemed *to be* had by all"—while *became* cannot be fitted into the sentence at all. There is, then, good reason for assuming that *be* can occur before past participles. On the other hand, *be* can also appear before adjectives, as in "The plate *is very hot*." If, in turn, we are faced with a construction like "He *is tired* of it," we can substitute *has* for *is*, which suggests that *tired* is here a participle. But contrariwise, we can expand to "He *is very tired* of it," which suggests that *tired* is an adjective.

In order to make decisions consistently we must give priority to the test of expandability by *very*. In "He is tired of it," *tired* is an adjective, since we can precede it by *very*. In "He is spanked by his father," *spanked* is a participle, since "He is **very spanked* by his father" is impossible. The form in which *has* occurs is, by this test, always a participle, since no construction such as "He has tired of it" is expandable by adding *very*. Whether *has* may be substituted for *is* does not constitute a reliable test. "He is spanked by his father" shows *spanked* as a participle, even though *has* cannot here be substituted for *is*. In "He is tired of it," *has* is substitutable, yet we must decide that *tired* is an adjective after *is*. *Tired* is a form which may be either participle or adjective; it is an adjective after *is*, a participle after *has*. These decisions, it is true, belong to the analysis of complete sentences rather than to description of verb phrases. At this point it is necessary only to point out that it is clear that *be* can occur in the type of phrase under discussion.

We have then, in accord with Hockett, limited the verbs which can appear in first position in this construction to three; *be, have, get*.[7] They can be fairly quickly described. With *be* and past participle, the same weak forms of the verb appear as have been described for sentences like *Jack's a man*. Syllabic forms with weak stress occur, as well as nonsyllabic variants, as described for the construction consisting of *be* and a verb in –*ing*. The negative forms are again the same as in the –*ing* construction. That is, they have the superfix tertiary-primary, and the juncture sequence is the same as that of *isn't going*.

The forms of *have* and past participle require some further description. First, this form does not contain *have*-1 ("possess": "I have three dollars"), or *have*-2 ("be under obligation [to . . .]": "I have to go"), but, as stated earlier, it contains a form to be called *have*-3, the only one of the three *have* verbs which is a genuine negative verb in American English. That is, only in this construction do we have forms like "He *hasn't* gone." Thus, it is the forms of this verb which were described in Chapter 9 as belonging to class VII, 1*b*. The verb we are now describing, *have*-3, has different stress and juncture patterns from those found for *have*-1 and *have*-2. This verb, like *will, be*, and occasionally *do*, has weak allologs which consist in the last consonant of the total form. Thus, we have *I've gone* and *we've gone* and a further set in the gender form which is /s/, /z/, or /ɨz/ distributed exactly like the weak forms of *is*. The juncture conditions for these forms are also like those for the weak forms of *be*. That is, *I've gone* is /àyv + góhn #/, with loss of juncture after the pronoun, but in *John and Mary've gone*, the juncture is preserved, giving /jân + in + mêriy + v + góhn #/ or /jân + in + mêriy + ɨv + góhn #/. In the gender forms, *Jack's gone*, the juncture is regularly preserved after nouns and again lost after pronouns. *Jack's gone* is then /jæk + s + góhn #/, and the construction is completely homonymous with the weak form of *is* in *Jack is gone*. The F3 form of *have*-3 is /d/ with loss of juncture after pronouns, giving /àyd + góhn #/. After nouns the juncture is usually preserved as /jân + d + góhn #/ or /jân + ɨd + góhn#/. After /d/ and /t/ the weak form is /ɨd/ with or without the preceding juncture. Thus we have *it had gone* without juncture as /ìtɨd + góhn#/, but *Pete had gone* with it /pîyt + ɨd + góhn#/. Besides these various nonsyllabic forms

---

[7] "English Verb Inflection," *Studies in Linguistics*, No. 2, 1942, pp. 1–8.

and forms with loss of the initial consonant, there are also forms with /h/ and weak stress. These forms, however, always preserve the preceding juncture. Thus we can say *Jack has gone* in the shape /jæk + hiz + góhn #/ or /jǽk | hiz + góhn #/. Correspondingly, we can also say *Jack had gone* with /jæk + hid + góhn #/ or /jǽk | hid + góhn #/. The forms with the vowel /æ/—/hǽv/, /hǽd/, etc.—occur only with one of the stronger grades of stress. The negative forms are /hæ̀vint/, /hæ̀zint/, /hæ̀dint/, and with these forms the phrase takes the superfix tertiary-primary. The final consonant of the negative forms is subject to assimilatory loss when the following juncture is absent.

In contrast with the complexity of the forms of *have-3* the forms of *get* in this construction are simple. Forms like *get taken* take the superfix secondary-primary and preserve the full set of junctures.

2. Structural semantic components

The description that we have given of the infinitive, *-ing*, and past participle phrases has been formal throughout, with no attention to meaning and function. In contrast, the semantic approach is typified by Sweet, who describes verb phrases as part of the English tense system.[8] He thus includes among the tenses of the verb simple forms like *saw* and phrases like *have seen*. Some phrases, like *try to do*, are not described at all. The traditional approach is not, however, without some justification, and Sweet's semantic observations are, as always, acute. There are many sentences where a phrase is required, and the use of a simple verb is a mistake in structure. A typical sentence where a phrase is required is "I am writing now"; the form "I write now," unless it is in a context such as an answer to "Do you print or use script nowadays?" is a mistake which would mark the user as a non-native speaker. Such required phrases make up a systematic part of structure, but belong to syntax rather than to morphology. In other instances, however, as in the contrast between "Run!" and "Keep running!" the phrase is required by nothing in the structure of the sentence and is a part of semantics only, not of syntax.

In describing the meaning and function of verb phrases, we shall limit ourselves to those which have some structural importance, even though many of those which have semantic importance only have peculiarities which are surprising. Thus for instance *keep* in "Keep running!" has no function

---

[8] *New English Grammar*, Part I, Pars. 274 ff.

that could be predicted from that of *keep* in "Keep it!" The meaning of *keep* followed by an *–ing* is to be referred to forms like "Keep cool" rather than to *keep* when followed directly only by a noun or pronoun.

The group of verbs which are followed by an infinitive without *to* are traditionally called modal auxiliaries, with *shall* and *will* described as making a simple future, and *may* as making a subjunctive. These forms do indeed translate many simple futures or subjunctives in languages like Latin or Spanish, but if a form like *may go* is to be described as a special mood, then a form like *must go* should also be described as a mood form, possibly a "necessitous mood," and so on throughout the whole list, an obviously wasteful procedure. Nor, to return to *will go*, is it quite true that future time requires it. There are future uses of the non-past tense, as in "He goes to Chicago tomorrow," and many other phrases besides *will go* which can occur in such a sentence: "He can go to Chicago tomorrow," "He wants to go to Chicago tomorrow," and so on.

A sentence used by a speaker of German background is here instructive. In describing arrangements for the coming evening he said, "I tell you what I do tonight." Any native speaker would feel that such a sentence is a mistake. Also, the corrections are almost always similar. We usually say the sentence should have been "I'll tell you what I'll do tonight." Yet the correction in this form is not the only way of making the sentence acceptable. First, *I'll tell* is not necessary, since *I tell*, though less common, can here be used as the future of the non-past. Second, any other of the verbs directly followed by an infinitive would make a syntactically satisfactory sentence, *can do*, *must do*, *may do*, and so on. Even such other phrases as *have to do*, *want to do*, *want done*, *plan to do*, *am doing* are equally satisfactory. The syntactic requirement then is merely that a phrase must be used in place of a simple verb. Exactly what combination is employed is a matter of the meaning of the individual phrase. In short, all the phrases made up of verbs and infinitive without *to* contain a semantic component which makes them acceptable with such an indicator of future time as *tonight* in the situation described above; and many others like *want done* and *am doing*, though not *used to do* or *have done*, contain the same semantic component.

Phrases of the verb-*to*-infinitive type need no further explanation, though "He *is to speak*" is semantically unpredictable. The sentence is appropriate in such a context as "We have made all the plans, and John *is to speak*." It contains a component which can be at least roughly transcribed as "future action in accord with already set arrangements." The phrase "It is to laugh" is an idiom, on the other hand, whose meaning is not inferable from its parts.

In phrases of the verb–*ing* type, only those of the *am going*, *is going* pattern need special description. For most verbs, there is a sharp distinction between forms such as *goes* and *is going*.[9] The difference is very clear in such a pair as *he drinks* and *he is drinking*. The one is habitual action and is required in such a sentence as "He —— everyday," where the blank can be filled by *drinks, shaves, studies*, and many more. The other is non-past, non-habitual action, and if our sentence is "He —— right now," we would fill the blank with *is drinking, is shaving*, or *is studying*. For most verbs the requirement is as given, and the distinction between the simple form and the phrase is meaningful, even when there is nothing in the context to require it. Not all verbs act in this way, however, since we say "I understand it now" and "I see it now." Forms like "I am understanding it now" are so rare as to be abnormal, and "I am seeing him now" is a form with different meaning. For one large group of verbs which do not require the *-ing* form in non-habitual action, Martin Joos has coined the apt name "private verbs." That is, no one but the speaker himself is a competent witness to such action as seeing or understanding, while with an action such as looking at, the hearer can verify what is occurring. There are, then, interesting variations, such as "I see the President over there," where *see* is a private verb, and "I'm seeing the President at ten," where *see* is a public verb meaning "meet for consultation." Yet, while the distinction between private and public verbs is a useful teaching device and makes clear to learners of the language why we say "I like apple pie now," but "It is raining now," it is not a sufficiently accurate description to take care of all cases. For instance, none of the negative verbs (or verbs homonymous with negative verbs) except *do*, *be*, and *have*-1 ("possess") have developed non-habitual forms commonly used. To these, *need* can certainly be added in some constructions, since "I'm always needing money" is perfectly possible. In other constructions, however, a non-habitual form is not possible in all dialects. Thus in my idiolect, I do not vary "I *needn't* do it" by "I'm *not needing* to do it," though this is a form which I have heard. For other verbs, the occurrence of a construction which is non-habitual in form is sufficient to identify the phrase as one which does not contain the negative verb. Thus *I'm willing* is a construction which might be filled out either with "I'm willing my books to the library" or with "I'm willing to do it." In either case, the construction *I'm willing* is shown not to contain the negative verb *will*. Still another group which does not have the non-habitual form is *call, say, declare*, as in "I call it an outrage," "I say it's an outrage," and "I declare I never heard of such a thing!" Thus, while setting up two categories such as public and private verbs is not an adequate description of English structural differentiations,

---

[9] The fullest discussion of these forms is in Anna Granville Hatcher, "The Use of the Progressive Form in English: A New Approach," *Language*, XXVII, 1951, pp. 254–80. The article should be consulted entire, particularly since the results are markedly different from those presented here.

it is still true that it gives us a number of interesting observations. If the two forms *he drinks* and *he is drinking* are called habitual and non-habitual, it is then true that Joos's group of private verbs are ordinarily given the syntactic treatment characteristic of habitual action. Without carrying such a statement to the lengths that similar observations were pressed by Whorf,[10] it is still possible to see in the treatment of verbs like *believe, understand, love, fear* a characteristic of English structure which may well correlate with the culturally determined value system, though it must be freely admitted that the statement is at present no more than a guess. Again, with a number of verbs where the non-habitual form is not specifically required, its use is possible with a resulting semantic distinction which is impossible in languages which do not have such contrasting forms. If we say "We *have* a lot of trouble at the office nowadays," the habitual form is less sharply distinct than it is for a verb like *avoid*, since *have* often occurs with habitual forms where the non-habitual might be expected. On the other hand, if we say "*We're having* a lot of trouble at the office nowadays," we have clearly specified that we did not always have it and that we do not expect to have it always in the future. Finally, there is a difference in treatment of the non-past simple form for those verbs which are regularly treated as if habitual and those which are not. It has been said several times that the simple non-past can occur in contexts which mark the action as belonging to future time. In a verb like *go*, this statement applies both to the simple non-past and to the non-habitual form. That is, we can say both "I go to Chicago tomorrow" and "I'm going to Chicago tomorrow." In such verbs, then, with markers of future time like *tomorrow*, the distinction between habitual and non-habitual is blurred, the non-habitual occurring where the habitual form would be expected.

With a regularly habitual verb like *understand*, the situation is different. If we have a sentence like "When I have finished the problem tomorrow, he —— it," we cannot fill the blank with *understands*, but must use some phrase which contains a component of futurity. If on the other hand we use a verb which ordinarily has a non-habitual form, like *copy*, the simple non-past is quite satisfactory. That is, with habitual verbs, the use of the simple non-past with future time is clearly more restricted than it is with verbs which have a non-habitual form. These statements must be taken as tentative, however, since there are unexpected forms whose distribution has not been fully studied. Thus Jespersen pointed out that future use of the

---

[10] Compare Whorf's statement in "The Relation of Habitual Thought and Behavior to Language" (1939), in *Language, Thought and Reality*, ed. by John B. Carroll, John Wiley, New York, 1956, p. 138: "It also became evident that even the grammar of Hopi bore a relation to Hopi culture, and the grammar of European tongues to our own 'Western' or 'European' culture."

simple non-past is common after *hope*, as in "I hope she *plays* one of Mozart's sonatas."[11] In this construction we can use the simple non-past even with a normally habitual verb, "When I have finished the problem tomorrow, I *hope he understands* it."

The past form of a phrase in *–ing* also requires special attention, and unfortunately the relationship between the simple past, like *wrote*, and the phrase, *was writing*, cannot be directly inferred from the relation between *writes* and *is writing*. The difficulty in arriving at the meaning of a phrase like *was writing* is that there are few situations in which it is required and many in which we can use either *was writing* or *wrote*. A first observation is that those verbs which lack the *is . . . –ing* construction also lack the *was . . . –ing* form. That is, in many idiolects in a sentence frame like "When the teacher was explaining the problem, Mary —— it," the only form of a verb like *understand* which will fill the blank is *understood*. If *copy* is used, the form may be either *copied* or *was copying*.

Perhaps a clear example of a sentence which requires the *was . . . –ing* form is one of this type: "When John came home, Mary —— the dinner, but it wasn't done." With any verb which is not habitual, the only form which will fill the blank is an *–ing* phrase—*was cooking*, *was preparing*, *was arranging*, and so on—though for a habitual verb like *see*, the form is the simple past, *saw*. The fact that the sequence *but it wasn't done* requires *was cooking* can then be used to isolate at least one component of the *was . . . –ing* construction, namely, that the action indicated is not complete, though in this sentence incompleteness necessarily means incompleteness with reference to a point in past time. The same notion can be found without past reference in a variation of the same frame: "Whenever John comes home, Mary *is cooking* the dinner, but it's never done." Both the *is . . .–ing* and the *was . . . –ing* phrases contain this component of incompleteness. It is usually said that the *–ing* phrases contain a component of action which has duration, but this does not seem to be primary. For instance, the question "What were you doing between ten and eleven this morning?" clearly defines action with duration, yet the answer can be either "I *played* the piano" or "I *was playing* the piano." On the other hand, if we assume that incompleteness is the basic component, then it seems natural to assume that duration can be easily correlated with it, at least in our language frame. Action going on is not punctual, but covers at least the immediate past and a small segment of the immediate future. It is this component of incompleteness that makes it possible to diagram the relations of two-part sentences in terms of the duration of the action in each part, as a number of students have done:[12]

---

[11] *A Modern English Grammar*, Winter 1931, Vol. IV, Par. 2. 47.
[12] *Ibid.*, Par. 14.94.

The band was playing ———
  while I wrote. •

The band played •
  while I was writing. ———

The band was playing ———
  while I was writing. ———

The band played •
  while I wrote. •

The diagram is in general accurate, but it seems to me to exaggerate the nondurational quality of some of these actions. In the second sentence it is certainly possible to vary by saying "The band played for an hour, while I was spending the afternoon writing." Such a sentence would be diagrammed:

The band played for an hour   (———)
  while I was spending
  the afternoon writing.   ———

That is, the simple past may have duration as well as the *–ing* phrase, but the duration is ended and so measurable. It is the measured duration (or repetition) of perfect action which explains a number of sentences where the simple past is required:

When the teacher came in, Mary ——— *once.*
                                    three times.
                                    several times.
                                    for five minutes.

In all of these sentences, if *cough* is used to fill the blank, the only form possible is *coughed*, not *was coughing*. That is, each of these sentences measures the action and so requires a perfect form. On the other hand, a frame like the following requires the *–ing* phrase:

When the teacher came in, Mary ———, *and she kept right on.*

The concluding sentence part defines the action as incomplete, so that *was coughing* is required.

The component of incompleteness, secondary in the *is . . . –ing* forms, can be used to explain some anomalies in the distribution of that construction. The *is . . . –ing* was called a nonhabitual form. Yet the form can occur with a form like *always*, which would seem to imply habitual action, as in "He's always talking nonsense." The explanation seems to be that such sentences are incomplete, and can be filled out by such a sentence element as "and he still is." If this analysis is correct, there are two distinct functions for the form *always*. Added to a habitual verb form, it means "without fail," as in "The sun always rises in the East," but added to a nonhabitual form it indicates that the action is repeated and incomplete, as in "The sun is always rising when John gets up."

If we assume that the basic component of the simple past, over and above that of belonging in past time, is completeness, we are then not surprised to find that the simple past can be used for forms either with or without duration, as in "I coughed once yesterday" and "I taught English for twenty years." It is the lack of explicitness as to duration which explains the occurrence of the phrase *used to*. This phrase is like the simple past in indicating perfect action but is explicit in stating that the action had duration, as in "I used to teach English, but now I'm in business." The *used to* phrase is therefore never required, the simple past being always substitutable for it; it is a semantic alternative which underlines duration.

Of the three common phrases in which the second verb is a past participle, two, those in *get* and *be*, belong together and are relatively easily analyzed. Both are traditionally called passives, which means that they fit into a frame which consists of noun (which selects the proper verb form), verb phrase, *by*, and second noun. A typical example is "John —— by Mary." Only phrases like *gets scolded, got scolded, is scolded, was scolded* will fill the blank; no simple verb form will do.[13] All such sentences can be interchanged with sentences in which the *by* is omitted, and the position of the nouns is reversed, whereupon a simple verb form is required, as in "Mary scolds John." It is a commonplace that in the type "John is scolded by Mary," though *John* is the subject since it selects the verb form, *Mary* is the actor. There are slight semantic differences between *gets scolded* and *is scolded*, which are in general parallel to the difference between *gets* and *is* in such sentences as "John gets hot every day" and "John is hot every day." In almost all sentences employing one of these passive constructions, the other can be substituted without noticeable difference.

More complex to analyze than these two phrases are those in *have* and a past participle. One of the first observations which can be made about this phrase type is that in *when* sentences, *have* with participle is substitutable with the simple non-past before a future time indicator. Thus we can say either "When I *finish* this book tomorrow . . ." or "When I *have finished* this book tomorrow . . ." In sentences not of the *when* type, however, where the non-past can be used with future time indicators, the *have* phrase cannot occur. That is, we can say only "I speak in Chicago tomorrow," not "I **have spoken* in Chicago tomorrow." There is thus some overlap with the non-past, but the overlap is not complete.

---

[13] The reader is reminded that "John drove by Mary" is a different construction, with a different stress pattern.

Have phrases, with many if not all verbs, may be put into sentences which indicate that the action is still going on. Thus: "*I have been* hungry all day, and I still am." If in this sentence the frame is varied to "I —— hungry all day, until I ate my supper," the *have* phrase will not go into the blank (at least in my idiolect), and the only possible form is *was.* Similar frames are "I —— lived in Washington for ten years, and I still do" or "I —— English for many years, and I still do." Both these blanks are fillable with *have* phrases, *have lived* or *have worked* for the first, and *have taught* or *have spoken* for the second. If the frames are varied by substituting *now I don't* for *and I still do*, the expected forms become *lived, worked,. taught, spoke.* These facts led Sweet to say that the "perfect [i.e., *have* and past participle] therefore expresses an occurrence which began in the past and is connected with the present, either by actual continuance up to the present time, . . . or in its results."[14] Yet, though this has become the accepted analysis, it is not strictly accurate. Thus, suppose we have a frame like "I *have read* that book twenty times, but I'm not reading it now," it is clear that the action is not still going on. Even in Sweet's own example, "I have come to see you," where he argues that *have come* is used because the speaker is at the moment carrying on his visit and that therefore the results of action are continuing, it is possible to vary the frame so as to show that continuing results are not a necessary condition for the use of *have come.* Suppose I am writing a note of apology to a person whom I have not succeeded in visiting. I can well use the sentence "I *have come* to see you three times this week, but you were not at home." There is still another variation in the use of the *have* phrase which also needs to be taken into account. Suppose there is the question "Do you live in Washington?" A possible answer is the sentence "I have lived in Washington," with the primary stress on *have* and secondary on *lived.* If the question is answered thus, a normal way of expanding the answer would be to add "but now I live in New York." That is, primary stress on *have* breaks any connection with action going on at the present time.

In the sentence frames we have so far examined, namely, "When I *have finished* this book tomorrow . . ." and the type represented by "I *have been* hungry all day," it is possible to find a component of completeness, together with a second component which is non-past action. The completeness, however, is to be associated only with the past participle, and the non-past component only with the non-past first verb, *have.* Our first sentence, "When I *have finished* . . .," is then a normal future use of the non-past *have*, with the notion of completeness carried by the form *finished.* It is, however, a limitation on the phrase that it cannot occur in future time unless there is

---

[14] *A New English Grammar*, Part I, Par. 275.

a time indicator like *when* or *by the time that*. Even though the phrase is thus syntactically limited, it would not be possible to explain its occurrence in future time without associating that occurrence with the usual non-past use of the form *have*, which is thus shown to be an inherent component of the phrase.

In "I have been hungry all day," there is the same component of non-past time, but it is more difficult to arrive at the component of completeness, since as has been said, the action is still going on. Completeness, however, is still there, though it is now translated from the action to the period of time. That is, whenever a *have* phrase occurs with a time indicator which indicates a period, like *all day, two hours, twenty years*, or the like, it is this period which is complete. As a result, the phrase is thus often used with action still going on, though we have seen that shift in the stress pattern changes this relationship. There is good justification for one of the traditional names for the phrase, *present perfect*, though as I have tried to show, it is not necessary to assume that the notion of action continuing into the present is a necessary component.

It is the semantic component of completeness, also found in the simple past tense, which is responsible for the fact that there are so many sentences which can employ either the *have* phrase or the simple tense, as in "I *have fallen* down twice today" or "I *fell* down twice today." Yet these sentences also suggest a form which can be used to explain those instances in which the simple past is required and the *have* phrase is impossible. If the sentence frame we have just used is varied to "I —— down twice *yesterday*," we then fill the blank with *fell*, not *have fallen*. That is, with time indicators like *today*, which are normally consonant with non-past action, the *have* phrase is possible since it has a non-past component. With time indicators like *yesterday*, consonant only with past action, the simple past only can be used. The *have* phrase occurs or does not occur in answer to a question like "Have you finished your lesson yet?" strictly in accord with the time indicators, not in accord with any components of duration. Thus, one answer to this question can be "Yes, I've finished it already," since *already* can be used with non-past forms ("I like him already, though I don't know him well yet"). Another answer is "I finished it at ten this morning." *At ten this morning* is usable as a future time indicator ("I go to Chicago at ten this morning") or, more frequently, as a past time indicator ("The accident occurred at ten this morning"). If then, the two components in the phrase are non-past action and completeness as shown by the time indicators which occur with the construction, it results that the phrase carries these components even when the time indicators are absent. Thus, in writing this chapter, I found myself using the phrase "the explanation which we *have presented*." No time indicator was given, but the sentence could easily have been expanded by the addition of "in the present chapter." Had the normal expansion been "in an earlier chapter," the sentence would more likely have read "the explanation which we *presented*." That is, *in the present chapter* can be used with non-past action, *in an earlier chapter* normally calls for past action.

If the explanation given for the *have* phrase as composed of the two basic components non-past and completeness is acceptable, then a phrase like *had presented* can be guessed to contain the components past action and completeness. The guess is correct, but is not the whole picture. A typical *had* phrase sentence is one in two parts, like "Mary had cooked the dinner before John came home." The occurrence in one part of the sentence of *before* and a past verb places the completion as antecedent to the time of the past verb. This antecedent relationship seems always present in these forms, since it is present also in sequences like "Mary had cooked the dinner when John came home" and "Mary had cooked the dinner. John came home," where there is no explicit statement of the relation in the time indicators. I should therefore redefine the components of the *had* phrase as not completeness and simple past action but completeness and past action antecedent to past action.

Curiously, there are no good examples of sentences in which either the *had* phrase or a simple past is required, and all situations in which one is possible can employ the other. We cannot therefore use our usual method of analysis, that of finding a meaningful element in the sentence which requires one of these constructions and assigning components in accord with such requirements. We can, however, fall back on a type of sentence in which both constructions occur, but with a clear contrast in meaning. If the sentence is "Mary cooked the dinner when John came home," there is no notion of antecedent completion in the first verb. That is, Mary may have begun the cooking at the instant when John marched in the door. This sentence is expandable to "Mary began to cook . . ." If the sentence is "Mary had cooked the dinner when John came home," there is an antecedent completion, and for *when* we can substitute the explicit *before*.

We can now give a survey of the syntactically defined semantic components of the several types which have already been described. Phrases, like *stop talking*, which occur only in accord with semantic requirements are not here described. A phrase like *is talking*, on the other hand, is syntactically required in such a sentence as "John *is talking* with the teacher right now." It is these syntactically required phrases which are analyzed below. They form only a selection from the total number of verbal constructions which are possible and meaningful.

TYPE A₁
F1(2,3)Inf.

The verbs which stand in first position in this construction are nearly all verbs which take the negative suffix *-nt*, as in *will go, can go, may go, shall go, must go,* and *do go.* The whole group of phrases have a component of future time, except for the last, *do go.* The component of futurity is syntactically required if the second verb is habitual, for instance, *understand,* and there is an indicator of future time. Thus, we do not say *"I *understand* it tomorrow," but rather, "I *will understand* it tomorrow." The requirement is only for the phrase type, not for a specific phrase, however. That is, we can also say "I *can (may, shall, must) understand* it tomorrow."

The occurrence of a past form for the first verb does not remove the component of futurity, as one might expect. We say "I *may understand* it tomorrow" or "I *might understand* it tomorrow." The past form adds a component of improbability, however, since "I *can go* tomorrow" pairs naturally with an expansion like "and I probably will," while "I *could go* tomorrow" pairs commonly with "but I probably won't."

Not all phrases which conform to the F1(2,3)Inf. type have the syntactically required component of futurity. Thus *do go* lacks it, and is shown to be a differing construction by its differing stress pattern. Similarly, stereotyped phrases in which the first verb is not one which takes the negative suffix also lack the element of futurity. That is, *let go* and *hear tell* occur only in accord with semantic requirements.

TYPE A₂
F1(2,3)*to*-Inf.

Many of these phrases, as for instance *want to understand,* have the same component of futurity as is found in the phrases just described from type A₁. Thus, we say "I *want to understand* it tomorrow" or "I *plan to understand* it tomorrow." That is, these phrases also occur with habitual verbs and indicators of future time, and as with phrases of the A₁ type, no specific phrase is required. Parallelism to A₁ phrases is also found in the fact that a past form for the first verb does not remove the future component, since we say "I *wanted to understand* it tomorrow" or "I *planned to understand* it tomorrow." The past suffix must therefore apply only to the first verb, not to the whole phrase.

Not all phrases which conform to this type of construction have a future component, however. One which does not is *used to* /yúwstə/, since we do not say *"I *used to understand* it tomorrow."

TYPE B
F1(2,3)F4

Of the many phrases which conform to this type, *stops shaving, starts shaving, keeps shaving,* etc., only one, *is shaving,* is syntactically required. That is, the distinction between "John *shaves* every day" and "John *is shaving* right now" is one which is regularly required as a syntactic distinction which must always be observed. Other phrases occur when their semantic content is appropriate to the situation, as when we say "The motor *stops going* when the gas is cut off."

The syntactically required *is shaving* type indicates non-habitual action and incomplete action. Past forms of *be* indicate action incomplete in the past, as in "John *was shaving* when the doorbell rang." The component of duration, sometimes described as the principal element in these phrases, is a secondary result of incompleteness.

TYPE C
F1(2,3)F5

1. *Be* and *get* followed by F5, *is wounded, got wounded* are examples of this type. These can be lumped together, since both have a component of passive action; the subject of the first verb is not the actor, the actor being indicated by a phrase in *by*. "John was wounded by the enemy" or "John got wounded by the enemy."

2. *Have* followed by F5, *have taken* illustrates the second subgroup of this type. For the non-past forms of the first verb, the components are non-past action and completeness, as in "I *have taken* that course twice this year," in contrast to "I *took* that course twice last year." For the past forms of the first verb, the components are antecedent action and completeness, as in "I *had* already *taken* that course twice before I entered the University."

13.... VERB PHRASES, II

Larger Constructions

1. Multiple-verb constructions

While verb phrases most often occur in the two-verb shapes, which have already been described, they can be expanded to much larger proportions. A sentence such as "I *don't want to have to be forced to begin to try to make* money," with no less than eight successive verb forms, and no nonverbal material other than the allolog *–nt* of the negative and the successive *to*'s, may seem somewhat awkward perhaps, but is perfectly understandable and in accord with normal rules of construction. There is, in short, no theoretical limit on the number of verb forms which can be strung together in this way, but as with other open-ended constructions, such sequences become rarer in proportion to the number of forms which are added. The construction we have just given probably comes at least close to the maximum which would be found in ordinary language use.

Expanded constructions of this sort are, however, not on quite the same level as minimal verb phrases like "I *can try.*" The minimal sequences of two verbs normally contain no juncture higher than /+/ within their boundaries and may be marked off from the other elements of the sentence by the occurrence of terminal junctures, such as single bars. These phonological characteristics mark such a sequence as *can try* in "I can try" /áy | kin + tráy #/ as a genuine phrase capable of being treated as a terminal juncture group, with all the features which mark such a nominal phrase as *the dog*, in "Cáll | the dóg #". A long construction such as our eight-verb sequence, however, is almost certain to be interrupted somewhere by the occurrence of one or more single or even double bars, with consequent occurrence of more than one primary stress within the sequence. If our sentence comes out then as something like /ày + dôwn + wóhnt | tə + hǽftə + bìy + fóhrst | tə + bigìntə + trây + tə + mêyk + mə́niy #/, it is clear that it has been broken up into several phonological phrases and, indeed, that the phonological marks of the boundary of the total verbal construction are somewhat blurred. The multiple sequence, then, is a construction parallel to such nominal sequences as *wise good man*, which contains two adjectives of the same order class and so requires /||/ after *wise*. Both these types of constructions can be defined as units by their syntactic characteristics, in that they can be replaced by a single free form, as "He is a *wise good man*" can be exchanged for "He is a *man*" and as our long verbal sequence can be exchanged with "I *make* (or *like* or *despise*) money." Such maximal sequences as our eight-verb sentence characteristically make up major sentence elements and will therefore be described further in our treatment of the relations of such units to each other.

Other than the fact that these maximal sequences can be interrupted by terminal junctures, and can thus be broken into more than one phonological phrase, there is little to add about their phonological characteristics. Thus, for instance, when *have to* occurs in such a sequence, it preserves its usual characteristic of loss of juncture and consequent consonant assimilation. Similarly, if the first verb in such a sequence is a form which takes tertiary or weak stress or has a nonsyllabic weak form, it preserves these characteristics. Generally, also, the verb forms which occur after the first verb preserve the normal secondary stress, or primary stress if final. Yet there are occasional reductions like the reduction of *begin* to tertiary stress in the example quoted. These reductions seem not to be predictable, except stylistically, and to be describable only by saying that if the phrase contains a primary stress and more than one secondary, one or more of these secondaries is likely to be reduced.

The internal syntax of these constructions is rather more interesting than their stress and juncture characteristics. First, they are characteristically built up by adding forms from back to front, in sequences like:

> I *make* money.
> I *try* to make money.
> I *begin* to try to make money.
> I *am forced* to begin to try to make money.
> I *have* to be forced to begin to try to make money.
> I *want* to have to be forced to begin to try to make money.
> I *don't* want to have to be forced to begin to try to make money.

There is only one instance in the build-up as here given where two verb forms seem to be added as a unit, namely *am forced*. That is, "I **forced to begin* to try to make money" is not a normal construction, since this particular verb requires a personal object and, if not introduced in the form "forced *him* to begin" must be introduced in one of the two passive forms, *am forced, get forced*. If, on the other hand, we try to build up the construction by adding forms after the first verb, we run into many more impossible constructions, such as "I **don't money*," "I don't want to **have* (have-2 /hæf/) money," "I don't want to have to **be forced money*," and "I don't want to be forced to **begin money*."

As was noticed in building up the construction, it is only the first verb which appears in form 1, 2, or 3; all forms which follow are infinitive, *–ing*, or participle. That is, as each new verb is added the forms following are changed thus: "He *makes* money," "He tries *to make* money," "He begins *to try to make* money," and so on. Further, as a verb becomes non-initial after an addition before it, it becomes an infinitive, an *–ing*, or a participle, in accord with the type of construction that the initial verb can enter into as first member. If the initial verb can enter into more than one type of two-verb construction, there is more than one possible form for the second verb. Thus if *keeps* is added to "He makes money," the resultant construction is "He *keeps making* money," since *keeps* does not appear as first member in an infinitive construction. That is, we do not say "He **keeps to make* money." If *decides* is the added form, then the resultant construction is "He *decides to make* money." If the added form is *tries*, on the other hand, the resultant construction may be either "He *tries to make* money" or "He *tries making* money." The non-initial verbs continue to affect the forms which follow them, however. If *keeps* is added to "He decides to make money," the resultant construction is "He keeps *deciding to make* money." That is, *keeps* takes *deciding* after it, and *deciding* takes *to make* in the third position, quite as if *deciding* were still initial.

Another limitation on these constructions is also in accord with the structure of two-verb phrases. Verbs like *can, may, ought, must,* and so on, which do not have infinitive, *–ing*, or participle forms, do not appear in any other position than first in phrases, whether of two or more than two verbs. Thus, we can construct sentences of the type "He can try to go," but if *wants* is added to the construction, a phrasal substitute—usually *to be able*—must be resorted to in place of the missing **to can.*

It is beyond the scope of this study to give a complete analysis of the semantic components of all types of multiple-verb phrases of the sort here described. Rather we shall give some specimens with comments which it is hoped will make the underlying principles clear:

I. John *is* good.
   Simple non-past, the habitual form.

II. John *is being* good.
    Non-past, the non-habitual form.

III. John *has been being* good all day.
     Constructed from *is being*, plus *has been*, so to speak telescoped to *has been being*, so that a way of representing the construction is to set up the sentence with overlap, thus:

John has been . . .
    . . . *is* being good all day.

Is being represents non-habitual action; *been,* of *has been,* represents completed action (in this phrase transferred to the period of time which completes the sentence); and *has* represents non-past action.

IV. John *is scolded* by Mary.
Passive action, habitual form.

V. John *is being scolded* by Mary.
Passive plus non-past, non-habitual action, equivalent to a non-habitual form for the simple passive phrase.

John is being . . .
    . . . *is* scolded by Mary.

VI. John *had been being scolded* by Mary for some time before the neighbors heard the quarrel.
Passive action *(is scolded),* plus non-habitual action *(is being),* plus completeness *(been),* plus antecedent action *(had).* It should be mentioned that this type of phrase maintains a maximum number of distinctions, and that it is often reduced to *had been scolded* by dropping out the form which indicates non-habitual action.

John had been . . .
    . . . *is* being . . .
      . . . *is* scolded by Mary . . .

VII. John *will have been being paid* by the same company for twenty years, next Tuesday.
Passive action *(is paid),* plus non-habitual action *(is being),* plus completeness and non-past action *(has been),* plus future action *(will have).* This phrase also is often reduced by dropping out the non-habitual indicator.

John will have . . .
    . . . *has* been . . .
      . . . *is* being . . .
        . . . *is* paid by the same company . . .

It will be noticed that in the examples which are given here, we have confined ourselves to combinations of those phrases which were previously defined as syntactically required. That is, we gave no account of multiple verb phrases like *began to try to make,* which is a combination of *tried to make* with *began to try.* These phrases follow the same rules of construction as those we have exemplified above but are not syntactically required in any of their occurrences. They are usually sum totals of the semantic components of the separate verbs of which they are made up, and so need no structural explanation.

In analyzing a verb sequence such as *will have been being paid* into its successive layers of constituents, the normal procedure is to reverse the order of accretion. That is, the first cut is after *will*, giving this as one constituent and *have been being paid* as the other. When this process is followed, however, it is also necessary to retransform second and later position verbs to the forms they have in first position. Having analyzed *have been being paid* as one constituent, we must rewrite in some fashion before going on to cut into further constituents. A device for this purpose might be to put the normal first-position form in parentheses after the form actually found, thus:

have (has) been being paid

This gives the constituents:

have (has) and *been being paid*

This in turn is:

been (is) being paid

And this gives the constituents:

been (is) and *being paid*

There are, however, maximal sequences in which the process of cutting is more complex. Such a sequence is "Johnny'*ll seem to be being* good, even when he's really up to mischief." That is, such a sequence contains within it the syntactically nonrequired *seems to be* even though the surrounding material consists of syntactically required phrase combinations. Such sequences are often broken into two by /||/ after *seem*, so that the first cut gives the constituents '*ll seem* and *to be (is) being good*. Thereafter, the cutting in each part of the maximal phrase follows the usual order, with the cuts falling always after the first form.

There is one other type of maximal verb sequence which has not yet been mentioned but which can be disposed of quickly. These are sequences of verbs in which there is no infinitive, *–ing*, or participle. Examples are "He *came and got* it" and "He *cleaned, cooked, and ate* the fish." It will be noted that these verbs are typically united by the nonverbal *and*, though this is often dropped except between the last two of a multiple series. These sequences may occur without any intervening juncture other than /+/, as often happens in *came and got*, yet the characteristic form is occurrence of /||/ between each pair of verbs. The sequences are then to be defined as several phrases, and not at all as the kind of minimal phrase which is composed of only one inflected verb form followed by an infinitive, *-ing*, or participle.

2. Verbal constructions containing nonverbal material

Up to this point we have been considering verb phrases which have no nonverbal material other than the allolog *-nt* and *to*, as in *don't want to go*. Yet all the types of verb phrases which we have described can be expanded by the addition of nonverbal material over and above the forms we have already mentioned. This material can consist of single forms or can itself constitute a potential phrase, so that the resultant verb phrase is maximal. The typical form of expansion is by the addition of constructions ending in the postbase *-ly* /liy/, which has been called {-liy}2, the form used to construct adverbs. We can use, as a typical example, the adverb *really*. If our basic phrase is *can run*, we then get expansions of the following types: "He really can run" /hìy + rìhliy + kǽn + rɔ́n #/ and "He can really run" /hìy + kìn + rìhliy + rɔ́n #/. It is also true that the sentence can be said in two other forms: "Really, he can run" and "He can run, really." In both these forms, however, a terminal juncture is required to set off *really* from the rest of the sentence, which then does not form part of the verbal phrase. We can then make a first generalization. When an adverb is added either immediately before a verb phrase or inside it, the adverb forms a part of the maximal verb phrase.

If we take a larger phrase, like *don't want to have to be forced to make* in "We *don't want to have to be forced to make* money," *really* can be added before *don't*, after *don't*, before or after *to have*, before or after *to be*, and after *forced*. The only limitation is that it cannot be added before *money*. It is also true that *really*, in informal English, can be added after any one of the three *to*'s in the phrase, though such constructions represent the celebrated "split infinitive," which has been long frowned on. In all these positions, *really* can be said with tertiary stress and without any stronger juncture than /+/ to set it off, so that it forms part of the phonological verb phrase. When treated in this way, the adverbial material always modifies what follows, just as adverbs in noun phrases modify what follows. But a sentence of the sort we have been discussing does not have to be said with /+/ and tertiary stress on the added *really*. We can have forms like "We don't want, really, to have to be forced to make money." Here, *really* is set off by /||/ and receives primary stress. It is interesting that in this construction, the adverbial material always modifies the preceding rather than the following material. Further, of course, when *really* is thus set off by terminals, it constitutes a separate minimal phrase, though it is still a part of the verbal sentence element.

Really was chosen as a first example of adverbs since it is very considerably freer in position than most. There are several classes within the large group of adverbs, not all of which are as yet fully investigated, though Fries has given a very valuable first list.[1] One order class within the adverb group can be illustrated by *badly*, defined as an adverb, be it noted, by the occurrence of {*-liy*}2. With many verb phrases, such as *has spoken, was speaking*, or *may speak*, *badly* can be added only at the end of the phrase and cannot occur either before it or within it. There are, it is true, other phrases like "It *was badly painted*" which varies with "It *was painted badly*." In spite of the variation, *badly* can be defined as an adverb of which end position is characteristic, and which thus represents a different subclass from that exemplified by *really*. In end position, adverbs like *badly* tend to receive the primary stress and are never given tertiary or weak stress. Furthermore, they are not set off from the preceding verb phrase by a terminal juncture. We can thus make a second generalization. Any adverb which, like *badly*, takes its characteristic position following the verb phrase without intervening terminal juncture forms a member of the maximal verb phrase.

In addition to recognizable adverbs like *badly*, there is another class of words which are not themselves verbs but can in some occurrences form part of extended verbal constructions. The class, called prepositions, is represented by such monosyllabic forms as *to, on, by*. These can occur between a first and a second verb, as in *try tǒ go* or *keep òn going*. In this situation, they form part of the verb phrase and receive either weak stress, as in the first example, or tertiary stress, as in the second. In this situation, no terminal juncture falls normally before the preposition. Words of this class can also occur after the verbal material and before the nominal material, as in "He teaches by examples." In this situation they are distinguished from adverbs by their stress and juncture characteristics. In the example just given, *by* is unstressed and is apt to be preceded by /||/. The stress marks it as a preposition, and the juncture assigns it to membership in the following construction rather than to the preceding verbal material.

Forms like *by* vary in their stress and juncture characteristics, and are not always prepositions nor always members of the following nominal construction. Thus, as written, the following sentence is ambiguous: "He passed by the bridge." It may represent either:

$$\text{/hìy + p\'æst | b\u{a}y + ð\u{3} + br\'ij \#/}$$

with stresses: 2   3 2   2   31   or, less probably,

---

[1] Charles Carpenter Fries, *The Structure of English*, Harcourt, Brace, New York, 1952, pp. 227–33.

$$
\begin{array}{cccc}
2 & 3\ 2 & 2 & 3\ 1
\end{array}
$$
/hìy + pǽst + báy | ðɔ̌ + bríj #/

In either of these two sentences the /||/ may be omitted, with consequent stress modification, so that the sentences become:

$$
\begin{array}{cc}
2 & 31
\end{array}
$$
FIRST SENTENCE   /hìy + pǽst + bǎy + ðɔ̌ + bríj #/ or
$$
\begin{array}{ccc}
2 & 3 & 1
\end{array}
$$
/hìy + pǽst + bǎy + ðɔ̌ + brîj#/

$$
\begin{array}{cc}
2 & 31
\end{array}
$$
SECOND SENTENCE   /hìy + pᷮst + bây + ðɔ̌ + bríj #/

The distinction is a double one, since if there is a /||/, it occurs before the unstressed *by*, though after the form of *by* with primary stress. If /||/ is absent, the distinction is reduced to stress alone, the two forms differing by the contrast between /˘/ and /^/. We have, then, a stress distinction which is, in one sense, not quite minimal, since it is a distinction between stresses removed from each other by two grades, weak and secondary, rather than by only one.

In occurrences between verb and noun, therefore, a stress distinction may distinguish not only between preposition and adverb but also the boundaries of the two potential phrases. In postverbal, pre-terminal position, however, a stress distinction distinguishes only whether a final form is adverb or preposition—both are members of the verbal construction. Notice "This is the bridge they passed by." If the stress pattern is /pǽst + bày #/, the sentence means "This is the bridge by means of which they passed." If the stress pattern is /pᷮst + báy #/, the sentence means "This is the bridge they overlooked, or decided not to take." Again, the distinction is one of stress, but this time the differing stresses are tertiary and primary. In both instances, the more weakly stressed form is a preposition. The form with stronger stress can be called an adverb.

These relatively strongly stressed adverbs are peculiar, however, and constitute a subclass of adverbs sufficiently well marked so that they might justify identification as a separate form class. If we compare such a form as the stressed *by* with a form like *thoroughly*, we find that the chief distributional situation which the two have in common is that both occur postverbally under primary stress before the terminal. That is, we have sentences like:

$$
\begin{array}{cc}
2 & 31
\end{array}
$$
John washed thoroughly.   and   *John passed by.* /jâhn + pᷮst + báy #/

In most other situations, one form or the other is impossible, or there is a difference in secondary characteristics which separates them. The forms in –*ly* occur freely in nominal phrases, characteristically under tertiary stress, as in *a thòroughly Amêrican áccent*. Forms like stressed *by* do not occur here at all. In sentences like "John passed by," stressed *by* can be followed by an unstressed pronoun object, as in

$$\overset{2}{} \qquad \overset{3}{} \quad \overset{1}{}$$
John passed by it. /jâhn + pæ̀st + báy + it #/

without an intervening terminal. Constructions of the same sort, but with a differing form in place of *by*, can be terminated by noun objects in the same way:

$$\overset{2}{} \qquad\qquad \overset{31}{}$$
John passed out cards. /jâhn + pæ̀st + âwt + kárdz #/

It will be noted that here, where the primary stress falls on a following noun, *out* receives secondary stress and is not reduced further to tertiary or weak. These situations are not shared by the adverbs in –*ly*; we do not say "John washed **thoroughly it*" or "John took **quickly cards*," though the latter sentence would be possible if broken by a terminal before *cards*.

Both types are possible in preverbal position in sentences in which the subject follows, as in "Quietly flows the Don" or "Down came baby, cradle, and all." But though both are possible here, there are still marked differences. The forms like

$$\overset{2}{} \qquad \overset{3}{} \quad \overset{1}{}$$
Down came baby. /dâwn + kêym + béybiy #/

are quite common in utterance, but of limited types. The verb in such a construction is always one which can be roughly described as one of motion. That is, we can say either "Jôhn câme úp" or "Ûp câme Jóhn," but with a sentence like "Jôhn clêaned úp," initial position for *up* does not occur. Nor do all of the group of adverbial forms occur in the construction. A typical adverbial form of the type we are discussing is stressed *to*, in such a sentence as:

$$\overset{2}{} \qquad \overset{3}{} \overset{1}{}$$
John came to. /jâhn + kêym + túw #/ (regained consciousness)

For this sentence, "**Tó câme* John" is quite as unnatural as "**Úp clêaned* John."

Sentences of the type "Quietly flows the Don" are created much more freely but are much less common in utterance. They occur under limited conditions of style, which might be typified by the rather tired literary flavor of "Quietly came the dawn," at one time a cliché in movie captions. "Quietly flows the Don" is itself a slight modification of a book title, one of the situations in which the construction is particularly likely.

The most striking feature of forms like *by* and *to*, which we have called adverbs when they are relatively strongly stressed, is precisely that they are identical with forms called prepositions when they are relatively weakly stressed. The fact that stress (and secondarily, juncture) alone distinguishes adverb and preposition becomes important when we realize that in a number of situations the stress is fixed, so that no possibility of contrast exists. Morphemes of the type *by, with, over, under, out* are common in fixed phrases—another one of the ways in which they contrast with the adverbs in *–ly*, which are characteristic of free phrases. Typical fixed phrases with these morphemes are *withstand, overtake, understand, outdo.* All have, as citation forms, a superfix consisting of {`} {+ ´} or {` ˇ} {+ ´}. All show that they are fixed phrases by the fact that they are inseparable units. As we should expect, they also sometimes show assimilation of their parts, as in a pronunciation /ən + stǽnd/ or /ənistǽnd/ for *understand.* Again, as we should expect of fixed phrases, they are semantic units in which the meaning of the construction is not a mere sum total of its parts, as in *understand, withhold, overtake.* Moreover, the type is not now very freely constructed, though there are occasional formations like "Mary wanted to *ùp-swêep* her hairdo." Commonest are forms in *out, under,* and *over.* Examples for *out* are *òut-thínk, òut-éat, òut-séll,* and even *òut-gíve* in such a sentence as "In this contest in generosity, John *out-gave* Mary." Constructions similar to these are also found for *under* and *over.* It is more interesting that forms like *crŷ óut* cannot be freely transformed into *òut-crŷ* without change of meaning, as in "Mary cried out," but "Mary *òut-críed* Jane." That is, *òut-crŷ* is immediately referred to the pattern of *òut-thínk.* A similar shift in meaning occurs with variation in the superfix alone. Note "Mary oûtràged Jane," but "Mary òut-râged Jane."

These phrases all have the superfix tertiary-primary, though necessarily varying with tertiary-secondary when they occur in larger phrases with the primary stress elsewhere. This pattern is not the only superfix which occurs with verbal fixed phrases and first elements like *up, by, in,* etc. Fixed phrases with primary-tertiary are also common, as in *óutlòok, óutràge, íncòme, óutgò, úpsèt, dównfàll,* and many more. This second type of fixed phrase is regularly nominal, as all of these forms are. Occasionally, however, one of these nominal fixed phrases can also occur as a verb, as with *by-pass,* where we can have either "He took the *bý-pàss*" or "He *bŷ-pàssed* the town." It should be noted, however, that it is primary-tertiary which identifies the fixed phrases as primarily nominal, as in *income,* which can be inflected like any normal noun—"He had several *íncòmes.*" As said earlier, in fixed phrases the inflectional morpheme can be added to a base morpheme which would not take it were the phrase free.

The fixed phrases we have been discussing are of importance in two ways. As we have said, the adverbs formed by postbases or prebases do not characteristically appear in fixed phrases. Second, in fixed phrases, as indeed in situations like "Up came John" where there is no stress contrast possible, the morphemes we have been discussing cannot be identified as specifically prepositions or adverbs. One other observation can be made about the stress distinction between adverb and preposition. A sentence such as "This is the place John *cáme tó*" can be defined as having the adverbial *to*, with the meaning "regained consciousness." Yet the prepositional *cáme tò* can, under contrastive stress, be made homonymous with the adverbial form—"Is this the car John *cáme bỳ*?" "No, this is the car John *cáme tó*."

It has become a firm tradition in grammatical analysis to distinguish adverb and preposition on the basis of stress. Yet, as we have seen, the positions in which stress makes a distinction between the two types are limited at best. The point is not one worth pressing very far, but it would seem that a preferable approach to the problem would be to set up a separate cover name for the group of segmental morphemes which can occur under either type of superfix, without insisting on referring the stressed type to the class of adverbs. Such a name might be a hyphenated form, adverb-preposition, which leaves the exact definition of each type of occurrence open. The stressed occurrences of the adverb-prepositions would then be adverbial uses, the weakly stressed occurrences prepositional uses. In those situations in which stress contrast is not possible, we would describe the morphemes as adverb-prepositions without distinction. As long, however, as the reader is in possession of all the facts, the type of terminology used is not of sufficient importance to warrant breaking with tradition.

If we distinguish between adverb and preposition primarily on the basis of stress, it should be pointed out that pre-terminal stress is a surer diagnostic than is stress when the form in question falls within a nominal phrase. The commonest stress morpheme for prepositions which begin nominal phrases or fall within them is {+ ˇ}, but there are instances of other grades. Note what happens to the sentence "Here's *one for you*" if it is a response to some such statement as "I need two pencils." Under these circumstances we may have:

óne fôr you #

In general, also, prepositional constructions which are fixed phrases, like *into, behind, between*, preserve tertiary stress on one of their members even in nominal phrases.

Thus, with a form such as *like*, occurrence under tertiary stress in final position in the sentence which follows is conclusive:

What did the picture *lóok lìke*?

Like is here a preposition, and the fact that it occurs under tertiary stress in nominal phrases—*lìke fáther | lìke són*—does not contradict that classification. It should be mentioned, however, that *like*, as do a number of the adverb-prepositions, occurs also under stress after the verb *be*, a position which is adjectival rather than adverbial:

> This picture is *vèry líke.*
> His number is *úp.*
> New York is a good place to be *fróm.*
> John is *óut.*

We shall return to prepositions in dealing with modifying phrases. At the minute it is sufficient for us to point out that they form members of verb phrases only when they follow a verb and are not preceded by a terminal. We are, then, ready to conclude our discussion of adverbs in relation to the two types of phrases in which we have found them. Adverbs can appear in maximal sequences consisting of a set of modifiers and a following noun, as in "the ten *thoroughly* American men." Here they characteristically receive tertiary stress and need not be set off by terminals. They are here limited in position in that they cannot occur immediately before the noun, and in function they can be said always to modify the following modifier, with which they always make up a unit capable of being set off by terminals.

Adverbs can also enter into verb phrases. If placed initially or internally within the verb phrase without being set off by terminals, they characteristically receive tertiary stress and once again form a unit with what follows. If occurring within the verb construction, but set off by terminals and given primary stress, they are still members of the maximal verb sequence but function with what precedes. If an adverb falls at the end of a verb phrase, it forms a part of it if it is not set off by a terminal. Such end-position adverbs are normally given primary stress.

As has been intimated, there are various classes of adverbs. A major distinction is that there is at least one adverb, *very*, which is nonverbal. That is, it can enter freely into nominal phrases, as in "very young American men," but cannot enter into verbal phrases unless it is itself followed by another adverb. Thus we can say "He has *very nearly* spent his money," but not "He has **very spent* his money."

In verb phrases, not all adverbs can occur in end position. An example is *really*, which does not occur at the end of a verb construction unless it is preceded by a terminal. Others are characteristically end-position forms. Most noticeable among these are the forms which also appear as prepositions, from which they are distinguished by differing stress and often by differing juncture distribution. These end-position adverbs are characteristically unit morphemes, like *by*, or are formed by prebases, like the initial of *away*, *ahead*. Some adverbs formed by {–liy}2 may appear in end position, like *badly*, but these may also appear in internal position.

The typical end-position adverbs of the group which also serve as prepositions, like *out, off, by*, do not appear in nominal phrases, except in situations like "an *ôff-whìte* dress" or "an *ôff-còlor* story." These forms are all to be regarded as fixed phrases. These characteristics give us several adverb classes: those which are possible in nominal sequences and in all positions in verbal constructions, like *thoroughly*; those which are only nominal, like *very*; those which are nominal and verbal, but which do not occur in end position, like *really*; those which occur characteristically in end position and are unit morphemes capable of functioning also like prepositions, like *by*; and a final group of end-position adverbs formed by means of prebases, like *away*. This last group, to which we will return in describing postverbal phrases and sentence elements, can also serve as adjectivals.

Besides these characteristics, Fries has pointed out that there are normal sequences of adverbs when more than one occurs.[2] Thus we can say "The ball went away out," but not normally *out away*. In place of this latter we can use the informal *out aways*, or use a connective, as in *out and away*. These order classes when there are sequences are strikingly reminiscent of the order classes of modifiers in nominal phrases and would be a worthwhile object of further study, particularly since many adult learners of English find the intricacies of order classes in adverbs one of the greatest difficulties in the language.

[2] *Ibid.*, pp. 85 ff.

14.... MODIFYING PHRASES

1. Phrases syntactically and morphologically adjectival

The phrases we have been describing up to this point have been nominal or verbal, in that the sequences could be exchanged for simple nouns or verbs. There are phrases which occur after the verb and before the terminal juncture, and which have no nominal or verbal component. In these phrases the end position is occupied by a modifier, and the phrase as a whole functions in accord with the characteristics of the end word.

It will be remembered that we set up a model nominal phrase and numbered the order classes in accord with it:

VI   V   IV   III   II   I   N

all the ten fine old stone houses

It will also be remembered that descriptive names were adopted for most of these groups: group VI was called the predeterminatives, group V the determinatives, group IV numerals, and group I nominal modifiers. Groups II and III are the true adjectives, and for these only the numeral designation was used.

If we return to our model phrase, the most striking fact about it is that we cannot transform it by putting the final noun before the verb, using the remaining sequence as a postverbal modifier. We do not say "Houses are *all the ten fine old stone.*" Prenominal and non-prenominal sequences differ rather considerably in structure. There is, for instance, a group of modifiers and modifying phrases which can occur only postverbally, never prenominally. A typical if somewhat bookish example is *content*. All idiolects use "The men were content," but not all use "a content man." A form like *content* immediately raises the question of classification, since both adjectives and adjectivals, on the one hand, and adverbs and adverbials, on the other, can occur in this position. We shall put off final decision on these postverbal forms and phrases until all their characteristics have been brought together. In the meantime, however, we can speak of an adjectival function for such forms when they occur after *be,* as in the example given above, and an adverbial function for postverbal modifiers when they occur freely after other verbs, such as *talk, study, write,* etc. The reason for the distinction in function is that position after a form of *be* is one that is possible for a recognizable adjective, as in "Jack is young," but not for a recognizable adverb, such as *rapidly,* unless of course, there is a terminal before the adverb. More interesting than the occasional forms like *content* are forms like *asleep, afire, abroad, ajar.* Postverbal position and impossibility of assuming prenominal position are characteristic of all these forms. Further, all occur freely after *be,* and less freely after other verbs, though we can have forms like "The door swung ajar." They are a group, then, which often have adjectival function. They are always printed as one word but nonetheless contain more than one segmental morpheme, since they are characterized by a plus juncture after the first vowel, as in /ə + jár/, which is therefore homonymous with the phrase *a jar.* We shall return to these forms in connection with others which function somewhat more freely as adverbs, like *afterwards.*

Having set up a special class of postverbal modifiers, we can return to the prenominal group and consider how many of them can occur in postverbal position. First, it was said that group I of prenominal modifiers contains a number of adjectivals derived from nouns, like *stone* in *stóne hóuses.* It might be thought that when such forms are found with no noun following they automatically revert to their noun status. This is not the case, however. We can say, for instance, "This house is stone" or "These houses are stone," in contrast to "This lump is a stone" or "These lumps are stones." That is, forms like *stone* after *be,* but without an article or plural suffix, are to be identified as group I nominal modifiers in postverbal position. These tests usually distinguish nouns from nominal modifiers of group I fairly sharply, as in "This man is *American*" (modifier) and "This man is an *American*" (noun). Ambiguities arise chiefly with uncountable nouns like *bread* or *milk,* which lack the indefinite article and do not normally have a plural. That is, in phrases like *good old bréad púdding* or *nice hot mílk púnch, bread* and *milk* are acting as group I modifiers, with the characteristic secondary stress of adjectivals. Thus, when a sequence of this sort is transposed, giving a statement like "This pudding is bread," there is a mild structural ambiguity, since the structure is indistinguishable from that of "This stuff is bread." As always with such ambiguities, the hearer solves them in accord with the interpretation which is most common and therefore most probable. In a situation like "This pudding is bread," it can be argued that the commonest type of expansion would be "This pudding is made of bread," an expansion in accord with the meaning of a group I modifier. In an ambiguous context like "This is bread," the hearer will decide whether the expansion "... is the bread ..." or "... is made of bread ..." is the more likely. In the one case, we are dealing with a noun, in the other with a group I nominal modifier. Needless to say, the hearer is guided by the structure of other sentences, that is, by stylistics, and by the nonlinguistic situation. It is rather interesting that many uncountable nouns do not appear as group I modifiers before other nouns, but instead take a stress superfix which makes them the first member of a fixed noun phrase. Thus *milk punch*, which has the superfix secondary-primary, contrasts with *mílkshàke* which has primary-tertiary and is a fixed noun phrase. The pattern of *milkshake* is found in *meatloaf, moneybags, breadsticks, sugarplum, sandlot,* and many more phrases where the first member is an uncountable, though not in *ríce púdding, wâter hýacinth,* and *ôil dréssing.* It would be interesting to know if uncountable nouns are more frequent in the pattern primary-tertiary than in secondary-primary and how their frequency with these superfixes compares with the distribution of the two superfixes with countable nouns, like *stone,* when placed before other nouns. It is noticeable, for instance, that *Stónewàll* acquires primary-tertiary only when it is a nickname. The structural ambiguity here discussed is often not very important to the meaning and can therefore be left unresolved in many instances. Yet there are instances where the meaning is signaled by the identification marks of nouns and nominal modifiers of group I. Thus, in "This is stone," the absence of an indefinite article means that the sentence is to be expanded as *made of stone,* as in "This statue is (made of) stone." In "This is a stone," we signal that two nouns are being equated, as in "This thing in my hand is a stone." With countable nouns, the distinction between the noun as noun proper and the noun as nominal modifier is certainly useful in explaining to foreigners some of the mysteries of our use of articles.

A less troublesome type of problem arises from the fact that unmodified proper names also appear as group I modifiers, as in *the good old Smíth hóuse.* Here it is immediately noticeable that we cannot transpose to something like "This good old house **is Smith,*" as we can say "This good old house is stone." In place of the hypothetical transposition given above we must say "This good old house is *Smith's,*" where *Smith's* is shown by its suffix to be a determinative. In short, proper names do not appear as group I nominal modifiers in postverbal position, and any proper name so appearing must be taken to be a noun.

We are now ready to describe the maximal limits of a postverbal phrase composed of adjectivals. If the head of the phrase is composed of a nominal modifier of group I, this can in turn be preceded by predeterminatives and adjectives, as in:

VI   III   II   I

The houses are *all fine old stone.*

It is clear that there can be no determinative in such a phrase, since such a modifier is a clear signal that the final form in the phrase is a noun and that the whole phrase is thus nominal rather than adjectival. A clear example is:

V III II N

This jewel is *a fine old stone.*

Somewhat the same kind of limitation applies to the occurrence of a postverbal phrase with a numeral. Number morphemes characteristically demand a plural suffix in the last word of the phrase, so that the phrase is thereby identified as a noun. Thus we have:

IV III II N

These jewels are *ten fine old stones.*

This characteristic of numerals is responsible for a structural requirement which is sometimes troublesome to foreigners. In our description of noun phrases we pointed out that phrases which contain number morphemes but which are not a part of the decimal counting system often appear as group I modifiers, as in:

V III II I N

a good old *five-cent* cigar

If such phrasal group I modifiers are moved to postverbal position, they always become fixed noun phrases, with the last word requiring a plural suffix:

IV N

This good old cigar is *five cents.*

There is but one notable exception to the rule here given. One type of nominal phrase is:

V III II I N

a nice little *six-year-old* child

In a phrase of this type *sîx-yèar-ôld* receives secondary-tertiary-secondary, and the whole sequence is a phrasal group I modifier, to be distinguished by its stress pattern from

sîx yêar-òld children

where *six* is a group IV modifier, that is, a numeral, and *year-old* with secondary-tertiary is a different phrasal modifier of group I. That *six-year-old* is a fixed phrasal unit is shown by the fact that *old*, normally a group II modifier, is here preceded by a modifier of the structure type of group I, but without the terminal juncture which is required when the order classes are reversed.

When this type of phrase is placed postverbally it becomes:

> This child is *síx yèars óld*.

And the stress pattern is now secondary-tertiary-primary, at least in some idiolects, though there may be others in which it is secondary-secondary-primary without intervening terminals. We can now state the exception to the rule, given above, that a plural suffix indicates that a postverbal phrase is nominal. Prenominal phrases of the type *"six-year-old* child" become in postverbal position "This child is *six years old*" without thereby losing their character as postverbal group I modifiers. As is characteristic of group I modifiers in postverbal position, the whole phrase can readily be transformed into a nominal phrase, as in "This child is a *six-year-old*" or "These children are *six-year-olds*." It is interesting that a plural suffix, or the possibility of a plural suffix, on the last form in the construction, *old*, requires that the plural of *years* be dropped. There is, then, a slight inconsistency in the retention of a plural suffix in a postverbal phrasal modifier of group I. It is therefore quite interesting that another phrase of the same type, "a *six-foot-tall* man" has in dialectal speech a postverbal variant without the plural suffix, namely "This man is *six foot tall*."

The sequence predeterminative, adjectives of groups III and II, and nominal modifier is, then, the maximal postverbal adjectival phrase. But such multiple adjectival phrases cannot be constructed with all group I modifiers at their head. Both *wood* and *wooden* are group I modifiers, as can be seen from these sequences:

III II I		III II I
fine old wood tables	and	*fine old wooden tables*

Yet, only *wood* can enter into any multiple adjective phrase in postverbal position. That is, we say "These tables are all *fine old wood*," but we do not use *wooden* in this position. The limitation is that only those group I modifiers which are homonymous with simple noun bases can appear in this position. Any group I modifier which consists of a noun base followed by a postbase, like *wooden*—or, for that matter, like *American*, where the resultant construction can still be treated as a noun—is impossible in a multiple adjectival phrase in postverbal position. The same limitation applies to phrasal modifiers of group I, like *six-year-old*, or more exactly, its postverbal form, *six years old.* These statements, however, do not indicate any limitation on complex nominal modifiers of group I in postverbal position when they are not preceded by modifiers of other groups.

If we can have the sequence predeterminative, adjectives of groups III and II, and nominal modifier, we should expect that we might have the sequence predeterminative, adjective of group III, and adjective of group II when the nominal modifier is absent, but this is not the case. We can have VI-III (predeterminative and adjective of group III) as in:

VI III

The houses were *all fine.*

Or VI-II, substituting *old* for *fine.* We have no sequence involving both III and II, however. That is we do not say:

III   II

The houses were **fine old.*

The rules of occurrence can be most simply stated by saying that if the sequence is not VI-III-II-I (where I is one of the permitted simple noun bases), then the maximum number of modifiers is two, and the first one is a predeterminative of group VI. That is, we have:

VI   III   VI   II   VI   I
all fine   *all old*   *all wooden*

But we have no combination involving two of the second members of these groups.

If there are any two (or more) adjectives or adjectivals which do not fall into the permitted patterns, they are connected by words of the type of *and* or *but* (a class not yet defined). Further, they do not then belong to the same minimal phrase, since they are usually separated by a terminal juncture, as in "The houses were *fine* | *ănd óld.*" Under these circumstances, order of groups is no longer of structural significance, and it is possible to say either *fine, and old* or *old, and fine.* An interesting feature, however, is a colloquial construction involving *good and* and a following adjective in postverbal position. This is often spoken with *good* reduced to tertiary stress and no terminal juncture preceding *and.* When this happens *good and* is a sort of intensive, so that "This book is *gòod ănd bád*" means that the book is very bad. In this construction *good and* is treated like an adverb and is quite distinct from the adjectival form in *góod* | *ănd bád.*

Adjectival phrases in postverbal position can be expanded by comparative and superlative postbases more or less according to expectation, though there are some minor irregularities. In a maximal postverbal phrase of the type VI-III-II-I, as in

VI   III   II   I

The houses were *all fine old stone.*

the postbases of comparison can be added to the modifiers of groups III and
II, giving:

III   II   I

all *finer older* stone

No type of comparison can be added to *all* (group VI), a type of limitation
which is also found in prenominal position, where a construction like "**more
all* the boys" is similarly impossible. A rather more interesting limitation
appears in the fact that we do not say "The houses were all fine old **more
stone.*" That is, the type of group I modifier which can appear in a maximal
postverbal phrase cannot be compared. The limitation applies also to group
I modifiers of this type when they are occurring alone in postverbal position.
That is, we do not say "This is **mòre stone,*" with adverbial *more.* Rather,
we say "This is *môre stóne,*" where *more* is shown by its stress to be an
adjective.[1]

The type of group I nominal modifier which cannot appear at the head
of a maximal postverbal phrase, however, can be compared, and when this
is done, it is always by means of adverbial *more* and *most,* as in "These men
are *mòre Américan.*" Phrasal group I modifiers in postverbal position are
only rarely compared, but the construction is at least possible, as in "I never
saw a girl who was *mòre thirtêen yèars óld.*"

Comparison of adjectives or adjectivals introduces one further exception
to the rules we have already given, however. It was stated earlier that the
appearance of any determinative in a postverbal phrase identifies the phrase
as nominal. The rule does not apply to a phrase containing a definite article
and a following adjective which is compared or to an adjectival preceded by
adverbial *more* or *most.* Phrases of this type can appear either with a recognizable noun at their head or with the comparative alone. That is, we can
say either "The houses were *all the older*" or "The houses were *all the older
types.*"

Finally, as has been suggested in dealing with material like adverbial
more and *most,* maximal adjectival phrases can be further expanded by
adverbs, and, indeed, simple postverbal adjectives can be expanded into
potential phrases by the same type of addition. It is here that Fries' observa-

---

[1] An apparent exception to the statement just given is the occurrence of sentences
of the type:

These houses are *mòre stóne|* thàn wóod #

The occurrence of *mòre* in this sentence is correlated with the separable *more. . .than*
sequence, which must be treated differently from *more* alone.

tion that there are subclasses of adverbs marked by characteristic order sequences is most useful.[2] Fries points out that when two adverbs belong to the same order group, they do not occur together unless separated by such words as *and* or *but* (and a terminal). Thus, following his principle, though using a different type of construction as illustration, we can have a sequence such as "These houses are *vèry mùch mòre expénsive*," where *very, much,* and *more* are all identified as adverbials by tertiary stress and are all shown to belong to differing order classes by the absence of connectives and, even more importantly, by the fact that order is fixed. Fries intimates rightly that there are more order classes of adverbs than the three he mentions. It is at least notable that one can build up a sequence of five, without intervening terminal junctures or connectives, e. g., "Jack is *vèry mùch mòre nèarly complètely* stûpid than Bill." Here also the order is fixed, and none of the positions occupied by the five adverbs can be shifted. An example of a construction involving two adverbs of the same order class is "Jack is *thóroughly | and complétely |* stupid." Here the order can be reversed as long as the connective is present. An addition to the statement made by Fries, however, is that in this situation at least, the two successive adverbs of the same order class may be set off by terminals alone, as in "Jack is thóroughly | complétely | stupid." An example of adverbs in reverse order is "The book is wármly | and génerally | líberal" or "The book is wármly | génerally | líberal." Even if the adverbs are in normal order, the sentence is usually "The book is génerally | wàrmly líberal," with a terminal after *generally*.

The order classes and other characteristics of adverbs in phrases of this sort have not been thoroughly investigated, though a number of unpublished doctoral dissertations on adverbial constructions have been completed. At present it seems possible only to make a relatively limited number of statements. The adverbial components of a phrase like *"very much more nearly thoroughly* stupid" are accretions built up by successive additions at the front, as with verb phrases. There are, however, unsolved problems of immediate constituent analysis in these phrases. For instance, neither *more* nor *much* can be dropped from the construction singly without producing impossible sequences, such as *very more* and **very much nearly*, though both can be dropped without trouble, as in *very nearly completely stupid*. It would seem, then, that the cutting should move from end to beginning but that at one cut *much more* would have to be recognized as a constituent. As for the order classes themselves, it would seem that those adverbs formed by the postbase *–ly* tend to come closest to the adjective at the end and head of the phrase, though as we have seen, there are further order classes within the *–ly* group. In the group of adverbs without this postbase, *very* is in a class by

---

[2] *The Structure of English*, p. 85.

itself and tends to occur first of all. If it is placed somewhere within the sequence, as in "Jack is much *more nearly very* stupid," stress and juncture shifts occur. The construction can be *mòre néarly | véry stûpid*, or it may be *mòre néarly | vèry stúpid*, both of which preserve the position of *very* as first in its (now minimal) phrase.

Up to this point we have been describing series of adverbs placed before a recognizable adjective as head word. Yet constructions of the type *very much more nearly thoroughly stupid* are probably not very common. More common are constructions of the type *very much more nearly thoroughly frightened*. That is to say, constructions in which the end position is occupied by a past participle. In this construction, however, there is a structural ambiguity, since forms constructed with any of the allomorphs of the suffix used for the past participle may be adjectives rather than verbal forms. Thus, for instance, *golden* employs the same suffix as that found in *taken* but is an adjective since there is no underlying verb **to gold*. Similarly, the dental suffix appears with fixed adjectival phrases like *a tôwhèaded bóy*, where though there is a verb *to head*, there is no fixed verbal phrase **to tówhèad*. The ambiguity between past participles and adjectives formed with similar suffixes is not very important, since the two groups act almost exactly alike. In some instances, however, pure past participles do not enter into the postverbal or prenominal modifier position. These are the so-called intransitives, verbs like *come, die, look*. For none of these do we use a form like "Jack is **thoroughly died*," except as an occasional nonce form like the following bit of conversation—"What do you mean, he's one of our coming men? He's one of our *come men*." In other instances, there is a distinction in meaning between the form which can enter into modifier positions and that which cannot. Thus, we can say "The cat walks," but not usually "The cat **is walked*." But the use of *walk* which occurs in "Jack walks the dog" easily permits the construction "The dog is thoroughly walked."

With forms like *frightened, loved*, which certainly appear as past participles (*has frightened, has loved*) and which also appear in modifying positions, there seems to be only one test which can be applied to determine whether we are dealing with participle or with adjective. It is a general characteristic of *very* that it does not occur immediately before a verb in the same phrase. We do not say "I **very will* go," as we say "I surely will go." We can therefore say that any modifier, like *frightened*, where we say "a *very frightened* man" or "The man is *very frightened*" is an adjective or adjectival, as are *golden* and *towheaded* mentioned above. A form like *spoken*, as in "*spoken* Latin" or "Latin was *spoken* in Rome," cannot thus be expanded by the addition of *very* and is thus a past participle.

A characteristic of phrases which consist of a series of adverbs and a past participle is that they may interrupt a nominal phrase of the type taken up in Chapter 11. That is, we can place such a phrase as *very newly painted* within the sequence *all the ten fine old stone houses*. When this occurs the participial phrase remains a unit, since it is set off by terminals. Further, there is great freedom of position, since the participial phrase can occur almost anywhere in the nominal sequence, though position between a determinative and a numeral seems to be less likely than the others. Moreover, the same kinds of statements, both as to the distinction between verbal and adjectival forms and as to position in nominal phrases, can be made about the forms in *–ing*. That is, since we can say *very boring*, *boring* is adjectival, but since we do not say **very shouting*, *shouting* is verbal. The forms in *–ing* fall into the same positions in nominal phrases and have the same juncture characteristics as the past participles, for example, the following:

II   I

âll thĕ tên strông yóung | vèry lòudly shóuting | Amêrican mén

2. Phrases syntactically and morphologically adverbial

The first group of modifying phrases are those in which an adjective or participle occupies the end position and is the head. There are others in which there is no such head word and in which the end position is occupied by an adverb. A typical adverbial phrase of this sort is "Jack studied *vèry mùch mòre nèarly thóroughly* | than John did." As can be seen, this phrase has exactly the same construction as *very much more nearly thoroughly stupid*, except that the head is now the recognizable adverb *thoroughly*. The same order groups are found in these sequences as are found in those sequences of adverbs where the head of the phrase is an adjective or participle. Little need be said of these phrases, therefore, except to point out that a phrase ending in an adverb marked by the adverbial postbase *–ly* does not occur after *be*, a situation which is characteristic of adjectival function.

As intimated earlier, constructions like *asleep, ahead, abroad* need more description. We have seen that this group are at least nonminimal words, characterized by an initial morpheme {ə} followed by /+/. The morpheme which characterizes the group can be added to a nominal base, as in *asleep*, to an adjectival base, as in *abroad*, or to an unclassifiable bound form, as in *akimbo*. Historically, as is well known, the initial morpheme of these phrases is an unstressed variant of *on*, but there is no reason to classify it so in present English. The group will therefore be described as constructions consisting of prebase and base. The whole group have a number of characteristics in common. All occur after *be:* "John is asleep," "John is ahead,"

"John is abroad," "John is away." All can occur after other verbs than *be:* "John fell asleep," "John continued afraid," "John pounded ahead," "John stood akimbo,"[3] "John traveled abroad." All have the further characteristic that they can stand immediately after a noun or nominal without intervening terminal juncture, a position in which they can then be defined as nominal modifiers. Examples are *"Children asleep* are a pretty sight," "The *road ahead* was rough," "The *trouble abroad* was reflected at home." All have the further negative characteristic that they do not stand immediately before a noun or nominal in the same phrase. That is, a construction like **the abroad trouble* is impossible.[4] Most of the group also enter into verbal phrases, as when we put *ahead* into "John wênt wálking." In such a sentence, of course, there is a difference between "John wênt ahéad | wálking" and "John wênt ahêad wálking." It is, finally, important to note that all of the group also often stand at first or last of a sentence, set off from the rest of it by a terminal juncture, as in:

> *Abróad | the trouble was worse than ever # * or
> *The trouble was worse than ever | abróad #*

From this description it will be seen that this group shares many characteristics with adverbs, and indeed they are usually grouped with them, as they are by Fries. Yet, if we compare the distribution of a form like *abroad* with the distribution of a form like *thoroughly,* which is clearly defined as an adverb, a number of differences emerge. *Thoroughly* does not stand immediately after *be* in the same phrase, as *abroad* does in "John is abroad." *Thoroughly* does not stand immediately after a noun in the same phrase, as does *abroad* in *the troubles abroad. Abroad,* on the other hand, does not stand in a sequence of modifiers with a noun, adjective, or participle at their head. That is, we can have a construction like *thòroughly expênsive nêw hóuses* or *expénsive | thòroughly nêw hóuses*—though the latter usually is interrupted by a terminal. We do not have *abroad* anywhere in the prenominal sequence, however, no matter what we do with stress and juncture.

While it is logically defensible to describe this group as adverbs, it is true that their special peculiarities must be taken account of, and when this is done, the group seems to have more characteristics shared in common by its members than characteristics shared with the class we have called adverbs. It is therefore more economical to set up still another form class, which is marked by syntactic characteristics alone and which will include *adjuncts* and

---

[3] "John stood akimbo" is certainly a rather rare form, yet a similar form "His yeoman ancestors, went of a Sunday to stand akimbo . . ." is quoted in *Webster's,* from Galsworthy, as the only contemporary citation.

[4] As expected, **an ahead job* is impossible, but *a straight-ahead job* is normal enough. *Straight-ahead* is a phrasal modifier of group I.

adjunctivals.[5] An adjunct proper is, then, a form like *content*, which is a word rather than a phrase and which is to be distinguished from constructions like *far ahead*, called adjunctivals since they are phrases. The use of the names "adjunct" and "adjunctival" does not prevent us from distinguishing various functions of members of the group. We can thus speak of an adjunct in adjective function in "John is abroad" and of the same adjunct in adverbial function in "John studied abroad." In *the troubles abroad* we can speak of the adjunct as functioning as a modifier of the preceding noun; and in initial position, or in final position set off by terminals (as in "Abróad | the troubles were worse than ever #" or "The troubles were worse than ever | abróad #"), we can describe them as functioning as sentence modifiers.

The adjunctival we have so far mentioned has been the phrase *far ahead*, but this is not the only phrase which belongs to the group. Other examples are the fixed phrases *thereafter, hereafter, afterward, afterwards, meanwhile*, and a good many more. Notice constructions like "Meánwhile | the fire burned steadily," "The fire burned steadily | méanwhile," "The fîre méanwhile | burned steadily." While such examples are enough to establish *meanwhile* as an adjunctival rather than an adverbial it is not to be thought that *meanwhile* functions in all ways like every other member of the group or, indeed, that there are not minor differences among most other members of the group. Thus *meanwhile* is rare in adjectival function, though such a sentence as "The examination is meanwhile" is probably possible. *Afterwărd*, on the other hand, is relatively common in adjectival function, as in "The examination is afterward."

The largest and probably the most important group of adjunctivals are phrases like *on the table*, but these will be separately described in Section 3 of this chapter. Here it is important to take up a relatively small but very common group of adjuncts which can be exemplified by *there, where, then, when*, and *now*. A first group can be set up as:

here	*there*	*where*
	then	*when*

These have been described in Chapter 9 as pronominals, since the repeated initial variation {h}: {ð}: {hw}, though it is not paradigmatic, is closely similar to the structure of pronouns. It is not necessary to deny our earlier

---

[5] The term "adjunct" as here used is not to be confused with the use of this term in Jespersen (*A Modern English Grammar*, 1914, Vol. II, Par. 1.21), where constructions are divided into heads or principals, primary modifiers or adjuncts, and secondary modifiers or subjuncts. In Jespersen's terms, *extremely hot weather* contains the principal (*weather*), an adjunct (*hot*), and a subjunct (*extremely*).

The terms "adjunct" and "adjunctival" are here used with acknowledgments to Henry Lee Smith, Jr.

description, even though in the present discussion we will redefine the group distributionally as adjuncts. Notice that a form like *here* occurs immediately after a noun:

The bôoks *hére* | are blúe #   or   The bóoks *hêre* | are blúe #

After *be:*

My interests are *hére* #

And after other verbs:

Washington slépt *hêre* #   or   Washington slêpt *hére* #

Here can also occur in initial position followed by a terminal, as in:

Hére | the trôuble rèally stárts #

Or in final position, preceded by a terminal:

Râin is scárce | *hére* #

There are minor differences between the members of the group, such as that we can treat *then* as a pure adjective in:

the *thên* Président #

Or that *when* does not commonly occur in final position preceded by a terminal.

These characteristics are enough to define the group we have been discussing as adjuncts. Yet in Chapter 9 they were described as pronominals, with the statement that the syntactic characteristics which justify that name would be given later. The most important syntactic characteristic that this group shares with pronouns is that they are very frequent as sentence beginners, as in "When is the show?" and "Here comes the train." Pronouns also occur in this position of course, but there are differences. In "He saw the train," the characteristic stress of the pronoun is tertiary. The adjunct group characteristically receive secondary stress, though there are a few exceptions to both of these statements. *Who* has been defined as a true pronoun since it has pronoun suffixes. In a sentence like

Whôse wás it #

the stress is secondary, as is usual with the adjuncts. An adjunct with tertiary stress is found in:

Thère's tróuble ahêad #

This use of *there* with tertiary stress constitutes a contrast with the use of *there* in:

Thêre gôes the tráin #

The tertiarily stressed initial *there* is the mark of the construction which can be called impersonal.

The similarity of these forms to pronouns has led a number of analysts to class them among the pronouns. Yet, not only are there differences in stress pattern, there is an even more important syntactic difference which prevents grouping these forms with true pronouns. A pronoun in preverbal position regularly selects the form of the following verb, as in a pair of sentences like *"He is* American" and *"They are* American." With a form like *here* or *there*, on the other hand, it is not the initial word but the following noun which selects the verb form, as in "Here *comes the teacher"* contrasted with "Here *come the teachers."*

The forms like *here, there, where* are like pronouns in their construction, their function as sentence beginners without a following terminal, and their occasional tertiary stress, but are like adjuncts in the rest of their distribution. We can, then, call them pronominal adjuncts, recognizing both sets of characteristics. The whole series characterized by the alternation {h}: {ð}: {hw} can be referred to the same group, the pronominal adjuncts.[6] There are differences among the group, of course, but notice that a typical pair like *then : when* are sentence beginners, as "Then came the dawn" and "When is it?" A complete list of the {h}: {ð}: {hw} group follows:

here	*there*	*where*
	then	*when*
hence	*thence*	*whence*
hither	*thither*	*whither*
		whether
		what
		which
		why
		how

There is, of course, an apparent irregularity in the list given above, in that *how* is listed in the last column, as if its pronunciation were */hwaw/. The irregularity is only apparent, however, since it is a morphophonemic rule that the morpheme {hw} cannot occur before a vowel nucleus in /w/, as is shown by the development of *who*, which still shows in its spelling the initial sequence it once had before the vowel nucleus became /uw/. Since *how* is like *what* and *why* in its general distribution, it is economical to describe the

---

[6] In describing this series as containing {h}, {ð}, and {hw}, no account is taken of dialect variation. In my own idiolect a number of the bases take {θ} rather than {ð}, as /θéns/ and /θíðər/. In a large part of America, {hw} is regularly reduced to {w}. In my idiolect, on the other hand, only unstressed occurrences—all relative uses—of forms in {hw} are thus reduced.

initial /h/ as an automatic alternant of /hw/. It should be remembered that *who* has been defined as a true pronoun, since it has the case forms *whose* and the now rare *whom*. Thus, though it is constructed with the same initial morpheme as are these forms and is generally like them in distribution, it does not appear in this list of pronominals.[7]

The three initial morphemes have meanings which can be described as near in space or time, {h}; distant in space or time, {ð}; and question indicator, {hw}. The last morpheme, however, has a second quite different function, since it also occurs in constructions like "The book *which I bought yesterday* was written by Smith." That is, the {hw} morpheme occurs in initial position in certain dependent sentences, indicating repetition of a nominal which occurs in the major sentence. These forms are traditionally called relatives and will be described more fully in Chapter 20. At the moment it is sufficient to define relativity as a second meaning of the {hw} morpheme.

There remains only one other difficulty in the list. This is the form *now*, which in general is distributed as if it were the missing member of the *then : when* series, yet does not have the expected */hen/ shape, though a form like *hence*, morphemically {h–en–s}, shows that the sequence {h–en–} is perfectly possible. It would seem simplest to recognize that *now* belongs to the series and to say that the form *{h–en} has been replaced by a suppletive portmanteau *now*. There is no real justification for cutting *now* into morphs, such as initial {n}, which replaces {h}, and {aw}, which replaces {en}. Such cutting of *now* would be more complicated than to leave it as an unanalyzed portmanteau, and also arbitrary, since there are no other forms with which to compare *now*.

The whole series of pronominal adjuncts, of course, can stand as the heads of adjunctival phrases, as in *just here*, or *just now*, or *from here*, *from whence*, and the more complex *from about here*, as in "From about here the road gets rough." There are also forms like *hitherward* /hiðər + wərd/, constructed with the bound *–ward* of *afterward*.

3. Prepositional phrases

We have several times referred to the last major phrase type, that which begins with a preposition. A typical prepositional phrase is *of England* in *King of England*. We shall use *of* as a conveniently typical preposition and will be able to take its characteristics as diagnostic of all members of this form class. Prepositions in nominal phrases are typically without stress and, in accord with other forms so treated, appear frequently with reduced forms,

---

[7] See previous discussion in Chap. 9, Section 2, p. 150.

as *of* may in the phrase quoted, /kíŋ | víŋglənd #/. While a preposition in a phrase like *of England* is typically without stress, we have seen that in post-verbal, pre-terminal position, the characteristic prepositional stress is ter-tiary. Even in nominal phrases, there is a situation where prepositions also have tertiary stress. This is when prepositions appear in sequences, as in *ìntŏ, òut ŏf:*

$$\text{òut ŏf Éngland} \mid \text{ìntŏ Fránce} \#$$

The preservation of one tertiary in a sequence of two prepositions occurs also in postverbal position, as in:

$$\text{a bôok to réad òut of} \#$$

The latter form is one which appeared a few years ago in a poem in a popular magazine:

"What did you bring that bôok to réad *òut ŏf* | *úp fòr?*"

That is, in this sentence, there is a sequence of two prepositions, the second with stress reduced to weak, followed by an adverbial (and stressed) *up*, followed in turn by prepositional *for*.

Prepositions are to be defined as words on account of their relative freedom in position. They are typically invariant bases. They are commonly phrase initials, with a following form which is noun, or nominal. They also occur internally in verb constructions, as does *to* in "I *want to go*" or *on* in "He *kept on going.*" We have also seen that prepositions occur postverbally before a terminal, where they receive tertiary stress. At this point, then, it is important to realize that in a situation where a form like *by* occurs between a verb and a following noun, it is not only the stress distinction which is important. There is also a juncture distinction, or more exactly a differing juncture point. In the sentence "John tried to pass by the road," the written form is ambiguous, not only as to whether *by* is preposition or adverb but as to the boundaries of the major sentence elements:

$$\overset{2}{} \qquad\qquad\qquad \overset{3\ 1}{}$$
$$\text{/jâhn + trâyd + tə + pǽs + bây + ðə + rówd} \#/$$

As long as *by* is thus stressed, there is a point after it at which a terminal is likely to occur, so that there is a variant form:

$$\overset{2}{} \qquad\qquad \overset{32}{}\ \overset{2}{}\ \overset{3\ 1}{}$$
$$\text{/jâhn + trâyd + tə + pǽs + báy} \mid \text{ðə + rówd} \#/$$

If stressed otherwise, the sentence may be:

$$\overset{2}{} \qquad\qquad\qquad \overset{3\ 1}{}$$
$$\text{/jâhn + trâyd + tə + pǽs + bay + ðə + rówd} \#/$$

In this form, the point at which a terminal is likely is before *by*, giving the variant:

$$\overset{2}{\text{/jâhn}} + \text{trâyd} + \text{tə} + \overset{32}{\text{pæs}} \mid \overset{2}{\text{bay}} + \text{ðə} + \overset{31}{\text{rówd}} \#/$$

That is, the relatively stressed forms which are adverbs belong with the verbal sequence of which they are components. The weakly stressed forms are prepositions, which in this sort of situation belong in the same construction with the following noun. We have had to refer several times to the stress distinction between preposition and adverb. It should be said in passing that the distinction has been noticed and discussed by a number of scholars, for instance, Jespersen,[8] but the further distinguishing juncture characteristics have been fully discussed only by H. L. Smith, in a work not yet fully published.

If, then, we define a prepositional phrase as one beginning with a preposition, it is a natural next step to inquire what comes after the beginning word. First, a preposition can occur before a noun, or before a noun phrase made up of any of the possible sequences of modifiers with a noun at the end. If we return to our specimen noun phrase,

VI V IV III II I   N

all the ten fine old stone houses

we immediately see that *of* can be placed before the whole sequence or before any partial sequence ending in *houses*. One or two examples will suffice:

VI V IV III II I   N

This is the best *of all the ten fine old stone houses.*

V IV I   N

This is the best *of the ten stone houses.*

This is the best *of houses.*

The whole sequence is a single potential phrase, and we can define the last word in it as its head.

Rather more interesting is what happens when *houses* is absent. We can now have sequences of preposition and any of the modifying groups except the adjectives of groups III and II. An example is:

P VI

This house is the best *of all.*

We cannot construct such a phrase ending in *the*, since it is a rule that an

---

[8] *A Modern English Grammar*, Winter 1931, Vol. III, Par. 13.9.

article cannot stand before a terminal. We can, however, use another member of group v and get:

P   v
This house is the best *of these.*

It is a point of interest that some of the pronoun modifiers of group v have a separate form before a terminal juncture, so that these modifiers signal the end of the phrase redundantly. Notice the following, written without punctuation:

This house is the best of all mine Mary chose it.

Even without any signaling of stress and juncture pattern, it is clear that there must be a terminal after *mine* and that it cannot fall after *all.* The same redundancy appears, but with the terminal placed differently, if we write:

This house is the best of all my Mary chose it.

We can easily construct the sequence preposition-iv:

This house is the best *of ten.*

And we can again have the complete sequence of three modifiers:

P   vi   v   iv
This house is the best *of all those ten.*

With modifiers of groups iii and ii, however, we do not construct phrases where the modifier stands finally. That is, we say neither "This house is the best **of fine*" nor "This house is the best **of old.*"[9] There is only one type of situation in which something like this seems to occur. We can construct sentences of the following two types, both of which have a terminal immediately after a prepositional phrase ending in a modifier of iii or ii:

If you take *âll of the fíne* | I'll take *âll of the óld* | *hóuses.*
If you take *all of the fíne hôuses* | I'll take *all of the óld.*

In both of the sentences, by the way, *houses* is apt to be set off by terminals and to receive primary stress. In neither of these sentences, however, is the modifier the head of the maximal construction. The rule is that when there are two parallel nominal phrases, one or the other of the occurrences of an identical noun head can be represented by zero. An even commoner arrangement, of course, is that in Modern English, we now represent the second occurrence of the identical noun by *one:*

If you take *all of the fine houses,* I'll take *all of the old ones.*

---

[9] The phrase "in days *of old*" is an idiom parallel to *of yore,* both of which require separate listing.

Mention of a nominal modifier of group I as a possible phrase head in prepositional constructions was deliberately avoided above, since whether or not a group I modifier can stand at the head of such phrases is debatable. It is clear that group I modifiers constructed with postbases, like *wooden* or *American*, do not occur as heads, any more than do modifiers like *fine* or *old*. The difficulty arises with nouns of the type of *stone*, which can occur as group I modifiers with secondary stress. It would be tempting to describe a sentence like "These houses are *of stone*" as containing a prepositional phrase with a group I modifier, rather than a true noun, at its head, since there is no overt mark of nominal status accompanying *stone*. First, however, it should be pointed out that in sentences which consist of noun, verb *to be*, and noun, English frequently requires that the two nouns be in the same number, as in "The dog is an animal" and "Dogs are animals." In such sentences, then, we have a formal distinction between a noun and a modifier in postverbal position. A sentence such as "Dogs are animal" must then contain a nominal modifier, not a noun. If, however, the sentence is of the pattern noun, verb *to be* (or any verb), and prepositional phrase, there is no necessity for agreement. We can say either "These stories are *of a man*" or "These stories are *of men*"—both contain nouns, as the article and the plural prove. Thus, one mark of distinction, that of agreement or lack of agreement, cannot here be used to decide the status of forms like *stone* after prepositions. It might, of course, be possible to use the occurrence or nonoccurrence of articles as a diagnostic, but the result would be to complicate description. Are we to say that "stories *of man*" contains a modifier? Then what do we do with *man* in "*Man* wants but little"? In short, there are many situations in which forms which are clearly nouns lack articles. Nor can transformations be used to decide the issue. It is true that in *a box of glass* we can transpose to /glǽs + báks/, with the stress pattern of a modifier, and that with *box of glasses* we can transform only to the pattern of a fixed nominal phrase /glǽsiz + bàks/. But while in this particular instance there seems to be a distinction between the marked noun and something that might be called a modifier, the distinction breaks down with many forms, and it turns out to be impossible to predict whether a transformed noun followed by preposition and noun gives the secondary-primary stress pattern or that of primary-tertiary. Thus both *heap of ash* and *heap of ashes* give only /ǽš + hìyp/, and *sack of wool* gives both /wúl + sæ̀k/ and /wûl + sǽk/. Regretfully, therefore, it must be decided that there is no precise distinction between a nominal group I modifier and a pure noun as head of a prepositional phrase. It must therefore be decided that in all sentences like "These houses are *of stone*," we are dealing with nouns, since it is clear that nouns can occur here, and it would be arbitrary and unnecessary to add group I modifiers as a second possibility.

Before we leave the occurrence of nominal phrases after prepositions, we should point out that prepositions may be repeated in the sequence, but only at two points. Prepositions may be repeated before predeterminatives and determinatives, but not elsewhere in the maximal series, as in:

VI   V   IV III II   I

He told me *of all of the ten fine old stone houses.*

Notice that this rule holds even if the sequence is minimized to *all houses.* We can then have *of all houses,* but if a second *of* is added, it requires a determinative after it:

VI   V

of all of the houses

There is a third position at which a preposition is in a sense possible. This is before the nominal modifier, *stone.* But if the preposition is added, a shift in order is required, giving:

He told me *of* all *of* the ten fine old houses *of stone.*

This characteristic offers some confirmation of the conclusion, reached above, that any nominal form after a preposition is a noun, not a group I modifier. That is, the behavior of *stone* is exactly like the behavior of *glasses* in "a fine old box *of glasses,*" where not only is *glasses* marked as a noun, but it is impossible, as we have seen, to shift it into the position and stress pattern of a modifier.

The most frequent heads for prepositional phrases are those which have been described, nouns and nominal phrases. Another form class which can occur as the head of prepositional phrases are the pronouns, as in *of me, of him.* We have already mentioned the occurrence of forms like *of mine, of hers* in describing the occurrence of prepositions in nominal phrases. The form here described as head of the prepositional phrase is form 2 of the pronoun paradigm, whereas constructions like *of mine* contain form 4. The phrases constructed with form 2 are generally simple and, except when the pronoun is *me,* do not very freely admit modifiers between the preposition and the head. *Me* will permit forms like *for poor little me* and perhaps even other modifiers, as in *for smart fat me.* Similar forms can occasionally be found for other pronouns, but in my own idiolect they are much more limited than with *me.* The distribution of *me* is, however, out of line with that of other pronouns even when no preposition occurs, as *dear me* shows.

Still another class which can stand as head of prepositional phrases are the pronominal adjuncts of the {h} : {ð} : {hw} group, as in "The books *ŭp thére* | are blue." The pronominal adjuncts, like pronouns, do not very freely admit modifiers between the preposition and the head, though we have forms like "He went *to right there*" and "It came *from just here.*" Other modifiers, such as *beautiful* or *suddenly*, do not go into these phrases.

The final type of head word which can occur after a preposition is a verb form. The first of these is *to* plus the infinitive, as in "I want *to go,*" a type which has been fully described already. The only addition that need be made now is that *to* is unique in distribution since it is the only preposition used in this type of phrase. It has already been mentioned that interposition of an adverb between *to* and the verb is a construction which occurs but is sometimes objected to as a "split infinitive." It is perhaps more interesting to note that though constructions like "John is *to readily go*" occur, a construction like "John is **to ready go,*" in place of "John is ready to go," is impossible. That is, *to* and infinitive is a construction like preposition and pronoun, in that modifiers do not readily occur between the preposition and the head of the phrase.

The second type of verbal form which can be head of a prepositional phrase is the *–ing.* The number of prepositions which occur before an *–ing* is much less limited; curiously *to* is rare in this situation, though it does occur, as in:

> Put it down *to learning* the business.

Much more common are sentences like:

> This is a fine night *for sleeping.*   or   He convinced me *by talking.*

Prepositional phrases in *–ing* differ from the *to* plus infinitive in that intervening modifiers can be freely added. These may be adverbs, adverbials, adjectives, or adjectivals, as in:

> He convinced me *by really talking.*
> He (the dog) convinced me *by just about talking.*
> He convinced me *by smart talking.*
> He convinced me *by lawyer-like talking.*

Up to this point no description of the distribution of prepositional phrases in larger sentence units has been given. Their distribution can be rather quickly described. They can occur as sentence beginners followed by a terminal, as in:

> *With her father's consent* | Mary married John.

They can also occur in final position, preceded by a terminal:

> Mary married John | *with her father's consent.*

They do not occur prenominally, except for a special situation which will be described below; rather, their most typical situation is postnominal, as:

The top *of the fine old wooden table* | is dusty.

It is to be noted that there is normally no terminal before the preposition in this particular construction, though in other sentences the prepositional sequence is regularly both preceded and followed by terminals, as in:

Máry | *wìth her fâther's consént* | *mârried Jóhn* #

In this sort of situation, the difference between a prepositional phrase preceded by a terminal and a prepositional phrase not preceded by one is meaningful. Note:

Jêannie with the líght-bròwn haír | *mârried Jóhn* #

The difference in meaning can be defined by stating that a prepositional phrase not separated by a terminal from a preceding noun is a modifier of that noun. If separated, the prepositional phrase has the same kind of relatively loose sentence modification that it would have in first or last position.

The distinction in structure also applies to situations like the following:

The books on the table are white.
/ðə + bûks + ɔn + ðə + téybəl | àhr + hwáyt #/
The books, on the table, are white.
/ðə + búks | ɔn + ðə + téybəl | àhr + hwáyt #/

The contrast in meaning here is frequently taken up in school grammars and handbooks under the terms "restrictive phrase (or clause)" for the first and "nonrestrictive" for the second. The distinction has represented a perennial difficulty for freshmen, since the distinction is usually presented in semantic terms, in that the restrictive material is stated to identify the particular object talked about, whereas the nonrestrictive material is stated to apply to all objects in the class, and the students are then told to punctuate accordingly.[10] There are several difficulties in this procedure. First, it is usually difficult to analyze semantically, unless the analyst has a clear idea of how the semantic difference is signaled. In the absence of some understanding of terminal junctures, the student has nothing to work with, and

---

[10] On the semantic approach found in handbook definitions, note the following definition of a nonrestrictive clause: "Adjective clauses . . . are nonrestrictive (set off by commas) when they merely *add information about a word already identified.*" (John C. Hodges, *Harbrace College Handbook*, 4th ed., Harcourt, Brace, New York, 1956, p. 126. Italics supplied.)

The italicized words indicate material which applies to all members of the class.

the placing of commas seems merely arbitrary. More important, however, the two sentences as written above are not perfectly clear, and it has been my experience that native speakers do not react to them without hesitation. That is to say, the juncture in the second form can be lost, suppressing the difference. It seems that the junctureless first form is reinforced, so to speak, by giving a pitch four on the stressed syllable of *table*, by over-loudness, or by both. When this is done, the first sentence clearly indicates a situation in which there are books elsewhere in the room, not on the table, and not necessarily white. The second sentence, with *on the table* set off by terminals, is apparently ambiguous in meaning no matter what is done to it by variations of pitch, vocal qualifiers, or junctures. The second sentence makes of the prepositional phrase a loose sentence modifier, like *with her father's consent* in contrast to *with the light-brown hair*. As is usual in such loose modifiers, they will be interpreted in whatever fashion seems most probable, just as will initial or final phrases like the following:

On the table | the books are white. and *The books are white | on the table.*

In short, with prepositional phrases, presence or absence of a juncture signals a structural difference, but the correlation with meaning differences is not absolute. The difference in meaning, however, is clearer with the so-called relative clauses and will be returned to later.

A final point in the general distribution of prepositional phrases is that they may be preceded by adjectives and adjectivals within the same juncture group. Thus we have:

Mary is *ready for the party*.

Here also, there may be a terminal after ready, making *for the party* a loose sentence modifier. The probable interpretation of the form with a terminal is that she is ready for the party only, not for something else. Prepositional phrases are occasionally preceded by adverbs, though often not in the same juncture group, as in:

Certainly with American students | this kind of discipline fails.

A terminal after *certainly* is probably more common here than its absence.

The general distribution postnominal-postverbal, set off by terminals at the start or end of the sentence, is recognizably that of elements which we have called adjunctival. They are, then, typically postposed modifiers, and are to be distinguished from phrasal modifiers of group I, which may be preposed, as in:

We sell *ready-to-wear* clothing.

It is worth noting, of course, that *ready-to-wear* contains a prepositional potential phrase but is not itself a phonological phrase. The fact that it is not is proved by its distribution—it can be preposed, where the prepositional phrase *to wear* must be postposed. That is, we say "We sell clothing *to wear*" and do not say "We sell **to wear* clothing."

Some books contain statements to the effect that phrasal modifiers must be postposed in English. The statement is true for prepositional phrases and adjunctival phrases generally, but does not take account of the group I phrasal modifiers and of modifiers of other groups which happen to take fixed-phrase form, as with *fórty-òdd*, or *líght-gràgy*. Probably the most interesting, and certainly the most complex, of preposed nominal modifying phrases are the so-called group genitives, a typical, though colloquial example of which is the previously cited:

Shè góes | *wìth thĕ bôy ŭp thĕ strêet's* bróther #

This sentence is a sort of Chinese box, in which there is one long prepositional phrase, *with . . . brother*, which itself contains a second prepositional phrase, *up the street*. The group offers an opportunity for detailed immediate constituent analysis, since the order and position of successive cuts must be carefully decided upon and then rigidly justified. Our first cut will be before *with*. This is determined by the fact that *with* is recognizable as a preposition by its lack of stress and by the possibility of a terminal before it. Were the cut to be after *with*, the form would have to be adverbial and so marked by stress. It is a rule of English structure that while prepositional phrases as whole units are often to be construed with what precedes, the preposition itself is to be taken with what follows.

Our next cut, in turn, is after *with*, giving the preposition as one constituent and the long nominal phrase, *the boy up the street's brother*, as the other. This cut is justified by the fact that it gives a second constituent which is a possible phrase, whereas to cut before *brother* gives an impossible phrase, and to cut so as to make a discontinuous constituent *with . . . brother* requires two cuts rather than one. Another possibility, of course, would have been to cut after *boy*, giving the constituents *with the boy* and *up the street's brother*. This is to be rejected because there is no possibility of producing an understandable variety of the sentence if a terminal is put after *boy*, proof enough that *up the street* must be construed with the noun that precedes.

At this point, however, we must reverse the direction of our cutting, working now from the end so as to give *the boy up the street's* and *brother*. At first sight, this may seem surprising, since it gives one constituent which is impossible as a free form. But we have already seen reason to believe that *up the street* forms a constituent with *the boy*, so that we cannot here accept a cut after *boy* any more than we could previously. The occurrence of the {s}-suffix, on the other hand, is a signal that we are dealing with a determinative, as is proved by the fact that as usual with nominal phrases, we cannot expand by the addition of another group v modifier, such as "*the* brother." We can, however, easily add another modifier of a lower group, such as "*older* brother." If then, *the boy up the street* is a constituent, and the {s}-suffix proves that there is a group v modifier, it must be this whole constituent which is the modifier, forcing the cut before *brother*.

The next cut is easy and has been suggested already. That is, we cut off the suffix, giving {s} and *the boy up the street*. We are now finally ready to make a cut before the prepositional phrase *up the street*, leaving that for one constituent, and *the boy* for the other. It might still have been possible to put off this cut, by cutting after *the*, leaving *boy up the street* as the other constituent. This, however, has been avoided since *the* does not have full freedom, whereas such a phrase as *the boy* can appear in almost any position. Further, with nouns of this class, a group v modifier is always required unless the noun is plural, which also suggests that article and noun make up a constituent. The fact that a cut after *the boy* is finally justified, though we have insisted that on all previous levels the prepositional phrase made a constituent with the preceding noun, is shown by the fact that *up the street* contains a second *the*, something that cannot occur in English unless the second part of the phrase is a differing construction from that which precedes.

We need not go further with analysis of this particular phrase, since the remaining cuts are now obvious. I can, however, point out that the so-called group genitive, which we have here been describing, consists of the treatment of a noun and following prepositional phrase as a phrasal group v modifier by the addition of suffix {s}. The only other type of group genitive is a noun and following relative clause in *who, which,* or the like, treated in the same way. It is worth noting that the sentence we have been analyzing is a simplification of a sentence which was actually recorded from normal conversation and which was of the relative type—"She goes with the boy who lives across the street's brother." Constructions of this sort constitute an exception to the general statement that English segmental morphemes are usually constituents of words rather than of free phrases. As has been shown, the {s}, spoken of rather loosely as a suffix, is actually a morpheme which is a constituent only of the free phrase, not of the preceding word, *street*, and is not itself a word since it is completely bound rather than free. The only alternative to such an analysis would be the very cumbersome one of assuming that *the boy who lives across the street* is a word, a solution that would enormously complicate the lexicon and contradict any sensible phonological basis for defining the limits of words.

Prepositional phrases do not generally occur as actor forms for verbs except in one rather curious construction and with a following infinitive in *to:*

> *For a man to marry* | is better than to burn.

The history of the form has been discussed at length by Jespersen, but more important than the history is a distinction in meaning carried by the position of *for*. We can arrive at the distinction in the following pair:

> *For the man to marry* | is what Mary is hoping.
> The man to marry | is what Mary is hoping *for*.

That is, preservation of the normal sequence is here a signal that *man* is the actor for the following infinitive; the separated position of *for* in the second sentence indicates that *man* is the goal. It is in relative sentences of the type found in this second example that the troublesome overlap between adverbs and prepositions occurs, as in a pair like:

> PREPOSITION   This is the place that Mary *cáme tò*.
> ADVERB   This is the place that Mary *câme tó*.

In the first of these sentences we find a preposition falling immediately after a verb, without an intervening terminal. Does this indicate that a preposition is normally a constituent with a preceding verb? There would be some advantage in so considering it—we habitually think of verb and following preposition as a unit in meaning, and we speak, for instance, of *look at* in *look at Mary* as the "transitive form" of *look*. We have seen, however, that the juncture situation when there is a following noun strongly suggests that the preposition goes with what follows. The relative type of sentence, with the noun or noun phrase in the first half can, and I think should, be brought into accord with the usual statements. In sentences with a final preposition, there is always an initial noun or nominal construction. This construction can be stated to be the displaced head of the prepositional phrase, and the final preposition can be stated to be at the start of a prepositional phrase where displacement has given a construction headed by zero. When a preposition occurs in a phrase headed by zero, terminal juncture before the preposition is regularly lost.

15 .... MAIN SENTENCE ELEMENTS, I

Subject and Subjectival

1. Juncture points and linkage of pitch morphemes in relation to sentence element boundaries

We have seen that segmental morphemes are often, though not always, bounded by junctures, and have set up a larger unit, the phonological phrase, which is a unit bounded by terminal junctures. With sequences of segmental morphemes we have also found situations in which a /+/ was likely to occur but was not stringently required. One such situation is in a stress sequence of primary-tertiary, as in the noun *content*, which may be either /kán + tènt/ or /kántènt/. That is, a juncture point occurs between the two stresses. The stress sequence does not minutely define the location of the juncture point. For instance, a sequence such as *won't it* with primary-tertiary would also have a juncture point, but if a /+/ occurred, it would be likely to fall after the cluster /-nt-/ rather than between the /-n-/ and /-t-/ as in *content*. In phrasal units we find a similar set of juncture distributions. It will be remembered that, as well as the phonological phrase, we set up a second unit, the potential phrase, consisting of a construction not marked by terminals at its boundaries but of such a morphological nature that terminals at the boundaries were possible.

Just as with a sequence of primary-tertiary, there is a juncture point in a sequence of primary-secondary or secondary-primary. But in such a sequence, the juncture point is different. In my idiolect, these stress sequences do not occur without a /+/, and the variation possible is that such a sequence can always be broken into two phrases divided by a terminal. The stress sequence contains two potential phrases. Thus, such an utterance as "Nice eats!" may be either:

$$\begin{array}{cc} 2 \quad 31 & 332 \quad 441 \\ \text{/nâys + íyts }\#/ \quad \text{or} & \text{/náys} \mid \text{íyts }\#/ \end{array}$$

When broken into two phrases, as in the second transcription, there are necessarily modifications in pitch and stress as well. The stress sequence of secondary-primary does not define the exact location of the juncture, any more than the sequence of primary-tertiary does. The utterance just given corresponds, in its segmental material, to the much less probable *nigh seats*. Here the juncture point would fall before, rather than after, the first /s/. But though the stress sequence does not define the location of the juncture point, the location is still predictable. In *nice eats* there is a /+/ after the /s/, and if a terminal occurs, it must replace this /+/. Similarly, if the utterance is *nigh seats*, a possible terminal must replace the /+/ before the /s/. We can then define an internal juncture point as one at which a /+/ is likely to appear in a sequence not marked by any juncture, and a terminal juncture point as one at which a /+/ is likely to be replaced by /|/, /||/, or /#/. An internal juncture point is one at which a single stress morpheme is likely to be broken into two, and a terminal juncture point is one at which a single pitch morpheme is likely to be broken. A terminal juncture point necessarily falls at the boundary of a stress morpheme, and this fact is one of the demonstrations of the stratification of suprasegmental material. The pitch morphemes are located in terms of the boundaries of the stress morphemes, which constitute the level next beneath them.

Not all terminal juncture points are alike, since the surrounding pitch phonemes may differ. That is, it is not enough to say that a terminal is likely to replace a /+/ at some point in the sentence; we must also describe the totality of the pitch morphemes which are likely to occur if the sequence is broken by a terminal. For that reason we shall give here a preliminary description of the phenomenon of linkage of pitch morphemes, though this is a matter to which we shall return more fully, and from a different point of view, in Chapter 19, Section 1.

There are three types of linkage of pitch morphemes into a single superfix. One of these, which is characteristic of complex sentences, can be called extension of contour by addition of a monotone morpheme in which the monotone level is the same as the level of the final pitch phoneme of the preceding morpheme. This is the only type of linkage which can take place across a /#/. A typical example is the sequence {2 3 1 #} {1 1 1 #} of the following:

$$\begin{array}{cccc} 2 & 3\ 1 & 1 & 11 \\ \textit{Nô indéed} \ \# & \textit{Jôhn sáid} \ \# \end{array}$$

This type of linkage will be spoken of as linkage by addition of a monotone morpheme.

The second type of linkage can best be illustrated by what happens to a unified construction, such as a noun phrase, which is for any reason broken into two or more phrases. An example is a construction which has already been discussed:

$$\begin{array}{ccccccc} 2 & & 2\ 2\ 33 & 2 & 44 & 2\ 2 & 3\ 1 \\ \textit{The Port of New York Authority} \mid \textit{ticket book} \mid \textit{sales office} \mid \textit{is over there} \ \# \end{array}$$

The morphemes in question are the series $\{2\,2\,2\,|\}$ $\{3\,3\,2\,|\}$ $\{4\,4\,2\,|\}$; the $\{2\,3\,1\,\#\}$ of the final phrase is not here under consideration. The sequence of three morphemes, their high points successively /2/, /3/, and /4/ can be, as Stockwell has said,[1] described as the equivalent of a single morpheme of $\{2\,3\,2\,|\}$, which would fall on a simpler construction, like the following:

2 3   2 2   31
The ticket office | is over there #

This kind of linkage can be called linkage by complex contour. It normally takes place across a /||/, but may also take place across a /|||/. A complex contour can be described by saying that a pitch morpheme whose peak is /4/ is linked to a preceding morpheme whose peak is /3/, and a morpheme whose peak is /3/ may be linked to a preceding morpheme whose highest point is /2/. The morpheme which contains /2/ is always a monotone. Linkage by complex contour is, in what follows, always taken as a signal of unity in a construction consisting of two or three phrases.

The third kind of linkage occurs when the final pitch phoneme of the preceding morpheme is identical with the initial pitch phoneme of the following morpheme. It is necessary to add that the second morpheme may not be a monotone; if it were, the linkage would be of the first type described. This type of linkage takes place across a /||/ or /|||/ and is usually characteristic of the morphemes which mark the boundaries between main parts of a sentence. A typical example is the sequence $\{2\,3\,2\,|\}$ $\{2\,3\,1\,\#\}$, as in:

2   32 2   31
Poor little old John | he nearly died #

This last type of linkage will be spoken of as minimal linkage.

In each of the three types of linkage, we have seen that there is a correlation between the types of pitch morphemes which occur and the nature of the underlying segmental material. Characteristically, a juncture point defined merely by such a sequence as /ˆ + ˇ'/ will give rise to a complex contour if the /+/ is replaced by /||/ or /|||/. An example might be:

2   31
Jôhn + Depéw #

If this name is broken into two phrases, we get

332   2 41
/jáhn | dipyúw #/

with a typical complex contour. If, on the other hand, the sequence /ˆ + ˇ'/ characterizes separate parts of a sentence, breaking it into two phrases

---

[1] See above, p. 113.

produces minimal linkage. If the stress sequence characterized "John appeared," we should expect the two-phrase treatment to give:

$$\text{332} \quad \text{2 31}$$
$$\text{/jáhn | əpíhrd \#/}$$

If the stress sequence characterized separate sentences, separate phrase treatment might be expected to produce extension by a monotone, as in:

$$\text{331} \quad \text{1} \quad \text{11}$$
$$\textit{"Go!" he said.} \quad \text{/gów \# iy + séd \#/}$$

The type of linkage produced merely by the succession of stress morphemes can be spoken of as phonologically controlled; the other two, in which identification of morphological content of the construction is necessary before the linkage can be predicted, can be spoken of as morphologically controlled. We can also, obviously, speak of phonological and morphological juncture points.

Since this chapter deals with the main parts of sentences, we shall be concerned with terminal juncture points and will most often base decisions on whether a possible terminal gives pitch morphemes linked by complex contours or by minimal linkage. If there is a complex contour, we shall assume that the two pitch morphemes belong to a single part of the sentence. If there is minimal linkage, we shall decide that the two pitch morphemes belong to different parts of the sentence. The type of linkage represented by addition of a monotone morpheme, since it characterizes the parts of a complex sentence, will be of primary importance to us only when we describe sentences of that type.

The elements of the sentence are familiar under such names as subject, predicator (or verb), and complement. Since there is no generally accepted name for the whole class, we shall call them sentence elements. We shall define them in detail in the sections of this chapter which follow. At present a general definition is sufficient. They are constructions within the sentence characterized by pitch morphemes with minimal linkage or by juncture points where such minimal linkage is possible. They are characteristically not bounded by pitch morphemes which form part of a complex contour.

2. Simple subject and subjectival

The first main sentence element is the subject. It is a construction bounded by a juncture point with minimal linkage, and must occur in a sentence in which there is a verb. No nominal sentence element can be identified except in terms of its relation to other sentence elements, so that minimal sentences like "John!" or even "Good boys!" do not contain identifiable elements and will be called elementless sentences.

When the sentence contains recognizable verb material and nonverbal material as well, this nonverbal material can be identified as the subject by the fact that the subject is linked to the verb by the process known as selection. In Chapter 9, Section 3, on verb morphology, we stated that the suffix {-z}4 occurs in sentences like "He goes," "She goes," "It goes," or "John goes." The suffix occurs in all sentences with a non-past verb and pronouns or nouns with gender, or possibility of replacement by a gender form. Unfortunately for the symmetry of the verb paradigm, a past tense suffix (except in the verb *to be*) does not occur together with the {-z}4, and in a number of negative verbs, the {-z}4 is represented only by a zero allomorph. In defining the subject, the term "selection" means that a gender-bearing noun or pronoun requires the {-z}4 suffix in any verbal situation where that suffix is possible, and it is this requirement which identifies a noun or pronoun as subject. Thus, in the sentence "Man makes laws," there are two nouns, but only one of them can be replaced by a gender-bearing pronoun: *man* can be replaced by *he*, but *laws* only by the genderless *them*. It is therefore *man* which bears gender and which has selected the verbal suffix.

In the sentence we have been discussing, it is clear that *man* is the subject. The instances in which a subject selects a distinctive verb form are limited, however. Thus, our sentence can be varied to give:

> *Men make law.   Men make laws.   Men made laws.   Men made law.*
> *Man makes law.   Man made laws.   Man made law.*

That is, out of eight possible variations in gender-bearing or non-gender-bearing nouns and non-past and past verbs, only two forms have any selection distinguishing which noun is the subject. Selection clearly marks the subject when only one of the nouns can be expressed by a gender pronoun and when the gender suffix is not suppressed.

Thus, it is possible to find a distinctively selected morpheme in only two out of eight sentence types. The result is that any such sentence as "Man made laws" can be made distinctive only by varying it to one of the forms which shows which noun is the selector. This process of variation is expected of the analyst, and we have used it as the basis of our definition of the subject. Yet, in ordinary language use, we interpret sentences without resort to variation. If our sentence is "The whale swallowed Jonah," we do not try *whale* in singular and plural and *swallow* in the two forms of the non-past to discover that variation in the form of *whale* controls the variation in the form of the verb.

In sentences of this sort we rely on sentence element order alone, and the significance of sentence element order is quickly shown by variation to "Jonah swallowed the whale." The new order gives us a different subject. The significant order of sentence elements is an important fact of major syntax, which deals with the relation of main sentence elements. The relation of words within sentence elements and phrases, the type of syntax we have previously described, belongs to the area of minor syntax. Significant sentence element order is probably responsible for the often repeated statement that English is a language primarily characterized by word order. Yet sentence element order is a somewhat limited phenomenon. As identifier of the subject, it applies only in sentences where the three elements are noun, verb, and noun. In sentences of other types, the selector can come after the verb, and the preverbal element is therefore not the subject. Notice:

Here comes the teacher. Here come the teachers.

Further, even in sentences of the noun-verb-noun type sentence element order is less important than selection and differences in the superfixes. A sentence like the following is at least possible and can be found in poetic language, though it is not common in conversation:

$$\overset{2}{}\quad \overset{3}{}\quad \overset{1}{}$$
Two loves has Mary. /tûw + lávz + hàz + mêriy #/

If this sentence is varied by replacing *has* with *have*, even without change in stress and pitch, the subject, and consequently the meaning, of the sentence changes.

Again in poetic language, difference in pronoun forms can differentiate the subject from something which is not a part of the subject. Usually the difference in morphology is accompanied by a difference in superfixes, as in the following pair:

$$\overset{2}{}\qquad\qquad \overset{31}{}$$
Two loves have I. /tûw + lâvz + hæv + áy #/

$$\overset{2}{}\qquad \overset{3}{}\quad \overset{1}{}$$
Two loves have me. /tûw + lâvz + hǽv + miy #/

Yet, if for any reason the stress is shifted on one of these sentences, they become minimal contrasts, different in only the pronoun forms:

$$\overset{2}{}\qquad \overset{3}{}\quad \overset{1}{}$$
Two loves *have* I. /tûw + lâvz + hǽv + ày #/

This is a normal contrastive sentence in response to something like "Did you have two loves?"

The sentences we have been quoting are rather rare, and even unnatural; but in literary language a rather common variation of the pattern is to place the subject pronoun between the two verbs of a verb phrase as in:

Strange fits of passion *have I known.*

This then gives a pattern of noun-verb-pronoun-verb.

Yet even if sentence element order can be shown to be thus secondary to selection, it is still a real part of the English signaling system. The order subject-verb-complement is so normal and expected that we automatically interpret in accord with it and are more or less frustrated when we cannot. Thus, in written sentences where the stress and juncture pattern is not indicated, a departure from the common pattern causes trouble. This is the reason for difficulty with sentences like these from Browning:

Irks care the crop-full bird? Frets doubt the maw-crammed beast?

Our first attempt may be to read these with some such pattern as:

2   31
/ə́rks + kêhr + ðə + krâp + fùl + bə́rd #/

The pattern suggests improbable items, such as *an irk*, and an improbable verb, *care*, with immediately following noun phrase, whereas the common verb *care* is usually followed by *for* or *about*. At that point, of course, the careful reader backs up and tries again, probably as:

2   33   2   33
/ə́rks + kéhr || ðə + krâp + fùl + bə́rd |||/

If we define the primary identification of the subject as its features of selection and its sentence element order as secondary, we can use these characteristics to make a useful distinction. This is the distinction between subject and subjectival. Sentence elements made up of nominals or pronominals which occur in preverbal position but which do not affect the verb form are to be defined as subjectivals. A genuine noun or pronoun will be taken as subject in preverbal position, unless that interpretation is contradicted by the features of selection, in which case the noun or pronoun will be defined as part of the complement, not as a subjectival. In short, genuine nouns and pronouns are either subjects or complements in preverbal position, never subjectivals.

An instance of a subjectival occurs when a pronominal such as *here* occurs before a verb, as in "Here goes!" Such pronominals are extremely common as subjectivals: "Which is?" "What does?" None of these are true subjects, since no selection occurs, as variations such as "Which are?" "What do?" prove. When the first position is occupied by a subjectival, there may then be a genuine subject in postverbal position, as in "Here comes the teacher" and "Here come the teachers." Both these sentences are then to be analyzed as subjectival-verb-subject.

There are a number of distinctions, however, in the behavior of the pronominals which can appear as subjectivals. *Which* and *what* can be used as subjectivals with no true subject following. We can say "Which is?" or

"What is?" but not *"Where is?" or *"Why is?" For forms like *here, how, why, where,* a following subject is generally required, as in "Here's the car," "How was it?" "Why is it?" "Where was it?" For *here,* however, there is an isolated construction in "Here goes!" which must be treated as an idiom, since other constructions like *"Here is," *"Here does," and so on, are not found. With *how* there is a similar idiom in "How come?" and the very much rarer "How goes?" Even with *what* and *which* the number of following verbs is somewhat limited, since we do not ordinarily say "What kills?" or "What explains?"[2] It is this limitation which gives the faint flavor of the unusual to passingly popular constructions like "What cooks?" and "What gives?"

We can in general define a pronominal in immediate preverbal position as a subjectival, since these forms do not select the verb form. There is, however, a genuine pronoun, *who,* which also occurs in immediate preverbal position and without variation in any way related to variation in the verb form. Thus we have sentences like "Who is?" "Who are?" and "Who is he?" and "Who are they?" These forms seem exactly like "How is he?" "How are they?" yet a distinction can be made. *Who* is a genuine pronoun, since it has pronoun suffixes in *whose* and *whom,*[3] even though the paradigm is not complete. It is therefore possible to describe *who* as a pronoun having a plural form with a zero allomorph, just as *sheep* was described as a noun with a plural formed by a zero allomorph. Sentences like "Who is that man?" and "Who are those men?" therefore contain morphemically different forms of *who.* In the first sentence *who* is morphemically {h} (the allomorph of {hw} which occurs before a nucleus containing /w/) and the base {uw}. It is without suffix for number and so is a gender-bearing form which can be replaced by *he.* It is therefore the subject and the selector of the verb form with gender suffix. In the second sentence *who* consists of the same two morphs, followed by a zero allomorph of the plural suffix, and *who* is therefore genderless and the subject of the verb without gender suffix. The distinction may seem fine drawn, but it has the virtue of making it possible to say that the two classes of forms, nouns and pronouns, which have inflection for number, are alike in their relation to verbs. That is, these forms have inflections correlated with the gender suffix in verbs. The uninflected forms which act as subjectivals are not thus correlated with

---

[2] With forms like "What kills . . ." a following noun or pronoun is required, as in "What kills the shrubs" or "What kills them," but these postverbal forms are not subjects, as the lack of selection proves. They are rather complements.

[3] A secondary distinction implied in the description of *who* as a true pronoun and *which, what* as pronominals only is that *whose* does not properly belong to the paradigmatic set of *which, what,* but to that of *who.* That is, when we say "That is the book *which* I read, but *whose* name I have forgotten," we are borrowing a form from the *who* paradigm to fill a gap in the paradigm of *which, what.*

verb forms. We therefore conclude that a noun or pronoun in preverbal position is always either a complement or a subject. If we do not make such an assumption, the analysis of sentences like

$$\begin{array}{ccc} 2 & 3 & 1 \end{array}$$
Two loves have I. /tûw + lóvz + hæ̀v + ây #/

is greatly complicated.

In dealing with pronoun subjects, it is worth returning to the bookish sentences which place the pronoun subject in noninitial position. Though a sentence like "Two loves have I" is rare at best, and the normal form is "I have two loves," the form in abnormal order is still of some importance. A pronoun subject in postverbal position preserves the form which would be characteristic of preverbal position; the use of forms like *me, him* in postverbal position indicates that the pronoun belongs to the complement.[4] This statement has implications for the unnecessarily vexed question of "It is I," as opposed to "It is me." A speaker does well to choose the one of these constructions which is employed in the common usage of the educated speakers of the community in which he finds himself. It is ironical, however, that thus analyzed, "It is me" turns out to be more in accord with general structure than "It is I." Neither *I* nor *me* can be the subject, since *it* selects the verb form. Both second pronouns must therefore be complements; the form "It is I" then requires a supplementary statement that, in dialects which employ the construction, a pronoun complement after the verb *to be* preserves its subjectival form.

We have implied in discussion up to this point that uninflectable material in preverbal position may constitute a subjectival. The statement immediately introduces another problem. What about sentences like "Red sets the sun," "Redder sets the sun," and "Redly sets the sun"? The forms are uninflectable, but it is clear from the postbases that we are dealing with adjectives and adverbs. The difficulty arises from the fact that adjectives can form a part of a following subject:

$$\begin{array}{cccc} 2 & 32 & 33 & 1 \end{array}$$
Rêd clóuds | gáthered #

And adverbs can form part of a verb phrase:

$$\begin{array}{cccccc} 2 & 32 & 2 & 32 & 2 & 31 \end{array}$$
Mìster Smíth | quìetly pícked úp | the chéck #

---

[4] There are occasional non-bookish response sentences which preserve a similar distinction between postverbal subject and complement pronouns. Thus:

$$\begin{array}{cc} 2\,2 & 3 \end{array} \qquad\qquad \begin{array}{cc} 22 & 3 \end{array}$$
Did they? /díd + ðèy |||/ and *Did them?* /díd + ð̀im |||/

The latter is an incredulous response to some such statement as "Mary did the dishes."

Furthermore, adverbial material can appear as adjunctival:

2   3   2   2   31

Mòre and mòre quíetly | the crôwd begàn to dispérse #

Both adjunctival material and subjectivals are bounded by juncture points with minimal linkage, so that the juncture pattern cannot be used to distinguish adjunctival and subjectival sentence elements. The simplest procedure is to follow the rule tentatively given above, that uninflectable material in immediate preverbal position constitutes a subjectival. The distinction between adjunctival and subjectival is then a matter of sentence element order. A sentence like

2   32   2   31

Brìghter and brìghter réd | sêts the sún #

has subjectival, verb, and subject. If the subject precedes, as in

2   32   2   32   2   31

The sún | brìghter and brìghter réd | sêts in the wést #

we have an adjunctival phrase. Similarly if the order is

2   32   2   31

Brìghter and brìghter réd | the sûn sêts in the wést #

we again have an adjunctival phrase.

Quite similarly, adverbial material placed before a subject is adjunctival, as in:

2   3   2   2   31

Mòre and mòre rédly | the sûn sêts in the wést #

Simple adverbial material in postsubject position can be treated as an adjunct set off as a separate phrase, as in:

2   32   33   2   2   31

Mìster Smíth | quíetly | pícked ûp the chéck #

If however, it is merely preceded by a juncture, it then forms part of the following verb phrase. Some of these problems will be returned to in discussing complex subjects composed of more than one phrase; at the moment it is enough merely to reiterate our rule that noninflectable material in initial position immediately before a verb is subjectival. Made in this form, the statement can now be used to solve a number of questions which have caused discussion. For instance, "Once is enough" and "Now is the time" are now both reasonably clear. The preverbal material in each is a subjectival, though in the first the postverbal material is a complement, whereas in the second it is the subject, as such variation as "Now are the times" clearly shows.[5]

The decision that uninflectable material before the verb constitutes a subjectival leaves us free to assign phrasal material, and even dependent sentences to this category. Thus, we have a prepositional phrase containing verbal material as a subjectival in *"For a man to marry,* is better than to burn." In the following, a complete sentence is the subjectival, with a true subject following:

2   3   1   1   1 1

Russian is a difficult language # *said Mr. Smith* #

A form like "'Yes,' said he" is essentially similar. It will be noted that *yes* has the superfix pattern

331

/yés #/

which marks it as a sentence, while *said he* has the pattern

1   1 1

/sèd + híy #/

which marks it as the concluding material of the larger, complex sentence. This latter type is very common; notice "Pop! goes the weasel," "'Ouch!' yelled John," "'Fiddle, diddle, dee,' goes the big burly bumbo," and many more.

The only caution necessary at this point is to point out that prepositional phrases may contain inflected material, but this material never selects the verb form and so is never the subject. Prepositional phrases are therefore always subjectivals in preverbal position. Thus, in a sentence like

2   3   2 2   3   1

In the window | ìs a cándle #

we have subjectival, verb, and subject. We have the same construction in:

2   3   2   2   3 1

From the windows | shînes a líght #

Just as in the handbook favorite *"Over the fence* is out," we have subjectival, verb, and complement.

---

[5] This analysis, as part of a complete study of English structure, differs in some details of terminology from my earlier discussion of "Now is the time" and "Once is enough" in the "English Forum" of *College English*, XII, 1950, pp. 168–69.

3. Subject and actor

In the discussion of both subjects and subjectivals, nothing has been said about the fact that the difference between subject and complement often distinguishes the difference between actor and thing acted upon, or goal. In English, actor and subject are by no means in a one-to-one correspondence, though in sentences like "The dog bites the man" and "The man bites the dog," the subject does indeed signal which is the actor. Subjectivals, however, do not ordinarily signal the actor, though forms like "What popped?" or "Which goes?" have subjectival actors as a result of the fact that these pronominals are relatively close to true pronouns. No one would argue that a subjectival phrase like *"For a man to marry*, is better than to burn" is an entity performing action. Again, as is obvious, in sentences like "John was loved by his parents," it is the prepositional phrase which signals the actor, and *John*, the subject, is signaled as the recipient of action. Furthermore, in a good many subject-verb-complement sentences, actor and goal of action are not clearly signaled at all. Thus, a sentence such as "This chicken eats well" can be said in two contexts. If we are describing chickens in a coop, we presumably mean that the chicken in question eats with a good appetite, and *chicken* is here the actor. If, on the other hand, we are talking about the chicken served at a banquet, we mean that we enjoy eating it. There are a good many sentences like this one, where the subject and actor are in an unusual relation: "This portion serves two people," "This room sleeps three men," and so on, not to mention the fact that the actor in "John saw Jack," from the point of view of optical science, is erroneously identified. In subject-verb-complement sentences, the actor is not definitely and structurally signaled. When signaling occurs, it is largely a lexical matter, determined by the kind of items contained in the sentence.

The prepositional phrase *by* and following noun is a definite actor signal, though it is not a subject. There are at least two other types of actor signal. One of these we find in the pair of sentences:

> *For the man to marry, is what Mary wants.*
> *The man to marry, is what Mary wants.*

The phrase *the man* is actor in relation to the following *to marry* in the first sentence, while in the second sentence *the man* is in goal relation to what follows. To describe the relation more exactly, we should add that in some sentences the absence of initial *for* leaves the actor-goal relation ambiguous. The *for*, on the other hand, is an explicit actor signal. "The house to rent, is what Mary wants" may mean either that she wants to rent the house or that she wants it to be rented. "For the house to rent, is what Mary wants" is clear. This use of *for* as an actor signal should not identify the following noun as a subject. No variation is possible in the following verbal phrase, and consequently the preceding noun or pronoun does not select as does a true subject.

The second actor signal is one of order. Note the contrast in the position of *them*, and the resultant difference in meaning in the following:

$$\begin{array}{ccc} & 2 & & 3\ 1 \\ I\ helped\ them\ work. & /\grave{a}y\ +\ h\hat{e}lp\ +\ \eth im\ +\ w\acute{\jmath}rk\ \#/ \end{array}$$

$$\begin{array}{cccc} & 2 & & 3 & 1 \\ I\ helped\ work\ them. & /\grave{a}y\ +\ h\hat{e}lp\ +\ w\acute{\jmath}rk\ +\ \eth im\ \#/ \end{array}$$

The distinction is not so clear when *to* is required. Notice:

$$\begin{array}{ccc} & 2 & & 3\ 1 \\ I\ wanted\ them\ to\ study. & /\grave{a}y\ +\ w\grave{\jmath}nt\dot{\imath}d\ +\ \eth im\ +\ t\partial\ +\ st\acute{\jmath}diy\ \#/ \end{array}$$

In this form the sentence is ambiguous, since *them* can be in either actor or goal relation to *to study*. The ambiguity can be solved by placing a terminal either before or after *them*. But while this position of the pronoun is ambiguous, the position in which the pronoun occurs last is clear, and indicates only goal. "I wanted to study them" is unmistakable with any stress, pitch, and juncture pattern. Position before form 1 in these verbal phrases signals at least the possibility that a pronoun is actor for the following verbal material. It is not a true subject, however, because of the lack of selection.

A following form 5 acts quite differently, and with pronouns at least, subject and complement can be signaled by different forms even when the pronoun occurs between the parts of the verb phrase. Note the following sentence, clear enough, even though poetic:

$$\begin{array}{cc} 2 & 3\ 1 \\ A\ cruel\ tyrant\ |\ h\hat{a}d\ h\grave{e}\ k\acute{\imath}lled\ \# \end{array}$$

This contrasts with:

$$\begin{array}{cc} 2 & 3\ 1 \\ A\ cruel\ tyrant\ |\ h\hat{a}d\ h\grave{\imath}m\ k\acute{\imath}lled\ \# \end{array}$$

If a noun is used, the sentence becomes ambiguous:

$$\begin{array}{cc} 2 & 3\ 1 \\ A\ cruel\ tyrant\ |\ h\hat{a}d\ J\hat{o}hn\ k\acute{\imath}lled\ \# \end{array}$$

It is an accident that these sentences also carry variation in the meaning of *had*. The same relationship can occur in poetic style without this variation:

$$\begin{array}{ccc} 2 & 31 & \qquad\qquad 2 & 31 \\ Strange\ countries\ |\ h\hat{a}ve\ \hat{I}\ kn\acute{o}wn\ \#\ \text{and}\ Strange\ countries\ |\ h\hat{a}ve\ m\hat{e}\ kn\acute{o}wn\ \# \end{array}$$

The actor, to sum up, is signaled not by identification of the subject but, insofar as it is signaled at all, by other devices: by prepositions, by order, or by variant superfixes. "Subject," on the other hand, remains a purely formal term, selector of the verb or, in some instances, pronoun with subjectival suffix. The meaning of the term "subject," or more exactly its semantic content, will be clear only as we take up the total pattern of the sentence.

4. Complex subjects

Up to this point we have been discussing subjects which consist of a single phrase. With subjectivals we have given examples of complete sentences as subjectivals, though the examples given have also consisted of only one phrase. We shall, therefore, go on to subjects consisting of more than one phrase but will omit further discussion of complex subjectivals, except to point out that they exist, as in:

For a man to marry, even at the cost of sacrifice, is better than to burn.

2   3 2   2   4

/fərə + mǽn + tə + mǽriy | ìyvin + it + ðə + kɔ̀st + əv + sǽk +

2 2   3 1

rifàys | ìz + bêtər + ðin + tə + bɔ́rn #/

In such constructions, the sum total of uninflectable preverbal material constitutes a subjectival, though it may consist of several phrases, with linkage by complex contour.

The simplest form of complex subject is that which consists of two nouns treated as separate phrases:

Sugar and honey are both sweet.

Normal forms of this sentence are:

33 2 2   4 2   2   31

/šúgər | in + hɔ́niy | ər + bôwθ + swíyt #/ or

22 2 2   3 2 2   3 1

/šúgər | in + hɔ́niy | ər + bôwθ + swíyt #/

Even though the forms in this sentence are both normally without plural suffixes, their form class is readily identifiable, since they can be preceded by such noun markers as *the*. We have, then, two nouns in preverbal position. Several things can be said about this type of construction, the most important of which is that when a terminal occurs between the nouns, as here, linkage of the pitch morphemes into a complex contour is possible. Our transcriptions gave two forms of complex contour, both of which are normal, though it must be added that the minimal linkage of {3 3 2 |} {2 3 2 |} could also characterize this type of subject. There are other characteristics as well. Order is nonsignificant. The construction could as well have been *honey and sugar* as *sugar and honey*. Also, if a terminal is present as here, the verb form selected is normally the nongender form. Finally, the two nouns are connected by *and* or some equivalent, forms which belong to a syntactically defined class which we have not as yet discussed.

In a number of constructions of this type, the order is relatively fixed, as in:

$$\overset{2}{} \qquad \overset{3}{} \overset{1}{}$$
sticks and stones /stîks + in + stôwnz #/

In such fixed-order constructions, the terminal juncture is commonly absent, but if the fixed order is reversed, the terminal is then required. It would seem that all of these phrases in which the order is fixed and in which the terminal juncture is absent ought to be considered as units and treated as lexical items to be learned separately and recorded in dictionaries, just as phrasal items such as *White + House* are learned and recorded. Dictionary makers have not generally recorded them, though an item like *sticks and stones*, which has the same fixed order in German as in English, must be a very old feature of the language.

In items where the order is fixed, there is often a lexical distinction between those forms of the phrase which select the verb form as if the phrase were a single gender-bearing unit and those which do not. The distinction can be shown by "*Jack and Jill* are children" and "*Jack and Jill* is a nursery rhyme." The same distinction is shown in "*Tom and Jerry* are brothers" and "*Tom and Jerry*'s a drink." In other fixed-order phrases only one type of selection is found, as in "Sticks and stones *are* dangerous" and "Bread and butter *is* nice."

The same type of construction can be extended to more than two nouns. When this occurs, the connecting *and* is frequently, though not necessarily, dropped between all but the last two in the series, the others being separated by nothing more than terminal junctures. In constructions of this multiple type, the terminals are commonly present, even when the order is fixed. As a consequence, the construction consists of several phrases, though there is often linkage of the pitch morphemes by complex contour. The selection is usually that of a genderless subject. An example with fixed order is:

$$\overset{222}{} \quad \overset{232}{} \quad \overset{2}{} \quad \overset{4}{} \overset{1}{}$$
Tom, Dick, and Harry /táhm | dík | ən + hǽriy #/

If there were following verbal material, it might be something like ". . . *are* brothers."

A complex subject is defined as one which contains more than one phrase, but a subject may contain many items without being complex, as long as the several items do not require interruption by a terminal juncture. All the familiar order groups of modifiers before a noun can, for instance, occur as a single-phrase subject:

2   3 2   2   3 1
Âll the tên fíne ôld stône hóuses | were sóld #

If, however, the order of modifiers is such as to require a terminal, the subject necessarily becomes complex, as in:

2   22   232   2   4   2   2   3 1
Âll the tên óld | fíne | stône hóuses | were sóld #

The transcription here given shows linkage of the pitch morphemes in a complex contour. The subject also becomes complex if, for reasons of emphasis, any one of a series of modifiers is set up as a single phrase.

Such a use of terminals gives a device of stylistic variation which can be effectively used in both writing and speech, as in this from a recent bit of academic composition, in which the variation occurs, it is true, in the complement rather than in the subject. The relationships would have been the same, however, in subject position:

The saga is told in a—deceptively—simple style . . .

It is clear that the final prepositional phrase has been broken into three:

2   22   2 3   2 2   4 1
/ìn + éy | disép + tivliy | sîmpəl + stáyl #/

The device, here indicated by the punctuation alone, reminds one of Swift's famous instance of reversal of order:

. . . I cannot but conclude the bulk of your natives to be the most pernicious race of *little odious* vermin. . . . (*Gulliver's Travels*, Part II, Chap. 6.)

Swift does not punctuate in order to indicate the pitch morpheme pattern; it is carried by the reversal of order alone:

2   2 2   33   2 44   1
/əv + lítəl | ówdiyis | vɔ́rmin #/

In both instances, the effect is one of sharp emphasis.

A distinction must be made between a complex element of the type found in the sentence from Swift, where adjectives precede the noun in such a sequence as to require breaking up into separate phrases, and sentences in which a phrase or phrases containing adjectives or adjectivals follows a noun. In the former construction we have a complex subject—or, as the case may be, a complex complement—while in the latter the modifying material constitutes an adjunctival phrase. An example is such a sentence as:

The boys, tired and hungry, at last went home.

2   32   33 2 2   3 2   2   32

/ði + bóyz | táyərd | in + hə́ŋgriy || .../   or   /ði + bóyz || .../

In this sentence, as the transcriptions show, linkage by complex contour does not occur, and, furthermore, *the boys* may be followed by /|||/ instead of by /||/. The sequence *tired and hungry*, also, may be varied in its position so as to give:

Tired and hungry, the boys at last went home. or
The boys at last went home, tired and hungry.

The order and superfix characteristics are enough to identify *tired and hungry* as adjunctival material, whereas the pitch linkage which occurs in the sentence from Swift indicates a unified construction. It is, of course, true that the adjunctival phrase or phrases belong semantically to the noun they follow, but the fact that they are noun modifiers is signaled only by the form classes of the contained material. Had the adjunctival phrase contained adverbs, we would group it semantically with the verb.

16.... MAIN SENTENCE ELEMENTS, II

Predicator and Predicatival

1. Simple predicator and predicatival

The second main sentence element is the verb, or verbal construction, which we can call the predicator. This sentence element has necessarily been discussed to a considerable extent already. The paradigmatic sets which define verbs and the phrases made up of complex verbal material have been described, but no attention has been paid to the syntactic characteristics of verbal material as a sentence element. Syntactically, the predicator can be defined as that sentence element whose form is selected by the subject. Thus we have no difficulty in recognizing the predicator in the following pair of sentences:

Man makes laws.　　Men make law.

Logically, there is an apparent difficulty in that we have defined the subject as that which selects the verb and are now defining the predicator as that which is selected by the subject. The difficulty disappears if we remember the procedure and its steps. In sentences such as "Man makes laws" or "The little girls are going to school," the initial elements are first examined as words or phrases and are identified as containing nouns or nominal constructions. The borders of the construction are further identified by juncture points, the positions at which a terminal can occur without pitch linkage by complex contour. The following material is similarly examined and identified as verbal. Only then are the two constructions considered as sentence elements, and since their content has been shown to be different, our definitions are more accurately statable in some such form as "The subject is that noun or pronoun material which selects the form of the verb" and "The predicator is that verb or verbal material whose form is selected by the subject."

When the predicator is defined in this way, it follows that it is useful to make a distinction which is parallel to that between subject and subjectival. There are forms in the verb paradigm which do not vary with a nominal sentence element which is in the position of subject. Note the lack of variation in the following pair:

The window *being* open, John felt cold.

The windows *being* open, John felt cold.

If the initial material is treated as an independent sentence, the noun construction is clearly the subject, as in:

The window *was* open. John felt cold.

The failure of such forms as *being* to vary as the noun form varies will not prevent us from identifying *the window* and *the windows* as subjects, since the sentences are fully variable with constructions in which selection occurs. A verb consisting of an *–ing* form, on the other hand, will be defined as a predicatival rather than as a predicator, since, though the *–ing* form belongs to the verb paradigm, the resultant sentence element does not show selection. A second instance of a predicatival, rather than a true predicator, is the verbal material which appears in subjectless sentences of the type described as imperative. Examples are "Open the window," "Open the windows," "Be a good boy," "Be good boys." All of these are subjectless, since the nominal material does not select the verb form. The nominal material must therefore belong to the complement.

A third verbal form which shows no selection is the past participle. The past participle characteristically appears in phrases which consist of participle, preposition, and following noun and which act as adjunctivals. Note the possibilities of order in the following, in which the three positions are those characteristic of adjunctivals:

Badly driven by a hired chauffeur, Jack's car left the road.
Jack's car, badly driven by a hired chauffeur, left the road.
Jack's car left the road, badly driven by a hired chauffeur.

It is interesting that the last sentence introduces a structural point where ambiguity can occur. Participial phrases (containing either form 4 or form 5) as adjunctivals tend to associate themselves with any immediately preceding noun, so that such an adjunctival in final position will be taken to modify the noun in the complement if that relation is at all likely. Notice:

Previously driven by a chauffeur, Jack finally learned to drive the car.
Jack, previously driven by a chauffeur, finally learned to drive the car.
But:
Jack finally learned to drive the car, previously driven by a chauffeur.

In the last sentence it makes no difference whether or not *car* is followed by a terminal, the following participial phrase is still associated with *car*, not with *Jack*. The behavior of adjunctivals made up of participial phrases can be summarized by saying that their function as modifiers of nouns takes precedence over their function as independent sentence modifiers. The conflict which results, needless to say, is why handbooks give rules about "dangling participles." There is need for such warnings, yet most handbooks give the rules in unrealistically rigid terms, not recognizing the fact that lexical probabilities modify the interpretation put upon a participial phrase. A further point about handbook rules on participial phrases is that a good many of their comic examples seem made up for the occasion. In some years of composition reading, the only genuine example of a funny dangler I encountered was:

This factory is five miles beyond Lynchburg, going South.

Lexical probabilities have affected the interpretation. The sequence *is . . . beyond Lynchburg* strongly suggests movement, so that we visualize a traveling factory.

We can sum up this part of our discussion by saying that both form 4 and form 5 can act as syntactic predicativals. A form 4 can act, however, as the predicatival in a linked sentence, while a form 5 is usually only the predicatival in an adjunctival sentence element. The past form of verbs, like the participles, has no morpheme selected by the subject. Yet, there are two reasons for calling past verbs predicators rather than predicativals. First, form 3 covers exactly the range of forms 1 and 2 taken together and is therefore parallel with them. Second, there is one verb, *to be*, which shows a selected morpheme in its past forms. A predicator, then, must contain a form 1 (the common non-past form, not the infinitive), 2, or 3. As we have seen, if there is more than one verbal form, it is only the first verb which shows a selected morpheme. The following verbal material is always form 1 (the infinitive), form 4, or form 5.

2. Complex predicator and predicatival

A predicator, like a subject, may be made up of more than one phrase. A typical example is:

$$\overset{2}{}\quad\overset{3\ 2\ 2}{}\quad\overset{4\ 2\ 33}{}\quad\overset{1}{}$$
John hates and despises algebra. /jâhn + héyts | in + dispáyziz | ǽljibrə#/

As with complex subjects, complex predicators are often connected by unstressed words of the class of *and* or *but*. As with subjects, *and* is often dropped between all but the last two of a series. Order is not significant, except in set phrases which then become units, with stress modification and loss of juncture. An example is:

$$\overset{2}{}\qquad\qquad\overset{31}{}$$
Mary ran and hid. /mêriy + rǽnin + híd #/

The predicator can also consist of verbal material together with adverbs or adverbial material. As one might expect, adverbial material in normal order sequence produces a predicator with several items in it, but does not necessitate a construction of more than one phrase:

Mr. Smith *very quietly opened* the door.

2   31
/mìstər + smîθ + vèriy + kwàyitliy + ôwpin + ðə + dór #/

The resemblance to nominal sentence elements is completed by the fact that if modifiers are in abnormal order, or for any other reason set off by terminals, we have a sentence element of more than one phrase, though with pitch linkage:

2   3   2 2   4 1
The car ran quietly, almost. /ðə + kâr + ræn + kwáyitliy | òl + mówst #/

The normal order here, which would not require a terminal, would be *ran almost quietly*. A form in which the terminal is a stylistic variant, with difference in emphasis, is:

He didn't want to be so—rudely—forced to leave.

2   2 2   2 3   2 2   41
/hìy + dìdin + wɔ̂nə + bìy sów | rúwdliy | fɔ̂hrs + tə + líyv #/

A more normal way of pronouncing this sentence would be to treat all of the material following the subject pronoun as a single phrase, or possibly to break the phrase only after *forced*.

3. Discontinuous predicator

Up to this point in the description of complex predicators, the resemblance to complex subjects is exact, but in the rest of their syntactic characteristics, predicators are quite different. We have already seen pairs of sentences of the type:

I helped work them. and *I helped them work.*

The difference in order is the signal, it will be remembered, that *them* in the second sentence is the actor for the following form 1, though it will also be remembered that it cannot (as is traditionally done) be called the subject, since there is no selection of variant verb forms. The chief problem in handling such a construction is that of cutting into constituents.[1] Since there is no doubt that the initial pronoun is the subject, the first cut would be before *helped*, giving a maximal verb construction consisting of all that

---

[1] See below, Section 4.

follows. Yet, considered thus, the maximal verb construction is discontinuous, containing a pronoun which is identical with the complement form of "I helped work them." On this first level of cutting it must, then, be recognized that predicators can be interrupted by nouns and pronouns in various relations to the surrounding material. The fact that such intrusive nominal material does not break up the structure of the predicator is shown by the fact that "I *helped them work*" can be, and often is, treated as a single phrase not interrupted by terminals.

Sentence elements discontinuous in this sense are not unusual in other languages, notably Latin, which gives such sentences as the Horatian:

> *Dianam tenerae dicite virgines.* (Praise Diana, O ye maidens tender!)

Here the noun sentence element, *tenerae virgines*, is interrupted by the verb in a fashion thoroughly un-English, since we cannot say *"O ye tender, Praise! maidens." Yet foreign to English as most Latin discontinuous sentence elements are, and impossible as it is for us to introduce discontinuity for stylistic variation, the inclusion of noun and pronoun material in the predicator is still a faint reminder of the characteristic Latin constructions.

When we advance to the next stage of cutting in such a sentence as "I helped them work," we have a more serious problem. One possibility would be to cut out *them*, leaving *helped . . . work*. Such a cut is tempting, since it sorts out the pronominal and verbal material promptly and neatly, but it is nevertheless to be rejected. Such analysis has a distinct theoretical disadvantage, in that to accomplish it two cuts are necessary, one before and one after *them*. Unless there is some compelling reason to the contrary, cuts in English are more economically made if they are single. The real alternatives, then, are a cut before *them* or a cut after it. There are several formal reasons for preferring a cut after *them*, the most important of which are the juncture points. The sentence often takes the shape:

$$\text{2} \qquad \text{3} \qquad \text{2} \quad \text{4 41}$$
$$\text{/ày} + \text{hélp} + \text{təm} \mid \text{wɔ́rk} \;\#/$$

Here there is no juncture at all before the reduced form of *them*, though there is a phonologically required $/+/$ before the suffix of *helped*. However, a terminal, if it occurs, is likely to fall after *them* rather than before it.

If we look further at the possibilities of substitution and omission, we discover that "I helped them" is a perfectly possible utterance, whereas something like "*Them work*, is what I helped do" is impossible. The sequence *them work* does not act as a unit and cannot normally be said alone or freely varied in position. For all of these reasons we can then say that there is a juncture point after *them*, which therefore belongs with what precedes. If this is done, our cuts fall into order. *Helped them* contains verb and complement in normal order, and *work* is then a separate minimal sentence element, to be defined as verbal and linked to the preceding pronoun in the way already described.

There are several types of predicators interrupted in this way by an intrusive noun or pronoun, each with its own characteristics. The type we have so far been describing can be defined as a maximal predicator which consists of form 1, form 2, or form 3, followed by a noun or pronoun, followed in turn by form 1. The material which intervenes may be expanded to give a noun construction, as in "I helped *the little boys* work." Pronouns, since they do not normally stand at the head of such phrases, obviously are not thus expanded in this position. Furthermore, any pronoun which occurs in this position must be in the nonsubjectival form. We do not say *"I helped *they* work." There are, however, two subdivisions of the construction, determined by whether or not *to* occurs before the form 1. The verb which we have used to illustrate the construction, *help*, is one which can occur with or without a *to* before the second verb form, since we can say "I helped them to work" as well as "I helped them work."

Two verbs which regularly occur without the *to* are *see* and *hear*, as in "I saw him fall" or "I heard him fall." Rather rarer are such sentences as "I noticed him fall" and "I felt him fall." The verbs without *to* make up a fairly tightly knit semantic group, but a verb like *perceive*, closely allied semantically, does not behave in this way. A sentence like "I perceived him fall" is perhaps a little more natural than *"I perceived him to fall," but in many idiolects both constructions are avoided, and "I perceived that he fell" or "I perceived him falling" is substituted. A verb which is similar in syntactic distribution, but which falls outside the semantic group above, is *make*, as in "I made him fall." The group which suppresses the *to*, therefore, can be described only by listing. The convenient semantic label "verbs of perception" does not take care of either *help* or *make*. The great majority of verbs, if they can enter into this construction at all, require the *to*, as in "I got him to study" and "I ordered him to study."

There are a number of other characteristics of this type of construction. One is that it is not related to the type of construction, described earlier, in which a verb phrase is made up of a form like *can*, *may*, *will*, or the like and a following form 1 not preceded by *to*. With a verb like *can* and a following verb, the normal form is:

$$\text{I can see him.} \quad /\grave{a}y + \overset{2}{kin} + \overset{3}{si}\overset{1}{yim} \#/$$

The form

$$\text{I can him see.} \quad /\grave{a}y + \overset{2}{k\hat{æ}n} + h\grave{i}m + \overset{3}{si}\overset{1}{y} \#/$$

is so rare and bookish as scarcely to be possible in normal contemporary English. Furthermore, this bookish sentence does not signal the usual relation between the pronoun form and the following form 1. The pronoun is here the complement rather than a possible actor for the following form. Therefore, if the verb after *can* is one which does not take a noun or pronoun as complement, the order of "I can him see" is impossible. That is, since we do not say *"I can die him," we also do not say *"I can him die." The distinction between verbs which act like *see* and those which act like *die* is familiar under the names "transitive" and "intransitive." It is interesting to note that there are fewer genuinely intransitive verbs than one might suppose. Many which are thought to be intransitive take noun complements in somewhat limited constructions or with change of meaning. A standard example is *walk*, often called intransitive, though sentences like "Mary walks the dog every day" and even "John walked two miles" are transitive forms. Another form usually called intransitive is *go*, though there are idiomatic sentences like "Go it!"

A final peculiarity gives a point of at least possible ambiguity. A sentence like

$$\overset{2}{}\qquad\qquad\overset{31}{}$$
I cooked them to eat. /ày + kûk + təm + tə + íyt #/

may be structurally indistinguishable from

$$\overset{2}{}\qquad\qquad\overset{31}{}$$
I ordered them to work. /ày + ɔ́rdərdəm + tə + wɔ́rk #/

though the probabilities of interpretation are very different in the two sentences. With a sentence like

$$\overset{2}{}\qquad\qquad\overset{31}{}$$
I got them to eat. /ày + gâtəm + tə + íyt #/

the ambiguity is greater than in the two sentences quoted. The amount of overlap is still slight, however, as we can see if we substitute nouns for the pronoun in the above type of sentence. If we take the homonymous pair *ham* and *Ham* (proper name), we get:

$$\overset{2}{}\qquad\overset{3}{}\qquad\overset{1}{}$$
I got ham to eat. /ày + gât + ˌhǽhm + tə + îyt #/
$$\overset{2}{}\qquad\qquad\overset{31}{}$$
I got Ham to eat. /ày + gât + hæ̂hm + tə + íyt #/

The ambiguity in "I got them to eat" is produced by the fact that a pronoun complement is normally lightly stressed. To give it full stress produces only a contrast form

$$\overset{2}{}\quad\overset{3\ 1}{}$$
/gât + ðém #/

(i.e., this set of items, not that set) without clearing up the nature of the construction. In nearly all instances of sentences with the ambiguous construction, the probabilities involved in the lexical sequences force one interpretation or the other, as they do in the sentences "I cooked them to eat" and "I helped them to eat."

A second type of discontinuous predicator is that in which we find a form 1, 2, or 3; a noun or pronoun; and a following form 4 (the *-ing* form). An example is "I heard him shouting." The constituent analysis of such sentence elements is the same as that of the previous type, and the relation of the pronoun to the following verbal is also the same. These constructions —or some forms of them—are sometimes objected to as "fused participles." The reason for the objection is a belief that an *-ing* form should always clearly indicate a distinction between nominal and verbal use. The sentence given above can be varied to "I heard his shouting," where *shouting* is a noun and might be inflected for number. "I heard *his shouting*" is therefore felt to be more clearly marked than "I heard *him shouting*." A form such as "He is falling" is equally clearly not a nominal use of *-ing*. It is not usual, however, to object to pronominal forms like "I heard *him shouting*." What is most often condemned is a sentence like "Eisenhower winning the election was good for the party." The objection is largely a priori, and does not take account of the fact that *Eisenhower winning the election* can be taken as a subjectival, so that it is unnecessary to assume that there is a more narrowly defined subject in either *Eisenhower* or *winning*. Moreover, no account is taken of sentences like "I saw him falling," where it would be unnatural to vary to *"I saw his falling." The pronoun here falls within the predicator and, as usual, stands in the relation of actor to the following verbal. If such sentences are acceptable, there is no reason for insisting that "I noticed John winning the race" should be made over to "I noticed John's winning the race." Nor is there reason to object to subjectival constructions in which the noun is actor for a following *-ing*.

The third type of discontinuous predicator is that in which we find a form 1, 2, or 3; a noun or pronoun; and a following form 5 (past participle) as in "He saw them taken." This construction follows the constituent pattern of the other discontinuous constructions, but there is a peculiarity if the contained form is a pronoun. With the construction *have* and form 5, in poetic language, an intervening pronoun in form 1 is the subject of the preceding verb and the actor of the whole construction. We have already quoted "Strange fits of passion *have I* known" and have pointed this out as a variant of the more prosaic "I have known strange fits of passion." Similar sentences can be constructed by making use of contrasting *I* and *me:*

Many strange cities have *I* known.
Many strange cities have *me* known.

Moreover, the contrast is minimal, since the two sentences are (or may be) as follows:

$$
\begin{array}{llll}
2 & \quad\;\; 3\;\; 2 & \;\; 2 & \qquad 3\;1 \\
\end{array}
$$

/mêniy + strêynj + sítiyz | hǽv + ày + nówn #/

$$
\begin{array}{llll}
2 & \quad\;\; 3\;\; 2 & \;\; 2 & \qquad 3\;1 \\
\end{array}
$$

/mêniy + strêynj + sítiyz | hǽv + mìy + nówn #/

The second sentence is bookish in the extreme, but presumably possible in poetry, and is of interest in being one of the rare instances in which distinction between subject and complement can be carried by the pronoun forms alone. The distinction is not carried over to other verbs. Thus we say "The troops saw *him taken*," but we do not use *he* in this sequence. A sentence such as "The troops saw him shot" contrasts, indeed, with "The troops saw he shot" in some such situation as ". . . but he didn't hit anything." In this construction, however, *shot* is form 3, not form 5, and the sentence may be replaced by "The troops see he shoots."

A second point of interest in this construction is the relation of the intervening noun or pronoun to the following verbal. Commonly a form 2 pronoun in this position is the goal of the following verbal, as in the sentence already quoted, "The troops saw him taken," which like any passive construction can be expanded by a prepositional phrase indicating the actor, as in ". . . by the enemy." If however, we construct a sentence of the type "I saw him fallen by the wayside," we have a sentence which seems to have the same form as "I saw him taken by the enemy." So far as there is any ambiguity of meaning, it is as usual solved by lexical probability, though this does not answer the question whether the two constructions are of the same type or not. As far as the prepositional phrases are concerned, *bỳ thě énemy* and *bỳ thě wáysìde*, the construction is indeed identical. The meanings of agent and location are carried by the same construction, and it is only probability which distinguishes one content from the other. The more difficult question is whether *him fallen* is a sequence in which a pronoun and a form 5 are in the relation of actor and verbal, thus contradicting the kind of relation signaled in *him taken*. The answer seems to lie in the fact that if we try the construction with the past participles of other intransitive verbs,[2] such as those of *look* and *die*, we find that we cannot say "I saw *him looked*," or "I saw *him died*." A form like *fallen* may be either an adjectival, as in "the fallen angels," or a participle, as in "The angels have fallen." Since no other intransitive past participles can appear in the construction we are examining, it is a relatively simple solution to call *fallen* an adjectival in the normal position with a pronoun, as is the adjective in "I saw him *flat* by the wayside."

---

[2] See above, p. 238.

Our description of verb phrases pointed out that, except for *to be* and some others like *seem* and *become*, the only verbs which can appear immediately before a past participle are *get* and *have*, as in *get known* and *have known*. Further, of these several forms which appear immediately before a past participle, only the type found in *have known* can be followed by a noun or pronoun complement. We can say "I have known the man" or "I have known him," but no forms of *be, seem, become,* or *get* will replace *have* in these sentences. For *be, seem, become,* not only the construction "John **is known him*" but also the variant "John **is him known*" is impossible. For *get* and all other verbs the only position in which a complement occurs is before the past participle, as in *get him shot, heard him shot, ordered him shot,* and so on. Only *have* varies the position of the complement, and it is noticeable that variation occurs only with the relatively strongly stressed forms. A sentence like "They've known him" must put the complement in final position. The verbs like *saw* require the complement in immediately following position in these phrases, thus signaling the relation to the verbal in unambiguous fashion. These phrases are therefore a second list of first position verbs which can occur with a following past participle, and a list like that given earlier in that it, too, is limited. We cannot put verbs like *say* or *try* into the blank in such a frame as "I —— him taken" or any similar frame. An accurate and exhaustive list of the verbs which will fill such a blank has not been drawn up.

A final apparent exception to the rule that verb phrases like *saw taken* do not occur without an intervening complement can be mentioned. The exception is exemplified by "The man I saw taken was set free yesterday." Constructions of this type are dependent sentences which have their own syntactic rules and which will be described more fully later. At present we need merely say that such sentences are variants of the order of independent sentences of the type "I saw the man taken."

We have up to now been considering discontinuous predicators of the type which usually appears after a subject, though in one instance—"Strange fits of passion have I known"—the initial element was a complement. Far commoner than most of the sentence types which we have so far discussed are those in which a list of special verbs, all of which can take the negative suffix *–nt*, appear in the order verb-subject-verbal. These are, of course, the familiar question forms, as in "Is he going?" "Has he gone?" "Is he gone?" and "Does he go?" A first observation about these forms is that they acquire a different stress pattern in question order from that found in non-question order. "He can go," the non-question form, is:

$$
\begin{array}{c}
231 \\
\text{/hìy + kin + gów \#/}
\end{array}
$$

While "Can he go?" is:

$$\overset{2}{/\text{kæn}} + \text{hiy} + \overset{3\,3}{\text{gów}} \,|||/ \quad \text{or} \quad \overset{2}{/\text{kæniy}} + \overset{3\,3}{\text{gów}} \,|||/$$

That is, the verbs in question order are usually given tertiary stress, though "Is he going?" may occur with no stress at all in the form:

$$\overset{2}{/\text{zìy}} + \overset{3\ 3}{\text{gówiŋ}} \,|||/$$

These sentences employ all three of the verbals (forms 1, 4, and 5) in second position. All of these sentences, when the inflected verb is initial, signal a question sentence, though the sentence type in which there is an initial complement is not such a signal. The order verb-subject with this list of verbs also signals a question, even when there is no following verbal, as in "Can he?" "Is he?" In everyday English the question type here described is limited to the negative verbs, though in older English, and in bookish style today, it is also found with other verbs, as in the line quoted from Browning:

Irks care the crop-full bird?

These question forms follow the usual constituent patterning, so that a sentence like "Did John buy a new car?" cuts first into a complex predicator, *did John buy*, and the complement, *a new car*. The next cut is after *John*, giving constituents which consist of a minimal predicator and its subject, and a following minimal predicatival. In all of these predicators, the intervening noun or pronoun is the subject of the first verb, and for all of them, except the type "Was he taken?" it is also the actor for the following verbal. As was explained in our treatment of verb phrases, the subject of this construction is a goal rather than an actor.

The remaining type of discontinuous predicator is both common and important. The type consists of a verb (or verb phrase), a complement, and a following adverb. Before we give examples of the construction, we should return to a type of sentence we have discussed previously. In writing, the following sentence is ambiguous:

We passed by the road.

In speech the sentence is clear enough:

$$\overset{2}{/\text{wìy}} + \text{pæst} + \text{bày} + \text{ðə} + \overset{3\,1}{\text{rówd}} \,\#/ \quad \text{(We passed by means of the road.)}$$
$$\overset{2}{/\text{wìy}} + \text{pæst} + \text{bày} + \text{ðə} + \overset{3\,1}{\text{rówd}} \,\#/ \quad \text{(We overlooked the road.)}$$

The two sentences also have juncture points in different locations, giving for the first:

$$\overset{2}{/\text{wìy}} + \overset{3\,2}{\text{pǽst}} \mid \overset{2}{\text{bày}} + \text{ðə} + \overset{31}{\text{ŕówd}} \#/$$

And for the second:

$$\overset{2}{/\text{wìy}} + \overset{32}{\text{pǽst}} + \overset{2}{\text{báy}} \mid \overset{31}{\text{ðə}} + \text{ŕówd} \#/$$

It will be remembered that the forms of the class of *by*, with tertiary or sometimes weak stress, were defined as prepositions and described as being a part of the following construction, as the juncture point demonstrates. The forms with secondary stress, or primary stress in final position, were defined as adverbs and assigned to the preceding verb construction. In these sentences, however, there are ambiguous pronunciations whenever the stresses are shifted. Thus, for instance, a primary stress on *by* gives:

$$\overset{2}{/\text{wìy}} + \overset{3}{\text{pǽst}} + \overset{1}{\text{báy}} + \text{ðə} + \text{ŕôwd} \#/$$

In this form, the contrastive stress destroys the distinction between the normal tertiary on a preposition and secondary on an adverb, so that the adverb-preposition difference is obliterated.

There are sentences in which the stress may vary, causing confusion. The difficulty can be illustrated by the pair:

He ran up a bill. He ran up a hill.

The first sentence is normally either:

$$\overset{2}{/\text{hìy}} + \text{rǽn} + \overset{31}{\text{ə̂pə}} + \text{bíl} \#/ \quad \text{or} \quad \overset{2}{/\text{hìy}} + \text{rǽn} + \overset{31}{\text{ə̂pə}} + \text{bíl} \#/$$

The second is:

$$\overset{2}{/\text{hìy}} + \text{rǽn} + \overset{31}{\text{ə̂pə}} + \text{híl} \#/$$

These forms are clear enough—the first sentence contains an adverb, the second a preposition. Yet, unfortunately for clarity, my idiolect contains also the pronunciation:

$$\overset{2}{/\text{hìy}} + \text{rǽn} + \overset{31}{\text{ə̂pə}} + \text{bíl} \#/$$

Such a sentence—and there are analogous pronunciations in many idiolects —forces a choice. If we assume that the sentence must contain an adverb, we are then forced to say that stress difference is not a sure guide as to which construction is occurring. If we assume, on the contrary, that stress difference is always distinctive, then we are forced to say that either adverb or preposition can occur in this particular sentence. Of the two, the second is the preferable alternative, since otherwise we are ultimately making an appeal to meaning and are in danger of confusing the formal differences. Moreover, there are undoubtedly other instances in which a form that is normally given adverbial stress and juncture characteristics is treated instead as a preposition without essential change in the meaning. For instance, recently a student was called on to read the poetic line:

My lips writhed back in a grimace.

The pronunciation given was:

$$\overset{2}{M\grave{y}} + \overset{3\ 2}{l\acute{\imath}ps} + writhed \mid \overset{2}{b\grave{a}ck} + ina + \overset{3\ 1}{grim\acute{a}ce} \,\#$$

The reading is somewhat surprising, but was natural. In such a pronunciation, there can be no doubt that *back* is treated as a preposition. More normally, however, *back* would receive primary stress and be followed by /||/, in which case it would necessarily be an adverb. A somewhat similar sentence is:

John drove by the house.

This may be either:

$$\overset{2}{/j\hat{a}hn} + dr\hat{o}wv + \overset{3\,1}{b\hat{a}y} + \eth\partial + h\acute{a}ws \,\#/ \text{ or}$$
$$\overset{2}{/j\hat{a}hn} + dr\hat{o}wv + \overset{3\,1}{b\grave{a}y} + \eth\partial + h\acute{a}ws \,\#/$$

In neither case is the meaning affected, though the first form contains an adverb, and the second a preposition. On the other hand, the sentence "John drove by the rules" usually has tertiary stress on *by*, which is therefore a preposition. Moreover, in this sentence there is a juncture point before *by*, giving:

$$\overset{2}{/j\hat{a}hn} + \overset{3\ 2}{dr\acute{o}wv} \mid \overset{2}{b\grave{a}y} + \eth\partial + \overset{3\ 1}{r\acute{u}wlz} \,\#/$$

Exactly the same form can be given for the sentence "John drove by the house." That is, a juncture point can be established as occurring before the form with tertiary stress. In turn, therefore, when we have

$$\overset{2}{/j\hat{a}hn} + dr\hat{o}wv + \overset{3\,2}{b\acute{a}y} \mid \overset{2}{\eth\partial} + \overset{3\ 1}{h\acute{a}ws} \,\#/$$

the occurrence of the /||/ without linkage by complex contour can be used to establish a juncture point after the forms with secondary stress. The adverbial forms, therefore, form a part of the verb construction, and so differ from the adverbs in *–ly*. An adverb in *–ly* is not fixed in postverbal position, since we have sentences like "He apparently forgot the name," as well as "He forgot, apparently, the name," and "He forgot the name, apparently." The adverbs in *-ly*, or in other adverbial postbases, are normally set off by terminals when they occur between the verb and the complement, and so do not belong to the same phrase with the verb. It is only the adverbs without postbases which are thus regularly made a part of the preceding verb phrase.

With adverbs lacking a postbase, the complement often occurs immediately after the verb, placing the adverb in final position. In final position the adverb normally gets primary stress, and there is no juncture point without pitch linkage before it. Thus we may have either:

$$\overset{2}{He\ ran\ a\ bill}\ \overset{31}{up.}\quad /h\grave{\imath}y\ +\ r\grave{\ae}n\partial\ +\ b\hat{\imath}l\ +\ \acute{\partial}p\ \#/$$

Or with pitch linkage:

$$\overset{2}{}\quad\overset{2\,2\ \ 331}{}\quad\overset{2}{}\quad\overset{3\,2\ \ 441}{}$$
$$/h\grave{\imath}y\ +\ r\grave{\ae}n\partial\ +\ b\acute{\imath}l\ \mid\ \acute{\partial}p\ \#/\ or\ /h\grave{\imath}y\ +\ r\grave{\ae}n\partial\ +\ b\acute{\imath}l\ \mid\ \acute{\partial}p\ \#/$$

The phonological evidence, therefore, is that in these sentences we have a discontinuous predicator which contains the complement.

Sentences involving verb, adverb, and complement offer several kinds of ambiguity. When the sentence is written, there is ambiguity as to whether it contains adverb or preposition. This sort of structural ambiguity is cleared up as soon as the sentence is spoken. In some sentences, even if spoken with adverb stress, the meaning may not be clear, as it is not in such a sentence as:

$$H\grave{e}\ l\hat{o}oked\ \hat{o}ver\ her\ h\acute{a}t.$$

Stressed in this fashion, it is clear that *over* is an adverb, yet the sentence may mean either "He examined her hat" or "He directed his gaze above her hat." Even with verb and preposition combinations there are similar semantic ambiguities. Thus, "Jôhn gôes with Máry" may mean that he accompanies her or that he is paying court to her. Of all the situations, however, that of verb, complement, and adverb is clearest. A sentence such as "John looked her *hât óver*" can only be one containing an adverb and can only mean "examined it." Yet, it should be emphasized that ambiguities can be resolved in other ways than by adopting discontinuous order when it is possible. For instance

$$\overset{2\ 3\ 2\ \ 2\ \ \ \ 31}{H\grave{e}\ r\acute{a}n\ \mid\ \grave{u}p\ a\ h\acute{o}use\ \#}$$

makes clear that *up* is a preposition and that the sentence presumably means that some creature such as a mouse ran up the side of a building. Similarly

$$\overset{2\ \ \ \ 32\ \ 2\ \ 3\ 1}{H\grave{e}\ r\grave{a}n\ \acute{u}p\ \mid\ a\ h\acute{o}use\ \#}$$

identifies the adverb, and indicates the meaning "He built a house quickly."

These sentences offer verb-adverb combinations which are semantic units, so that they should properly be recorded as units in dictionaries. Since verb-preposition combinations are separated by a juncture point, they should not be thus recorded, even though sometimes their meaning is surprising. Further, the entries for combinations such as *look over* ("examine") should be marked for their stress pattern and indicate that *over* is an adverb.

There are peculiarities of order, however, in the verb-adverb sentence elements. We have been dealing with a group of them which often assume discontinuous order. In point of fact, these constructions fall into three groups: those which have either continuous or discontinuous order; those which have only one order; and those which have both orders but with a distinction in meaning between the two. The first class is exemplified by:

$$\overset{2}{\text{He picked up the books.}} \quad /\text{hìy} + \text{pîkt} + \overset{31}{\hat{\text{ə}}\text{p}} + \text{ðə} + \text{búks} \,\#/$$

$$\overset{2}{\text{He picked the books up.}} \quad /\text{hìy} + \text{pîkt} + \text{ðə} + \overset{31}{\text{bûks}} + \text{ə́p} \,\#/$$

The class which can have only one order has two subdivisions, those for which only continuous order is possible and those for which only discontinuous order is possible. A clear example of the first type is *come off*, as in:

$$\overset{2}{\text{John came off his high-horse.}} \quad /\text{jâhn} + \text{kèym} + \overset{3}{\hat{\text{ɔ}}\text{f}} + \text{iz} + \text{háy} + \overset{1}{\text{hɔ̀rs}} \,\#/$$

That is, such sentences as "John came *his high-horse off*" do not occur.

There is more variation among the sentences in which the normal order is discontinuous, but in many idiolects the following sentence does not vary its order:

$$\overset{2}{\text{It shook the car apart.}} \quad /\text{ìt} + \text{šûk} + \text{ðə} + \text{kâr} + \overset{31}{\text{əpárt}} \,\#/$$

A clear example in which difference in order gives a difference in meaning is to be found in the pair:

$$\overset{2}{\text{John drove by the car.}} \quad /\text{jâhn} + \text{drôwv} + \text{bây} + \text{ðə} + \overset{3\ 1}{\text{kár}} \,\#/$$

$$\overset{2}{\text{John drove the car by.}} \quad /\text{jâhn} + \text{drôwv} + \text{ðə} + \text{kâr} + \overset{31}{\text{báy}} \,\#/$$

It is to be noted, of course, that the first of these sentences has a different stress pattern from "Jôhn drôve by̆ thĕ máp," where *by* is a preposition.

At least as common as the type in which order is a clear signal of difference in meaning is the type in which one order is ambiguous but the other is explicit. An example of this latter class is the pair:

$$\begin{matrix} & 2 & & & 3\ 1 \end{matrix}$$
John got off the letters. /jâhn + gàt + ɔ́f + ðə + létərz #/
$$\begin{matrix} & 2 & & & 31 \end{matrix}$$
John got the letters off. /jâhn + gât + ðə + lêtərz + ɔ́f #/

The first sentence could be expanded either by "... he was sitting on" or by "... in the early mail." The second sentence could be expanded only by the latter sort of addition. The ambiguity in the first sentence disappears, however, if the complement is a pronoun:

$$\begin{matrix} & 2 & & 3 & 1 \end{matrix}$$
John got off them. /jâhn + gàt + ɔ́f + ðɨm #/

In this pattern, the meaning can only be "removed himself from them." A peculiarity of order is that the first class, that represented by "Pick up the books" and "Pick the books up," where either order is possible without change of meaning, permits only one order with a pronoun complement. Thus:

$$\begin{matrix} & 2 & & & 31 \end{matrix}$$
John picked them up. /jâhn + pîk + ðɨm + ɔ́p #/

A pronoun complement after the adverb is perhaps possible, but in my idiolect only as a contrast form treated as a separate phrase:

$$\begin{matrix} 2 & & 32 & 44\ 1 \end{matrix}$$
/jâhn + pîk + tɔ́p | ðém #/

The order classes when the complement is a noun are therefore less precise than they are when the complement is a pronoun, and variant order with pronouns is always significant. In the instances in which the order of adverb followed by noun complement is ambiguous, the ambiguity is solved by lexical probabilities as usual. Notice the following pair:

$$\begin{matrix} & 2 & & & 31 \end{matrix}$$
John got down the plate. /jâhn + gàt + dâwn + ðə + pléyt #/
$$\begin{matrix} & 2 & & & 3 & 1 \end{matrix}$$
John got down the mountain. /jâhn + gàt + dâwn + ðə + máwntin #/

The two sentences are structurally alike, but the lexical items which fill the complement position make differing interpretations likely for each. Yet, if *John* is sufficiently supplied with earth-moving equipment, the second sentence might mean the same thing as the first. Also, of course, discontinuous order is more likely for the first than for the second, and if the complements are replaced by pronouns, the first will probably have "John got it down," while the second will be "John got down it." In these sentences, ambiguity is resolved by the items within the sentence. Sometimes the ambiguity is more troublesome and could only be settled by probabilities on a span wider than the sentence. Such a situation is found in:

$$2 \qquad\qquad 31$$
John got over his ideas. /jâhn + gàt + ôwveriz + ày + díhz #/

The sentence may mean either "John recovered from his ideas" or "John got his ideas over."

4. Constituent analysis of predicators, and linear transcription

As well as presenting ambiguities, some of which are not resolvable structurally, verb-adverb combinations present difficulty in constituent analysis. When the order is verb-adverb-complement, procedure is simple enough—the cuts are such as to give the verb-adverb construction as one constituent and the complement as the other. Trouble arises only with constructions like *picked the books up*. It seems inescapable that the constituents are *picked . . . up* and *the books*, especially since a variant of the construction is *picked up the books*. The double cut before and after *the books* which would be necessary to arrive directly at a constituent *picked . . . up* is a kind of cutting which we have tried to avoid if possible. Even more, a process of normalizing, by transposing to continuous order, is to be avoided since such transposition does violence to the actual facts of the language.

A process of cutting and reassembly which offers a possible solution of the difficulty in all discontinuous predicators is the following:

John picked the books up.

The first cut is after *John*, giving:

John and *picked the books up*

The second cut is before *up*, giving:

picked the books and *up*

This cut is justified primarily by the fact that *picked the books* is a more likely independent construction than *the books up* and by the analogy of *helped them work* which we have cut (see p. 277) into *helped them* and *work*.

The third cut is after *picked*, giving:

picked and *the books*

At this point we have sorted out the sentence elements, and *picked* and *up* can now be reassembled as the parts of a discontinuous predicator. The justification for reassembling them is the occurrence of the variant construction in which they are in continuous order.

The juncture points in this sentence do not, at first sight, offer evidence which supports our process of cutting. One juncture variant is clear enough:

$$\begin{array}{cccc} 2 & 32 & 2 & 31 \\ \end{array}$$
$$/\text{jâhn} + \text{pík} + \text{t} \mid \text{ðə} + \text{bûks} + \text{ə́p} \; \#/$$

Since no complex contour occurs, we have a juncture point which is morphologically conditioned. It is occurring at a boundary between main sentence elements. Yet, to make our first cut at this point would give us rather needlessly complex constituents.

A second variant is the following:

$$\begin{array}{ccc} 2 & 32 & 441 \\ \end{array}$$
$$/\text{jâhn} + \text{pîk} + \text{ðə} + \text{búks} \mid \text{ə́p} \; \#/$$

We have a typical complex contour, indicating that a unified construction has been broken up. The phonological evidence would seem to indicate that our cuts are wrongly placed and that *up* is dependent upon *the books*.

I should rather take this evidence as pointing to the necessity of reassembly after the cutting has been done. We shall therefore assume that the steps of cutting, based primarily on procedural consistency, are justified and shall pass on to the possibility of reassembly, hoping that reassembly will solve the peculiarities of juncture distribution.

What we are about to do is an extension of the technique of linear transcription which was applied to stress and pitch morphemes in Section 6 of Chapter 7. There, we were able to write pitch morphemes in linear sequence with the underlying stress and segmental material, since if the terminal junctures were properly placed, the pitch phonemes could be located by rule. The same principles can be applied to discontinuous predicators. The sentence "John picked the books up" offers opportunity to restate the position of the predicator in linear fashion as follows:

John   the books   picked up.

If we do so, however, we must first satisfy certain conditions. We cannot transpose to the order found in "John picked up the books," since such a transposition would obliterate a distinction found in actual sentences. We must therefore transpose only to an order which is not actually found. We must also be able to state by simple rule where the transposed parts of the predicator actually occur.

The transposed order given above satisfies these conditions. The order "John   the books   picked up" is not found in English under the single

pitch morpheme {2 3 1 #}, which is the normal form for the actual sentence
with which we started:

$$\overset{2}{\text{/jâhn}} + \text{pîk} + \text{ðə} + \text{bûks} + \overset{31}{\text{ə́p}} \text{#/}$$

In the transposed order, in which *picked uṗ* is given last, we can state that
in actual occurrence the verb *picked* always precedes the complement.

There are several things accomplished by such a linear writing. The
first is the obvious one of bringing together the discontinuous elements of
the predicator. A more important result is that a variation in order, such
as that shown in "Jôhn drôve bŷ the cár" and "Jôhn drôve the câr bý,"
which might seem to be a variation in the order of words only, is shown
to be a variation in sentence element order. It is therefore in line with
distinctions like that between "The whale swallowed Jonah" and "Jonah
swallowed the whale." As a principal result of this type of transposition,
we reach a conclusion that there are three types of order variation in English.
There is the type found in such variations as "The man was strong but old"
and "The man was old but strong," which can be defined as stylistic and
without linguistic significance. A second type can be found within phrases
and sentence elements, as in *two very fine old houses* and *two fine, very old
houses*. This type of order variation can be said to belong to minor syntax.
The third type of significant order is that of sentence elements, the only
factor of order that belongs to major syntax.

Our proposal of controlled transposition, it is believed, offers a final
solution to the difficulties of achieving a consistent immediate constituent
analysis in relation to the evidence of the juncture pattern. If we have in
picked the books up a discontinuous predicator which contains the complement, it is not strange that the juncture pattern suggests that a major break
occurs before the first part of the predicator and that a juncture before *up*
occurs in such a fashion as to indicate that *up* is not independent of the
preceding material. Our transposition makes it clear that *up* is ultimately
linked to *picked* and is linked to *the books* only because this is contained
within the predicator.

17.... MAIN SENTENCE ELEMENTS, III

Complement and Adjunct

1. Single complement

We have been forced to use the term "complement" rather often in dealing with the sentence elements already described, though we have not given a definition of it. We begin our discussion with the type of construction which forms the core of this class of sentence element.

Probably the commonest sentence type—certainly commonest if we exclude the sentences which are used as responses only—consists of a noun or noun construction, a verb, and a following noun or noun construction. Under normal conditions, we expect the initial noun or noun construction to be the subject and the final noun construction to be the remaining principal component of a three-part sentence, the complement. A preliminary definition of a nominal complement, then, is that it is a noun or noun construction which is not the subject and which has its normal position immediately after the predicator. There are a great many sentences where it is the sentence element order alone that signals which of two nouns or noun constructions is subject and which complement. These are sentences like most of the variations on the type "Men make laws," which were used in discussing subject and subjectival sentence elements (see p. 260). In three-part sentences, it is the subject which is most clearly marked; the second noun or noun construction is then automatically the complement.

A noun complement, further, can duplicate the internal structure of a noun subject. A simple noun complement can therefore contain all the normal sequences of modifiers, as in:

> The company sold *all the ten fine old stone houses.*

The complement may also be composed of more than one phrase if the order requires a terminal. When the complement is thus complex, there is linkage by a complex contour, just as there is in a complex subject.

> *The company sold all the ten old fine stone houses.*

2
/ðə + kə́mpəniy + sôwld + ɔ́hl + ðə + tên + ówld | fáyn | stôwn + háwziz #/

Like a subject, the complement may be composed of more than one noun construction, again with possible linkage by complex contour and often with connectives of the class of *and:*

The company sold *all the old houses and all the new lots.*

$$
\overset{2}{|ð\vartheta} + k\hat{\vartheta}mp\vartheta niy + s\hat{o}wld + \hat{\vartheta}hl + ðiy + \hat{o}wl + \overset{3\quad\;2}{h\acute{a}wz\grave{\iota}z} \; |
$$
$$
\overset{2}{in} + \hat{\vartheta}hl + ð\vartheta + \overset{41}{ny\hat{u}w} + l\acute{a}hts \; \#|
$$

A complement may consist of a pronoun, just as may a subject. We have seen, however, that a subject pronoun is in form 1; a pronoun in the complement is in form 2. With pronouns there is, then, a paradigmatic difference between subject and complement. In most instances the inflectional difference is redundant, since the difference is also signaled by order. But when the normal sentence element order is departed from, the form of the pronoun may be a signal which identifies the subject or complement:

SUBJECT   Two loves have *they.*

The contrasting sentence has normal order, giving the sequence subject-verb-complement:

COMPLEMENT   Two loves have *them.*

These sentences do not usually contrast minimally in terms of forms alone, since there are differences of stress and pitch:

$$
\overset{2}{|t\hat{u}w} + \overset{31}{l\hat{\vartheta}vz} + h\underset{}{\ae}v + ð\acute{e}y \; \#| \quad \text{and} \quad \overset{2}{|t\hat{u}w} + \overset{3}{l\hat{\vartheta}vz} + h\underset{}{\ae}v + \overset{1}{ð\grave{\iota}m} \; \#|
$$

It was said in Chapter 11 (see p. 188) that *all* and *both* can act as modifiers of preceding pronoun forms. Thus the complement forms are *them all* and *them both,* corresponding to the subject forms *they all* and *they both.* The variants *all of them, both of them, half of them,* and *some of them* do not, of course, change in form when they appear as complements rather than subjects.

Before we go on to complements of other types than simple nouns, noun constructions, pronouns, and pronoun constructions, it will be useful to make a distinction between complement and object (or, as it is sometimes called, goal) just as we made a distinction between subject and subjectival, on the one hand, and actor, on the other.

The type of construction called object or goal is a subtype of the complement. Further, the distinction between non-object and object within the class of complements is semantic and is not formally signaled. That is to say, sentences such as "This seems a big price" and "This brings a big price" are formally indistinguishable, though it is traditional to say that only the second contains an object. Only in those dialects which use construc-tions like "It is I" and "It is they" do we have a formal distinction between an object and a non-object form for pronoun complements. In these dialects, "It *is they*" contrasts with "It *feeds them*," and the contrast *they : them* is therefore meaningful. While, in general, we have called the pronoun form found in *them, him, me,* etc. a complement form, there is no reason to narrow it to the designation "object form" in general English structure. Nor should it be thought that the complement is the only situation in which the form which we designate thus can appear. We have already seen that the com-plement form appears after prepositions, as in *of them.* It also appears, somewhat unexpectedly, in the minimal sentences used as responses, as in reply to a question such as "Who's there?" To this question the normal response in most dialects is "Me." A similar use of the form which is normally a complement appears in extended examples of response sentences, as in a recent magazine advertisement which shows an astonished gentleman gesturing toward himself, with the caption "WHO, *ME* FLY? My own airplane!" Presumably this spelling and punctuation indicate a total pattern for the utterance more or less as follows:

$$\begin{array}{cccccc} 3\,3\,4 & 4\ 4 & 3 & 3 & 4 & 4 \\ \end{array}$$
/húw ‖ míy + flây ‖ màyôwn + éhr + plèyn ‖/

It would probably be usual to analyze the part of this found in "Me fly?" as containing an aberrently shaped subject. Since the pronoun does not have subject form, this analysis can scarcely be satisfactory. There is, clearly, a juncture point before *fly,* and the sentence has the same shape as such other response utterances as "Me? a genius?" which are of a special equational type which contains no true subject.

2. Double complement

Within the class of sentences containing a nominal or pronominal complement are sentences in which there are two complements. A typical example of this construction is:

$$\begin{array}{cccc} 2 & 32 & 2 & 31 \\ \end{array}$$
I gave John a book. /ày + gêyv + jáhn | ə + búk #/

In the transcription of the sentence, one of the several forms with a terminal before the second complement has been chosen, though there are many occurrences of this sentence type with no terminal. However, the fact that, if there is a terminal, it falls after *John* is indication that the two nominal forms do not belong to the same phrase. Whether they belong to the same sentence element can be settled only by further analysis.

One distinction can be set up rather easily on a formal basis, and the signal identified. Suppose we write the following without any punctuation:

I bought Sandy a dog

The probability is that it will be read as:

$$\overset{2}{/\text{ày}} + \text{bɔ̂ht} + \text{sǽndiy} + \overset{31}{ə + \text{dɔ́hg}} \#/$$

In this form the sentence will be interpreted as "I bought a dog for Sandy." Another reading is possible, however:

$$\overset{2}{/\text{ày}} + \text{bɔ̂ht} + \overset{3}{\text{sǽndiy}} \# \overset{1}{ə} + \overset{11}{\text{dɔ́hg}} \#/$$

In this form the utterance is probably to be interpreted as "I bought a dog called Sandy." The signals seem to operate in this fashion with all sentences where there is any real likelihood of alternative interpretations. If there is conflict between the lexical probabilities and the formal signal, however, the result seems to be hesitation. Thus, in the sentence which can be written "I called John—a fool," where the punctuation indicates

$$\overset{2}{/\text{ày}} + \text{kɔ̂hld} + \overset{31}{\text{jáhn}} \# \overset{1}{ə} + \overset{11}{\text{fúwl}} \#/$$

the result is usually confusing. That is, the lexical sequence *call John a fool* has so much more frequency in the sense of "call him names" that we hesitate to take the less frequent interpretation, even though the stress and juncture pattern signals it. The hesitation, however, does not mean that the probabilities override the juncture patterns. A typical reaction is that the sentence pronounced in this fashion "sounds like a mistake." That is, it is the sequence appropriate to another set of probabilities and therefore makes the sentence sound unintelligible.

These sentences, then, in which the second nominal group is set off by /#/, can be referred to a special type of the equational situation and the second nominal group then excluded from the complement. An interesting result is that we have discovered a situation in which a juncture point cannot have /#/ instead of /|/ or /|||/ without changing the character of the utterance.

We are left with sentences of the following type:

I gave John a book. and *I call John a fool.*[1]

---

[1] There is a sort of hint of interpretation, signaled by something in the form, in this second sentence as given. The sequence *I call* uses the simple non-past, defining *call* as the habitual verb "to declare that something is." After this verb we expect to find a name. If the form were *I am calling*, the non-habitual form characteristic of the verb *call* meaning "summon," the probabilities would be considerably affected.

Both can have /|/ or /||/ after John, and both second nouns are given with the pitch morpheme {2 3 1 #}. In each sentence, both noun groups are complements, but the question as to whether they are parts of the same sentence element is left unanswered. There is another type of sentence which is now helpful. The type is that found in:

> *I called John and Jim.*
> *I called John, Bill, and Jim.*
> *I called John, Bill, Jim, all three.*

These forms we have already described as having single complements made up of more than one phrase. The signal is, in the first two, the presence of the connective *and*; and in the third it is *all*, which is here postposed. Apparently the postposed position of sequences beginning with *all* or *both* (*all three, all of them, both of them*) is related to the fact that these two group VI modifiers can be used to make pronominal phrases in postposed position. If these sentences, then, are defined as complements of more than one phrase, we can further test by leaving out the *and*, which we have defined as the formal signal of the relationship. The result is to transform our first sentence into:

> *I called John Jim.*

2   3 1   2   3   2 331
/ày + kɔ̂hld + jâhn + jím #/ or /ày + kɔ̂hld + jáhn | jím #/

In either case the result is the same. We are dealing with a different sentence, and not only is the reality of the signal proved, but it is clear that we do not now have a single complement of two phrases. We can therefore come to the conclusion that two complement noun groups, separated by a juncture point without linkage by complex contour, constitute two-complement sentence elements, and that the presence of two-complement constructions is meaningful.

The presence of two complements is familiar under such names as "indirect object" and "direct object" for sentences of the type of "I gave John a book," and "object" and "objective complement" for "I called John a fool." It should be emphasized that these names indicate semantic distinctions only and that nothing in the formal structure distinguishes one relationship from the other. English signals both relationships in the same way, leaving the proper interpretation to the probabilities involved in the lexical sequences. We shall therefore avoid the traditional terminology.

It is not quite true, however, that both of two successive complement sentence elements are formally alike. It is, for instance, a usual though not quite universal rule that only the first of two complements can be expressed by a personal pronoun. That is, we have sentences like "I gave him a book," but not usually "I gave *John it*" or "I gave *him it*." This limitation does not apply, however, to the pronominals *this* and *that*, which can occur as second complements, whether or not the first complement is in the form of a personal pronoun. That is, we say "Don't call John that" or "Don't call him that," and "I bought John that" or "I bought him that."

The limitation just described does not apply to British English, however, in which sentences like "I sent it you yesterday" and "Please give it me" seem to be natural. They are unknown, however, except as bookish forms in many American idiolects. An exception which is established in my idiolect, but so isolated as to constitute an idiom, is "Give me it," always used in the form:

$$\begin{array}{cc} 33 & 1 \\ /\text{gímiy} + \text{it} \# / \end{array}$$

In one form, the limitation seems to be universal. In no dialect known to me is it possible to express both complements by the same pronoun. In all forms of the language "I *gave them them*" and "I *call it it*" are impossible. It is this limitation, in both British and American English, which prevents using *it* for both complements in "He gave the house a roof." The only substitution possible is "He gave it a roof." Similarly, if the sentence is "He gave the houses roofs" or "He gave his children houses," it is only the first complement which can take the pronoun *them*. It would seem that American English either has extended this universal rule against identical pronouns to the more stringent rule that only the first complement can be a pronoun in any case, or is in process of so extending the rule. Further, it is interesting that the English forms which have been quoted prefer the order of "Give it me," that is, with the *it* complement in first position, while in the idiomatic American English "Give me it," it is the *me* complement which occupies this position. The British pattern, though older, is the more complex of the two, since it involves an order shift. If the complement expressed by *it* in the sentence quoted is replaced by a noun, in both British and American English, the order must be "Give *me a book*." Neither form of the language can have "Give *a book me*." Thus the British pattern means that the entities expressible by *it* and *me* must reverse their position if both pronouns are used.

Another feature of the double-complement sentence type is a matter of probability, not of formal characteristics. A frequent situation in these sentences is that one complement will be a "thing," that is, something expressible by *it*. The other complement will be a "person," that is, something expressible by one of the other pronouns. When this happens, the almost universally predictable order is person complement first, thing complement second, as in "I gave *John the book*." It is just barely possible to reverse the order and say "I gave the book John," which could mean only something like "I contributed a character called John to the contents of the book we were describing."

When the first complement is a thing, and expressed by *it*, it is nearly always true that the second complement is also a thing, as in "He gave it a new roof" or "He gave the house a new roof." There are also sentences in which both complements are persons, as in "She gave John a son." In sentences of this type, the rule that only the first complement can take the shape of a pronoun seems to be universally observed both in British and American English. It is rather rare that we have two person complements, both of which are proper names, though it is possible to construct examples which are natural, as in "When the war took her sons, it left *Mary only John*."

The situation in which there is a person complement and a thing complement is so common, and the order person-thing, with only the first complement in pronoun shape, so nearly universal that one can use it to explain another type of construction. That is, a sentence of the type "I gave *John it*" is so uncommon that we can say that if for any reason the thing complement is given pronoun shape, we normally use an alternate construction in which the person complement is made the head of a postposed prepositional phrase: "I gave it to John."

We can sum up our results so far by saying that two complements signal the type of semantic relationship found both in "I gave John a book" and in "I call John a fool." The most useful names are the purely formal ones, first complement and second complement. The order of complements can be shown to be significant in contrasting sentences like:

> *He gave the building the library.*
> *He gave the library the building.*

The significance of the first complement can be loosely described by calling it the complement which is the more distantly related of the two to the preceding predicator. The British sentences with two pronoun complements of the type "Give it me" reverse this relationship, leaving the semantic contents of the sentence to be signaled only by the difference in pronouns. In British as well as American English the sentence "Give me that" follows the normal order, however. As always, the loosely describable semantic content of a first complement cannot be used as a means of definition. The formal nature of the difference between first and second complement means also that the distinction does not exist unless two complements are present. That is, there is no formal difference between "I wrote *it*" and "I wrote *you*," both of which contain single complements, though it is true that the verb *write* and the pronoun *you* give a highly probable interpretation differing from that in *wrote it*. It could be interpreted in the same way as *wrote it* only in this highly unlikely situation—"Well, my little book, I wrote you!"

3. Complements containing adjectival material

In dealing with complements, we have thus far described only those which consist of nominal and pronominal material. In describing adjectival material earlier, however, we pointed out that adjectives can occur in post-verbal position. Such adjectives and adjectivals are also complements. Thus sentences like "My house is white," "We are seven," "His face went white," all contain complements. *White* is a true adjective, so defined because it can be compared, while *seven* is adjectival, so defined because of its position in modifier groups and its lack of comparison. Adjective and adjectival complements are commonest, perhaps, after the verb *to be*, but it is by no means true that they are rare or strange after other verbs.

As well as the sentence "His face went white," which has an adjective after *went*, other common examples are:

> He always talks *big*.
> I feel *bad*.[2]
> He gradually became *old*.
> They finally came *clean*.

All of these complements are true adjectives. We have also seen that nominal modifiers of group I, whether they are adjectivals formed from nouns or true adjectives, can occur as complements. "These fields are stony" contains an adjective of group I, while "The election went Republican" and "These houses are stone" are complements containing group I adjectivals which in other situations are used as nouns. It will be remembered that forms like *Republican* and *stone* were identified as adjectivals here because of the absence of noun markers. In the sentence "The election went Republican," articles or plural inflection are impossible; in "These houses are stone," inflection produces a highly improbable statement. Recognition of the occurrence of group I modifiers as complements solves the difficulties of analysis in such sentences as "Buy British," just as analysis is simplified if we assume that "Drive slow" contains an adjective complement. The dis-

---

[2] An interesting detail of American usage is that many speakers now solve the old argument about whether to say *feel bad* or *feel badly* by differentiating the two constructions, using *bad* in "I felt bad because my stomach hurt," and *badly* in "I felt badly when the old house burned."

tinction between noun and group I modifier in complement position can also be brought to bear on another vexed question of analysis, namely the form class of *home* in such sentences as "John went home" and the somewhat more colloquial "My books are home." It is true, of course, that *home* in other situations is a noun and is proved to be so by its inflectional characteristics, as in *the homes of the great.* Yet in the sentence "John went home," *home* cannot be inflected, nor can it be preceded by a definite or indefinite article. The difficulty has been handled in various ways. Curme calls *home* in *go home* an "old adverbial accusative of goal,"[3] a phrase which implies that he analyzed it as still a noun, in spite of the absence of nominal markers. The other usual position is that taken by Jespersen that "In 'Come *home* . . .' *home* . . . [was] originally [a substantive], but [is] now generally called [an adverb]"[4]—a position which he later modifies slightly to speak of such constructions as "nouns used adverbially."[5] Curme decides on historical, Jespersen on semantic, grounds, criteria which would not be used in more modern analysis. Nonetheless, the decision that *home* is noun or adverb is still the usual position. It is to be observed, however, that a decision that *home* is an adverb does not cover the sentence "My books are home," at least without further discussion, and that to call it a noun does violence to its formal characteristics. There is a relatively simple third possibility. *Home* is in origin a noun, but it is used as a modifier in *home fires* /hôwm + fáyrz/, *home study* /hôwm + stɔ́diy/, and the like. If "The election went Republican" and "These houses are stone" can be spoken of as containing modifiers of group I as complements, there is then no reason why *home* cannot be called a group I modifier acting as complement in both "John went home" and "My books are home." In line with this analysis, constructions like *the hunter, home from the hill* are to be analyzed as containing *home* as a group I modifier, since here also it is impossible to inflect it. This last construction is therefore of the same pattern as *a soldier, proud of the uniform* and is of a different pattern from *these houses, homes of the great.* We analyze both "They are home" and "They are homes" as containing a complement following the verb, though only the second contains a noun. In other words, whether we are dealing with modifier or noun makes no difference in the first level of constituent analysis of such sentences. It is only when we try to define the contents of the complement sentence element that the distinction becomes important.

Since, as we have seen, past participles are often homonymous with adjectives, there is another situation in which decision as to form class is

---

[3] George O. Curme, *Syntax,* Heath, Boston, 1931, Par. 16.4a.

[4] Otto Jespersen, *The Philosophy of Grammar,* Allen & Unwin, London, and Holt, New York, 1924, p. 98.

[5] *Ibid.,* p. 159.

important. Here, however, the distinction is important not only to the constituent analysis but to the meaning as well. A form shown to be an adjective following an inflected verb is part of the complement; a form shown to be a participle in such a situation is part of the predicator. If we have such a sentence as "He was bearded," the probability is that it will be interpreted as containing an adjective and analyzed accordingly. If so interpreted, the sentence is capable of being expanded by adding *heavily*, a construction which would prove conclusively that *bearded* is an adjective and a complement. Actually, however, the quoted sentence is ambiguous, since a second and less probable way of expanding it is to add "... in his den." If this is done, *bearded* will be taken as a participle of the verb *to beard*, since this verb is frequent in the sequence *beard ... in his den*. In such a situation, the predicator is *was bearded*, while in "He was bearded," the probable predicator is *was*, and *bearded* is the complement. The pitch morphemes do not offer a very sure guide in these two sentences, since a /‖/ is about equally possible before *bearded* in both. Yet the following is certainly a normal variant:

$$\text{2} \qquad \text{32} \quad \text{33} \quad \text{1}$$
He was bearded. /hìy + wə́z | bírdïd ‖/ (had a beard)

That is to say, before an adjective complement breaking into two phrases does not produce a complex contour. If our sentence is

$$\text{2} \qquad \text{32} \quad \text{44} \ \text{1}$$
He was bearded. /hìy + wə́z | bírdïd ‖/ (in his den)

we are perhaps more likely to have a complex contour, as shown. Both statements are made with hesitation, however, and may not be true for all speakers.

One juncture situation can be used to differentiate a somewhat similar sentence from one of the pair:

> *He was bearded in the spring.*
> *He was bearded in his den.*

In the first of these, *in the spring* is a sentence adjunct, and consequently is regularly set off by terminals. In the second, *in his den* is not such an adjunct, and so is rarely preceded by a terminal.

If the material which immediately follows the predicator is nominal or pronominal and that which follows thereafter is adjective or adjectival, we have another structurally ambiguous situation. Since adjectival material can itself act as a complement, such constructions may contain a double complement. On the other hand, adjectival material can frequently appear in postposed position in the complement and stand in a modifying relation to the preceding noun or pronoun. Unfortunately for the clarity of the signaling system, both a postposed modifier and an adjectival as second complement are preceded by juncture points (but see below, p. 304), so that the juncture pattern cannot be used to distinguish the two constructions. The structural ambiguity can be more sharply realized if we give a pair of sentences where the probable interpretation would differ·

2   31
She told him all. /šìy + tôwld + ìm + óhl #/
2   31
She told it all. /šìy + tôwld + ìt + óhl #/

If we interpret the first sentence in the most probable form, we would assume that it could be transformed into something like "She told all [of it] to him." Conversely, we would transform the second to "She told all of it." Yet the second sentence could at least conceivably be interpreted differently. If the stylistic situation makes it clear that the reference of *it* is to some such object as a diary, it would be possible to interpret the second sentence as a variation of the first. The structural ambiguity is here resolved by the frequencies of sequences. A sequence such as *he all* is extremely rare—we do not ordinarily say "He all went away." It is also rare in complement position, though it is possible in some such sentence as "He let the sun tan him all." In contrast, *it all* is a frequent sequence in subject position and elsewhere: "It all went away," "I ate it all," and so on. *All* is generally more frequent in situations where it acts as a modifier, though there are also situations in which it is a nominal, as in "He lost *his all.*" Putting these probabilities together, as the human mind so frequently does, we interpret the sequence *him all*, in the sentence quoted, as more probably a double complement, consisting of pronoun and following nominal use of the adjectival *all*. In the second sentence we interpret, still in terms of probable sequences, as pronoun and following adjectival modifier. I have here deliberately chosen two sentences in which the lexical sequences strongly influence the interpretation, removing any practical ambiguity. It is easy to construct sentences in which probabilities based on lexical sequences within the sentence fail us. Such a sentence would be "She told them all." Here, as long as we stay within the borders of linguistics, that is, within the borders of the sentence, there is real ambiguity. It is only when we take the structure and content of surrounding sentences into account that we get probabilities which enable us to interpret such sequences as *them all.* Such sequences are linguistically ambiguous, but may be stylistically clear.

The discussion of adjectivals as possible second complements demonstrates, at least, that there are two kinds of constructions, necessitating a different analysis for the sentence and often affecting the meaning. We have also seen that there are sentences in which the linguistic signals leave the possibility of either interpretation open. Yet, it is not true that all kinds of nominal or pronominal material followed by all kinds of adjectival material offer as much ambiguity as the sentences we have been discussing. Some relatively specific principles governing interpretation can be given.

If there is either nominal or pronominal material followed by the group VI modifiers *all* or *both*, the ambiguity is real, since these modifiers often occur postposed in both complements and subjects, and also appear as nominals. All such sentences must then be interpreted in accord with probable lexical sequences, either linguistic or stylistic. Examples which are linguistically ambiguous are:

> She told *them all*.　　He brought *the Thompsons all*.
> She told *them both*.　　He brought *the Thompsons both*.

Somewhat surprisingly, *half*, the third group VI modifier, does not produce ambiguity when postposed. In this situation it is always a second complement, never a modifier of the preceding nominal or pronominal material:

> He gave John *half*.　He gave him *half*.

If the postposed modifier is of group V (determinatives) or group IV (numerals), the resultant construction is like *half*; the modifier forms a second complement. It must be remembered that not all group V modifiers can occur when no noun follows; the articles never occur in this position at all, and the pronominal modifiers like *my, our, their* have special forms— *mine, ours, theirs*—when they occur here. The group V modifiers which occur without following nouns are *this, that*, and inflected forms of nouns, like *Jack's*. Examples, all to be interpreted as second complements, are:

> He gave *Mary that*.
> He gave *her that*.
> Mary wanted John's book, but they gave *her Jack's*.

Examples of group IV modifiers as second complements are:

> He brought the *boys ten*.　He brought *them ten*.

The first sentence is striking, since to transpose *boys* and *ten* gives a quite different statement:

> He brought the *ten boys*.

The rule that a postposed modifier of group IV is normally a second complement applies even to the idiomatic sequence *make it* with a following numeral, where the first complement refers to no noun in the preceding material:

John counted twelve, but I *make it* ten.

Modifiers after pronouns in the complement generally constitute second complements. However, there are a number of characteristics of order, as well as superfix characteristics, which have to be taken into account. When we are dealing with sequences containing a pronoun, it should be remembered that no modifier of any of the six groups stands before a pronoun in the same phrase. Furthermore, in subject position the group VI modifiers *all* and *both* are the most frequent after pronouns, as in *they all* and *they both*. It should be added that a limited number of numerals (group IV) also stand after subjectival pronouns, as in *we two, we four*, etc., though the possibilities of this type of construction cannot be very accurately described. Some limitation there is, since *they ten* is certainly less likely than the examples given. Pronoun constructions like *them all, them two*, which correspond to these subjectival types, are of course common in complement position, and may, as just said, be modifiers in a single complement. There are, however, complement sequences involving pronouns and following modifiers of other groups, like *it hot* or *it fine* in:

$$\overset{2}{\text{She likes }} \textit{it hot.}\ \ /\text{šìy} + \overset{}{\text{lâyks}} + \overset{3}{\text{ìt}} + \overset{1}{\text{hát}} \#/$$

$$\overset{2}{\text{She likes }} \textit{it fine.}\ \ /\text{šìy} + \overset{}{\text{lâyks}} + \overset{3}{\text{ìt}} + \overset{1}{\text{fáyn}} \#/$$

The second sentence, it is true, is ambiguous, since it could be interpreted as either "She likes it very well" or "She likes it to be fine." The ambiguity need not concern us at the minute. What is more interesting is that there is a juncture point before *fine*, and one which can be quite precisely described. There are a number of variant pronunciations, all of which would be recognized as versions of the sentence just quoted. They are:

2	3	3	331
/šìy +	láyks +	ìt |	fáyn #/
2	3	2	222
/šìy +	láyks +	ìt |	fáyn #/
2	3	1	111
/šìy +	láyks +	ìt |	fáyn #/

2	3	2	441
/šìy +	láyks +	ìt |	fáyn #/
		or	
2	3	3	441
/šìy +	láyks +	ìt |	fáyn #/

On the other hand, certain combinations of terminals and pitches produce different utterances:

$$\overset{2}{\textit{She likes it?}} \overset{3}{\textit{Fine.}}\ \ /\text{šìy} + \overset{}{\text{láyks}} + \overset{3}{\text{ìt}} \,\|\, \overset{231}{\text{fáyn}} \#/$$

$$\overset{2}{\textit{She likes it.}} \overset{3}{\textit{Fine.}}\ \ /\text{šìy} + \text{láyks} + \overset{1}{\text{ìt}} \,\#\, \overset{231}{\text{fáyn}} \#/ \quad /\text{šìy} + \text{láyks} + \overset{1}{\text{ìt}} \,\#\, \overset{111}{\text{fáyn}} \#/$$

The sentence has been given in so many variants for the reason that it is one which gives us an opportunity to describe a juncture point more precisely than we have as yet done. That is, as long as the utterance remains a single sentence and does not become a main sentence and dependent sentence, a terminal may fall before *fine*, and pitch linkage either by means of a single contour or a complex contour shows that the sentence is still unified. Separate contours with /|||/ or /#/ break the utterance into two sentences. The same variations would have been possible with "She likes it hot," except that a two-sentence utterance such as "She likes it. Hot" is less likely, thus dictating the choice of our example. Having demonstrated that there is a juncture point—with pitch linkage—before the adjective, we can then dispose of this sentence type by describing it as a sentence with first and second complement. The decision we have just made is based on two facts: the juncture situation we have just described and the further fact that sequences such as *it all* and *it hot* have different distributions. *It all* can appear in both subject and complement position, *it hot* can appear only in complement position. A sequence involving *it all* is then structurally ambiguous and may be either pronoun and following modifier in the same construction or a two-complement construction. With *it hot* there is no ambiguity, and we can call the construction an instance of two complements without inconsistency. Yet it must be specified that in such two-complement constructions, *hot* remains in the semantic relation of modification to the preceding pronoun and is still an adjective, as can be proved by such a sentence as "She likes it *hotter*." The structural relations and semantic relations, as often, are different. One other point about constructions of this sort can also be made. It is sometimes possible to leave out either one of the complements and still have a natural sentence. In other sentences only the second complement can be omitted. An example of the first sort is "She got it hot," where we can say both "She got it" and "She got hot." The second sort is represented by "She likes it hot," where we can have "She likes it," but not "She *likes hot*." This sort of distinction is not unknown in other two-complement sentences. In "She gave them books," either complement can be omitted, but in "She gave them shivers," only the first complement is likely to be found alone.

When we pass on to noun complements followed by forms which belong to the various classes of modifiers, we can use the decisions which have just been made for pronouns as our guide. That is, such a sentence as "She brought the teachers both" is genuinely ambiguous, since we have the same sequence in subject position: "The teachers both came." As with pronoun sentences, sentences involving forms like *all* and *both* may be either single-complement or double-complement constructions. In conversational English, none of the numerals of group IV are thus ambiguous after nouns, as they may be after pronouns. A numeral after a noun is a second complement, as it is in "She brought the teachers three."[6] As with pronouns, the forms like *all, both,* and numerals as second complements are no longer in modifying relation to the preceding noun but are rather independent nominals.

With modifiers of all groups except *all* and *both,* only position before a noun is possible in the subject, while position both before and after the noun is possible in the complement. Often enough there is no very sharp distinction in meaning between the two orders, as in:

John likes *hôt cóffee.*   and   John likes *côffee hót.*

There are other situations in which the two orders are markedly different in meaning, as in:

They got the *hôt drínks.*   and   They got the *drînks hót.*
Mary found *Jôhn háppy.*   and   Mary found *hâppy Jóhn.*

It is not possible to give a precise definition of the difference in meaning between the two differing orders, but the fact that there is difference is sufficient to prove that the two orders are not mere variants. As we should expect, also, there are sentences in which one order or the other is very much more probable:

Mary kissed her *old father.*
Mary thought her *father old.*

The construction, then, in which a modifier follows a noun complement is an example of a second complement, unless the modifier is an ambiguous *all* or *both.* The decision is strictly parallel to that which we made for pronouns. Before we go on to semantic discussion, it will be well to give a set of clear examples and examine them for stress, pitch, and juncture characteristics:

John is always knocking Jack.   (speaking badly of him)
2   31
/jâhn + z + ᵊlwɨz + nâkiŋ + jǽk #/

John is always knocking silly Jack.
2   31
/jâhn + z + ᵊlwɨz + nâkiŋ + sîliy + jǽk #/

---

[6] Literary language occasionally has a sentence with a postposed numeral involving some ambiguity. Often, however, the sentence is one in which the ambiguity is slight, as in "He *saw the Wise Men three.*" A verb such as *see* does not occur in more than a few limited types of double-complement sentences, such as "I was seeing Nellie home," so that in the sentence above, the interpretation that *the Wise Men three* is an order variant of *the three Wise Men* is forced.

The two sentences are examples of single complements, though the second contains a modifier.

John is always knocking Jack silly.

The sentence now means "striking him so as to deprive him of his senses" or, figuratively, "producing a great impression on him." It may occur as either:

$$\overset{2}{/\text{jâhn}} + z + \text{ôlwɨz} + \text{nâkiŋ} + \overset{3}{\text{jǽk}} + \overset{1}{\text{síliy}} \#/ \text{ or}$$

$$\overset{2}{/\text{jâhn}} + z + \text{ôlwɨz} + \text{nâkiŋ} + \overset{22}{\text{jǽk}} \mid \overset{33}{\text{síliy}} \overset{1}{\#/}$$

That is to say, there is a juncture point with linkage by complex contour. If we give the sentence the following form, we produce a different utterance:

$$\overset{2}{/\text{jâhn}} + z + \text{ôlwɨz} + \text{nâkiŋ} + \overset{31}{\text{jǽk}} \# \overset{111}{\text{síliy}} \#/$$

The latter form would be punctuated:

John is always knocking Jack. Silly.

In the form not punctuated as two sentences, there is a juncture point before *silly*, and one which shows by the pitch linkage which occurs that there is unity with what precedes. Moreover, exactly the same sort of pitch linkage can occur in:

Mary is always giving John books.

$$\overset{2}{/\text{mêriyz}} + \text{ôlwɨz} + \text{gîviŋ} + \overset{22}{\text{jáhn}} \mid \overset{331}{\text{búks}} \#/$$

As far as juncture points are concerned, then, the sequence *knocking Jack silly* seems to act exactly as a double complement should. There are distinctions between the several types of double complements, however. The type in which there is a modifier after the noun is one in which the semantic relation between the second complement and the first is still one of modification, while the double complement composed of two nouns or nominals has no such relation. The difference between the two types is found only in the form class to which the material in second-complement position belongs. Beyond this distinction, often shown by noun or adjective markers, the constructions are indistinguishable. Notice:

It made the water ice. $\overset{2}{/\text{ìt}} + \text{mêyd} + \text{ðǝ} + \overset{22}{\text{wótǝr}} \mid \overset{331}{\text{áys}} \#/$

It made the water icy. $\overset{2}{/\text{ìt}} + \text{mêyd} + \text{ðǝ} + \overset{22}{\text{wótǝr}} \mid \overset{33\ 1}{\text{áysiy}} \#/$

She made the guests ices. $\overset{2}{/\text{šìy}} + \text{mêyd} + \text{ðǝ} + \overset{22}{\text{gés}} + \text{s} \mid \overset{33\ 1}{\text{áysɨz}} \#/$

Each type of construction, further, leaves narrower semantic relations unsignaled. There are obvious semantic differences between "He ran the team ragged" and "He thought their play ragged," just as there are differences between "He called John a fool" and "He called John a taxi."

Our statement that a modifier following a noun complement is itself a second complement, yet is still in modifying relationship to the preceding material, is not without parallel in phrases which modify a preceding subject. Thus, the following sentences all contain modifying material set off by terminals from the subject and the predicator, but in all, the semantic relation is still one of modification:

$$2 \qquad 22 \quad 232 \quad 2 \qquad\qquad 3\,1$$
These books—both—are in French. /ðìyz + búks | bówθ | àr + ɨn + frénc #/

$$2 \qquad 22 \quad 2\,32 \quad 2 \qquad\qquad 31$$
Some dogs—Jack's—began to bark. /sɜ̀m + dɔ́gz | jǽks | bɨgǽn + tə + bárk #/

$$\qquad\qquad\qquad\text{\textit{The Thompsons, all three, came to the party.}}$$
$$2 \quad 2 \qquad 2 \quad 2 \quad 32 \quad 2 \qquad\qquad 3\,1$$
/ðə + táhm + sɨnz | ɔ̀l + θríy | kêym + tə + ðə + pártiy #/

All three of these sentences have been shown with pitch linkage, though the forms here transcribed are not intended to indicate that these are the only pitch morphemes which might be used in these sentences.

If it is granted that a noun-adjective sequence in postverbal position is indistinguishable from a noun-noun sequence except for the form class of the material following the first noun, a number of troublesome problems are easily solved. Yet, there remains the problem of immediate constituent analysis. There is no doubt that *knocking . . . silly* and *ran . . . ragged* in the sentences "John's always knocking Jack silly" and "He ran the team ragged" are both semantic units, replaceable by single words like *stunning* or *exhausted*. A cut into such discontinuous constituents presents the same problem as was found in cutting "John picked the books up" and is to be solved in the same way. That is, all double-complement sentences are to be cut so as to make verb and first complement into one of the first constituents, and second complement into the other. Thereafter the first complement is to be cut off, and at that point the verb and second complement in such sequences as *knock . . . silly* or *run . . . ragged* can be reassembled into semantic units.

The procedure of cutting just outlined is consistent, since it treats all double-complement sentences alike. If we should, on the other hand, have cut into units like *Jack silly* or the discontinuous *knocking . . . silly* we would have been inconsistent with the treatment of such sentences as "She told her husband a story." All analysts would be agreed that in this latter sentence, *a story* should be cut off as first constituent. We must therefore follow the same procedure with *knocking Jack silly*. As often, semantic linkages and structural units are different.

One of the formal distinctions which we are now ready to handle is that between an adjective or adjectival in second complement position and an overtly marked adverb. The following sentences make such a distinction:

> *Mary and John ate their dinner cold.*
> *Mary and John ate their dinner coldly.*
> (in a hostile manner toward each other)

The first sentence contains a second complement, and since *cold* is recognizable as an adjective, it is not surprising that it still may stand in modifying relation to the preceding noun. *Coldly*, on the other hand, is a recognizable adverb and consequently does not stand in a close modifying relationship to the preceding noun.

A somewhat similar problem is raised by the ambiguity in the sentence "She likes them fine," a type mentioned on page 304. One normal meaning might be "She likes them small," the other, "She likes them well." The usual analysis, making use of meaning to define the form class, assigns one use of *fine* to the class of adjectives, the other to that of adverbs. Such an analysis is to be rejected, and since the sentence is ambiguous, we must decide that *fine* is either adverb or adjective in both interpretations of the sentence, with exact meaning left to be cleared up, if at all, stylistically, as in:

> *John likes them coarse, but Mary likes them fine.*

If, then, there is no formal mark which distinguishes the function of *fine*, it must be assigned to a form class on the basis of those other situations in which its syntactic characteristics make it clear. Situations which are clear can be found in sentences like:

> *Jóhn rûns fíne #*
> *Fíne féathers | mâke fíne bírds #*
> *Mâry lîkes them fíner #*

In the second of these, *fine* cannot be an adverb, since it is occurring with secondary stress immediately before nouns in the same phrase. In the third, *finer* is shown to be an adjective by its postbase. In the first, it is not necessary to regard it as an adverb, since we have seen adjective complements in this position, as in "The stream *rûns réd.*" There is therefore no reason for calling *fine* an adverb at any time. It is an adjective of group III and is so in "She likes them fine." As with other adjectives of groups III and II, its exact relation to the rest of the sentence is left unsignaled when it is not in prenominal position. Even when the form class is clearly marked, by the addition of postbases to *fine*, there are uses which are semantically confusing, though the structure is clear. Notice:

> *She ground them finely.*
> *She ran it finer.*

The final word in each sentence is formally clear: the first is an adverb, the second an adjective. In accord with this distinction, each sentence has a probable meaning: the first is probably "She ground them well"; the second, "She ran it [so that it was finer than it had been]." Yet, in spite of probabilities, each sentence is somewhat ambiguous, and less probable interpretations are possible. For instance, the first might occur in such a situation as the following:

> *John gave them a coarse grind, but she ground them finely.*

And the second might be:

> *She may not have run it so cheap, but she ran it finer.*

In short, the several types of material which can follow a first complement are all characterized by semantic overlapping.

One group of double complements needs further discussion, and the formal characteristics which they show are often of importance to meaning. It will be remembered that a modifier of group I was defined as a noun placed in position immediately before another noun, as in "a stône house," thus becoming a nominal modifier. The group also contains true adjectives derived from nouns, as in "a stôny field." The nominal modifiers also were found in postverbal phrases, as in "All the houses were stone," where a noun proper would show inflection. That is, the sentence just quoted is now sufficient to establish nominal modifiers as complements. They can also serve as second complements, and since they are modifiers, they preserve this semantic function when they serve so. When such forms are treated as nouns—that is, inflected or accompanied by articles or the like—they then show the semantic characteristics of second nouns in double-complement constructions. A clear example of a distinction in meaning is the following pair, where the first shows *home* as a nominal modifier serving as second complement, and the second shows *home* as a true noun:

> *Mary found John home.*
> *Mary found John a home.*

Other examples of nominals of group I as second complements are:

> *Mary believed the dishes china.*
> *I like my cars American.*
> *Mary drove John west.*

Sometimes an uninflected form in such a position is structurally and semantically ambiguous, particularly if the noun form is one which can be treated as a mass noun, without an indefinite article. Notice the following:

>*Augustus found the city wood, but left it stone.*

The probability of interpretation is that *wood* and *stone* are nominal modifiers as second complements, but it is possible that the sentence might be expanded so as to give nouns:

>Augustus found the city *sòme wóod*, but left it *sòme stóne.*

A characteristic which nominals of group I show as second complements is correlated with the fact all these forms also occur as nouns. In many sentences omission of the first complement immediately forces the interpretation that the nominal is now a true noun. This shift occurs in "Augustus found the city wood." If *the city* is omitted, we immediately interpret *wood* as a noun, capable of being preceded by an article. The statement is by no means universally true, however, since often it is impossible to omit the first complement and still have a natural sentence. Notice that *John* cannot be omitted from "Mary found John home." Such a limitation, preventing occurrence as a complement unless preceded by a first complement, is true of many modifiers as second complements, though there are a good many exceptions correlated with the preceding verb. As we have said above, we can treat *hot* as a single complement by omission of the noun in "They got the drinks hot," but with *like*, omission of the first complement is not possible. The exceptions might be investigated by first listing those verb-adjective combinations where the adjective is a complement. That is, if we can have "John froze stiff," we should expect to find "John froze his fingers stiff," also. The type has been a good deal discussed, usually with a belief that adjective complements are somehow peculiar. The subject needs investigation from a more rigorously formal point of view.

We can now summarize our results for adjectives and adjectivals as complements. All adjectives and adjectivals, except the nonfinal forms of group v (determinatives) can stand as single complements, though as just intimated, not after all verbs. All can occur as second complements, though the type represented by *all* and *both* can also occur as postposed modifiers in the same construction with a preceding noun or pronoun. The *all, both* construction is structurally and semantically ambiguous, as in "She told them all." With all other modifiers, position after a noun complement always indicates that they are serving as second complements, though this fact does not prevent them from being still in the semantic function of modifiers. Structural ambiguity is produced only when there is doubt as to whether the second complement is an adjective (or adjectival) or a noun. Such structural ambiguity can be exemplified by "He found them wood." For all modifiers, however, there is semantic ambiguity since the relation of second complement to first, and to the whole of the sentence, is not narrowly signaled. Thus, we have semantic ambiguity, though the structure is clear in "She likes them fine."

We have thus far considered complements made up of nominal, pronominal, or adjectival material, either in single- or double-complement constructions. To the list of materials which can appear in complement position, we can briefly add that a complement may consist of some more or less isolated form, which is sufficiently outside the phonemic and morphological structure of the language so that it cannot be assigned to any form class. An instance of such an isolated form is the /b/ followed by a long trilled [r] which we conventionally use to indicate that we are cold. Such a form can occupy the position of a complement, or for that matter of a subjectival, as in:

He said "brr!" or *"Brr" is what he said.*

In general, such nonlinguistic forms do not occupy the position of the predicator or appear as integrated modifiers within a phrase. Their occurrence is limited to subjectival or complement function within the sentence, and though they are certainly not nouns, their limitation to positions in the sentence where nouns occur freely gives them a sort of quasi-nominal character.

4. Complements and adverbs

As well as nominal, pronominal, and adjectival material, forms which are recognizable as adverbs can occur in postverbal position. As a result, there are situations in which such an adverb might be analyzed as the complement, but before we pass on to sentences where this is so, it will be convenient to summarize the limitations on possible adverbial complements. First, an adverb preceded by a noun or pronoun never makes up a second complement. In this situation, an adverb made with the postbase {–liy} is preceded by a juncture point and is to be interpreted as adjunctival. Many adverbs in {–liy} are quite free in position, like *really*, which can occur before the subject, after it, after the verb, or after the complement, though in all these positions it is characteristically set off by terminals. Not all adverbs have equal freedom, but all can at least vary from postcomplement position. The following is a typical arrangement:

Really, I like John.

I really like John.   *I thoroughly like John.*

I like—really—John. (rare)

```
     2    3 2  23  2  33 1
```
/ày + láyk | ríhliy | jáhn #/

I like John, really.   *I like John thoroughly.*

Thoroughly is far more limited in position than *really*, but it still can occur elsewhere than in final position. It will be remembered that adverbs which can thus occur outside the sentence frame of subject, verb, and complement were spoken of as sentence adjuncts. *Really* is therefore such a form. Since *thoroughly* occurs in postcomplement position, with a juncture point before it, it is simpler to call *thoroughly* also a sentence adjunct than to set up a distinction on the basis of order characteristics alone.

A second position in which adverbs in {–liy} may appear is between verb and noun complement. Here, also, the adverb is set off by terminals and is a sentence adjunct. Notice the following examples:

He whispered, quietly, a name.
```
    2       3 2   2 2  2 2    31
```
/hìy + hwíspərd|kwáyitliy|ə + néym #/

The magician produced, suddenly, a rabbit.
```
    2                    3 2  22  2 2   3 1
```
/ði + məjišin + prə + dúwst|sádinliy|ə + ræbit #/

Adverbs in {–liy} are somewhat uncommon in this position, as the somewhat bookish flavor of the quoted sentences might suggest. Far commoner is an adverb before an adjective or adjectival which in turn is placed before a noun or prepositional phrase. Examples are:

```
    2                    31
```
He shôt nèarly twênty dúcks #
```
    2              3      1
```
He âte pràctically áll of thèm #

The juncture pattern of these sentences demonstrates that we are dealing with a different type of construction. If there is a terminal, it will normally fall before the adverb:

```
    2 32    2            31
```
He shôt | nèarly twênty dúcks #
```
    2 32    2         3      1
```
He âte | pràctically áll of thèm #

That is, in this normal arrangement, the adverb is to be construed with what follows and is therefore a part of the phrase which makes up the complement. Variant treatment is possible, though unlikely, even for sentences employing these particular adverbs. Notice:

$$\text{He áte} \mid \text{práctically} \mid \text{áll of thèm} \#$$
2 32   22   2 33   1

In such a treatment, the adverb would be a sentence adjunct, not a part of the complement. I should gloss such a sentence as meaning much the same thing as "He practically ate all of them," that is, *practically* cannot modify *all* unless it is in the same phrase with it.

A remaining position in which an adverb can occur is immediately before the verb, or before a verbal form preceded by a first verb. Here the treatment varies, since adverbs in this position may be set off by terminals or may be without them:

He quietly whispered a name.

Such a sentence, if the juncture points which set off the subject and complement are filled, may be either:

```
232      2          3    2    2    31
/híy | kwàyɨtliy + hwíspərd | ə + néym #/ or
222     23   2     33   2    2    31
/híy | kwáyɨtliy | hwíspərd | ə + néym #/
```

The alternate treatment here produces no particular change in meaning, but does produce a change in structure. That is, when the adverb is set off by terminals, it is to be treated as a sentence adjunct, similar to the treatment of such an adverb when it occurs initially or finally. When there is no such isolation from the following verb by means of terminals, it is then to be treated as part of the verb phrase. When the adverb appears within the verb phrase, we have a somewhat similar juncture situation, as in:

He was nearly killed by the accident.

Here *nearly* can be given tertiary stress and be treated as part of the verb phrase, to be construed with what follows. If, however, it is set off by terminals and given full stress, we cannot very easily call it a sentence adjunct, since to do so gives us a discontinuous predicator, a type of analysis which we have tried to avoid whenever it is possible to do so. But though stress and juncture conditions do not solve the difficulty for us, fortunately pitch linkage does. The sentence we have just quoted has several forms:

```
2                        32    2        3    1
/hìy + wɨz + nìhrliy + kíld | bayðiy + ǽksɨdɨnt #/
```

This form, in which *nearly* is not set off by terminals, offers no difficulty; we have a single predicator which happens to contain an adverb.

$$2 \qquad 32 \quad 2 \qquad\qquad 4\,2 \quad 2 \qquad\qquad 3 \qquad 1$$
/hìy + wáhz | nìhrliy + kíld | bayðiy + ǽksidɨnt #/

In this form, the complex contour of {2 3 2 |} and {2 4 2 |} indicates that we are still dealing with a unified construction, though one now consisting of two phrases. In this particular juncture arrangement, *nearly* is placed in the same phrase with *killed* and is therefore to be construed as modifying it. In the first form, the relation of *nearly* to the surrounding verb forms is less explicitly signaled, but would normally be interpreted as the same as in the second form of the sentence. A third form of the sentence is:

$$2 \qquad 22 \quad 23 \quad 2 \quad 442 \quad 2 \qquad\qquad 3 \qquad 1$$
/hìy + wɔ́z | níhrliy | kíld | bayðiy + ǽksidɨnt #/

In this form we have *nearly* treated as a phrase, but with pitch linkage, showing that the predicator is still a unified construction. In this form, the sentence offers some ambiguity in my idiolect, since it is impossible to say whether *nearly* is to be construed with what follows or with what precedes. It is not to be thought that these variant pronunciations are all that are possible for this particular sentence. Those given are merely typical, and intended to show that the possibility of pitch linkage can be relied on to indicate that an adverb which interrupts the parts of a predicator need not be taken as the same thing as a sentence adjunct, even when it is set off by terminals.

In dealing with adverbs in {-liy} we have then discovered several possibilities. The adverb may be an independent sentence adjunct, in which case it may be set off by terminals but without pitch linkage. If an adjunct, it may appear initially, finally, before the verb, or before the complement. If the adverb appears within the parts of the predicator, it remains a part of the predicator construction even if set off by terminals, since in this construction pitch linkage is possible. Negatively, we have also said that a postposed adverb never forms a second complement. By implication we have also made it clear that an adverb between a verb and a noun complement does not form a first complement, since in this situation we have called the adverb a sentence adjunct.

There is one situation in which it might be possible that an adverb could form a complement—a situation in which there is a verb, an adverb, and no following nominal or pronominal complement. Sentences of this type are, of course, extremely common:

He talked quietly.   *He died suddenly.*
He bought extravagantly.   *He sang loudly.*

For interpretation of these sentences we have a precedent in the analysis we gave to preverbal adverbs. In that situation we interpreted the structure differently, in accord with whether or not there was a terminal present. We shall do the same here, since all of these sentences can be pronounced with or without /||/ and without pitch linkage if /||/ occurs:

2   3   1   2   3 2   3 3   1
/hìy + tɔ̂hk + kwáyìtliy #/ or /hìy + tɔ́hk + t | kwáyìtliy #/

Thus, when verb and adverb form a single phrase, with characteristic final position of the primary stress, it would seem simplest to define the adverb as a member of the predicator and the sentence as an order variant of a predicator with preceding adverb, where the stress again falls finally. Such sentences are then made up of subject and predicator, with no complement.

When the sentences of this type contain a final adverb preceded by /||/, it is clear that the adverb cannot be a member of the predicator. On the other hand, it is certainly in a position where we would expect a complement, and we have furthermore stated that a complement is preceded by a juncture point. We have, however, found no other situations in which an adverb can form a complement, and we have already seen a situation in which a sentence-final adverb can occur, not as a complement, but as a sentence adjunct. We will therefore produce a consistent analysis if we also call these final adverbs in sentences without a nominal complement sentence adjuncts. Our final position must then be that an adverb can form a member of a noun phrase as complement, but can never form a complement alone, even when set off by terminals. Thus, a set of sentences such as the following are of different structure:

> *He sang loud.*
>
>   2   3   1
> *He sang loudly.*   /hìy + sæ̀ŋ + láwdliy #/
>   2   32   33   1
> *He sang, loudly.*   /hìy + sæ̀ŋ | láwdliy #/

The first sentence contains subject, verb, and adjective complement. The second contains subject and predicator made up of verb and following adverb. The third contains subject, verb, and sentence adjunct.

The adverbs so far discussed are those formed by the postbase {–liy}. As well as these forms, there is a second set called adverbs much more limited in position than adverbs in {–liy}, namely, the forms like *up*. These forms, further, are not marked by postbases and are (as we have said several times) homonymous except for stress characteristics with prepositions. Like other adverbs, these forms can never act as complements, and such a sentence as "John drove up" is therefore without a complement, just as "John drove slowly" is without a complement. There is a striking difference between adverbs like *up* and adverbs like *slowly*, however. No juncture point without pitch linkage falls before the adverbs without postbases. "John drove up" is always either:

$$\begin{array}{ccccc} 2 & 31 & 2 & 32 & 441 \\ \end{array}$$
/jâhn + drôwv + ə́p #/ or /jâhn + dró̇wv | ə́p #/

In such sentences, therefore, the adverbs without postbase are always members of the predicator, whereas the adverbs in {–liy} are not members of the predicator unless preceded by no terminal juncture. In line with this difference is the fact that the final adverb in "John drove slowly" may be preceded by *very*, whereas such expansion does not occur in "John drove up." Further, the adverbs without postbases only rarely occur in other positions, the only variation in this particular sentence being "Up drove John." The order found in this variation gives a sentence of a somewhat surprising superfix pattern, since it is either:

$$\begin{array}{ccccc} 33 & 1 & 33 & 2 & 331 \\ \end{array}$$
/ə́p + dròwv + jâhn #/ or /ə́p + drôwv | jáhn #/

It is also striking that the number of sentences in which this variation in order occurs is limited. Thus, such a sentence as "John acted up" cannot be transposed. Further, the order in these sentences is not that of "Quietly, he talked," where the adverb is placed before the subject. The "Up drove John" type can then be described as idiomatic, rather than one which is possible for all verb and adverb combinations. Since there is no juncture point after the adverb, the *up drove* construction can be defined as a special sort of predicator with preposed (and stressed) adverb.

In dealing with adverbs like *up* it will be remembered that we analyzed the sentence "John picked the books up" as containing a discontinuous predicator,[7] so that these sentences do not contain double complements. The adverbs like *up* are then like the adverbs in {–liy} in not forming double complements, even though there are syntactic and semantic differences between "John picked the books up" and "Mary found John up." Both have discontinuous predicators, though there is no example of a continuous *find up* to compare with the continuous *pick up*. The semantic difference is paralleled, however, by that in an ambiguous sentence frame like "John found —— out." If the blank is filled by *Mary*, the interpretation may be either "John found that Mary was out" or "John discovered the truth about Mary." The forms of the class of *up*, which we have treated as adverbs or prepositions according to their stress, can occur in two other types of constructions, however. They can occur after forms of the verb *to be* in sentences

---

[7] See above, Chap. 16, Section 4.

like "John is up," and they can occur before nouns, with secondary stress, as in *the úp tráin*. In neither of these situations is an adverb in {-liy} possible. We must add to our list of the functions of the group of forms like *up* that many of them can occur in positions which identify them as adjectivals or adjectives. In *the up train*, *up* is to be identified as adjective, since we have parallel forms like *the upper layer*; in "John is up," *up* would be identified as adjectival or adjective according to whether such a sentence as "John is upper than he usually is" is regarded as possible or not. Such adjective and adjectival occurrences are not possible for all of the adverb-preposition forms; *by* is one of the adverb-prepositions, but it does not occur before nouns with secondary stress; that is, *bypass* has, in my idiolect, only the compound stress /ˊ ˋ/. Yet *by* can still appear in complement position, as in "Don't pass through until the funeral *is by*." Apparently single-complement position is characteristic of the whole group, constituting a final syntactic difference between them and adverbs in {-liy}.

5. Complements and prepositional phrases

A set of problems somewhat similar to those found with adverbs arises with the analysis of prepositional phrases in relation to main sentence elements. A first statement, however, can be made about one class of prepositional phrase, in line with what has already been said about predicators. A prepositional phrase consisting of *to* and a following infinitive is normally a part of the predicator, as in "John *tries to be* kind." A second such preliminary statement is that there are a number of prepositional phrases consisting of an adjectival, *of*, and following pronoun which function as sentence elements, either subjects or complements. Examples of one of these constructions as subject are:

All of it goes away.   and   *All of them* go away.

It is clear here that the phrase is a true subject, since there is selection of the verb form in accord with *it* and *them*. Examples as complements are then:

John ate *all of it*.   and   John ate *all of them*.

The most interesting characteristic of these constructions is that it is the pronoun which forms the head, since in subject position it is the pronoun which selects the verb form. In other prepositional phrases, such as those in which the first and last forms are nouns, it is not the noun which follows the preposition which thus selects, but rather the noun which precedes, which is therefore the head:

The house with the seven gables is in Salem.

The type represented by *all of it, all of them* is found when the first member is any one of the three group VI adjectivals, that is, *all, both*, and *half*, though of course, *both* does not occur in this construction with a following singular form. This type also occurs with the prenominal form *some*[8] as in:

> *Sóme of ìt* is red.   and   *Sóme of thèm* are red.

The type is also found if the final member of the phrase is a noun, as in:

> *Âll of the hôuse* is stone.   and   *Âll of the hôuses* are stone.

Prepositional phrases beginning with other adjectives and adjectivals also make up single phrases, but it is the first form which is then the head. Notice:

> *One of the houses* is red.   and   *Two of the houses* are red.
> *Each of the houses* is red.

With adjectives and adjectivals of the other groups, however, the group of modifier-preposition-noun (or pronoun) does not stand as subject, but only as complement. Examples are:

> That was *kind of them.*   That was *fine for Jack.*
> John was *afraid of him.*   Milk is *good for children.*

With this last group, junctures are possible before the prepositions. In every instance, introduction of a terminal not only modifies the stress pattern but gives the possibility of a different construction, with changed possibilities of order and some difference in meaning. The normal pattern for the first sentence is:

$$\overset{2}{/ð\text{æt}} + \text{wiz} + \overset{3}{\text{káyndəv}} + \overset{1}{ð\text{im}} \#/$$

If a single bar is introduced, we then get:

$$\overset{2}{/ð\text{æt}} + \text{wiz} + \overset{32}{\text{káynd}} \mid \overset{2}{\text{əv}} + \overset{31}{ð\text{ém}} \#/$$

This can then be transposed to:

$$\overset{2}{/\text{əv}} + \overset{32}{ð\text{ém}} \mid \overset{2}{ð\text{æt}} + \text{wiz} + \overset{32}{\text{káynd}} \#/$$

Or even:

$$\overset{232}{/ð\text{æt}} \mid \overset{2}{\text{əv}} + \overset{32}{ð\text{ém}} \mid \overset{2}{\text{wiz}} + \overset{31}{\text{káynd}} \#/$$

---

[8] The prenominals *each* and *some* are not fully described, though their characteristics can be summarized by calling them adjectivals which do not fit into the series of modifier groups. See above, pp. 188–89.

In these sentences, the variations in order, with minimal linkage, suggest that we are dealing with sentence adjuncts. Further, there is at least some change in meaning, since all of these sentences treating *of them* as a separate phrase introduce contrast, suggesting that for others, not named, the same actions might not be kind. The contrast in meaning comes out much more sharply in a sentence like the following:

They gave him a seat by Jupiter.
2   3   1
/ðèy + gêyvimə + sîyt + bày + júwpitər #/

Suppose now we introduce a terminal before *by*, modifying the stresses as required but leaving the pitches unmarked:

/ðèy + gêyvimə + síyt | bày + júwpitər #/

This particular transcription is ambiguous, and has been deliberately chosen, since it gives us a chance to be more explicit about pitch linkage than we have been as yet. Suppose the pitch morphemes are either {2 2 2 |} {2 3 1 #} or {2 3 2 |} {2 4 1 #}, then the sentence is a variation of the one we have already given, with the meaning "They gave him a seat beside Jupiter." If, on the other hand, the pitch morphemes are {2 3 1 |} {1 1 1 #}, the sentence is quite different, and would be written "They gave him a seat, by Jupiter!"

Of these several forms of pitch linkage, the third is clearest. This monotone morpheme, continuing the final pitch of the preceding, is characteristic of dependent sentences. Thus, we can describe "by Jupiter!" in the last utterance as a dependent, elementless sentence, rather than a sentence adjunct. It is to be noted that this kind of linkage characteristically makes the monotone morpheme dependent on the preceding morpheme.

The sequence {2 3 2 |} {2 4 1 #} is a typical complex contour. Such a sequence, like the one described above, makes the second pitch morpheme dependent on the first, but indicates that a unified construction has been broken into two phrases. It should not be thought, however, that all instances of morphemes containing /4/ are examples of linkage. For instance, a pitch ·/4/ occurs without attachment to a previous /4/ and without linkage when it occurs isolated or following the morpheme {2 3 1 #}. In such a situation, such a morpheme as {2 4 1 #} indicates merely an emphatic statement, as in:

2   41
It's good! /ìt + s + gúd #/

The remaining form of the sentence we have been discussing is that with the morphemes {2 2 2 |} {2 3 1 #}. That is to say, a form in which the monotone morpheme precedes a morpheme with a contour rather than follows a morpheme with a contour. In this situation, where {2 2 2 |} is preceded only by silence and followed by a morpheme beginning with /2/, the simplest interpretation is to assume that it indicates dependence on what follows. To do so, in this situation, is to make the sequence {2 2 2 |} {2 3 1 #} another instance of a single contour, {2 3 1 #}, which has been broken into two phrases. In situations where {2 2 2 |} is preceded by silence, this is an unambiguous interpretation. There are, however, instances of {2 3 2 |} {2 2 2 |} {2 3 1 #}, as in the previously quoted "He didn't want to be so—rudely—forced to leave." In such instances, the monotone {2 2 2 |} does not demonstrate on which of the surrounding morphemes it is dependent. It merely demonstrates dependence, and in such instances interpretation must therefore depend on the expected forms of the construction when no terminals set off parts of it.

The ambiguity in interpretation is due to the fact that /2/ frequently ends phrases and even more frequently begins them. There are still possibilities in linkage of pitch morphemes into larger unified pitch superfixes which have not been investigated. It is clear that linkage can occur across the boundary of phrases separated by /|/. Linkage can occur across a /#/, as has been said, if the following morpheme is a monotone. An instance can be found from one of the previously quoted sentences, which has not been transcribed—"Milk is good for children." This might have the form:

$$\begin{array}{ccccc} & 2 & 31 & 1 & 1 & 1 \end{array}$$
Milk is good—for children. /mîhk + iz + gúd # fər + cíldrin #/

Linkage can also occur across a /|||/. An example can be found in the following:

$$\begin{array}{ccccc} & 2 & 33 & 3 & 3 & 4 \end{array}$$
What's that? A house? /hwât + s + ðǽt || ə + háws |||/

This pronunciation, of course, is somewhat special, since the normal sequences would be the unlinked {2 3 1 #} {2 2 3 ||}, or the like. The linkage is to be described as of the complex contour type in which a morpheme containing /4/ is related to a previous morpheme containing /3/.

We can now use these characteristics of pitch linkage to return to the group of sentences containing prepositional phrases and to make some formal decisions about them. We have already seen that a sentence like "That was kind of them" can be pronounced with no contained terminals. When this type of pronunciation is given, the final prepositional construction is a part of the complement. We have also seen that the sentence could be pronounced with a /|/ before *of* and the minimally linked morphemes {2 3 2 |} {2 3 1 #}. This type of pronunciation can be used for the whole

group of sentences, and whenever used, it indicates that the final prepositional phrase is now a sentence adjunct, capable of being varied in position
as any sentence adjunct is.

The whole group of sentences can be treated as more than one phrase,
with minimal pitch linkage. Yet, if given pitch linkage, there may be two
types, resulting in different structural interpretations. Suppose the linkage
is of the following type:

$$\begin{array}{cccc} 2 & 32 & 2 & 41 \end{array}$$
$$/ðæt + wiz + káynd \mid əv + ðém \#/$$

The complex contour indicates that a unified construction has been broken
into two phrases, so that we must suppose that in this pronunciation the
prepositional phrase is a part of the complement. Finally, the sentence may
have:

$$\begin{array}{cccc} 2 & 31 & 1 & 11 \end{array}$$
$$/ðæt + wiz + káynd \# əv + ðém \#/$$

In this form, we have a following dependent sentence of the elementless
type, exactly like "They gave him a seat, by Jupiter!"

There are instances of sentences in which there is a final prepositional
construction where the freedom in juncture and pitch is not so great. Such
a sentence is "He sailed north by east." For this sentence the normal
pronunciation is:

$$\begin{array}{cc} 2 & 3\ 1 \end{array}$$
$$/hìy + sêyld + nɔ̂rθ + bày + íyst \#/$$

If it is broken into two phrases, there is pitch linkage of the complex contour
type, {2 3 2 |} {2 4 1 #}, or the equivalent, {2 2 2 |} {2 3 1 #}. That is, it
is impossible to treat "by east" as a dependent sentence of the "by Jupiter"
type.

There are a number of miscellaneous sentences which involve linkage
of sufficient interest to warrant further discussion. One of the most interesting
is the following supplied by a friend:

$$\begin{array}{cccccc} 2 & & 3 & 2 & 44 & 1 \end{array}$$
Thânk whoêver brôught the tówel dòwn | fór mè #

The linkage type is familiar, a complex contour which merely indicates
that a unified construction has been broken into two phrases. The surprising
thing about the construction is the meaning. In several idiolects on which
the sentence has been tested, it means "Thank for me the person who
brought the towel down." There seems to be nothing in the nature of the
construction that requires such an interpretation. What has happened is
apparently that a construction has been extended to a greater length than

a single morpheme will bear, forcing breakup. This, in turn, requires an interpretation that is different from the interpretation of a sentence in which the prepositional phrase is attached to the nearest possibility. That is, the sentence is merely different from:

$$
\begin{array}{ccccc}
2 & & 3 \ 2 & 2 & 3 \ 1 \\
\end{array}
$$

Thânk whoêver brôught the tówel | dòwn fór mè #

This kind of overweighting and consequent breakup is of course, the phenomenon that H. L. Smith treated in his example *air-raid warden | defense post | stairway* or *the Port of New York Authority | ticket book | sales office* discussed by Weinreich and Stockwell.[9] All of the constructions show pitch linkage by complex contours.

Another sentence of some interest is:

John left Mary with the children.

If given as a single phrase with $\{2\ 3\ 1\ \#\}$ the sentence is ambiguous and may mean either that he left her at home or elsewhere temporarily or that he deserted his family. If it is given with $\{2\ 3\ 2\ |\}\ \{2\ 4\ 1\ \#\}$ the structure is clear, but the ambiguity remains, as indeed it also does if the pitch superfix is $\{2\ 4\ 2\ |\}\ \{2\ 2\ 2\ \#\}$. A final possibility is the contrastive $\{2\ 4\ 2\ |\}$ $\{2\ 4\ 1\ \#\}$, which may at first sight seem semantically clear but turns out, I believe, to be no clearer than any of the others when given closer examination. That is, ambiguity remains no matter what type of structure is given to the sentence. Nor, for that matter, have the two interpretations we have suggested for the sentence exhausted all the semantic possibilities. Does the sentence mean, for instance, that the children were taken by John or that they are still with Mary?

Thus the signals which the language gives for prepositional constructions of this sort are limited to identification of the prepositional material as part of the complement, whether it consists of one or two phrases; as sentence adjuncts set off by terminals with minimal pitch linkage; or, finally, as dependent elementless sentences. Each type of construction involves semantic ambiguities, and as usual these can be resolved only by choosing the stylistically most probable interpretation. We need go no further with these ambiguities except to point out that the following two sentences are of the same constructional type, yet involve different semantic relations:

The snow was piled high by the wind.
The snow was piled high by the door.

Before we leave the noun-preposition-noun construction, we can point

---

[9] See above, p. 113.

to one other mark of difference between, on the one hand, the sequence which either has no included terminal or has it only with linkage by complex contour and, on the other hand, the type where a terminal may occur with minimal linkage. A contrasting pair is:

> *I dream of Jeannie with the light-brown hair.*
> *I dream of Jeannie with delight.*

The first sentence contains no juncture point without linkage by complex contour. The second may be broken into two minimally linked phrases. The first may receive a {–z} suffix, giving something like "I dream of Jeannie with the light-brown hair's marriage." The sentence may be awkward, it is true, but is still possible. On the other hand, "I dream of *Jeannie with delight's* marriage" is impossible, since it makes a sort of pseudo proper name of *Jeannie-with-delight.*

We have, then, at least established that a prepositional construction following a noun, pronoun, or adjective which is in complement position does not act as a second complement. If a terminal is present, the treatment of the prepositional material is various, and there is considerable semantic ambiguity.

The remaining position in which a prepositional construction may occur is following the predicator, when there is no preceding complement form. A pair of examples, somewhat different in their behavior, are:

> *John went to town.*
> *John sings in the shower.*

Both sentences may be without terminals:

$$
\begin{array}{l}
2 3\,1 \\
\text{/jâhn + wên + t\partial + táwn } \#/ \\
2 3 1 \\
\text{/jâhn + sî\eta z + in + ð\partial + šáwər } \#/
\end{array}
$$

If the first receives a terminal, there is very apt to be linkage by a complex contour:

$$
\begin{array}{l}
2 2\,2 2 3 1 \\
\text{/jâhn + wént | t\partial + táwn } \#/
\end{array}
$$

A terminal in the second sentence is much less likely to produce a complex contour:

$$
\begin{array}{l}
2 32 2 3 2 \\
\text{/jâhn + sí\eta z | in + ð\partial + šáwər } \#/
\end{array}
$$

In accord with this difference in pitch and juncture behavior, the prepositional construction in the second sentence can be called a sentence adjunct. As we should expect, it is then a sentence in which the order "In the shower, John sings" is quite possible. Its status as a sentence adjunct explains why it is possible to introduce a complement before it, as in "John sings sentimental songs, in the shower." Complements can be introduced into the first sentence, it is true, but they are rather semantically limited, all being nouns having to do with distance:

$$
\begin{array}{cc}
2 & 3\,1 \\
\textit{John went} \mid \textit{twô mîles to tówn} \,\#
\end{array}
$$
$$
\begin{array}{cc}
2 & 3\,1 \\
\textit{John went} \mid \textit{the lông wây to tówn} \,\#
\end{array}
$$

Thus far, we have found no difference between the two prepositional sentences except one of pitch linkage. But if we now vary the position of the prepositional constructions and the added complement, we find another distinction. The first sentence becomes:

2   3 2   2   3 1
John went to town, two miles. /jâhn + wèn + tə + táwn | tûw + máylz #/

John went to town, the long way.

2   3 2   2   3 1
/jâhn + wèn + tə + táwn | ðə + lɔ́ŋ + wéy #/

The second sentence becomes one in which a terminal before the prepositional construction is not merely possible but required:

John sings, in the shower, sentimental songs.

2   3 2 2   3 2   2   3 1
/jâhn + síŋz | in + ðə + šáwər | sêntimèntəl + sóhŋz #/

The only variation possible on this type of structure, when this order is used, is to break the utterance into two sentences, giving:

2   3 1   2   3 1
/jâhn + sîŋz + in + ðə + šáwər # sêntimèntəl + sóhŋz #/

The same two-sentence form is, of course, possible for the first sentence:

2   3 1   2   3 1
/jâhn + wèn + tə + táwn # tûw + máylz #/

Since the two-sentence shape is possible for both sequences, it is of no diagnostic value. What is significant is the required terminals setting off *in the shower* when a noun complement follows. The sequence *in the shower* acts, therefore, exactly like an adverbial adjunct, which in the same position would also require terminals:

2   32   23 2   2   3 1
/jâhn + síŋz | láwdliy | sêntimèntəl + sóhŋz #/

In the shower, however, is different from *to town*. A terminal is possible before *to town*, but certainly less likely than before *in the shower*. But since a terminal is possible in both sentences, the juncture situation cannot be safely used as a diagnostic of the difference between the two constructions. The difference would seem to lie in the substitution characteristics of the two forms. In the sentence "John went to town, two miles" it is quite possible to place a sentence adjunct, such as *quietly*, before *to town*, setting the adjunct off by terminals. Such an arrangement suggests that *to town* is at least not a part of the predicator. It is also not a sentence adjunct, since it does not occur in such a pitch pattern as the following:

$$\text{2 \qquad 32 \quad 2 \quad 32 \quad 2 \qquad 31}$$
$$\text{*/jâhn + wént | tə + táwn | tûw + máylz #/}$$

That is, it does not have the pattern we have found for *in the shower* when it is placed before the complement. If *to town* is not a part of the predicator and not a sentence adjunct, the remaining possibility is that it is a complement. Our analysis will be simplified if we adopt this decision. If we say that when it follows the predicator immediately, it is a complement, we then have no difficulty in explaining the appearance of a sentence adjunct before it. It should be emphasized, however, that the problem we face in analyzing *went to town* is less important than that of separating this sequence from *sang in the shower*. For this separation, once more, we must rely on the characteristics of the phrase under examination when a noun complement is added. The juncture and pitch characteristics of *in the shower* in that situation are what identify it as an adjunct. Once thus identified, its greater freedom of order becomes understandable.

There are a number of questions left over, however. A typical prepositional phrase which acts as a complement is *at Mary* in "John looked at Mary." It is not a sentence adjunct, since if we add a complement such as *three times*, we get:

$$\text{2 \qquad\qquad 3 \ 2 \quad 2 \qquad 31}$$
$$\text{/jâhn + lûk + tit + méhriy | θrîy + táymz #/}$$

That is, there is no required juncture before *at Mary*, as there would be were it an adjunct. We must then assume that it is a complement, and since *three times* is also a complement, the sentence must be one which contains two complements. What happens, however, if the noun complement comes first, as in:

$$\text{2 \qquad\qquad 3 \ 2 \quad 2 \quad 3 \ 1}$$
$$\textit{Jôhn lôoked dággers | at Máry #}$$

In spite of the semantic linkage between *look* and *at*, established by the fact that a single form like *see* is often substitutable for the sequence, *at Mary* in this sentence is treated differently from the treatment it gets in a sentence without such a preceding noun complement. The possibilities now are that it could form a modifier of the preceding complement, a total phrase *daggers at Mary*. This possibility can be ruled out, on the grounds of the juncture and pitch pattern. The second possibility is that *at Mary* is now a sentence adjunct, which is suggested by the juncture and pitch pattern and borne out by the fact that it is now possible to vary the position of the phrase.

Suppose we now have two prepositional phrases, as in the set:

2   3 2 2   3 1
Jôhn lôoked at Máry | wìth compássion #
2   32   2   3 2   2 3 1
Jôhn lóoked | wìth compássion | at Máry #
2   3 2   2   3 1
Wìth compássion | Jôhn lôoked at Máry #
2   3 2 2   3   1
Àt Máry | Jôhn lôoked wìth compássion #

It is clear, both from the juncture and pitch pattern and from the order characteristics, that *with compassion* is not a second complement but is rather a sentence adjunct. Thus our first sentence contains a single complement, *at Mary*. The same complement is contained in the third sentence, but there the adjunct is placed in initial position. In the second sentence, *with compassion* is still an adjunct, and the position which *at Mary* assumes in the fourth sentence shows that it also is an adjunct when it does not immediately follow the predicator.

We can now put several of these statements together into two general rules. First, a prepositional construction does not form a complement if it is separated from the predicator by an intervening phrase or sentence element. Second, there cannot be a double complement consisting of two prepositional constructions. An instructive example of the first rule is the following contrast, where the difference in structure is reflected in a difference in meaning:

John looked right at Mary.
2   32 2   3 1   2   3 1
/jâhn + lúkt | ràytìt + méhriy #/ or /jâhn + lûkt + ràytit + méhriy #/

With or without /||/ after the predicator, this sentence has a single complement consisting of *at Mary* preceded by an adverb. It is to be interpreted as "directly at Mary."

2   32   23 2 2   3 1
John looked—right—at Mary. /jâhn + lúkt | ráyt | ət + méhriy #/

Right is here a first adjunct, meaning "to the right," and *at Mary* then becomes a second adjunct.

The only instance, then, in which there can be a double complement, one of which is a prepositional phrase, occurs when the prepositional phrase immediately follows the predicator and is in turn followed by a noun complement. The example already given is:

John looked at Mary, three times.

Other examples are:

John puts on the dog—a lot.
John gave to his work—years of devotion.
John brought up his children Americans.

The examples are sufficient to show that this kind of construction can signal very different kinds of semantic relations, depending on the kind of semantic material which fills it. Such diversity of meaning is no more surprising with this set of constructions than it is with the following pair:

John brought the bacon home.
John brought home the bacon.

Both are double-complement sentences, structurally alike. For the first the meaning is clear. For the second the meaning may be the same as for the first, but may also be "John had an important success." It is the change in order which alone produces the semantic difference.

Double-complement sentences have a special relation to sentences containing both a complement and a prepositional phrase. That is, the double-complement sentence "John gave Mary a book" is a semantic equivalent to "John gave a book to Mary." But though there is semantic equivalence, the two sentences are structurally different. It is a serious mistake to equate the two structures, by any such procedure as describing *Mary* as "the object of the preposition *to*, understood." Such a procedure takes no account of the difference in order between the form of the sentence without preposition and that with it. In our analysis, "John gave Mary a book" ends with a second complement which is invariant in order. The sequence *to Mary* has the freedom of order we should expect of a sentence adjunct, since though it usually falls in final position, "To Mary, John gave a book" and "John gave, to Mary, a book" are both possible. Moreover these forms have the juncture and pitch pattern of a sentence adjunct.

Our treatment of prepositional phrases concludes our survey of complements. We can now give a final definition of the term, since we now know what kinds of material can form sentence elements of this type. Complements can consist of nominal or pronominal material, which normally follows the predicator. The nominal or pronominal material must be more narrowly defined as that which lacks the selectional characteristics of the subject and, with pronouns, that which lacks the subjective case form. Again, while it is normal for the nominal or pronominal complement to follow the predicator, if it is otherwise distinguished from the subject or subjectival, it may vary in order, as in "Two friends have I." Adjectives and adjectivals are complements when they follow the predicator in a position where they cannot be taken as members of a larger complement. This statement is taken to cover not only such sentences as "His hair turned white" but also sentences with group I modifiers, as in "They seemed American" and "He went home."

Prepositional constructions can act as complements only if they immediately follow the predicator, and under rules which we have just given. Adverbs, on the other hand, never function as complements, since they appear only as sentence adjuncts or as parts of the verb or complement.

Double complements, finally, consist of two noun constructions or of pronoun and noun. It is a point which has not been emphasized that double-complement constructions include sentences such as "He studies law nights," "He drove the car three miles," "He eats an apple a day," "It comes to a dollar a pound," and many more, as well as the sentences like "John gave Mary a book." That is, in our analysis of double complements we made no distinction between so-called adverbial uses of nouns and second complements, since the language offers no structural signal by which they can be distinguished.

Double complements can also consist of a limited number of group I modifiers with an additional noun complement, as in "He drove the car west," "He drove the car home," and "He brought home the car." The remaining double-complement construction consists of a prepositional construction immediately after the verb, with a following noun. In this last type, the prepositional phrase has a juncture point before it, and if the juncture occurs the linkage is minimal. If the juncture is required, the prepositional phrase is a sentence adjunct.

We do not take up those instances in which a construction which has all the characteristics of a sentence occupies the position of a complement, just as we did not take up this type of construction fully under subjectivals. These constructions will be handled in dealing with dependent sentences, in Chapter 19. Some instances of unclassifiable and usually extralinguistic material can, however, appear as complements, in sentences like "John went 'brr!'"

6. Adjuncts

Much of the discussion of adjunct sentence elements has been anticipated in discussing sentence elements of the three other types. Stated most briefly, sentence adjuncts are words or phrases not definable as subject, verb, or complement or as parts of those three sentence elements. They are characteristically set off by terminals with minimal linkage, and these terminals are required except when the sentence adjunct follows the complement, in which case the juncture may be lost. When lost, however, the juncture point remains. Characteristic sentence adjunct material consists of prepositional phrases and overtly marked adverbs. In a sentence consisting of the normal elements of subject, verb, and complement, an adjunct has four possible positions, since it may occur initially, finally, or between any two sentence elements. Thus, if we take the sentence

SUBJ.   VERB   COMPL.

The council   holds   meetings

we can add to it an adjunct consisting of the adverb *frequently*, or the prepositional phrase *in our town*. We get, then, the following sets:

> *Frequently, the council holds meetings.*
> 3   3   2   2   3   1
> /fríykwìntliy | ðə + kâwnsil + hôwlz + míytiŋz #/

> *The council—frequently—holds meetings.*
> 2   3   2   3 3   2   2   3   1
> /ðə + káwnsil | fríykwìntliy | hôwlz + míytiŋz #/

> *The council holds—frequently—meetings.*
> 2   3 2   3 3   2   33 1
> /ðə + kâwnsil + hówlz | fríykwìntliy | míytiŋz #/

> *The council holds meetings frequently.*
> 2   3   2   3 3   1
> /ðə + kâwnsil + hôwlz + míytiŋz | fríykwìntliy #/ or
> 2   3   1
> /ðə + kâwnsil + hôwlz + mîytiŋz + fríykwìntliy #/

Exactly the same set of order variations occurs with the prepositional phrase *in our town*, but with slightly different juncture conditions. With the adverbial adjunct, the sequence *frequently holds* becomes a single predicator, with *frequently* reduced to a component of it if the juncture is absent and the proper stress pattern is given. With the prepositional phrase, it is the sequence *the council in our town* which is thus subject to juncture loss, with change of status for the prepositional group, which then becomes a component of the subject. It is to be noted that for both adjuncts, loss of juncture when they occur in final position does not change their status. The fact that juncture may be lost here is apparently the reason that native speakers do not always react clearly to a distinction in meaning based on the presence of a juncture at this point. Notice such a pair as:

2	3	1	2	3	2	2	3	1

Hè côunseled mỳ bróther-in-lâw #   Hè côunseled mỳ bróther | in láw #

The essential distinction here is whether or not there is a /||/ before *in law*. The two sentences are clear, however, only because the juncture distinction is often more than that between /||/ and /+/, since *brother-in-law* often lacks any juncture at all before *in*, and also because the juncture distinction is reinforced by an even clearer distinction in stress and pitch. With another sentence, clarity is somewhat lessened. Thus, with

2   3   1
He took the path at the corner. /hìy + tûk + ðə + pǽθit + ðə + kɔ́rnər #/

the form given is ambiguous and could be the structural equivalent of either "The path at the corner is the one he took" or "At the corner, he took the path." With some other sentences semantic ambiguity remains, even though the structure of sentence components may be quite clear. This is notably true of a sentence discussed by Martin Joos—"I'll take the big one upstairs."[10] There are three ways of pronouncing this sequence, and all remain ambiguous:

2   3   1
/àyl + têyk + ðə + bîg + wə̀n + ə̀p + stéhrz #/
2   3   2   2   3   1
/àyl + têyk + ðə + bíg + wə̀n | ə̀p + stéhrz #/
2   3   1   2   3   1
/àyl + têyk + ðə + bíg + wə̀n # ə̀p + stéhrz #/

The first is ambiguous structurally, since in the absence of a juncture we do not know whether the phrase *upstairs* is a sentence adjunct or a part of the complement. The second is clear structurally, since *upstairs* is now a sentence adjunct. But sentence adjuncts (and even more, dependent sentences, as in the third form) do not signal exactly what their relation to the other elements is, so that we still do not know whether to interpret as "I'll take the big one, [which is] upstairs" or as "I'll take the big one up [the] stairs." The sentence remains one which is ambiguous, even for the most sophisticated user of the language.

We have summarized the positions of adjunct sentence elements as if all four of them were equally likely. Actually, however, initial and final position are much the most frequent locations. Internal position is so infrequent that it can be described by saying that it occurs only under stylistic pressure. Further, there are some adjunct sentence elements which

---

[10] Review of *Machine Translation of Languages : Fourteen Essays,* ed. by William N. Locke and A. Donald Booth, John Wiley, New York, 1955, in *Language,* XXXII, 1956, pp. 297–98.

can only occur in initial position. A prepositional group which frequently acts as an adjunct sentence element is *for me*, as in "Thàt was góod—fòr mé." In this simple form, the phrase has the freedom characteristic of an adjunct. But if we expand it by the addition of *as*, we get:

$$2 \qquad\qquad 3\ 2 \quad 2 \qquad\qquad\quad 3\ 1$$
As for me, that was good. /æ̀z + fər + míy | ðæ̀t + wɨz + gúd #/

In this form, there is no possibility of change from initial position. The introductory form *as*, by the way, belongs to a form class which it is convenient to discuss in connection with dependent sentences, since it characteristically occurs in utterances like "As I was saying, John likes coffee." At present it is enough to give the class a name, preliminarily. They will be called by the generic title of conjunctions, and separated from prepositions by their stress and order characteristics. The fixed order of the adjunct quoted above is inherent in the sequence *as for*—— and does not apply to other sequences, like *as in*——.

The occurrence of adjunct sentence elements fixed in initial position leads naturally to a type of adjunct sentence element not yet mentioned. We have analyzed sentences like "John looked at Mary three times" and "John drove the car three miles" as containing double complements. It must have occurred to the reader, however, that there are other possibilities of order in these sentences, namely:

> *Three times, John looked at Mary.*
> *Three miles, John drove the car.*

But not:

> John drove **three miles, the car.*

At first sight it might seem possible to analyze these sentences as containing double complements, but with the second complement placed in unusual order. There is difficulty in the way of such an analysis. It springs from the typical double-complement sentence "John gave Mary a book." It does not seem to be possible to vary the order of this sentence to "A book John gave Mary" as a fully independent sentence. This order occurs only in situations like "That is the book John gave Mary," or possibly in stylistically varied sentences like "John gave Mary the book. The book John gave Mary." The same limitation seems to apply to other types of double-complement sentences, like "John brought the car home." Neither "Home John brought the car" nor "The car John brought home" are possible as fully independent sentences unless there is something in the stylistic situation which explains them. With the sentence "Three times John looked at Mary" there is no such limitation as there is for "Home

John brought the car." The fact that *three times* in initial position gives a normal rather than a dependent sentence is justification enough for rejecting the explanation that it is a sentence with a displaced second complement.

If we return to adjunct sentence elements, we can now sum up by saying that in any situation in which an apparent second complement is freely capable of being placed in presubjectival position, postsubjectival position, or both, it is preferable to analyze it as an adjunct sentence element. Displaced genuine second complements are to be recognized only under stylistic conditions which explain their occurrence. Our rule can be stated from a different angle, in order to take care of still other variations.

Suppose we take as our starting point the bookish but possible sentence:

> *I died a thousand deaths.*

It is clear that *deaths* is the head of the complement, and these relations are not changed if the order becomes "A thousand deaths I died," since in this order the pronoun is still identified as subject, and we have a displaced complement. If instead of this sentence we had used "I died a thousand times" and "A thousand times I died," we would be again forced to say we are dealing with a single complement, capable of being displaced. Our rule for treating noun material as a sentence adjunct is dependent on the recognition of other noun material as a complement. It is only a noun phrase which occurs initially, or preverbally, set off by terminals, and followed by a verb and complement which can be called a sentence adjunct. The rule can now be applied not only to "Three miles he drove the car," "Three years she grew in beauty," and others of the same type, but also to sentences in which we have a noun placed first, with a normal sentence following it, and a pronoun replacing either the subject, the complement, or both. Examples are:

> *The cookies—John ate them.*
> *The dishes—they washed them.*
> *John—he ate the cookies.*

If such a noun is placed finally, it may be treated in two differing ways:

> *John ate them—the cookies.*

2	3	1	2	3	1		2	3	1	1	1	1

/jâhn + éyt + ðìm # ðə + kúkiyz #/ or /jâhn + éyt + ðìm # ðə + kúkiyz #/

Both superfixes are characteristic of sentences, though in the second utterance the monotone morpheme marks a dependent rather than a main sentence. The important fact is that final position produces, for these sentences, a structure quite different from that characteristic of a double-complement sentence. To pronounce "John ate them—the cookies" with the superfix of "John gave them the books" would be quite abnormal.

The same analysis applies to subjectless sentences like "Open the windows!" If we have "Open them—the windows," we have the superfix characteristics of linked sentences. If we have "The windows, open them!" there may be superfix characteristics marking a sentence adjunct. But for all sentences of this type, in which there is a noun set off as a separate phrase, followed by a normally constructed sentence containing pronoun subject or complement, there is always a possibility of treatment as separate sentences, though with linking. If the superfix pattern is {2 3 2 |} {2 3 1 #} or the like, we have a sentence adjunct. If the pattern is {2 3 1 #} {2 3 1 #}, we have separate sentences, linked stylistically by the pronoun reference.

Adjunct sentence elements are typically made up of adverbial material, of prepositional phrases, and, under limited conditions, of nominal material followed by a normal sentence structure of three or two elements. The only remaining type of adjunct sentence element is made up of single forms which are characteristically capable of standing alone as complete sentences and which are not capable of inflection, or of taking postbases, or of fitting into any of the form classes we have set up. A typical example is *yes*. Examples of it as an adjunct are the following:

> *Yes, it's hot.*
> *It—yes—is hot.*
> *It's—yes—hot.*
> *It's hot, yes.*

If *yes*, in initial or final position, is given {2 3 1 #}, it becomes an independent sentence. If given /||/ or /|||/ in these situations, together with minimal pitch linkage, it is an adjunct sentence element, as it is in internal position, where a terminal other than /#/ is required. Exactly the same treatment can be given to forms like *oh*, *gosh*, and *ouch*. We should add that a sentence like "They oh'd and ah'd," no longer contains the adjunctival forms, but contains verbs derived from them.

We have implied throughout that a sentence adjunct must be a form not identifiable with one of the other types of sentence element, though we have shown that this statement does not mean that an adjunct sentence element needs to be semantically unrelated to subject or complement. Our sentence "The cookies—John ate them" contains two items presumably referring to the same thing, but the formal complement is *them*. The rule that an adjunct sentence element cannot contain one of the other elements gives rise to a natural extension. Even though a form like the following is independent in position, and set off by /||/, it is not an adjunct sentence element:

$$\overset{2}{Burning}\ \overset{32}{thèm}\ |\ \text{Mary spoiled the cookies.}$$

The initial element here contains a verbal and a complement and so must be treated as a dependent sentence. Our rule, in short, is that an adjunct sentence element cannot itself consist of more than one element; anything containing more than one sentence element is a sentence, dependent or independent.

18.... SIMPLE SENTENCES

1. Definition of sentence types

A sentence, as has been implied in what has gone before, is a sequence of segmental material occurring under a single pitch superfix. The superfix may or may not contain more than one pitch morpheme, but if there is more than one pitch morpheme, the pitch morphemes must be linked. A sentence must also have a stress superfix, which also may consist of several stress morphemes. Obviously, also, a sentence must contain one or several segmental morphemes.

The reader must by now be aware that the simplest type of sentence is a single segmental morpheme like *yes*, treated with the superfix material which identifies it as a sentence:

$$\overset{331}{Yes.}\ /y\acute{e}s\ \#/\quad \{'\}\ \{yes\}\ \{3\ 3\ 1\ \#\}$$

In such a construction, both the stress superfix and the pitch superfix are minimal, in that each consists of a single morpheme.

Considered from the point of view of pitch superfixes, there is but one combination of morphemes which clearly distinguishes a sentence type. This is the sentence with extension of a single contour by addition of a monotone, which we have met in such examples as:

$$\overset{2}{Russian}\ is\ a\ \overset{3}{difficult}\ \overset{1}{language}\ \#\ \overset{1}{Dean}\ \overset{11}{Smith\ said}\ \#$$

Such a sentence is phonologically marked as complex by its superfix. We have seen that the same type of superfix occurs with sentences where the second pitch morpheme does not fall on material which contains recognizable sentence elements. An example is:

$$\overset{2}{He}\ \overset{3}{talks}\ \overset{1}{too}\ \overset{111}{much}\ \#\ Silly\ \#$$

This example is also a complex sentence, though the second part of it is elementless.

In most situations, however, the difference between a simple and a complex sentence is shown only by the content, so that a complex sentence must usually be defined morphologically rather than phonologically. A morphologically simple sentence is one which contains no more than one pattern clustering around a predicator. That is, it may have subject, predicator, complement, and second complement, with an indefinite number of adjuncts. A morphologically complex sentence has two or more patterns, each clustering around a predicator. That is, subject-predicator plus subject-predicator, and subject-predicator-complement plus subject-predicator-complement are typical complex sentence patterns. The complexity of the subject-predicator-complement elements of which a sentence is made up has no effect on whether or not the sentence is simple. The following is a simple sentence:

ADJUNCT
In our beautiful country

SUBJECT
many wise statesmen, sturdy pioneers, and adventurous merchants

PREDICATOR
have consciously and unconsciously combined to give

FIRST COMPLEMENT
our youthful nation

SECOND COMPLEMENT
its wealth, freedom, and greatness.

In contrast, the following is a complex sentence:

If Mary washes the dishes, John will dry them.

Here there are two subject-predicator-complement constructions, the first being marked as linked by the introductory *if*.

In the present chapter our task is to survey the simple sentence as a complete structure, as we have already surveyed its parts. Our first task is to describe those entities which mark the ends of sentences.

2. Junctures as sentence enders

A sentence composed of such pitch morphemes as {2 3 2 |} {2 3 1 #} has been spoken of as containing a superfix with minimal pitch linkage. The statement is justified, though before it can be finally accepted, it is necessary to consider the fact that such a morpheme as {2 3 2 |} occasionally occurs in utterance final position, where it cannot be linked to anything following:

$$\overset{2}{} \qquad \overset{32}{}$$
It's good enough. /ìt + s + gûd + inɔ́f ‖/

Unless it is possible to show that {2 3 2 |} is normally linked to following morphemes beginning with /2/, we find ourselves in the uncomfortable position of saying that one of the commonest pitch morpheme sequences, characterizing many morphologically unified sentences, is not a unified superfix.

The answer to this problem lies in the nature of the junctures. We shall now reclassify the junctures into hierarchies. Of the four junctures, /+/ never occurs at utterance final, and so can be spoken of as lowest. The juncture which is commonest at utterance final is /#/, which can therefore be spoken of as highest. Double bar is commoner at utterance final than /|/, so that /‖/ is higher than /|/. In line with these distributional features are the phonemic qualities of the junctures, which are arranged in a similar series from /+/, which is shortest, to /#/, which is longest. All investigators, whether their measurements are impressionistic or by machine, agree with this statement of the relative durations of the three terminals, though their exact duration in terms of average phoneme length is not fully settled. Second, it seems clear that duration as defining the various terminals must normally mean the amount of time allotted by each to elongation of preceding segmental material. That is, duration of a terminal can scarcely mean the total duration of the period before the same speaker begins to talk again, since otherwise we should have the preposterous result that some terminals might stretch out into periods of hours, days, or even years. The silence that follows, or may follow, a terminal is then to be distinguished from the tempo features of the terminal itself. This silence, unlike the elongation of the terminal, is an extralinguistic feature. Yet it can be set up as a hypothesis, reasonable enough, but as yet unchecked, that the occurrence and duration of pause has some relation to linguistic features. Henry Lee Smith has called attention to the fact that in the total communication situation, a speaker somehow gives recognizable signals to another speaker indicating when the second speaker is expected to say something.[1] It would seem that these signals are primarily pauses following terminals. Such pauses can be at least roughly defined as of two durational types. A pause following /|/ or /‖/ sufficient to bring the sum of the terminal elongation and the pause up to the elongation characteristic of a /#/ indicates that these terminals are functioning as units equivalent in total to a /#/. A pause after any terminal, including /#/,

---

[1] See below, p. 342, note 3.

sufficient to bring the sum total of time up to more than is characteristic of /#/ is indication of the end of utterance. Generally, however, in conversational interchange, short responses such as *yes, go on, really,* and so on, which do not interrupt the flow of the first speaker's discourse, are given after terminals together with pauses which add up to being equal to the duration of /#/. Longer, completely articulated utterances by the second speaker are not normally given unless the second speaker has waited long enough to know that terminal and pause are greater than the duration of /#/. The two types of pause phenomena can be designated by the symbols (p) and (P), where parentheses indicate that these are extralinguistic phenomena, not included in the phonemic and morphemic system, and the lower case letter indicates the relatively shorter, the upper case letter the relatively longer, pause.

It is this concept of following pause which we can use to solve the problem posed by the pitch-morpheme sequence $\{2\ 3\ 2\ |\}\ \{2\ 3\ 1\ \#\}$. The morpheme $\{2\ 3\ 2\ |\}$ does not occur as a sentence ender unless accompanied by the extralinguistic phenomenon of (p) or (P). The normal use of $\{2\ 3\ 2\ |\}$, then, is as a morpheme linked to the morpheme which follows to make up a unified superfix. There is indeed a minimal degree of pitch linkage, since the preceding morpheme ends in /2/, the same phoneme on which the following morpheme begins. In general, the occurrence of a /#/ can be taken as indicating the end of a sentence, except for pitch linkage of the type $\{2\ 3\ 1\ \#\}\ \{1\ 1\ 1\ \#\}$, which we have seen in such sentences as:

"Let's go," John said.

It has been said that (p) and (P) are extralinguistic, yet that they belong to the total communication situation. It is therefore necessary to define the area of communication to which they belong. Sentences belonging to the same utterance are linked by (p)'s; sentences belonging to different utterances are separated by (P)'s. It therefore follows that these entities define relationships between sentences, rather than between parts of sentences. They therefore belong to the area of stylistics, and we have isolated a juncture and pause hierarchy which also belongs in this area. In this stylistic hierarchy, /|/ plus (p) and /|||/ plus (p) add up to an equivalent of /#/; and any terminal plus (P) is an utterance ender, something which /#/ alone is not. The stylistic hierarchy gives the investigator, therefore, both a first foothold in the area of stylistics, and measureable entities which can be used in stylistic analysis.

The discussion which we have just completed has been focused on 'he two morphemes $\{2\ 3\ 2\ |\}$ and $\{2\ 3\ 1\ \#\}$. We should therefore add at east a word about morphemes ending in /|||/. It is a commonplace by now that such a morpheme as {2 2 3 ||} normally stands alone as a question, so that the expectancy is that it is a sentence ender. It is to be noted, however, that pitch linkage can occur across the /|||/, as we saw in the sentence quoted on page 321:

$$\begin{matrix} 2 & 33 & 3 & 44 \end{matrix}$$
Whàt's thát || a hóuse ||

Further, if my own observations are correct, such linked questions assign a shorter duration to the interval between them than occurs when the two juncture groups are question and reply. In such a linked series, therefore, the total time involved between morphemes is comparable to that which would occur in the material set off by double bars in the following:

$$\begin{matrix} 2 & 32 & 2 & & 3 & 2 & 2 & & 3 & 1 \end{matrix}$$
The boys || tîred and húngry || at last went home #

In other words, /|||/ as a sentence ender is also accompanied by (p), and as utterance ender by (P). Moreover, a sequence consisting of {2 3 2 ||} and {2 3 1 #} also constitutes a unified superfix, just as does a sequence in which the first morpheme is {2 3 2 |}, and the second {2 3 1 #}.

Before we turn more specifically to the pitch superfixes which mark sentences, we should discuss still further the arrangements of junctures. It will be remembered that we defined morphological juncture points as those places in the sentence where a /+/ might be replaced by a terminal without pitch linkage by a complex contour. It will also be remembered that we defined phonological juncture points as those at which a /+/ would be expected between a tertiary and stronger stress, or in which a /+/ might be replaced between secondaries or between a secondary and a primary. These points, unless morphologically conditioned, would give a terminal across which linkage by complex contour would be expected to occur. If we now know the general behavior of junctures in relation to pitch and to segmental material, it will be useful to introduce another type of concept in connection with junctures. This is the concept of juncture range.

A juncture range is to be defined as the sum total of junctures likely at a given juncture point. The first and least important range is that which falls at a phonological juncture point defined only by a tertiary preceded or followed by a stronger stress, as in *cóntènt* or *cón + tènt*. The range is from no juncture to /+/. The second phonological juncture point is that conditioned merely by sequences of stresses stronger than weak. The range is from /+/, which is always present, to /||/ and /|||/, with linkage by complex contour, and to /#/, always with linkage by addition of a monotone. The third type of juncture point is that which falls at a morphologically defined main sentence element. If a terminal is present at this point, normally only minimal pitch linkage occurs. The range is from no juncture to /+/, /‖/, and /‖‖/. The statement that there may be no juncture at such a point is perhaps surprising, but it should be remembered that there is often no juncture after the subject in "I'm a man." The instances of a junctureless boundary between main sentence elements are limited, however, to pronoun subjects ending in a semivowel with following weak allologs of negative-suffix verbs. In all other instances, a /+/ must always be present. When /‖/ or /‖‖/ occurs at such a point they have no more than minimal pitch linkage across them.

The remaining juncture range is that at the end of utterance, which has already been described, but can be briefly recapitulated as running linguistically from /‖/ to /‖‖/ and /#/, but stylistically falling into two series—a lesser one of /‖/ (p), /‖‖/ (p), and /#/; and a greater one of /‖/, /‖‖/, and /#/, all followed by (P).

The juncture points and the ranges characterizing each have been described in terms of their occurrence at the boundaries of sentences and sentence elements—at the points, in short, at which the utterance would be successively cut in constituent analysis. There is another sort of juncture occurrence, however, which is not at all predictable in terms of constituent boundaries. This type of juncture occurrence can be illustrated by a sentence which I recently heard, and can therefore record accurately:

> *Oh look, I've found my . . . card.*
> 2   31   2   2   2   331
> /ôw + lúk # àyv + fâwn + mày | (P) kárd #/

In point of fact, the pause was long enough for me to address a question to the speaker, and only after my query was the second phrase, together with utterance final /#/, given. There are two interesting facts about this kind of juncture occurrence. One is that it may occur without upgrading of the stress or pitch on the material after which the first terminal juncture falls, so that we have in this kind of utterance an exception to the rule that a primary stress must fall somewhere between any pair of terminal junctures. The second fact is that the point at which this kind of juncture and pause will fall is largely predictable, though not in terms of linguistic structure. It will fall where there is a boundary, marked by a /+/, but before that morpheme or construction which represents the point in the sentence where there are the greatest number of lexical choices; and it will not occur at those points in the sentence where the structure limits the choices. Thus, it cuts across the borders of constituents, leaving an apparently impossible construction like "I've found my," which never occurs as a normal independent utterance. This kind of juncture use is, therefore, more predictable in terms of communication theory than in terms of linguistic analysis.

Communication theorists usually measure the amount of information as a function of the number of alternatives; thus, this type of juncture will fall at the point where there is most information, measured lexically, in the technical information theorist's sense. It will not fall at any of those parts of the sentence where there is little information, that is, where redundancy is high.[2] The fact that such juncture occurrences are not part of the linguistic signaling system is shown by the fact that they produce phrases often abnormal in stress and pitch, and by the fact that they almost always produce sequences with morphemes standing quite abnormally before final junctures. They are often accompanied by long pauses, but may finally produce a sentence normal enough if the terminal and subsequent pause are disregarded. The pause, incidentally, may be filled with semantically vague terms which cover the majority of the alternatives and so reduce the information—terms like *so-and-so*, *what's-his-name*, *thing*. The pause may also be filled with a vowel nucleus, often /əh/, accompanied by drawl, with or without pitch variation, but usually without a recognizable pitch morpheme. All this description makes it probable that many of these pause and juncture occurrences can be summed up under the rather vague name of hesitation, but while many of them may be so described, there are others that cannot be. A friend has reported to me overhearing a conversation between two young women. One said, "I should have worn a . . . ," with terminal juncture and no upgrading of stress, the juncture apparently coinciding with the point at which my friend's nearness was observed. Some seconds later, after both young women had turned a corner, came the conclusion, "girdle." It would therefore seem that these phenomena occur at those points where self-interruption is most likely, and that we cannot firmly predict the reason for the interruption by what happens to the utterance. This occurrence of pause and juncture is one of the points at which information theory and linguistics most clearly meet. The occurrences are in general predictable in terms of concentration of information, but are at least partially controlled by linguistic structure, since the interruptions do not often fall at points where there is no juncture.[3]

---

[2] For these concepts, consult George A. Miller, *Language and Communication*, McGraw-Hill, New York, 1951, p. 41.

[3] This section on juncture occurrences owes a very heavy debt to the work of Henry Lee Smith, Jr., particularly to a paper given by him before the Linguistic Society of America, December 1954, but also to many conversations with him. The concept of juncture hierarchies differs, however, from his "marking" and "determining" junctures, and my juncture points differ from his also, at least in detail. Without Smith's pioneering in this field, syntactic analysis would have been immensely retarded, yet at the same time it is to be hoped that his first formulations can be still further improved. It is in that spirit that this section has been written, though needless to say the blame for faults found here belongs to me rather than to Smith.

3. The boundaries of pitch superfixes

In the preceding section we have considered junctures together with
(p) and (P) as enders of sentences and superfixes. In this section we will
take up the totality of pitch phonemes, terminal junctures, and pauses, as
marking sentence and superfix limits. It is obvious that if we are to define
the sentence as a sequence characterized by a single superfix, we shall have
to be as clear as possible about the boundaries of superfixes in order to be
clear about the boundaries of sentences.

One of the principal marks of a superfix boundary turns out to be
simple. If we for the minute disregard junctures and pauses, it can be
said that a superfix ends when a pitch morpheme has a different pitch
phoneme from that which begins the following morpheme. The statement
can be illustrated by the following:

$$2 \qquad\quad 31 \qquad 2 \qquad\qquad 3\,1$$
John went to town. Mary stayed home.

As given, the utterance contains two pitch superfixes, and so contains two
sentences. The final of the first superfix is /1/, the first phoneme of the
second is /2/. If the utterance had been given the sequence /2 3 2/ /2 3 1/,
there would have been a superfix of two morphemes linked by the same
final and initial phoneme. What results might be considered a complex
rather than a simple sentence, but since it is a sentence phonologically
marked as such, we need not consider its exact type at this point. A different
situation is found in:

$$2 \;\; 23 \quad 2 \qquad 23$$
Ahead? Or behind?

The pattern is one of two superfixes and, thus, two separate question
sentences. The same final-initial difference in phonemes identifies a
question sentence followed by an answer, as in:

$$2 \qquad\;\; 23 \;\; 2\; 31$$
Do you see? I do.

A break between a final /4/ and an initial /2/ may be found in the same
situation:

$$2 \qquad\;\; 24 \;\; 2\; 31$$
Do you see? I do.

The only exception to the statement that a difference in final-initial
phonemes is a primary signal of the end of the superfix occurs when the
second pitch morpheme is one in which the initial and middle pitch points
coincide because the initial syllable is also that with primary stress. Such

a situation can be illustrated by an utterance like "Certainly." The commonest pronunciation for such a form seems to be

33   1

/sə́rtɨnliy #/

though there are also instances of

23   1

/sə́rtɨnliy #/

That is, utterances in which the initial syllable is also that with primary stress frequently, but not always, assimilate the usual initial pitch /2/ to the usual middle pitch /3/. Whenever this assimilation takes place, the statement that difference of final-initial phonemes constitutes the end of a superfix is upset. For instance, notice the following:

2   32   331

The boys went—out. /ðə + bôyz + wént | áwt #/

The form transcribed is without the type of linkage represented by a complex contour, which if it had occurred, would clearly have indicated linkage. In this form of the sentence, there is a final-initial difference in phonemes, occasioned by the fact that the last phrase shows coalescence of the initial and middle pitch points. If the sentence were the following:

2   32   2   31

The boys went—away. /ðə + bôyz + wént | ə + wéy #/

the fact that the final phrase has a separate initial and middle pitch point immediately restores the final-initial linkage.

Coalescence of the initial and middle pitch points can also produce the appearance of linkage. Note the following slogan of World War I:

2   3 3   331

Are we downhearted? No! /àr + wìy + dâwn + hártɨd ‖ nów #/

There would have been no linkage had the final phrase been "Of course not," with {2 3 1 #}. The form of this transcribed utterance is one in which the parts were ordinarily spoken by the same person. Often enough, however, such successive pitch morphemes offer prima-facie evidence that they are separate superfixes because question and reply are given by different speakers. When spoken by the same person, the pitch phonemes alone do not define whether or not the morphemes are linked.

If final-initial difference or identity is the first mark of separate or linked pitch morphemes, a second is the terminal which ends the first morpheme. In all but one situation, /#/ can be taken as ending a superfix. The one exception is such a sentence as:

$$\underset{\text{\textit{They gave him a seat}}}{\overset{2}{}}\ \#\ \underset{\text{\textit{by Jupiter}}}{\overset{31\ \ 1\ \ 1\ \ 1}{}}\ \#$$

That is, /#/ does not end a superfix if the following morpheme is a monotone linked to the final phoneme of the preceding. This situation is that characteristic of a complex sentence, since as we have said, it is also found in situations like:

$$\underset{\text{\textit{Let's go to the movies}}}{\overset{2}{}}\ \#\ \underset{\text{\textit{John said}}}{\overset{3\ \ 1\ \ 1\ \ 11}{}}\ \#$$

In all other situations, the occurrence of /#/ marks the end of the superfix, and takes precedence over final-initial linkage. It is still not certain that such a morpheme as {2 3 2 #} is actually found, but if the terminal which may occur after such a pitch sequence can be shown to be an allophone of /#/ in contrast with ///, such an occurrence would mark the end of a superfix, even if the following morpheme begins with /2/. A possible example would be:

$$\underset{\text{\textit{I'd like a cup of coffee}}}{\overset{2}{}}\ \#\ \underset{\text{\textit{I don't want more}}}{\overset{3\ \ 2\ \ 2\qquad\quad 31}{}}\ \#$$

The other terminals, /|/ and /|||/, do not normally end superfixes, unless accompanied by a final-initial difference. Thus the slogan quoted above, "Are we downhearted? No!" might have either {2 3 3 ||} {3 3 1 #} or {2 3 3 |} {3 3 1 #}. Both sequences of pitch morphemes would be presumed to represent linking into a single superfix. So also would be a sequence such as {2 3 2 |} {2 3 1 #} or {2 3 2 ||} {2 3 1 #}, which would be characteristic of "Tired and hungry, the boys went home." On the other hand, such a sequence as {2 3 3 ||} {2 3 1 #}, which would occur in "Are we downhearted? Of course not," would normally be taken as making up two superfixes. Similarly, any sequence consisting of {2 3 1 |} {2 3 1 #} would make two superfixes, as in:

$$\underset{\text{\textit{Take the first crossing}}}{\overset{2}{}}\ |\ \underset{\text{\textit{it's paved}}}{\overset{3\ \ 1\ \ 2\ \ \ \ 3\ \ 1}{}}\ \#$$

The third type of signal which can end a superfix is pause, either (p) or (P). These signals take precedence over final-initial linkage and the junctures. Thus the sequence {2 3 3 ||} {3 3 1 #} of "Are we downhearted? No!" was stated to be one which shows linkage. If this sequence becomes {2 3 3 ||} (p) {3 3 1 #}, it is then two superfixes. If the pause were (P), the superfixes would characterize two utterances; with (p) the superfixes are those of two sentences within the same utterance. Similarly, an utterance such as the following would contain two superfixes rather than one:

$$\text{2} \qquad\qquad\quad \text{3 2} \quad\;\; \text{2} \qquad\qquad \text{3 1}$$
I'd like a cup of coffee | (p) *I've already eaten* #

From the above discussion it is clear that the linguistic signals of the boundary of a superfix are absence of phonemic linkage in pitches and the terminal which ends the first morpheme. The third, nonlinguistic, signal is following pause. All three act together, often producing redundancy. The clearest possible signal of superfix boundary would be a situation like the following:

$$\text{2} \qquad\qquad\quad \text{3 1} \qquad \text{2} \qquad\qquad\qquad \text{3 1}$$
Mary washed the dishes # (P) *John scrubbed the floor* #

If this same utterance is given the superfixes {2 3 1 #} {2 3 1 #}, the redundancy is reduced, and if the superfixes are {2 3 1 |} {2 3 1 #}, there is no redundancy at all.

The occurrence of {2 3 2 |} in utterance-final situation, though not very common, is normal, and can be used to explain the bit of dialogue which was quoted in Chapter 2 (p. 23). The passage was:

". . . Johnny had to get his car—"
Her voice ended on an upward inflection, letting the explanation hang
suspended on the air.

Presumably the quoted sentence of dialogue had a superfix of one morpheme, {2 3 2 |}, but with following (P). Strictly speaking, the description of this situation as "upward inflection" is wrong; only in the fact that the distinct fall of {2 3 1 #} is absent can the inflection be called "upward." A more accurate description would have been "level inflection." "Letting the explanation hang suspended" is an apt description and is a good indication of the effect of {2 3 2 |} (P). The sequence can be said to represent stylistic completeness, contradicting the linguistic incompleteness.

An exhaustive description of superfixes has not yet been made, so that it is impossible to give a list of all the superfixes. Indeed, the rigorous analysis of pitch phonemes considered as components of morphemes and these, in turn, as components of larger constructions dates no further back than the appearance of the Trager and Smith *Outline* in 1951. Consequently it is not possible to define the exact meaning of pitch morphemes and superfixes, though we can often point to a social response appropriate for one or another of the superfixes. Even though we are reasonably certain that the kind of meaning they will eventually be shown to have is that of appropriate social response, it will probably never be possible to say that a specific social response is appropriate to all occurrences of a given superfix. We shall content ourselves, therefore, with a single instance of such a specific social response. I once asked a Spanish speaking waiter for a napkin, and received the reply "Si, si, si" in a form which I automatically interpreted as the pattern of English "Yes, yes, yes," with {1 1 1 |} {1 1 1 |} {1 1 1 #}. In consequence, the response seemed to me to be a rude one, though the waiter's conduct amply proved that it was, as it would not be in English, a properly friendly and respectful one.

4. Morphological types of simple sentences

The absolutely minimal construction which can be called a sentence is an utterance like "Oh!" Its total shape is:

$$\text{3 3 1}$$
$$/\text{ów} \#/ \quad \{'\} \ \{\text{ow}\} \ \{3 \ 3 \ 1 \ \#\}$$

The utterance is minimal on all three levels: it has a single segmental morpheme, composed of the minimal number of phonemes; it has a minimal stress superfix, composed of only one morpheme, and the morpheme composed, in turn, of only one phoneme; and it has a minimal pitch superfix composed of only one pitch morpheme. The last statement is another way of saying that this utterance is a sentence which contains only one phrase. The fact that both the pitch and stress superfixes are in the minimal form consisting of only one morpheme should not blind us to the fact that the utterance has superfixes as well as suprasegmental morphemes.

The utterance is, then, the irreduceable minimum of the type of sentence which may be called the single-construction type. In all but a few single-construction sentences, it is impossible to identify the content of the sentence with any one of the sentence elements such as subject, predicator, complement, or adjunct. In many instances, it is also impossible, as here, to identify the content of the sentence with any one of the major form classes, such as noun or verb. It is possible, on the other hand, to subdivide the single-construction sentences in various ways. The example we have given conforms to a class of sentences employing forms which are common as unit sentences, which rarely enter into larger constructions and seldom employ suffixes or postbases that identify them with the regular form classes. The description of the type has a certain practical usefulness, and these forms may be called sentence words. Yet the description lacks rigor, since most of the sentence words appear in occasional forms which identify them as capable of entering into the normal structure of the language. Such a form for *oh* is the sentence "They *oh'd* and *ah'd* when they saw it."

For what it is worth, then, here are some typical examples of elementless sentences, all employing forms which commonly appear without identifying marks in minimal sentences: "Yes." "No." "Ouch." "Golly!"

Only very slightly different are elementless minimal sentences employing forms which may elsewhere be identifiable as to form class, but which, since they occur in minimal sentences without postbases or suffixes, are unidentifiable in the quoted forms. Such sentences are: "Help!" "Out!" "Swell!"

The elementless sentence may be expanded. When this happens, what results is a phrasal construction which can be recognized as nominal, adjectival, or the like, though the sentence remains without a classifiable or identifiable sentence element. Such forms are "Nice day!" "A pleasant party!" where we have no difficulty in recognizing a nominal phrase. The sentences are without a recognizable sentence element, since in the absence of a predicator, we cannot call the nominal material either subject or complement.

Elementless sentences may be of more than one form, since they may be statements or questions. Thus "Coffee?" with the form

$$2\ 2\ 3$$
$$/\text{kɔ́fiy} \ |||/$$

is a question, equivalent to "Do you want coffee?" or something else, such as "Is this coffee?" When elementless sentences have the minimal superfix $\{2\ 3\ 1\ \#\}$, they are in the form usually associated with statements, though one of the commonest occurrences of sentences in this shape is that of citation forms. What has just been said about the possibility of elementless sentences as either statements or questions applies equally well to the expanded elementless sentences, as in "A pleasant party?" with $\{2\ 3\ 3\ |||\}$.

Another type of elementless sentence is the type found in "A big book, a big evil." The sentence superfix such forms receive is usually either $\{2\ 3\ 2\ |||\}$ $\{2\ 3\ 1\ \#\}$ or $\{2\ 3\ 2\ |\}$ $\{2\ 3\ 1\ \#\}$. It is easy to identify the two phrases of which this sentence is composed as nominal, but it would be arbitrary to identify one as subject and the other as complement, since our definition of these sentence elements turns on the presence of an identifiable predicator. The type has often, and quite properly, been called equational. Usually, as here, it consists of two phrases united under a single sentence superfix. The utterance may easily become two independent sentences, with only stylistic linking between them, as it would be if pronounced with $\{2\ 3\ 1\ \#\}$ $\{2\ 3\ 1\ \#\}$. Other examples of the type are "Cold hands, warm heart" or, with negatives, "No money, no dinner." The type is by no means limited to equated nominal phrases, since we may have forms like "Unlucky at cards, lucky in love." The construction is particularly common in pro-verbial material, as the examples show, and it is also very frequently marked by parallelism in the equated phrases. Examples which are neither pro-verbial nor in strict parallel construction can be found, however. An example is "Ten dollars; two dollars apiece."

If such elementless sentences are extended to more than two phrases, they become lists. The only mark of difference between an equation and a list is, then, the number of items, so that a sentence like "One, two" is an equation, while "One, two, three" is a list. The simplest form of a list is found in the counting situation, as in:

3 32   33 2   33 2   33 1

One, two, three, four. /wɔ́n | túw | θríy | fɔ́hr #/

The sentence may also have {3 3 2 ||} for the first three phrases, and the type frequently occurs in other situations than numerical counting. It can occur as simply a list of items:

Books, paper, pen, ink.

Or the items may be phrases:

Writing tablet, fountain-pen ink, a pair of pencils, three erasers.

This pattern is extremely common in speech but is often objected to in formal writing, where elementless sentences are rather generally avoided. No real limitation—other than that just mentioned—occurs on this type of sentence, except the rather vague and essentially stylistic one that usually the enumerated items belong to similar semantic categories. That is, such a sentence as the following is rare and would occur only in a stylistic situation where the lack of semantic parallelism could be explained:

Two books, a subject and predicate, great courage.

These three types represent the total of elementless sentences in English. It is a curiosity of English structure that there can be only one type of sentence which contains only a single sentence element. This is because there is only one type of sentence element which can be fully identified by the morphemes contained within it, namely the predicator, since nominal material is identified as subject or complement solely by its relation to a verb. Nominal material without a verb is therefore elementless, as we have said.

Examples of single-element sentences are, as a result, limited to verbs and verb phrases. The type is rather rare and presents a few minor difficulties. A clear example of it, however, might be such questions as "Murdered?" "Was going?" Each of these verbal sentences contains morphemes which indicate that the construction is verbal. If there is no such morphemic indication, it may be quite impossible to identify the sentence type without recourse to the stylistic situation, as in "Fire!" where it is impossible to define the form class to which the single segmental morpheme belongs. Yet, if this same sentence occurs in a stylistic sequence such as "Get ready!" "Take aim!" "Fire!" the stylistic situation fully defines it as verbal, and so as a single-element sentence, here imperative. The commonest form of the single-element sentence is the imperative, but it should be pointed out again that many imperatives are identifiable only stylistically. Thus "Run!" is much more likely to be an imperative than anything else, but it is at least conceivable that it might be an answer to such a question as "Was the battle fought at Bull Branch?" The imperative, since it uses only form 1, naturally cannot be inflected in ways that prove its verbal character. Occasionally, however, a given morpheme or construction occurs only as a verb, so that a single-element sentence is lexically identified. Such sentences are "Come!" or "Listen!"

Two-element sentences consist of subject and predicator, or predicator and complement. The subject-and-predicator type is a pattern of which we have seen many examples. Any verb can occur in this pattern, though there are some such as *murder*, which are rare in it. Such a sentence as "John murders" is possible, however. The only structurally important limitation on the type is that the group of verbs which have weak or nonsyllabic forms (allologs), do not use these weak allologs unless there is a complement or a second verbal form following. That is, "John is going" may appear as:

$$2 \qquad \quad 3 \; 1$$
$$\text{/jâhn} + \text{z} + \text{gówiŋ } \#/$$

But if there is no such following material, only the fuller allolog, {iz}, with one of the stronger grades of stress, occurs. A difficulty, of a type which we have already met, arises over the relation of statement sentences with subject and complex predicator to the corresponding question sentences. The statement "John's going" becomes "Is John going?" in the question form. That is, we have a discontinuous predicator. Our procedure will be the same as that which we have used in other instances of discontinuous predicators. That is, we will make our first cut so as to give *is John* and *going*, without regard to sentence elements. Thereafter, when we have cut out *John*, we reassemble linearly. In doing so, however, we do not reassemble into the normal subject-predicator order of "John is going," since the question order must not be confused with the normal order. Our reassembly is into the artificial:

Is . . . going   John?

The same procedure is followed with those verbs which make special

question forms with *do*, as in "Does John dance?" Reassembled this form
would be:

$$Does \ldots dance \quad John?$$

It can be said in passing that such reassembly isolates a significant factor of
sentence element order, which brings these sentences into accord with the
archaic sentence element order of the previously quoted sentence, "Irks care
the crop-full bird?" (see p. 262).

The second type of two-element sentence is predicator and complement, the form typical of the imperative. An example is "Listen to the
mocking bird!" Little need be said of the sentence type, except to remind
the reader that imperative uses of the verb are uninflected, so that sentences
of this sort may be formally indistinguishable from others, except in a
stylistic situation which makes the interpretation clear. Thus a childish joke
is the answer "I can't; they fly too fast," to the sentence

2   31
Time flies. /tâym + fláyz #/

willfully taken as an imperative. There are occasional sentences consisting
of predicator and complement which are not imperatives, but are rather to
be interpreted as instances in which the subject (though not necessarily a
specific subject) has been replaced by zero. Such a sentence is the social
formula "I'll be seeing you" in which the subject *I* and the weak allolog of
the first verb are both often lost. These forms are identifiable as forms with
a zero subject by their stylistic situation and the fact that often the subject is
readily restorable. The predicator-and-complement sentence may have a
second complement, as in "Give him the book."

The typical three-element sentence is, of course, the favorite subject-
predicator-complement pattern, much more frequent in our structure than
any other. Examples are commonplace: "John likes apple pie," "The English
settled Jamestown," "Boys will be boys," and many more. At the moment we
need make only one distinction. There are two types of sentence when both
subject and complement are nouns or nominals. In one the subject selects
the number of the complement; in the other, there is no relation. In the first
type, the typical verb is *be*, though there is a small list of others, such as
seem and *become*. Examples of the first type are "These houses are palaces"
and "This house is a palace." We have already mentioned that in such a
sentence as "These houses are stone" we have a different construction, in
which *stone* is to be taken as a group I modifier. There are still other sentences like "This man is two different persons," in which there is lack of
agreement. With the lack of agreement going in the other direction we have
"These books are a bargain." That is, the verb *be* can link sentences where

the subject and complement agree and sentences where they do not. The justification for setting up a sentence type characterized by the subject's selection of the number of the complement is that in such a sentence as "This man is a teacher," it is impossible to vary the number of subject and complement independently. There is a semantic guide in that disagreement in number is possible when the second noun is a class which includes the items designated by the first noun as its members. A typical member-class sentence is "These soldiers are a squad." Stated the other way round, of course, lack of agreement between two nouns thus linked by *be* is a signal of the member-class relationship. The meaning of the sentence type where the subject selects the number of the complement is equation (though the sentence is not of the type we have called equational); and in English equation is the principal meaning of the verb *be*. Other languages frequently signal this relationship without verbs.

Of the sentence which consists of subject, predicator, and complement where there is no selection by the subject and where the complement can therefore freely disagree with the subject, we have already given copious examples. "John met the girls" is a sufficient exemplar of the type at this point. We need only point out that the complement does not have to be a noun but can be pronominal, as in "John saw her," or adjectival, as in "John got angry."

The rare three-element types which consist of subjectival, predicator, and subject have already been described. The typical example, it will be remembered, was "Here comes the teacher." There can be a four-element type, however, in which there is subjectival, predicator, subject, and complement. An example is "There goes the train home!" The remaining four-element type is subject, predicator, complement, and adjunct. An example is "They have two bus lines, in our town." Of these also we need say little, nor do we have to state the relationship of adjunct clauses to sentences of two elements. The type is adequately described by the simple statement that adjuncts can be added freely to all sentences containing recognizable sentence elements.

19.... COMPLEX SENTENCES, I

Linking Devices other than Lexical

1. Sentence linking defined

Complex sentences consist of two sentence structures which are placed under a single pitch superfix of two or more morphemes. The two sentence structures may be two subject-predicator-complement constructions (or any one of the subvarieties of these constructions); or the two patterns may be a single subject-predicator-complement construction together with a single-construction sentence, or even an elementless sentence. An example of this latter type is the sentence we have several times quoted:

They gave him a seat, by Jupiter!

2   3 1   1   1   1

/ðèy + gêyvimə + síyt | bày + júwpitər #/

Complex sentences involve two processes, linking and downgrading. We shall discuss linking first. Linking occurs when two or more constructions otherwise capable of receiving the phonological treatment characteristic of sentences are so modified in form as to show that they are parts of a single, larger sentence. The simplest form of linking is modification of two pitch superfixes so that they become a single superfix, giving therefore a single, though complex, sentence.

A simple example might be the following:

John likes coffee. Mary likes tea.

2   3 1   2   3 1

/jâhn + lâyks + kófiy # mêhriy + lâyks + tíy #/

As given, this utterance consists of two sentences, with the independent superfixes {2 3 1 #} and {2 3 1 #}. As said in the last chapter, these superfixes are independent not only because of the occurrence of /#/ at the end of the first but also because of the difference in final and initial pitch phonemes. The sentences are obviously stylistically linked by their close parallelism of structure and content, but linguistically they are independent.

In order to produce a linked, complex sentence, the pitch morphemes are modified to the following:

$$\text{2} \qquad \text{3 2} \quad \text{2} \qquad \qquad \text{31}$$
/jâhn + lâyks + kóhfiy | mêhriy + lâyks + tíy #/

That is, the superfix {2 3 2 |} {2 3 1 #} is unified both by the final-initial linkage and by the normally nonsentence-final juncture.

The sentence "They gave him a seat, by Jupiter!" shows linking by extension of a single pitch contour across a terminal and following monotone pitch morpheme. The type has been called a complex sentence rather than a single sentence with a following sentence adjunct for two reasons. First, a following linked monotone pitch morpheme is a pitch construction characteristic of following quotative sentences, such as:

$$\text{2} \qquad \qquad \text{3 1} \quad \text{1} \qquad \text{11}$$
Russian is a difficult language # Dean Smith said #

In such a situation, obviously, the monotone morpheme covers an utterance containing·subject and predicator, forcing the conclusion that the sentence is complex. Second, though a construction like "By Jupiter!" does not contain a recognizable sentence element, it is perfectly capable of standing alone as an elementless sentence. Thus, our utterance is best described as a complex sentence, consisting of one fully articulated subject-predicator-complement construction and a following elementless construction. A further typical situation in which a following linked monotone is found is in sentences with a final vocative, as in:

$$\text{2} \qquad \text{32} \quad \text{222}$$
Let's go | John #

These also, then, are to be described as complex sentences, though in other situations a vocative, like the construction "By Jupiter!" may occur either as an independent sentence or as a sentence adjunct. Note the pitch morpheme in the following, which contains a sentence adjunct:

$$\text{232} \qquad \text{2} \quad \text{31}$$
John || let's go #

Here, it is occurring under the morpheme {2 3 2 ||} with final-initial linkage, a characteristic morpheme for sentence elements when they are treated as separate phrases.

The instances of complex sentences so far given show the two constructions following each other. There is a second possibility; they may occur in nonsequential order, with one construction contained in the other. A clear, if somewhat unusual, example of such a sentence occurs in a recent poem by Ogden Nash:

She's got the wrong, she murmurs, bag . . .

In my own reading of the line, a natural rendering would be:

2   32   2   2   2   441
She's got the wrong || she murmurs || bag #

There are several interesting things which happen to the pitch morphemes here. First, *she murmurs* has a morpheme which, it has often been observed, is found in parenthetical material. Second, for me at least, it is more natural to surround *she murmurs* with /|||/ rather than /||/. That is, in such a situation, it seems normal to use a juncture higher in the phonemic hierarchy than /||/. Third, perhaps the most striking feature of this construction is that if *she murmurs* is lifted out of it, the pitch morphemes which remain are {2 3 2 ||} {4 4 1 #}—a typical complex contour. The complex contour seems, here at least, to be related to the fact that a more normal order for the sentence would be "She's got the wrong bag, she murmurs." The situation can be used to establish a phonological distinction between genuinely parenthetical material and such other material as sentence adjuncts or contained sentences. If we assume that the superfix in this sentence is typical, the parenthetical material shows linkage in final-initial phonemes with the preceding morpheme, while the preceding morpheme shows its unity with the morpheme following the monotone by the fact that it makes up an interrupted complex contour with it. Other, perhaps more common, examples of similar constructions are:

2   3 2   2   22   44 1
Mary shops | we believe | wisely #
231   1   1 1   441
Get | John shouted | out #

The parenthetical element need not be a subject-predicator construction:

2   32   22 2 441
John got || quietly || out #/

A sentence adjunct, on the other hand, may show a monotone morpheme or a morpheme with a peak, but the discontinuous complex contour surrounding it is absent. The sentence we have just quoted might also have *quietly* treated as an adjunct:

2   32   22   2 331
John got | quietly | out #

Phonological linking always distinguishes a main sentence from a dependent sentence, and the characteristics of main and dependent sentences can now be summarized. In a superfix in which one of the morphemes is a monotone, the monotone morpheme characterizes the dependent sentence. A sequence such as {2 3 1 #} {1 1 1 #} is the only device by which a following sentence can be made dependent on a preceding one. If both pitch morphemes have normal contours, as in such a sequence as $\{2\ 3\ 2\ |\}$ $\{2\ 3\ 1\ \#\}$, the initial morpheme characterizes the dependent sentence, since it has the normally nonsentence-final $/||/$, with a final pitch phoneme which links it to the following morpheme. In the sentence quoted above,

> 2 3 2 2 31
> *John likes coffee | Mary likes tea #*

the first sentence is dependent, the following is the main sentence. A following monotone morpheme is the device by which a final sentence is made dependent, and linkage by final pitch phoneme and by use of $/||/$ or $/|||/$ is the means by which an initial sentence is made dependent.

Phonological linking may be accompanied by other devices, which are secondary. Thus, there may be morphological linking as in the use of an *–ing* suffix for the verb form:

> 2 3 2 2 31
> *The windows being open | the room was cool #*
> 2 3 2 2 3 1
> *The room was cool | the windows being open #*

As the superfixes show, the secondary linking device may occur in either the phonologically main or the dependent sentence. In the type of analysis used in this book, it has been our practice to grant priority to phonological signals in analysis of constructions. Thus, for our purposes, the two sentences quoted above would be described as follows: the first consists of a dependent sentence with secondary linking, followed by a main sentence; the second consists of a dependent sentence, followed by a main sentence with secondary linking. This type of analysis, the reader will recognize, differs from the conventional, in which phonological characteristics are left out of account, and in consequence the sentence containing *–ing* would be described as dependent in either position.

Other secondary devices of linking are lexical, as in:

> 2 3 2 2 3 1
> *Because the windows were open | the room was cool #*
> 2 3 2 2 3 1
> *The room was cool | because the windows were open #*

A third type of secondary linking may be syntactic, in that the sentence element order of one sentence may depart from the normal subject-predicator-complement sequence, as in:

> 2 3 2 2 3 1
> *The dinners she gives | they're really something #*
> 2 3 2 2 3 1
> *They're really something | the dinners she gives #*

In each of these examples, order has been reversed to show the secondary linking device falling in both the main and the dependent sentences. We shall return to these types of secondary linking later and in more detail. In our preliminary and general description, we are now ready to go on to the second process characteristic of complex sentences, downgrading.

2. Downgrading defined

Downgrading consists in a reduction of status, for instance, from that of independent sentence to that of a sentence element within a larger sentence. Thus, the following subject-predicator-complement sentence is complete and independent:

2   3 1
The man came to dinner #

It can be downgraded to the status of a single sentence element by the addition of *who* and placement in a larger construction:

2   3 2   2   31
The man who came to dinner | broke his leg #

The construction is now serving merely as the subject and no longer as an independent sentence. Downgrading can also occur even when the construction remains an independent sentence. Thus, "The man came to dinner" can be modified by the addition of *who* and become a different type of construction, used independently as the title of a play, *The Man Who Came to Dinner*. In this form it can still be described as downgraded by the addition of *who*, since it is no longer a fully articulated subject-predicator-complement sentence, but an elementless sentence which is a nominal construction with following modifier. The addition of *who* gives the sentence much the semantic status of a proper name or title, like *Ethan Frome, The Tragic Comedians*, or *The Man Who Was Thursday*. In the sentence we have been describing, we might also describe the result of the addition of *who* as downgrading *came to dinner* from predicator and complement to the status of modifying construction.

Still another type of downgrading occurs when something which might otherwise be a dependent sentence is reduced to the status of a part of a sentence element in a larger sentence. A reasonably clear example of such downgrading is found in the following contrasting sentences:

2   3 2   2   3 2   2   3 1
The only man || who spoke || was ejected from the ladies' meeting #
2   3 2   2   3 1
The only man who spoke | was ejected from the ladies' meeting #

The distinction is familiar from traditional grammar under the names "non-restrictive" and "restrictive" clauses. In our terms, *who spoke* in the first sentence is a minimal dependent sentence of subject and predicator, and in the second is a modifying construction forming part of the subject. It should be noted that the main sentence is discontinuous but that the included dependent sentence is not given the superfix treatment which we have described above as that which characterizes a parenthesis. The included sentence is thus phonologically indistinguishable from a sentence adjunct and is identifiable as a dependent sentence only by the nature of the material it contains. The superfix given to the first version of the sentence, where *who spoke* is set off by /|||/, is not the only one which might be employed. There are evidently dialects in which the junctures employed would be /||/; some of the difficulty teachers experience in teaching the difference between the two sentence types is caused by this variation and by the fact that for a speaker to whom the use of /|||/ is natural, the use of /||/ will seem ambiguous.[1]

A similar example of downgrading, which is even more striking, is found in the following:

$$\overset{2}{} \qquad\qquad \overset{3\ 1}{}$$
the boy who lives across the street #

Even in this form, the sentence has been downgraded, since the occurrence of *who* reduces what would otherwise be a fully articulated sentence of three elements to an elementless sentence. But in a conversational sentence recorded by a field worker for the *Linguistic Atlas of New England* the construction was downgraded a second time:

$$\overset{2}{} \qquad\qquad\qquad \overset{3\ 2}{} \qquad \overset{44\ \ 1}{}$$
She goes with *the boy who lives across the street's* | brother #

In this sentence what might otherwise be a sentence has been downgraded to the status of a long modifying construction.

Downgrading can also affect sentence elements, since something which might be a sentence element, such as a sentence adjunct, may be downgraded to the status of part of a larger sentence element. An example is the following pair:

$$\overset{2\ \ 3\ 2}{} \quad \overset{2}{} \quad \overset{3\ \ 2}{} \quad \overset{2}{} \quad \overset{31}{}$$
The books || on the table || were blue #
$$\overset{2}{} \qquad\qquad \overset{3\ \ 2}{} \quad \overset{2}{} \quad \overset{31}{}$$
The books on the table | were blue #

The situation is essentially the same as that described two paragraphs above. The material is again nonrestrictive or restrictive according to its superfix

---

[1] See below, pp. 359–62, for a more extended discussion of a similar problem.

treatment. The only difference is that in this contrast, the form which is not downgraded is identified by its content as a sentence adjunct rather than as a contained dependent sentence. The same dialect differences exist here also, in the junctures used to mark the first sentence. As for meaning, the first sentence can be glossed as "The books, all of which were on the table, were blue." The second sentence can be glossed "Only those books which were on the table were blue." In more structural terms, the first sentence has *the books* as its subject, while the second has *the books on the table*.

Downgrading, like linking, can be accomplished by several types of devices. Phonological downgrading is accomplished by the pitch super-fixes, as our examples have shown. An example of morphological down-grading is found in the addition of –'s to *the boy who lives across the street*, above. Lexical downgrading has been shown by the addition of *who* to forms like *the man came to dinner*. As with linking, the phonological process is primary; lexical and morphological downgrading is secondary. Syntactic downgrading, finally, is shown in the sentence already quoted:

$$\overset{2}{}\qquad\overset{3\ \ 2\ \ \ 2}{}\qquad\overset{31}{}$$
The man who came to dinner | broke his leg #

Here the syntactic downgrading is also secondary to the superfix treatment; and the first construction is shown to be the subject by the immediately following verb. Had we had

$$\overset{2}{}\qquad\overset{3\ \ 2\ \ \ 2}{}\qquad\overset{31}{}$$
The man who came to dinner | *he* broke his leg #

we should have had an example of linking of an elementless first sentence to a normally constructed main sentence.

Before we go on to discuss the devices of linking and downgrading in detail, it is necessary to discuss further the phonological distinctions between downgraded and relatively independent elements. The distinction is a perennially troublesome one in composition classes and is almost equally troublesome to the analyst. In our discussion we shall make no particular distinction between the various types of construction which may be down-graded. Up to this point, we have spoken confidently of a difference, phonologically signaled, between the two types of construction. Yet, if a pair of sentences such as "Take the first crossing which is paved" and "Take the first crossing, which is paved" is used as a test with native speakers of English, a surprising amount of hesitation emerges from their responses. The hesitation which natives show is in marked contrast to their responses to a pair like *bríefcàse* and *bríef cáse*, which even the most linguistically naive can distinguish sharply.

It is not altogether easy to design a thoroughly satisfactory test which would show whether or not native speakers respond to a superfix morpheme marking off an independent element and to its absence marking a downgraded construction. A proper test should call for a differential response, not a description of meaning. The test I have used is as follows:

Informants were given a map showing a road with two crossings, one paved and the other unpaved. Two cars were represented as traveling along this road in opposite directions, car A so as to approach the unpaved crossing first, car B so as to approach the paved crossing first. After proper explanation, the informants were given a test sentence, and asked to respond by saying whether the sentence would have been appropriately addressed to A or to B. The test sentence—shown here unpunctuated—was a direction, such as a bystander might have given:

Take the first crossing which is paved

When the sentence was given in the form immediately following, response was unanimous:

$$\overset{2}{} \qquad\qquad\qquad\qquad\qquad \overset{31}{}$$
$$/têyk + ðə + fôrs + krɔ́siŋ + wìciz + pévd \#/$$

All informants agreed that this sentence was addressed to A, who came to the unpaved crossing first. If, however, the sentence was next given with /||/ after *crossing* and the proper changes in pitch and stress, most informants also said that it applied to A. With separate groups, the order of sentences was varied, the /||/ variant being given first. The result was still the same; the /||/ variant applied to A. Next the sentence was tried with /|||/ after *crossing*. The result was confusion, informants replying A or B in a fashion approaching random. At this point a good many informants volunteered a quite common bit of verbalization. The two sentences involved a point in grammar which they had never understood—they said the distinction "ought to mean something," but it was a matter for experts. Finally, the sentence was given with fully separate superfixes, that is, with only stylistic linking:

$$\overset{2}{} \qquad\qquad \overset{3\ \ 1}{} \quad \overset{2}{} \qquad\qquad \overset{3\ \ 1}{}$$
$$/têyk + ðə + fôrs + krɔ́siŋ \# hwìc + ìz + péyvd \#/$$

The response to this sentence was clear—it applied to B.

The test has also been reversed to make it a test of production. Asked to produce the sentence so as to make it apply to A, most informants gave the whole as a single phrase with no terminals. Asked to make it apply to B, a good many gave $\{2\ 3\ 2\ |\}$ $\{2\ 3\ 1\ \#\}$. But, as if the confusion were not enough already, when those who gave /||/ were asked whether the sentence was the same as or different from one with no /||/, a good many replied that it was the same.

At first sight such results are startling and seem to add up to inability to respond to presence or absence of /||/ and /|||/. If this were the only interpretation, it would force us to conclude that these entities are not English phonemes. Fortunately there are other situations in which informants react to these signals clearly, so that their phonemic status need not be questioned. The explanation for the confused response must be assumed to lie in the particular situation tested, not in all occurrences of juncture or its absence. The explanation offered by the informants, that they did not know proper English structure, can also be disregarded. Pretty certainly what was meant was that they did not understand a handbook rule. They were in fact reacting normally for speakers of English. On the other hand, their reactions, when they were asked to pronounce, indicate clearly that there is a basis in phonology for the handbook distinction.

While I do not regard the tests I have given as fully satisfactory, they suggest, even if they do not prove, the following tentative conclusions:

1. In many situations, the presence or absence of the terminal is a stylistic choice, involving no distinction in meaning for any speaker. A sentence like "Turn at a crossing which is paved" implies several crossings, some paved, some unpaved. So far as my testing goes, speakers react to this sentence indifferently, putting in a terminal or not at random.

2. There are some signals which are clear, others ambiguous. In my tests, *the crossing which is paved* was a clear signal if there was no terminal and there was thus a single pitch morpheme. It was also clear if there were two superfixes, each {2 3 1 #}. With /||/ and /|||/, the signal was ambiguous.

3. Ambiguity of the signals was decreased if there was a vocabulary item which directed attention to a difference in meaning and so indicated that the presence or absence of the juncture would be significant. Thus, informants respond more clearly to juncture or its absence if the sentence is in the following form than they do to the sentence in the form previously described:

Turn at the *only* crossing which is paved.

These conclusions can be further interpreted. Some part of the confusion is due to the previously mentioned differences in dialect, that is, the minimal signal for the sentence without downgrading may be /||/ in some dialects, /|||/ in others. Another part of the difficulty is that situations in which there is a meaning distinction, in terms of differing nonlinguistic response, are rather infrequent. Informants have therefore had little experience in verbalizing about the distinction unless they have been trained in grammar. More important, however, is genuine ambiguity of a superfix like {2 3 2 |} {2 3 1 #} in a situation such as this, where the construction *which is paved* is final. That is, in accord with a general rule of English structure such postposed elements can still be treated as modifiers when occurring under separate pitch morphemes, as long as there is linkage. When such an element is essentially a dependent sentence, rather than a mere modifier, it may have exactly the same treatment. It is a clearly separate sentence, with stylistic linking only when there are two clearly separate superfixes, {2 3 1 #} {2 3 1 #}.

Tentative as these conclusions may be, they have implications for the teaching of composition. In the face of student perplexity, teachers have attempted to avoid teaching the distinctions between restrictive and non-restrictive by meaning alone and have resorted to teaching it "by ear." The results have not always been good. They cannot be expected to be good unless teachers and students both understand fully what the signals are, and what the ambiguities are, also.

3. Phonological linking and downgrading

We have given several examples of phonologically linked sentences, but all have been in continuous order. Main sentences may be discontinuous, containing the dependent sentence within them, as in:

John, who likes coffee, had to drink tea.

33 2   2   3   2   2   31
/jáhn | hùw + lâyks + kóhfiy | hæd + tə + drîŋk + tíy #/

In all such sentences, the phonological linking of the several pitch morphemes still leaves us with differing possibilities of interpretation. One interpretation might be that we do not have a discontinuous main sentence, but rather three continuous linked sentences. Under that interpretation, the first would be a dependent elementless sentence, the second a dependent sentence of three elements, and the third a main sentence of two elements. The phonological characteristics do not distinguish between a possibly discontinuous main sentence and three linked sentences. Nevertheless, we can still distinguish between the two types of construction and thus reject the interpretation that the sentence above contains two dependent sentences and one main sentence. We can state as a normal rule of procedure, that interpretations which yield elementless sentences and two-element sentences are to be avoided if interpretation as a discontinuous and contained sentence gives a sentence of the normal three sentence elements.

Phonological downgrading is, as we have seen, clearest when the downgraded material is treated as part of the same phrase with the preceding material. The characteristic of this type of downgrading that we have discussed has been the absence of any terminal juncture before the downgraded construction. It must here be added that when this occurs, the rest of the superfix pattern is modified as well. There is only one pitch morpheme, the normal treatment of a single phrase, instead of the two which would be found in two phrases. There is also reduction of one primary stress to secondary, since as has been said throughout, only one primary stress occurs between terminal junctures. Downward modification of the terminal to /+/ or no juncture never occurs alone as a minimal signal, but is backed up by other modifications which can be described as redundant, since they are dependent on the juncture modification.

Downgrading, as we have also seen, cannot be proved to have occurred by any formal characteristics when the downgraded (or possibly downgraded) construction is preceded by an ambiguous terminal juncture. In practical language use, the interpreter makes his decision in accord with which construction is stylistically or referentially more probable. In analysis, the student can test by substitution, at least as long as the utterance is his own. If the utterance is not his own, he may be able to induce his informant to substitute, in either case, with the purpose of finding out what range of junctures is possible at the juncture point being studied. If the range is known, the student may then adopt some convenient, nonphonemic symbol indicating the range, since the range will be different for the two types of sentence. Thus, in the sentence we have been discussing

$$\overset{2}{\text{/têyk}} + \eth\text{i} + \text{fôrs} + \text{kr}\acute{\text{o}}\text{siŋ} + \text{hwìc} + \text{iz} + \overset{3}{\text{pé}}\overset{1}{\text{yvd}} \text{ #/}$$

the /+/ which follows *crossing*—even though it is phonemically indistinguishable from any other /+/—might be recorded with an arbitrary symbol indicating that it could be replaced by the other members of its range, namely /||/ and /|||/. To be more exact, such an arbitrary symbol would be a convenient way of recording that this sentence has two other variants:

$$\overset{2}{\text{/têyk}} + \eth\text{i} + \text{fôrs} + \overset{3}{\text{kr}}\overset{2}{\acute{\text{o}}}\text{siŋ} \mid \text{hwìc} + \text{iz} + \overset{3}{\text{pé}}\overset{1}{\text{yvd}} \text{ #/ and}$$

$$\overset{2}{\text{/têyk}} + \eth\text{i} + \text{fôrs} + \overset{3}{\text{kr}}\overset{2}{\acute{\text{o}}}\text{siŋ} \parallel \text{hwìc} + \text{iz} + \overset{3}{\text{pé}}\overset{1}{\text{yvd}} \text{ #/}$$

If, on the other hand, the sentence is known to have been that which contained a second, dependent sentence, but one ambiguously pronounced as

$$\overset{2}{\text{/têyk}} + \eth\text{i} + \text{fôrs} + \overset{3}{\text{kr}}\overset{2}{\acute{\text{o}}}\text{siŋ} \mid \text{hwìc} + \text{iz} + \overset{3}{\text{pé}}\overset{1}{\text{yvd}} \text{ #/}$$

the structurally ambiguous /||/ might be recorded with a different non-phonemic symbol, to indicate that the juncture range now runs from /||/ through /|||/ and /#/. This symbol would then be a short device for indicating that this sentence also had two variants, namely:

	2		3 2	2	31

/têyk + ði + fôrs + krósiŋ || hwìc + iz + péyvd #/ and

	2		3 1	2	31

/têyk + ði + fôrs + krósiŋ # hwìc + iz + péyvd #/

The device of indicating junctures by differing symbols according to the ranges possible at differing juncture points is essentially that devised by Henry Lee Smith, who has for some time been concerned with these problems and has done very valuable work on them. It must be emphasized, however, that the device employs nonphonemic symbols and that differing symbols for differing "marking junctures," to employ a phrase Smith has used,[2] are symbols which record in convenient form the result of comparison between differing versions of the same sentence. If the symbols are used before such a comparison has been made, they are used only as the result of an appeal to meaning. Without comparison, the sentence is ambiguous as to structure, unless one of the two clear signals has occurred.

4. Morphological and syntactic linking and downgrading

The order adopted in this section of this chapter departs from normal procedure in moving through the language hierarchy. The normal hierarchy moves through phonology, morphology, lexicon, and syntax in succession. We therefore should take up linking and downgrading devices in that sequence. Lexical linking and downgrading are the most complex of the several processes and involve identification of a major form class which has not yet been described. For that reason, we bring together the relatively easily described processes of morphological and syntactic linking and downgrading, treating lexical linking and downgrading out of order, and separately.

Morphological linking most frequently occurs in the verb form and consists in the use of a verb uninflected for gender or tense, the forms which have previously been called predicativals rather than predicators. The forms in question are form 1 (the infinitive), form 4 (the –*ing*), and form 5 (the past participle). As said earlier (see p. 274) the nominal or pronominal form which precedes such a predicatival can still be called the subject, since the construction is fully variable with constructions containing

---

[2] See p. 342, footnote 3.

inflected verb forms, in which the subject is readily identifiable. The sentence in which there is the secondary linking device of an uninflected predicatival may be either the dependent or the main sentence. Examples of two- and three-sentence-element linked sentences with –*ing* follow:

SUBJECT AND PREDICATIVAL

2   3   2   2   31
John hesitating | Mary made the decision herself #
2   32   2   3   1
Mary made the decision herself | *John hesitating* #

PREDICATIVAL AND COMPLEMENT

2   3 2   2   31
Being windy | the day was cool #
2   32   2   3   1
The day was cool | *being windy* #

SUBJECT, PREDICATIVAL, AND COMPLEMENT

2   3 2   2   31
The window being open | the room was cool #
2   32   2   3 1
The room was cool | *the window being open* #

Examples with a past participle and the superfix $\{2\ 3\ 2\ |\}\ \{2\ 3\ 1\ \#\}$ follow:

SUBJECT AND PREDICATIVAL

Their commander taken, the enemy forces surrendered.
The enemy forces surrendered, *their commander taken*.

PREDICATIVAL AND COMPLEMENT

Taken prisoner, the enemy commander surrendered.
The enemy commander surrendered, *taken prisoner*.

SUBJECT, PREDICATIVAL, AND COMPLEMENT

Their commander taken prisoner, the enemy surrendered.
The enemy surrendered, *their commander taken prisoner*.

Examples with *to* and an infinitive and the same superfix follow:

SUBJECT AND PREDICATIVAL

A chance to marry, Mary wanted most of all.
Mary wanted most of all, *a chance to marry*.

PREDICATIVAL AND COMPLEMENT

To marry Mary, John traveled to her home.
John traveled to her home, *to marry Mary*.

SUBJECT, PREDICATIVAL, AND COMPLEMENT

The man to marry Mary—John knew he was the chosen candidate.

John knew he was the chosen candidate, *the man to marry Mary.*

The three types of predicatival constructions, *-ing,* past participle, and infinitive, are found in constructions which are still further downgraded, in that they serve as single sentence elements, or parts of single sentence elements:

		2	3	2	2	3	1
SUBJECTIVAL	*Being flirtatious* | was good for John #

	2	3	1
COMPLEMENT	John feared *being flirtatious* #

	2	3 2	2	31
SUBJECT	*A man driven crazy* | is what John is #

	2	3 1
COMPLEMENT	John is *a man driven crazy* #

	2	32	2	31
SUBJECTIVAL	*To be wise* | was John's hope #

	2	32	2	31
COMPLEMENT	John hoped | *to be wise* #

In the third and fourth of these examples, *driven crazy* is itself a downgraded construction. That is, it contains predicatival and complement, but can here be described as downgraded to the status of modifier of the preceding subject, *man.*

A more striking example of downgrading is found in the following pair:

The natives, ready to wear clothing, came to the Mission.

2   3 2   2   3 2   2   3 1
/ðə + néytivz ‖ rêdiy + tə + wêhr + klówðiŋ ‖ kêym + ti + ðə + míšin #/

The natives' ready-to-wear clothing came to the Mission.

2   3 2   2   3 1
/ðə + nêytivz + rêdiy + tə + wêhr + klówðiŋ | kêym + ti + ðə + míšin #/

Ready to wear clothing in the first sentence must be described as a dependent sentence rather than as a sentence adjunct, since it contains more than one recognizable sentence element, namely, subjectival, predicatival, and complement. The two utterances are perhaps not quite strictly parallel, since *natives* and *natives'* in the two sentences contain different, though homonymous, suffixes. Yet *ready to wear clothing* in the first example is a dependent sentence; in the second, it is downgraded to the status of a part of a sentence element, the subject.

Constructions containing predicativals of this type are downgraded when they occur as sentence elements, or parts of sentence elements, by the phonological treatment they receive—as *ready to wear* is, above. Yet all of these predicativals occur as downgraders in independent sentences, though such sentences are rather limited in occurrence. They are usually either titles or response sentences, like the following:

2   3 1
Marching Through Georgia
2   3 1
Angels Fallen
2   31
To Catch a Thief
             2   31
What is John doing? *Being good.*
             2   31
Where has John gone? *To get the car.*
         2   3 1
Was John caught? *Taken red-handed.*

In formal composition, such sentences are objected to unless they are of the special sort found in:

2   3 2 2   31
Better to marry | than to burn #

All of these sentences are downgraded to the status of elementless sentences. The one just quoted is an example of the equational type of sentence, in which two constructions of the same type are linked. It is closely similar to:

2   32 2   31
Better a live dog | than a dead lion #

There is primary phonological linking in that the two pitch morphemes are linked, but there is in addition a secondary linking device, the *-er . . . than* construction, which will be described below.

The only morphological downgrader which is always found in downgraded constructions, never in merely linked constructions, is the movable {z} of nouns, already illustrated in "She goes with *the boy who lives across the street's* brother." This particular construction may remind the student of the process found in such constructions as "an *unforgettable* experience" or "an *un-get-at-able* man," the latter a rare form. These types of compounding, however, are to be distinguished from downgrading, in that the prebase *un–* and the postbase *–able* are added to words or fixed phrases, whereas the downgrading form is added to material capable of standing as nonminimal sentence element or sentence.

The features of sentence element order which appear in dependent sentences are primarily downgraders rather than linkers. The most important of these order devices is the sequence noun-noun-verb, as in:

2   3   1
The dinner Mary gave #

The two constructions which precede the verb need not be nouns, but may be nominal constructions, nominals, pronouns, or pronominals. The construction just quoted is downgraded in the sense that it is now an elementless sentence, in which *Mary gave* is a modifying construction. As we should expect, therefore, sentences of this type appear frequently as titles:

The Woman Thou Gavest Me

It is rare for both the forms which precede the verb to occur as pronouns, but it is possible:

Him I love. or *He I love, is comely.*
Whom I teach, stays taught. or *Who I teach, stays taught.*

This order is common with pronominals in first position, as in:

what Mary thought

At least one of the constructions is particularly common as a response sentence, as in:

Did Mary go to town? *That she did.*

All of these constructions occur as members of larger sentences, as in:

The book he wrote was quite long.
Mary saw *him she loved.*

As should be evident from the examples we have given, this sequence consists in complement, subject or subjectival, and verb. The complement, as always, need not be an object or goal, however. Note:

The boy John had been still showed in his appearance.

Though these constructions can occur in linked sentences, it is still possible to describe this order sequence as a pure downgrader. A sentence in which it might be thought that the noun-noun-verb construction is merely linked is the following:

2 3   2   2   3   1
The book John wrote | it was really long #

Yet *the book John wrote* is a sentence downgraded to a single construction, here linked as a dependent, elementless sentence to a normally constructed main sentence. We have much the same kind of construction in :

2   32 2   3   1
John's book | it really was something #

The initial element might be thought of as an adjunct sentence element, but if it is put last it can occur with a monotone morpheme:

> *It really was something—John's book.*
> 2   3   1   1   1 1
> /ìt + rìhliy + wáhz + sə̂mpθiŋ | jâhnz + búk #/

In final position, such an element gets the treatment that is usual for a dependent sentence. It may therefore be called a dependent sentence in initial position.

Downgrading by order also occurs in constructions placed immediately before or after the verb, in which situation the downgraded construction serves as subject or complement:

> 2   3 2   2 31
> *The book John wrote* | is long #
> 2   31
> I bought *the book John wrote* #

These constructions are readily expandable by the addition of a pronominal, as in:

> The book *which* John wrote is long.

This expandability has led some analysts to treat the simpler construction *the book John wrote* as containing a zero form of the pronominal. Such analysis is to be avoided, since it is unpredictable from the simple form whether the expanded form will contain *which* or *that*, and the order sequence alone will serve as a downgrader adequately enough, as we have seen.

20 .... COMPLEX SENTENCES, II

Lexical Linking and Downgrading

1. Pronominals

We have identified a group of forms called pronominals, which are characterized by stress treatment like that of pronouns and are differentiated by initial elements, as pronouns are, but which are not pure pronouns because they lack the paradigmatic structure of pronouns. The set is imperfect, since most bases are not found carried throughout the series, and there are other irregularities as well. The series is:[1]

{h–}	{ð–}	{hw–}
here	*there*	*where*
hither	*thither*	*whither*
		whether
hence	*thence*	*whence*
	then	*when*
	that	*what*
		why
		which
		while
		how
		who

The chief irregularities here are, first, that we have included in the list one true pronoun, *who*, which has the paradigmatic characteristics of pronouns but which in all its other characteristics belongs with this group, even in its initial morpheme. Second, we have listed *how* and *who* as containing the morpheme {hw–}, though the form actually found is an initial {h–}. This initial {h–}, therefore, is described as an allomorph of {hw–} which occurs before any base containing /–w/. The necessity for so classifying these forms is their strong syntactic similarity to the whole list of forms with initial {hw–} and their lack of similarity to the forms with initial {h–}. A third irregularity is that *while* is not only not supported by forms in {h–}

---

[1] See above, pp. 148–49.

and {ð-} but also lacks the interrogative functions of the rest of the group. Since it shares other functions, it has nonetheless been included. A final irregularity in distribution, which we shall see as we go on, is that *that* unexpectedly has many of the functions and much of the distribution that we should expect of *what*.

It has been stated that the forms with {hw-} have interrogative function. It will therefore be necessary to describe the various distributions which have interrogative function and to distinguish these from the distributions which have linking and downgrading function. A place to begin this distinction is with the pair "What man?" and "Which man?" These forms have secondary stress and are modifiers of group v, as is proved by such a sequence as:

V   IV   III   II   I

What ten fine old stone houses?

The forms "What man?" and "Which man?" are normally pronounced:

2   31   2   31
/hwât + mǽn #/ and /hwîc + mǽn #/

But they may receive the question superfix {2 2 3 ‖} and may also vary in the stress pattern, receiving /′ ˆ/ instead of /ˆ ′/. It is the secondary stress which is the minimal distinction marking these interrogative uses. Also, only *which* and *what* occur thus as group v modifiers.

We can go on to distinguish a different use of *what* placed before a noun. The first of these sentences is interrogative:

What man does?

2   31   2   3   1
/hwât + mǽn + dɔ́z #/ or with different meaning /hwât + mǽn + dɔ̂z #/

In contrast is:

What man does, woman can do.

2   3   2   33   1
/hwàt + mǽn + dɔ̂z | wúmən + kɪn + dûw #/

The construction is now not interrogative, but a linked dependent sentence. The minimally distinctive signal is the stress, here tertiary. We can now set up a primary distinction: a pronominal in {hw-} is interrogative if it receives secondary stress, a linker if it receives tertiary (or weak) stress, though we shall meet at least one exception. The distinction can be immediately used with two other forms. We pointed out above that *that* acts as we should expect *what* to. That is, *that* is often used as a linker and downgrader. It is therefore necessary to distinguish the linking *that* from the

form that is a group v modifier and has the plural form *those*. A written
sentence which may be interpreted in two ways is:

Mary can do anything that woman does.

2   2   2   2   31
/mêhriy + kɨn + dûw + énɨθɨŋ | ðǽt + wûmən + dɔ́z #/

The first pitch morpheme may also occur as {2 3 2 |} rather than as a
monotone. The meaning of this form of the sentence is "Mary can do
anything which that woman does":

2   3   1   2   ʻ 31
/mêhriy + kɨn + dûw + énɨθɨŋ | ðɔ̀t + wûmən + dɔ́z #/

In the second, *that* may also appear as /ðǽt/, rather than as the form given.
The meaning of the second sentence is "Mary can do anything which
women do." The second sentence contains the linking *that*, here occurring
in a downgraded sentence, serving as part of the complement. The first
sentence contains the group v modifier, here occurring in a normal subject-
predicator sentence. Both forms may occur in the same sentence:

Mary can do anything *that that* woman does.

The stress sequence will then be /... ðət + ðǽt.../.[2] Here also stress
establishes the distinction between the group v modifier and the linker.

A second form in which stress establishes a distinction is *how*. If the
sequence is *how big*, two treatments are possible:

2   31   2   31
/hàw + bíg #/ and /hâw + bíg #/

Both are minimal, elementless sentences, but the first contains the linking
and downgrading *how*, the second the interrogative.

Even though the linking and downgrading forms are thus distinguished
from the interrogative by stress, there are secondary distinctions in syntax,
which need description. There is one general type of order which occurs in
both interrogative and downgraded sequences. This is:

{hw–}   VERB   NOUN

---

[2] The piling up of *that*'s gives one of the peculiar constructions used in many
languages as catches:

That that that that means . . .
/ðǽt | ðət + ðǽt + ðǽt + míynz . . . /

The first *that* is a group v form used as subject of a discontinuous sentence. The
second *that* is a linker introducing the dependent sentence. The third is a normal
group v modifier, and the last is *that* used as a noun (the word *that*), capable of
having a plural, as in the first phrase of this note.

There are two types which conform to this pattern. The first is:

{hw–} SUBJECTIVAL	VERB	NOUN (SUBJ.)
Where	*was*	*Cock Robin?*

The fact that the following noun is here the true subject is proved by its selection of the verb form, as in:

Where were the Hittites?

The second type of this order is:

{hw–} SUBJ.	VERB	NOUN (COMPL.)
Who	*killed*	*Cock Robin?*

Both subtypes appear, then, in interrogative sentences. Only the second appears also in downgraded constructions, as in:

He told us *who killed Cock Robin.*

If the first type is downgraded it assumes the order:

	{hw–}	NOUN (SUBJ.)	VERB
He asked	*where*	*Cock Robin*	*was.*

This pattern, then, conforms to that order which has been called syntactic downgrading, namely noun-noun-verb. In this pattern, it will be remembered, we described the first noun, nominal, pronoun, or pronominal as the complement and the second noun as the subject. The relationship holds here, also. Notice the order in the following:

who Cock Robin killed   or   *whom* Cock Robin killed

In this sentence, *who* is not only the complement but, more narrowly, the goal, and *Cock Robin* is not only the subject but, more narrowly, the actor.

This shift from interrogative order to downgraded order when the noun is subject is one of the points which is perennially troublesome to learners of the language. The shift is very common in normal conversational English, and so is a point in structure that has to be taught. It is possible, however, to avoid the shift by treating the construction beginning with a form in {hw–} as a linked, rather than a downgraded sentence:

He asked us, "Where was Cock Robin?"

2   3   2   2   3 3

/hìy + ǽst + ǝs | hwêr + wiz + kâk + rábin ‖/

This linking treatment is what is indicated by the use of quotation marks in written composition. It is also true that bookish and poetic style does not follow the normal rules. Thus a poetic interrogative is:

Whence comes the dawn?

2   3 3

/hwêns + kə̂mz + ðə + dóhn |||/

The transcription here given with {2 3 3 ||} seems to be a common pitch in such rather unnatural constructions, though it is certainly possible to give them the more normal {2 3 1 #}. In bookish style this order can also be used in linked and downgraded constructions, the sole necessary difference being in the stress given *whence*:

John looked toward the East, whence comes the dawn.

2   32   2   3 1

/jâhn + lûk + tò̄hrd + ðiy + íyst | hwèns + kə̂mz + ðə + dóhn #/

Structurally, though not semantically, this particular form of the sentence is somewhat ambiguous. The final construction can be interpreted as downgraded, forming a modifying construction for *East*, or it can be interpreted as a linked main sentence. Since a linked sentence, however, should be capable of standing as either main or dependent sentence, and this construction is not normal in first position, it seems best to call *whence comes the dawn* a dependent sentence downgraded to the status of modifying phrase.

To return to distinctions between interrogative and downgraded order, we can point out that for sentences containing the verb *to be*, the order {hw-}-verb-subject (noun or pronoun), all with the superfix {2 3 1 #}, is normal for the following, though they may also have {2 2 3 ||} on occasion:

<table>
<tr><td>When is it?</td><td>Why is it?</td></tr>
<tr><td>Where is it?</td><td>How is it?</td></tr>
<tr><td>Whence is it?</td><td>Which is it?</td></tr>
<tr><td>What is it?</td><td>Who is it?</td></tr>
</table>

In general, the same list of forms in {hw-} tend to occur in interrogatives of this pattern with the verbs *can*, *will*, *shall*, *may*, *must*, and *do*. There are individual limitations, such as that *whence* occurs rarely with any of these forms, but it seems not worthwhile to give an exhaustive list. For all these interrogative forms, the corresponding downgraded order is normally a reversal of the position of verb and subject. A single example will do:

Why must I? That is the reason why I must.

The use of this pattern with any other verbs than those in the list given above is always bookish, and now rare. There are degrees of difference, however, in the freedom with which such constructions occur. With verbs, such as *kill*, which are normally used with a complement which is the goal, and with forms in {hw–}, such as *what*, which can stand as subject, we would then have in this order, a form like "What killed he?" I should hesitate to say the form is impossible, but it is certainly very rare, so rare indeed that it almost produces the impression of a mistake for "What killed him." A form such as "When died he?" is certainly commoner, and forms like "Whither goest thou?" and "Whence comes it?" are commoner still, presumably because *whither* and *whence* are themselves somewhat bookish, so that bookish syntax is in accord with bookish vocabulary.

For all these verbs, then, the normal question order is:

{hw–}	1ST VERB	SUBJ.	2ND VERB
When	*did*	*he*	*die?*

The form in {hw–} is to be interpreted as a complement but is by no means always the goal. The decision that *when* in a sentence like that quoted immediately above is a complement, rather than a subjectival, is based on the fact that another type of interrogative order, not here described since it has no relation to downgrading, is "He died when?" In this second form, *when* would clearly have to be analyzed as a complement, since it occupies the normal complement position. The semantic difference between the pronominal as complement alone and the pronominal as complement which is also a goal is shown in such a pair as the following:

When did he die?   What did he eat?

For all these question forms, the corresponding downgraded order is:

{hw–}	SUBJ.	VERB	
What	*he*	*ate*	was apple pie.

If the sentence is one in which the verb is in the form of a combination consisting of inflected first verb with light stress and uninflectable second verb, the correspondences are threefold. In a statement the order is:

SUBJ.	1ST VERB	2ND VERB	COMPL.
John	*can*	*drive*	*a car.*

In question form, this is:

1ST VERB	SUBJ.	2ND VERB	COMPL.
Can	*John*	*drive*	*a car?*

The question order is also used when an interrogative is added at the start:

INTERR.	1ST VERB	SUBJ.	2ND VERB	COMPL.
How	*can*	*John*	*drive*	*a car?*

The downgraded order (with initial {hw–}) is the same as that of statement:

{hw–}	SUBJ.	1ST VERB	2ND VERB	COMPL.
I found out *how*	*John*	*can*	*drive*	*a car.*

We have been considering the order of elements in these several sentences, but it must be pointed out that the various orders are accompanied by differences in stress. In the order of simple statement, the first verb usually receives weak stress. In question order, it often receives tertiary or even stronger stress. If an interrogative is added, however, the interrogative receives the usual secondary stress, and the following first verb is then ordinarily weak. In downgraded order, the initial {hw–}-form gets tertiary or weak stress, as does the first verb.

These then are the characteristics which define certain uses of the form in {hw–} as interrogative. We should add that *whether* and *while* do not occur as interrogatives, and are therefore linkers and downgraders only. The same is true of *that*, which unexpectedly, as we have said, acts as a linker, but never as an interrogative.

Who, which, and *what* can occur in downgraded constructions as the subject, with the order:

	SUBJ.	VERB	COMPL.
I know	*who*	*killed*	*Cock Robin.*

In the sentence just given, we can substitute either *which* or *what* for *who*. This fact of distribution is the reason why these three forms constitute a fairly well-marked subgroup within the total list of forms being considered. If the order is

	SUBJ.	DOWN-GRADER	VERB	COMPL.
It was	*the sparrow*	*who*	*killed*	*Cock Robin.*

the unity of the subgroup is broken by the fact that *what* does not occur in this construction type in standard speech. In place of the expected *what*, we have *that*.

Who, which, and *that* (rather than *what*) occur also in the order:

	NOUN	DOWN-GRADER	NOUN	VERB	NOUN
It was	*Cock Robin*	*whom*	*the sparrow*	*killed.*	
It was	*Tuesday*	*that*	*the sparrow*	*killed*	*Cock Robin.*

It is interesting that these two sentences establish a distinction between *that*, on the one hand, and *who* and *which*, on the other. All three forms may occur in the first sentence, but *who* and *which* do not occur in the second. The first noun in such a sequence is the complement of the preceding verb and is followed by a juncture point. As the sentences indicate, the first noun may be in variant relation to the following verb. Thus, "It was Cock Robin that the sparrow killed" is semantically, but not structurally, different from "It was Tuesday that the sparrow died." It is not even true that a noun following the verb of the downgraded construction must be a true goal, since we can have "It was Cock Robin that the sparrow killed Tuesday." This last sentence, however, has a juncture point, though not necessarily a juncture before *Tuesday*; while a juncture before *Cock Robin* in "It was Tuesday that the sparrow killed Cock Robin" is less likely and, conversely, more likely to be accompanied by linkage by a complex contour, should the juncture occur. The sequence noun-downgrader-verb-noun is found not only with *who, which,* and *that* but also with most of the other downgraders:

> The time *when* the sparrow killed Cock Robin was long ago.
> The place *where* the sparrow killed Cock Robin was in the forest.
> The place *whence* Tommy Stout pulled Pussy was the well.
> The place *whither* Tommy Green threw Pussy was the well.
> The question *whether* the sparrow killed Cock Robin is settled in
>   the rhyme.
> The reason *why* the sparrow killed Cock Robin is not given.
> The country *while* Old King Cole ruled it was merry.
> The way *how* the sparrow killed Cock Robin is described.

The last sentence is not, perhaps, of as common a type as the others, and indeed can be reduced by dropping off the material before *how*. Common or not, however, it is a type which occurs. Even *what* can be found in a sentence of this type, though in my idiolect it requires a contrastive stress on *what*:

$$\overset{2}{\textit{The qu}}\overset{3}{\textit{êstion wh}}\overset{2}{\textit{át J}}\overset{2}{\textit{ôhn d}}\overset{3}{\textit{îd}} \| \overset{1}{\textit{ìsn't impórtant}} \, \#$$

In formal composition, where stress is not indicated, such a sentence is often revised to "The question *of what* John did is not important." In other postnominal situations, *what* is uncommon and often occurs with vocabulary or syntax which suggest a non-English sentence type, as in such a possible sentence as "This is the best Hasenpfeffer what gives." Rare as postnominal *what* now is, it was once widespread. The English *Dialect Dictionary* quotes examples from many English counties, the United States, and Australia.[3] One of its examples is sufficient:

> I've got a *letter what she wrote.* . . .

---

[3] Joseph Wright, *The English Dialect Dictionary*, Frowde, London, 1898 ff., Vol. VI, pp. 492–93.

Sentences like this, now definitely regarded as substandard, have structural justification, nevertheless. They bring *what* into line with the other forms in {hw-}.

The fourth type of downgraded order consists in:

{hw-}	COMPL.	SUBJ.	VERB			
2			3 2	2		3 1
Whàt	*dêvil*	*Mèphistôpheles*	*wás* || Mârgaret dìdn't knów #			
2			3 2			
Whàt	*a dêvil*	*Mèphistôpheles*	*wás* || Margaret didn't know #			
2			3 2			
Whàt	*the dêvil*	*Mèphistôpheles*	*wás* || Margaret didn't know #			

All three sentences have the same superfix patterns, and have been chosen primarily because they indicate the rather surprising semantic differences which can emerge without change in structure. The last two have special, idiomatic meaning, and the last also has rather special social connotations. But special as they may be, they still indicate that *what* in this particular prenominal position can be followed by an article, that is, a modifier of group v. We have seen that the interrogative *what* has secondary stress, and the linking and downgrading *what* has tertiary stress. The form in the sentences just quoted is therefore the linking *what*. It differs from the interrogative *what* not only in its stress characteristics but also in the order group to which it belongs. The secondarily stressed, interrogative *what* belongs to group v, and so cannot be followed by such group v forms as *a* and *the*, as can the linking *what* with tertiary stress. The linking *what*, then, belongs to group vi, along with forms like *all* and *both*. The placing of this particular *what* in group vi is borne out also by addition of *all* to such a sentence as the following:

> *What money John had was not enough.*

If *all* is added, the result is usually:

> *All of what* money John had was not enough.

That is to say, *all* and *what* act as we should expect if they belong to the same order group, since group vi is one of those which permit only one example in a single construction. The introduction of *of* is therefore explained as breaking the sequence in two, by making what follows it a prepositional construction.

Which is the other form in {hw-} which occurs in this order under the conditions we are describing. Yet, it is a question whether *which* is to be described as belonging to group vi as *what* does. In my own speech, there seems to be some reason for assigning it to vi, but I should be surprised if this were true of all idiolects. The following three sentences are natural to me:

> *Whìch bôok Jôhn wróte, Mary didn't know.*
> *Âll of whìch bôok Jôhn wróte, Mary didn't know.*
> *Whìch the dêvil Jôhn wás, Mary didn't know.*

The distribution of *which* is like *what*, therefore, not only in the stress it receives, but in its relation to group VI forms preceding and in the possibility of a definite article—limited in occurrence as such constructions may be— after it. *Which* is unlike *what* only in that *which a* does not occur.

Even though the assignment of linking *which* and *what* to group VI solves a number of problems of analysis, some others remain. One of them is that in sentences like the following, *what* and *which* are interchangeable with forms which clearly belong to group V:

> *Whàt* môney Jôhn hád | was not enough.
> *The* money John had | was not enough.

If we construct a pair of sentences with such a noun as *book*, we get variant substitute forms. If *book* is in the plural, the normal substitute is *the:*

> *Whàt bôoks* Jôhn wrítes | are always good.
> *The books* John writes | are always good.

If *book* is in the singular, a normal substitute is *a:*

> *Whàt bôok* Jôhn wrítes | doesn't matter.
> *A book* John writes | doesn't matter.

In short, *what* and *which* are related to group V forms, even though they are not members of that group. The group V forms, also, are themselves linkers in sentences like these and will therefore be described among the list of lexical linkers in our next section.

A more troublesome problem arises from a stress situation which seems to contradict what we have just said. We have described *what* with secondary stress as belonging to group V, and *what* with tertiary stress as belonging to group VI. Yet note the stress in the following:

> *What the book John wrote was, was brilliant.*
> 2   32   2   3 1
> /hwât + ðə + bûk + jâhn + rôwt + wáhz ‖ wɨz + brílyɨnt #

The stress is secondary, but the form following is *the*, which would not be expected were the *what* of group V found here, as the stress seems to indicate. The *what* found here, also, rather obviously has parallels with the *what* of sentences like:

> 2   32 2   3 1
> Whàt the bôok wás | was brílliant #

In this sentence, *what* has tertiary stress and is clearly the linking rather than the interrogative *what*. It would seem that the peculiarities of the sentence "Whât the bôok Jôhn wrôte wás, was brílliant" are due to the fact that it has two immediately successive verbs and that this occurrence is a special one in which the *what* takes secondary stress but remains the linking form, that is, a member of group VI. A key to the construction is in the statement that such group V forms as *the* themselves occur in downgraded constructions. That is to say *the book John wrote* is itself a downgraded form, with downgraded order, normally introduced by a group V modifier. This downgraded construction stands as a modifier between the subject *what* and its verb *was*, an interpretation borne out by the fact that the superfix is often a complex contour:

$$2 \qquad\qquad\qquad\qquad 3\,2 \quad\ 4\,4\,2$$
$$\text{/hwât} + \text{ð\textschwa} + \text{bûk} + \text{jâhn} + \text{rówt} \mid \text{wáhz} \mid \ldots/$$

We thus have what amounts to two downgraders, *what* and *the*, in succession. Under these circumstances it seems reasonable to assume that the first receives an otherwise unusual secondary stress, instead of the expected tertiary. Semantically the construction is different from that found in:

What the devil Mephistopheles was, Margaret didn't know.

This simpler construction has the formula:

VI	V	NOUN	NOUN	VERB
What	*the*	*devil*	*Mephistopheles*	*was* . . .

The more complex construction has the formula:

VI	V	NOUN	NOUN	VERB	VERB
What	*the*	*book*	*John*	*wrote*	*was* . . .

The difference is then in the fact that the longer construction has a second verb. This longer construction is therefore doubly downgraded. The whole construction is acting as a single sentence element, the subjectival of the verb which immediately follows the terminal juncture. The subjectival construction itself contains the construction *the book John wrote was*, which in turn contains the subjectival construction *the book John wrote* and its verb, *was*. The whole is downgraded to the status of a modifying construction. Even more like a Chinese box, this construction further contains *John wrote*, which consists of subject and verb, again downgraded to the status of modifier of the preceding noun.

These constructions with final double verbs constitute then a fifth type of linked and downgraded order, distinct from the fourth type, which has only a single verb in final position. The fifth type permits other forms than *what* in first position:

> *Whích the bôok Jôhn wróte wás, I don't know.*
> *When the day they were married was, I don't remember.*
> *Where the place John lived was, I don't remember.*
> *Whither the plane John took went, I don't know.*
> *Whence the plane John took came, I don't know.*
> *Who the man Mary married was, I don't know.*
> *How the plan John formed worked, I don't know.*
> *Whether the plan John formed worked, I don't know.*
> *While the plan John formed worked, it was effective.*
> *Why the plan John formed worked, I don't know.*

That is, the whole group of forms in {hw–} can occur here. However, the group are here occurring in linked rather than downgraded sentences, since what follows in every case is a normal sentence type of subject and verb, with or without complement. All but one of these forms in {hw–} also occur when this sequence is downgraded to the status of subjectival sentence element:

> *Whât the hôuse Jôhn bûilt wás, was expensive.*
> *Which the house John built was, was evident.*
> *When the day they were married was, was Tuesday.*
> *Where the place John lived was, was Paris.*
> *Whither the plane John took went, was evident.*
> *Whence the plane John took came, was evident.*
> *Who the man Mary married was, was important.*
> *How the plan John formed worked, became plain.*
> *Whether the plan John formed works, is important.*
> *Why the plan John formed works, is important.*

In short, all of the forms except *while* occur in downgraded constructions as well as in linked sentences. To the list should be added *that*, which here also acts as linker and downgrader:

> *Thât the plân Jôhn fôrmed will wórk, I don't know.*
> *That the plan John formed will work, is evident.*

The most firmly fixed phonological characteristics of these constructions are the primary stress on the last verb form and the following terminal, always either /|/ or /|||/. At this juncture point, then, the range of junctures is relatively fixed and does not include /+/ or, normally, /#/. A feature of the analysis is that if we follow the successive cuts as we have described them, we are left with main sentence frames for all the downgraded sentences which would look like this:

> *What . . . was expensive.*
> *Which . . . was evident.*
> *When . . . was Tuesday.*
> *Where . . . was Paris.*
> *Whither . . . was evident.*
> *Whence . . . was evident.*
> *Who . . . was important.*
> *How . . . became plain.*
> *Whether . . . is important.*
> *Why . . . is important.*
> *That . . . is evident.*

A number of these skeleton sentences do not occur, or scarcely occur as independent sentences, or, as with *when was Tuesday*, occur commonly only with the superfixes of a question. Yet, since there is no structural difference between *which* and *whether* in these sentences, it seems best to assign the whole group of {hw–} forms to the status of subjectivals in these downgraded constructions. These downgraded sentences with piled-up verb forms must receive the superfix pattern described above to be intelligible. Since the writing system does not indicate the superfixes accurately and they are therefore puzzles for the reader who has to sort them out, sentences of this sort are usually avoided in written composition. It is possible, for instance, to construct a sentence which is a real problem when read, but is plain enough when pronounced:

> *What the house John had had had had, had had its importance.*
> 2   3 2   2   4 2
> /hwàt + ðə + hâws + jâhn + həd + hǽd | həd + hǽd ||
>   2   3   1
> həd + hǽd + ìts + impórt + əns #/

The sentence is a freak in writing, which no writer in his senses would use. Spoken, it is only mildly queer, and is at least intelligible. Even though these sentences are understandably rare in writing, the reader should not suppose that they are either uncommon or unnatural in speech.

The discussion of these sequences has happened to turn on instances where the sequence was serving as a subjectival sentence element. It should be added that they can also serve as complement constructions, as in:

>   2   3 1
> *I don't know | whàt the hôuse Jâck bûilt wás #*

Again all of the forms in {hw–}, together with *that*, occur in this type of downgraded construction, except for *while*. We need not illustrate them further, but it is interesting that sentences where the downgraded sequence serves as complement seem to be commoner in writing than sentences where it serves as subjectival. A possible reason is that in the former there can be only two verbs in sequence, whereas in the subjectival type, the two verbs of the downgraded construction are followed by a third.

The two-verb constructions constitute the fifth type of linked or downgraded order. The sixth consists in the relatively simple one of subject, verb, and complement, with the form in {hw–} in first position. Examples of linked sentences, as dependent or as main sentences, are:

> *When Mary left the house, it was already late.*
> *It was already late, when Mary left the house.*

Examples of downgrading as subjectival and complement, respectively, are:

> *When Mary left the house* was Tuesday.
> I don't know *when Mary left the house.*

The chief difficulty in analysis of this type of construction is in assigning the pronominal in {hw–} to its proper sentence element. A clue can be found in such a sentence as the following:

> *What John left his son was little enough.*

This sentence can be transposed so as to give:

> 2   22   2   3 1
> *John left his son* | *what was little enough* #

Such a transposition suggests that *what was little enough* can be treated as a single phrase, a second complement. If we substitute another entity, the relationship may be clearer:

> *The money John left his son was little enough.*

In this instance, we have a typical downgraded order; complement, subject, verb, and again complement. We should have no hesitation in calling *the money* a second complement, even though it occurs in initial position, since it can readily be transposed to independent order, and then becomes "John left his son the money." There seems to be no reason, therefore, why we cannot follow the rule we have used elsewhere and interpret all pronominals in {hw–} when followed by subject, verb, and complement as second complements. The decision is formal and therefore may be strange to those who analyze in terms of semantics. Thus, traditional analysis treats the initial elements of the following pair quite differently:

> *When John left his wife* . . .   *What John left his wife* . . .

When is stated to be an adverb, because "it qualifies the verb as to time."

What, on the other hand, is stated to be a pronoun, because "it stands for a noun." To recapitulate our present analysis, all the forms in {hw–} have been called pronominals, primarily because of the way in which they are constructed, secondarily because of their stress characteristics. As pronominals, therefore, they may be interpreted as forming subjectivals, subjects, or complements just as do nouns. The two partial sentences we have just quoted, then, are structurally alike, consisting of second complement, subject, verb, and first complement. The difference in meaning between the two sentences is inherent in the meaning of the items contained, not in the structure.

All of the forms in {hw–} occur in linked sentences of this sixth type. It is unnecessary to illustrate them in both dependent and main positions.

Where John shot the bear, it was cold.

This particular sentence frame can be used to illustrate several of our forms; *when* and *while* both fit into the position occupied by *where.*

Whether Mary found her way, John didn't know.

Into this sentence *whither, whence, why,* and *how* can all be fitted.

What in this construction can be illustrated by a sentence we have already used, with a slight modification:

What John left his son—it was little enough.

In connection with this sentence it is worth returning for a moment to a stress distinction:

What men leave their wives . . .

As written, this construction is ambiguous. Aside from the pitch and juncture distinctions, it is only the degree of stress which *what* receives which identifies the form as an interrogative belonging to group v or as the linking *what* with tertiary stress, which belongs to group vi.

Who and *which* seem to be the most difficult to fit into this construction, but the following is at least not unnatural:

Who Mary paid ten dollars—it made a lot of difference.

Which occurs more naturally in the main sentence, as in:

One was expensive, which John bought Mary.

In the dependent sentence, the place of *which* is usually taken by the fixed phrase *whichever:*

Whichever Mary drove home, one was left behind.

<pre>
      2   3 1   2   31
/wicêvər + mêhriy + drôwv + hówm | wə̂n + wɨz + lêft + bɨháynd#/
</pre>

One of the general features of pronominals as linkers is that often one of the linked sentences will be introduced by a form in {hw–}, the other by the corresponding form in {ð–}. Under these circumstances, the form in {ð–} is therefore also acting as a linker:

> *When Mary washes the dishes, then John scrubs the floor.*
> *Then John scrubs the floor, when Mary washes the dishes.*
> *Where the Bee sucks, there suck I.*
> *Whither he goes, thither I go.*
> *Whence comes luxury, thence comes wealth.*
> *What you learn in college, that's important.*

The correlation is at best somewhat loose, since often the forms in {ð–} and {hw–} do not have the same base, as in:

> *There I cowch when Owles doe crie.*   or
> *Whither he goes, there I go.*

These forms, also, often pile up, so that one gets sequences like *here where*, *there where*, and so on. It is a minor feature of order that in such sequences it is always the form in {hw–} which is last. The forms are often open to more than one analysis, since the position and number of terminals will vary. Thus, with the following sentence, a number of different forms are possible:

> *Here where the shore is smooth, let's go ashore.*

This can be pronounced as:

```
2                              3 2    2                  3 1
/hìr + hwèr + ðə + šɔ́hr + iz + smúwð | lêt + s + gòw + ə + šɔ́hr #/
              or /híhr | hwèr . . ./
```

In instances like the second, it is possible to regard the main sentence as the discontinuous sequence *here . . . let's go ashore.* If the first pronunciation is used, it would seem that both linkers are occurring in the dependent sentence. The interpretation is borne out by what happens if we adopt the following less common order:

> *Let's—here where the shore is smooth—go ashore.*

In this situation, for me it would be quite strange to set off *here* by a following terminal, so that it becomes necessary to regard *here where* as a sequence belonging to the dependent included sentence. If, on the other hand, the following order is adopted, there are still more possibilities:

> *Let's go ashore here where the shore is smooth*

The sentence has been left unpunctuated, since there are three possibilities: there may be only one terminal, placed either before *here* or after *here*, or there may be two terminals, placed before and after *here*. In the last arrangement, then, it would be necessary to regard the utterance as composed of three linked sentences: the first dependent sentence composed normally of more than one sentence element; the second, an elementless sentence; and the third, the main sentence, composed of pronominal linker, subject, verb, and complement.

When pronominals pile up thus within a single sentence or sentence element, we get sequences such as the following:

PRONOMINAL	PRONOMINAL	NOUN	VERB
here	*where*	*John*	*works*

We have seen that when we have the sequence of single pronominal followed by the subject and verb, it is best to interpret that pronominal as the complement. If we have two pronominals there is a difficulty. Are both of them complements, or only one? It would seem that the best answer that can be given is that, both forms being of the same class, they together make up a compound complement, rather than a first and a second complement of the type found in "Give him the book," where characteristically only one of the complements can be a pronoun.

The pronominals also cluster in dependent sentences downgraded by being without terminal junctures. Typical examples are:

Where the river's smooth, *there's where* we'll go ashore.
What you learn in college, *that's what's* important.

There is, of course, a difference in the analysis of the two sentences, since the second contains two forms of the verb *to be*—"*that's what's*." There is a whole series of sentences in the order:

SUBJ.	VERB	COMPL.
{hw–}, {ð–}, or {h–}	*to be*	{hw–}

These occur as independent sentences, though usually with stylistic dependence on sentences preceding: *that's what, that's why, that's how, here's where, here's why, here's how* (the latter is also an idiomatic and unpredictable sentence used as a toast), *then's when, that's who*.

The only one of the {hw–} forms which never seems to occur as complement in these sentences is *while*. There are a fair number of sentences also in which the same form occurs as both subject and complement—*that's that, who's who, which is which*. Except for these forms, which are identified as questions or statements by the superfixes they receive, forms in which a form in {hw–} is the subject are normally questions, as in "What's that?"

We noted above that we can have linked sentences like "That's what's important." The first pronominal is serving as subject of the immediately following verb, and *what* is its complement. The whole sentence, *that's what*, is then downgraded to the status of subjective sentence element for what follows. In "There's where we'll go ashore," *there* is again subject for the immediately following verb, but the following construction is *where we'll go ashore*, which is a typical downgraded sentence consisting of pronominal as second complement, subject, verb, and complement. The whole construction serves as the complement of the preceding verb. The construction which might be generalized as $\{ð \ldots iz + hw \ldots\}$ is downgraded so that it acts as a linker with just about the same function as one of the pronominals alone.

Not only do pronominals pile up in constructions like *here where*, they enter into combinations with other forms. These combinations can either be treated as free phrases, with normal stress and juncture, or be treated as fixed phrases with modification of stress and often loss of $/+/$. The pronominal in these combinations often shows itself to be the head of the construction, in that the pronominal could occur alone, while the second form could not. Yet even when this is true, the pronominal does not necessarily get the heavier stress. A typical example is *whatever:*

Whatever John saw was green.
2   32 2   31
/hwatèvər + jâhn + sɔ́h | wɨz + gríyn #/

Here *whatever* is a fixed phrase, with weak rather than the normal tertiary on the first member and loss of $/+/$. It can be treated as a free phrase, however, but still with the heavier stress on *ever:*

2   3   2   2   31
/hwàt + évər + jâhn + sɔ́h | wɨz + gríyn #/

Yet, no matter which form is given, *what* remains the head, since we may have "What John saw was green," but not "*Ever* John saw was green."

Ever is the commonest of these second elements, occurring not only in *whatever* but also in *whoever, wherever, whenever, however,* and *whichever.* For the distribution of these forms, it is only necessary to point out that *however* differs from the others in occurring frequently as a separate adjunctival sentence element rather than as a linker. The distinction is real, and once produced a ludicrous student mistake in punctuation: "I do not like fish; however, it is cooked." The student had evidently been following a model mechanically, perhaps that of a sentence like "I do not like fish; however, it is a good food."

While *ever* is the commonest second element, there are a number of others, as in *whereas* and *whereupon*. While I shall not attempt to list all these forms, a brief comment on these two may be made. *Whereas* has stress on the second element as usual and may be either fixed or free phrase. It is different from *whereupon* in that in most of the situations where it occurs, both of its elements can also occur separately:

> Mary washed the dishes, *whereas* John scrubbed the floor.
> Mary washed the dishes, *where* John scrubbed the floor.
> Mary washed the dishes, *as* John scrubbed the floor.

In fixed phrases of this sort, where distribution does not indicate which member is the head of the construction, it would therefore seem necessary to rely on stress and speak of *as* as the head. With *whereupon* the situation is different. If we have "Mary washed the dishes, *whereupon* John scrubbed the floor," only the first element can occur alone, and *where* is accordingly the head.

The only other class of fixed phrases involving pronominals that need be mentioned are those in which the pronominal is the second element. *Nowhere* has essentially the distribution of *where* and is therefore simply a negative compound of *where*. *Somewhat*, however, has neither the distribution of *some* nor the distribution of *what*, but has rather the distribution of *very*, as in:

> *a tall, somewhat fat man* compared with *a tall, very fat man*.

Somewhat is therefore an adverbial fixed phrase. The various fixed phrases have to be identified, therefore, individually, according to the distribution which each has.

We can conclude this long, though still far from exhaustive, discussion of the pronominals as linkers and downgraders with mention of the fact that they often occur with constructions which are of lower status than linked or downgraded sentences. For instance, *while* can occur as merely the introductory element in an adjunctival sentence element or as the initial linker in a dependent sentence. Notice the distinction in the following, shown in writing by the comma, in speech by a terminal:

> *While young, John worked the farm; his father taught.*
> *While young John worked the farm, his father taught.*

In adjunctival sentence elements, *while* can also link two adjectives or two adverbs:

> John, *intelligent while illiterate*, could express himself in painting.
> John, *gracefully while firmly*, declined the task.

A peculiarity of distribution in these adjunctival sentence elements is that when *while* occurs before two adjectives, a second linker is required before the second adjective, even if the adjectives are in normal order. Thus:

> While *strong and young*, John worked the farm; his father taught.

This contrasts with:

> While *strong young* John worked the farm, his father taught.

Though rarer, we also find constructions in which *while* introduces an adjunctival sentence element which consists of a noun:

$$\overset{2\ \ \ \ 3\ \ \ \ 2\ \ \ \ 2}{\textit{Wh\'ile pr\'esident} \mid \textit{John initiated many measures}} \overset{3\ \ \ 1}{\textit{}} \#$$

Notice that here also there is a stress and juncture distinction between *while* as linker and *while* as the initial of an adjunctival sentence element:

$$\overset{2}{\textit{Wh\`ile pr\^esident J\^ohn in\^itiated m\^any m\'easures}} \overset{3\ \ \ 2\ \ \ 2}{\textit{}} \parallel \textit{president}$$
$$\overset{3}{\textit{Jack initiated very few}} \overset{1}{\textit{}} \#$$

The group of pronominals which share the distribution we have just described for *while* are *when* and *where*. To these can be added *whether*, since the distribution found in *while strong and young* is closely similar to one use of *whether*:

> *Whether strong or weak*, John worked the farm.

In other adjunctivals introduced by *whether*, the noun, adjective, or adverb is followed by *or not*, elements which do not necessarily occur with *while*, *when*, and *where*:

> *Whether president or not, John initiated many measures.*
> *Whether strong or not, John worked the farm.*
> *Whether gracefully or not, John declined the task.*

But notice:

> *While president or not, John initiated many measures.*   and
> *Where understood or not, the doctrine is salutary.*

The distribution of this subgroup is closely similar to that of adverbs, and for that reason our subgroup are often defined as belonging to that form class. We, on the contrary, have chosen to define them once and for all as pronominals, on account of their formal construction and over-all distribution, though the similarity of some of their occurrences to those of adverbs must be recognized.

2. Prepositions and adverbs

Among the secondary linkers, a number of the weakly stressed and uninflected words that we have called prepositions are fairly common. It is to be remembered that words like *for*, *by*, and *to* were distinguished from adverbs by their stress. Since these forms as linkers are typically unstressed, they are therefore to be classed with prepositions.

Examples are the following:

> *For someone to rent the house, Mary hunted every day.*
> *With men stumbling into each other, the confusion was terrible.*
> *By John fighting his battles, Jack saved his skin.*
> *To John going off to war, we gave good wishes.*
> *In John going to war, we all found sorrow.*

As has been mentioned earlier (see p. 280), there is a purist belief that a number of these sentences are "incorrect," and should be in the form, for example, of *by John's fighting his battles*. All the sentences we have given certainly occur, however, and the general tendency toward relaxation of normative rules has given them recognition.

All of the forms we have given occur in the dependent sentence, and though our list is not complete, it would be possible to construct dependent sentences which use all the prepositions in the language. It is interesting that in the dependent sentence the verb is always one of the uninflectable forms. In the main sentence it may also be uninflectable, as in:

> *We gave good wishes* | *to John going off to war.*

Yet with one prepositional use of *for*, the main sentence can have an inflected verb, so that *for* becomes a linker:

> 2   3 1
> *He spoke good French* | *fòr hè had stûdied it wéll* #

We need not describe these forms as introducers of adjunctival sentence elements, or of modifying constructions which form parts of sentence elements, since the contrasting types found in "He married Jeannie with the light brown hair" and "He married Jeannie, with her father's consent" have been fully taken up already. At the present point we need only point out that the position of the terminal is decisive for the structural interpretation of many of these sentences. Notice:

> *She looked* | *at John going off to war.*
> *She looked at John* | *going off to war.*

Again, as is usual with sentences containing linking devices, we have followed a rule of interpretation which would make the order of subject, verb, linked construction an example of downgrading, since under these circumstances the linked construction is a complement. Thus, in the first sentence above, *at John going off to war* is downgraded to the status of complement, since we give preference to the normal pattern of subject, verb, and complement. When the order is reversed, so that we have a construction with a linking device followed by subject and verb, we have preferred to speak of the construction with the linking device as linked, rather than downgraded. The decision may seem arbitrary, particularly since there is at best a stylistic distinction rather than a purely semantic one between a pair like:

> *Why he did it, Mary didn't know.*
> *Mary didn't know why he did it.*

We have chosen to call the first type a linked sentence for the following reasons. The range of junctures at the point represented by the comma is greater than at the corresponding point in the second sentence. It is abnormal for me to reduce the juncture in the first sentence to $/+/$, whereas in the second sentence there may be $/+/$ or no juncture. While it may be possible to speak of the first sentence type as following the order complement-subject-verb, it will be remembered that this has been described (see p. 368) as a downgraded order. If we spoke of the first sentence as containing a construction downgraded to the status of complement, it would then be necessary to speak of the whole sentence as downgraded, which it is not.

Adverbs as linkers are not very important, since in most instances the occurrence of an adverb in a linked sentence is merely a part of one of the constructions or sentence elements of which the sentence is made up, and would still occur in that position were the sentence independent. There are a few forms, however, that need discussion. It will be remembered that *only* is one of those forms for which adjectival and adverbial uses are both possible, as in *an ónly chíld* and *he ònly whíspered*. It will also be remembered that the phonological distinction between adverbs and adjectives which are otherwise identical is one of stress—the adverbs characteristically receiving tertiary stress, the adjectives secondary in comparable situations. The distinction holds for *only* in a sentence like the following:

> *It was a nice party, only John stayed home.*

This may be:

$$2 \qquad\qquad\qquad 3\ 1\ \ 2 \qquad\qquad\qquad\qquad 3\ 1$$
$$/\text{ìt} + \text{wìzə} + \text{nâys} + \text{pártiy} \mid \text{ôwnliy} + \text{jâhn} + \text{stêyd} + \text{hówm} \;\#/$$

With this stress pattern, *only* is an adjective, and the meaning is "Everyone came but John." Or the sentence may be:

2   3 1 2   3 1

/ìt + wìzə + nâys + pártiy | òwnliy + jâhn + stêyd + hówm #/

Here *only* is an adverb, and the meaning of the sentence is "It was a nice party, except that John stayed home." It should be added, of course, that *only* can be given primary stress, and set off by terminals, without changing the meaning—however it may change the structure—from that found in the second version. The tertiarily stressed *only* is then like *quietly* in "Quietly John lit his pipe," though there is a difference in that this *only* is not as freely placed elsewhere in the sentence as is a form like *quietly*. But most important for our purposes at the moment, *only* in initial position in sentences like that we have quoted seems to be a genuine linker. Not only may it be freely varied with other linkers, like *but*, but sentences of this type do not seem to occur without some sort of linkage to a preceding dependent sentence, linkage which is either linguistic or stylistic. In short, *only* acts at least as much like a linker as *but*. It is not known whether the linking function of *only* with tertiary stress has anything to do with the fact that it so regularly tends to occur at the first of the sentence, but its two commonest positions, before and immediately after the subject, are like the distribution of the linking *that*. In any event, however, the adverbs that *only* is most like are forms like *certainly*, *surely*, which occur very frequently before the subject. Others such as *suddenly*, *quickly* occur in that position less frequently, and others such as *nearly*, *very*, though they may occur before or as a part of a subjectival construction, do not occur at all immediately before a noun subject. Clearly the order characteristics of adverbs need further study, and it is possible that such a study would reveal still other linking functions of adverb forms.

A form which needs rather careful discussion at this point is *so*. The form occurs under varying stress conditions, and in various distributions in relation to surrounding segmental morphemes, so that there are uses of it which have to be described as belonging to differing form classes. Some of these various uses have linking function, some do not. We shall begin our discussion with an attempt to separate the various uses of *so*, then go on to discuss each in relation to linking function.

There are occurrences of *so* which are clearly adverbial. In the following pair, *so* has the stress and positional characteristics of an undoubted adverb like *quietly*:

Sò swímming | he reached the bank.

Swìmming só | he reached the bank.

So may also occur with a following adjective, with tertiary stress, in positions where such forms as *really* may occur:

I'm fond of dear Pussy, her coat is *sò wárm.*

It is true that *so* does not occur within a single adjectival group headed by a noun, such as *all the ten fine old stone houses*, but this is true also of other adverbs, like *suddenly*. Introduction of either *so* or *suddenly* usually requires breaking the construction into two phrases. Like other adverbs, *so* can be placed before a noun phrase beginning with or containing an article:

Sò all the men went to town.
Neàrly all the men went to town.
Sò the men went to town.
Sùrely the men went to town.

So also occurs in various kinds of independent sentences, but in describing them it is, as always, necessary to distinguish carefully between forms with different degrees of stress. One characteristic set uses *so* before nouns, pronouns, pronominals, and adjectives, with secondary or even primary stress on *so* and the {2 3 3 ‖} superfix:

$$\begin{array}{cc} \overset{2}{} \quad \overset{3\,3}{} & \overset{2\,2}{} \quad \overset{3}{} \\ \textit{So John?} \ /\text{sôw} + \text{jáhn} \,\|/ \text{ or } /\text{sów} + \text{jâhn} \,\|/ \\ \overset{2}{} \quad \overset{3\,3}{} & \overset{2\,2}{} \quad \overset{3}{} \\ \textit{So you?} \ /\text{sôw} + \text{yúw} \,\|/ \text{ or } /\text{sów} + \text{yûw} \,\|/ \\ \overset{2}{} \quad \overset{3\,3}{} & \overset{2\,2}{} \quad \overset{3}{} \\ \textit{So what?} \ /\text{sôw} + \text{hwát} \,\|/ \text{ or } /\text{sów} + \text{hwât} \,\|/ \\ \overset{2}{} \quad \overset{33}{} & \overset{2\,2}{} \quad \overset{3}{} \\ \textit{So big?} \ /\text{sôw} + \text{bíg} \,\|/ \text{ or } /\text{sów} + \text{bîg} \,\|/ \end{array}$$

The second variety described here is a somewhat unusual combination of pitch and stress patterns but is like *really* with the stress sequence /ˊ ˇ/ and the pitch morpheme {2 2 3 ‖}, which has been described earlier. It should also be mentioned that if the element following *so* is polysyllabic, my own idiolect requires treatment as two phrases, a form which also exists as a variant for the forms given above:

$$\overset{222 \quad 33 \quad 3}{\textit{So, Johnny?} \ /\text{sów} \mid \text{jáhniy} \,\|/}$$

So, when it occurs as a separate phrase or even a sentence, is very often accompanied by the vocal qualifier of drawl.

It is clear that this particular *so*, occurring as it does with secondary stress and immediately before nouns, is not an adverb.[4] A tentative assignment for it is as a modifier, but if so, it belongs to a special group. Notice such sentences as:

Sô âll the mén? and *Sô bôth the mén?*

---

[4] It must be added that there are at least two possibly adverbial forms which occur in this position. They are *really* and *nearly*, as in "Really men?" and "Nearly men?" In my idiolect, however, these forms occur here with the characteristic secondary stress of adjectives.

That is, in both these sentences, *so* occurs before group VI and does not occur elsewhere. It must then be described as a member of a class with one member only, which can be called VI*a*. These forms are not properly interrogatives, since if the {2 2 3 ||} superfix is not given, the sentences cease to be questions. Notice:

$$\overset{3\ 3}{So\ Big.}\ \overset{1}{/\text{sów}\ +\ \text{bîg}\ \#/}\ \text{(a title)}$$
$$\overset{2}{So\ what.}\ \overset{31}{/\text{sôw}\ +\ \text{hwát}\ \#/}$$

A result of this assignment is that we have a means of handling the distinction in the following sentence, in which the written form is ambiguous:

I've always liked John, since he was so big.

The main sentence here can be either:

$$\overset{2}{/\text{sìnsiy}}\ +\ \overset{3}{\text{wɨz}}\ +\ \overset{1}{\text{sów}}\ +\ \text{bîg}\ \#/\ \text{or}\ \overset{2}{/\text{sìnsiy}}\ +\ \text{wɨz}\ +\ \overset{3}{\text{sòw}}\ +\ \overset{1}{\text{bíg}}\ \#/$$

With this particular adjective, it is the first sentence which is perhaps the more probable; it means roughly "since he was little." The second sentence means "because he was so big." The first form is our group VI*a* modifier, the second is the adverb. These instances of group VI*a* can be dismissed from this discussion with the statement that the whole group of two-word sentences we have quoted are examples of elementless sentences.

We may now return to the definitely adverbial *so*. There are certainly instances in which a construction containing adverbial *so* occurs either as a main sentence or as an independent sentence:

I'm fond of dear Pussy, her coat is *sò wárm.*
This dinner's *sò níce!*

There are also instances in which linked elementless sentences occur, all with adverbial *so*'s:

Sò róund, sò fírm, sò tíghtly pácked.

In spite of sentences like this, it used often to be maintained that in written composition the construction containing *so* was always to be followed by a main sentence to which it was to be linked, as in:

$$\overset{2}{\text{He was}}\ \overset{3\ 2}{sò\ póor}\ |\ \overset{2}{\text{he went}}\ \overset{3}{\text{hungry}}\ \overset{1}{\#}$$
$$\overset{2}{\text{He was}}\ \overset{3\ 2}{sò\ póor}\ |\ \overset{2}{\text{that he went}}\ \overset{3}{\text{hungry}}\ \overset{1}{\#}$$

The contradiction between the rule and the types of sentences which occur in speech or in informal writing would seem to be resolvable in terms of differences between linguistic and stylistic linking. Conversational sentences like "This dinner's *sò níce*" are normally linked stylistically to preceding or following sentences. In formal written composition, closer linguistic linking is demanded. We are therefore justified in calling this type of *so* a linker, at least as much so as forms like *if* and *but*, which also occasionally occur in stylistically rather than linguistically linked sentences. The composition rule, however, is mistaken in one particular. The construction with *so* is more characteristic of the dependent sentence, but does not have to occur there, as our quotation from the nursery rhyme shows.

There are instances in which *so* occurs alone, as a complement. Here again there are stress distinctions. We can have the following as an independent sentence:

$$\text{2} \qquad\qquad \text{3 1}$$
John works so. /jâhn + wə̂rks + sów #/

The meaning is "John works in this fashion." It would seem to be necessary to identify this occurrence of *so* as our group VI*a* modifier, used as a complement, here receiving primary stress because of its final position. Beside this form there also occurs:

$$\text{2} \qquad\quad \text{3} \qquad\quad \text{1}$$
/jâhn + wə́rks + sòw #/

A sentence of this type is clearly linked, occurring in larger utterances such as:

> Mary never lacks money, *Jôhn wórks sò #*
> *Jôhn wórks sò* | [that] Mary never lacks money.

Or downgraded as in:

> Mary is pleased *Jôhn wórks sò.*

These sentences can then be described as containing the adverbial *so*, again occurring as a linker. An interesting feature of the distribution is that it is only the group VI*a* modifier which occurs as sole complement after the verb *to be*. If *so* receives tertiary stress, the complement is completed by the addition of an adjective:

$$\text{2} \qquad\qquad \text{3 1}$$
It was so. /ìt + wɨz + sów #/ (It was true.) but
$$\text{2} \qquad\qquad\qquad \text{31}$$
It was so long. /ìt + wiz + sòw + lɔ́hŋ #/

The adverbial forms we have been describing are, in my speech, normally given tertiary stress, but it should be added that they can on occasion receive weak stress, something which is unusual for adverbs. Yet, the only sentence in which *so* regularly receives weak stress is the idiomatic "So long."

So occurs not only in the complement but also before the subject when there is a following verb with or without complement. As usual, there are stress distinctions which must be observed. We illustrate with a sentence which is ambiguous without punctuation:

Mary said it was good so it was

| 2 | | | | 32 | 2 | | | 3 | 1 |

/mêhriy + sêdit + wɨz + gúd ‖ sòw + ìt + wáhz #/

| 2 | | | | 32 | 2 | | | 3 | 1 |

/mêhriy + sêdit + wɨz + gúd ‖ sôw + ìt + wáhz #/

The first sentence means approximately "It was good because Mary said it was," and the second, "Mary said it was good, and it really was."

As our discussion might suggest, the secondarily stressed form is the group vɪa modifier, giving an independent sentence, but one with downgraded order, since the order is that of complement-subject-verb. As with other such independent sentences in downgraded order, this is interpreted as an elementless sentence. With other modifiers one finds the same type in a form like:

Did you say six? *Six it is.*

The form with tertiary stress, on the other hand, is once again our adverbial linker. This use of the adverbial linker more often occurs in the main sentence, though it is not at all strange in the dependent sentence:

| | | | | | 2 | | 3 1 |

Mary cooked the dinner herself | *sò it would be góod* #

| 2 | | 3 2 |

Sò it would be góod ‖ Mary cooked the dinner herself.

This type of construction may also be downgraded:

Mary always cooks *so it's good.*

| 2 | | | | | | 31 |

/mêhriy + ɔ̀lwɨz + kûks + sòw + ìt + s + gúd #/

Notice that this is quite a different sentence if there is a terminal after *cooks*.

This discussion of *so* can be summarized by saying that there are two main uses of the form; one with secondary or even primary stress and distributional characteristics which have led us to call it a group vɪa modifier; the other with tertiary stress, which we have called an adverb. It must be admitted, however, that *so* with tertiary stress may occur in final, postverbal position, a position in which most adverbs receive primary stress. *So* is then a special type of adverb, to be distinguished both from those with the postbase *–ly* and the forms, like *up*, which are either adverbial or prepositional, according to the stress they receive in final position. In any event, it is the form of *so* with tertiary stress which functions as a linker.

After this fairly full discussion of *so*, the somewhat similar *such* can be more quickly handled. There is, first, a secondarily stressed modifier, which can occur immediately before a noun, as in *sùch thíngs, àny sùch thìng, nò sùch thìng*. This modifier belongs to group v, since it can be preceded by *all*, does not occur with other group v forms, and may precede other modifiers of lower groups. This form can serve as a sentence element, as in "Such is life!" or with linkage:

$$\overset{2}{I} \overset{3\ 2}{\text{còuldn't dò sùch}} \mid \text{'cause I loved her too much.}$$

There is a second form of *such*, seen in "They were sùch nîce bóys." It is this form which occurs in *sùch a nîce bóy* and which can be called an adverb. As an adverb, however, it is extremely limited in distribution, occurring always before the group v indefinite article except in constructions where the indefinite article itself cannot occur. Limitation in the order characteristics is common in other adverbs, however, so that though the limitation on *such* is extreme, it need not prevent us from assigning it to the adverb class. The variation in stress would seem to be what accounts for the variation between *nò sùch thìng* and *nò sùch a thìng*.[5]

In complement position, adverbial *such* is like *so*, though the two forms have one bit of complementation in their distribution. *Such* is expected if the complement is headed by a noun; *so* is expected if the complement is adjectival, not so headed:

The boys were *so* nice, they were always polite.
They were *such* nice boys, they were always polite.

In initial position adverbial *such* seems to have little linking function—that is, it is a stylistic linker at best. Its linking function in this position is taken over by a compound linker, *such as*, usually /sə̀ciz/, though it may be treated as a minimal phrase particularly in the question:

$$\overset{2}{\text{Such}} \overset{3\ 3}{\text{as?}} / \text{sə̀c} + \text{ǽz} \mid\mid\mid /$$

This form is used also as a linker between phrases in a complex sentence element consisting of several nouns. Both uses can be illustrated as follows:

---

[5] The construction *nò sùch a thìng* resembles the order of *sò wíse a mán* and *hòw wíse a mán*. In both types of construction, the placing of the articles is unusual. The stress conditions are different, however. The *so wíse a man* construction seems to be related to the fact that *so* and *how* do not occur in unified constructions of adjectives headed by nouns. It is in line with this interpretation that *very*, which enters freely into adjectival constructions headed by nouns, does not occur in place of *so* in the *so wise a man* construction. It would seem that this construction constitutes a minor type of equational sentence, to be differentiated from the elementless, single-construction type of *such a wise man*.

> *Such as* the dinner is, we'll eat it. or the rarer
> *Such as* is the dinner, we'll eat it.
> Food, *such as* bread and milk, was on the table.

In complement position, adverbial *such* is a linker like *so*. Such sentences as the following are characteristic:

> They're *such* nice boys, they couldn't have done it.
> They couldn't have done it, they're *such* nice boys.

A detail in which *such* and *so* are alike as linkers when placed in the complement is that the merely stylistically linked sentences tend to show shifts of stress:

2   3   1

They are so nice! /ðèy + ər + sów + nâys #/

2   3   1

They are such NICE boys! /ðèy + ər + sə̀c + náys + bôyz #/

2   3   1

They are SUCH nice boys! /ðèy + ər + sə́c + nâys + bôyz #/

3. Conjunctions

In the usual approach to English grammar, all the "parts of speech" are given first. We have departed from this procedure for the reason that the form class we are now about to describe is one which cannot be understood fully except in terms of complex sentences. Some of the forms which fall here are among the commonest in the language, and the reader must therefore have wondered why no attention has up to now been paid to words like *and*, *if*, and *but*. In dealing with these words, our first task is one of definition, which as usual will be done in terms of formal characteristics and distribution. The name we shall use for the class is the traditional one, "conjunction." We can use the three examples we have given above as a starting point for definition and description and then go on to build a more extensive—though not exhaustive list—of forms belonging to the class.

Conjunctions are one of the classes of invariant words—that is, they take no suffixes and no prebases and postbases. They do, however, admit of compounding, in that there are constructions belonging here which contain more than one morpheme which elsewhere appears as a base. A typical compound form is *although*, usually /ɔlðòw/, which recognizably contains the bases *all* and *though*, even though the distribution, function, and content of the compound form could not be predicted from the distribution, function, and content of the separate bases. Apart from variation by compounding, conjunctions have only allologs resultant from variant stress and morphophonemic situations.

The fact that these forms are not varied by the addition of prebases, postbases, or suffixes makes them resemble such other invariant classes as prepositions and adverbs formed without postbases. Stress characteristics also produce a similarity to adverbs and prepositions, since these forms also are normally lightly stressed. Adverbs in nonfinal position are given secondary stress, as in:

The wînd tôre ôff the róof #

Or, in adjectival sequences, tertiary stress:

A vèry fíne ôld hóuse #

Adverbs are very rarely weak, though we have seen reason to speak of the idiomatic "So long!" as containing an adverbial form reduced to weak stress. Conjunctions are often given tertiary stress, as in:

John'll wash the floor | if Mâry wâshes the díshes #

Conjunctions, however, frequently appear without stress, as the weak allolog of if written 'f in the following testifies:

'f I had some money, I'd go.

Adverbs are given primary stress in final position and are common there. Conjunctions do not normally fall before terminal junctures, so that the only instances in which they receive /'/ are occurrences of contrastive stress. In stress, therefore, conjunctions are more like prepositions than like adverbs, since both prepositions and conjunctions range from weak to tertiary. Indeed, the dividing line between the two classes is blurred even in distribution, since we have seen that a form like for, which we have called a preposition, occurs as a linker and therefore shares some of the distributional features of conjunctions.

Yet, it is in distribution that the sharpest distinctions between conjunctions and the related classes are found. One distinction we have already given: a conjunction does not fall before a terminal, while both prepositions and adverbs can appear in that position.[6] In linking sentences, the most usual place for a conjunction is initially in one or the other of the two linked constructions. This is a place which can also be occupied by an adverb or a preposition, but it is not the primary location of either class. Adverbs, as we have seen, can occur before or after the verb and after the complement. They can also occur between the adjectives in a construction

---

[6] An exception to this rule for words like but is the colloquial "I won't do anything else but."

of modifiers headed by a noun. We can illustrate these adverbial positions by a series of sentences with *therefore:*

> *Therefore John loved Mary.*
> *John loved Mary therefore.*
> *John therefore loved Mary.*
> *John loved beautiful, therefore popular, Mary.*
> *It is a fine old, therefore expensive, house.*

As we have also seen, adverbs are often limited in distribution, not all of them occurring in all the positions possible for the group as a whole. Yet, even such a positionally limited adverb as *very* occurs in a number of adverbial positions and is without nonadverbial characteristics of distribution. In the sentences we have just given, a form like *therefore* has the distribution of such a form as *certainly*, which is marked as an adverb by its postbase. In consequence, *therefore* is to be classed as adverbial.

Considerable confusion results, however, from the fact that the whole group of adverbs such as *therefore, also, thus, indeed, consequently* produce at least stylistic linkage. That is, a sentence like "John consequently loves Mary" is certainly more natural if placed in a stylistic situation where there is some such preceding sentence as "John always falls for a pretty girl." Since all these forms have the characteristic distribution of adverbials, whether constructions of more than one base or unit morphemes, they are not conjunctions and should not be classed with them. The fact that they produce an impression of less than full independence in the construction in which they occur is then merely a part of the semantic content of these forms, not a structural property.

There are other characteristics which differentiate conjunctions and prepositions besides the non-occurrence of conjunctions in final position. Both prepositions and conjunctions can link constructions of lesser status than sentences, but a number of these lesser linking functions are distinct. Both prepositions and conjunctions can link nouns in the same sentence element and phrase:

> We saw John *and* Mary.   We saw John *with* Mary.

Both prepositions and conjunctions can occur within the predicator, but with slightly different distributions. The prepositions occur between the inflected first verb and the uninflectable second verb.

> John wants *to* talk.   John keeps *from* talking nonsense.

A detail of this distribution, however, is that a preposition does not occur before a past participle in this type of construction. Conjunctions do not occur in this position, but do occur between two inflectable or two uninflectable verbs, where in turn, prepositions do not occur:

> John cooked *and* ate the fish.
> Mary wanted to work *and* play.
> Mary was laughing *and* crying.
> The car was taken *and* driven by John.

In modifying constructions, whether or not they are parts of a single phrase, two modifiers may be linked by a conjunction:

> Two young *and* beautiful girls came in.
> Two beautiful, *if* silly, girls came in.
> No men, old *or* young, flocked to the cause.

This position, though open to adverbs, is one in which prepositions do not occur.

Both prepositions and conjunctions can introduce adjunct sentence elements, though there are again differences. The most common prepositional adjunct is a phrase headed by a noun. The typical conjunctional adjunct is a phrase headed by a participle, an adjective, or an adverb:

> John, *with* great difficulty, reached the shore.
> John, *if* elected, will be a good president.
> John, *if* young, is still wise.
> The men—*if* quietly—still left rapidly.

There is, however, one area where there is overlap. Conjunctional adjuncts can be constructed where a noun is the head. The following pair illustrate first the conjunctional adjunct, then the prepositional:

> John, *if* president, will initiate the measure.
> The faculty, *to* a man, came to the party.

Using this set of diagnostic characteristics, we can set up a list of conjunctions, all of which occur in the following sentence frames:

> *John will wash the car —— Mary will wash the dishes.*
> *Mary, beautiful —— young, had great success.*
> *The car will be wrecked —— driven by John.*

The frames are meant to distinguish conjunctions from prepositions, on the one hand, and adverbs, on the other. A preliminary list of forms all of which are conjunctions since they fit here are: *and, as, but, if,* and *or.* We are here taking no account of the presence or absence of phrasal boundaries within the constructions linked by these conjunctions.

Within this list of rather closely similar conjunctions, there are still distributional differences. Two of the forms, *as* and *if*, will occur in either the dependent sentence or the main sentence:

> *As* John washes the car, Mary washes the dishes.
> Mary washes the dishes, *as* John washes the car.

The other three, *and*, *but*, and *or*, occur only in the main sentence. *As* and *if* again belong together, since they can introduce a postnominal adjective phrase consisting of a single adjective, which the others do not do:

> Mary, *if* young, was wise.
> Mary, *as* young, was wise.

Negatively, *if* and *as* again act alike in that they do not occur between two inflected verbs, where the others do.

> John shot *and* wounded the deer.
> John shot *but* wounded the deer.
> John shot *or* wounded the deer.

There remains a group of conjunctions which are more easily confused with adverbs than with prepositions. If we go back to the diagnostic list of sentence frames, we find a number of words like *because* which also fit all three:

> John will wash the car, *because* Mary will wash the dishes.
> Mary, beautiful *because* young, had great success.
> The car will be wrecked *because* driven by John.

Among the forms which fit here are *till, until, although, unless,* though it must be admitted that to fit each into the particular sequences chosen here produces some occasional semantic strangeness, as with *beautiful unless young*. These difficulties are, obviously, easily removed by substituting other forms of the same class, as *beautiful unless angry*. The five forms we have now added are like *if* and *as* in occurring in either the dependent or the main sentence. All can be distinguished from adverbs in that they do not occur in final position and do not occur before or after the verb in simple subject-verb-complement sentences.

It is interesting, when we look at forms of this type, to find that *since*, which is closely associated semantically with *because*, and *though*, which is associated both formally and semantically with *although*, do not properly belong to this group. Both have the varied position typical of adverbs:

> His house is in the village *thóugh*.
> I have never done it *since*.
> I háve | *sínce* | nèver dóne ìt.

Since and *though*, therefore, are to be assigned to the subclass of adverbs which have, as one of their semantic properties, an indication of stylistic linkage.

We have not attempted to give an exhaustive list of the forms which can be assigned to the class of conjunctions, nor of the adverbs often confused with conjunctions. Our purpose has been to give a representative list; exhaustive listing belongs to lexicography rather than to description of structure. As for the stress characteristics of conjunctions, it is perhaps safest to say that they have a relatively wide range of stress. Until more is known of the stress characteristics of the group and of how these characteristics differ from dialect to dialect, the order distribution of these forms may be said to be their most clearly identifying feature.

One other form should be mentioned—*like*. In popular speech it certainly occurs in linking functions:

> Dôn't dô *like* I dó, dô *like* I sáy.

Such sentences are often regarded as substandard, though they certainly occur in the speech of educated persons. If such sentences are admitted for analysis—as they should be—it is tempting to speak of *like* as a conjunction, but such an assignment does not solve all problems. For instance, *like* occurs in some final positions:

> What did it lóok *like*?

Also, if it is a conjunction, it is limited in that it does not unite verbs or adjectives, but only nouns as in:

> We treated *John like Mary.*

It would seem that there are several *likes*, but none of them is a conjunction. There are, first, forms which are adjectives:

> John is *like* to his father.
> These children are very *like*.
> This portrait is very *like*.

The other uses of *like* have the distribution of prepositions and, like prepositions, can act as downgraders, as in the sequence "Do like I do," where *like I do* is the complement. We have also seen, with *for*, that prepositions can be linkers. All of these prepositional uses of *like* are peculiar only in that they regularly have the higher of the two grades of stress which prepositions receive, namely tertiary. There is one use of *like* which can receive primary stress in final position and which must therefore be called an adverb. This decision is an extension of the one made in downgraded sentences like

"What are you *crying for?*" where *for* is an adverb if fully stressed, a preposition if given tertiary or weak stress. Notice the similar distinction in:

> What was the picture *páinted lìke?*
> What was the picture *pâinted líke?*

The answer to the first question can be much the same as if it were "How was the picture painted?" The second requires an answer like that to "What was the picture painted to resemble?"

Conjunctions, like other linkers, often pile up, or occur in correlated pairs. A typical example of piling up is *as if:*

> John washed the dishes *as if* he hated the job.

A number of the correlations are more interesting. One of these is *either . . . or* and its negative *neither . . . nor.* Both can link sentences, as in:

> *Either* John goes to work *or* I quit.
> John *neither* goes to work *nor* does he quit.

They can also serve as linking material in constructions of lesser status:

> John was *either* sick *or* lazy.
> John was *neither* sick *nor* lazy.

The correlation is of interest in several ways. First it is a correlation of words from different form classes, since *either* is an adverb and *or* a conjunction. Second, the correlation is closely similar to that found in *whether . . . or,* also one between words of different form classes, since *whether* is a pronominal. The correlation gives some evidence, therefore, for the morphemic analysis of *whether.* The initial element is the usual pronominal {hw–}, and there is a final element repeated in *either* and *neither.* The element would seem to be, in its morphemic norm, {iyðər}, but to have assumed the allomorph {–eðər} after {hw–}. Finally, the *nor* of *neither . . . nor* requires a downgraded order after it—one elsewhere characteristic of questions.

Another of the frequent correlations is *as . . . as.* As a linking correlation in sentences, this sequence usually falls on two dependent sentences followed by a main sentence, often with a pile-up of *and* and *as* in the second dependent sentence:

> *As* John washed the floor, *and as* Bill washed the dishes,
>   Jack washed the car.

More common, however, is the use in which it precedes an adjective and again precedes a subject and verb *to be:*

> Mary is *as tall as I am.*

It also occurs merely linking a noun, pronoun, or pronominal as part of the complement:

Mary is *as tall as John.*

One of the points on which usage is not fixed is the form of a pronoun which should be used in such sentences:

Mary is *as tall as I.*   or   Mary is *as tall as me.*

A good deal of ink has been spilled on the subject, but since both forms are found in educated usage, both are acceptable.

One particular device does not strictly belong here, since neither of its correlated members is a conjunction. It is, however, so closely similar in distribution to the correlated *as . . . as* that it is convenient to mention it at the same time. This device consists of a comparative in *more* or *–er* followed by *than.* It is thus a correlation between adverb, or postbase, and adverb. Most of its distinction is like the downgrading uses of *as . . . as.* Notice:

Mary is tall*er than* I am.
Mary is *more* intelligent *than* I am.
Mary is tall*er than* I (or me).
John is *more* sinned against *than* sinning.

As a linker, note:

John runs *more* to muscle *than* Mary does to flesh.

Throughout the discussion of the various sorts of lexical linkers, we have found correlated constructions, like *when . . . then* or *as . . . as.* The type is frequent with all the classes of words which act as linkers. There can be no doubt that these correlations constitute constructions which have to be taken account of at some point in the analysis of sentences into their constituents. Yet, since they are discontinuous, it often follows that in orderly cutting into immediate constituents, we will have cut so as to put the first member, say *when*, into the dependent sentence and the second, say *then*, into the main sentence. A transcriptional device which will meet this problem, as with other problems of discontinuous constructions, is to write the whole of the construction at the point at which its unpredictable member occurs. If we apply this method to the following sentence, our analysis would go like this:

When Mary washes the dishes, then John dries them.

PRONOMINALS	SUBJ.	VERB	COMPL.
When . . . then	*Mary*	*washes*	*the dishes*
	John	*dries*	*them.*

21.... BEYOND THE SENTENCE

1. Stylistics

All the material which has gone before has dealt with what linguists, following Trager, have come to call microlinguistics. It is the area which begins with phonemes and ends with sentences. Microlinguistics has been described at length, primarily because it has been less than fully explored, but also because most modern students would agree that it is the foundation on which all other study of language must rest. Microlinguistics does not cover the whole of language activity, and since it covers neither the correspondence between the symbol and the object designated nor the artistic structures of literature, it does not cover those parts of language activity which have the most importance for us as members of society. In this chapter we can do little more than point to some of the important phases of language activity which fall outside the subject of this book.

It has several times been said that there is a close relation between linguistics and stylistics, that is, between language and style. The definition of stylistics which has been implied in preceding chapters is one which has gained considerable currency among linguists. It is by no means the only definition possible, nor is it the usual one among students of literature. As we go on studying communication in its entirety, we may find that there are many phenomena and relationships to which the name "style" is now indiscriminately applied, each to be defined in its own way. In the meantime, the definition we are about to offer can be described as a definition of an area capable of being studied, to which it is convenient to apply the name "style." The definition is not intended to preclude the possibility of other definitions, of other types of study, or of the existence of other phenomena.

The definition in question is that stylistics concerns all those relations among linguistic entities which are statable, or may be statable, in terms of wider spans than those which fall within the limits of the sentence. It is immediately necessary to add that there is quite a different definition of style also in use among linguists. It is possible to define the sum total of style as all the choices of equivalent items which the language offers the user in each linguistic situation. Stylistics, under this second view, is the collection and tabulation of these alternatives, sentence by sentence throughout the corpus under study. There have been many valuable attempts to gather such knowledge, most notably in studies of poetic diction.

Different as the two definitions might appear to be, they can be reconciled and are no more than obverse and reverse of the same coin. If I hear the sentence "This is my hat," I may hear an unexploded or a fully exploded final [t]. If the sentence is one that is without context—perhaps a scrap from a tape recording—I can only say that to explode or not explode a final [t] is a choice which the language offers to every speaker. Suppose, on the other hand, that I have heard enough of the context to realize that the speaker was giving consistently higher rather than lower junctures at all juncture points, was giving full rather than reduced forms of unstressed morphemes, and was consistently avoiding assimilations. In such a situation, I would say that he was using a markedly formal style, and I should expect him to accord with it by exploding his final stops. Stylistically considered, what was an unpredictable choice within the sentence becomes something explainable in terms of the wider span.

Similarly, a sentence I once concocted was "Prolapsed, the semidorsal spherophore made surreptitious, progressive, peristaltic movements." The sentence says no more than that "The ball-carrying halfback was crawling." The stylistic situation was obviously one in which the game of five-dollar words was being played. The situation is similar to that described on the phonemic level. Linguistically, *spherophore* and *ball-carrier* are different items, but under conditions in which the stylistic situation is fully known, the occurrence of one or the other can be predicted.

The situation offers, however, a number of problems. For instance, suppose we decide that exploded and unexploded final stops are stylistic variants, and so place them in the same phoneme. Does this mean that we have mixed levels because we have had to go to the much higher stylistic level in order to make a statement about the lowest—the phonemic—level of linguistics? The answer to this paradox is a double one. First, we have not so much mixed the levels as merely widened the corpus; we have not so much appealed to higher-level structures as considered phonemics in several sentences. It is a commonplace, of course, that this is essentially the way any wise phonemicist proceeds. He does not attempt to derive the whole of phonemics from a single sentence or from a succession of single sentences without comparison. Furthermore, in working on the phonemic level, the student begins to observe that such differences are without the normal phonemic function of distinguishing one morpheme from another. From this he can make the prediction that the variation is stylistic, a prediction which he can then proceed to verify. That is, "free variation," linguistically considered, is variation without function; stylistically considered, it is (or perhaps it is safer to say, is presumed to be) predictable. Or put another way, "free variation" is contrastive linguistically, but stylistically complementary. In operating with such higher entities as words and constructions, the same kind of relationship holds. Within the boundaries of the sentence, *spherophore* and *ball-carrier* are in contrast, stylistically they are in complementation. We would ordinarily say they "mean the same thing," or "have the same reference," which are loose ways of saying that the difference is without linguistic function—the two forms do not keep separate phrases and sentences apart. They are synonyms, in short.

We have been saying, to turn our discussion still another way, that the function of stylistics is to reduce the area of linguistic arbitrariness by explaining as much as possible of linguistic variation. It is not, of course, believed that all variation is controlled—it will never be possible to predict all that a man might say before he says it. Nonetheless the area of scientific stylistics is exactly the area in which explanation, and therefore predictions, of linguistic choices can be made.

If the preceding statements have given some general notion of the field covered by stylistics, it is still true that they have given no notion at all of the specific content of stylistic study, or rather of what is likely to be its content as such study, still in its infancy, becomes more mature. First of all, it is clear that there is more than one kind of stylistics. That which is most likely to interest the academic and artistic worlds is the stylistics of literature, though ultimately the stylistics of ordinary speech will also have to be thoroughly investigated. A field in which stylistics is beginning to be practiced is the investigation of poetic structure, not only in the nonlinguistic, conventional ornamentation of poetry by rhyme and meter but also in the relation of poetic sentences to each other and in the relation of content, often expressed in analogical statements, to the various parts of the poem. There have been, also, a number of promising investigations into the characteristic sequences of items which mark the whole of an author's work.

A part of communication activity which is outside the area of microlinguistics, but is not on the straight line which leads from sentences to style, is what can be called paralinguistics. The chief investigator here has been Henry Lee Smith and, for a second part of the field, Ray Birdwhistell. Neither has carried his work as far as might be wished, but each has at least demonstrated that there is an intimate relationship between the expressive features, which accompany speech, and speech itself, and that these expressive features pattern in a way similar to linguistic patterns and are learned rather than innate. It is not possible at the moment to give a good outline of material the investigation of which is so fluid. Smith, however, has concerned himself primarily with the manner of speaking, as an expressive feature. The material, or rather a part of the material, which he deals with, he has called the vocal qualifiers. These are to be defined as exaggerations of features usually a part of the normal signaling system, arranged in pairs. Thus, among the vocal qualifiers are overloudness and its paired opposite, over-softness. A second pair is exaggerated pitch, called singsong, and its opposite, tonelessness. It is thus possible to think of the vocal qualifiers as continuous axes which bisect the microlinguistic area and extend outward from it like spokes from a wheel. The paralinguistic area investigated by Birdwhistell has been called by him kinesics. It is the system of facial and body movements which accompany speech and which are distinct from the formalized gestures, such as the crooked finger of beckoning. What Birdwhistell is investigating is rather the things like raising of the eyebrows, pursing of the lips, hunching the shoulders, and so on. These movements have been shown to differ from one language group to another, and so, like vocal qualifiers, to be learned behavior. The vocal qualifiers together with kinesics make up the paralinguistic system, which accompanies individual sentences. These, in turn are arranged in larger sequences, characteristically like those of stylistics. These larger structures constitute parastylistics—an area of obvious literary and dramatic importance, to name only two ways in which knowledge of the area might be useful.

2. Semantics

Undoubtedly important though paralinguistics may be, the field which is most important to all of us is that of meaning. The reader cannot have failed to observe that meaning has been little discussed in this book and has never been used as a primary tool of analysis. It is to be hoped that no reader has gained the impression that meaning is either unimportant or unreal to the linguistic analyst. The attempt has been to lay some of the foundation on which a study of English meanings might be built. Linguists, further-more, are now hopeful that there can be a genuinely scientific semantics—we no longer share the pessimistic view expressed ten years ago by no less a linguist than Edgar Sturtevant that meaning will forever be beyond the reach of orderly investigation. The term "meaning" has been used through-out this book, but no definition of the term has been given. It is now time to remedy the omission, though instead of a definition, I shall attempt a description.

In terms of the familiar three-level map of linguistics, meaning exists only on the metalinguistic level. As long as one operates strictly within the microlinguistic, only what has been called "differential meaning" is relevant. By this term is meant no more than identity and difference—microlinguis-tically we can say that two items are "sames" or "differents" and nothing else. Same and different, in turn, are identity or difference in speaker-hearer behavior. Meaning proper is ultimately correspondence between a linguistic item and an item in the nonsymbolic world, or between a linguistic structure of many items and a similar structure in the nonsymbolic world. If we can leave this statement as a first approximation, we can go on to some of the ways in which meaning can be studied.

The identity-difference which constitutes microlinguistic meaning can be studied by the process of observing whether substitution of one item for the other produces identity or difference in a larger structure. That is to say, in studying phonemics, we substitute one sound for the other and observe whether the substitution produces identity or difference in morphemes. In studying morphemics, we substitute entities which produce identity or difference in words and fixed phrases, and so on through the hierarchy. In coming to conclusions about phonemic structure, a suspected pair of sounds like [b] and [p] are proved to be "differents" because substitution of one for the other produces the different morphemes *bat* and *pat*. Conversely, exploded and unexploded final /t/ does not produce such morphemic difference, and these items are then "sames." Exploded and unexploded final /t/ have already been discussed, and it has been pointed out that on the stylistic level, they can be presumed to be predictable variants. There is no contradiction between the two statements. The two sounds produce equivalents—capable of being chosen—on the level immediately above phonemics. Their predictability does not appear until we have reached a level many stages above phonemics.

In morphemics we can also apply the technique of substitution to observe whether sames or differents are produced on the next higher level. An example is the variation between {nt} and {nat} after the verbs like *can, are, must*, etc. On the morphemic level, the two forms occur in the same environments, and so constitute a choice. If we go to the next higher level, that of phrases and constructions, we find there is no phrase in which *cannot* occurs in which *can't* may not be substituted. We conclude, therefore, that {nt} is a mere variant of {nat}.

A somewhat more complex situation can be described by reference to a quotation famous in linguistic history. In the late eighteenth century, Sir William Jones inaugurated comparative Indo-European studies with the statement that no "philologer" could doubt the historical identity of the Indo-European tongues. The term "philologer" is strange to modern usage, but no one would have any hesitation in substituting the current *philologist* for it. The postbases *-er* and *-ist* certainly occur in the same linguistic environments, since we have not only *philologer : philologist* but also *telegrapher : telegraphist*. Most forms ending in *-er* are more or less interchangeable with forms in *-ist*, but there is at least one pair which is distinct, namely *exhibitioner : exhibitionist*. Speaker-hearer behavior is not the same for the sentences "John was an *exhibitioner* at the University" and "John was an *exhibitionist* at the University." To state that *exhibitioner : exhibitionist* are differents is a legitimate appeal to differential meaning; it is unnecessary to say that they are different *because* one means "holder of a scholarship," the other "a practitioner of exhibitionism." The two forms, *–er* and *–ist*, are then differents on the morphemic level, since they produce a difference at the word level.

The fact that *–er* and *–ist* are different morphemes does not settle the status of *philologer : philologist* except as we look downward from the word level. As we look downward, we must say that *philologer : philologist* are differents because they contain different morphemes. It is also possible to look upward, examining the distribution of *philologer : philologist* in phrases, sentence elements, and sentences. When the pair are examined thus, we find that there is no phrase or construction where one cannot be substituted for the other. As words, measured by their behavior on the next higher level, the two forms are sames. In ordinary language, we describe *philologer* as a variant of *philologist*.

With words, acceptable substitution should properly produce identity on the phrase and construction level, not merely on the sentence level. A word substitution which produces a satisfactory sentence alternate only, without first producing satisfactory phrasal substitution, is misleading. An example of satisfactory substitution, leading to the conclusion that we are dealing with synonyms, can be drawn from the sentence "That's *so*." A probable substitution is "That's *true*." The forms *so* and *true* occur under the same stress, are both acting as minimal complements, and so may be said to produce sames on the phrase level. A satisfactory sentence substitute for "That's *so*" might be "That's *the truth*." Yet obviously, *truth* and *so* appear in quite different phrase types and are therefore not synonyms.[1]

The description of this kind of substitution technique is here deliberately simplified, since there are many intermediate levels which have to be taken into account, as when we say that /iy/ and /ay/ are morphophonemic equivalents in *either*, but not phonemic equivalents, since they produce a difference in *beat* and *bite*. It should be said that the substitution technique is an age-old common-sense method of investigating meaning. All that the linguist can do to improve the method is to use it more rigorously, as I have tried to do in rejecting *the truth* as a substitute for *so*.

The substitution technique can also be applied in a fashion which is

---

[1] The statement that *so* and *true* are synonyms is not a contradiction of the statement below (p. 412) that synonyms are to be found only in individual situations. Note that there are situations in which one is not substitutable for the other, as in *the true and the beautiful*.

experimental and verifiable. The method is a major contribution to linguistics, and is the work of Zellig Harris.[2] Harris presented sentences to a group of native speakers acting as experimental subjects. In any sentence, perhaps the "That's so" which was used above, he asked each subject to make a list of substitutions. If all put *true* first on their lists, this was the substitute of highest probability. Since communication theorists have shown us that human speech is understood by a process of treating the highest probability of occurrence, position by position, as if it were absolute, Harris was therefore safe in saying that the most probable substitute was the right substitute. Harris' experiment is of importance in two ways. First, he was investigating substitution itself and not why substitutes are acceptable. The *why* of substitution can be put off until a later stage, as long as there is a satisfactorily objective method of identifying the substitutes. Second, the experiment offers a parallel to the relations of phonetics and phonemics. It was an important statement of nineteenth-century phonetics that no two sounds are ever physically identical. Phonemics has resulted in a revision of this postulate, and now states that physically unlike sounds can be structurally the same. Similarly a long-standing result of linguistic study, of whatever period or school, is the denial of the existence of perfect synonyms. Harris has shown a way in which synonyms can be set up. Synonyms are the most probable substitutes, in any given situation—but in one situation only, which is an important limitation. The attempt to set up perfect synonyms fails because the substitution is studied without reference to particular situations; when it is limited to single situations Harris has shown that it succeeds.

Meaning can be investigated, somewhat less satisfactorily, on the stylistic level. To perform this investigation with ideal perfection, an all-knowing investigator would have before him a corpus which includes the whole of the language, that is, all the sentences which are produced in it. Such an ideal is impossible, and what the investigator does, in fact, is to try to handle a sufficiently broad sample so that his results will be statistically reliable. When the investigator has such a stylistic sample at hand, he then investigates, tabulates, and describes all the linguistic and stylistic environments in which a given form appears—and by implication all those environments in which it does not appear. A linguistic and stylistic definition of meaning results. That is, stylistically considered, meaning is the sum total of environments to which a form is appropriate. This book contains a good many such environmental statements. For instance, one way of describing the large form class composing nouns, nominals, and nominal phrases is to say that most members of the class can occur after the definite article.

---

[2] The experiment was reported to the Linguistic Society of America in 1948, as part of a continuing investigation of discourse analysis, but has not been published.

The last method of studying meaning is the extralinguistic one of studying correspondence. This method is that which is practiced in all language-learning and -using activity; it is what happens to us when we learn what objects can be correlated with the linguistic item *table*, and what cannot. It is a method which somehow works on the practical level, but which is nevertheless frustrating to the scientific analyst. Unfortunately for the linguist, investigation of correspondences is the method of semantic investigation which inevitably occurs first to anyone. The linguist, impressed with the difficulty of finding a thoroughly satisfactory defining characteristic which draws a sharp line between the objects of the class *table* and all objects of such other classes as *desk* and *bench* has in the past been more pessimistic about correspondence meaning than is strictly necessary. His pessimism, as is now abundantly evident, has made the linguist seem to the layman the perfect example of the impractical scholar who retreats from important issues.

There are two hopeful statements which can be made about the study of correspondence meaning. First, if the investigation of identity-difference and stylistic environments is exhausted, it is unthinkable that these preliminary investigations will fail to clarify in abundant measure the still formidable task of investigating correspondences. The second statement is that structural parallelism is a powerful and reliable tool for the investigation of correspondences, whether in meaning or elsewhere. In limited areas we are able to point to parallelism between structures of linguistic and nonlinguistic items, and are therefore able to make limited but secure statements about correspondence meaning. As Murray B. Emeneau has pointed out, one of these areas of structural parallelism is that between chemical terminology and the structure of chemical compounds.[3] As our knowledge of structures in cultural behavior and in noncultural objects increases, so will our knowledge of meaning.

3. Language and predictability

It is now possible to give a quite different definition of meaning, which will supplement rather than contradict the first approximation given above. Meaning can be defined as partial predictability. By predictability is meant systematically describable occurrence. Anything is totally predictable if its conditions of occurrence are so rigidly describable that its presence or absence can be known before the event. Anything which is totally predictable is thus incapable of distinguishing alternatives and is therefore redundant, or meaningless. For instance, on the phonemic level, the occurrence of nasal

---

[3] "Language and Non-linguistic Patterns," *Language* XXVI, 1950, pp. 201–02.

quality on any /æ/ placed immediately before a nasal consonant is totally predictable in the speech of millions of Americans. It is therefore redundant and must be left out of a description of distinctive features.

Anything which is totally unpredictable is correlated with nothing linguistic or nonlinguistic. It fits into no structure at all, and so cannot be responded to. It is, for instance, within the realm of possibility that an American might produce a sound, somewhere during the course of his language activity, identical with the ejective labial stop employed in many non-Indo-European languages. At present, however, if the adult is not a student of phonetics, the occurrence of such an ejective is something which is unpredictable. It therefore follows that no one who hears such an unpredictable sound can react to it as meaningful.

If meaning is thus defined, we can now separate three levels of meaning, the linguistic, the stylistic, and the extralinguistic. All linguistic items which belong to the system at all are partially predictable. An ejective consonant such as that described above is totally unpredictable in English, and so does not belong to the system. The nasalized vowel described above is an example of a redundant element. In terms of meaningful items of the sound inventory, we can say that phonotactics describes the partial predictability of phonemes, identifying the impossibilities and the alternatives. Morphotactics gives us the partial predictability of morphemes and allomorphs, and syntax in turn gives us the partial predictability of larger items.

Even if we accept the idea that phonemic occurrences are partially predictable, and so meaningful, it may not be clear how their meaningful qualities operate. Their chief function, in terms of this kind of analysis, is to identify the linguistic context more sharply than is possible within the limits of what is actually heard. For instance, suppose I hear a scrap of sound that I can identify as /ŋər/. Assuming that this is English, I know that there must have been a preceding vowel, perhaps that of *singer*. Nor do linguistically meaningful items have to be phonemes alone. A sentence which was discussed above (p. 341) was "Oh look, I've found my ——." The occurrence of *my* before (P) was a clear signal that eventually a nominal construction of some sort would close the sentence. That is, the partially predictable items let us make predictions about a wider corpus, here linguistic.

An item which is partially predictable on the stylistic level may be said to have stylistic meaning. To be partially predictable on the stylistic level, its occurrences must be partially describable in terms of spans wider than the sentence. An example can be drawn from the use of the definite article in a pair of sentences:

When I went down town, I met *a man*. *The man* was an old friend.

We can generalize that one stylistic consideration governing the occurrence of the definite article is that it occurs with any noun which has been mentioned before within the same corpus. Even in these terms it is not, however, totally predictable, since the second sentence might have been something like this:

Another man was with him.

That is, the mere recurrence of the same linguistic item does not completely control the appearance of *the*, since some recurrent items have identical reference, others do not. Nor is this the only way in which the presence or absence of *the* is less than totally predictable. Our second sentence might have been:

He was walking along *the* street in *the* sun.

Neither street nor sun has been mentioned previously in our small corpus of two sentences, yet both occur with a definite article. It is usual to define the use of *the* with *street* as meaning "the particular street nearest the speaker or person spoken of," and the use of *the* with *sun* as controlled by the fact that *sun* is a class of one member only. Yet, in different terms, it is possible to describe both these uses of *the* as uses of the particular nouns whose references are most likely to have been previously mentioned had the corpus been more widely extended. From this point of view, therefore, the definite article enables us to reconstruct more of the stylistic corpus than we have actually heard.

We have been dealing with material partially predictable within the linguistic framework, which then gives us information about the sentence, and with material partially predictable within a stylistic corpus composed of sentences, which in turn gives us information about the larger stylistic corpus. Extralinguistic meaning has been defined as consisting of linguistic and nonlinguistic correspondences; if this is true, it is necessary to show that the occurrence of linguistic items is at least partially predictable in relation to nonlinguistic items and, further, that partial predictability enables us to predict in the nonlinguistic world.

Perhaps the easiest way of showing the partial predictability of which we speak is to relate the linguistic activity of a speaker to the physical situation in which he is talking. Suppose that our speaker is a teacher in a classroom and that he and his students are both speakers of English. A number of nonlinguistic items are present as stimuli in the environment. Among them are the objects called pens, pencils, erasers, chalk. Since the stimuli are present, sooner or later it is extremely likely that a sentence employing one or more of these words will be spoken. Such a sentence might be "Give me a piece of chalk." Furthermore, in reply to such a sentence, one of the students would hand over a physical item and would assume from the teacher's response that he had identified it correctly. That is to say, a partially regular relation between language item and nonlanguage item is set up.

It is not, of course, true that we can predict how many of the physical stimuli will give rise to language responses, nor can we predict their order of occurrence. It is also true that our teacher can talk about things not present in the environment. He can mention shoes and ships and sealing wax or cabbages and kings. Suppose, however, that he does. His hearers can then be said to be predicting about the nonlinguistic world. Having observed the stimulus-response relation between an object for writing on the blackboard and the language item *chalk*, they conclude that the same relation would hold for other nonlinguistic items and the language responses, were the physical situation larger. That is, they are predicting about the physical world, the area in which language has extralinguistic meaning.

Each of these levels of meaning is important to normal language users. The linguistic level of meaning is what enables us to hear our native tongue and understand it, even when redundancy is reduced to a minimum. The native hearer is trained to make full use of partially predictable items and sequences—he can hear a sentence which is pronounced as

$$331$$
$$/s + gwíyt \#/$$

and recognize it for "Let's go eat." Our difficulty in understanding a foreign tongue, even after long study, is largely that we do not make full use of partial predictability. We cannot, in other words, make use of prediction to reconstruct a partially heard sentence or to recognize which of two possible interpretations is the more probable.

The stylistic situation is similar. Having arrived at probable interpretations and identifications within a sentence, we assume that these probabilities will hold for wider bodies of material. We thus construct a stylistic corpus which is often more than was actually heard—we have, to use the technical term, extrapolated from the probabilities of the known to arrive at the unknown. A famous book on linguistics used as a type sentence "The farmer kills the duckling." The two definite articles were not accounted for by previous mention. Yet, if the reader had been asked "Why *the* farmer and *the* duckling, not *a* farmer and *a* duckling?" a very likely answer might have been "Because these were the farmer and the duckling Sapir had been thinking about." If such is the answer, it is clear that the reader is using probabilities to construct a corpus which includes unobserved, even unknowable, utterances.

When we pass to correspondence meaning, we once more construct a wider structure in terms of the probabilities observed in the narrower setting which is before us. We assume that the associational tie between stimulus and response in the immediately present situation will also hold for stimulus and response not a part of the immediate situation. We construct, therefore, a much wider nonlinguistic situation in accord with the probabilities of what is directly observable. It is by this process that we give language its semantic structure, and in very large measure learn the structure and entities of the world in which we live.

The study of semantics, which has enjoyed a considerable vogue in recent decades, has concerned itself largely with an attempt to improve the processes of extrapolation from known symbol-object relations, so that knowledge may be increased and not contaminated by extrapolations falsely made. Composition teachers have for centuries concerned themselves with improving special kinds of communication, and literary artists have always striven for newly vigorous and beautiful utterances. All these activities are worthy. Yet there is a study more worthy than all of them, a study the aims and methods of which we can at last begin to plan. It is how human communication works in its entirety, how it forms us as men, and how it gives us glimpses of a world beyond experience without which we cannot live. If the study of linguistics can prepare us for the full study of symbolism and communication, it will have accomplished more than its founders would have dared to claim for it.

APPENDIXES

The two appendixes which follow are given on the principle that "he knows not England who only England knows." They are meant, therefore, as short sketches for the purpose of throwing a little further light on the structure of English by contrast with two languages whose entities and framework are significantly different from those of English, and from each other. It should be stated emphatically that both sketches have necessarily been done at second hand and that I cannot pretend to a profound writing, reading, or speaking knowledge of either language. Both sketches are therefore structural reformulations of data gathered by others. The brevity of each indicates that neither is a grammar, but that they are sketches—structural statements and analyses of sample material, in no instance exhaustively listed.

The two languages have been deliberately chosen. Eskimo and Latin are at opposite ends of a scale of what is to us cultural prestige and importance. Eskimo, though a living language, is remote, and is the medium of a culture quite apart from the Western European tradition. Latin is of immense cultural importance and prestige and, though very different from English, is genetically related to our own tongue, whereas Eskimo—in spite of some attempts to state the contrary—is without any evidence of relationship. Latin is, furthermore, a historic state of the Romance tongues, a knowledge of whose structure therefore involves the problems of reconstruction. Finally, I have not been uninfluenced by the fact that among scholars whose acquaintance with modern linguistics is not exhaustive, it has become something of a commonplace to speak of structural linguistics as a reversal of the old policy of analyzing Eskimo as if it were Latin, by attempting to analyze Latin as if it were Eskimo. Such statements constitute a challenge. If even Latin can be made to respond to structural analysis, then the ghost of Latinizing grammar for languages unlike it is finally laid. The attempt here has accordingly been to analyze a little of the structure of each language, neither one from the point of view of the other, but both from the point of view of techniques and attitudes which should be useful for all languages, or for none. It is hoped that the sketches will be read in the spirit in which they are meant, as suggestions for further study, not as dogmatic formulations or attacks on previous scholarship.

APPENDIX A

ESKIMO: *A Grammatical Sketch*

1. Introduction

The Eskimoan stock comprises a group of dialects spread along the arctic coast of North America, with an extension in Siberia, ranging therefore from Greenland in the east to the mainland of Asia. The number of speakers of Eskimo in its various forms was estimated at "hardly forty thousand" by Thalbitzer in 1911.[1] The estimate is, if anything, rather generous.

The varieties of Eskimo are reasonably close to each other, in spite of the isolation under which the various tribes have lived for a long period of time, and this closeness suggests an interesting contradiction of the belief that under primitive conditions languages necessarily differentiate themselves very rapidly. Eskimo is fairly closely similar in structure to Aleut, the language of the Aleutian Islands, which with Eskimo, makes up the larger family Eskimo-Aleut.[2]

Swadesh divides the Eskimo dialects into two groups, which he christens the Yupik, found in Southern Alaska, and the Inupik everywhere to the east.[3] The names are drawn from the name for human being in the two groups of dialects. Swadesh further estimates that the extremes of difference are a little less than those which separate English and German, and consequently that "1500 [or] 2000 years ago the linguistic predecessors of all present-day Eskimos spoke one language." The period of a unified Proto-Eskimo-Aleut must be some thousands of years farther back in the past.

In general, the most striking characteristic of Eskimo is the construction of long "words" consisting of one morph which always occurs after silence or a terminal juncture, a series of morphs which never stand after silence or terminal and never before silence or a terminal, and one or more morphs which never occur after silence or a terminal but may occur before

---

[1] Thalbitzer, "Eskimo," p. 971. (Full publication data for this reference and others applying specifically to Appendix A will be found in the Bibliography for Appendix A, p. 440.)

[2] Harry Hoijer, "Introduction," *Linguistic Structures of Native America*, pp. 10–11.

[3] Swadesh, "Kleinschmidt Centennial III: Unaaliq and Proto Eskimo," pp. 66–70.

silence or a terminal. These complexes differ from English words in that they can be freely created, much as we can treat the elements of free phrases and sentences. Furthermore, an Eskimo construction thus freely created and limited by the one initial morph and the one or more potential final morphs may on occasion constitute all of a sentence, with elements which correspond, semantically at least, to the several sentence elements of an English sentence. Yet, it is also true that the usual Eskimo sentence consists of several words, or even of a main sentence and one or more dependent sentences, since Eskimo has well-marked devices of linking.

The most striking characteristic of Eskimo is that each word contains one and only one initial—the base. Following the initial there may be a large number of postbases, which are normally followed by a small number of suffixes. These terms are to be defined in Eskimo as they are in English, and so should be clear. It is striking that Eskimo makes use of neither prebases nor prefixes. There is, apparently, no theoretical limit on the number of postbases which may occur in a given word, except the fact that bases are rather more numerous than postbases in the total lexicon. The fact that Eskimo makes use of successive morphs added after the base as the sole means of building up complex words means that the analyst has a simple task in cutting compounds into their constituents. The cutting always proceeds by cutting off the last morph, until finally the base is reached. There is no necessity of deciding whether a postbase or a prebase is to be cut off first, as there is in English.

2. Phonemics

Eskimo possesses fewer phonemes than many languages do, so that its phonemics is relatively simple. In contrast to such a language as Chinook, however, the morphophonemics of the language is complex, since there are many phonemic modifications in morphemes under conditions of contact. The morphophonemics is sufficiently complex so that a student of the language often finds it hard to recognize the underlying morphemic norms, since there are many unpredictable portmanteaus.

The phonemics here presented is that of Greenland, as given by Swadesh, on the basis of material from Thalbitzer and Kleinschmidt.[4] I have modified the symbols for convenience.

Consonants are, as usual, a class of sounds to be distributionally defined, a task which is easily performed in Eskimo. Consonants are segmental

---

[4] Swadesh, "South Greenlandic (Eskimo)," pp. 30–32. Swadesh adopts a number of characters more phonetically accurate than those I have chosen. More curiously, he gives a single symbol for a voiced midpalatal spirant, and for a velar spirant. Presumably his intention was to indicate that this phoneme had midpalatal and velar allophones, but the presentation is far from clear.

phonemes which cannot occur doubled initially. Vowels in Eskimo are the class of phonemes which may appear doubled in such a position.

Among the consonants, there are two sets in symmetrical arrangement with each other:

$$/\text{m} \quad \text{n} \quad \text{ñ} \quad \text{ŋ}$$
$$\text{p} \quad \text{t} \quad \text{k} \quad \text{q}/$$

Of these symbols, /m n ñ ŋ/ represent nasals, their points of articulation being bilabial, dental, palato-velar, and uvular, respectively. They are normally voiced, even when geminate, a position in which a number of other phonemes assume voiceless allophones. The symbols /p t k q/ represent voiceless stops with similar points of articulation. The stops have aspirate allophones before the high allophones of the vowels /i/ and /u/, but are otherwise smooth.

There is also a pair of spirants which can be conveniently written /b g/, though the reader is warned that this writing is not to be confused with the voiced stops indicated by these symbols in English phonemics. These spirants are voiced when intervocalic, but voiceless when geminate. Their morphophonemic alternations are with /p/ for /b/, and /k/ and /q/ for /g/. In some dialects /g/ also alternates with /ŋ/.[5] There is thus a certain amount of skewness in the relation of these phonemes to the stops. The spirants show reduction from four articulatory positions to two, but judging from morphophonemics, the front spirant, /b/, is still bilabial, whereas the back spirant, as we should expect, is relatively intermediate in position between the two back positions of stops.

There are also a set of four other consonants, all to be defined as lingual, in which the differentiation is rather in manner than in position. These can be written /y l s š/. The first, /y/, is a slit spirant, approximately the same as the English /y/ in *yield*, but the Eskimo phoneme occurs only in intervocalic position. It there contrasts with /i/, which makes it necessary to set it up as an independent phoneme. The second, /l/, represents a lateral as in English, though it is spirantized in clusters, and voiceless if geminate. The pair written /s/ and /š/ are apical groove and dorsal slit spirants, respectively.

The pattern of consonants, in its totality, is therefore:

$$/\text{m} \quad \text{n} \quad \text{ñ} \quad \text{ŋ}$$
$$\text{p} \quad \text{t} \quad \text{k} \quad \text{q}$$
$$\text{b} \qquad \text{g}$$
$$\text{y}$$
$$\text{l}$$
$$\text{s}$$
$$\text{š} \qquad /$$

---

[5] Thalbitzer, *A Phonetical Study*, pp. 83–86.

In contrast with English, the distinction between voiced and voiceless sounds is nowhere a distinctive feature.

The vocalic system is again one with few entities, there being only three phonemes:

$$/i/ \qquad /u/$$
$$/a/$$

The range of allophones, as might be expected, is wide. A number of the allophones are written in older grammars, though it is curious that Kleinschmidt long ago recognized the essentials of the vocalic structure.[6] The most important allophones are [e] and [o], which occur for /i/ and /u/ finally and before uvulars.

The juncture phenomena of Eskimo have not been investigated. Morphophonemic modifications do not extend over the boundaries of words, but seem to take place without limitation within these boundaries. It is possible that the transitions between phonemes on each side of the limits of words are not characterized by any form of juncture phenomenon, but unlikely. It will therefore be assumed that the spaces which in texts are written before and after words represent some form of juncture, though its nature is unknown. It is also highly probable that there is some form of terminal juncture at the ends of main sentences and dependent sentences, but Thalbitzer's descriptions are too meager to reveal it. There may or may not be some form of juncture within the limits of words, but in the absence of any evidence on the question, it will be ignored.

Stress would seem to be closely bound up with the phonemic structure of syllables, syllables of like structure receiving equal stress. Closed syllables and long syllables receive greater stress than do short syllables and open syllables.[7] Stress is therefore not significant. Thalbitzer's description of pitch patterns does not reveal any pitch phonemes. The syllable does not seem to play any important part in Eskimo structure, since there is no evidence that the syllable division is phonologically significant, and in morphology, morphemes may be monosyllabic, polysyllabic, or nonsyllabic.

3. Phonotactics

Only vowels and the consonants /s m n p t k q/ can occur after juncture, and no consonant clustering is possible in this position. Before juncture only

---

[6] Kleinschmidt, *Grammatik*, pp. 2 ff. It is interesting that Kleinschmidt's description of the "sounds" of Eskimo is nearer to modern procedures than is the minutely accurate differentiation of Thalbitzer.

[7] Thalbitzer, *A Phonetical Study*, pp. 127–28.

the vowels and /p t k q/ can occur. Again no consonant clustering is possible in this position.

Any vowel can cluster with any vowel, including itself. Clusters of more than two vowels are found, but no polyvocalic cluster can contain more than two like vowels. This feature in the clustering habits of vowels, together with the fact that vocalic clusters facilitate morphemic analysis, makes it preferable to analyze long vowels as a cluster of two like vowels, rather than to set up a phoneme of length for either vowels or consonants.

Consonant clusters must be intervocalic and never contain more than two consonants. The commonest clusters are geminates, all consonants forming such clusters except /y/. The only nongeminate clusters in which the first member is a stop are /ts/ and /tl/. Normally the first member of a nongeminate cluster is /b/ or /g/. The phoneme /b/ will cluster with all consonants except /m ñ ŋ y/, and /g/ with all but /ñ ŋ y/. The only nongeminate nasal cluster is /ñm/.

The rules governing permitted clusters are of great importance in Eskimo morphophonemics, since unpermitted clusters frequently arise in combinations. When this happens, the unpermitted cluster is assimilated to one of the permitted ones, thus forcing the morpheme out of shape. Among the more important rules of assimilation is the replacing of /k q/ by /g/ and of /p/ by /b/ in the first position in clusters. In other instances assimilation gives a geminated cluster, as in */-tp-/ > /-pp-/, and */-mn-/ > /-nn-/.

Applying the detailed statements which have just been given on clustering habits, we can arrive at a number of general conclusions. Vowels are a group of phonemes which may begin an utterance. Consonants—or rather one group of them—may also be initial, but in Eskimo, vowels are distinguished from consonants by the fact that if the initial phoneme is a vowel, the second may also be a vowel, indeed, the same vowel as the initial. If the first phoneme is a consonant, the second must be a vowel. This statement is a more rigorous way of stating what was said earlier: that vowels are sounds which cluster in initial position.

In contrast with English, there is more limitation on consonant clustering, and less on vowel clustering, since the maximal consonant cluster is two, which must be intervocalic, while vowel clustering is possible in groups of three. Apparently, therefore, consonant clusters are distributed between two syllables, and in the absence of knowledge about a possible /+/, it cannot be established that two consonants ever fall in the same syllable. The fact that sequences of two clusters are ambisyllabic does not prevent the classification of such sequences as clusters, since in Eskimo as in English, a cluster is a sequence of two or more phonemes of the same class without an intervening phoneme of another class.

Distributionally, therefore, there are two clearly established phoneme classes—vowels and consonants. The third class is junctures, of which two are presumed, though not identified.

4. Morphemics

There are two main classes of morphemes, both segmental. Since we do not know the suprasegmental phonemes, we cannot usefully speculate about suprasegmental morphemes. The two classes which we can identify are bases—those forms which appear after juncture or silence—and nonbases—those which do not. Each class contains subdivisions. Bases are divided into those forms which are not followed by nonbases, like {iiq} (Ouch!), and those more common forms which may be followed by nonbases.

Nonbases are divided into the classes of postbases and the more limited group of suffixes, characteristically the final forms. Suffixes are arranged in paradigmatic sets, and the number which may occur in any single word is limited, whereas the number of postbases is not.

In addition, there is a still more limited class of nonbases which may be called postphrases. These are distinguished by the fact that they occur after the suffixes, which are the normal construction closers. An example of a postphrase is {–lu} (and), which is added to the end of a word and indicates that this word forms part of a phrase with a preceding word or words. Such a construction is {tigu–b–ak–ka quya–bu–ŋa–lu}[8] (I received them and I give thanks). Ordinarily, the personal suffix {–ŋa} would close the second of these constructions, though a second personal suffix might be added. The morpheme {–lu} thus acts as a mark of the phrase boundary.

By far the most striking type of morpheme is the postbase, the extensive development of which gives the language its special character. It is impossible to predict from anything in its semantic content whether a given morpheme will be a base or a postbase. Here, for instance, are some postbases which will seem strange to speakers of English, where the corresponding morphemes would be bases:

1. {–ŋiag–} (because; because of), as in {igpi–ŋiag–a–a} (He is troubled because of it.)
2. {–qag(pu)–} (have; possess), as in {qaya–qag–pu–ŋa} (I have a boat.)
3. {–u(bu)–} (be; is), as in {iglu–u–bu–q} (It is a house.)

---

[8] In this chapter a slightly variant convention of morphemic transcription has been adopted for purposes of convenience. Morphemes are divided by hyphens, and the whole of a series of morphs enclosed in a single pair of braces: { }. Word boundaries are indicated by spaces.

While there is, as we have said, no theoretical limit on the number of postbases which may be added to an initial, Eskimo words are not, on the average, as long as some of the freaks commonly exhibited for the benefit of the beginner.

Suffixes are not nearly so numerous, and there are never more than three (with one exception) in any one construction. The suffixes are number morphemes, personal morphemes with pronominal reference, case morphemes, and a set of highly irregular paradigm formatives, called verb signs, which appear in each of the several forms of the verbs.

5. Words and word classes

As already said, the most general division which can be made in Eskimo words is into bases not followed by postbases and suffixes; and bases capable of having postbases and suffixes after them. The bases which do not receive postbases and suffixes may be called particles, and the class has already been illustrated with the base {iiq} (Ouch!). At this point we can add that there is a second class of forms which can also be called particles. These are bases which may be followed by postbases, but not by suffixes. Such a form is {usi–ubba}, literally "now," the base, plus "there," the postbase. The construction, however, is to be idiomatically rendered "I thought that. . . ." The particles which can be thus modified by the addition of postbases may be called complex particles.

A normal base—one capable of modification by postbases and suffixes— may also appear without any such modification. One of the ways in which Eskimo resembles English and is different from Latin is that the Eskimo noun paradigm leaves one form unmarked, that is, without any suffix. Postbases may always be present or absent. An example of a normal base without either postbase or suffix is {qimmiq} (dog). A generalized formula for the type of word which may take full sets of modifying morphemes (the class that we can call inflectable words) is then:

$$B^1 \ PoB^{\emptyset-n} \ S^{\emptyset-3} \ PoP^{\emptyset-1}$$

In this formula, B stands for base, PoB for postbase, S for suffix, and PoP for postphrase. The superscript numbers indicate how many of each type of morpheme may be present in a single word. Thus, the superscript 1 in B^1 indicates that there is always one and only one base, and $PoB^{\emptyset-n}$ indicates that there may be no postbases, or an indefinite number of them. A construction which conforms to this formula is:

B   PoB PoB S PoP
{aglag –ag–siag–tit–lu} (pattern-thing characterized by preceding-secured-your-and)

The whole is to be idiomatically rendered "and the letter you have received."

The formula above, which states that there is always only one base, emphasizes one of the differences between Eskimo and both English and Latin. There are no fixed phrases having more than one base, like English *hothouse* or Latin *magnanimus*. Eskimo has phrases, as the morpheme class called postphrases demonstrates. The phrases of Eskimo are always free, however. A minor difference is that Eskimo postphrases are always sharply distinguished from suffixes, whereas in English grammatical suffixes can also function as postphrases, as in "the King of England's crown."

There are two classes of inflectable words. These can be called nouns and verbs. Each has its own formula of construction, which will be given below. It should be pointed out that there is some limitation on bases as to whether the suffixes for nouns and verbs can be freely and directly added to them or whether only noun suffixes or only verb suffixes can be added. Thus, for instance, a base like {qimmiq} (dog) cannot be given verb endings and made to mean something like "He is a dog." There is nothing in the meaning or form of bases which enables the analyst to predict such limitation. Further the situation is met by the postbases which can be added. For instance, the verbal postbase {–u–bu–} can be added to {qimmiq}, giving {qimmi–u–bu–q}, which is "He is a dog." As in English, the nominal or verbal character of the whole complex is determined by the last postbase added, without respect to the morphemes which precede. There is probably less of this limitation of bases to nominal suffixes only, or to verbal suffixes only, than the dictionaries of Eskimo would lead one to suppose, but there can be no doubt that it exists.

As is to be expected in a language possessing only three major form classes, the range covered by each is much larger than the range of English classes with corresponding names. Thus, particles of Eskimo contain not only morphemes which we should translate as particles but also a good many which we should translate as adverbs, conjunctions, and interrogatives. Nouns cover the range of our nouns, adjectives, and pronouns. Only verbs correspond fairly closely in range to our verbs.

Eskimo nouns are words which can be inflected as follows: There are three numbers, a singular, which except in one instance is unmarked and is therefore shown only by the absence of any suffix, and a dual and a plural, each with distinct suffixes. Next in order of addition, there follows a complete set of forms with personal reference, roughly equivalent to the "possessor," though the use of the term "possessor" is more nearly a convenient label than an accurate translation. There are twelve of these forms, since there are four persons and three numbers. The forms for pronominal reference are portmanteau morphs, which do not analyze readily into two morphemes, one for person and one for number, making it simpler to set up twelve suffixes, each, however, with two components. Finally there are seven modifying or "case" suffixes, normally added in last position, though the first of these, the so-called relative, appears in an abnormal position which will be later described. This statement then gives us a positional type of inflection, in which any or all positions may be empty, and in which all may be filled, though there is the further limitation that only one of the possible suffixes may be present in each position in any one construction.

With some additions to the symbolism we have already used, we can devise a formula for noun constructions. The new symbols are as follows: N stands for number suffix, P for personal suffix, and C for case suffix. For the suffixes, two sets of numbers are provided, written as fractions. The numerators indicate the number of such suffixes which may be present in a single noun, and the denominators indicate the total number of suffixes in each set:

$$ B^1 \quad PoB^{\varnothing-n} \quad N_{2}^{\varnothing-1} \quad P_{12}^{\varnothing-1} \quad C_{7}^{\varnothing-1} $$

The formula is somewhat generalized and does not take account of certain peculiarities and limitations which will be given in the analysis which follows.

In the examples of Eskimo forms here given, no attempt will be made to list complete paradigms. The forms will be illustrations of types of constructions rather than a reference tool for translating Eskimo.

Eskimo nouns, when uninflected, may end in any one of the phonemes which can stand before juncture,[9] with the exception of /-p/:

{iši} (eye)	{inuk} (man)
{iglu} (house)	{qimmiq} (dog)
{nuna} (land)	{aŋut} (male person)

The norms for dual and plural suffixes are {-k} and {-t}, respectively. The morphophonemic rules of addition are that these norms are added directly to a base or stem ending in a vowel, but replace the final consonant of a base ending in any consonant except /t/. When a base ends in /t/, the suffix allomorphs {-ik} and {-it} are added directly:

{iši} (eye)	{iši–k} (two eyes)	{iši–t} (eyes)
{iglu} (house)	{iglu–k} (two houses)	{iglu–t} (houses)
{qimmiq}(dog)	{qimmi–k} (two dogs)	{qimmi–t} (dogs)
{sannat} (tool)	{sannat–ik} (two tools)	{sannat–it} (tools)

---

[9] See p. 430 below.

Besides the relatively automatic and predictable allomorphs, there are others which are unpredictable, which have been here omitted.

The second position is that of the twelve personal suffixes. As was said earlier, most of these are portmanteau morphs containing two components, person and number. In spite of the fusion which has occurred, there is occasionally enough similarity between forms in the same person but in different numbers to suggest that there may be an underlying type of construction in which there are separate morphemes for person and number. An example of this similarity is the following:

{–a} (his, hers, its)   {–k} (belonging to them two)   {–at} (theirs)

In this set the expected {–k} and {–t} of dual and plural appear, and the person morpheme can be found in the vowel, though it must be pointed out that the person morpheme would have to be said to be occurring as a zero allomorph in the dual. More typical of the usual difficulty of analysis are the forms for the fourth person:

{–ni} (his own)   {–gtik} (their own)

Examples of the pronominal inflection, without number morphemes for the noun preceding, are given below:

{iglu–ŋa} (my house)   {iglu–gput} (our house)
{iglu–a} (his house)   {iglu–at} (their house)
{iglu–ni} (his own house)   {iglu–gtik} (their own house)

If the noun possessed is inflected for number, so that both positions are filled, further fusion takes place. Sometimes, however, this fusion is the result of regular morphophonemic rules and is thus capable of explanation. Thus, the endings for "my two" and for "my several" are both {–kka}. There is good comparative evidence for supposing that the suffix for "my" given above as {–ŋa} is derived from *{–ga}, which has become {–ŋa} between vowels. If, then, the forms for dual and plural with following first person possessor had been formed as expected they would have been *{–k–ga} and *{–t–ga} respectively. Both */–kg–/ and */–tg–/ are unpermitted clusters and have been regularly assimilated to /–kk–/. A specimen of this double paradigm follows:

{iglu–ŋa} (my house) {iglu–k–ka} (my two houses) {iglu–k–ka} (my houses)
{iglu–a} (his house)   {iglu–k} (his two houses)   {iglu–ii} (his houses)

In the above forms, {iglu–k} has a zero allomorph of the possessor, instead of the expected {–a}, so that the form is identical with the simple dual, without possessor. The plural, furthermore, is quite unpredictable and totally fused, showing no trace of the {–t} which is the usual form of the plural suffix.

The last position is that of the case suffixes. As stated earlier, one of the suffixes, that called the relative, has irregular order characteristics and will therefore be described separately later. Those which occur in the expected third position also have some peculiarities, the chief of which is that when they are added to a base it is always inflected for number. Further, it was said earlier that there was an exception to the fact that the singular is normally unmarked. The exception occurs when these case suffixes are added, since the singular now acquires an observable suffix, namely {–m–}. The form of the plural suffix also undergoes modification, appearing in the allomorph {–n–}, instead of the norm {–t–}. Specimens follow:

ALLATIVE   {–ut} (to)   {iglu–m–ut} (to, or into, [a] house)
LOCATIVE   {–i} (in; at)   {iglu–m–i} (in, or at, [a] house)
PROSECUTIVE   {–kut} (through; over)   {iglu–k–kut} (through, or over, [a] house)

In the last form it will be noticed that the unpermitted cluster */–mk–/ has been assimilated to /–kk–/.

{iglu–n–ut} (to, or into, [the] houses)
{iglu–n–i} (in, or at, [the] houses)
{iglu–ti–ŋut} (through, or over, [the] houses)

The prosecutive is irregular, the plural suffix having assumed the unpredictable allomorph {–ti–}, and the prosecutive suffix appearing as {–ŋut} rather than {–kut}.

With the exception of those forms which contain the relative case suffix, the last inflectional type is that in which personal suffixes and case suffixes are both present. When this happens, inflection for number is absent, and the same forms are used for singular, dual, and plural of the noun possessed. Curiously enough, however, the suffixes for the cases in this double inflection are all in an allomorphic shape characterized by the addition of an initial /–n–/, which immediately suggests that it is the plural morpheme described above. Whatever its origin, it cannot now be regarded as a plural sign, since were it a plural suffix it would have to appear before and not after the personal suffix. This particular paradigm, which admits of seventy-two theoretically possible forms, is highly irregular and shows a great deal of fusion and homophony.

{iglu–a–ni} (in his house, or houses [locative])
{iglu–an–ni} (in their house, or houses)

In the last form given, note that the suffix {-at} (their) has been assimilated to {-an-} before the following nasal.

Since the inflectional types so far described represent considerable complexity, it may be well to summarize the types of construction possible. Omitting that type in which there is no suffix of any sort present, there are five types:

1. Number suffix alone, personal and case suffixes both absent
2. Personal suffix alone, number and case both absent
3. Number suffix followed by personal suffix, case absent
4. Number suffix, personal suffix absent, case present
5. Number suffix absent, personal suffix present, followed by case suffix

The most striking limitation here is that not all positions can be filled at once, though any combination of two is possible. A further limitation follows from the fact that when the case suffixes are present, there is a unique suffix for the otherwise unmarked singular. As a result, number is always present with case suffixes unless the personal suffixes replace it. In other words, the case suffixes cannot occur alone.

The relative suffix has been referred to a number of times, with the statement that it has peculiarities of order. It has certain other peculiarities as well. It has not usually been classed with the case suffixes, but since it has basic syntactic similarities to these suffixes and since the relative suffix never occurs in the same construction with another case suffix, it becomes possible to set it up as an irregular example of case, with a resultant clearer and simpler analysis. Its peculiarities are the following: First, it does not occur in final position but immediately after the stem, preceding all other grammatical suffixes, even those for number. Second, it alone occurs in the maximum inflectional type, that with number, personal, and case suffixes, though, as just said, the order is then actually case, number, personal suffix. Third, when the relative suffix is present, it occurs either alone or with the maximal type just described. There are no combinations of two.

The norm of the relative suffix is {-p}, and any noun form which ends in this phoneme contains the relative morpheme. This is the reason for the exception stated above that an uninflected noun can end in any phoneme capable of standing before juncture, except /-p/. In morphophonemic distribution, the suffix acts like the suffixes for number, being added directly to a stem ending in a vowel, but replacing final consonants except /-t/, in which case the relative suffix has the allomorph {-ip}, which follows the /-t/. There is a third and unpredictable allomorph, {-up}. The relative is usually translated as "of or to," but more exact statements about its meaning will be given later:

{iši–p} (of, or to, an eye, or eyes)
{iglu–p} (of, or to, a house, or houses)
{nuna–p} (of, or to, a land, or lands)
{qimmi–p} (of, or to, a dog, or dogs)
{aŋut–ip} (of, or to, a male person, or persons)
{inu–up} (of, or to, a man, or men)

It will be noted that these forms are without a number suffix, so that such a form as {nuna–p} can be variously translated as singular, dual, or plural.

When the relative is present, the only other type of inflection is that in which number and personal suffix both follow. The case, number, and personal suffixes are thoroughly fused and must be treated as portmanteau morphs. Thus, the endings of the third singular possessor for the simple singular, dual, and plural of the noun are given below, and the corresponding relative endings under them. It will be seen that the relative endings are quite unpredictable:

{–a} (his)   {–k} (his two)   {–ii} (his more than two)
{–ata} (of, or to, his) {–kit} (of, or to, his two) {–isa} (of, or to, his more than two)

These forms give the following examples:

{iglu–ata} (of, or to, his house)
{iglu–kit} (of, or to, his two houses)
{iglu–isa} (of, or to, his houses)

6. Verb forms

Verb forms in Eskimo present something of a paradox in that the number of possible forms is very much greater than that for nouns, there being over nine hundred verb forms, at the same time that the construction of verbal complexes is essentially simpler than the construction of nouns. Verbs are always constructed by means of the addition of a rather irregular morpheme, called the verb sign, and one or two pronominal suffixes. There are a total of seven modes of the verb, largely differentiated by the verb signs, but also in part by the use of variant pronominal suffixes. The pronominal suffixes are often irregular, but are sufficiently like the pronominal suffixes of noun forms to make it clear that they are basically the same. A formula for verb forms can thus be given:

$$B^1 \ PoB^{\emptyset-n} \ VS_7^1 \ P_{12}^1 \ P_{12}^{\emptyset-1}$$

The only unfamiliar symbol here is VS, which equals verb sign, of which there are seven (with allomorphs), distinguishing the seven modes. It will be noted that there must be one set of personal suffixes, and there may be two. It is usual to refer to verb forms with a single personal suffix as "intransitive," those with two as "transitive." The names are not perfectly accurate and are here replaced by the terms "simple" and "complex." When a single suffix occurs, it merely indicates a person connected with the action, without specifying whether this person is actor or goal. When a double suffix occurs, the first indicates the actor, the second the goal. As will be described in more detail later, the first three of the verb modes are those which characterize independent sentences, the last four dependent sentences. As with noun forms, there is very great fusion and irregularity in the suffix morphemes which occur, so that the basic structure is considerably obscured, even though still analyzable. The verb forms will be merely illustrated, rather than given complete.

The independent modes are as follows:

I. INDICATIVE

A. SIMPLE

The base chosen for illustration is the verbal morpheme {kapi–} (stab, stick, or sting). The verb sign for this inflection is {–bu–}, which has the allomorph {–pu–} after consonants, often with assimilation of the final consonant of the preceding morpheme:

> {kapi–bu–ŋa} *stab*-VS-*I* (idiomatically, I stab, I am stabbed,
>   I stabbed, or I was stabbed)

The form, in short, does not specify time.

An example of a consonant stem, with allomorph of the verb sign is:

> {katak–} (drop, or be dropped)
> {katap–pu–ŋa} *drop*-VS-*I* (I drop, or I am dropped)

B. COMPLEX

The verb sign is {–ba–}, with the allomorph {–pa–} after consonants:

> {kapi–ba–a–ŋa} *stab*-VS-*he-me* (he stabs, or stabbed, me)
> {kapi–ba–a–tit} *stab*-VS-*he-thee* (he stabs, or stabbed, thee)
> {kapi–b–a–a} *stab*-VS-*he-him* (he stabs, or stabbed, him)

The last form given illustrates one of the rules of Eskimo morphophonemics. Not more than two like vowels can occur in succession. Therefore the expected *{–ba–a–a} is reduced to {–b–a–a}.

II. INTERROGATIVE

A. SIMPLE

The verb sign is {–b–} with the allomorph {–p–} after consonants:

{kapi–b–a} *stab*-VS-*he*, or *him* (does he stab? or is he stabbed?)

B. COMPLEX

The verb sign is {–bi–} with the allomorph {–pi–} after consonants:

{kapi–bi–si–ŋa} *stab*-VS-*you*(pl.)-*me* (do you stab me?)

III. OPTATIVE AND IMPERATIVE

A. SIMPLE

The second person simple forms are to be translated as imperatives. In the second person, the verb sign is {–ŋ–}, in other persons {–la–}:

{kapi–la–ŋa} *stab*-VS-*I* (I wish I might stab, I wish
I might stab myself, or I wish I might be stabbed)
{kapi–ŋ–it} *stab*-VS-*thou* (stab thou!)

B. COMPLEX

The verb sign is zero in second person of the actor, and the second person actor forms are to be translated as imperatives. In other persons, the verb sign is {–l–}:

{kapi–si–ŋa} *stab*-[VS ø]-*you*(pl.)-*me* (stab [you] me!)
{kapi–l–i–ŋa} *stab*-VS-*he*-*me* (I wish him to stab me)

In the last form given, the third person suffix is irregular, having been analogically carried over from the third person plural and plural of object possessed, so that the expected translation would be "they" rather than "he."

The dependent modes are:

IV. CONTEMPORATIVE PAST

This mode indicates that the action takes place at the same time as the main action, but is placed in past time.

A. SIMPLE

The verb sign is {–ga–}, which becomes {–ka–} after consonants, and {–a–} after /–g–/. A third allomorph, {–mm–}, appears in third singular:

{kapi–ga–ma} *stab*-VS-*I* (when I stabbed, stabbed myself, or was stabbed)

B. COMPLEX

The verb sign is {–mm–}:

{kapi–mm–a–ŋa} *stab*-VS-*he-me* (when he stabbed me)

In the dependent modes the personal suffixes frequently appear in the form appropriate to nouns in the relative, as in {kapi–ga–ma}, above. Parallelism between relative forms of the noun and dependent modes of the verb is understandable, since the relative nouns may be regarded as subordinate nouns.

V. SUBJUNCTIVE

A. SIMPLE

For both simple and complex forms the verb sign is {–gu–}, except for third person simple forms and third person actor forms in the complex inflection. In these forms the verb sign is {–pp–}:

{kapi–gu–ma} *stab*-VS-*I* (when, or if, I stab myself or am stabbed, etc.)

B. COMPLEX

{kapi–pp–a–ŋa} *stab*-VS-*he-me* (when, or if, he stabs me)

VI. FIRST PARTICIPIAL

This inflection is always simple, and the single personal suffix can indicate actor or a passive or reflexive goal. The action, however, is not thought of as directed toward a specific goal. Thus, the form below may be translated as "I stabbing" or "I stab in generalized fashion." It may not be translated "I stab something," which would require the second participial. The verb sign is {–glu–}:

{kapi–glu–ŋa} *stab*-VS-*I* (I being stabbed, I stabbing, or I stabbing myself)

VII. SECOND PARTICIPIAL

This mode may be either simple or complex, but even when simple the action is thought of as directed towards a specific goal.

A. SIMPLE

The verb sign is {–šu–}:

{kapi–šu–ŋa} *stab*-VS-*I* (I stabbing [something], I who stab [something])

B. COMPLEX

The verb sign is {–gi–} varying with {–ki–} after /–q/ which is in turn assimilated to /–k/, except in third person actor forms. Here the verb sign is {–ga–}, varying with {–ka–} as above:

{kapi–ga–a–ŋa} *stab*-VS-*he-me* (he stabbing me)[10]

In the above specimens of paradigms, it has proved convenient in most instances to give brief notes on the semantic components of the suffixes as they were described. The following section will give additional material on semantic components, syntactic characteristics, and characteristics of selection.

7. Semantic content of suffixes

The number morphemes are essentially familiar and offer no real difficulty. However, in contrast to many languages which have a dual number, Eskimo tends to substitute the plural for the expected dual in nouns referring to items which habitually come in pairs,[11] like the nouns *eye, hand*, etc. As with many languages, however, the dual is less frequent than the other two numbers and may indeed be passing into disuse.

---

[10] The verbal scheme here given follows that laid down by Kleinschmidt (pp. 16–17) and adopted by Swadesh, though I have modified the terminology. I have rejected the more complex and wasteful scheme of Thalbitzer, "Eskimo," (pp. 1031–46), which gives a total of twelve modes. Since, however, Swadesh and Thalbitzer, the two most accessible treatments of Eskimo, differ rather confusingly in the analysis of verb forms, it is worthwhile to give a table of equivalents.

KLEINSCHMIDT-SWADESH	THALBITZER
mode I, indicative	mode II (intransitive) and mode III (transitive)
mode II, interrogative	mode IV
mode III, optative-imperative	modes I and V, which are split into two by Thalbitzer
mode IV, contemporative-past	mode X
mode V, subjunctive	mode XI
mode VI, first participial	mode VI
mode VII, second participial	modes VII and IX, split by Thalbitzer into a simple and a complex mode

Thalbitzer's modes VIII and XII, both of which are abstract nouns built on verbal stems, are omitted, since there are many nouns built from verbs, and there is no reason to include this pair in the paradigm unless all others are also included. It should be noted that Thalbitzer fails to make any distinction between independent and dependent modes.

[11] Swadesh, "South Greenland (Eskimo)," p. 40. This practice is in contrast to the treatment of the relatively rare dual in the older Germanic languages, where the dual was common with nouns which normally appear in pairs.

In person forms the first three are familiar enough, but the fourth requires explanation. The fourth person ties the possessor of a noun to the personal reference of a verb form. Thus, if the actor of a verb is in the third person, and that same actor is referred to as the possessor of a noun in the same sentence, the fourth person is then used:

> {qimmi–p taku–b–a–a iglu–ni} (dog-relative see-indicative-he-it
>   house-his own; i.e., "The dog sees his own house.")
> {qimmi–p taku–b–a–a iglu–a} (dog-relative see-indicative-he-it
>   house-his; i.e., "The dog sees someone else's house.")

In verb forms, the fourth person is used to indicate that a third person actor is the same as a third person actor in a preceding construction. In these uses, the fourth person performs a function a good deal like that of our relative pronouns in sentences like "A man is patriotic *who* loves his country":

> {kapi–b–a–a taku–ga–mi–iuk} (stab-indicative-he-him see-verb sign
>   of contemporative past-he himself-him; i.e., "He stabbed him,
>   when he [same person as stabber] saw him.")

This grammatical device obviates a difficulty inherent in English, where the normal form of the corresponding sentence, "He stabbed him when he saw him," is ambiguous.

8. Case suffixes and sentences

Those suffixes which appear in final position generally indicate that the noun to which they are added is in a modifying relation either to a verb or to a noun which occurs in the same sentence. They generally, therefore, can be translated by English prepositional phrases, as the translations of the examples given indicate.

The relative case is both more important and more complex. It ties the noun to which a relative suffix has been added to another noun or a verb occurring in the same sentence. For speakers of English, the relationship between a relative noun and a second noun uninflected for case is the easiest to understand. If there is a noun in the relative case and a second noun uninflected for case, but provided with personal reference, the relative noun is the possessor and the personal reference is to the relative noun, agreeing with it in person and number:

{qimmi–p niqa–a} (dog-relative meat-his; i.e., "the dog's meat")

The relative is also used for the actor with complex verbs, the actor suffix of the verb then agreeing in person and number with the noun in the relative. Needless to say, the goal suffix will then agree in person and number with the uninflected noun:

> {qimmi–p taku–b–a–a} (dog-relative see-verb sign of indicative-he-him (or her, or it); i.e., "The dog sees him.")
>
> {qimmi–p agnaq taku–b–a–a} (dog-relative woman see-verb sign of indicative-he-her; i.e., "The dog sees the woman.")
>
> {qimmiq–agna–p taku–b–a–a} (dog woman-relative see-verb sign of indicative-she-him; i.e., "The woman sees the dog.")

The relative of nouns does not occur, however, with simple verbs. Thus, as has been said, it becomes impossible to distinguish between actor and goal, the single pronominal reference being then simply to a noun somehow connected with the action without further specification.

The order of words within the sentence is without significance, though words cannot be taken out of dependent sentences and placed in the main sentence, or vice versa, without producing confusion. The order of post-bases within a construction sometimes affects the meaning of the construction, but not in a way which can be systematically stated at present. The order of personal suffixes in verbs, however, distinguishes between actor and goal.

Any free form—that is to say, a morpheme or series of morphemes surrounded by junctures—can stand alone as a complete utterance. There are, however, differences in the degrees of freedom. Some forms are normally bound, in that they usually occur only as parts of larger constructions. These forms will be described in more detail in the discussion of linking below, but these normally bound forms can still occur in complete response utterances.

Sentence types are then:

1. Single noun sentences, as in {nuna} (Land!)
2. Nominal sentences consisting of more than one noun, both un-inflected for case, as in {nuna–gput qaqqa–li–šuaq} (land–ours mountain-provided with-intensive; i.e., "Our land is very mountainous.") These sentences are equational in type, and often correspond to English sentences consisting of noun, verb *to be*, and adjective.
3. Verbal sentences, with or without independent nouns, as in {qimmi–p agnaq taku–b–a–a} (The dog sees the woman.)

Eskimo has a number of devices of linkage and downgrading, which affect independent words in their relation both to phrases and to sentences.

In general, the phrasal types of downgrading are those morphemes which mark a given word as forming part of a larger construction of a phrasal type.

In nouns, the case forms all perform the function of marking the inflected noun as the modifying member either of a nominal or verbal phrase. Thus, in the description above of the uses of the relative, a typical phrase of this sort was given:

{qimmi–p niqa–a} (the dog's meat)

Again, it can be pointed out that when the relative marks the noun actor in a phrase containing a complex verb, the whole constitutes a verbal phrase in which the relative noun is occupying the position of a sort of modifier. Similarly, a sentence of the sort found in {taku–b–a–a iglu–m–i} (see-indicative-he-him house-singular-in; "He sees him in a house") can be thought of as a verb phrase, where the noun occupies a modifying position.

Sentence downgrading is accomplished by the use of one of the four dependent verbal modes. An example of this type is the sentence above translated as "He stabbed him when he (same person as stabber) saw him."

Linking is accomplished in at least two ways. One is the linking of two successive sentences by the use of the fourth person, which has been described above. This type can become an example of downgrading if the verb form in the fourth person is placed in a dependent mode.

The second type of linking is that marked by the occurrence of the syntactic suffixes described above:

{tigu–b–ak–ka quya–bu–ŋa–lu} (I receive them and I give thanks.)

This sort of linking occurs when there are two nouns, or two verbs, essentially parallel grammatically, and it does not mark either form as downgraded.

SPECIMEN TEXT

{kaasasu–guyu–ŋuaq}
Kaasasuk, proper name, nominal base
{–guyu–} nominal postbase, (wretch)
{–ŋuaq} nominal postbase (little) The two postbases together often contain the notion of "dear little." The whole complex given above is an uninflected noun, and means approximately "Dear little Kaasasuk."

{agli–niq}
{agli–} verb base (grow)
{–niq} nominalizing postbase used with verbs (state indicated by preceding verb base) The whole complex is then again an uninflected noun, and may be translated "growth."

{ayug–mm–at}

{ayug–} verb base (be bad, be unable to perform)

{–mm–} verb sign, mode IV, contemporative-past, simple form, a dependent
mode

{–at} relative third person singular suffix used with this dependent mode
(he) The complex can now be translated "when he was unable to
perform growth."

All the material given up to this point constitutes a single dependent sentence, marked as dependent by the presence of a mode IV verb. It should also be noted that since the verb is simple, both nouns which occur with it are without case, though we should think of the first as actor, the second as goal. As has been said, with simple verbs it is impossible to distinguish actor and goal. The whole of this clause may now be idiomatically translated as "When dear little Kaasasuk was unable to grow . . ."

{tigu–mi–šag–aluag–glu–ŋu}

{tigu–} verb base (take)

{–mi–} nominal or verbal postbase (with arm or hand)

{–šag–} verb postbase (be obligated)

{–aluag–} verb postbase, concessive (although)

{–glu–} verb sign, first participial, a dependent mode, and without any
specific goal of action

{–ŋu} personal suffix, irregular third person singular found instead of the
expected {–a}. As usual with simple verbs, the personal suffix can
indicate either an actor, or a passive or reflexive goal. Here the stylistic
situation suggests a passive goal. The whole complex constitutes a
second dependent sentence, and is to be translated ". . . although he
ought [to have been] taken up in arms . . ."

{atta–n–ut}

{atta–} noun base, occurs only in plural (piece of dung)

{–n–} plural suffix, the allomorph which occurs before case suffixes

{–ut} suffix of allative case (onto)

This form is an example of the use of adverbial cases to form modifiers. The form begins the main sentence. It is to be translated "onto the dunghill."

{iŋi–tagp–pa–at}

{iŋi–} verb base (throw)

{–tagp–} verb postbase (be accustomed)

{–pa–} verb sign, mode I, indicative, complex, in allomorph appropriate
after consonants. This form is then the main verb of the whole sentence.

{-at} portmanteau morph meaning "they-him," apparently by loss of the morpheme meaning "him." The whole complex is to be translated "They used to throw him."

Bibliography

The bibliography which follows is a selection of useful books, which have been the principal sources for this study.

1. Samuel von Kleinschmidt, *Grammatik der grönländischen Sprache*, G. Reimer, Berlin, 1851. This work probably represents the earliest realistic and scientific grammar of any American language and, in spite of its age, is still an almost indispensable tool.

2. William Thalbitzer, *A Phonetical Study of the Eskimo Language*, Vol. XXX, Meddelelser om Grönland, Copenhagen, 1904. An excellent study of the details of pronunciation and dialect variation, but too old to have made use of phonemic theory. There is a fairly extensive body of texts and some interesting material on the difficulties of Greenland natives in learning to spell properly according to the narrow spelling introduced by Europeans.

3. William Thalbitzer, "Eskimo," *Handbook of American Indian Languages*, ed. Franz Boas, Bureau of American Ethnology Bulletin 40, 1911, pp. 967–1069. Full paradigms and good information on sound changes, but little material on syntax or semantic components of paradigms.

4. C. W. Schultz-Lorentzen, *Dictionary of the West Greenland Eskimo Language*, Vol. LXIX, Meddelelser om Grönland, Copenhagen, 1927. A full and very usable Eskimo-English vocabulary. In the Kleinschmidt-Thalbitzer orthography. Gives many illustrations, but does not distinguish morpheme boundaries very rigorously.

5. Morris Swadesh, "South Greenlandic (Eskimo)," *Linguistic Structures of Native America*, ed. by Cornelius Osgood, Viking Fund, Publications in Anthropology, No. 6, New York, 1946, pp. 30–54. An excellent structural restatement, containing the only phonemicization of Eskimo.

6. Morris Swadesh, "Kleinschmidt Centennial III: Unaaliq and Proto Eskimo," *International Journal of American Linguistics*, 17, 1951, pp. 66–70. The only estimate as to the time depth of the Eskimo stock, and a new division of the dialects.

7. John Hinz, *Grammar and Vocabulary of the Eskimo Language*, The Moravian Church, Bethlehem, Pa., 1944. The fullest and most reliable source of information on Alaskan Eskimo. Since Hinz follows the structural outline of Kleinschmidt, his material is unusually good.

APPENDIX B

LATIN

1. Phonemics

Latin had the following fourteen segmental phonemes, which will be provisionally called consonants, though the definition of the term will not be given until we describe the phonotactics:

$$
\begin{array}{ccc}
/\mathrm{p} & \mathrm{t} & \mathrm{k} \\
\mathrm{b} & \mathrm{d} & \mathrm{g} \\
\mathrm{m} & \mathrm{n} & \eta \\
\mathrm{f} & \mathrm{s} & \mathrm{h} \\
& \mathrm{l} & \\
& \mathrm{r} & /
\end{array}
$$

The first column can be assumed to have had labial position (bilabial for all but /f/), the second column had position against the back surface of the upper front teeth, and the last column had palato-velar position. The phonemes /l/ and /r/ were apical, the /r/ a trill. Since these two were apical, it is also likely that /s/ was apical, but there is no evidence.

The /h/ was a spirant, and at no time the type of semivowel found in English. It was present only in the early stages of the language and was lost in classic Latin, though graphemic traces of it remained.

The /ŋ/ was inherited as an allophone of /n/, but in Latin came to contrast with /n/, since there were clusters of /ŋn/ and /nn/. The Roman name for this sound was *agma*.

Structurally, the most interesting features here are that the characteristic arrangement is into threes rather than fours, as in English, and that only in the stops is the contrast between voice and voicelessness a significant feature. The voiceless stops were smooth, rather than aspirated as in English.

Latin had the following vowels:

$$
\begin{array}{ccc}
/\mathrm{i} & & \mathrm{u} \\
\mathrm{e} & & \mathrm{o} \\
& \mathrm{a} & /
\end{array}
$$

In early Latin, /i u/ had consonantal allophones [y w], but in imperial Latin, these allophones had become the contrasting phonemes /y/ and /w/. All the vowels had close and open allophones.

Latin had at least three junctures, which can be written /+/, /|||/, and /#/. It is at present not known whether it had any entity corresponding to /||/. As well as the phoneme of /+/, which was as in English a phoneme of time, there was a second time phoneme, length, which can be written /:/. Length occurred only after vowels. Latin also had phonetically long consonants, but these are better analyzed, largely for morphemic reasons, as geminate clusters.

There were three grades of stress, which can be written /'/, /`/, and /ˇ/, with weak stress omitted in transcriptions unless there is reason to write it. The general arrangement of Latin phonemes into sets of threes suggests (but does not prove) that there was no fourth stress. There were certainly pitch phonemes, which as in English formed sentence patterns rather than word patterns. Since they cannot be accurately reconstructed at present, they will be disregarded. Much discussion has been devoted to whether the Latin "accent" was phonetically a stress or a pitch contrast, or both together. The argument is here passed over in silence, since it is clear that there were two kinds of contrast, one, characteristic of both words and sentences, which we call stress without committing ourselves as to its exact phonetic nature, and one, characteristic of sentences, which we call pitch, with the same reservation.

2. Graphemics

The evidence for the phonemic entities listed above is essentially that the spelling system provides contrasts corresponding to most of these entities. For their nature we have guesses based on comparison with related and descended languages, and occasionally, as with *agma*, descriptions by contemporary grammarians. There are still other types of evidence for reconstruction, but these are the principal ones.

The graphemic correspondences—taking account primarily of the norms—are as follows.[1] Among the stops the graphemes corresponded to the phonemic symbols we have used, except for /k/, the graphemic norm for which was ⟨c⟩. The sequence /ks/ was written ⟨x⟩, and the sequence /ku-/ before vowel (later /kw-/) was written ⟨qu-⟩. The phoneme /ŋ/ was written ⟨n⟩ before palato-velars, but ⟨g⟩ in the cluster /ŋn/. Otherwise

---

[1] A grapheme can be defined as a letter or other visual symbol (or sequence of symbols) considered in its relation to a phoneme. Graphemic symbols are enclosed in angle marks (⟨ ⟩), whereas mere spelling forms from Latin are given in italics.

the nasal graphemes and phonemic symbols corresponded, as did those for the spirants and liquids.

The vowel phonemes and graphemes corresponded almost exactly in the stage when [y] and [w] were not yet separate phonemes, the only exceptions being the writings ⟨æ⟩ and ⟨œ⟩ with ⟨e⟩ instead of ⟨i⟩. Latin never provided graphemic symbols for the phonemes /y/ and /w/, but modern editors have normalized by using ⟨j⟩ and ⟨v⟩, originally mere allographs of ⟨i⟩ and ⟨u⟩, for /y/ and /w/ respectively. Neither stresses nor pitches were provided with graphemic symbols. The stresses can be reconstructed from later developments, but as we have seen, the pitches cannot.

The grapheme for /+/ was normally the blank space left between words, but in internal position in classic Latin, a graphemic ⟨h⟩ was often the symbol for /+/, as in ⟨uehō⟩ /wé + o:/. In a few instances, such as the spelling ⟨lacue⟩ (or milk), the unusual sequence spelled the phonemes /k + w/, in contrast with the sequence /kw/ of ⟨aqua⟩. The other junctures are not spelled, but can be inferred from the later developments. Length has been normalized by editors as a macron over the vowel, though the manuscripts frequently employed double vowels.

3. Phonotactics

The phoneme classes of Latin are five: consonants, vowels, time phonemes, stresses and pitches, and terminal junctures. In contrast, the classes of English are four: consonants and semivowels, vowels, junctures, and stresses and pitches.

The first phoneme class are the terminal junctures. Every complete utterance must end in one of these. Every utterance must also have a phoneme of stress and one of pitch, or combinations of stresses, or combinations of pitches. These are distributionally defined as a class by the fact that they are the only phonemes which occur at the same time with other phonemes—they are the suprasegmentals. Stresses and pitches are also grouped by the fact that they are co-occurrent and co-extensive.

Every utterance must have one of the five phonemes which have been called vowels. These three classes (terminals, stresses and pitches, and vowels) are then those which necessarily occur in every utterance.

The two remaining classes are the time phonemes and the consonants. They are distributionally distinguished by the fact that the consonants may be initial, whereas the time phonemes must be preceded by other segmental phonemes.

The two segmental classes, the members of which occur in clusters, are the vowels and the consonants. We shall take up the vowels first, and describe the clustering conditions true at the time when [y] and [w] had only allophonic status. A true vocalic cluster is a diphthong. Characteristic of early Latin was the limitation that in any diphthong, at least one member had to be an /i/ or /u/, which we shall hereafter describe as the high vowels. If the first member of a diphthong was a high vowel, it always became a consonantal allophone. This rule applied also when both members of the diphthong were high vowels. On the other hand, if only the second member were a high vowel, it was this second phoneme which became the consonantal allophone. It will be seen that as long as these rules held, the occurrence of vocalic or consonantal allophones was predictable, and it is this distribution which is responsible for the statement that there were at that time no separate [y] and [w] phonemes. We can list the diphthongs as follows, beginning with those which had a high vowel as first member:

[yi] /ií/ ⟨adiiciō⟩ /adiíkio:/
[ye] /ié/ ⟨iecur⟩ /iékur/
[ya] /iá/ ⟨iam⟩ /iám/
[yu] /iú/ ⟨iūs⟩ /iú : s/
[yo] /ió/ ⟨iocus⟩ /iókus/
[wi] /uí/ ⟨uicis⟩ /uíkis/
[we] /ué/ ⟨uĕr⟩ /ué : r/
[wa] /uá/ ⟨uagus⟩ /uágus/
[wu] /uú/ ⟨uulgus⟩ /uúlgus/
[wo] /uó/ ⟨uolens⟩ /uólens/

Those diphthongs in which only the second member was a high vowel were:

[ey] /éi/ ⟨hei⟩ /(h)éi/
[ay] /ái/ ⟨aes⟩ /áis/
[oy] /ói/ ⟨Oenus⟩ /óinus/
[ew] /éu/ ⟨euge⟩ /éuge/
[aw] /áu/ ⟨aut⟩ /áut/
[ow] /óu/[2]

These two lists give all the vowel clusters occurrent at this time. All other apparent clusters of vowels consisted of vowel, juncture, and vowel. Furthermore, the series of true diphthongs given here contrasted with the same sequence of vowels interrupted by a juncture. An example of such a contrast is ⟨aes⟩ /áis/ (brass), given above, and ⟨ais⟩ /á + is/ (thou sayest). The evidence for this distinction is that the second form was counted by the Romans as two syllables—that is, both phonemes had vocalic allophones.

The habits of vocalic clustering we have described are strikingly unlike

---

[2] This diphthong disappeared in classic Latin, becoming /u:/, but there are inscriptions which show it, e.g., ⟨LOVCOM⟩ /lóukom/, later ⟨lucum⟩ /lú:kum/.

those of English. It is therefore interesting that a later change produced a state of affairs which was rather more like that of our own tongue. In imperial times, forms like the older /hóik/ became, by a process of assimilation, /(h)úyk/. That is, the older rule that only the first of two high vowels was phonetically consonantal no longer held. As a result, consonantal quality was no longer predictable, and [y] and [w] became everywhere the phonemes /y/ and /w/.

Thus, at a blow, a class of semivowels was set up. All diphthongs became combinations of vowel and semivowel, so that vocalic clustering no longer occurred, just as it does not occur in English. Yet some phonotactic differences between the two languages remain. The Latin sequences of vowel and semivowel continued to contrast with vowel and length, which, in current phonemic analyses, is not the interpretation given for English. In Latin, also, both the sequence semivowel-vowel and the sequence vowel-semivowel were distributed in positions where vowel alone or vowel and length were also possible. In English, on the other hand, only the sequence vowel-semivowel has a distribution like that of a simple vowel. In the sequence semivowel-vowel, the English semivowel is distributed like one of the consonants.

Consonant clustering, except for the difference, mentioned just above, that a prevocalic semivowel does not form a part of a prevocalic consonant cluster, is rather strikingly like that of English. The maximum initial cluster is three, and there are order groups as in English; the first group consists of spirants, the second of stops, and the third of linguals and nasals. In initial position the order must be 1-2-3, but in medial and final position, it may also be 3-2-1 as in English. The mixed and special sequences found in English are absent. Intervocalic geminate clusters occur, as do clusters involving two phonemes of the same order group. The latter, but not the former, type is also found in English.

The number of theoretically possible clusters is reduced by phonotactic rules:

1. No two stops, one of which is voiceless and the other voiced, occur in clusters.
2. The nasals cluster only with non-nasal consonants of the same articulation order; that is, /ŋ/ clusters only with palato-velars; /m/ clusters only with labials; /n/ only with dentals.
3. Among the spirants, /f/ occurs only in two-consonant clusters, and /h/ did not cluster at all, even before its disappearance.

Even after the reduction of the numbers of clusters by these rules, it is striking that many of the theoretically possible clusters do not occur.

We shall illustrate only with the initial three-consonant clusters, since these will serve to illustrate both the similarities and the differences between Latin and English. In a three-consonant cluster, position 1 must be filled by /s/, and position 3 only by a lingual. Position 2 must be filled by a voiceless stop, as in English, but there seems to be no theoretical reason why this should be so in Latin. Five clusters occur (figures in parentheses show the total number of dictionary entries):

/spl–/ ⟨splendeō⟩ (9)
/spr–/ ⟨sprētiō⟩ (2)
/stl–/ ⟨stloppus⟩ (3)
/str–/ ⟨strabo⟩ (75)
/skr–/ ⟨scribō⟩ (31)

The lexical frequency is immediately suggestive. Thus, /spl–/, which is frequent in English, occurs in only two morphemes, that found in ⟨splēn⟩ (spleen) of Greek origin, and that found in ⟨splendeō⟩ (shine). All other dictionary entries are examples of these same two morphemes in differing constructions. The other rare clusters are found either in borrowed words or in forms with very special meanings, like ⟨stloppus⟩ (the noise of a slap on the inflated cheeks). The suggested conclusion is that only /str–/ and /skr–/ are thoroughly established in the Latin clustering pattern. The clusters themselves are very like those of English, but distribution is very different.

4. Morphemics and morphotactics

Latin has the following classes of segmental morphemes: bases, pre-bases, postbases, and suffixes. It is sometimes said that there are also infixes, as in the /–ŋ–/ characteristic of a tense form like ⟨pungō⟩, but since these nasals are found in only a few forms and since there is always a set of distinctive suffixes with which the nasal forms are associated, there is no reason to analyze /puŋg–/ as anything more than an allomorph of the base. Infixes were once doubtless a living type of morpheme, but they are not so in historic Latin.

Bases are to be defined as possible initial morphemes. Some bases are also possible finals, as in forms like *haud*. In this connection, "initial" is taken to mean postjunctural, and "final" is taken to mean prejunctural, where "junctural" means terminal juncture. Most Latin bases do not occur as finals, since they are followed by one or more suffixes, before which there may also be one or more postbases. The fact that most Latin bases are normally followed by suffixes is a significant difference from English.

Many English bases, even when inflectable, are without following postbases or suffixes in many of their occurrences, and many English bases are never followed by suffixes in any occurrence.

A prebase is a possible initial which occurs before other possible initials, themselves either prebases or bases. A postbase is not a possible initial but is a form which occurs either after a base or after another postbase. Prebases and postbases are alike in that constructions occur frequently without them, since a common shape of Latin construction consists only of base and suffix.

A suffix is characteristically a possible final, and is added to either a preceding postbase or a preceding base. Suffixes have the further characteristic of occurring in the partially symmetrical sets called paradigms. There are instances of more than one suffix, but this is rare except in verb forms. Usually a single suffix closes the construction.

Constructions can, as intimated, have more than one postbase, but the number of postbases added to a single base is normally much more limited than it is in English. Constructions can also have more than one base. When this happens there are two types, either the construction consists of base, base, and suffix or it consists of base, suffix, base, and suffix. Anything consisting of two bases is a fixed phrase, but within that class it is convenient to speak of the class where there is no suffix intervening between the bases as a compound. These fixed phrases and compounds may have been interrupted by a plus juncture, but were never interrupted by terminals.

Examples of these several types of morphemes follow:

PREBASES

{ad–}, which is added to the possible initials of *moneō* and *optō* to give *admoneō* {admone + o:} and *adoptō* {adopto:}.

BASES

Final bases are forms like *haud* {(h)aud} and *enim* {enim}, which are regularly invariant. Nonfinal bases can be illustrated by the two verb forms already given, of which the base morphemes are {mone–} and {opt–}, respectively.

POSTBASES

{–tik–}, added to the allomorph {akwa:} of the base *aqua* to give *aquāticus* {akwa:tikus}. Multiple postbases, {–ment–} and {–a:ti–} added to the base {argu–} found in the verb *arguō*, to give {argu–ment–a:ti–o} (bringing of proof).

magnānimus, which consists of the base {maŋn–} followed by the allomorph {a : nim–} of {animus} (soul). With the suffix {–us}, this gives the form cited (great-souled).

iurisdictio (jurisdiction). Consists of the allomorph {iur–} of the base found in {iu : s} (law), plus the suffix {–is–} plus the base {dik–} found in *dīcō* (say), plus the postbase {–ti–}, and the suffix {–o :}.

Suffixes have already been fairly freely illustrated. A simple additional illustration might be the noun *arx* (citadel), three of whose case forms are {ark–s}, {arke–m} and {ark–e}.

To the four primary classes of segmental morphemes which we have described and illustrated, it might be possible to add a fifth, the so-called enclitics like *–que* in *puerīsque* (and about boys) or the *–ue* of *lacue* (or milk). These forms would seem to be, however, no more than invariant bases, which preserve a plus juncture before them, but are unique in having no juncture stronger than a plus as well as in having lost normal stress characteristics. They are thus distinct from forms like *haud* and *enim*, but are best handled as a subclass rather than as a separate group. These enclitics are somewhat like the postphrases of Eskimo.

5. Paradigmatic classes of words and fixed phrases

Latin possesses more paradigmatically marked form classes than either English or Eskimo. These classes are nouns, pronouns, adjectives, and verbs. Eskimo, it will be remembered, possesses nouns and verbs as classes characterized by paradigms, and English possesses nouns, pronouns, and verbs.

Nouns in Latin are marked by forms for the categories of number and the set of syntactic relations called case. Pronouns have these categories and, in addition, the categories of person and the selection (or agreement) category of gender. Adjectives have the case and number categories of nouns, and also the gender category found in pronouns. Verbs have categories of number and person, and a set of special categories not found elsewhere in paradigmatic sets, those called tense, mood, aspect, and voice. These paradigmatic characteristics mean that form classes are much more clearly marked in Latin than in English and at least as well marked as, though much more complex than, those of Eskimo.

In describing Latin, we shall by no means cover all the inflected form classes but shall confine ourselves to some instances of nouns and verbs, since these will suffice to illustrate the nature of the structure and its complexities.

If we survey the whole series of Latin nouns, we can make a number of general statements before going on to illustrate the forms of any single noun. If we count the distinctions in the category of case, we find a maximum of six, though no single noun makes all these distinctions. There are two numbers—singular and plural. This should give us a total of twelve distinctions, but in actuality there are only ten, since two case distinctions are lost in the plural in all nouns. These ten distinctions could be made with six suffixes, were the system rigorously analytical in structure; that is, the six cases could be indicated by leaving one case unmarked and providing distinctive suffixes for the other five, and similarly the two numbers could be indicated by leaving one unmarked and providing a distinctive suffix for the other. The first fact of importance in a general description of Latin noun inflection is that the system is not analytical in the fashion we have just set up as a possibility. If we compare the case forms in the two numbers in the paradigm of any Latin noun, we get forms like the accusative singular *mēnsam*, in which the suffix is {–m}, and the accusative plural *mēnsās*, in which the suffix is {–: s}. The two suffixes contain no phoneme in common; there is consequently no element within the suffix which can be associated with the case alone. Analyzing in another way, if we list all the plural forms for this noun, we find the suffixes {–y}, {–: s}, {–i: s}, and {–: rum}. While two phonemes, /:/ and /s/, occur in more than one of these suffixes, these phonemes occur in no fixed order, and neither one is found in all the plural suffixes. There is thus no element in these suffixes which can be associated with number alone. This type of relationship is found throughout the whole of the noun inflection and is therefore a fundamental property of the system. In Latin, therefore, the number and case forms are formally fused so that a total of ten suffixes, or nine if one were left unmarked, would be required to make the ten distinctions. In fact, this fusing of intersecting categories has long been recognized as one of the most striking features of languages like Latin and, in attempts at generalized language typology, has been used to define what is meant by calling Latin an "inflectional" language, in contrast to a language which does not thus fuse its intersecting categories and is called "agglutinating."

In Latin nouns, there are also two selection classes—genders—which are formally differentiated: a non-neuter class and a neuter class. This double distinction would then mean that with the Latin system of fusing intersecting categories, a total of twenty suffixes would be needed to make all distinctions. A count of the number of suffixes which are different phonemically, taking no account of their distribution and leaving out of account rare and foreign suffixes, yields a total of only twenty-four phonemically distinct suffixes, and among these twenty-four, there are at least three which are clearly no more than automatic variants scarcely needing separate listing. This number of suffixes corresponds strikingly with the number of distinctions which the system provides for, and it is plain that if the suffixes were systematically distributed, we should have a noun inflection of very little complexity. Yet the suffixes are in fact so distributed as to give an inflection which is indeed complex; there are, again leaving out of account rare and foreign nouns, at least twelve differing paradigmatic noun sets. The Latin noun inflection has therefore a property which we have called "skewness," that is to say, lack of symmetry in distribution of elements, with resulting complexity.

The skewness in the noun inflection shows in a number of different ways. First, the inflection of nouns is out of alignment with the inflection of other classes to which it is related. Thus, in adjectives and pronouns, there are three selection or agreement sets, conventionally called masculine, feminine, and neuter, though these classes are by no means rationally connected with notions of sex and sexlessness. In nouns, on the other hand, there are only two such sets, which we have already called non-neuter and neuter. Since it is a commonplace that every Latin noun is either "masculine, feminine, or neuter," this statement may sound like a contradiction of common knowledge. What is meant is this: Nouns like *mēnsa* and *agricola* are declined alike, yet one is "feminine" and one "masculine" in its agreement characteristics. Even the set like *servus*, which schoolboys usually think of as a "masculine" declension, contains some feminine nouns. The only sets in which any of the suffixes reliably indicate the gender are the forms like *bellum*, which are neuter. Thus, whether a noun will take a feminine or a masculine adjective in agreement with it is unpredictable from the way in which it is declined, though the paradigmatic sets do enable the analyst to predict whether or not a noun will take a neuter adjective. That is, the masculine-feminine distinction is a property of the noun base, not of the paradigmatic suffixes or arrangement.

Skewness is also shown in the fact already mentioned that the singular and plural cases do not agree with each other, there being six case distinctions in the singular and only four in the plural. These rather general examples of skewness do not indicate at all the most important complexities. The real complexity is perhaps best indicated by a statement of how many of the possible ten distinctions are made in individual nouns. No more than eight are made in any one noun, and the minimum is five. Furthermore, not all the nouns that have the same number of distinctions have the same distinctions. It is, then, primarily this differing and nonsymmetrical reduction in the number of distinctions which is responsible for the fact that there are so many paradigmatic sets of nouns.

Having described where the skewness lies, we now also know the problem which faces the analyst. It is to analyze the skewed sets so as to be able to state them with accuracy and with a minimum number of separate statements. The first problem is that of placing the boundary between base and suffix. One general principle governing such cuts can be seen from a comparison of a few forms:

| NOM. SING. | *mēnsa* | *acus* | *stirps* | *turris* |
| ACC. SING. | *mēnsam* | *acum* | *stirpem* | *turrim* |

An unwary step would be to assume that the suffix of the first form here is {-a}, added to a base {me : ns-}, though to do so would be to make all bases in this set regular. It would, however, make eight different suffixes, which with the four bases make a total of twelve morphs. A better cut would be before the final consonant. We have now one ending for the accusative, {-m}, two endings for the nominative, {-ø} and {-s}. We have five base forms, since we must add the variation between {stirp-} and {stirpe-}. This type of cut then gives us a total of eight morphs, a saving of four. Another conclusion that we can come to from these forms is that the nominative singular of *mēnsa* is not a form without suffix but rather one with a zero allomorph of the ending which appears in the other forms. Similarly, {stirpe-} can be assigned allomorphic status, so that from a morphemic standpoint, this set of eight forms can be reduced completely to the minimum number of morphemes necessary for the differentiation, four base morphemes and two suffix morphemes. This procedure does not solve all difficulties in cutting, since there are forms like the dative plural of our set:

mēnsīs   acubus   stirpibus   turribus

There are obviously two endings, and several base forms. *Acubus* gives us no trouble; we cut {aku-bus}, and follow the same procedure with {turri-bus}. We cannot cut *{mé : nsi : -s} in the same fashion, since a form with final {-s} occurs elsewhere in the paradigm of this noun, *mēnsās*, accusative plural. Therefore to cut here before the consonant would be to increase the troublesome homonymity in the suffixes and to throw the distinction back into the base, where it certainly does not belong. We must therefore cut into {me : ns-i : s} and make the assumption that {me : ns-} is a base allomorph which has lost its vowel before a vocalic ending. We cannot resort to the same analysis for *stirpibus*, however, because if we

452 INTRODUCTION TO LINGUISTIC STRUCTURES

assume a general ending *{–ibus}, we have trouble in explaining why the vowel of the base, rather than a hypothetic vowel of the ending, has been preserved in {aku–bus}. We must then assume a third allomorph {stirpi–} for this base.

These principles of cutting are not meant to be a complete statement, but rather an illustration of the kinds of difficulties met. Assuming that we now know how to cut, we next proceed to a stage of normalization. Basically, this is a process of removing the skewness which we have described by setting up an arrangement of suffixes which would accomplish all the distinctions found in the actual paradigmatic sets with a rational distribution. The process is accomplished simply. The ending most frequently found in a given case-number form in the several sets will be associated with that case-number as its norm. Simple counting is departed from only when a less common form must be chosen as the norm if the distinctions found in the paradigms are to be preserved in the normalized set. An illustration is the norm for the vocative singular, {–e}. This occurs in only one set—*domine*—but must be chosen because this is the only distinctive vocative singular ending. The normalized set of endings follows:

NON-NEUTER NOUNS

VOC. SING.	{–e}
NOM. SING.	{–s}
ACC. SING.	{–m}
ABL. SING.	{–:}
DAT. SING.	{–i:}
GEN. SING.	{–is}
VOC.-NOM. PL.	{–y}
ACC. PL.	{–: s}
ABL.-DAT. PL.	{–bus}
GEN. PL.	{–um}

Only one of these forms requires special comment. This is {–y}, chosen as the norm for the vocative-nominative plural. This morph occurs in only one group of nouns, those like *mēnsae*, and the morph {–: s} is far commoner. This morph, however, must be associated with the accusative plural, leaving {–y} among the morphs found in the vocative-nominative plural as the only one not associated with some other case-number.

The same principles of normalization can be applied to the neuter nouns. All but one of the neuter suffixes are identical with the norms of the non-neuter nouns. The special neuter suffix is {–a} for the vocative-nominative-accusative plural. The appearance of this unique morph justifies the contention that the neuter nouns are a special paradigmatic class.

NEUTER NOUNS

VOC.-NOM.-ACC. SING.	$\{-m\}$
ABL. SING.	$\{-:\}$
DAT. SING.	$\{-i:\}$
GEN. SING.	$\{-is\}$
VOC.-NOM.-ACC. PL.	$\{-a\}$
ABL.-DAT. PL.	$\{-bus\}$
GEN. PL.	$\{-um\}$

It is to be noted that the first suffix in this list, $\{-m\}$, is identical with that found as the norm for the accusative singular in the non-neuter nouns. In the neuter nouns the distinction between vocative, nominative, and accusative is absent, so that the morph has a wider range of case-number occurrences when added to a neuter noun base than when added to a non-neuter base.

The sets of normalized endings are abstractions, since no Latin noun is inflected in accord with the normalized arrangement. Abstract as the sets may be, setting them up has accomplished two things. We have associated individual morphs with individual case-numbers by a process sufficiently rigorous so that it may be readily verified. We have also distinguished in a similarly rigorous fashion between the neuter and the non-neuter classes.

More important than these results, however, is the usefulness of the normalized forms for further description. When norms have been chosen, the suffixes actually found in any noun paradigm can be described either as instances of the norms or as departures from them. The departures fall into two main distributional types. The first is simple variation, and such a morph will be called a variant. The term indicates a suffix different from all case-number norms. The second type of departure is an ending identical with a case-number norm, but one which appears in a case-number different from that associated with the norm, thus destroying a distinction. Loss of distinction in case-number forms has interested Latin scholars, who have described the loss with the term "syncretion." We can slightly modify this traditional term and call our second type of variant a syncrete.

An illustration of a variant is found in the ending of *mēnsārum*, genitive plural. The norm for this case-number is $\{-um\}$, and the morph which appears with this noun is a variant since it is different from the norms of all case-numbers. A syncrete can be illustrated by an ending which is common in the vocative singular. The norm for the vocative singular is the rare morph $\{-e\}$. Most nouns have the morph $\{-s\}$, which is the norm for the nominative singular. The vocative form in $\{-s\}$ is therefore a syncrete.

The forms thus described as norms, variants, and syncretes are morphs, and assignment of them to the status of allomorphs or morphemes is a separate operation. The sum total of morphs which appear in a given case-number constitute a paradigmatic family, and syncrete and norm therefore belong to such a family. In general it can be said that norm and variant usually are allomorphs of a single morpheme, whereas it must be assumed that a syncrete belongs to the morpheme of the norm with which it is homonymous, even though we have just said that a syncrete belongs to the same paradigmatic family with the other endings for a given case-number. The conclusion that a syncrete belongs with the norm with which it is identical is based on the decision that phonemic identity is a criterion which takes precedence over meaning in classification of morphs into morphemes. The case-number identification carried by a suffix is its meaning and so is not a criterion to be applied in classification. It should also be pointed out that if all morphs found in a given case-number were assumed to be members of a single morpheme, the result would be to produce many phonemically indistinguishable morphs which would be members of more than one morpheme; that is, morphemic overlapping would be increased. The alternative chosen here minimizes such overlapping, though it does so at the expense of recognizing overlapping in the semantic content of morphemes.

Terms such as "norm," "variant," and "syncrete" are distributional and descriptive terms, and carry no implication as to how the distributional arrangement they are meant to describe came into being. Thus, for instance, a form called a variant may, in point of fact, be older than the norm, so that in a historical sense the term "departure" would be more applicable to the norm than to the variant. It is true that complete understanding of a distributional arrangement should include knowledge of its history. It is also true, however, that exact description of an arrangement should normally precede historical study and is separate from it.

The three terms we have set up for morphic analysis of paradigms are basic, but as we shall see, some morphs fall into subdivisions of one of the three classes. We can then proceed to problems of actual analysis as found in a pair of typical non-neuter nouns.

In the following paradigms, the forms are first given in conventional spelling, then in phonemic transcription, followed in turn by a morphic transcription which omits stress. The morphemic status of the morphs is discussed after the paradigm has been given.

NON-NEUTER   *mēnsa* (table)

VOC. SING.	*mēnsa* /mé : nsa/	{me : nsa}	{ø}.
NOM. SING.	*mēnsa* /mé : nsa/	{me : nsa}	{ø}

ACC. SING.	*mēnsam* /mé: nsam/ {me: nsa} {m}
ABL. SING.	*mēnsā* /mé: nsa :/ {me: nsa} {:}
DAT. SING.	*mēnsae* /mé: nsay/ {me: nsa} {y}
GEN. SING.	*mēnsae* /mé: nsay/ {me: nsa} {y}
VOC.-NOM. PL.	*mēnsae* /mé: nsay/ {me: nsa} {y}
ACC. PL.	*mēnsās* /mé: nsa: s/ {me: nsa} {: s}
ABL.-DAT. PL.	*mēnsīs* /mé: nsi: s/ {me: ns} {i: s}
GEN. PL.	*mēnsārum* /me: nsá: rum/ {me: nsa} {: rum}

The base offers little difficulty in this paradigm, there being only two allomorphs, a base norm, {me: nsa}, and an allomorph, {me: ns}, which appears before the one suffix which begins with a front vowel.

The first two endings here introduce a problem. The paradigms of Latin nouns do not normally leave one form without suffix, yet vocative and nominative of this noun have no material following the base which can be interpreted as a suffix. The familiar device for handling such a situation is to assume that these forms contain a zero allomorph of some suffix. The device is justified, and has been adopted, but it immediately brings a further problem with it.

The zero allomorph appears as a variant of the norm for nominative singular, and also appears in the vocative, a case frequently not distinguished from the nominative. In other words, we have an example of syncretion between variants, whereas our previous description envisaged only syncretion between a variant and a norm. It would be tempting to say that such syncretional variants constitute independent morphemes, defined by their special range, in this instance, vocative-nominative. Yet the example before us is instructive, since it is one which clearly makes such an independent classification impossible. The reason is that if we set up this zero allomorph as a morpheme, we would be setting up a morpheme whose only allomorph is zero, a procedure inadmissible since it would open the door to the most arbitrary kinds of analysis. Therefore our zero allomorph must belong to a morpheme which contains an observable suffix. It is preferable not to assign this zero to both the vocative and nominative norms, since overlapping allomorphs are to be avoided if possible. We must, in consequence, find a criterion for classifying it with one or the other. The criterion can be found in the distribution of syncretes. When vocative and nominative are distinguished, the vocative suffix is {-e}, and the nominative suffix is {-s}. There are many nouns with {-s} in both nominative and vocative, none with {-e} in both cases. This distribution indicates that the direction in which syncretion moves is from nominative to vocative, not the reverse. Unfortunately, the language in which such a distribution is described is necessarily one of process, but the reader is again reminded that no historical implications are intended. We are merely searching for a means of deciding whether our zero allomorph belongs to the morpheme whose norm is {-s} or to the one whose norm is {-e}, and this purpose has been achieved. Since the distribution shows "movement" from nominative to vocative, our zero suffix will be assigned the status of an allomorph of the nominative norm. As a form for the vocative, it is then a fourth type of suffix beyond the three we have set up, a type which can be called a homonymous variant. Such variants will always be assigned allomorphic status in a single case-number form, and the distributional arrangement will be used as the criterion on which decision will be based.

We can now conclude the description of the suffix forms for this noun. Vocative and nominative show the homonymous variant {-ø}, which is an allomorph of {-s}, the nominative singular norm. The accusative singular and ablative singular show the norms for the two case-numbers. The dative singular, genitive singular, and vocative-nominative plural all show a syncrete, {-y}, identical with the norm of the vocative-nominative plural. The accusative plural {-:s} is the norm. The ablative-dative plural {-i:s} is a variant of the norm {-bus}. The genitive plural {-:rum} is a common variant of the norm {-um}.

The discussion of the syncretes and homonymous variants which appear in this noun probably makes clear the reason for an operation which has been performed on the paradigm, but which has not been mentioned. That is, the familiar order of cases, as given in school grammars, has been departed from. The arrangement given here is for the purpose of bringing those case-numbers which are alike into juxtaposition. It is worth mentioning that such a rearrangement is one which has pedagogical value. If paradigms are to be learned, an arrangement which brings the similar forms together is easier than one which does not.

NON-NEUTER   *dominus* (master)

VOC. SING.	*domine*	/dómine/	{domin} {e}
NOM. SING.	*dominus*	/dóminus/	{dominu} {s}
ACC. SING.	*dominum*	/dóminum/	{dominu} {m}
ABL. SING.	*dominō*	/dómino:/	{domino} {:}
DAT. SING.	*dominō*	/dómino:/	{domino} {:}
GEN. SING.	*dominī*	/dómini:/	{domin} {i:}
VOC.-NOM. PL.	*dominī*	/dómini:/	{domin} {i:}
ACC. PL.	*dominōs*	/dómino:s/	{domino} {:s}
ABL.-DAT. PL.	*dominīs*	/dómini:s/	{domin} {i:s}
GEN. PL.	*dominōrum*	/dominó:rum/	{domino} {:rum}

The inflection of this noun differs from that of the first noun not only in the suffixes but in the allomorphs of the base. There are the following base allomorphs: {domin-}, {dominu-}, and {domino-}. The first of these allomorphs appears before all suffixes beginning with a front vowel, the second before consonantal suffixes, and the third before suffixes beginning with /:/.

Vocative, nominative, and accusative singular are the norms for these three case-numbers. The suffix of ablative and dative singular is a syncrete, identical with the norm of the ablative.

The forms of the genitive singular and vocative-nominative plural are peculiar. These case-numbers have a syncrete identical with the norm of the dative singular. It is to be noted that the norm of the dative singular does not, however, appear in this paradigm, since as just said, the ending of the dative is a syncrete identical with the norm of the ablative. The syncrete which appears in genitive singular and vocative-nominative plural is therefore not identical with any form elsewhere in the paradigm of this noun, yet the ending remains a syncrete, since it is identical with a norm. The ending is therefore not a new type of variant, though it is a type of distribution which we have not previously met. Syncretes distributed thus can be said to be displaced, though as always, such a statement is a description of distribution, not history.

The remaining forms offer no difficulty. The accusative plural is the norm, and the ablative-dative plural has the same variant which we saw in *mēnsīs*. The genitive plural is also a variant and the same one which appears in *mēnsārum*.

NEUTER   *bellum* (war)

VOC.-NOM.-ACC. SING.	*bellum* /béllum/	{bellu}	{m}
ABL. SING.	*bellō* /béllo:/	{bello}	{:}
DAT. SING.	*bellō* /béllo:/	{bello}	{:}
GEN. SING.	*bellī* /bélli:/	{bell}	{i:}
VOC.-NOM.-ACC. PL.	*bella* /bélla/	{bell}	{a}
ABL.-DAT. PL.	*bellīs* /bélli: s/	{bell}	{i: s}
GEN. PL.	*bellōrum* /belló: rum/	{bello}	{: rum}

The base allomorphs are {bellu-}, {bello-}, and {bell-}. The first appears only before the nasal ending, the second before all endings beginning with /:/, and the third before all endings beginning with a vowel.

The suffix here written for vocative-nominative-accusative singular needs some comment. It is a syncrete, identical with the norm of accusative singular in the non-neuter nouns. Its morphemic status is thus clear. Yet it has a special distribution in nouns of this class, best expressed by the statement that all noun bases which have neuter selection characteristics when occurring with adjectives or pronouns and which have the morph {-a} for vocative-nominative-accusative plural also have the syncrete {-m} for the same cases in the singular. Thus, distribution of this syncrete constitutes a secondary characteristic of the paradigmatic class of neuter nouns, and the paradigm is shown with the three cases lumped together because there is never a distinction.

The ablative and dative singular have a syncrete identical with the norm of the ablative. The genitive singular has a syncrete identical with the norm of the dative. As in *dominus*, the syncrete which appears in the genitive singular is displaced. The morph which appears in the vocative-nominative-accusative plural has already been classified as the norm and the chief identifying characteristic of this paradigmatic class. The ablative-dative plural has the same variant which we have met in other nouns, and the genitive plural likewise has a common variant.

NEUTER   *murmur* (murmur)

VOC.-NOM.-ACC. SING.	*murmur* /múrmur/ {murmur} {ø}
ABL. SING.	*murmure* /múrmure/ {murmur} {e}
DAT. SING.	*murmurī* /múrmuri:/ {murmur} {i:}
GEN. SING.	*murmuris* /múrmuris/ {murmur} {is}
VOC.-NOM.-ACC. PL.	*murmura* /múrmura/ {murmur} {a}
ABL.-DAT. PL.	*murmuribus* /murmúribus/ {murmuri} {bus}
GEN. PL.	*murmurum* /múrmurum/ {murmur} {um}

In this noun, the base allomorphs are simple, there being only one departure from the norm, the occurrence of {murmuri-} before the suffix of the ablative-dative plural. The suffixes are also relatively simple, except for the zero allomorph which appears in vocative-nominative-accusative singular. It will be remembered that we have once before met a zero allomorph, occurring in vocative and nominative (but not accusative) singular of *mēnsa*. There the zero allomorph was assigned to the same morpheme as the norm of the nominative singular. The zero allomorph which occurs in neuter nouns like *murmur* must, on the other hand, be assigned the status of an allomorph of the accusative singular norm. The reason for this statement is that, as we have just seen, the movement of syncretion is from the accusative singular to the other cases, whereas in the differently distributed zero allomorph of *mēnsa* the movement of syncretion was from the nominative form. These two zero allomorphs constitute, therefore, an unavoidable instance of overlapping allomorphs.

The morph {-e} which appears in the ablative singular is a syncrete, identical with the norm of the vocative singular. It is here a displaced syncrete. The dative singular and genitive singular show the norms. The vocative-nominative-accusative plural has the norm for neuter nouns, and the ablative-dative plural and genitive plural have the norms for all nouns, the first paradigm in which these norms have been met.

It is hoped that the approach to paradigmatic analysis and the several entities set up (norms, variants, syncretes, homonymous variants, and displaced syncretes) offer a reasonably rigorous and economical description of an inflection as remarkably skewed as is that of Latin nouns. We have also given a sort of generalized approach to the problems of morphemic classification when the morphs have been identified. It should be pointed out that if classification into morphemes is to be rigorous, a good many problems of detail remain. Indeed, in any study of a historical state of language, where records are always less than complete, some of these details will remain unsolvable. If, for instance, a variant always appears after a given base, or list of bases, it can be confidently assigned the status of allomorph of the norm, since it is then in complementary distribution with the norm. On the other hand, it often happens that a given base appears either with the norm or with the variant whose status we wish to settle. A typical example is the proper name *Aenēās*, the accusative singular of which appears with both the morphemic norm, as *Aenēam* {ayne: a–m}, and with a differing morph, as *Aenēān*, {ayne: a: –n}. Considered in terms of paradigmatic distribution alone, such alternate forms would have to be called instances of contrastive distribution. In many instances, such as this one, it is possible to guess that there is a stylistic explanation. With this particular name, the form with {–n} is of Greek origin, and so might be more likely in any stylistic corpus where Greek items tended to cluster. In many other instances of variant endings, no such guess can be made. In past states of language, we can call variant endings instances of that troublesome term "free variation," by which we mean linguistic contrast without function and, because without function, believed to have a stylistic explanation—variation contrastive on the linguistic level but complementary on the stylistic level. All such variants can be arbitrarily assigned to allomorphic status, but with the frank admission that such assignment is no more than an approximation necessary because of the fragmentary nature of the corpus which is our evidence.

A collection of noun paradigms is a distributional statement of suffixes, but a severely limited one. All that is given is the morphotactic distribution of the suffixes in question. That is, it is a statement only of the bases and postbases with which they occur in words or fixed phrases. These words and phrases, in turn, have syntactic distribution since they occur in still larger constructions. A given suffix has several levels of distribution and meaning, several levels on which partial predictability occurs. If we use our four nouns once more as an illustration, we find that an allomorph in {–ø} limits (among these four nouns) the case-number possibilities to vocative singular, nominative singular, and accusative singular. If the morphotactic situation is given, there is some further limitation. If the preceding form is the base *murmur*, the possibilities are the same three case-number forms, but if the preceding form is the base *mēnsa*, the possibilities are only vocative or nominative. In general, therefore, the combination of base and suffix only limits the case possibilities. It is meaningful, since there is partial predictability, and its meaning is all the possible case-number forms for the particular combination of base and suffix in question.

Suppose now we have a larger syntactic distribution:

Mēnsa exstructa est. (The table is loaded [with food].)

This is a syntactic situation which finally defines the exact case-number form, nominative singular. The case-number form now has another level of meaning—in this situation it defines *mēnsa* as the subject of the verb.

In terms of our particular problem, the assignment of morphs, the separation of levels of distribution means that we can avoid the necessity of having to redefine suffixes as something else than morphemes or of having to redefine morphemes in terms of something else than distribution. On the first level, suffixes are morphemes with morphotactic distribution. Their meaning is the sum total of possible case-number forms for a given morphotactic combination. The case-number forms thus limited are identified by the syntactic situation, giving one single case-number form, which then has wider meaning in that it clarifies the structure of the utterance as a whole. It is thus possible to refer every Latin ending to a comparatively few morphemes, but to represent distribution in such a way as to show the skewness. This might most graphically be done in diagrammatic lists, like the following pair:

	mēnsa		*dominus*
VOC. SING.	⎫ allomorph {–ø}	VOC. SING.	{–e} norm
NOM. SING.	⎭ of nom. sing. norm	NOM. SING.	{–s} norm
ACC. SING.	{–m} norm	ACC. SING.	{–m} norm
ABL. SING.	{–:} norm	ABL. SING.	⎫ {–:} norm of
DAT. SING.	⎫	DAT. SING.	⎭ abl. sing.
GEN. SING.	⎬ {–y}, norm of	GEN. SING.	⎫ {–i:} norm of
VOC.-NOM. PL.	⎭ voc.-nom. pl.	VOC.-NOM. PL.	⎭ dat. sing.
ACC. PL.	{–: s} norm	ACC. PL.	{–: s} norm
ABL.-DAT. PL.	{–i : s} allomorph of norm for this form	ABL.-DAT. PL.	{–i : s} allomorph of norm for this form
GEN. PL.	{–: rum} allomorph of norm for this form	GEN. PL.	{–: rum} allomorph of norm for this form

Our endeavor up to this point has been to simplify the structure of suffixes so far as possible. We have emphasized that we were making a descriptive, not a historical, statement. The descriptive statement sometimes parallels the best statements of historical origins and processes now available, sometimes is at variance with them. Thus, in the genitive plural, the form {–um} is indeed the older form of the ending, and the allomorph {–: rum} is an analogical extension from the pronoun forms. On the other hand, the statement that in *dominī*, vocative-nominative plural, we have a displaced syncrete identical with the norm of the dative singular has nothing to do with the historical facts, since the dative has not replaced the plural ending. The long {–i:} here is not a dative form, but a development of the same form found in {me: nsa–y}, by a sound-change which coalesced the semivowel with the preceding vowel of the base. Both endings, however, were analogical in origin, having been extended from the pronouns.

In simplifying the system of suffixes, also, we have neglected to speak of the nature and distribution of base allomorphs. It is interesting that by the process of cutting so as to simplify the number of suffix allomorphs, there emerges a series of classes of base morphs which is in general agreement with the statement of base classes made by historical students. The class of bases represented by *mēnsa* is describable as all those in which the base ends in /–a–/. *Dominus* represents a class in which the last phoneme of the base was originally /–o–/, though developments before some of the endings have obscured this terminal to some extent. There is also a class represented by *acus* (needle)—of which the ablative-dative plural is *acubus*—which represents all those bases in which the last phoneme is /–u–/. There is no recognizable set in which the last phoneme is /–e–/, but supplying its place is a set, represented by *diēs* (day), in which the base ends in /–e : –/. There are, finally, two classes which have become sufficiently confused so as no longer to remain clearly separate, those like *arx* (citadel), in which the base, originally at least, ended in any consonant, and those like *turris* (tower), in which the base originally ended in /–i–/. The Latin system of base construction is fragmentary but suggests quite clearly an earlier system in which there were types corresponding to the five vowel phonemes, with or without following /–: –/, and a sixth type in which the final was a consonant. In general, there is enough left of the system of base structure in Latin, so that it is of considerable use in stating morphemic norms of bases. One minor detail of base allomorphic structure is that final base vowels, if high, do not assume consonantal quality before a vowel of an ending. When they thus preserve their vocalic quality before a vowel, there is then a juncture between base and ending, which is not a part of either base or suffix, but a part of the superfix structure of the construction, and which, as in English, defines the boundaries of the morphs.

The base allomorphs must be handled by listing. Thus, for *dominus* the norm of the base is *domino–*. Allomorph *a* is *domin–*, and allomorph *b* is *dominu–*. In such a list, automatic variations, such as the stress shift in the genitive plural, *bellōrum*, need not be given, since they are provided for by general morphophonemic rules. In such a compressed statement of forms as we are here envisaging, suffixes can also be handled by listing and numbering. The morphemic norms can each be given a number, and the allomorphs of each given a letter. In addition, each non-neuter base must be labeled with an indication of its selection class, masculine or feminine. A sample of such compressed description is given for a noun not yet described:

flōs, masculine (flower)

The base belongs to the class of consonant-finals. The base norm is therefore the commonest allomorph ending in a consonant, namely *flōr–* {flo : r–}. Base allomorph *a* is *flōs* {flo : s} (the usual citation form). The other allomorphs are vocalic: *b, flōre–* {flo : re–}, and *c, flōri–* {flo : ri–}.

The differentiated forms, with their constituents, are then as follows:

I. VOCATIVE AND NOMINATIVE SINGULAR
Base allomorph *a* followed by allomorph A of suffix 2, which is zero. Expressed in a formula: *a*-2A = {flo : s}

II. ACCUSATIVE SINGULAR
Allomorph *b* of base, followed by suffix 3: *b*-3 = {flo : rem}

III. ABLATIVE SINGULAR
Norm of the base, followed by suffix 1, a syncrete: *n*-1 = {flo : re}

IV. DATIVE SINGULAR
Norm of the base, followed by suffix 5: *n*-5 = {flo : ri :}

V. GENITIVE SINGULAR
Norm of the base, followed by suffix 6: *n*-6 = {flo : ris}

VI. VOCATIVE-NOMINATIVE-ACCUSATIVE PLURAL
Allomorph *b* of base, followed by suffix 8: *b*-8 = {flo : re : s}

VII. ABLATIVE-DATIVE PLURAL
Allomorph *c* of base, followed by suffix 9: *c*-9 = {flo : ribus}

VIII. GENITIVE PLURAL
Norm of the base, followed by suffix 10: *n*-10 = {flo : rum}

The information here given is useful in that it gives a systematic picture of what constitutes base, and what suffix. Traditional presentations do not, leaving the student in doubt, for instance, whether the final of /flō : s/ is base-final or suffix. This information would be most properly given, in suitable tabular form, in the lexicon rather than in the grammar, and with suitable cross references to forms like *mōs* (custom), which has a similar arrangement of base allomorphs as well as of suffixes.

In describing the paradigmatic structure of Latin nouns, we have used the traditional names of the cases and numbers as merely convenient labels, with no attempt at definition. Nor do we need even here to be exhaustive in either definition or description of the syntactic distribution of these forms. Singular and plural are familiar to us from English, and need no discussion —semantically, they are "one" and "more than one." For the cases, we can give brief descriptions, with the statement that they are meant as no more than identifications, which would be greatly amplified were we presenting a complete Latin syntax. In systematic presentation, also, it should be pointed out that only the case forms belong in morphology, but for purposes of convenience the syntactic information on case forms is usually anticipated, as here:

1. VOCATIVE. The case of "direct address." That is, a form used for the person spoken to. It is a separate phrase, which is then an adjunct sentence element.
2. NOMINATIVE. Primarily the case of the subject. It is, further, used in sentence adjuncts and single sentence element sentences containing only the noun and its modifiers, when these are not direct address forms. It is also the form used for complements which are not goals.
3. ACCUSATIVE. Primarily the case used for a complement which is a goal of action. Latin, therefore, makes a structural distinction between non-goal and goal complements, which is absent in English.
4. ABLATIVE. A case which defines a noun as neither subject nor complement, covering the range of a good many prepositional phrases in English. It is also used as an adjunct sentence element, always a separate phrase. These sentence adjuncts—"ablative absolutes"— consist in noun and following entity, which may be participle, adjective, or second noun. The ablative adjunct sentence elements differ structurally from nominative and vocative adjuncts in that there must always be two elements in the ablative construction, noun and equated second noun, or noun and equated adjective or participle. Examples are:

Patre vīvō, Johannēs agricola erat.
([While his] father [was] alive, John was [a] farmer.)

Mēnsā exstructā, Johannēs cēnam ēdit sumptuōsam.
([The] table [having been] loaded [with food], John ate [a] luxurious dinner.)

Johannē agricolā, vitam miserrimam dēgit.
([While] John [was a] farmer, [he] led [a] most miserable life.)

The accusative and ablative are also the cases used after prepositions, which are a form class therefore definable in Latin as invariant forms which select accusative or ablative in a (usually following) noun.

5. DATIVE.   Primarily the case of the second goal. Latin thus makes a sharp distinction between two goal complements, a distinction made only syntactically in English.

6. GENITIVE.   As in English, a modifying case of nouns. It differs from the corresponding English case in not having fixed order characteristics.

6. Verbs

In dealing with Latin verbs, we shall simplify the task of dealing with the many base and suffix allomorphs by confining our analysis to only one verb, chosen because it is full enough and typical enough to reveal the general structure of the system. The verb system is more complex than that of English, since the usual school grammar lists over two hundred forms, instead of the mere five we have found in English. The usual listing of Latin verbs is not quite accurate, since a number of the forms listed are verbal constructions rather than inflected forms, and there is some duplication. Nevertheless, the number of forms is impressive, and it is in this richness of forms that the complexity of the system lies. The verb forms are not characterized by the skewness which marks the nouns.

The minimal Latin verb form consists of two parts, a base and a suffix for person. The personal suffixes agree with the subject, normally the actor. A notable minor difference between English and Latin verb syntax is that Latin very frequently uses verb forms alone, without demanding a separately expressed subject form. This fact makes it necessary to describe the Latin relation between verb and subject as one of agreement rather than selection, since subjectivals and verbs can each occur alone. The personal suffixes are for the familiar three persons and two numbers, giving a total of six forms. As in nouns, it is not possible to analyze the six forms into recurrent partials, one for person and one for number. A list of these suffixes, with their allomorphs follows:[3]

$$1. \{-o:\} \sim \{-m\}$$
$$2. \{-s\} \sim \{-sti\}$$
$$3. \{-t\}$$
$$4. \{-mus\}$$
$$5. \{-tis\}$$
$$6. \{-nt\} \sim \{-: runt\} \sim \{-: re\}$$

---

[3] The symbol $\sim$ is to be read "alternating with."

As well as this set of endings, there is another set of six which, like the first set, agree with the subject, but in which this subject stands normally as the goal of action. These goal-agreeing suffixes are called passive, and the distinction between normal subject and goal-subject is called voice. The names are not very good, but will be used since they are generally familiar. The endings are as follows:

1. {–or} ~ {–r}
2. {–ris}
3. {–tur}
4. {–mur}
5. {–mini:}
6. {–ntur}

Like much else in Latin inflection, these forms are only partially systematic. All but one contain an /–r/ plus recognizable elements similar to the active endings. It is therefore a commonplace to speak of Latin as having a "passive in –r–"; yet, in spite of this very nearly common element, the forms resist analysis. The difficulty of analysis can be measured by the number of statements that would be necessary to present these forms as consisting of voice marker and the normal personal suffixes. If a voice marker were set up, it would have to have at least three allomorphs plus some provision for identifying what part of form 5 corresponds to the voice marker. There would have to be provision for at least two allomorphs of the suffixes plus another provision for identifying some part of form 5 with the suffix. There would also have to be at least five statements of order of occurrence. Such a total of thirteen statements would obviously be more wasteful than an analysis of the six forms as fused portmanteaus, capable of being stated with six statements only, by listing. It is possible, then, to say that there is discoverable in these forms a voice sign *{r}, which is combined with personal suffixes in a way which can only be stated by listing the results. Thus:

1. *{r} + suffix 1 = {–or}; or
5. *{r} + suffix 5 = {–mini:}

This fusion of forms is of some importance, however, since it is capable of a sort of generalized solution, statable as "voice marker plus personal suffix equals passive suffix." Stated in this fashion, the fused voice marker is parallel to other markers which we shall go on to describe, in that the suffixes which we shall call markers are forms which may be present or absent and which occur in fixed positions. The fact that the voice marker thus fuses with the personal endings indicates that it occupies the position immediately before them. In the voice contrast of active and passive, then, the active is the unmarked form, with absence of the element *{r}. A pair of contrasting forms would then be analyzed as follows:

amō (I love) consists of base allomorph and an allomorph of personal ending 1: {am–o:}

amor (I am loved) consists of base allomorph plus voice marker and personal ending (equals passive suffix 1): {am–or}

The marker which occurs in position immediately before the voice marker is one for a distinction called mood. The unmarked form is the so-called indicative mood, the marked form the subjunctive. The mood marker consists of an element in {–e: –} or {–e–} (there are other allomorphs more easily described later). It gives us two further contrasting forms:

amem (I may love) consists of base allomorph, plus allomorph of mood marker {–e–}, plus allomorph of personal suffix 1: {am–e–m}

amer (I may be loved) consists of base allomorph, plus allomorph of mood marker {–e–}, plus voice marker and personal suffix (equals allomorph of passive suffix 1 {–r}): {am–e–r}

Preceding the mood marker, there may be a time marker, the Latin verb having three different times, or tenses. The unmarked form is the present, the marked forms are past and future. The future marker and the mood marker are mutually exclusive—the subjunctive having no future tense. The allomorphs of these markers that we need to take up at this point are:

PAST TENSE   {–ba–} ∼ {–r–}

FUTURE TENSE   {–bi–} ∼ {–b–}

These give us a set of six forms, contrasting with those we have already given, all of which were from the unmarked present:

amābam (I was loving) consists of the norm of the base {ama: –}, plus the past tense marker {–ba–}, plus the allomorph {–m} of personal suffix 1: {ama: –ba–m}

amābar (I was loved) consists of norm of the base {ama: –}, plus past tense marker {–ba–}, plus fused voice marker and personal suffix 1, {–r}: {ama: –ba–r}

amārem (I may have been loving) consists of norm of the base {ama: –}, plus allomorph {–r–} of the past tense marker, plus allomorph {–e–} of the mood marker, plus allomorph {–m} of personal suffix 1: {ama: –r–e–m}

amārer (I may have been being loved) consists of norm of base {ama: –}, plus allomorph {–r–} of past tense marker, plus allomorph {–e–} of mood marker, plus fused voice marker and personal suffix 1, {–r}: {ama: –r–e–r}

amābō (I shall love) consists of norm of base {ama: –}, plus allomorph
{–b–} of future tense marker, plus personal suffix 1: {ama: –b–o:}
amābor (I shall be loved) consists of norm of base {ama:–}, plus allomorph
{–b–} of future tense marker, plus fused mood marker and personal
suffix 1, {–or}: {ama: –b–or}

It will be remembered that the reason there are only six of these marked
tense forms, instead of the expected eight, is that the subjunctive lacks the
future tense.

The remaining marker is one for a distinction in what has been called
aspect, the state of action. The Latin aspects are two, one which is unmarked
and indicates incomplete action, and the marked one which indicates
completed action. While I adopt the traditional name "aspect," I prefer to
use the terms "incomplete" and "completed" rather than the traditional
"imperfect" and "perfect," since these have been used in ways which tend to
confuse them with tense forms.

The aspect marker has a number of allomorphs, appearing as {–wi–},
{–we–}, and {–wis–}. In addition a number of allomorphs of other elements
appear in conjunction with the aspect marker. If the personal suffixes appear
immediately after the aspect marker, they assume the following shapes
(those not given remain unmodified):

> 1. {–:}
> 2. {–ti}
> 6. {–: runt} alternating freely with {–: re}

When the past tense marker appears immediately after the aspect marker, it
assumes two allomorphic shapes, {–ra–}, after vocalic allomorphs of the
aspect marker, and {–s–}, after the allomorph {–wis–}. The future tense
marker, immediately after the allomorph {–we–}, assumes the shape {–r–},
and the mood marker in turn assumes the shape {–ri–} after the same allomorph. The aspect marker and the voice marker are incompatible, as are
the future tense marker and the mood marker. There are thus no passive
forms, and as usual no future subjunctive forms. The result is that the
addition of an aspect marker produces but five additional forms, instead of
twelve as we should find were the system complete. In school grammar
presentation, the missing passive forms are supplied by constructions made
up of a participle and forms of the verb *to be*.

amāuī (I have loved) consists of norm of the base {ama: –}, plus completed
aspect marker in the allomorph {–wi–}, plus personal suffix 1 in the
allomorph {–:}: {ama: –wi–:}
amāuerim (I may have loved) consists of norm of the base, followed by the
aspect marker in the allomorph {–we–}, followed by the mood marker

in the allomorph {–ri–}, followed by the allomorph {–m} of personal suffix 1: {ama : –we–ri–m}

amāueram (I had loved) consists of norm of the base, plus aspect marker in the allomorph {–we–}, plus past tense marker in the allomorph {–ra–}, and the allomorph {–m} of personal suffix 1: {ama : –we–ra–m}

amāuissem (I perhaps had loved) consists of norm of the base, followed by the aspect marker in the allomorph {–wis–}, then the past tense marker in the allomorph {–s–}, the mood marker in the allomorph {–e–}, and personal suffix 1 in the allomorph {–m}: {ama : –wis–s–e–m}

amāuerō (I shall have loved) consists of the norm of the base, followed by the aspect marker in the allomorph {–we–}, the future tense marker in the allomorph {–r–}, and personal suffix 1: {ama : –we–r–o :}

The principal problem raised by these forms is the set represented by *amāuerim* and its relation to the set represented by *amāuerō*. As every para-digm-learning schoolboy has discovered, the two sets are very nearly homonymous, and in classic times only the forms with suffix 1 were distinct. There is historic evidence, however, that there was once more differentiation than there was later, the forms of *amāuerim* having generally had a long /i :/, the others a short /i/. In classic times, both sets seem to have had a long or short, as a free variant.[4] It is worth giving the inflections entire:

{ama : –we–ri–m}	{ama : –we–r–o :}
{ama : –we–ri–s}	{ama : –we–ri–s}
{ama : –we–ri–t}	{ama : –we–ri–t}
{ama : –we–ri–mus}	{ama : –we–ri–mus}
{ama : –we–ri–tis}	{ama : –we–ri–tis}
{ama : –we–ri–nt}	{ama : –we–ri–nt}

Displayed in this fashion, the nature of the problem is plain. Five forms have a morph {–ri–} identical in both sets, the other forms have {–ri–} followed by {–m}, opposed to {–r–} followed by {–o:}; in short, the sole differences are the sequences of phonemes /–im/ and /–o :/. The temptation is therefore to set up /–im/ as an independent morpheme and associate it with present subjunctive meaning. Such an analysis would confuse the structure and is fortunately unnecessary. The sequence {–ri–}, on the one hand, and {–r–} alternating with {–ri–}, on the other, are allomorphs of different morphemes, which happen to be homonymous in most of their occurrences. They are formally distinguished by the fact that one has one variant only, the other two. We can thus solve our difficulties by identifying one {–ri–} as the mood marker throughout, and the other

---

[4] For the historical statements, consult Ferdinand Sommer, *Handbuch der lateini-schen Laut- und Formenlehre*, Heidelberg, Winter 1914, Par. 364.

{–ri–}, alternating with {–r–}, as a future tense marker throughout. The difference in the endings {–m} and {–o:} remains allomorphic, since as usual, the {–o:} is associated with an immediately preceding future tense marker.

We have now surveyed that part of the Latin verb inflection which is most tightly and symmetrically constructed. Before we go on to survey the remaining forms in equally brief fashion, we can review the general structure we have so far presented. Latin has a verb paradigm which in its simplest form consists of base and personal suffixes alone, {am–o:}. This form, usually called the present indicative active, might better be called, on a formal basis, the unmarked paradigm. Latin has also a conjugation consisting of base and passive marker fused with personal suffixes to give a portmanteau set of passive suffixes, {am–or}. This set is usually called the present indicative passive, but again on a formal basis might be called the simple passive. Latin has two forms with the subjunctive marker, occurring with or without the voice marker already described, the simple subjunctive, {am–e–m}, and the subjunctive passive, {am–e–r}. If we add a past tense marker, we get a simple past tense, {ama:–ba–m}; a past passive, {ama:–ba–r}; a past subjunctive, {ama:–r–e–m}; and a past subjunctive passive, {ama:–r–e–r}. The addition of a future tense marker (which cannot occur together with a mood marker) gives us a simple future, {ama:–b–o:}, and a future passive, {ama:–b–or}.

The remaining forms are constructed with the addition of a completed aspect marker, which cannot occur together with a voice marker. The forms are then a simple completed {ama:wi–:}; a completed subjunctive {ama:–we–ri–m}; a completed past {ama:–we–ra–m}; a completed past subjunctive {ama:–wis–s–e–m}; and a completed future {ama:–we–r–o:}.

The most striking fact about this type of verb conjugation is that it is positional, with a total of six positions, of which one, base, and six, personal suffix, must always be filled. The other positions may be filled or empty, but no more than three of these positions may be filled in any one construction. These are statements typical of the description of any positional type of inflection, as can be seen if we go back to the preceding description of Eskimo. Indeed, it is possible to present a formula to express the construction of Latin verbs, different in detail from that for Eskimo, but generally similar.

We shall use the following symbols for the various classes of segmental morphs:

PrB, prebase
B,   base
PoB, postbase
AM, aspect marker

TM, tense marker
MM, mood marker
VM, voice marker
PS, personal suffix

In addition, the following numerical symbolism is used: superscript numbers indicate the possible numbers of each class of morph present in a single construction, so that a superscript $\varnothing\text{-}n$ indicates that a class of morph may be present or absent, and if present may have an indefinite number of representatives. A superscript $1\text{-}2$ indicates that there must be one representative of the class and no more than two. A superscript fractional number states in the numerator the number of representatives which may be present and in the denominator the number of morphs in the paradigmatic set. Thus $\frac{1}{6}$ indicates that, out of a paradigmatic set of six suffixes, one personal suffix only is present in a single construction. These symbols give us the verb formula:

$$\text{PrB}^{\varnothing\text{-}n} \quad \text{B}^{1\text{-}2} \quad \text{PoB}^{\varnothing\text{-}n} \quad \text{AM}^{\varnothing\text{-}1} \quad \text{TM}^{\varnothing\text{-}1}_{2} \quad \text{MM}^{\varnothing\text{-}1} \quad \text{VM}^{\varnothing\text{-}1} \quad \text{PS}^{1}_{6}$$

In addition, we can indicate the instances in which some of the theoretically possible inflectional forms are absent, by simple statements of incompatibility. The first of these is that when AM is present, VM is absent. The statement indicates that there is no passive for the form which contains the marker of completed action. The second statement of incompatibility is that when the future TM is present, MM is absent. This statement indicates that when the tense is future, there is no subjunctive marker and no subjunctive inflection.

The diagram we have given is of value if it presents the structure of the Latin verb with any increase of clarity. The Latin verb forms' general similarity to Eskimo verb forms is of some further interest, since it demonstrates something which has often been denied: language structures are alike or different, depending solely on the nature of the structures, not on cultural status. Often enough, as with Eskimo and Latin, cultural extremes make use of structures which resemble each other. There is no "civilized" type, and no "primitive" type.

Beyond this set of forms, which makes full use of personal suffixes and markers, there is another set often called a mood. This set is isolated from the forms we have described in that it uses personal suffixes and markers fragmentarily and in a different fashion. The set is the imperative, the forms of which follow:

SIMPLE IMPERATIVE

1. *amā* (love thou!) /áma:/ {ama:}
2. *amāte* (love ye!) /amá: te/ {ama:} {te}

FUTURE IMPERATIVE

1. *amātō* (thou shalt love!) /amá: to:/ {ama:} {to:}
2. *amātōte* (ye shall love!) /ama: tó: te/ {ama:} {to:} {te}
3. *amantō* (they shall love!) /amánto:/ {ama} {nto:}

PASSIVE IMPERATIVE

1. *amāre* (be thou loved!) /amá: re/ {ama:} {re}
2. *amāminī* (be ye loved!) /amá: mini:/ {ama:} {mini:}[5]

FUTURE PASSIVE IMPERATIVE

1. *amātor* (thou shalt be loved!) /amá: tor/ {ama:} {to} {r}
2. ——
3. *amantor* (they shall be loved!) /amántor/ {ama} {ntor}

In these forms, the singulars are without any observable element which could be analyzed as a personal suffix. They are usually said to be second person forms, even though the future forms are often found in syntactic situations which suggest that they are forms for the third person also. It therefore seems best not to interpret these forms as containing a zero allomorph of the second person singular suffix, but rather to assume that they are without personal suffix. These singular forms of the imperative therefore constitute an exception to the general rule that inflectable bases do not occur in Latin without a suffix of some sort. The fact that these suffixless bases are usually found in situations where the actor is also the person addressed is then to be explained as no more than the product of the probabilities of use.

The morph {te} which appears in the plural of the simple and the future imperative is different in form from the suffix of the second person plural which appears in *amātis* {ama:}{tis}, (ye love), and the morph {te} is therefore in contrast with {tis}. It is thus an independent morpheme, and since we have already defined the singular as without personal suffix, this morpheme is best described as a plural suffix similarly without personal reference. The forms of the future imperative and future passive imperative, in which the stem is followed by {–nto:} and {–ntor}, respectively, obviously have a personal reference which is absent from the rest of the imperative inflection. Both forms are portmanteaus, the first element of which is the third person plural ending, {–nt}, followed in the simple future by an allomorph, {–o:}, of the imperative future marker, {–to:}. The single /t/ which occurs can be assigned to the preceding morph on the ground that assimilation in Latin, as well as in English, normally modifies the second

---

[5] But see discussion below, p. 472.

rather than the first of a pair of consonants. In the future passive, the allo-morph of the future marker in the corresponding form is {-o-}, which in turn is followed by the passive marker. These third person forms do not contain the plural suffix {-te}, plural reference being carried by the personal endings. The forms are irregular in the order of morph occurrence, since the normal position for personal endings is at the end of the construction.

The second form of the simple future, *amātōte*, shows its suffix morphs in more normal order, with the future marker {-to : -} preceding the plural suffix {-te}. The singular of the passive imperative is of interest in that it shows us a morph, {-re}, which can be identified as the norm of the voice marker and the only form of the voice marker which occurs without fusion with some other suffix element. The second form of the passive imperative, *amāminī*, like the third person forms of the two future imperatives, clearly carries a personal reference in its suffix. The suffix is the portmanteau which appears as the normal fusion of voice marker and personal suffix. The form is clearly homonymous with a normal passive, whose meaning would be "ye are loved." Strictly speaking, therefore, the form does not belong to the imperative inflection but is an instance of special semantic development by which a form belonging to another part of the inflectional system has come to fill an empty position in a second set. The fact that this second form of the passive imperative does not properly belong in the imperative inflection is supported by the fact that the corresponding future passive imperative lacks a second form altogether.

The remaining forms of the inflection are verbals rather than true verbs, and are all either nominal or adjectival in character. Their chief interest is that in comparison with English, they are much more highly differentiated. There is a simple infinitive *amāre* {ama : -re} (to love), which shows the normal form of the infinitive suffix, homonymous with the norm of the voice marker which we have seen above. The infinitive suffix can be preceded by the marker of completed action, giving a form *amāuisse* {ama : -wis-se} (to have loved), where the infinitive suffix appears in the allomorph {-se}. There is also a passive infinitive, *amārī* {ama : -ri :} (to be loved), where the form {-ri :} is a fusion of infinitive suffix and passive marker. Another verbal noun is the so-called gerund, a noun with defective endings, formed with a postbase {-ndo-} to which noun endings are added, as in *amandum* {ama-ndu-m}, accusative singular, (to love). There is a so-called supine, a noun formed with a different postbase {-tu-} and differing noun suffixes, as in *amātum* {ama : -tu-m}. There is an active participle, formed with a postbase {-n-} alternating with {-nt-}, to which adjectival endings are added, as in *amāns* {ama : -n-s} (loving). There is also a passive participle formed with the postbase {-to-} and its allomorphs in the masculine and neuter, and with {-ta-} in the feminine, giving *amātus* {ama: –tu–s}. There is a future participle which seems to have the same postbase plus an allomorph of the future marker *amātūrus* (about to love), though there is not much evidence on which to base analysis, and the form is without passive meaning. Thus a conservative cutting would be into {ama: –tu: ru–s}. There is, finally, a future passive participle formed with a postbase {–ndo–}, *amandus* {ama–ndu–s} (to be worthy of love). We can leave this hasty survey with pointing out the fact that there are other forms of nouns or adjectives formed with postbases added to a base which appears in verb forms, such as *amor* (love) and *amātor* (lover), but as in English these form no part of the verbal conjugation, since they are unsystematic in their appearance with given bases and do not pattern as parts of verbal constructions as the others do.

We can say also a little more about meaning without going beyond the limits of a short sketch. I have given translations of a good many of the verb forms, but these were intended as not much more than convenient aids to memory. The Latin system being different from English, forms do not translate with one-for-one correspondence. Thus a complete form such as *amāui* corresponds to both "I loved" and "I have loved," Latin not making the same distinction as English does. English, in turn, makes no distinction like that between gerund and supine. In no set of forms are the translations more misleading than in the subjunctives. In general the Latin subjunctive is certainly more nearly a mood characteristic of linked and dependent sentences than a mood of wishing or doubting.

7. Remaining classes of words

Besides nouns and verbs, which we have taken up at some length, there are two other form classes, pronouns and adjectives, which are paradigmatically defined but which we shall omit. The remaining form classes are all without paradigmatic variation. Yet there are two groups within the invariant classes which are clearly marked. The first of these are the prepositions, which as we have already said, are defined by the fact that they select the ablative or accusative in nominals, which usually immediately follow and with which they make up a single construction. The second group are adverbs. These are often marked by characteristic postbases, such as the *–ter* of *graviter* (heavily), from the base which appears in *gravis* (heavy). Among the postbases which help to distinguish the class from the closely similar adjectives are the adverbial comparative, *–ius*, as in *altius* (more highly), which contrasts with the adjectival comparative *–ior*, *altior* (higher). Many adverbs are in origin simply case-number forms of adjectives or nouns and are thus, in their citation forms, indistinguishable from adjectives, as with *primō* (at first) from *prīmus* (first). For these forms, since order characteristics cannot be used as a diagnostic, a chief identifying characteristic is that they will appear in the same phrase with a verb where they are clearly not subjects or complements and even where a complement is impossible, as in:

Diū uiuēbat. (He lived a long time.)

In other instances, it is essentially the fact that adverb forms agree with nothing, and so do not vary for case-number, which distinguishes them from the inflectable word groups.

The remaining uninflectable forms can be most easily treated by lumping them, as is sometimes done, under the name "particles." It is possible, however, that a further study of Latin syntax would make it possible to distinguish words like *et* or *uel* as a class of conjunctions, but this is by no means certain. The usual definition of a Latin conjunction relies only on meaning. It should be pointed out, however, that some forms which in English are conjunctions, are in Latin enclitics (see above, p. 448), a class of morphemes, of lower status than words, which make up phrases with preceding free forms and which show their dependence by their stress characteristics. Such a form is the *-que* of the following:

oppida uīcōsque (towns and villages)

8. Latin sentence types

In Latin as in English, the favorite sentence types are (1) subject and verb and (2) subject, verb, and complement. The only difference is that Latin makes a distinction not made in English between subject, verb, and complement, and subject, verb, and goal-complement. Latin, again like English, can have sentences composed only of verb and complement, as in *matrem amā* (love [your] mother), an imperative, and sentences composed of a single sentence element, as in *En Priamus* (Lo, Priam!).

There are a number of sentence types not found in English, however. One difference is that a verb or verb construction often occurs alone, as in the daughter languages, with no separate indication of the subject. Thus, *amat* is a complete and normal sentence in Latin, though English "loves" is not. Thus, a single verb is not a one sentence element sentence, as it would be in English, but one of two sentence elements, subject and verb. The Latin verb, when it occurs alone, can be spoken of, however, as a downgraded sentence, since the subject is here reduced to the status of a mere suffix.

The second differing sentence type is the equation. These are not unknown in English, but are far commoner in Latin. Examples are:

Ego dux. (I [am the] leader.)
Summum ius summa iniūria. ([The] height of right [is the] height of wrong.)
Puella bona. ([The] girl [is] good.)

The common properties of these sentences seem to be that the initial is a noun or nominal and that what follows may then be noun, pronoun, or adjective. Under these circumstances we are justified in speaking of the first word or construction as a subjectival and the following as a complemental (not a true complement, since this would require a verb). There would seem to be a difference in order, therefore, in a pair like the following:

O fēstus diēs! (Oh happy day!)
Diēs fēstus. ([The] day [is] happy.)

If this conjecture is right, the first is a one sentence element sentence, and the other an equation. In the absence of knowledge of Latin superfix patterns, the conjecture must remain unprovable.

In dealing with complex sentences, which are quite as common in Latin as in English or Eskimo, we need only to cite one typical instance. This is the general appearance of the subjunctive as a linker and downgrader, much as is the *–ing* form of English or the dependent modes of Eskimo. The following is an example from a closing tag by a medieval scribe:

Qui scripsit scribat semper cum domino uiuat. Amen.
([He] who has written [this book] may he write [and]
may he always live with God. Amen.)

Since we do not know the superfix structure, we hesitate to be dogmatic about the relationship of these several constructions, but it would be natural to guess three linked sentences, the first linked by the pronoun, the second consisting of *scribat* alone, with the subjunctive as the linker, and the remainder again linked by the subjunctive *uiuat*.

9. Syntax

Two statements can be made at the outset. First, as Waldo Sweet has recently made abundantly clear, order of sentence elements is not a part of the Latin signaling system. That is, a subject-verb-goal sentence like "The girl loves her mother" can be expressed in Latin in any possible order:

Matrem puella amat.   *Amat matrem puella.*
Matrem amat puella.   *Puella matrem amat.*
Amat puella matrem.   *Puella amat matrem.*

Only the last is in English order. The subject of order has been confused by some older statements, such as this from a book excellent in its day: ". . . normal order . . . is subject, modifiers of the subject, modifiers of the verb, verb . . . But the so-called normal arrangement is really rare, since the speaker or writer generally has some special emphasis to put on some part of the sentence *(rhetorical order)*."[6] This particular statement confuses what is linguistically significant and what is not. Order of sentence elements is linguistically without significance in Latin, but is a feature controlled by the stylistic situation, and so meaningful on the stylistic level. If the unfortunate student hunts for English order signals in Latin, he will never be at home with the language.

A second general statement is that within the limits of the sentence, dependent or otherwise, the various parts of sentence elements are not necessarily continuous but can occur in discontinuous order. The following quotations from Horace will illustrate:

> *Non sum qualis eram bonae sub regno Cinarae* . . .
> (I am not what I was under the rule of the good Cinara.)
> *Lydia, dic, per omnes te deos oro* . . .
> (Lydia, tell [me], by all the Gods I pray thee . . .)

In the first, the construction which consists of *Cinara* and the adjective which agrees with it is interrupted by the preposition-noun construction. In the second, the construction *per omnes . . . deos* is interrupted by the goal-complement, *te*. Yet, it is to be noted that this variation does not extend beyond the limits of the dependent sentences. Thus, if in the first sequence we reverse the order of the verbs, we get a significantly different statement: "I was not what I am under the rule of the good Cinara." That is to say, these two verbs belong to two different, but linked, sentences. In terms of phonology, this fact makes it likely that there was a terminal juncture of some sort at the boundary of a linked sentence, though we have to guess at its location. In this particular Horatian line, a reasonable guess is that the terminal was after *sum*, since it seems likely that the *qualis* had the same linking function in initial position that the related {hw-} forms have in English. Again we do not know exactly what the terminal was, but a guess is that it was a rough equivalent of /|||/. Looked at from the internal point of view, the discontinuity of the parts of sentence elements

---

[6] W. G. Hale and C. D. Buck, *A Latin Grammar*, Ginn, Boston, 1903, pp. 334, 337.

makes it extremely unlikely that there were either junctures or juncture points between sentence elements as there are in English.

It should also be stated that, though discontinuous and highly variant orders occur, some things are fixed. Thus, in the first of these Latin quotations, the position of *sub* with respect to *regno* is fixed. It could not come before the adjective *bonae*, since the adjective does not belong to the same construction as *regno* (as its case form shows), nor could *sub* occur after its noun or before *Cinarae*.

The discontinuity of parts of sentence-elements introduces a problem in dealing with suffixes which show agreement. If we have a sentence such as *illa puella bona matrem amat*, the same case-number suffix, indeed the same allomorph of the nominative singular suffix, appears on each of the first three words. Such repetitive sequences have been called by Harris a single "broken morpheme," rather than a sequence of occurrences of the same morpheme.[7] Such a procedure of analysis would seem to be perfectly acceptable in languages like Bantu, where there are repeated suffixes of agreement but in which the members of the same sentence element are contiguous. In such a situation, the repeated suffix is redundant and has no other meaning than "of such and such class or classes." In Latin, however, it is the recurrence of these classes which sorts out the members of the sentence element or construction for us, so that the recurrence is not redundant, but significant. Thus, had the first quotation read . . . *bono sub regno* . . . instead of . . . *bonae sub regno* . . ., the adjective would have been a member of the prepositional construction, instead of part of the modifying genitive construction. It would seem necessary to regard the Latin suffixes then as separate morphemes, though they are indeed members of single long, and discontinuous, constructions.

The repeated suffixes are clearly enough one of the principal means by which Latin is understood, and order is not such a means. The statement is no more than a commonplace, yet, though it is true enough, it leads to problems in immediate constituent analysis. The first of the problems is simple and can be solved readily enough. Suppose our sentence is one composed of the sentence elements subject-verb-goal, in any order and with no parts of any sentence element occurring in discontinuous order. An example would be any one of our six forms of *matrem puella amat*. The orders here can be generalized by disregarding which noun is goal and which subject, as:

> VERB-NOUN-NOUN
>
> NOUN-VERB-NOUN
>
> NOUN-NOUN-VERB

[7] Zellig S. Harris, *Methods in Structural Linguistics*, University of Chicago Press, Chicago, 1951, pp. 165–66.

A simple rule for cutting is then to make the first cut so that one constituent always contains verb and noun. That is, the first example would be cut between the nouns, the second before the verb (we work by preference from the front, taking the first possible cut we come to), and the third again between the nouns. The justification for this apparently arbitrary rule is that by so doing we always arrive at one minor constituent and a major constituent capable of standing as a sentence—either *matrem amat* or *puella amat*, with their order variants.

The situation is quite different in constituent analysis of discontinuous sentence elements. Constituents are constructions, and no matter whether they occur in a linear order or not, there are many reasons why they should be presented in analysis in a linear fashion. Thus, some rearrangement is ultimately necessary, though obviously the rearrangement should be minimized. It must be limited to rearrangement of the discontinuous parts of the separate sentence elements—it would be doing violence to the structure of Latin if we arranged the order of sentence elements to produce any sort of nonexistent "normal order." As with the procedure for rearranging the discontinuous predicators of English, the rearrangement should be done after the cutting into constituents has been completed. Yet there is an important difference in procedure. Discontinuous sentence elements are rare in English, being limited to the predicator only. In Latin, on the other hand, sentence elements of all kinds may be discontinuous. Thus, English is a language in which double cuts, before and after a contained element, are to be avoided if possible. Latin would seem to be a language in which contained elements within a discontinuous sentence element are so common as to demand double cuts as normal procedure. By such a process, we shall see, the cutting itself largely accomplishes the needed rearrangement. But though double cuts would seem to be admissible, and useful, they must still be done in a consistent and orderly fashion.

Let us take a simple example:

Caesar Galliam uīcit omnem. (Caesar conquered all Gaul.)

A rule which has already been implied is that we work consistently from the start of the sentence, rather than from the end. The choice is arbitrary, perhaps, but is at least consistent. The first step is to hunt for any sentence element which is neither discontinuous nor contained within another sentence element. If there is more than one such element, we take that which is nearest the start of the sentence and cut this out by a first and single cut. We proceed next to any other continuous and noncontained sentence elements there may be.

We are left with discontinuous sentence elements which contain either wholes or parts of other sentence elements. If the discontinuous sentence elements contain a continuous sentence element, we give preference to the continuous sentence element, cutting this out by a double cut and leaving the containing sentence element now isolated.

These principles can be applied to our relatively simple sentence quoted above. The sentence element which is both continuous and nearest the start is *Caesar*. We cut after this, giving the two constituents *Caesar* and *Galliam uīcit omnem*. Out of this second constituent, we next cut out the continuous predicator, leaving *uīcit* and *Galliam . . . omnem*.

A typical more complicated situation can be exemplified by the following sentence from Horace:

> *. . . sunt quos curriculo pulverem Olympicum*
> *collegisse iuvat metaque fervidis*
> *evitata rotis palmaque nobilis*
> *terrarum dominos evehit ad deos . . .*

This is translated thus by C. E. Bennett:

> . . . some there are whose one delight it is to gather Olympic dust upon the racing car, and whom the turning-post cleared with glowing wheel and the glorious palm exalt as masters of the earth to the very gods.[8]

As usual with Latin, we must merely guess at the terminal junctures, but since there are two complete subject-predicate-complement constructions, we are safe in supposing that we have two linked sentences. The first cut will therefore be after *iuvat*, giving:

> *sunt quos curriculo pulverem Olympicum collegisse iuvat*, and
> *metaque fervidis evitata rotis palmaque nobilis terrarum dominos*
> *evehit ad deos*

We can proceed to further cuts on the first of these sentences: *Sunt* is the predicator, without subject other than the contained verbal suffix. Since it is thus the first complete sentence element, the next cut is after it, leaving *quos curriculo pulverem Olympicum collegisse iuvat* as the next constituent.

The next separate element is *quos*, which shows a kind of linking which is typical of Latin in that it agrees in person and number with the preceding verb but is not in the expected nominative case. As for its relation to *sunt*, it can then be called a subjectival, yet, in terms of what follows, it is also linked to the infinitive *collegisse*, for which it is not subject, but actor. Our next cut will be after it, leaving the next constituent as *curriculo*

---

[8] Horace, "Dedication to Maecenas," *The Odes and Epodes*, Loeb Classical Library, London, 1927, p. 3.

pulverem Olympicum collegisse iuvat. The next independent element is *curriculo*, which can be defined as a sentence adjunct. The remaining constituent, *pulverem Olympicum collegisse iuvat* should be cut after *Olympicum*, leaving *collegisse iuvat.* The last two cuts can then be made between the separate words of the complement and predicator.

The first sentence contains no discontinuous sentence elements, and so offers a minimum of difficulty in constituent analysis. The most striking feature of this sentence is the downgrading which it shows. All the material following *quos* is, in structure, an independent sentence, which, if isolated, would be capable of being translated as "It is pleasing to collect Olympic dust on the racing car." This sentence is downgraded by the addition of *quos*, in a fashion similar to downgrading by the addition of *who* in English. As a downgraded construction, the material beginning with *quos* serves as a single sentence element, the complement of *sunt*. It is a detail that the downgrader here is a cognate, in its initial consonant combination, of the series of {hw–} downgraders of English.

The second sentence was:

> *metaque fervidis evitata rotis palmaque nobilis terrarum dominos*
>   *evehit ad deos*

The first observation is that the *–que* of *metaque* must be assumed to be a sentence linker. Since it occurs after the first word of the new sentence, it cannot be taken as linking this word narrowly to something that precedes. It is therefore a sentence linker appearing in a different function from that of *–que* which appears as a postphrase when it links two nouns.

In this second sentence, there is a long, continuous first sentence element, the subject. It ends with *nobilis*, and consequently our first cut will be after this word, leaving, as the other constituent:

> *terrarum dominos evehit ad deos*

In the subject, we find a second *–que* which is this time functioning more like the *–que* in postphrasal uses of the form. Were there no adjective following *palmaque*, we should say that *–que* was marking the end of the subject sentence element. In the situation found here, it serves to indicate that *palma* is a part of the subject, but the subject is not bounded by the *–que*, and there could have been an indefinite number of following adjectives, all belonging to the subject, and shown to belong to the subject only by their agreement with it.

In further cutting of the subject, we look first for a continuous construction within it. The only such element is *palmaque nobilis*, and accordingly, our cut is before it. The other constituent is:

> *metaque fervidis evitata rotis*

The arrangement, as far as agreement is concerned, seems to be something which could be represented as *abab*, since the first and third and the second and fourth words agree with each other, suggesting that we have two dovetailed discontinuous elements. The conclusion is unnecessary, however. The form *evitata* is a participle, a typical downgraded form of predicator, downgraded because it serves as a modifier of the noun with which it agrees. It can, however, still be treated as an independent element. We therefore make our next cut after *metaque*, leaving *fervidis evitata rotis* as the other constituent.

We now for the first time reach a discontinuous construction and, in consequence, proceed by cutting out the contained element by a double cut, giving the constituents:

fervidis . . . rotis and *evitata*

These elements are to be defined as sentence adjunct and predicator, respectively.

In cutting this long subject, we have again met downgrading devices. One of these, the use of a participle as predicator, has already been mentioned. The second device is a factor of sentence element order. That is, the constituent *fervidis evitata rotis* is placed within the borders of the subject construction and so is not an independent predicator with adjunctival element. Had the constituent been **metaque fervidis evitata rotis*, we should have had an independent subject-predicator-adjunct construction, presumably to be translated as "The turning-post is avoided with glowing wheel." It is therefore not quite true that there are no instances of significant factors of sentence element order in Latin. In this sentence the contained predicator and adjunct are both downgraded and shown to be modifiers of the first part of the subject by their position. A subject for future investigation, therefore, is those factors of possibly significant sentence element order which are revealed by constituent analysis.

The constituent we have not yet analyzed is:

terrarum dominos evehit ad deos

This constituent was translated as "exalt as masters of the earth to the very gods." The translation is somewhat free, but stylistically justifiable since it gives a good English equivalent of the Latin construction. In point of fact, however, we have a discontinuous sentence element, a long prepositional phrase, interrupted by the predicator. Further, *terrarum* cannot be cut off from it first, since it seems to be a rule of Latin syntax that a genitive belongs to the same construction with the nearer of the two nouns, rather than to the more distant. We find, therefore, a second instance of a situation in which order is often significant.

Our cut must then be a double one, giving:

terrarum dominos . . . ad deos and *evehit*

The only remaining cut which needs to be described is in the discontinuous element we have just isolated. Since we have just said that the genitive belongs to the nearer noun, the cut should be into the two discontinuous parts rather than after *terrarum*.

We have offered this fairly extended example of constituent analysis partly as a sample text, but more importantly because it is believed that consistent constituent cutting, making use of double cuts when necessary, will minimize the necessity of rearrangement of sentence elements. It is also believed that constituent analysis will lead to significantly increased knowledge of Latin syntax. The two most important contributions which such analysis might make are, first, a knowledge of what variations in order are significant or possibly significant and, second, what variations in order are stylistic only. At present the two types of variation are not as clearly distinguished as full and precise statement requires.

INDEX